The Comingled Code

The Comingled Code

Open Source and Economic Development

Josh Lerner and Mark Schankerman

The MIT Press
Cambridge, Massachusetts
London, England

For information about special quantity discounts, please email special_sales@mitpress.mit.edu

This book was set in Palatino on 3B2 by Asco Typesetters, Hong Kong.
Printed and bound in the United States of America.

Library of Congress Cataloging-in-Publication Data

Lerner, Joshua.
The comingled code : open source and economic development / Josh Lerner and Mark Schankerman.
   p.   cm.
Includes bibliographical references and index.
ISBN 978-0-262-01463-2 (hardcover : alk. paper) 1. Open source software. 2. Computer software—Development. I. Schankerman, Mark. II. Title.
QA76.76.S46L46   2010
005.3—dc22   2010001730

10 9 8 7 6 5 4 3 2 1

To Carol and Ralph
To my mother Etta and my father Paul (Z"L), with love

Contents

Preface and Acknowledgments

Many a book has a tangled story behind it, and this one has a particularly long and twisted one. As a result there are a lot of people to thank.

This project has sought to understand the role of open source in economic development using several approaches. Given the early stage of open source software's development and the inherent difficulty of measuring these activities, only through taking multiple approaches can we do justice to this complex phenomenon.

The first approach was a careful review of the economic principles to shed light on the open source phenomenon and its implications for economic development. We prepared an analytical framework that highlighted how economics could guide us in understanding these complex issues. To do so, we drew on a diverse array of bodies of literature, including work on growth, the nature of innovation, and the literature on incentives and innovation in open source. When economic principles point in different directions—as they sometime do—we highlighted the open questions. The analytic framework underlies the work, and broadly informs how we approach the conceptualization of the demand and the supply sides in open source, as well as how we address the key policy questions.

The second approach was the preparation of a series of case studies of the open source phenomenon. We sought to understand the complexity of the role of open source in half a dozen nations in various stages of development. Rather than focus on the entire canvas of activities in each nation, we looked at different issues raised by specific situations in a number of emerging economies. Each study was based on interviews with Harvard Business School's case writers and secondary sources. The cases we studied were:[1]

---

1. A variety of supplemental material not included in the book is posted on-line at http://mitpress.mit.edu/comingledcode.

• In Brazil, a project called HackerTeen seeks to combine educating young programmers with the development of new software.

• In China, the CEO of a mobile telephone software company must decide whether to use Linux or commercial alternatives as the basis for his system.

• In France, a chief information officer must choose whether to recommend the Ministry of Finance will run on open source or proprietary software.

• In Singapore, the government considers whether to support a research initiative to promote research in open source.

• In South Africa, a vendor of software and services must decide how much effort to devote to developing expertise in open source.

• In Thailand, the government considers whether to promote a "People's PC," which would combine a low-cost hardware platform with open source software.

By focusing on a wide variety of actors in a diverse array of situations, we gained a rich picture of open source activity and its implications for development.

The third and final aspect of the project involved a large-scale survey of software users and developers in fifteen countries. (The developer survey alone had nearly 2,000 respondents.) The nations included many of the same ones on which we wrote cases, as well as other developing and industrialized countries, including Chile, Greece, India, Israel, Kenya, Mexico, Poland, Russia, and Turkey. We highlighted in the questionnaire not just questions about the utilization of open source software, but also about the respondents' attitudes and perspectives on the costs and benefits of this software. We further looked separately at developers and users of different types (for users, different sizes of companies, government agencies, and ownership; for developers, different sizes, ownership, software activities, etc.).

After we had conceptualized the project, we realized that the expense was so great that it was unlikely that we could fund it using our own resources: both the surveys and case studies proved to be extremely costly to implement. We discovered that Microsoft was interested in funding academic work into open source, with the goal of promoting a less ideological discussion of the pros and cons of software choices and public policy toward this sector, as well as providing the empirical evidence that could contribute to a more balanced and evidence-based formulation of public policy. We accepted their funding under stringent terms that ensured that the effort was characterized by intellectual independence and analytical rigor.

This work, and the conversations it engendered, led to the idea of developing this book. As always, the process of converting research into (at least what we hope is) readable prose proved to be a far more daunting task than we had initially envisioned.

First of all, we are very grateful for the contributions of Jacques Crémer of the University of Toulouse. In addition to being the co-author of chapter 6, Jacques was crucially involved in many discussions that led to the development and elaboration of the main themes and ideas of the book. His was an important contribution to the volume.

Next, our thanks must go to our long-suffering MIT Press acquiring editor, Jane Macdonald, for her patience with us. We also would like to thank David Evans, Anne Layne-Farrar, and Daniel Schwartz of LECG for their initial encouragement and help with the project, especially in the development of the survey questionnaires. Jacques Lawarree was the project's champion at Microsoft. We also benefited from considerable financial support from Harvard Business School's Division of Research. Mark Schankerman also thanks the British Academy and the Muzzy Chair in Entrepreneurship at the University of Arizona for their financial support of this research.

Sam Kortum of the University of Chicago was a member of the original project team and contributed a number of ideas. Brian DeLacey, Kerry Herman, and David Kiron played key roles in developing the case studies. Ivan Maryanchuk and Liat Oren provided excellent research assistance on the empirical analysis found in chapters 4, 5, and 6, and Kathy Han and Gabriel Fotsing provided invaluable research support on other aspects of the book. Maurie SuDock helped with the manuscript preparation and cleanup. While we are grateful for all the support, it is important to note that the ideas and recommendations represent our own opinions only.

As we discuss at more length in the introduction, there remains a considerable divide between the economics and open source communities. It is our hope that this book helps bridge this gap, by discussing the economic issues around open source in an accessible but tangible way based on systematic empirical evidence. We particularly hope that this approach leads to a less shrill (or less acrimonious) interaction between these communities, and a more informed, evidence-based public policy toward this sector.

Josh Lerner and Mark Schankerman
Boston and London
October 2009

1   Introduction

Open source software involves developers at many different locations and organizations sharing code to develop and refine computer programs that are then distributed at no or low direct cost. Over the past fifteen years open source software has experienced explosive growth around the world. The importance of open source software today can be illustrated by considering a few examples:

• The market for server software, which is used by the computers that make Web pages available to users through the Internet, has been dominated by the open source Apache project since the inception of systematic tracking by Netcraft in 1995. As of July 2009 more than half of servers employed Apache or other open source products, rather than commercial alternatives from Microsoft, Oracle, or other firms.[1]

• While definitive numbers are very hard to come by, a variety of survey evidence suggests that the open source operating system called Linux has rapidly outstripped Microsoft's Windows program as the operating system most frequently embedded into products ranging from mobile phones to video recording devices.[2]

• Open source software is dominant in a number of other areas as well; for example, PERL and PHP are the dominant scripting languages (programming languages designed specifically for instructing one computer how to communicate with others).

• Even corporations that have traditionally resisted open source, and the stringent General Public License (GPL) in particular, have seemingly changed their approach. Most visibly Microsoft, whose executives

---

1. http://news.netcraft.com/archives/web_server_survey.html (accessed August 23, 2009).
2. http://www.linuxfordevices.com/c/a/Linux-For-Devices-Articles/Snapshot-of-the-embedded-Linux-market-April-2007/ (accessed August 23, 2009).

once branded the GPL as "fundamentally undermin[ing] the independent commercial software sector,"[3] released two substantial blocks of code under this license in July 2009.[4]

• Open source software is not a phenomenon that is confined to rich countries. For better or for worse, the Brazilian and many other developing nation governments are promoting the use of open source software as an alternative to proprietary products. Significant numbers of contributors to open source software, in proportion to the population, can be found in countries with per capita income as low as $10,000.

Open source software may be poised for rapid growth in the future. The number of projects has exploded: the website SourceForge.net, which provides free services to open source software developers, has grown from a handful of projects in 2000 to well over two hundred thousand open source projects today.[5] Many of the projects seem to have room to expand: for instance, the operating system Linux has opportunities in the market for desktop operating systems; in 2009, only one percent of the Web queries tracked by Net Applications came from machines running Linux, although that share was gradually rising.[6] More generally, the economic downturn appears to have accelerated corporate interest in and adoption of open source solutions: for instance, IDC recently revised its projected growth in revenue from open source products through 2013 upward, to an annual rate of 22.4 percent.[7]

The growth of open source software is attracting considerable attention from the public sector as well. Government commissions and agencies have proposed—and in some cases implemented—a variety of measures to encourage open source developers, including R&D support, encouragement for open source adoption, explicit preferences in government procurement, and even mandates regarding software

---

3. http://www.microsoft.com/presspass/exec/craig/05-03sharedSource.mspx (accessed August 23, 2009).

4. http://www.microsoft.com/presspass/features/2009/Jul09/07-20LinuxQA.mspx?rss _fdn=Toppercent20Stories (accessed August 23, 2009). It should be noted that Microsoft's motivations for this step were hotly questioned and debated (e.g., http://blog.seattlepi .com/microsoft/archives/174828.asp; accessed August 23, 2009).

5. http://sourceforge.net/apps/trac/sourceforge/wiki/Whatpercent20ispercent20Source Forge.net? (accessed August 25, 2009).

6. http://marketshare.hitslink.com/report.aspx?qprid=8 (accessed August 23, 2009).

7. http://finance.yahoo.com/news/Open-Source-Software-Market-bw-400190557.html?x =0&.v=1 (accessed August 23, 2009).

choices. In 2008 the Center for Strategic and International Studies identified 275 open source public policy initiatives, 182 of which have been favorably enacted.[8] For instance, since 2003, Singapore has offered tax breaks to companies using GNU/Linux operating systems rather than proprietary ones in order to encourage the development of the local software sector. Many European governments have enacted policies to encourage the use and purchase of open source software for government use. Governments have even mandated the development of localized open source projects, as has occurred in China. But while the efforts are concentrated in Europe and Asia, the interest in open source is truly global.

Brazil, Mexico, and South Africa are just a handful of developing nations that have launched significant open source initiatives. In part the appeal of these programs is that they are typically available for free, or at a much lower direct cost than comparable proprietary products. But these nations also argue that a wide variety of economic development benefits can follow from the development of a vibrant open source community, including the development of local industries, an improved foreign trade balance, and a reduction in intellectual property piracy.

Policy discussions around open source, though, have frequently been characterized by more heat than light. While the question at the heart of the debate—what is the impact of open source on consumers, firms, and economic growth more generally—is an economic one, the discussion is frequently framed in nearly theological tones. Advocates of open source passionately assert its benefits, while critics denigrate its role. Missing from the debate has been rigorous economic analysis and systematic microeconomic evidence, which might help sort out these competing claims.

This paucity of rigorous analysis in part reflects the strong emotions that the subject engenders. But it also reflects the difficulty of conclusively answering these questions empirically. Open source software usage is difficult to track, and the economic impacts of software utilization hard to trace definitively. Moreover there is always the chicken-and-egg problem: Did the use of a certain type of software promote the growth of a software industry in a given country, or did the rapid growth of a nation lead to it turning to a given set of software?

---

8. http://csis.org/files/media/csis/pubs/0807218_government_opensource_policies.pdf (accessed August 23, 2009). All citations to these programs are provided in chapter 6.

About This Book

This book seeks to address these challenging issues. Building on a series of analyses, we hope to improve our understanding of how open source and proprietary software interact and the policy issues that this raises. In particular, we try to provide an economic perspective on a debate that has been largely conducted on other terms, and a new large-scale database that can support more informed discussion.

The prior paragraph, of course, suggests a question: Why should economists have anything to say about software at all? It is true that we have spent many a happy hour programming regressions in Stata and trying to make tables come out just right in LaTeX. But we certainly do not pretend to be expert programmers, nor have we ever organized an open source project or corporate software initiative.

Rather, the answer to this question lies elsewhere. The question might well be reasonable if the book's focus was on the nature of open source and/or proprietary programs. But our focus in this book is different. In particular, we will be concentrating on understanding the broader impact of open source software. And once we move beyond the programs themselves, and to how they interact with the rest of the world, an economic perspective can be indispensable. Among the questions we will examine are these four:

• How does software differ from other technologies when it comes to promoting economic development?

• What are the motivations that drive individuals and firms to contribute to open source projects?

• How do firms using and developing software view the trade-offs between proprietary and open source projects?

• What policies can governments adapt to ensure that open source effectively competes with proprietary software and contributes to economic growth, and which steps run the danger of backfiring?

It is our belief that in each of these arenas, an economic perspective adds essential value in shedding light on these questions.

In particular, we highlight several crucial insights that the application of an economic framework to the world of open source suggests:

• Traditional economic frameworks that prescribe that the market will solve the optimal allocation of activity do not apply very well to the software industry.

• Open source and proprietary software share many common elements, as well as differences, that economic analyses can illustrate.

• Based on studies completed to date, it is hard to draw unambiguous conclusions as to the superiority of open source versus proprietary software.

• There is not a strong foundation for the claim that the government should favor open source or proprietary software when purchasing for its own purposes.

• While governments in developing countries may have strong rationales for encouraging the development of a software industry in general, the desirability of encouraging open source is more circumscribed, and economic analysis help identify the conditions under which such support may be justified.

Ultimately, it is our hope that this book stimulates more conversations between the open source and economics communities. Each side, it seems, has much that can be learned from the other. Despite (perhaps because of) the extensive research that we have undertaken in this area, we are keenly aware of the limitations that economists have faced when studying the open source realm and the way in which a keener understanding of the technical and social aspects of open source communities could be valuable. At the same time we strongly believe, and hope to have shown in this book, that many of the conceptual and methodological tools in the economics "tool kit" can be valuable additions to many in the programming community interested in more rigorous, systematic studies of this important sector of the economy.

A Road Map to the Book

To give a sense of where we are going with the book, we will provide a brief overview of chapters 2 through 7.

An Initial Look at Software and Growth
The second chapter has an ambitious mandate. To help set the stage for an understanding of open source software, we begin by explaining why software is important from an economic perspective.

Traditionally economists studying economic growth focused on how physical capital accumulates over time. As the economy grows and people take some of their earnings and invest it in extra machines and facilities, there is greater output and hence economic growth. Later theories applied a similar principle to the accumulation of "human capital," where savings are used to accumulate more knowledge: some of labor time is used not directly for production but for schooling and training.

In recent years, however, there has been a dramatic change in the economists' perspective, growing out of the realization that we had "Hamlet without the prince." The "new growth theory" puts technological innovation at the center of the growth process: the ways that inputs (e.g., people and machines) are translated into outputs, both products and services. The special thing about an innovation is that it can be shared: everyone can use it at the same time (whereas a worker or a machine cannot be everywhere at once). Unlike a physical piece of equipment, the use of a recipe for a better mosquito repellant in one country or by one individual does not hinder its use in other countries or by other individuals. Economists call this the nonrivalry property of information. But one must also ensure that individuals and firms have incentives to invent better recipes. They might not have incentives to do so if the new knowledge they generate is immediately and freely made available to everyone who wants to use it.

Where does computer software, and open source software in particular, fit within this framework of growth theory? In many respects it is like other technologies: it allows people to produce more with the same amount of materials. Indeed software's reach extends far beyond the software industry. Much of the innovation in software sprang from firms in other industries that have embodied software into products and processes.

The same conundrum described in the new growth theory is present in traditional proprietary software. On the one hand, since a software program, once developed, can be distributed very cheaply via the Internet, it is socially wasteful for some firms and countries to use inferior software. And indeed software use (at least as evidenced by available evidence on diffusion of Internet and computers) and software production (measured using software patenting in the United States and by open source contributions) both vary with the level of development: many national information technology industries appear stuck at a lower level of development (these disparities appear to be much greater on the production side). On the other hand, as before, we need to worry about the incentives to develop better software.

Where does open source software fit within this framework? If the open source model of software development could deliver state-of-the-art and easy-to-use products for all applications, it would solve the conundrum of the new growth theory as it applies to software. On the one hand, it would make the best recipes available everywhere at essentially zero cost, hence taking full advantage of the nonrivalry property. On the other hand, the incentive problem would be solved by the fact that programmers (either as individuals or as firms) contribute voluntarily to the software development. This analysis suggests why open source is potentially so revolutionary, and the critical importance in understanding its economic development impact.

Lessons from History

To understand open source software, it is useful to understand where it has come from. In chapter 3 we explore the origins and evolution of this sector. We highlight how there have been three distinct eras of open source development:

• During the 1960s and 1970s many of the key features of computer operating systems and the Internet were developed in academic settings such as Berkeley and MIT, as well as in central corporate research facilities where researchers had a great deal of autonomy, such as Bell Labs and Xerox's Palo Alto Research Center. The sharing by programmers in different organizations of the source code for computer operating systems and for widely used transmission protocols was commonplace. These cooperative software development projects were undertaken on a highly informal basis.

• In response to the threats of litigation engendered by this lack of clear rules, efforts to formalize the ground rules behind the cooperative software development process emerged. These efforts ushered in the second era. The critical institution during this period was the Free Software Foundation, begun by Richard Stallman of the MIT Artificial Intelligence Laboratory in 1983. The foundation sought to develop and disseminate a wide variety of software at no cost. The Free Software Foundation introduced a formal licensing procedure, called a General Public License, for a computer operating system called GNU. This procedure ensured that all derivatives of the program would also be disseminated at low or no cost.

• The widespread diffusion of Internet access in the early 1990s led to the third era that saw a dramatic acceleration of open source activity. Because it became easier for developers at very distant physical locations to collaborate on the development of projects at low cost, the volume of contributions and diversity of contributors expanded sharply, and numerous new open source projects emerged. Other innovations in recent years have been the proliferation of alternative approaches to licensing cooperatively developed software and (not unrelatedly) the emergence of corporate contributors.

The history of open source software detailed in this chapter also anticipates many of the themes that will emerge later in the book. In particular, as we review the institutional features during and research insights about the evolution of open source, five critical themes have emerged. These are:

• The pace of change in the open source community. The industry today is very different from that even a few years ago, whether we examine the number and mixture, the actors involved, and the processes followed within the groups.

• The way in which the seemingly esoteric issues of open source licenses, with their detailed delineation of rights and responsibilities of the key parties, profoundly affect the nature of these projects.

• The increasingly important role of corporations and corporate contributors. While press accounts frequently highlight the image of open source programs being driven by graduate students and moonlighting computer administrators, for-profit firms have played an important and growing role in open source development. Frequently these activities are done alongside the development of proprietary software.

• The extent to which users of open source programs are concerned about the costs of moving across programs and from one version of a program to another. These worries often are important drivers of users' willingness to adopt open source programs.

• The increasingly important role of the public sector in influencing both the development and adoption of open source software, whether through subsidies, procurement decisions, or other means.

Who Develops Open Source Software?
In chapter 4 we return to the hypothesis we highlighted in the second chapter: that the great appeal, and potential importance, of open source lies in the fact that it might represent a solution to *the* fundamental challenge to promoting innovation. In particular, open source software might be able to solve the tension between the need to provide firms and individuals with the incentive to innovate and the desirability of encouraging widespread use of cutting-edge technologies.

By making the software available to anyone at essentially zero cost, open source projects ensure that cutting-edge projects will be widely diffused. And the incentive problem may not be there, as the voluntary contributors are rewarded in other ways. On top of that, spillovers of knowledge would be enhanced by the fact that the source code is available for many to build upon.

We examine this hypothesis in this chapter by looking closely at the development and marketing of software by firms. This investigation is made possible by the new and unique survey of software companies we conducted, covering nearly two thousand firms in fifteen countries.

Three key insights are highlighted in the chapter. Most surprisingly, firms extensively blend the development of open source and proprietary product, rather than specializing in one or the other. It is commonplace to see the same firm developing both open source and proprietary programs, or else making the same program available under both a traditional proprietary and open source licenses. We observe this comingling of open source and proprietary software development by firms in all of the countries we survey. In all likelihood this mixing by software firms suggests that there are substantial cost synergies, whether in product development or marketing, between open source and proprietary software.

Software companies diversify between open source and proprietary software in other dimensions as well. For instance, companies will frequently combine support services with product development: clearly, the insights from product development can translate into its installation. We find that larger firms are far more likely diversify along these lines than smaller ones, presumably because they can exploit cost synergies more readily without sacrificing economies of scale.

While as the two previous points suggest, open source and proprietary software are similar in many respects and are extensively comingled, they differ substantially when it comes to exports. While software firms of all kinds are likely to export products, firms that concentrate on the development of proprietary software are both more likely to export and are more intensive exporters than their open source-focused peers. This pattern may well change over time, but for now appears to be quite robust.

This empirical evidence suggests that the initial hypothesis formulated in chapter 2 was too optimistic. The same fundamental tension that is at the heart of innovation policy—how to encourage the development of new knowledge without sacrificing the social gains that can occur from the widespread diffusion of cutting-edge technologies —also characterizes the software industry. And given the extensive similarity between, and cohabitation of, open source and proprietary software, these challenges are likely to apply to open source as well as proprietary software. Sad to say, open source software offers no free lunch, no easy way to solve the innovation paradox.

Who Uses Open Source Software?

We then turn in chapter 5 to understanding who uses open source software and how they make the decision between open code and proprietary software. Once again, we undertake a unique survey, covering more than two thousand users in fifteen countries. The data provides many new insights into the structure of demand for software, and in particular how it relates to a number of user characteristics and to their perceptions of the various costs involved in adopting software.

The analysis suggests four main insights:

• Open source and proprietary software present users with differing costs. Not surprisingly, proprietary software presents users with a considerably higher upfront cost. However, the other costs associated with adopting any piece of software—the costs of switching (learning), interoperability (compatibility of different programs), and support services—are greater for users of open source software. These patterns are observed across a wide variety of countries, from the most to the least developed.

• Software users vary substantially. This variation is seen not just in the users' software needs, but also in how they evaluate costs. As a result of these different preferences and requirements, two users could make very different choices between open source and proprietary software.

• Mixing is commonplace. Across countries and all types of users, open source and proprietary software are frequently comingled. Mixing is more frequently practiced in settings where economic principles would suggest it should be, such as the greater prevalence among cost-constrained (small) firms.

Thus in many respects the insights regarding the survey of users and developers are quite complementary. Despite the substantial differences between the two families of software, open source and proprietary code do not live in two totally different worlds. Rather, there are extensive interactions. The same firms that market proprietary code are also likely to contribute to or sell open source code as product. Users are likely to be employing both open and proprietary software. Our detailed survey data on software development and usage have allowed us to document the extensive cohabitation between the open source and proprietary software worlds.

The Policy Challenge

As the discussion of the two prior chapters suggest, policy makers face a substantial challenge when it comes to setting policies for encouraging software development and diffusion. On the one hand, software has the potential to impact economic growth in a positive and substantial manner. And open source has properties that are likely to be particularly attractive, as we have discussed.

But as our survey has highlighted, many software developer firms sell proprietary software while contributing to open source development, and software users extensively mix and match the two types of software. The problem is not an either/or one —to choose between one form of software and the other—but rather to develop a policy framework that ensures that developers and users mix in an efficient manner, and one that contributes to innovation in both forms of software. How can a government develop a framework that facilitates the competitive interactions between open source and proprietary software in a manner that boosts efficiency and innovation?

In the sixth chapter we turn to the question of how public policy can address this question. We use economic reasoning to evaluate the key arguments for why the government should support open source software. We complement this analysis with our data from the fifteen-nation survey, which provides evidence on what kinds of regulatory and incentives schemes are available to users and developers.

We argue that government's role in procurement is fundamentally different from a corporate buyer. Because of the relative size and visibility of government purchases in many economies, the public sector can play a leadership role with its purchases that many others may not. Moreover the government must consider what is good for the economy as a whole (what economists call social welfare), rather than simply minimizing its own costs. These observations do not mean that the government should in every case design its procurement policies to play a leadership role: the proper decision depends very much on the

specific context, and we identify leading cases where this may be warranted. When such a role is not needed, the purchasing decision should
be based on an evaluation of the total cost of ownership, similar to that
which a corporate buyer would make.

When it comes to regulation, we argue that governments should encourage vigorous competition between open and proprietary software.
This does not mean, it should be noted, a hands off, or *laissez faire*,
approach. Rather, it means, first and foremost, taking the necessary
steps to ensure that commercial firms do not abuse the networks they
may have developed to disadvantage open source. Encouraging truly
open standards, to allow the most competition possible between forms
of software, is also important. Yet ensuring that private firms have real
economic incentives to innovate is also critical. This conclusion is borne
out in our survey of users and developers, which found a strongly
voiced preference for a regulatory regime that allows them complete
freedom to choose between open source and proprietary software,
rather than one that either requires or favors one or the other.

Regarding the plethora of other policies relating to encouraging
software development, whether open source or proprietary, clear
economic prescriptions are few and far between. The strongest case
can be built for the government playing a lead role in providing information to consumers about the features of different types of software, as well as demonstration projects of various types. While one
cannot make definitive statements on the basis of existing economic
analysis, the case for direct subsidies for open source appears to be
weaker.

There are, of course, many other policy choices that will need to be
addressed when shaping an information technology policy. Governments need to decide whether to finance local information technology
firms (or their financiers), whether to subsidize users of advanced technologies, how much to invest in education of information technology
professionals, and how to design an intellectual property regime that
is appropriate for software, which does not fit neatly into traditional
categories. Especially in developing countries, governments need to do
all this with limited human and financial resources. On all these issues,
much more research is needed to assist decision makers with the difficult choices they have to make. We hope that some of the energy that
has, in recent years, been directed at the rather polarized debate between open source and proprietary software will be redirected more
constructively toward these issues.

Lessons

We end in chapter 7 with a series of recommendations for the various key audiences, drawn from the discussions and analyses in the book. For government officials, we emphasize four lessons:

1. The danger of making choices: given the trade-offs between different technologies, and the frequent miscues that public efforts to "pick winners" have encountered, it is far better to let competition take its course than mandate a solution.

2. The many reasons for encouraging competition between open and proprietary software: as we highlight throughout the book, there are many trade-offs that mean that different users in different situations could come to diametrically opposed answers when choosing between software types. Recommending that governments should encourage competition, however, is not the same thing as arguing that they should not be involved in regulating the software industry.

3. The need for a different calculus when governments make decisions about software procurement as opposed to private entities: when funding the development of software, whether for their own use or as a more general R&D effort, government officials should use similar criteria as corporate users—but also take into account the likely benefits to society of adopting a leadership position.

4. Shared standards—technologies that facilitate communication with and from the users of public services, as well as with their suppliers— are essential, and they can be implemented both in proprietary and open source software.

We also highlight six implications for corporate managers:

1. There is no "right" answer in the choice between open source and proprietary software: different firms will make different choices, reflecting their circumstances.

2. Think carefully when making this choice: the "received wisdom" regarding the costs and benefits to corporations can be misleading here.

3. The appropriate mixture between open and proprietary software will vary with the firms' circumstances: for instance, firm size and market segment can lead to very different choices.

4. The local circumstances also matter: the choice between open and proprietary software will vary with the stage of development of the nation in which the firm is based.

5. Consumers have very different needs when it comes to software products: this suggests the desirability of offering both proprietary and open products.

6. Mixing between both classes of software, both among users and developers: mixing is the general rule across many different classes of firms operating in a wide variety of nations.

Finally, we end with a few suggestions for the research community, in the hopes of encouraging more work which combines economic frameworks with an understanding of the open source phenomenon:

1. Beware of simply "transporting" economic frameworks from elsewhere into the software arena, particularly when it comes to open source.

2. Much more research is needed to assist policy makers with the difficult choices they have to make with promoting the development of information technology sector, and open source in particular.

3. Researchers into the open source phenomenon must focus more on the dynamics of choices within software-producing and using firms— too much of the focus has been on the individual developer, rather than the complex setting in which firms operate.

4. The experience with "technology sharing" that the open source and proprietary software industries have grappled with over the past few decades has important implications for other industries.

It is our hope that the analysis in our book will have accomplished two things. First, we have tried to show the power of intellectual cross-fertilization—the way that economic ideas can be useful in shedding light on these important technological questions. Second, we have tried to be candid in highlighting how much we *do not know* about economic development and open source, and the substantial opportunities that await researchers who will explore these issues in the years to come.

2 Software and Growth

For the last twenty years information technologies in general, and software in particular, have played an important role in the growth of modern economies as a source of innovation. The choice of policies that affect the software industry—of which open source is a critical component—must consider the sector's consequences both for innovation and growth.

In this chapter we survey briefly the ways in which innovation is fostered in software, and its consequences for growth. This is, to be sure, a large topic but an important one that sets the stage for the material specifically on open source software that follows.

While we will discuss many papers that look at a variety of topics, of necessity two conclusions stand out most sharply:

1. Software is widely embedded in manufacturing (and nonmanufacturing) industries, both as a process and product. Rather than being isolated in an industry of its own, it is used by—and impacts—a wide variety of sectors.

2. Software use and software production both vary with the level of development across nations, but this link appears much stronger for the production side. This may reflect the more specialized skills associated with being at the frontier in the development of new software code.

Defining Software

Over the past decade economists have increasingly recognized that the economic laws governing software are somewhat different from those for the economy as a whole. This section will quickly review the key reasons why.

It may be helpful to begin with a few definitions. Wikepedia[1] defines software as follows: "Computer software (or simply software) refers to one or more computer programs and data held in the storage of a computer for some purpose. Program software performs the function of the program it implements, either by directly providing instructions to the computer hardware or by serving as input to another piece of software."

From the viewpoint of computer scientists, software can be divided into two big classes: system software and application software. All other subclasses belong to these two classes. System software helps run the computer hardware and computer system. It includes operating systems, device drivers, programming tools, servers, windowing systems, utilities, and more. Application software allows a user to accomplish one or more specific tasks. Typical applications include office suites, business software, educational software, databases, and computer games. These distinctions focus on software as it is delivered to the user, and forget an important class, "user-written software ... [which] tailors systems to meet the users' specific needs. User software includes spreadsheet templates, word processor macros, scientific simulations, graphics, and animation scripts. Even email filters are a kind of user software. Users create this software themselves and often overlook how important it is."[2]

These definitions are mostly applicable to software designed to work on general purpose computers, as opposed to embedded systems, which are "special purpose computer system[s], which [are] completely encapsulated by the device [they] control." Embedded systems are extremely important and are integrated in much of modern machinery from cars to machine tools, but in the discussion that follows we will focus on software designed for general purpose computers, although much of our discussion should carry over.

One thing is clear about the production of software: it is not just done by software firms. For instance, a tabulation by Bessen and Hunt

---

1. http://en.wikipedia.org/wiki/Software (accessed April 10, 2009). Wikipedia is a "free content" encyclopaedia. Free content is the equivalent of open source for functional work, art work or any other type of creative content.

2. According to the US Census Bureau (http://www.census.gov/prod/ec02/ec0251i06 .pdf) in 2002, US software publishers had sales of $40 billion for "system software" and $47 billion for application software. The rest of their revenues were mainly composed of consulting services, custom development and support services (for a total of $13 billion). Chapter 4 (on the supply of software) provides more detailed micro-level survey evidence on the mix of software activities across countries.

looked at who made software patent filings, using keywords to identify these patents. They found that of the software patent applications filed between 1994 and 1997, which had issued by 1999, traditional software publishers (e.g., Adobe or Microsoft) accounted for only 5 percent of the awards. Even when one added in firms that primarily undertook software consulting and IBM (which is often classified as a computer hardware firm), software firms only accounted for 13 percent of the software patents. Much of the patenting was taking place elsewhere, particularly within manufacturing firms that used software in some manner. In short, software innovation was everywhere, and today it is taking place in a variety in products and processes in a wide variety of industries.[3]

To this functional classification of software, one can add a classification according to usage (which we will refer to later in the book as the "demand side"):

• Software can do tasks for one individual (or group of individuals) using the computer. A word processor, for instance, provides tools to write; a scientific computation program helps the user solve a research problem. Traditionally the software was resident on the user's computer; in recent years software based on the Internet (e.g., Google Apps) have become commonplace.

• Software can also transform the computer into a communication tool, from email to accessing the web to collaboration software. Of course, most software programs have both features. For instance, a word processor can be primarily used as a writing tool but must also produce files that can be read by other computers or can be the basis for collaboration between different persons working on the same document.

Like all engineering, software engineering—the creation of software —involves many tasks. First, a customer need that can be solved by a program must be identified. After planning the program and selecting the tools, the source code of the program is written in a programming language. The source code is a human-readable description of the instructions given to the computer. This source code is then translated into a machine-readable "executable" code, which, for all practical purposes, cannot be read by human beings. This translation is conducted

---

3. Of course, there have been some very dubious patent awards issued in the software field. But even if we were able to somehow narrow the analysis to "important" patents, it is likely that the same pattern would hold.

by computer programs called compilers. The program must be tested, documentation must be written, and it must be delivered to the users for whom it is intended.

Although the preceding description is very linear, in practice the development of a computer program cycles through the different stages. For instance, a preliminary idea will give rise to a "quick and dirty" preliminary implementation, which will be tested by some potential users before being rewritten and polished. This process continues through the successive versions of the software.

Teams are responsible for the production of large programs. Some of their members are responsible for writing the code, whereas others will test it, manage the interaction with potential clients, or work on the compilation of the program. As we will see, all types of software require these different tasks, but the difference in the mode of licensing allows some open source projects to organize their teams or contributions in ways that are different from the ways in which teams of contributors to proprietary software are organized.

Computer programs do not function alone, but communicate with each other. The behavior of programs is often modified by other programs. For instance, word processors such as Microsoft Word or OOo Writer[4] can be used "straight out of the box," but they have also been designed so that other functionalities can be added through APIs, defined by Wikipedia as: "An application programming interface (API) is a set of definitions of the ways one piece of computer software communicates with another."[5] These functionalities can be added by an end user, by the support services in the organization where she is working, custom designed by outside firms, or purchased as added software. For sophisticated users, in particular large firms and government agencies, the ease with which diverse functionalities can be implemented (which is dependent on the quality of the APIs) is an important element of choice, and designers of new programs need to make sure that these added functionalities can be easily implemented.

Some Economics of Software

The characteristics of software as a product, and the way in which it is developed, give the economics of the software industry certain features

---

4. OOo Writer is the Word Processor of Open Office, the leading open source office suite.
5. http://en.wikipedia.org/wiki/API (accessed April 20, 2009).

that influence our analysis. We summarize them in this section. Many of these features are shared with other information technologies.[6]

Many analysts and policy makers, in particular competition authorities, have been worried that large fixed costs and the presence of network externalities make the software industry susceptible to "tipping," where one firm captures most of the market.

As is common in information industries, the production of software involves a large "fixed" cost that is independent of the number of users, as writing a program is expensive. But subsequent distribution to consumers is cheap. This implies that direct competition between two similar programs will generally be unstable: each of the two sellers would find it profitable to sell at lower than average cost in order to attract more customers, but this would imply that they would be unable to earn reasonable profits.

This "all or nothing" aspect is compounded by the presence of network externalities: a user will generally prefer to use software already used by many other users. This is true for a number of reasons: support and technical help are easier to find, complementary software is more accessible, and so on. The modern literature has stressed the fact that these benefits often are even more complex. One description is that there are "double-sided externalities": a user of the good prefers to use a product for which there are many other users, including those whose needs are somewhat different. For instance, a firm will choose an operating system in part because of the presence of a large number of developers who write for this platform, and a developer will choose to develop for an operating system because there are many users of this operating system, and hence many potential clients for his products.

In the software industry as a whole, network externalities also exist between users of different programs when these programs are used as communication tools. For instance, there are network externalities between users of different email clients because they can communicate with each other. There are network externalities between firms who use programs compatible with the XML standard, as they can more easily build applications that enable them to exchange data. This implies that the use of the standard becomes more valuable when there are more other users. It is also worth noting that there are indirect externalities between software developers who work on the same

---

6. For a general and accessible discussion of the economics of information technologies, see Carl Shapiro and Hal Varian (1998). For an academic discussion of the use of Linux in the public sector, see Shapiro and Varian (2004).

platform. For instance, if a "killer application" is developed for an operating system, the number of users will increase and the sales of other programs written for this platform will also increase.

Although both large fixed costs and network externalities would seem to make software markets prone to concentration, there are forces that favor competition. Modern software provides a combination of many different functionalities. For instance, a program such as Lotus Notes defines itself as providing an integration[7] of "email, calendars, journals, to do lists, directories, and other applications," "Integrated Lotus Instant Messaging functionality," "follow-up function, quick rules, and visual indicators to show users when they've forwarded or replied to email messages," and "industry-leading calendaring and scheduling." By providing different mixes or "bundles" of functionalities, firms can distinguish their products from others, and if the requirements of potential purchasers are sufficiently diverse, they will be able to serve different portions of the market and reduce the intensity of post-entry competition. For a given number of firms this increases the profits of firms. In turn this increase in profits will induce more firms to invest the costs of developing new variants of programs and will increase competition at the design stage.

Not only do consumers attach different relative values to different features and favor different bundles, they also are willing to pay different amounts for these features and for different quality. This is why software companies often propose different versions of the same program at different prices. For instance, in April 2009, Adobe was selling Adobe Acrobat Pro for $449 and Adobe Acrobat standard for $299. Sometimes it is different programs from different companies that occupy these distinct "niches" in the market. For instance, in statistical software SAS[8] is recognized superior in its capacity to handle large data sets, but is somewhat user unfriendly, whereas Stata[9] has a more user-friendly interface but is more limited when data sets become very large. Neither can be said to be better than the other in an absolute sense, and even if the price were exactly the same, different users would make different choices between the two of them. These features also are crucial in explaining why users mix software types and software firms differ in their business focus (type of software niche), an issue we will revisit when we turn to the survey results.

---

7. All the citations that follow in this paragraph are from http://www.lotus.com/lotus/offering1.nsf/wdocs/ibmlotusnotesvsmicrosoftoutlook (accessed April 1, 2009).
8. www.sas.com (accessed April 23, 2009).
9. www.stata.com (accessed April 23, 2009).

The software industry is also characterized by important switching costs. These take two forms. First, there are physical limitations. For instance, much of the user software developed for one application might not be transferable to other programs. These switching costs are even larger when different pieces of software are complementary and need to be changed simultaneously. Second, there are the soft costs associated with human learning: users can find it both difficult and costly to change the program they are using for a specific task because the cost of learning might be quite high. The way in which the program is designed can strongly affect both interoperability of hardware and software, and switching costs on the part of users (learning). Our survey, which we will discuss in subsequent chapters, provides lots of information about how users see the importance of these costs.

The presence of switching costs and network externalities create the danger of "lock-in," where consumers are reluctant to switch to a new software program. Suppliers can, at least in the short run, exploit this reluctance through higher prices. At the same time competitors will also realize that customers will be locked in if they adopt the competitor's own program, and hence these firms have strong incentives to displace the incumbent firm. This will put competitive pressure on the incumbent firm, which will not be able to take advantage "excessively" of its position. There will be "competition for the market," which will limit the advantages held by the incumbent firm.

This intuition is captured in a formal model by Chen, Doraszelski, and Harrington (2009). These authors show that in a simple setting, where two firms have roughly the same size market shares, they choose to make their products compatible. Even if one firm gains advantage and tries to dominate the market with a proprietary standard, the smaller firm may adjust its prices and product features to retain compatibility. Thus, even in a market with strong network effects, it need not be the case that one firm emerges as the dominant one.

Of course, all of these elements are affected by the fact that programs or parts of programs are easily copied, and the problems of the use and protection of intellectual property have been central to the development of the software industry. This is a vast, complicated, and controversial topic that we will discuss some aspects of later in this book.

Information Technology, Productivity, and Growth

Before turning to the specific question of how software affects innovation, and the consequences for the economy, we should look at the implications of the adoption of information technology in general. This area has attracted numerous studies by leading researchers, so of necessity we need to provide only a high-level summary.

For much of the past three decades, the relationship between information technology and productivity seemed paradoxical. US spending on information technology boomed during the 1970s, 1980s, and early 1990s, yet the economy seemed stuck in a pattern of low productivity growth. "You can see the computer age everywhere but in the productivity statistics," joked Robert Solow (1987, p. 36). But after 1995 the rate of productivity growth surged, averaging 2.8 percent from 1996 to 2000. This was widely attributed to the impact of information technology spending. But this view came into question again when the rate of productivity growth slowed after 2004, even as spending on information technology remained strong.

Economists have sought to understand the relationship between information technology spending and productivity in several ways. The first has been more "macro," economy-wide studies, which try to decompose the sources of productivity growth. Many of these decomposition analyses—perhaps the most influential of which was by Jorgenson and Stiroh (2000)—showed that the accumulated information technology spending seems to be associated with an accelerating growth rate. Not only has the investment in information technology boomed, but these technologies have become far more efficient: there has been rapid technological progress in the many computer-related sectors, as exemplified by Moore's law; that is, the proposition the number of transistors that can be placed inexpensively on an integrated circuit doubles approximately every two years, with the associated increase in quality and fall in price.

These authors have argued that information technology has indeed had a major impact on overall productivity economy-wide. These changes were not immediate—firms needed to invest in many skills before they could take advantage of the new technologies. Nor were the effects constant: the huge boom–bust cycle associated with the late 1990s boom in ".com" and telecommunications introduced many disruptions. But overall, the picture from the literature is a positive one. It is not so much that information technology is fundamentally different from other forms of innovation in spurring growth, these authors suggest: the primary difference is that the rate of progress in computer-related technologies has been so fast that it has had a huge economic impact. (Jorgenson, Ho, and Stiroh 2008.)

Other academics have taken a different tack, and instead sought to undertake micro-level analyses of how information technology affects individual firms and industries. Authors have taken different approaches to this question:

• Bartel, Ichniowski, and Shaw (2007) study the effects of new information technology on manufacturing by examining plants with a common production technology in a narrowly defined industry—valve manufacturing. Using detailed survey data, they look at the impact of the adoption of new technology, such as computerized machine tools, on product innovation, production process improvements, employee skills, and work organization. They show that the change was far more than a shift from one type of manufacturing technology to another: the falling cost of information technologies produced productivity gains, especially faster machine setup times, which favored the production of customized products instead of commodities.

• Bresnahan, Brynjolfsson, and Hitt (2002) look across a variety of industries at how labor practices and firm organization vary with information technology use. Their analysis suggests there is a relationship between computer-related spending and workforce skills. Information technology use is correlated with more decentralized decision-making and greater use of teams. Moreover those firms that have more trained personnel and more flexible organization structures are most likely to invest in information technology.

• Bloom and co-authors (2009) argue that the impact of information technology on organizational hierarchies is more complex. In particular, if the primary goal of management structures is to acquire and transmit knowledge and information, then information technologies can enable workers to acquire more knowledge and become empowered. If instead technologies replace workers' knowledge with directions from their managers, they can lead to centralization. The authors find that technologies such as CAD/CAM increase production workers' autonomy and control, while communication technologies such as data networks decrease them.

In short, there is today a compelling amount of information suggesting that information technology has transformed the economy in important ways. A natural follow-on question, given the focus of this book, is how much is attributable to software specifically? This is a challenging "chicken-or-egg" type question: without the hardware to run on, it is clear the software would not have had much of an impact, and vice versa! Nonetheless, we can make several observations about software, innovation and growth.

Software, Innovation, and Growth

The software industry has been extremely innovative over the last thirty years, and programmers have been required to adapt to a very fast-changing environment (to illustrate this point, it is sufficient to mention the seismic shift created by the development of the Internet). Despite these changes the development of software is cumulative, with products evolving over many generations. For instance, Linux has developed into its current version over nearly two decades, starting from a UNIX base through the Minix operating system. A program such as Microsoft Word has a twenty-five-year history. These developments are both internal to the programs, whose code is developed and in which new functionality is implemented, and external, as they can incorporate code from other sources or allow collaboration with new "add-on" programs.

To understand the concept of innovation better, it is useful to think of an economy as composed of two elements, a set of ingredients and a recipe by which these ingredients are combined to produce goods and services. The total value of these goods and services is the gross domestic product (or GDP), and the growth and innovation processes increase GDP as the economy acquires more ingredients and uses better recipes.

The ingredients, or inputs, are labor (number of workers), human capital (the skills of the workers, acquired through education or on the job), and physical capital (quantity and quality of buildings and machinery). A one percent increase in *all* the ingredients leads to a one percent increase in GDP (what economists call "constant returns to scale"). An example of physical capital would be personal computers, and figure 2.1 shows how the quantity of this ingredient varies with the development of countries. The recipe is the country's technology, that is, all the different techniques used to produce products and services. For a given set of ingredients, a better technology leads to higher GDP.

There is a fundamental difference between the recipe and the ingredients. The use of one of the ingredients by an economic agent prevents anyone else from using it. For instance, the use of a computer or an Internet connection by one firm implies that no other firm can use it.

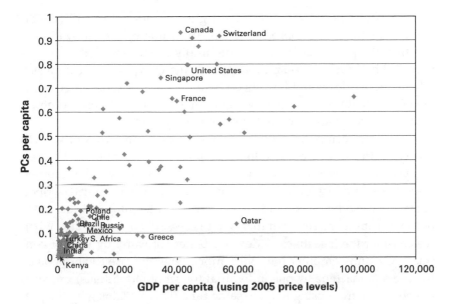

Figure 2.1
PCs per capita across the large set of countries in 2007 compared with GDP per capita

We express this in economic terminology by saying that the ingredients are rival goods, in the sense that there exists a fundamental rivalry between potential users. The recipe is very different: everyone can use it at the same time. Economists term this a nonrival good. The use of a new programming technique in one country or by one individual does not hinder its use in other countries or by other individuals.

Because the "recipe" is a nonrival good, once it is discovered, it is efficient to let anybody use it. On the other hand, one must also ensure that individuals and firms have incentives to engage in innovative activities. They will not have incentives to do so if the new knowledge they generate is immediately and freely made available to everyone who wants to use it. As economists have realized at least since Ken Arrow's seminal 1962 essay, "Economic Welfare and the Allocation of Resources for Invention," this implies that the free market will not result in an optimal outcome. Without the ability to protect ideas, small firms will have few incentives to produce new ideas. Even larger firms, which are in a better position to protect their ideas through secrecy, may be reluctant to invest in R&D.

Thus, in order to provide incentives for innovation, intellectual property rights are needed. These grant the innovator the right to charge for the use of the innovation. But these rights are not a "cure-all" either. Some potential users, those for whom the value of the innovation is less than the price that is charged or simply cannot afford the innovation, will be unable to use it even if, from the viewpoint of society as a whole, the world would have been better off if they did. Moreover, if we end up with many property rights that conflict with each other, a "patent thicket" may emerge that deters innovation.[10]

Where does computer software fit within this framework of growth theory? Better software is just like a better recipe in that it can be used everywhere at once. The cost of dissemination is tiny via the Internet. Thus the economics of software runs into the conundrum described above. Since software is nonrival, once it is written, it is a social waste not to distribute it freely, but this is not necessarily a good policy when we consider the incentives to develop better software. By way of contrast, PCs, and computer hardware more generally, are rival goods as the use of a machine by one individual (or set of individuals) prevents anybody else from using it at the same time. This explains why the policy issues associated with the hardware and software industries are different, although, of course, they influence each other. Note, however, that the *design* of computers is a "recipe," and raises the same type of policy issues that software raises.

For a long time economists stressed how the accumulation of physical capital over time led to growth: because the economy saves (i.e., consumes less than it produces), it can use some of its inputs to produce extra capital, which leads to a greater output. Later work applied a similar theory to the accumulation of human capital, where savings were used to accumulate more human capital: some of labor is used not directly for production, but for schooling and training. Human capital is also accumulated by participating in productive activities, through the process of "learning by doing."

Recently the "new growth theory" has integrated innovation activities into this framework. Arrow's insights about the dynamics of innovation and intellectual property have been subsequently incorporated into the literature on growth, most notably the works of Paul Romer and of Philippe Aghion and Peter Howitt. These authors have examined how the conflict described above between the need to encourage inventive activity and the need to encourage the use of innovations affects the way in which the "recipe" changes over time. They have

---

10. The impact of patent thickets has also attracted a substantial body of work, including Joseph Farrell and Carl Shapiro (e.g., their joint 2008 piece).

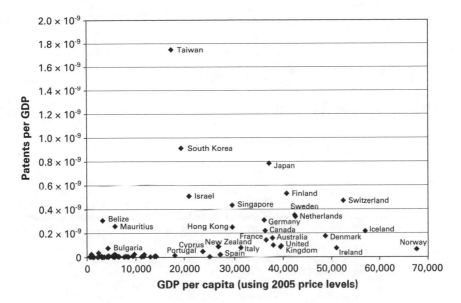

Figure 2.2
US patent awards compared with GDP per capita

also stressed the fact that the productivity of inventors is enhanced by "spillovers of knowledge" between them: the knowledge generated by one of them helps others discover new inventions. Because of these spillover effects, there is positive feedback, somewhat similar to network externalities, through which the inventive activity of one person facilitates innovations by others. This is consistent with the data presented in figures 2.2, 2.3, and 2.4, where one sees that inventive activity increases sharply when countries reach a certain level of wealth:

• In figure 2.2 the relationship between innovations, as measured by per capita US patent filings by those living in a given nation, and per capita gross domestic product is shown for 2008. It is clear that wealthier countries innovate more.

• Figure 2.3 depicts this relationship over time for the fifteen countries in the survey described below. While there has been some acceleration in patenting by emerging economies in recent years, the disparity remains substantial.

• Figure 2.4 shows that this relationship is not just confined to traditional manufacturing innovations. This figure presents the same relationship for patents involving computer software (which we define

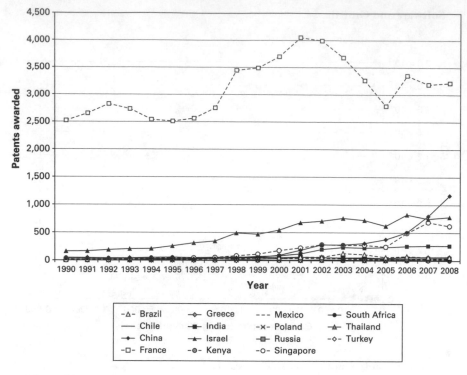

Figure 2.3
US patents over time for surveyed countries

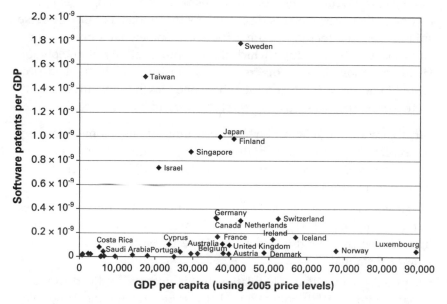

Figure 2.4
Software patents compared with GDP per capita for a large set of countries

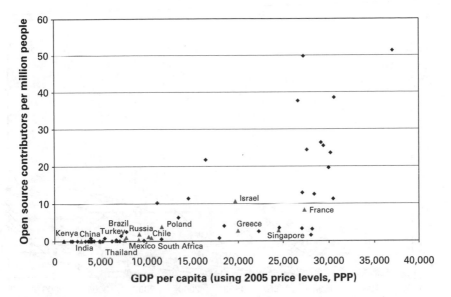

Figure 2.5
Contributions to open source software compared with GDP per capita across sixty countries (fifteen surveyed countries highlighted, and the United States dropped). Source: Lerner, Pathak, and Tirole (2005).

here as those awards assigned to patent classes 700 to 725), as in figure 2.2. Again, we see a strong relationship between GDP and patenting.

It might be thought that this was only a consequence of the nature of the patenting process. Filing for patents, particularly in foreign countries, can be a time-consuming and expensive process. The apparent lower innovativeness of less wealthy nations may be a consequence of these "transactions costs" rather than the fundamental innovativeness of the economy.

But, as figure 2.5 reveals, this relationship also holds for open source contributions, where these costs are not present. This figure looks at the contributions to open source software and the level of economic development across sixty countries. It shows that the relationship between contributions to open source software and the stage of economic development is similar to the relationship between inventive activity and development that was exhibited earlier in figure 2.2. It should be noted, however, that some middle-income countries, particularly in Eastern Europe, contribute a lot to open source development, while their innovative activity (measured by US patents) is modest. On the other hand, Asian countries contribute little to open source software.

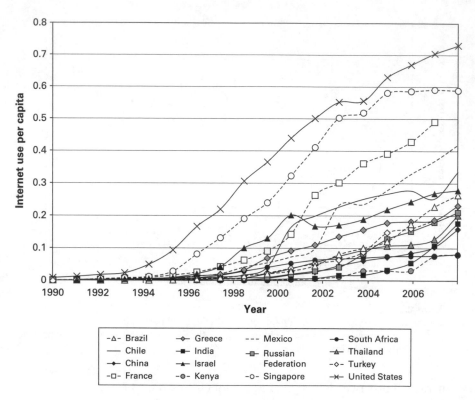

Figure 2.6
Internet use per capita, 1990 to 2007

The picture is somewhat different, however, when it comes to the diffusion of innovations. Often the differences across countries are far less dramatic when we compare the speed with which they adopt new ideas than when we compare the development of these ideas in the first place.

Of course, when a new innovation becomes available, it is not suddenly adopted by every agent in the economy for a number of reasons. First, at the beginning the new innovation will be expensive, and it may pay for buyers to wait. Second, knowledge is needed in order to make use of the technology (this is the spillover effect discussed above), and there are costs in adopting the invention (which are closely related to the switching costs discussed earlier). As a consequence new technologies spread progressively across the economies, as can be seen in figures 2.6 and 2.7. These figures also show that, as one would expect, poorer countries embrace new technologies (in these cases per-

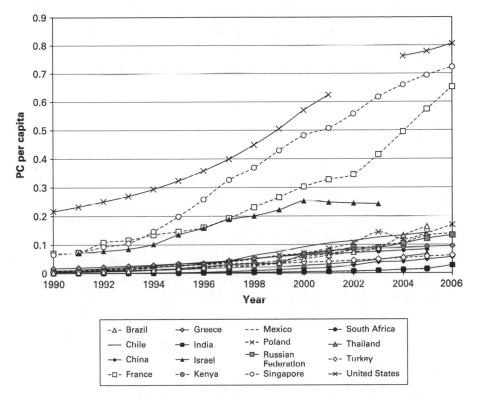

Figure 2.7
Personal computer use per capita, 1990 to 2006

sonal computers and the Internet, but many others exhibit a similar story) more slowly than richer countries.

At the same time these figures show that these technologies (and many others) are being adopted quite rapidly in a number of developing and emerging economies. For example, figure 2.6 reveals that Internet use in Mexico lags the United States by only a few years (whereas Mexico's GDP per capita has historically lagged the corresponding level in the United States by many decades). Even more extreme, the usage of cellular telephones in many developing countries far outstrips that of the United States.[11] The rapid adoption of some innovations in developing countries makes it important to think about the policies that they need to adopt with respect to these new technologies.

11. http://www.nationmaster.com/graph/med_tel_mob_cel_percap-telephones-mobile-cellular (accessed August 5, 2009).

Table 2.1
Open source and proprietary software usage across small set of countries (percent of respondents using)

	Only proprietary	Only open source
Aggregate	67.3	5.9
Country		
Brazil	51.0	12.9
Chile	73.5	1.9
China	79.2	6.9
France	66.0	8.8
Greece	72.3	0.0
India	62.7	2.5
Israel	79.6	3.2
Kenya	47.7	12.3
Mexico	65.4	8.3
Poland	67.5	6.4
Russia	46.1	12.8
South Africa	80.0	1.9
Singapore	87.7	1.9
Thailand	74.2	9.0
Turkey	56.1	0.0

The same patterns can be seen in the adoption of open source software. The survey of users, conducted as part of the research for this book and discussed in detail below, provides very useful data on the use of software by firms in the fifteen countries. We summarize some of the findings in this chapter, though we dig deeper into the survey in the chapters that follow. These findings enable us to evaluate the extent of use of different forms of software, and by implication to assess the relative strengths of the different types of software as reflected in market demand. More detailed information, as well as a description of the survey methodology, is available later in the book and in the online materials.

Table 2.1 shows the responses to the survey question, "Does the corporation or agency you work for use any of the following types of software?" in the fifteen countries in which the survey was conducted. A high percentage of respondents report using proprietary software, but there are strong variations across countries and these are not simply related to stage of economic development. In all countries very few respondents use only open source software; the highest percentages of

Table 2.2
Open source and proprietary software usage across small set of countries (percent of respondents)

	Embedding open source in high-tech manufac- turing	With open source embedded software out of all embedded software in following intervals			With revenues from embedded open source software in following intervals		
		<25	25–75	>75	<25	25–75	>75
Brazil	70.0	28.6	57.1	14.3	64.3	21.4	14.3
Chile	12.9	75.0	25.0	0.0	100.0	0.0	0.0
China	26.6	25.0	50.0	25.0	50.0	25.0	25.0
France	42.8	58.3	33.3	8.3	33.3	41.7	0.0
Greece	14.3	33.3	33.3	33.3	66.7	33.3	0.0
India	35.1	30.8	61.5	7.7	38.5	53.8	7.7
Israel	13.8	40.0	20.0	40.0	40.0	20.0	40.0
Kenya	60.7	0.0	91.2	8.3	8.3	83.3	8.3
Mexico	25.9	42.8	42.9	14.3	42.9	57.1	0.0
Poland	17.8	0.0	75.0	25.0	25.0	75.0	0.0
Russia	39.1	55.5	44.4	0.0	55.5	33.3	11.1
South Africa	6.9	0.0	100.0	0.0	0.0	100.0	0.0
Singapore	9.1	50.0	0.0	50.0	50.0	0.0	50.0
Thailand	45.9	5.8	88.2	5.8	0.0	94.1	5.9
Turkey	16.6	100.0	0.0	0.0	100.0	0.0	0.0

firms using only open source software are found in Brazil (12.9 percent), Kenya (12.3 percent), and Russia (12.8 percent). In addition, open source software is widely used in conjunction with proprietary software in Brazil, India, and Turkey.

Another tabulation, which suggests a similar conclusion, looks at the utilization of open source software in products. As we have mentioned, open source software is frequently embedded in products such as personal digital assistants, smart phones, and cars. The proportion of firms embedding open source software in high-tech manufacturing products varies widely across countries and is not strongly related to the stage of economic development. As table 2.2 shows, more firms embed some open source software in high-tech products in Brazil and Kenya, followed by France and Thailand. However, there is more of a tendency for firms to specialize in embedding open source software in Israel and Singapore: open source software accounts for more than 75 percent of all embedded software in 40 percent of firms in Israel and 50 percent in Singapore. By contrast, in Brazil and Kenya only 14.3

percent and 8.3 percent of firms, respectively, use open source for 75 percent or more of their embedded software. The main exceptions in our sample are France, and to a lesser extent Israel, Mexico, Russia, and Singapore. For 53.8 percent of these firms, revenues from products with open source software are between 25 and 75 percent of the total revenues from all products with embedded software.

These depictions might reassure us that technology can be quickly adopted across countries. But, as we noted above, there is an important distinction to be made between the adoption of new technologies and the *development* of innovative new ideas.

Final Thoughts

This chapter has had an ambitious mandate: before we turn to the specifics of open source software, it is helpful to understand what economists have had to say about software more generally. But as we have seen from this chapter, reflecting the complex nature of software, there is a large and somewhat disjointed literature about this industry.

Several conclusions emerge from this discussion:

• Software's reach extends far beyond the software industry. Much of the innovation in software sprang from firms in other industries that have embodied software into products and processes.

• Information technology, of which software is a crucial element, really matters. Studies on both the economy-wide and firm-level show that the adoption of advanced computer-related technologies has a substantial impact on both productivity and how production is organized.

• Software use (at least as evidenced by available evidence on diffusion of Internet and computers) and software production (measured both by evidence on software patenting by countries in the United States and by open source contributions) both vary with the level of development, but this link appears much stronger for production side. It may be that the barriers to being truly innovative in this realm are considerably greater than incorporating new programs into existing businesses.

3   The History of Open Source

As we discussed in the first chapter, open source software has experienced enormous growth in recent years. This might lead to the conclusion that the ideas behind open source are very new.

Reality is more complex. Software development has a tradition of sharing and cooperation. Many of the principles behind open source have been established for many decades. But in recent years both the scale and formalization of development have expanded dramatically with the spread of the Internet. In this chapter we will review the history of the development of open source. As we proceed, we'll highlight the key institutional features that make this activity so distinct and important and the research that has attempted to understand these patterns. To help organize things, we'll highlight that open source has gone through three eras.

The First Era

Many of the key aspects of computer operating systems and the Internet were developed in academic settings such as Berkeley and MIT during the 1960s and 1970s, as well as in central corporate research facilities. Even the corporate research laboratories resembled academic institutions in many respects: it was commonplace to allow researchers a great deal of autonomy to pursue topics wherever their intellectual curiosity led them, even though there was only a tenuous relationship with the products or services that the corporation offered. (Famous examples include Bell Labs and Xerox's Palo Alto Research Center). Reflecting this spirit of academic freedom, in these years, the sharing by programmers in different organizations of basic operating code of computer programs was commonplace.

Here we need to make a brief technical digression. Software can be transmitted in either *source code* or *object code*. *Source code* is the code written by programmers that uses languages such as Basic, C, and Java. *Object code* is the sequence of 0s and 1s that directly communicates with the computer; and hence it is often called *binary code*. Object code is difficult for programmers to interpret or modify. Most commercial software vendors today provide users only with object or binary code; when the source code is made available to other firms by commercial developers, it is typically licensed under very restrictive conditions. In the first era, sharing of the source code was commonplace.

Consider, for instance, the pioneering computer program FORTRAN, which was developed in the late 1950s by IBM researchers with some help from volunteer outside labor. The software allowed writing computer programs in a dramatically easier way than earlier efforts, which had relied on manipulation of "assembly language" that had been the standard earlier approach. Moreover it opened the door to allowing the same program to run on computers of different makes. Despite this strategic value, IBM did not prevent competitors from employing FORTRAN. Indeed IBM disseminated the critical information needed to run FORTRAN to its competitors. In part, this reflected the difficulty of protecting the software (copyright protection was not yet available for software). But it also reflected the fact that software was not perceived as having market value and the prevailing ethos regarding sharing software.[1]

Many of the cooperative development efforts in the 1970s focused on the development of an operating system that could run on multiple computer platforms. The most successful examples, such as Unix and the C language used for developing Unix applications, were originally developed at AT&T's Bell Laboratories. The software was then installed across institutions, and kept on being transferred freely or for a nominal charge. Many of the sites where the software was installed made further innovations that were in turn shared with others. The process of sharing code was greatly accelerated with the diffusion of Usenet, a computer network begun in 1979 to link together the Unix programming community. As the number of sites grew rapidly (e.g., from 3 in 1979 to 400 in 1982), the ability of programmers in university and corporate settings to rapidly share technologies was considerably enhanced.

---

1. This account is based on Campbell-Kelly and Garcia-Swartz (2008) and Schwarz and Takhteyev (2008).

These cooperative software development projects were undertaken on a highly informal basis. Typically no effort to delineate property rights or to restrict reuse of the software was made. This informality proved to be problematic in the early 1980s when AT&T began enforcing its (purported) intellectual property rights related to Unix, which had been widely shared across (and contributed to by) the research community.

Unfortunately, we know relatively little about this period, since the projects did not really leave a trail that can be analyzed. The events of the second two periods, however, have been much more scrutinized.

The Second Era

In response to these threats of litigation, the first efforts to formalize the ground rules behind the cooperative software development process emerged. This ushered in the second era of cooperative software development. The critical institution during this period was the Free Software Foundation, begun by Richard Stallman of the MIT Artificial Intelligence Laboratory in 1983. The foundation sought to develop and disseminate a wide variety of software without cost.

One important innovation introduced by the Free Software Foundation was a formal licensing procedure that aimed to preclude the assertion of intellectual property rights concerning cooperatively developed software (as many believed that AT&T had done in the case of Unix). In exchange for being able to modify and distribute the GNU software (as it was known), software developers had to agree to make the source code freely available (or at a nominal cost).

As part of the General Public License (GPL, also known as "copylefting"), the user had to also agree not to impose licensing restrictions on others. Furthermore all enhancements to the code—and even code that intermingled the cooperatively developed software with that developed separately—had to be licensed on the same terms. It is these contractual terms that distinguish open source software from shareware (where the binary files but not the underlying source code are made freely available, possibly for a trial period only) and public-domain software (where no restrictions are placed on subsequent users of the source code).

It should be noted, however, that some projects, such as the Berkeley Software Distribution (BSD) effort, did take alternative approaches during the 1980s. The BSD license also allows anyone to freely copy and modify the source code (as long as credit was given to the University of California at Berkeley for the software developed there, a requirement no longer in place). It is much less constraining than the GPL: anyone can modify the program and redistribute it for a fee without making the source code freely available. In this way, it is a continuation of the university-based tradition of the 1960s and 1970s.

This project, as well as contemporaneous efforts, also developed a number of important organizational features, which are as distinctive features of the open source process as the licenses themselves. In particular, these projects employed a model where contributions from many developers were accepted (and frequently publicly disseminated or posted). The official version of the program, however, was managed or controlled by a smaller subset of individuals closely involved with the project or an individual leader. In some cases the project's founder (or his designated successor) served as the leader; in others, leadership rotated among various key contributors.

This period also saw a substantial change in the mixture of contributors. Conventional wisdom is that open source development is dominated by myriads of individuals voluntarily contributing to thousands of open source projects out there, with no pecuniary compensation, driven largely by intrinsic motivation. While this view may have appropriately captured the nature of contributors in the early days of the industry (and even this is not clear), by the time of the second period, the picture was far more complex (see Lerner and Tirole 2002).

To understand the motivations of contributors to open source projects, it is helpful to step back a little. A programmer working on an open source software development project incurs a variety of benefits and costs, which she weighs against each other. The programmer incurs an opportunity cost of her time. This has two dimensions. First, a programmer who would work as an independent on open source projects would forgo the monetary compensation she would receive if she were working for a commercial firm or a university. Second, for a programmer with an affiliation with a commercial company, a university or research lab, the opportunity cost is the cost of not focusing on her primary mission. For example, the academic's research output may sag and the student's progress toward a degree may slow down.

Two immediate benefits may counter this cost. First, when fixing a bug or customizing an open source program, the programmer may actually improve rather than reduce her performance in the mission endowed upon her by her employer. This is particularly relevant for system administrators looking for specific solutions for their company.

Second, the programmer may discover how enjoyable the open source alternative is compared with the mission set by the employer. A "cool" open source project is likely to be more fun than a routine task.

There are also two distinct, although hard-to-distinguish, delayed rewards from participating in open source projects. The *ego gratification incentive* stems from a desire for peer recognition, and has doubtless been a driver of open source contributions from the beginning of these projects. The *career concern incentive* may be of more recent origin: it refers to future job offers, shares in commercial open source-based companies or future access to the venture capital market. Probably most programmers respond to both incentives. There are some differences between the two. The programmer mainly preoccupied by peer recognition may shun future monetary rewards and may also want to signal her talent to a slightly different audience than those motivated by career concerns. From an economic perspective, however, the incentives are similar in most respects. Not surprisingly, these motivations will be stronger, the more visible the performance is to the relevant audience (peers, labor market, venture capital community), the higher the impact of effort on performance, and the more informative the performance about talent.

Thus, to have an "audience," programmers will want to work on software projects that will attract a large number of other programmers. This suggests the possibility of multiple outcomes. The same project may attract few programmers because programmers expect that other programmers will not be interested; or it may flourish as programmers (rationally) have faith in the project.

To compare programmers' incentives in the open source and proprietary settings, we need to examine how the fundamental features of the two environments shape the incentives just reviewed. We will first consider the relative short-term rewards, and then turn to the deferred rewards.

Commercial projects have an edge on the current-compensation dimension because the proprietary nature of the code generates income. The profit motive makes it worthwhile for private companies to offer salaries.[2] This contention is the old argument in economics that the prospect of profit encourages investment, which is used, for instance, to justify the awarding of intellectual property rights to encourage invention.

---

2. To be certain, many commercial firms supporting open source projects are also able to compensate programmers, as discussed below.

By way of contrast, an open source project may well lower the cost for the programmer for two reasons. The first is an alumni effect. Because the code is freely available to all, it can be used in schools and universities for learning purposes; therefore it is already familiar to programmers. This reduces their cost of programming.[3] Second, and as we have already noted, the cost of contributing to an open source project can be offset if the activity brings about a private benefit (the ability to fix bugs and customize the product to one's own ends) for the programmer and her firm. Note again that this factor of cost reduction is directly linked to the openness of the source code. Commercial software vendors (e.g., Microsoft in its shared source initiative) have again tried to emulate this benefit by opening their code to selected users under a confidentiality arrangement.

When we consider the delayed reward (signaling incentive) component, the open source process also has some benefits over the closed source approach. As we noted, signaling incentives are stronger, the more visible the performance and the more attributable the performance to a given individual. Signaling incentives therefore may be stronger in the open source mode for three reasons. First, in an open source project the outsiders are able to see not only what the contribution of each individual was and whether that component "worked," but also whether the task was hard, if the problem was addressed in a clever way, whether the code can be useful for other programming tasks in the future, and so forth. Second, the open source programmer is her own boss and takes full responsibility for the success of a subproject she works on, with little interference from a superior. Finally, since many elements of the source code are shared across open source projects, more of the knowledge they have accumulated can be transferred to new environments.

These concepts have been tested in a variety of studies. Academics first attempted to understand motivations of developers through surveys. Given the inherent subjectivity of these assessments, the low response rates that many of these surveys have obtained, and the sensitivity of some of these questions, it is not surprising that self-reported motivations vary considerably across studies. Haruvy, Wu, and Chakravarty (2003) find that commercial objectives—particularly, the promise of higher future earnings—are an important driver of contributions to open source projects. Other surveys, however, have suggested alter-

---

3. Commercial firms also emulate this aspect of open source, licensing their software for educational purposes.

native motivations. For instance, Lakhani and von Hippel (2003) suggest that the overwhelming driver of open source contributors is to solve their own specific programming needs, while the Boston Consulting Group survey (2003) implies that intellectual curiosity is the most important determinant.

The empirical evidence has been largely consistent with this framework. The most comprehensive study, by Hann et al. (2004), suggests that economic incentives are the most important motivation for open source contributors. To analyze this question, they examine contributors to the Apache project, drawing on a wide variety of project records to assess contributions. The authors complement these data with a survey on employment that yields usable data for multiple years for 147 contributors to the project.

They then seek to explain the total compensation that the contributor received in 2000, including information on the contributions to the open source project as well as many controls. Not surprisingly, technical education pays off: contributors with a doctorate degree are paid about 20 to 22 percent more than college graduates. Similar, greater work experience increases the salary, but with increasing work experience, the increase in salary grows more slowly. Working for publicly traded firms, which are presumably larger, also pays more than private firms.

Interestingly neither the coefficient for the number of contributions to the Apache project in 1999 nor that for total contributions until through 1999 is significant: contributions per se do not seem to increase wages. On the other hand, those who have moved up the ranks of the open source project are paid more: the wages of contributors with rank "committer" or above is on average about 29 percent higher than that of developers after controlling for education, programming skills, work experience and history, and firm characteristics. These results suggest that employers of contributors do not reward participants for making contributions to open source project per se. But rank within the project, they note, may convey information that the individuals have sought-after characteristics that distinguish extraordinary programmers but are typically hard to observe.

The Third Era

Over the past fifteen years there has been a dramatic acceleration of open source activity. The volume of contributions and diversity of

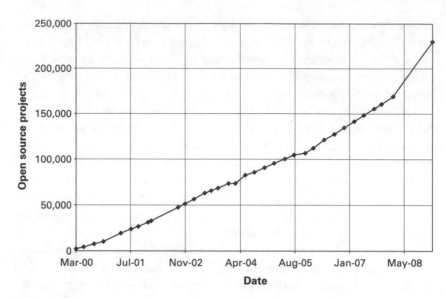

Figure 3.1
Number of open source projects registered on SourceForge

contributors expanded sharply, and numerous new open source projects emerged, most notably Linux (a UNIX operating system developed by Linus Torvalds in 1991).

As a result of these shifts the past fifteen years has seen unprecedented growth of open source software. Both the number and size of projects have skyrocketed. This growth can be illustrated through two charts.

Figure 3.1 shows the number of projects registered on SourceForge over time.[4] This measure, however, must be treated with caution: of the projects registered, most of are considered inactive or were stillborn, never attracting a critical mass of participants in the first place.

Most projects have little activity, apart from a few well known, large and admittedly important projects like Apache. Work by Sharon Belenzon and Mark Schankerman (2008) shows how infrequent contributions are for many projects: table 3.1 summarizes the distribution of activity in open source projects. Only a small fraction, 6.6 percent, of projects listed on SourceForge receive any contributions at all, either from project members or unaffiliated programmers. If we limit the

---

4. The source of this chart is archived versions of www.sourceforge.net (accessed August 28, 2009).

Table 3.1
Distribution of activity across open source projects

Percentile	All projects	Projects receiving at least one contribution
10	0	1
25	0	1
50	0	3
75	0	9
90	0	29
95	1	58
99	18	246
Average	1.4	21.3
Number of projects	61,514	4086

Source: Computed from SourceForge data covering the period 1998 to 2005. Contributions include both those by programmers who are registered members of the project and those not affiliated with the project. For more detail, see Belenzon and Schankerman (2008).

analysis to projects that receive at least one contribution, the mean project only receives 21 contributions. Moreover these averages are driven by a few exceptional cases: even among the projects that receive contributions, the median project receives three contributions.

Figure 3.2 presents an alternative approach, looking at the volume of contributions. This tabulation has been compiled by Amit Desphande and Dirk Riehle (2008) from the database of the open source analytics firm Ohloh.net, which has been crawling open source software code repositories since 2005. It examines on a weekly basis from 5,122 active and popular open source projects.

Ohloh.net provides data on each individual piece of code contributed or deleted from each project by every programmer, typically as far back as 1995 or the project's inception. This figure compiles the lines of source code added and deleted from each of the projects, omitting empty or commented lines of code. Using this data, they calculate the change in the size of a source code file by adding or subtracting the number of lines of code added to or removed from its existing size. This calculation again reveals a picture of dramatic growth.

This growth can be attributed to three factors. The first of these needs the least explanation. The widespread diffusion of Internet access in the 1990s meant that access was no longer restricted to a small, elite network of scientists and engineers. As a result the pool of people

Figure 3.2
Cumulative change in size of 5,122 open source projects (millions lines of source code).
Adapted from Deshpande and Riehle (2008, fig. 2).

who could work on these projects, and the ease with which they could
be organized, were greatly enhanced. Two other drivers of this growth,
however, deserve greater discussion: changes in licensing rules and the
corporatization of open source.

Changes in Licensing Rules

Another innovation during this period was the proliferation of alternative approaches to licensing cooperatively developed software. During
the 1980s the General Public License (GPL) was the dominant licensing
arrangement for cooperatively developed software. This changed considerably during the 1990s.

In 1998 a variety of open source leaders came together to establish a
consistent set of criteria for what constituted an open source license,
which they termed the "Open Source Definition." Among the requirements for the license of a program to be considered "open source"
were that:

• The source code for the program must be available at little or no charge.

• Redistribution of the program, in source code or other form, must be allowed without fee.

• Distributions of modified software must be allowed without discrimination.

• The distributions of those modifications on the same terms as the original program must be permitted.

This definition was broad enough to both encompass the GPL and those licenses that allow users greater liberty in how they use the code. These guidelines allowed licensees greater flexibility in using the program, including the right to bundle the cooperatively developed software with proprietary code. These new guidelines did not require open source projects to be "viral": they need not "infect" all code that was compiled with the software with the requirement that it be covered under the license agreement as well. At the same time they also accommodated more restrictive licenses, such as the General Public License. Thus today there is a real choice of license type. In each case the product originator gives users the right to employ the copyrighted code through a license. But the licenses differ tremendously in the extent to which they enable licensors and contributors to profit from the code that is contributed.

Lerner and Tirole (2005) show that firms strategically choose particular licenses. To illustrate the choices, the paper begins with a stylized depiction of reality: an entity, either an individual or a firm, is deciding (1) whether to make some software available under an open source license, and (2) if so, what type of license to employ. The interactions of the licensor with the community of programmers are then depicted. The programmers' benefits from working on the project may depend on the choice of license. The licensor must assess how its choice of license, together with project characteristics—such as the environment, the nature of the project, and the intended audience—impacts the project's likely success. Because the project needs to attract contributors to be successful, the decision is shaped not just by the preferences of the licensor itself but also by that of the community of users.

What drives the choice of license type? The critical trade-off is as follows: a more restrictive license involves fewer proprietary rights, that is, a reduced ability to make profits from commercializing the open source code. But the many contributors may prefer to work for projects with more restrictive agreements—at the very least, they are be unlikely to be more enthusiastic about unrestrictive agreements than the project founders. The rationale for this claim is that commercial benefits are likely to flow disproportionately to the project leaders: as we discuss in this volume, there are numerous examples where project leaders have parlayed participation in these projects into commercial opportunities.[5]

The model suggests that permissive licenses such as the BSD, where the user retains the ability to use the code as he sees fit, will be more common in cases where projects have strong appeal to the community of open source contributors—for instance, when contributors stand to benefit considerably from signaling incentives or when the licensors are well trusted. Conversely, restrictive licenses like the GPL will be commonplace when such appeals are more fragile. Examples of cases where we would expect a restrictive license are computer games, which are geared for end users who are unlikely to appreciate the coding, or projects sponsored by corporations, who potential contributors might fear would "hijack" the project.

An illustration of this argument was the dispute over licensing of the Mozilla Internet browser. When it sought to release its browser's code to the public, Netscape initially proposed the "Netscape Public License," which would have allowed Netscape to take pieces of the open source code and turn them back into a proprietary project again, according to Hamerly, Paquin, and Walton (1999). Ultimately the firm announced the "Mozilla Public License," under which Netscape cannot regain proprietary rights to modifications of the code: in fact the terms of the final license are even stricter than those of the General Public License.

Lerner and Tirole (2005) also present an empirical analysis of the prevalence of different types of open source licenses. Their analysis looks at the SourceForge database, a compilation of nearly 100,000 open source projects. SourceForge is a free service that since 1999 has offered hosting and project administration tools to software development projects. The site's operations have been funded since its in-

---

5. This assumption is addressed in Belenzon and Schankerman (2008), which shows how license type affects the number (and composition) of contributions from different developer types. In other words, the paper provides evidence that license type matters for the forthcoming contributions, as Lerner and Tirole argue.

Table 3.2
Tabulation of characteristics of projects with and without highly restrictive license provisions (in percent)

Intended audience	All licenses highly restrictive?	
	Yes	No
End users/desktop	62.3	42.0
Developers	57.3	78.5
System administrators	29.5	23.3
Software developers	12.2	29.6
Office/business employees	5.5	4.4
System operators	20.4	18.6
Games players	16.6	12.3

Notes: For all of the rows, the differences between the percentages in the first and second columns are statistically significant at the 1 percent level.

ception by VA Software (formerly known as VA Linux), which at the time of the site's creation was primarily selling computers optimized for Linux. Today VA has abandoned the hardware business; it intends to ultimately earn a profit by selling a version of the SourceForge service to corporations to manage the development of software for internal (proprietary) applications. SourceForge accepts listings of (and is willing to host) all projects that conform to the Open Source Definition discussed above, as well as selected projects operating under licenses that are not compliant with that definition. Not all open source projects, however, are hosted on SourceForge. Many of the largest projects instead have their own web sites. Other projects are hosted at smaller competing sites. These tend, however, to be much smaller.

Since all of the projects in this database are open source, the empirical analysis in the Lerner–Tirole paper focuses on whether the license requires that when modified versions of the program are distributed, the source code must be made generally available, and/or whether the license restricts modified versions of the program from mingling their source code with other software that does not employ such a license. (This condition, which the authors term "highly restrictive," is associated with the General Public License and several other types of licenses.)

That this pattern indeed holds is illustrated in table 3.2, which compares the features of projects that are with and without highly restrictive license provisions. The first column reports the features of the projects that employ highly restrictive licenses; the second column, those without such licenses. The table compares the projects based on their intended audience. It indicates that projects with more sophisticated end users—namely other software developers—are less likely to have restrictive licenses, while those geared toward unsophisticated consumers are more likely to do so. Projects geared toward games, business applications, and routine system tasks are more likely to have restrictive licenses, while those oriented toward software development are dominated by less restrictive licenses. These patterns are consistent with the theoretical predictions above.

In other, unreported tabulations, similarly consistent results hold. Restrictive licenses are also less common for projects operating in commercial environments, where the costs of such provisions would presumably be greater. Projects whose natural language is not English, whose community appeal may be presumed to be much smaller, are more likely to employ restrictive licenses. Moreover projects with less restrictive licenses tend to attract more contributors, suggesting that these provisions really matter.

The Corporatization of Open Source

A third driver of the rapid growth has been the increasing involvement of large and small corporations. Although initially the bulk of contributions to open source projects was made by individual volunteers, recent years have seen a rise in major corporate investments—for instance, IBM is reported to have spent $1 billion in 2001 alone on such projects. According to Forrester Research, "more enterprises are deploying open source databases than ever before," and "every enterprise should now consider open source databases as part of its overall DBMS strategy, as doing this delivers cost savings." (See Yuhanna, Gilpin, and Salzinger 2008 and earlier publications.)

Commercial firms have been increasingly active in this arena and interacted with open source projects in a variety of ways. While corporations have not received the same scrutiny from economists as individual contributors, we are gradually understanding their approaches.

Commercial companies may interact with an open source project in a number of ways. The simplest of these approaches is formally or informally encouraging employees to spend some working hours contributing to open source projects. While improvements in the open source software made by employees may not be captured by the firm, but instead benefit everybody, this strategy can still be beneficial for firms for several reasons:

• The activity may make programmers more effective employees: working on these problems may "sharpen the edge" of employees, just as employees often benefit from corporate-sponsored classes in advanced math and engineering.

• The tools used in the course of open source projects may in some cases be able to be incorporated into the firm's projects—particularly if the project is using one of the licenses that is more "permissive" of such adaptations than the General Public License. Just as a drug company may send employees to scientific conferences in the hope of gleaning approaches, so too can the tools developed in open source projects be adapted.

• Firms may temporarily encourage their programmers to participate in an open source project to learn about the strengths and weaknesses of the project's technical approach. For-profit firms may compete directly with open source providers in the same market, and participating in these projects may be a form of "competitive intelligence."

• Commercial companies may interface with the open source world because it generates good public relations with programmers and customers.

Other firms have chosen to interact with open source projects more directly. A common approach is to provide software or consulting services that are not part of an open source program but help it work more effectively. A for-profit firm that seeks to provide services and products that are complementary to the open source product, but not supplied efficiently by the open source community, can be described as "living symbiotically." IBM, which has made open source software a major focus for its systems integration and consulting work, exemplifies this approach. A company in this situation will want to have extensive knowledge about the open source movement, and may even want to encourage and subsidize open source contributions, both of which may cause it to allocate some programmers to the open source project. When firms invest in an open source project, however, they do not capture all the benefit: this consideration may limit to some extent how many contributions corporations are willing to make.

The code release strategy arises when companies release some existing proprietary code and then create a governance structure for the resulting open source development process. For example, IBM released half a million lines of its Cloudscape program, a simple database that resides inside a software application instead of as a full-fledged database program, to the Apache Software Foundation. Hewlett-Packard released its Spectrum Object Model-Linker to the open source community to help the Linux community write software to connect Linux with Hewlett-Packard's RISC computer architecture. This strategy is comparable to giving away the razor (the code) to sell more razor blades (the related consulting services that IBM and HP hope to provide).

When can it be advantageous for a commercial company to release proprietary code under an open source license? In general, it will make sense if the increase in profit in the proprietary complementary segment offsets any profit that would have been made in the primary segment, had it not been converted to open source. Thus the temptation to go open source is particularly strong when the product is lagging behind the market leader, but the firm sees a possibility that widespread use and further development will increase the profitability of the complementary product or service. If network effects and switching costs are very strong, the second-best commercial package might have a small and diminishing market share. In these cases the cost to corporations of releasing code may be very small. Moreover such a strategy may reassure present and potential users that the released software will never be withdrawn (i.e., they will always be able to maintain the product themselves).

This motivation can also depend on the evolution of vertical relationships between small and large firms in the software industry in commercial software environments. Indeed many small developers are uncomfortable doing business with leading software firms. They fear that the commercial platform owner has an incentive to introduce substitutes in the developers' segment in order to force prices down in that segment, and to raise the demand for licenses to the broad software platform. By contrast, when a large firm makes its platform available on an open source basis through a restrictive license, such as the GPL, the small firm need no longer fear being squeezed in this way. By using open source licenses when releasing new code, the firm can promise users that they will not be "held up" by a future price increase after adopting a technology and that they will always be able to tailor their technology to their own particular needs without depending on the good will or health of a vendor.

Numerous challenges appear, though, when a for-profit firm seeks to become the center of an open source development project. Leadership by a commercial entity may not absorb enough of the objectives of the open source community. In particular, a corporation may not be able to credibly promise to keep all source code in the public domain and to highlight important contributions adequately, especially when they go against the particular technological approach being promoted by the firm.

These difficulties help explain why Hewlett-Packard released its code through Collab.Net, a venture by leading open source programmers, which organizes open source projects for corporations who wish to open up part of their software. In effect Collab.Net offers a kind of stamp of approval, or certification, that the firm is committed to the open source project. (The Apache Software Foundation plays a similar role in the Cloudscape case mentioned above.) In a theoretical model, Wouter Dessein (2005) shows that a boss who can direct the activities of an employee generally gains by delegating control rights to an intermediary with preferences or incentives that are somewhere between the boss's and the employee's. The partial alignment of the intermediary's preferences with the employee's fosters trust and boosts his initiative, ultimately offsetting the partial loss of control for the principal. In the case of Collab.Net, the ongoing involvement of open source developers was assured by Hewlett-Packard through the employment of visible open source developers and the involvement of O'Reilly, a technical book publisher with strong ties to the open source community.

Thus corporations may emulate some of the benefits attached to open source production by getting involved in these projects. First, such involvement can simply enhance learning by the corporation. Second, selling of complementary goods and services that are inadequately provided by open source projects can be profitable. Finally, firms may contribute software to open source in the hope that the program will find widespread usage as a standard, as the HP case discussed above illustrates.

As a result today there is a real mixture of contributors to open source projects, with very different motivations. This point is illustrated in a paper by Belenzon and Schankerman (2008), which seeks to figure out what are the key motives behind open source innovation. Again using the SourceForge data-set, the authors seek to determine the drivers of software code contributions by focusing on distinct groups of developers.

In particular, the authors classify each developer according to the type of open source license governing the projects of which she is a registered member (programmers typically register to be part of proj-

Table 3.3
Distribution of code contributions by developer type and receiving project characteristics (in percent)

Receiving projects	Contributing developers		
	Highly restrictive	Unrestrictive	Mixed
License type			
Highly restrictive	66.8	26.9	1.2
Restrictive	21.0	23.2	28.3
Unrestrictive	12.3	49.9	30.5

ects on which they work). This yields four developer categories: highly restrictive, unrestrictive, mixed, and anonymous (i.e., with no registration). They investigate how the pattern of contributions from each developer type varies with the license type and other characteristics of projects.

The central empirical finding by Belenzon and Schankerman is that developers strongly "sort" on a variety of observed project characteristics, which suggests that software developers are heterogeneous with respect to their motivations. Highly restrictive developers (i.e., those registered to contribute to highly restrictive projects) almost exclusively contribute to projects with highly restrictive licenses, suggesting that these are motivated by the ideology of the open source movement. Unrestrictive developers primarily contribute to projects with unrestrictive (more commercial) licenses, which suggests that they are going to where reputation gains are likely to be obtained. They are also likely to contribute to larger projects and to those that are sponsored by corporations, again suggesting career concerns. Finally, restrictive developers are much more likely to contribute to projects aimed at end users (e.g., computer games), whereas unrestrictive developers target developer-oriented (programming tool) projects. Again, we might anticipate the latter to be more likely to attract programmers interested in displaying their talents to prospective employers.

These results are reported in table 3.3. This table reports the distribution of code contributions by developers of different types. (The authors exclude contributions by developers who are members of the receiving project, as we might expect that people would disproportionately contribute to projects where they are members.) The table presents the distribution of contributions by three types of developers:

• Highly restrictive—developers who are only members of projects with highly restrictive licenses.

• Unrestrictive—developers who are only members of projects with unrestrictive licenses.

• Mixed—developers who are members of both highly restrictive and unrestrictive projects.

The table reveals that the first type of developer is far more likely to contribute to projects with highly restrictive licenses, while the second type favors unrestricted projects. These are consistent with the argument that these types differ strongly in their preferences.

While there are no formal employment contracts between contributing developers and open source projects, the project license is itself a contract governing the subsequent use and openness of the contributed software code. Thus Belenzon–Schankerman's paper can be viewed as a contribution to the empirical literature on motivation and contracts, in that they show that contract design has strong sorting effects. In that paper, the contract choice is treated as something determined elsewhere (in the language of economics, exogenous). Lerner and Tirole (2005) study the choice of open source license, arguing that the relevant trade-off is between greater proprietary control with the more commercial, unrestrictive licenses and a potentially greater pool of contributors with more restrictive licenses. The sorting effects of the project license play a central role in their theory, and the Belenzon–Schankerman results provide econometric evidence supporting that perspective.

We will revisit the question of how firms interact with open source software—both in their roles as developers and distributors—in chapter 4, when we examine the question of what economic factors drive the creation of open source. We will present evidence that around the world, firms are intimately involved with the creation of open source programs. Moreover, far from being segregated from the remainder of the activities of the corporation, in many cases there is mixing between open source and proprietary code.

When we turn to considering the demand for open source products in chapter 5, we will again visit this territory. In particular, our survey results will highlight the fact that many software users of all types mix proprietary and open source programs. In addition to highlighting this phenomenon, we will discuss why this mixing is commonplace.

Ongoing Challenges

At the same time the movement has faced a number of challenges. We will highlight three of these here: the proliferation of projects, frequently in competing variations, the patenting of software, and the development of products for high-end users.

One issue that has emerged in a number of open source projects is the potential for programs splintering into various variants. In some cases passionate disputes over product design have led to the splintering of open source projects into different variants. Examples of such splintering are the Berkeley Unix program and Sendmail during the late 1980s.

More generally, most open source projects struggle to get a "critical mass" of contributors. Most projects have only a very small number of contributors: for instance, the analysis of tens of thousands of projects on SourceForge alluded to above suggests that the mean project only has three developers registered to write code for the project. It appears the distribution of contributors, and the number of contributions they make, is very skewed: a small number of projects account for the overwhelming amount of activity.

Thus the inherently entrepreneurial nature of the open source process can make the successful management of a project a daunting challenging. For the typical founder of an open source project, the experience is very different from that of Linus Torvalds, where the world beat a path to his project soon after he announced Linux's creation. Rather, it is a struggle to get the attention of programmers and users alike.

A second challenge, which instead has sprung up largely from outside the industry, is software patents.[6] This issue was first brought to the community's attention with the litigation launched by the SCO Group, which holds to (at least partial) rights to UNIX (acquired from Novell, who in turn had purchased them from AT&T). Beginning in 2003, the firm initiated a series of lawsuits against, among others, AutoZone, DaimlerChrysler, IBM, and Novell, alleging that they were violating SCO's intellectual property by contributing to or using

6. In this section we will avoid discussing the highly contentious and unsettled question of the economic impact of software patents more generally: for more on this topic, see, for instance, Bessen and Hunt (2003), Caillaud (2003), Graham and Mowery (2003), Hahn and Wallsten (2003), and Noel and Schankerman (2006).

Linux.[7] The allegedly detrimental impact of software patents on open source was also a frequently invoked reason for opposing software patents in the ongoing debate in the European Parliament on this question.[8]

Software patents create the possibility of holding up software producers. In the case of commercial software, individuals and companies that do not produce software themselves (e.g., hardware manufacturers and software users) but hold a software patent can try to obtain royalty payments from software vendors. (Large software vendors are less likely to engage in such behavior against each other, as they have accumulated patent portfolios that they can use for retaliatory purposes.)

The status of software patents was thrown into uncertainty by the ruling of the Court of Appeals for the Federal Circuit in the *In re Bilski* case in October 2008.[9] In a 9–3 decision the court upheld a ruling made by the Board of Patent Appeals and Interferences that denied a patent for a method of hedging in commodities trading developed by Bernard Bilski and Rand Warsaw. While disallowing this patent, the court made clear that business-related processes such as some software programs will still be patentable. In particular, it indicated that it would disallow patents where every step of the claimed process may be performed entirely in the human mind, rather than needing to rely on a specialized machine: "of course, a claimed process wherein all of the process steps may be performed entirely in the human mind is obviously not tied to any machine and does not transform any article into a different state or thing. As a result, it would not be patent-eligible." Press commentaries after the decision highlighted that the extent to which software decisions could still be patented and the status of existing awards were all uncertain, particularly in the light of the decision of the Supreme Court to review this decision.

Open source software is vulnerable in a different way. After all, the code is free of charge and the contributors hardly solvent for the most part, so attempting to collect royalties is not a powerful incentive.

7. Patent concerns have also slowed the adoption of Linux in the public sector: for a discussion of the impact of these concerns on the city of Munich's open source effort, see, for instance, http://www.informationweek.com/story/showArticle.jhtml?articleID =26806464 (accessed August 25, 2004).
8. See, for instance, http://news.zdnet.co.uk/business/legal/0,39020651,39116053,00 .htm (accessed March 26, 2004).
9. 543 F. 3d 943 (Fed. Cir. 2008) (*en banc*).

However, firms with software patents may seek damages from firms that service or use open source software. Software firms facing competition from open source alternatives may sue to enjoin utilization or distribution of open source code. It remains to be seen whether the open source movement will itself enter into defensive patenting, as large commercial vendors already do, or at least make a more concerted effort to forestall patenting by others by aggressively publishing. One intriguing initiative is the Red Hat Assurance Plan, in which the Linux distributor is offering partial protection against intellectual property litigation.[10]

Another interesting area of study concerns the consequences of users paying royalties for an open source program that also included some commercially patented material. Such royalty demands might trigger "sweet-heart" deals between firms, the splitting of open source projects into different branches (often termed "forking"), and the privatization of blocks of code. The General Public License seeks to address these problems by providing, "[I]f a patent license would not permit royalty-free redistribution of the Program by all those who receive copies directly or indirectly through you, then the only way you could satisfy both it and this License would be to refrain entirely from distribution of the Program." Many other types of open source licenses, however, do not address this issue.[11]

Another, less prominent, question relates to the impact of patents on the dynamics of information sharing and collaboration among open source contributors. To what extent will the ability of programmers to protect their discoveries with strong patent rights reduce their incentives to participate in open source projects?

To date, very little systematic analysis has examined the implications of patents for open source. However, a broader literature has scrutinized the impact of patenting on the generation and diffusion of scien-

---

10. http://www.redhat.com/about/presscenter/2004/press_blackduck.html (accessed August 24, 2004). One challenge is that the extent and dispersion of the patent holdings that may impact open source projects: the insurer Open Source Risk Management estimates that there are 283 patents that might be used in claims against the Linux kernel alone; see http://www.eweek.com/article2/0,1759,1631336,00.asp (accessed August 24, 2004).

11. A related danger is that programs will inadvertently infringe patents. Programmers may lack the incentives and skills needed to check whether their contribution infringes awards. As an effort to limit this problem, beginning in May 2004, Linux contributors were required to attest that they have the right to make that contribution. For a discussion, see http://www.computerworld.com/softwaretopics/os/linux/story/0,10801,93395,00.html (accessed August 8, 2004).

tific knowledge more generally, especially the augmented ability of academic institutions, government laboratories, and nonprofit institutions to patent the results of publicly funded research. This literature has sought to understand the pervasiveness and consequences of the "anti-commons" problem (see Heller and Eisenberg 1998): the concern that the patenting of scientific knowledge will lead to lower research productivity, and hence eventually to reduced economic growth.

Much of the discussion of these questions to date has featured broad assertions and anecdotal examples (see Bok 2003). But it is clear from the more careful studies that have been completed that institutions and researchers have responded to the increased incentives to commercialize products by engaging in more patenting and commercialization activities (see Jaffe and Lerner 2001; Lach and Schankerman 2008). Whether these commercial activities have detrimental effects on research and social welfare is much more ambiguous.[12] Given this preliminary and somewhat contradictory evidence, our ability to draw conclusions for consequences of formal intellectual property rights for open source software is quite limited.

Another challenge has been the apparently lesser emphasis on documentation and support, user interfaces,[13] and backward compatibility found in at least some open source projects. The relative technological features of software developed in open source and traditional environments are a matter of passionate discussion. Some members of the community believe that this production method dominates traditional software development in all respects. But many open source advocates argue that open source software tends to be geared to the more sophisticated users.[14] This point is made colorfully by one open source developer:

12. For instance, Thursby and Thursby's (2003) study of six major research universities suggests that while the probability that a faculty member will indicate to his university's technology transfer office that he has made a new discovery has increased tenfold over the past decade, research productivity in basic research journals has remained constant. On the other hand, Murray and Stern (2007) have shown that papers published in the journal *Nature Biotechnology* are somewhat less likely to be cited in other articles once the corresponding patent application issues. They find that the papers with corresponding patents are initially more heavily cited than those without, but then their citation rate declines more sharply over time.

13. Two main open source projects (GNOME and KDE) are meant to remedy Linux's limitations on desktop computers (by developing mouse and windows interfaces).

14. For example, Torvalds (1999) argues that the Linux model works best with developer-type software. Ghosh (1999) views the open source process as a large repeated game process of give-and-take among developer-users (the "cooking pot" model).

[I]n every release cycle Microsoft always listens to its *most ignorant customers*. This is the key to dumbing down each release cycle of software for further assaulting the non-personal-computing population. Linux and OS/2 developers, on the other hand, tend to listen to their *smartest* customers.... The good that Microsoft does in bringing computers to non-users is outdone by the curse that they bring on experienced users. (Nadeau 1999)

Certainly, the greatest diffusion of open source projects appears to be in settings where the end users are sophisticated, such as the Apache server installed by systems administrators. In these cases users are apparently more willing to tolerate the lack of detailed documentation or easy-to-understand user interfaces in exchange for the cost savings and the possibility of modifying the source code themselves. In several projects, such as Sendmail, project administrators chose to abandon backward compatibility in the interest of preserving program simplicity.[15] One of the rationales for this decision was that administrators using the Sendmail system were responsive to announcements that these changes would be taking place, and rapidly upgraded their systems. In a number of commercial software projects, it has been noted, these types of rapid responses are not as common. Once again, this reflects the greater sophistication and awareness of the users of open source software.

As the history in this chapter has suggested, one of the defining characteristics of open source software has been an ability to change, and it is by no means certain that open source projects will always be characterized by a focus on high-end users. Indeed, in several examples, contributions have been made not only to code but also to other aspects of the project. One of most visible and successful efforts was the marketing campaign to persuade consumers to switch to the Firefox Internet browser (see Krishnamurthy 2009). The volunteer community developed a site (www.switch2firefox.com) geared toward persuading consumers to switch browser, including both product comparisons and testimonials from switchers. The community also took out a two-page advertisement in *The New York Times*, which was funded by over ten thousand donors. In keeping with the open source norms, the advertisement featured the name of every donor. A variety of other marketing efforts drew on community members, such as a competition to develop the best short videos featuring Firefox. This ef-

---

15. To be certain, backward compatibility efforts may sometimes be exerted by status-seeking open source programmers. For example, Linux has been made to run on Atari machines, a pure bravado effort since no one uses Ataris anymore.

fort suggests that the single-minded focus on technical development that has traditionally characterized many open source projects may be evolving.

The debate about the ability of open source software to accommodate various users' needs has direct implications for the choice of license. The recent popularity of more liberal licenses and the concomitant decline of the GNU license are related to the rise in the "pragmatists'" influence. These individuals believe that allowing proprietary code and for-profit activities in segments that would otherwise be poorly served by the open source community will provide the movement with its best chance for success.

Open source software seems poised for continued growth in the future. The Internet has allowed open source software to operate extremely efficiently, both by facilitating the collaboration between programmers and by lowering the cost of distribution and support. As a consequence in a number of market segments the use of open source software is increasing, sometimes very quickly. IDC's report for the first quarter of 2007 says that Linux now holds 12.7 percent of the overall server market.[16] Surveys of chief information officers suggests that Linux will continue to increase its market share in enterprise software: for instance, a 2008 survey by *CIO Magazine* showed that more than half the respondents are using open source applications in their organization today, and an additional 10 percent plan to do so in the next year. For nearly half, open source applications are considered equally with proprietary solutions during the acquisition process.[17] The recession seems to be accelerating these trends, as cost-conscious firms trim spending.[18] While the prospects for desktop operating systems for consumers remain less certain, it is clear that open source will be an important part of the landscape for many years to come.

Final Thoughts

In this chapter we have followed the history of the development of open source software. We have highlighted the key institutional features that make this activity so distinct and important as well as the

---

16. As reported by www.linux-watch.com (accessed January 4, 2009).

17. http://www.cio.com/article/375916/Open_Source_is_Entering_the_Enterprise_Mainstream_Survey_Shows/1 (accessed January 3, 2009).

18. http://www.businessweek.com/technology/content/nov2008/tc20081130_069698.htm (accessed December 28, 2008).

three eras that open source has gone through. As we progressed, we digressed to consider the research that has documented and explained these patterns.

What kind of lessons can we draw from this history? In many respects, this account anticipates themes we will explore in much greater detail in subsequent chapters. Among the key lessons are the following:

• The proliferation of open source projects, and the subsequent maturation and formalization processes of many groups and organizations. As a result the sector today is very different from that of even a decade ago.

• The critical importance of licenses, as a way of codifying the rights and responsibilities of the contributors, users, and leaders of open source projects.

• The extent to which individual contributors and the private sector have been linked in the development of open source. Many proprietary firms have played a key role in developing open source technology, often in conjunction with the development of proprietary software, and such mixing is also seen among users.

• The great importance that users of open source software place on interoperability and "switching costs"—the ability to have programs that work across different platforms. This emphasis is considerably more dramatic than what is seen among users of proprietary software.

• The increased role of government in promoting one type of software over another, whether through subsidies, procurement, or property rights such as patents.

4   The Supply Side: Comingling Open Source and Proprietary Software

In chapter 2 we described the fundamental tension underlying innovation policies: it is socially wasteful for anyone to use anything but the best recipe, but it is impossible to give everyone access to the best recipe without sharply reducing incentives to invent. This tension applies to software as to all other innovation. Can open source software circumvent this trade-off between the creation and diffusion of innovation? In 2003 the respected weekly magazine *The Economist* gives the following description:

During that time, however, a rival universe to Microsoft started expanding. This is the movement for free software, whose code can be downloaded by anybody and is written and refined by a community of hobbyists.[1]

The picture conveyed is attractive: software free to users and supplied by volunteers. Yet this is one of the milder claims made for open source software. Raymond, one of the leading apostles of the "free software" movement, asserts that open source is something separate and fundamentally different than traditional software, a new and radical alternative that will largely displace the existing proprietary regime. As he puts it:

In a future that includes competition from open source, we can expect that the eventual destiny of any software technology will be to either die or become part of the open infrastructure itself. While this is hardly happy news for entrepreneurs who would like to collect rent on closed software forever, it does suggest that the software industry as a whole will remain entrepreneurial, with new niches constantly opening up at the upper (application) end and a limited lifespan for closed-IP monopolies as their product categories fall into infrastructure.... Finally, of course, this equilibrium will be great for the

1. "Now it's Novell," November 6, 2003, available at http://www.economist.com/displaystory.cfm?story_id=2199007 (registration required; accessed August 16, 2005).

software consumer driving the process. More and more high-quality software will become permanently available to use and build on instead of being discontinued or locked in somebody's vault.... The free market, in its widest libertarian sense including all un-coerced activity whether trade or gift, can produce perpetually increasing software wealth for everyone. (Raymond 1999, p. 163)

If these views were correct, open source software would solve the tension between providing incentives to innovate and encouraging efficient use. By making its software input ("recipes") available to anyone at essentially zero cost, it takes full advantage of the nonrivalry property, and the incentive problem does not exist as work is provided by volunteers. On top of that, spillovers of knowledge would be enhanced by the fact that the source code is available for many to build upon.

In this chapter we study the supply side of the software market, providing an in-depth look at how open source and proprietary software are licensed, developed, and sold. We will argue there is no sharp divide between the open source and proprietary worlds for software developer companies, in sharp contrast to the conventional wisdom that has taken over much of the debate over open source. The analysis reveals pervasive diversification by software developers, including a striking comingling of open source and proprietary development within firms. We will explain how economic analysis can shed light on the underlying factors that shape these business strategies and lead software firms to diversify in the ways we observe. In the next chapter we focus on the demand side of the market, analyzing the ways in which software users assess alternative open source and proprietary offerings in the market and how they make their choices among them.

Of course, not all firms diversify in the same way. There is a lot of variation among software companies, and we will show how business strategies and diversification depend on the characteristics of the firms. In addition, building on our international survey data, we will investigate how, and why, the comingling of open source and proprietary software development, and other aspects of diversification such as exporting, differs across countries. Finally, turning to the financing side, we show that external corporate funding for open source development is common and important, and that the form of open source licensing strongly influences this funding.

The chapter develops three main themes. The first is that firms extensively comingle their software development activities. This diversification takes a number of different forms. It is common for companies to develop both applications and operating systems software and, more interestingly, to engage in both open source and proprietary software development. Moreover firms follow business strategies that involve combining different types of software "business models" to make money. These include developing and selling unbundled software and software bundled in their own or other firms' hardware, and providing software support services. Even more striking is the fact that firms often comingle development and marketing of open source and proprietary software *within* these business models. This comingling of the open source and proprietary activities raises important questions about the advisability of public policies that treat them as distinct and separable, as we discuss in chapter 6.

The second major theme is that the comingling occurs in settings where firms have the most to gain. In particular, firms comingle where they can exploit opportunities to lower development and marketing costs (or "synergies"). Examples include combining development of customized software together with the provision of support services, developing both open source and proprietary software for operating systems, and greater comingling of open source and proprietary software in large firms where this can be done without sacrificing the benefits of economies of scale.

The final theme is that despite the comingling of open source and proprietary software, the two license forms differ in their export potential. Open source is less likely to be export oriented, and the evidence suggests that this reflects higher fixed costs of setting up the necessary marketing and distribution channels. This point is relevant in thinking about the policy debates over promoting open source, particularly in developing economies favoring an export-driven growth strategy.

Before we get started, a word is in order about why we focus on *firms* in open source development. After all, perhaps the most commonly held view about open source is that its development is driven by decentralized contributions by an army of individual volunteers. As we discussed in chapter 3, there are two points worth highlighting. The first is that the evolution of open source has involved a gradual shift toward greater firm-based development and funding. The second point is that while the community of contributors to open source development is widespread, the vast majority of open source projects are very small and contributions are highly concentrated on relatively few projects. Moreover the incentives driving such "volunteer" contributors are varied, and while intrinsic motivation plays a part, the evidence strongly points to an important role for market-oriented motivations, especially enhancing the developer's labor market prospects. Thus the long-term sustainability of open source contributions relies in part on the coexistence of a vibrant, market-based software sector.

One of the major challenges to the academic and policy debates around open source has been the dearth of information on how software developers actually behave, the business strategies they follow, and other aspects of "competition and cohabitation" between open source and proprietary software. This lack of information has led to a more heated, but less informed, debate. Our new survey of software developer firms is designed to help fill this gap, and in particular, to shed some light on the issues from an international perspective. Before turning to the core analysis of these issues, we take a brief detour to describe the methodology and scope of the survey which underpins the empirical analysis in this chapter.

Overview of the Developer Survey Methodology

To understand how open source and proprietary software developer firms interact, we conducted a cross-country survey of software developers. We created an extensive survey questionnaire that was translated into the language of each of the fifteen countries covered (and then back-translated into English to confirm accuracy), and administered by telephone by a professional survey company (Lieberman Research Worldwide).[2] The countries in the survey are Brazil, Chile, China, France, Greece, India, Israel, Kenya, Mexico, Poland, Russia, South Africa, Singapore, Thailand, and Turkey. These countries span a wide range in terms of the levels of economic development. Using the World Bank categories (WDR 2004), two of the countries are lower income (India and Kenya), six are lower middle income (Brazil, China, Russia, South Africa, Thailand, and Turkey), three are upper middle income (Chile, Mexico, and Poland), and four in the upper income category (France, Greece, Israel, and Singapore).

The sample design was the same in each country. Within each country the survey company constructed a nationally representative random sample of software developing firms to be surveyed. The list of

---

2. The complete questionnaire is provided in an on-line appendix. We thank Daniel Garcia-Swartz at Law and Economics Consulting Company for help preparing the survey.

companies was compiled from the registry of firms, and the survey company contacted the person responsible for making the decisions regarding software development for the company.[3] In cases where the respondent was unable or unwilling to respond, another user was added to the list until the quota was met. Our primary focus in this analysis was to understand how software companies diversify into both open source and proprietary activities, so we wanted to ensure adequate representation of different types of software developers. To do this, we defined four different categories of software companies: (1) "pure developers"—companies that develop new or original software which is either sold to final users or to computer hardware manufacturers for bundling; (2) "custom developers"—companies that specialize in customizing software either for end users or hardware manufacturers; (3) "bundle developers"—companies that manufacture hardware and either develop original software or customize software developed by others; and (4) "support developers"—companies specializing in providing software support services to customers using software developed by others (software development and customization may be involved in this process). In what follows we will refer to these categories as "business models." In the sampling process we imposed a minimum quota of 20 for each of these categories in each country. The company conducting the surveys extensively checked the data for outliers, and in some instances, contacted respondents to check the accuracy of responses.

Table 4.1 summarizes the composition of the developer sample. In total we have 1,894 responses, spread almost equally across the fifteen countries. The sample covers the range of sizes, with 62.0 percent being small firms (less than 25 employees), 33.4 percent medium-sized firms (between 25 and 250 employees), and 4.6 percent large firms (more than 250 employees). Domestic software companies account for 89.0 percent of respondents, with the remaining 11.0 percent being local subsidiaries of foreign corporations. The survey covers developers with a variety of business models: 38.3 percent of the firms focus primarily on development of pure software, 24.4 percent on customized software, 14.2 percent on software designed for bundling in hardware, and the remaining 23.1 percent on software support services. The

---

3. Among survey respondents, 46.3 percent were a senior executive, 23.5 percent were the head of the software department, 17.2 percent were the chief information officer, and 13.0 percent were a senior IT executive.

Table 4.1
Composition of the software developer sample (in percent)

Software developer	Sample
By size	
Small (<25 employees)	62.0
Medium (25–250)	33.4
Large (>250)	4.6
By ownership/size	
Domestic company	89.0
Small	65.3
Medium	31.6
Large	3.1
Foreign subsidiary	11.0
Small	36.3
Medium	47.4
Large	16.3
By business model	
Pure (original) software	38.3
Customized software	24.4
Bundled with hardware	14.2
Support services	23.1

composition of the developer sample is very similar across the fifteen countries.

Comingling Open Source and Proprietary Software Development

Our developer survey provides rich data about the development of proprietary and open source software. In this section we begin by looking at the central feature of these data: there is no sharp divide between the worlds of open source and proprietary software. Software firms comingle development of open source and proprietary, and this holds to varying extents across a wide range of firm characteristics. We develop this point by looking at various aspects of how developer firms extensively mix between open source and proprietary software activities. In later sections we will examine the patterns of diversification in greater detail and explain how economic forces influence this diversification.

To begin, table 4.2 presents information on the proportion of software firms that engage in open source development, and the extent to

Table 4.2
Specialization in some open source software development by firms (in percent)

	Firms developing some open source	Developer hours devoted to open source			
		<25	25–50	50–75	>75
Aggregate	39.6	38.5	29.5	16.9	15.1
	(1.1)	(1.8)	(1.7)	(1.4)	(1.4)
Size					
Small	38.0	39.8	26.4	17.2	16.6
	(1.5)	(2.3)	(2.1)	(1.8)	(1.8)
Medium	40.7	33.1	35.4	17.9	13.6
	(1.2)	(2.9)	(3.0)	(2.4)	(2.1)
Large	52.9	56.5	26.1	8.7	8.7
	(2.0)	(7.3)	(6.5)	(4.2)	(4.2)
Ownership					
Domestic	39.1	40.1	28.7	16.0	15.2
	(1.2)	(1.9)	(1.8)	(1.8)	(1.4)
Foreign subsidiary	44.0	27.2	34.8	23.9	14.3
	(3.4)	(4.6)	(5.0)	(4.4)	(3.6)
Business model					
Pure software	32.0	37.5	28.0	17.3	17.2
	(1.7)	(3.2)	(2.9)	(2.5)	(2.5)
Customized software	42.6	36.5	31.0	14.7	17.8
	(2.3)	(3.4)	(3.3)	(2.5)	(2.7)
Bundled with hardware	43.3	44.8	27.6	16.4	11.2
	(2.9)	(4.6)	(4.2)	(3.4)	(2.9)
Support services	46.8	38.1	30.7	19.0	12.2
	(2.2)	(3.4)	(3.2)	(2.7)	(2.3)
Export orientation					
Nonexporters	38.0	37.7	28.0	17.9	16.4
	(1.4)	(2.3)	(2.1)	(1.8)	(1.7)
Exporters	42.3	39.8	31.6	15.5	13.1
	(2.9)	(2.8)	(2.7)	(2.1)	(2.0)

Note: This table is read as follows (row 1): 39.6 percent of firms do some open source development, 38.5 percent of firms who do some open source development allocate between 25 and 50 percent of their total developer time to open source software, and so on. Multinomial standard errors are in parentheses. These are computed as $\sqrt{p(1-p)/n}$, where p is the reported proportion and n is the relevant sample size.

which these firms specialize in open source development, as measured by the percentage of their developer hours devoted to open source.[4] Open source development is not an isolated phenomenon—overall, 39.6 percent of the firms in our survey develop at least some open source software.[5] But the most striking, and important, fact is that companies that develop open source software typically also develop proprietary software. As the first row of the table shows, 68 percent of firms engaged in developing some open source software devote at least half of their development hours to proprietary software. Only 15 percent of these firms devote more than 75 percent of development input to open source. This extensive comingling of open source and proprietary software development is found in each of the fifteen countries covered by our survey (for brevity, we do not present the country detail).

The remaining rows of the table provide more detail about how this comingling varies for firms of different sizes, for domestic and foreign subsidiaries, and for different business models. While there are some differences in the extent of comingling, it is striking that all categories of firms exhibit broadly similar patterns. This commonality strongly suggests that there is some basic economic force underlying the decision to mix, and we will discuss this in more detail later.

The descriptive statistics in table 4.2 tell us that participation of firms in open source development, and the comingling of open source and proprietary software, are widespread. However, to pin down the determinants of these decisions, we turn to econometric analysis of the choice of whether to engage in open source development and the degree of diversification, which allows us to control for the effects of all of the relevant factors together. For the interested reader, the details of the results are reported in appendix 4.1. Here we limit ourselves to a summary of the three main key findings.

The first is that the propensity to engage in open source development varies across countries. A formal statistical test allows us to reject the hypothesis that countries are the same, once we control for the other factors. But it turns out that only three countries stand out as dif-

---

4. The measure based on developer hours is preferable to revenues because it is directly tied to the development effort. Nonetheless, it is reassuring that all of the key conclusions in the chapter also hold if we use the distribution of revenues to measure diversification.
5. Interestingly there is not much variation across countries in the proportion of firms doing open source (for brevity, we do not present country level detail). Only two countries stand out—Kenya, which has a much larger proportion, and South Africa, which is much lower than the others.

ferent from the rest: Kenya, Singapore, and South Africa. Software developers in Kenya have a significantly higher probability of engaging in open source than other countries, while the opposite is true for Singapore and South Africa. This finding shows that open source development activity is *not*, as some have claimed, a phenomenon particularly associated with, or concentrated in, developing countries. This is also what we found in chapter 2, looking at the per capita contributions to open source projects by individual developers.

The second finding is that large firms are significantly more likely to engage in some open source activity than either small- or medium-sized companies, but at the same time the large firms are less likely to specialize in open source. This is what we would expect to find if there is a fixed "entry" cost of engaging in open source development. It is more likely that large firms will be able to cover the entry cost and thus to do some open source, without the need to specialize in order to do so.

The third finding is that the decision to develop open source is related to the set of software business models the firm adopts. In particular, companies that work on customized software, bundled software, and (to a lesser extent) support services are significantly more likely to engage in some open source than pure software developers. This fact suggests that there may be some kind of cost savings or other advantages—"synergies" for short—that make it attractive to combine open source with particular business models. We will investigate this idea in more detail in the next sections.

A Closer Look at Diversification in Software Development

The evidence we presented in the previous section shows clearly that software firms typically mix open source and proprietary activities, and that the decision to comingle is affected by characteristics of the software firm. But what are the underlying economic forces that influence how firms choose to combine different development activities, including mixing between open source and proprietary software? In the next subsection we first briefly discuss these economic factors and then turn to a more detailed examination of the patterns of diversification in software development.

Economic Forces Shaping Diversification by Software Firms

The decision of software firms to diversify and the pattern of that diversification are driven by two main factors—cost synergies and demand factors. Cost synergies arise when doing two (or more) activities together is less costly than doing them separately. Economists refer to such cases as economies of scope. When they are present, we expect to see firms exploiting the opportunity for cost savings by diversifying into both activities. Economies of scope can take two forms— *cost synergies* in the development of software and *marketing synergies* in the distribution and sale of software. The pattern of cost synergies will depend on the particulars of the software development process, including how on-the-job programming experience is acquired and the extent to which it is "fungible," or of dual use. Similarly marketing synergies will depend on the extent to which marketing and distribution channels (e.g., the firm's reputation, often its most important asset) can be used for multiple purposes.

The second factor that determines the scope for diversification is demand, or size of the market. Adam Smith first observed that the division of labor is limited by the extent of the market. It does this because the size of the market affects the ability of firms to make money through specialization. If there are cost advantages to being larger (economies of scale), firms can only exploit them profitably (and cover their fixed costs) if the market is large enough. This also applies when there are both economies of scale and potential advantages to combining different activities (economies of scope). Thus both the level and composition of demand affect how firms diversify.

Since both open source and proprietary software are tradable goods, the relevant market is global, at least in principle. But in practice, national boundaries may still exert some influence on many firms. There are substantial fixed costs in marketing and distribution required to enter international markets. As a result small software firms are not well positioned to enter the export market, and for them the size of the domestic market may be more relevant. While this is not an insuperable barrier (we later show that small firms also export), there are advantages to size. In addition companies that provide software support services, and those developing customized software, are more likely to cater more to local needs. Finally, the composition of demand can matter, such as the mix of government, individual, and corporate users. If individual users are the dominant source of demand, and if they lack the technical sophistication required to adapt and use open source, the effective market for open source may be more limited. This is less likely to be the case when corporate demand is dominant.

To set the stage for the empirical analysis, we begin by identifying three distinct ways in which software firms can and, as we will see, do diversify. The first is what we will call "software focus," which refers to whether software is designed for operating systems or applications. The programming skills required for these two types of software are different, even if there is, of course, overlap. While operating system software is typically aimed at technically sophisticated users (e.g., in-house IT personnel), applications software is designed for less computer savvy, final users and, as such, needs to be more user friendly.

The second dimension of diversification is "license type," which refers to whether the software is distributed under proprietary terms or under some form of open source license. Firms can choose to develop operating system or applications software under the open source or proprietary mode, or both. As we have discussed earlier, there are strong claims made both in the academic and popular debates about open source and proprietary software development being separate and distinct realms, with little if any overlap. Our analysis will show that the reality is more complex, with firms frequently crossing the boundaries of license type in their software development activities.

The third and final dimension of diversification we study is the "business model." By this we mean the ways in which open source and proprietary software firms make their money. They can develop and sell original (packaged) software, customize software for users, develop software for bundling in computer hardware, and supply software support services. Of course, the business strategies firms adopt can and, as we will see, often do involve combining one or more of these business models.

While these three forms of diversification are distinct, they are not mutually exclusive. Companies can diversify using any combination of them—software focus, license type, and business model—and presumably do so in ways they expect to be most profitable. We will use our survey data to examine the extent to which software firms do this and what those patterns of diversification tell us about the economic factors shaping this process.

In view of this discussion, where would cost synergies most likely arise? We should expect them to be important in contexts where innovations in software architecture or code have dual (or multiple) purposes. This is particularly likely to be the case across different business models: such as between developing customized software and software for bundling in hardware, or between customized software (or software for bundling with other firms' hardware) and the provision of support services for that software. But cost synergies can also operate between open source and proprietary license types, since code innovations in open source might be usable in proprietary packages. Certain types of competencies acquired in writing software can have a similar dual-use character. Marketing synergies can also operate in any of these dimensions. However, we would expect it to be stronger between open source and proprietary software (where the broad customer base is more similar), as compared with different software functionalities (software focus) or business models.

Real-World Examples of Diversification and Comingling

Before we turn to the empirical analysis of the data on diversification and comingling of different types of software, we briefly consider some real-world examples of how companies make money from open source software, how they combine open source and proprietary software, and why some firms contribute to open source development rather than simply exploiting existing open source commercially.

Some firms that are in the business of selling software support services work primarily with open source software. Even if the source code is available at very low cost, implementing the software in specific situations can be technically challenging, and firms sell support services, or packages that include software from different sources, to provide a complete solution to the users. For instance, Novell sells its Novell Linux Desktop 9 by describing it as "A desktop operating system and office-productivity environment that enables businesses to use Linux and open source with confidence."[6] Of course, the fact that firms can package and sell open source software is not sufficient to understand why they contribute to its development.[7] Why not let others do the work, as they let you have the result for free?

To our knowledge, there are no systematic studies of the reasons firms choose to contribute to open source software rather than free ride on the work of others, but it seems that two main reasons come into play.[8] First, firms like the visibility of being a core contributor.

---

6. http://www.novell.com/products/desktop/ (accessed October 31, 2005).

7. Actually, under the GPL license, a firm must use the GPL licence for all the software that it wants to distribute along whatever open source software it distributes. However, it is common for firms to do much more than this and to actively contribute to the core functionality of the product itself.

8. A number of authors have argued that firms can benefit from such contributions, such as shaping the trajectory of open source developments, sustaining a regime of reciprocal contributions, and in other ways (e.g., Chesbrough, Vanhaverbeke, and West 2006). While there are many anecdotes along these lines, the hypotheses have not been subjected to rigorous testing, to our knowledge.

Part of this is public relations, but there are other more tangible reasons. In particular, their clients will be more willing to buy support from them if their employees are top contributors to the programs; this provides a guarantee of the depth of competence within the firm. Second, firms try to influence the development of the open source program. For instance, the press release announcing the acquisition of Suse Linux by Novell stated:

SUSE LINUX engineers will work closely with Novell's product teams to ensure they maximize their respective synergies in joint development efforts. "We're making a commitment to open source, not to a product we're selling," said Messman (chairman and CEO of Novell). "With SUSE LINUX and Ximian, we gain some of the best open source developers in the market, and we want to leverage those capabilities in our development efforts across the entire product line."[9]

In practice, the differences between open source and proprietary software developers and firms are less sharp than the preceding description (and many public discussions) makes it appear. Many firms have both proprietary and open source offerings. For instance, Zend is an Israeli company, created by Andi Gutmans and Zeev Suraski who "are the architects of PHP and creators of the open source Zend Engine.... Because of their internationally recognized authority, the company and its founders continue to play leadership roles in the PHP and open source communities, and are accountable for a central role in the explosive growth of PHP." On top of this role in the development of open source programs, Zend sells "commercial products and services that enable developers and IT personnel to deliver business-critical PHP applications, Zend is taking the power of PHP to the enterprise."[10] For instance, it sells Zend studio, which is an Integrated Development Environment for PHP. Similarly VA Software, which owns the website SourceForge.net that provides services to open source projects, sells a proprietary version of the functionalities of that site under the name SourceForge Enterprise Edition.[11]

One explanation for these strategies is simply that the profit-maximizing business model is different for the different products sold by the firm. Another is that the open source software serves as

---

9. http://www.novell.com/news/press/archive/2004/suse_archive/novell_closing.html (accessed March 28, 2005).
10. These two quotations are taken from http://www-03.ibm.com/systems/i/software/php/products.html (accessed March 28, 2005).
11. See Lyons (2005), who also provides other examples.

advertising or as a way to make potential users aware of the functionalities of the proprietary software. Finally, part of the explanation lies in our discussion of network externalities in chapter 2. By providing some software freely, the firms increase the demand for their proprietary products, which are made more valuable by the increased size of the installed base. Some of these benefits could be realized by freely distributing proprietary software, as with Adobe, which distributes the free program Acrobat Reader in order to increase the demand for Acrobat. Distributing under an open source license also has other advantages such as providing users with a guarantee that if the firm changed strategy, the product would still be available and furthermore could still be improved by others. All these explanations boil down to saying that there is some kind of cost or marketing synergies (economies of scope) that makes it profit maximizing to do open source and proprietary activities together. This idea was also discussed in chapter 3, when we dealt with the "third era" in the history of open source. Later in this chapter we will use our survey evidence to try to illuminate the patterns of diversification and what they say about the nature of these synergies.

Furthermore, although open source code is available for free, companies can go to much effort to prevent this code from being compiled and distributed in a version that competes with their own compiled version, making the program semiproprietary. For instance, Red Hat's Linux distribution includes programs beyond the core Linux programs. These programs are open source and can be downloaded from Red Hat's website, but Red Hat does not distribute freely a compiled version of its program and restricts the right of third parties to use the name Red Hat in a distribution that they would have compiled themselves.[12]

Not only do developers often belong to both the proprietary and open source worlds, but some programs also do, as they are distributed both under an open source and a proprietary license. For example, this is true of MySQL, the most prominent open source database, and of the mono-project.[13] The firm that owns the software releases

---

12. It is also subject to competition by those who recompile its software. See Stephen Shankland (2005).

13. MySQL was developed by MySQL AB and is available under a GPL license. It is also available as a commercial license: "Commercially licensed users are also free from the requirement of making their own application open source." See http://www.mysql.com/company/legal/licensing/ (accessed April 20, 2005). On the mono-project, see http://www.mono-project.com/FAQ: Licensing (accessed April 20, 2005).

the purchaser of a commercial license from some of the obligations that the open source license imposes on them. This is especially valuable for licenses like the GPL, which restricts the use of the open source code in conjunction with proprietary software. When these strategies do not enable firms to make profits, then they can choose to sell the product exclusively under a commercial license.[14]

What do these examples (and the list could easily be expanded) teach us? The most important lesson is that software companies frequently find it in their profit-maximizing interest to combine development and sale of open source and proprietary software. Indeed in some cases they release very similar programs under both license forms. This comingling occurs for three main reasons. The first is that there are synergies in the development and marketing of open source and proprietary offerings, which firms exploit by diversifying into both. The second reason is that software users are heterogeneous, differing in their technical sophistication and software requirements. Software firms can exploit this diversity, and capitalize on their reputation, by operating in both the open source and proprietary realms. Finally, users themselves often combine open source and proprietary software, as we demonstrate in the next chapter on the demand side of the software market. This mixing behavior of consumers gives firms another opportunity to exploit their reputational capital, and any available synergies, by operating in both realms.

Survey Evidence on Diversification by Software Firms

The examples given in the previous section illustrate a variety of ways in which software developer firms adapt their business strategies to mix open source and proprietary software. In this section we examine the evidence on diversification more formally, and discuss what it tells us about the form of the potential cost synergies in software development and marketing. We do this in stages, looking at each of the following dimensions of diversification:

1. *Software focus* Combining development of applications and operating system software.

---

14. *Forbes* describes as follows the reasons behind VA Software's decision to sell Source-Forge Enterprise Edition under a commercial license: "Officials at VA Software say they can't release SourceForge Enterprise Edition as an open source program, because, if they did, copycats could create knockoffs of the program, and that would hurt sales. 'Our own code could be used to compete against us,' says Colin Bodell, chief technology officer at VA Software."

2. *Software focus by license type* Combining open source and proprietary software for applications and operating systems.

3. *Business models* Combining development of separate (packaged) software, unbundled software, customized software, software bundled in hardware supplied by the firm, software bundled in hardware provided by other firms and support services.

4. *License type and business models* Combining open source and proprietary software within some set of the business models listed above.

For each of these four cases, we want to analyze the tendency of firms to combine certain activities. To illustrate how we do this, let's consider any two activities, which we denote A and B. If firms tend to do A and B together (but not all firms combine them), then knowing that a firm does A should tell us that it is also more likely to be doing B. All we do is to formalize this simple intuition. To illustrate, we consider the following simple case where the overall proportion of firms engaged in A is 40 percent (this is called the "marginal frequency"). Suppose that 80 percent of the firms that do A also are engaged in activity B (this is called the "conditional frequency" because it tells us the likelihood that firms do B, conditional on them doing A). If we draw a firm at random, the chance it is engaged in A is given by the marginal frequency, 40 percent. But if we randomly draw a firm from those that do A, the chances that firm does B is given by the conditional frequency, 80 percent. This comparison tells us that firms tend to do A and B together, which we interpret as evidence that there are positive synergies that lead them to do so.

In short, our procedure is to compare conditional and marginal frequencies in the data. When the conditional frequency is larger than the marginal frequency, it means that there is a positive synergy connecting the two activities (in economist parlance, "economies of scope")—firms tend to do the activities together. When the conditional frequency is lower than the marginal frequency, there is a negative synergy ("diseconomies of scope")—firms doing one tend not to do the other. Finally, if the conditional and marginal frequencies are the same, we draw the conclusion that there are no synergies connecting the two activities, either positive or negative.[15]

---

15. We recognize that any such empirical interpretations need to be qualified. Inferring that there are synergies from observed pairings of software or business activities is always subject to the concern that it may reflect unobserved characteristics of the firm that are correlated with their choices, rather than any kind of underlying synergy. With the available data, there is not much we can do to address this concern.

Table 4.3
Diversification by software focus and license type (percentage of respondents)

Panel A

	Operating systems	Applications
Operating systems	—	81.7
Applications	38.2	—
Marginal probabilities	43.0	92.1

Panel B

	Proprietary operating systems	Proprietary applications	Open source operating systems	Open source applications
Proprietary operating systems	—	79.9	34.3	32.2
Proprietary applications	31.1	—	17.2	30.6
OS operating systems	50.8	65.6	—	76.8
OS applications	30.1	73.7	48.5	—
Marginal probabilities	32.3	83.1	21.8	34.5

Comingling Development of Operating Systems and Applications Software

We start with the simplest case, the diversification into both applications and operating systems software. The 2 by 2 matrix in panel A in table 4.3 presents the relevant information for this case. Each element in this matrix tells us the frequency (empirical probability) with which software companies operate both in the activities denoted by the corresponding row and column. The numbers in the last row give the overall frequency of firms operating in the activity given the corresponding column ("marginal frequency"). Thus the last row shows that 43.0 percent of firms in the survey develop software for operating systems, and 92.1 percent develop applications software. The number in the first column of the matrix tells us that, of those firms doing operating systems software, 38.2 percent also develop applications software. The number in the second column says that, of those firms doing applications software, 81.7 percent also develop operating systems software.

These numbers tell us that it is *less likely* for a firm to be developing applications software if it also is doing operating systems software, and vice versa. Thus they indicate that operating systems and applications software are alternative, not complementary, areas of expertise for software firms.[16]

The analysis so far does not distinguish between open source and proprietary software within the operating systems and applications development. This aggregation may hide synergies. To analyze this, in panel B of table 4.3 we refine the analysis by breaking down the software focus into open source and proprietary. A simple comparison of the elements in the columns with the marginal frequencies in the last row and column shows that there are differences, indicating that the various activities are not independent of each other (a formal statistical test confirms this conclusion). Using the same approach as before (comparing conditional and marginal frequencies), this table reveals the synergies that appear to be operating. The first column shows that 32.3 percent of firms develop proprietary software for operating systems. The element in the third row of that column shows that, among companies that develop open source software for operating systems (identified by the row), 50.8 percent also develop proprietary software for operating systems (identified by the column). This conditional frequency is much larger than the overall frequency, indicating that firms are more likely to work both on proprietary and open source software for operating systems than would be predicted if these choices were independent.

Applying similar reasoning to column 2, we conclude that firms are substantially less likely to work on proprietary applications if they work on open source operating systems or applications (compare the conditional frequency of 65.6 percent to the marginal frequency of 83.1 percent). Column 3 reveals that companies are about twice as likely to develop open source software for operating systems if they also develop open source software for applications, and if they develop proprietary software for operating systems (compare 48.5 and 34.3 percent to the overall frequency of 21.8 percent). Finally, in column 4 we see that firms are more than twice as likely to develop open source applications if they also do open source work on operating systems (76.8 percent as compared to the marginal frequency of 34.5 percent).

These numbers indicate cost (or marketing) synergies operate in two dimensions: between open source and proprietary software for operat-

---

16. Using a standard statistical (chi-square) test, we strongly reject the hypothesis that the rows and columns in the table are independent of each other, which would be the case if operating systems and applications software development were simply independent. The evidence here suggests the stronger conclusion that there are actually diseconomies of scope—development is cheaper if they are not done together.

ing systems, and between open source software for operating systems and applications. To put this another way, there is an "operating system synergy" that links open source and proprietary activity, and an "open source" synergy that links operating systems and applications. Interestingly we do not find any evidence of synergy between open source and proprietary applications (i.e., no "applications synergy").

The evidence presented in table 4.3 uses all firms in the survey sample, pooling data from the different countries. But our examination of similar tables for individual countries, which we do not discuss here in detail, indicates that similar patterns hold at the more disaggregated level (where there is more noise in the data due to smaller sample sizes). This finding that the diversification patterns are broadly similar across countries is noteworthy because it suggests that the synergies revealed in these tables are cost-related synergies, rather than being driven by demand constraints, which we would expect to be more specific to individual countries.

Thus far we have examined diversification in software focus and license type. There is clear evidence that there are systematic forces (synergies) at work, as firms tend to combine some activities but not others. As we discussed earlier, software firms also adopt a variety of business models in their software development and marketing, and we turn next to whether there is any evidence of synergies among these business strategies.

Comingling Business Models

The survey asks software firms about the pattern of diversification of their software development activities in five distinct areas of operation: separate (packaged) software, customized software, software bundled in their own marketed hardware, software sold to other firms for bundling in their hardware, and software support services. Companies in the survey report in which of these five areas they operate. Table 4.4 summarizes the pattern of diversification.

Since the manner of interpretation will be clear by now, we simply summarize the key findings that emerge from this table. Overall, the table reveals that there are some synergies among business models, but they are weaker than those we found for license type and software focus.[17] The first finding is that the development of separate (packaged) software and customized software are substitutes rather than

17. As before, the formal statistical test strongly rejects independence between the rows and columns in the table (i.e., no synergies among business models).

Table 4.4
Diversification by business activity (percentage of respondents)

	Separate software	Customized software	Own bundled	Other bundled	Support services
Separate software	—	28.3	21.1	41.1	81.0
Customized software	50.2	—	22.8	50.1	83.5
Own bundled	63.2	38.4	—	50.9	82.6
Other bundled	59.7	40.9	24.7	—	91.9
Support services	60.9	35.4	20.8	47.7	—
Marginal probabilities	61.7	34.8	20.6	42.6	82.0

being paired activities. Second, customized software and software designed to be bundled in hardware tend to be paired in the data, indicating positive synergies (this holds both for hardware produced by the same firm and bundling in other firms). In addition there are positive synergies between the provision of support services and development of software sold for bundling in hardware by other firms. These linkages between software customization and bundling, and support services and bundled software, are not surprising. In fact there are many examples of such behavior among software firms, a leading one being the transformation of IBM during the 1990s from a pure mainframe computer company to one heavily diversified into hardware and software services (see Kirkpatrick and Tkaczyk 2004).

Comingling of Open Source and Proprietary Software within Business Models

Evidence presented thus far shows interesting synergies across specific software business models. But what about synergies between open source and proprietary software within these business models? Do we observe that companies integrate open source and proprietary software development either within or across business model—such as by developing both open source and proprietary packaged software, or by providing proprietary packaged software and open source support services? To examine this question, we now turn to more detailed information on diversification, broken down both by business model and license type.[18] The results of our examination are provided in table 4.5.

---

18. With this two-way breakdown, the survey does not allow us to distinguish between separate (packaged) and customized software; in the table "separate" refers to both of these categories.

Table 4.5
Diversification by business activity and license type (percentage of respondents)

	Proprietary software				Open source software			
	Separate software	Own bundled	Other bundled	Support services	Separate software	Own bundled	Other bundled	Support services
Proprietary software								
Separate software	—	26.9	33.2	69.8	25.0	9.9	12.0	21.8
Own bundled	80.4	—	49.1	72.0	32.9	30.9	23.3	31.6
Other bundled	75.4	37.3	—	72.8	27.5	15.7	31.0	29.8
Support services	76.2	26.3	35.0	—	21.2	10.5	13.8	29.9
Open source software								
Separate software	70.5	31.0	34.1	54.6	—	30.1	41.4	61.3
Own bundled	62.7	65.6	43.9	60.8	67.9	—	50.0	70.3
Other bundled	53.3	34.8	60.9	56.3	65.6	35.1	—	66.2
Support services	55.5	26.9	33.5	69.9	55.5	28.2	37.9	—
Marginal probabilities	71.1	23.8	31.3	65.2	25.2	11.2	15.9	27.9

Note: The symbols NW, SW, SE, and NE indicate the names of the quadrants.

Again, we begin by testing the hypothesis that there are no synergies whatsoever (i.e., whether the rows and columns in the table are independent of each other). The data decisively reject this hypothesis (the test statistic is highly significant). There clearly are synergies at work, but we would like to know more precisely where they are located. Are the synergies operating between different business models, or between open source and proprietary software within a given business model, or perhaps both?

To answer this question, we redo the test that there are no synergies, but this time separately for each of the four quadrants in the tables: (1) among business models for proprietary software (northwest quadrant), (2) among business models for open source (southeast quadrant), and (3) between open source and proprietary license types for a given business model (southwest and northeast quadrants). In each of these cases we strongly reject the hypothesis that there are no synergies. This shows that there are systematic links working both across software business models and between open source and proprietary software within business models. In the next part of the discussion, we pinpoint exactly where these synergies are coming from.

To do this, we have to examine table 4.5 in more detail, quadrant by quadrant. This could quickly become tedious, so instead of going element by element, we illustrate with a few leading examples and then summarize the main conclusions that emerge from the table. Consider first the diagonal elements in the southwest quadrant. These elements give us the proportion of firms that do a particular *open source* activity that also do that activity under the *proprietary* license form. This provides information about the synergies between open source and proprietary software, *for the same business model.* For example, 70.5 percent of the companies that develop separate open source software also develop separate proprietary software. This is very close to the overall proportion doing separate proprietary software (71.1 percent), which indicates that there is no synergy at work. Using similar comparisons, however, we see that there is a strong synergy between open source and proprietary licenses for software bundled in hardware. This holds both for software bundled in the same firm's hardware and in hardware produced by other firms.

We do not have enough information to pin down the explanation, but the following hypothesis looks plausible. In the case of bundled software there may be fewer issues associated with intellectual property rights to protect the software, since exploiting it requires adaptation to the specific hardware. Hence at both the development and mar-keting levels the different types of software are similar enough that having learned to develop one, it is relatively easy to develop the other. The diagonal elements in the northeast quadrant tell a similar story, but there the focus is on whether firms that do a particular pro-prietary activity also do that activity under the open source license form.

The next step involves the off-diagonal elements in the northwest and southeast quadrants. These tell us about synergies among different software activities, *for a given license form*. We turn first to the north-west quadrant, which focuses on proprietary software. Let's start with the conditional frequency of 80.4 percent, the element in the first col-umn and second row of the table. This says that 80.4 percent of firms that develop separate software are also engaged in doing software for bundling in hardware. Yet the marginal frequency for separate soft-ware (given at the bottom of the first column) tells us that overall, only 71.1 percent of firms are engaged in developing separate (pro-prietary) software. This comparison between the conditional and marginal frequencies reveals that it is more likely that firms are devel-oping separate software if they are also doing software for bundling. We infer from this evidence that that separate software and software designed to be bundled in hardware exhibit synergies. By making sim-ilar comparisons, we learn from the second and third columns that software for bundling by the developer and software sold to others to be bundled in hardware are also linked by such synergies. Finally, pro-prietary support services are typically paired with proprietary soft-ware for bundling by other firms. In short, this evidence indicates substantial synergies working across some, but not all, business mod-els within the proprietary license form.

We turn to the southeast quadrant of the table, and the story that emerges for open source software is similar to, but stronger, than that of proprietary software. Notice that all of the conditional frequen-cies in this quadrant are far higher than the marginal frequencies (in the columns). This shows that there are strong synergies linking all four of the different software activities under the open source license. In other words, there is a strong "open source synergy" at work across all business models.

The information presented in the last three sections is the first sys-tematic evidence on the cost synergies in software development. We showed that there are strong synergies working in several dimensions, particularly between different business models and between open source and proprietary license forms within business models. The evidence is indirect in the sense that we infer cost synergies from the observed diversification behavior of firms rather than estimate it econometrically from direct measures of inputs and outputs (what economists felicitously call "multi-product production functions"). But as long as it reasonable to assume that software companies formulate their business strategy and diversification decisions to exploit opportunities for cost and marketing synergies—in other words, as long as firms diversify "rationally"—then this indirect evidence tells us something useful about these opportunities.

Diversification by Sources of Revenue
The evidence on diversification we have presented so far is based on simply identifying which software development activities a company is active in, without reference to the importance of each area to the firm. It is possible that developers operate under various business models but focus on only one or two. As we will now show below, however, this is not the case. The revenue sources are also diversified, and the distribution of revenue from the different sources is very similar for open source and proprietary software.

Table 4.6 shows that the revenue sources for firms that sell open source and proprietary software, under various business models, are much more similar than one might have thought. For the sample as a whole, proprietary software sales account for 78.3 percent and open source the remaining 21.7 percent, of total revenues. This dominance of proprietary sales is not surprising. What is more noteworthy is that this breakdown is very similar in nine of the fifteen countries in our survey (not reported here for brevity). The countries where open source accounts for a distinctly higher proportion of revenue are Kenya (57.2 percent), France (28.5 percent), and Thailand (28.5 percent); those at the low end include Brazil (11.1 percent), Israel (12.1 percent), and South Africa (14.1 percent). There are both low- and high-income countries in both groups, confirming that open source activity by software firms (measured in terms of revenue generation) is not concentrated in less developed countries.

Moreover the distribution of revenues for the various business models is strikingly similar for proprietary and open source software. For proprietary software, software for final users (separate software) and support services are the main sources of proprietary revenues. Together these two categories account for 78 percent of all revenues

Table 4.6
Sources of revenues from open source and proprietary software development (percentage of revenue)

Revenues from	Proprietary				Open source			
	Separate software	Other bundled	Own bundled	Support services	Separate software	Other bundled	Own bundled	Support services
Aggregate	37.6	6.4	10.3	24.0	7.7	2.6	3.4	8.0
	(1.1)	(0.6)	(0.8)	(1.1)	(1.1)	(0.7)	(0.8)	(1.1)
Size								
Small	39.4	5.9	10.6	23.3	7.5	2.4	3.1	7.8
	(1.5)	(0.8)	(1.0)	(1.3)	(1.4)	(0.9)	(1.0)	(1.4)
Medium	35.0	7.0	10.0	24.9	8.0	2.6	4.0	8.5
	(2.0)	(1.1)	(1.3)	(1.9)	(1.9)	(1.3)	(1.5)	(1.9)
Large	37.6	6.4	10.3	24.0	7.7	2.6	3.4	8.0
	(5.3)	(3.5)	(3.5)	(5.1)	(5.0)	(4.1)	(4.2)	(4.9)
Ownership								
Domestic	38.2	6.1	10.4	24.1	7.8	2.2	3.2	8.0
	(1.2)	(0.7)	(0.8)	(1.1)	(1.1)	(1.1)	(0.8)	(1.1)
Foreign subsidiary	33.1	9.1	9.4	22.6	7.5	5.3	5.2	7.8
	(3.4)	(2.3)	(2.3)	(3.2)	(3.1)	(2.8)	(2.8)	(3.2)

Note: Multinomial standard errors are in parentheses. These are computed as $\sqrt{p(1-p)}/n$, where p is the reported proportion and n is the sample size.

derived from proprietary software sales, the remaining 22 percent being generated by software bundled in hardware either by software firm itself or by hardware firms. The pattern is nearly identical for open source, with sales of software for independent use and support services accounting for 72 percent of open source revenues. Not only that, but these patterns are highly similar across firms of different sizes, and for domestic and foreign companies.

What emerges from this evidence is the striking similarity in the ways open source and proprietary software companies exploit market opportunities to make money. Not only do they use the same broad business models, but the importance of different revenue sources is surprisingly similar for the two. Our analysis of revenue sources in this section aggregates domestic sales and exports. Next we investigate whether the similarity between open source and proprietary software extends to exports.

Diversification into Exporting: How Similar are Open Source and Proprietary Software?

One of the central themes in this chapter is that the differences between the development and marketing of open source and proprietary software are much less sharp than is often thought, and that software firms typically cross boundaries and operate in both. The evidence we have presented thus far strongly supports this perspective, showing extensive diversification and comingling. Does this perspective also apply to exporting? Is export behavior similar for open source and proprietary software, or does the license under which software is distributed affect its propensity to be exported? Our survey provides the first available detailed information about software exporting activity that allows us to study this issue.

This question is important for policy-making, as it is sometimes claimed that only proprietary software is amenable to export activity and that policies to promote open source development will retard software exports. This view is loosely based on the idea that open source is somehow antithetical to profit-making and market activity. While this chapter has demonstrated that profit-oriented firms can, and do, engage in open source development, it is still an open question whether open source is as export-oriented as proprietary software. Here we will show that it is not, and explain what appears to be driving the difference between the export orientation between open source and proprietary software.

Table 4.7
Patterns of software export activity (in percent)

	Firms with some software exports	Sales derived from exports
Aggregate	37.1	28.2
	(1.1)	(1.0)
Size		
Small	30.6	24.5
	(1.3)	(1.3)
Medium	45.3	29.9
	(2.0)	(1.8)
Large	65.5	42.2
	(5.1)	(5.3)
Ownership		
Domestic	33.9	23.9
	(1.2)	(1.0)
Foreign subsidiary	62.7	46.7
	(3.3)	(3.5)
Software focus		
Develop only proprietary	35.4	28.5
	(1.4)	(1.3)
Develop only open source	30.3	21.7
	(3.3)	(2.9)
Develop both proprietary and open source	42.9	29.2
	(2.1)	(1.9)

Note: Multinomial standard errors are in parentheses. These are computed as $\sqrt{p(1-p)/n}$, where p is the reported proportion and n is the relevant sample size.

Table 4.7 presents information on the proportion of software firms that export and the intensity of their exports (measured by the percentage of sales derived from exports), broken down by firm characteristics. The first thing to notice is that export activity is widespread among software firms. Overall, 37.1 percent of software firms do at least some exporting and, among those firms, sales from exports account for 28.2 percent of their total revenues. Moreover export behavior is not limited to proprietary software. Among firms that develop only open source, 30.3 percent do some exporting, which accounts for 21.7 percent of their overall revenues. However, firms developing proprietary software are both more likely to export and more intensive in their export activity than open source firms.[19] It is interesting that the

19. The companies in our survey that do open source development may be contributing to international open source projects. In this sense they may be "exporting" but without any direct financial reward. The survey does not have any information on this issue.

strongest involvement in exporting is evident among those firms that develop both open source and proprietary software (42.9 percent of such firms do some exports). This fact suggests that there may be some synergies by combining open source and proprietary software that may give advantages to such firms in exporting. As we showed earlier in this chapter, there is evidence of such synergies in the diversification patterns of software firms.

In addition to the software license form, export activity varies with the characteristics of firms. First, firm size is an important determinant of *whether a firm exports*—the proportion of medium-sized and large firms that export (45.3 and 65.5 percent, respectively) is much higher than for small software companies. Yet nearly a third of small firms also export. However, the table shows that firm size is not as strongly associated with *export intensity*. There is no difference between small and medium-sized companies and, while the average export intensity is higher for large firms, the difference is not very statistically significant.

This evidence has a straightforward economic explanation—"entry costs" for exporters. If there is a large sunk cost required to enter an export market, such as those associated with setting up a foreign distribution network, small firms will be less likely to enter this market for fear of not being able to recover the entry cost. While sunk costs would affect the decision of whether to enter the export market, it plays no role in determining how much exporting to do once the firm has entered.[20]

Second, the table shows that foreign subsidiaries are nearly twice as likely to export as domestic firms, and this is also true for their export intensity. This finding shows that foreign subsidiaries are not set up primarily to cater to local software demand; if they were, we would not expect such a large difference between them and domestic firms. Other factors—especially labor costs of software developers—are likely to be important considerations for foreign subsidiaries.

The descriptive statistics in table 4.7 tell us that export behavior is related to the mode of licensing and firm characteristics. However, to pin down the determinants of export behavior, we use econometric analysis of the decision to export and of export intensity, which allows us to control for the effects of all of the relevant factors together. In addition to the size and ownership of the firm, we take into account the busi-

---

20. This finding is consistent with many studies of exporting behavior by firms (e.g., Roberts and Tybout 1997).

ness strategies the firm adopts—namely whether the firm develops open source and/or proprietary separate (packaged) software, software for bundling with hardware, or support services. For the interested reader, the details of the results are reported in appendix 4.2. The multivariate regression analysis confirms the key findings about the role of firm size and ownership revealed by the simple descriptive table. In addition, however, the regressions deliver three new results that we summarize here.

The first is that the decision to export is shaped by the software business models adopted by firms.[21] Exporting is most strongly associated with firms that develop separate (both original and customized) software, followed by software for bundling in hardware. As one would expect, firms providing software support services are the least likely to be involved in exports. It is not surprising that separate and bundled software are more export oriented, since they involve less close and ongoing interaction with clients than support services, which is difficult and costly to set up and maintain. But while the business model affects the decision to export, it does not affect the export intensity of those firms that do enter the international market. This evidence also shows that it is more difficult for an open source firm to find export outlets, but when it has found one, the firm is able to exploit it as intensely as would a proprietary software firm. In other words, the fixed setup costs of exporting are higher for open source software than for proprietary software.

Both the type of software license and the business strategies of software firms affect the decision of firms to engage in exports. But is the effect of the business models the same for open source and proprietary software? The regression analysis shows that the answer is no. It is *only proprietary software* models that increase the likelihood of export activity, in particular strategies to develop separate software and software for bundling in other firms' hardware. The choice of an open source business model has no significant impact on whether a company exports.

Finally, the regression analysis reveals differences across countries both in the propensity to export and in export intensity. The countries in which firms are most likely to export are India, Israel, Kenya,

---

21. Of course, over the long run the choice of exporting and business models are both under the control of the firm, and are shaped by more basic factors such as the technical and marketing competencies of the firm. With our survey information, which observes firms at only one point in time, we cannot examine the causal links between exporting and business strategies.

and Singapore. The countries in which exporting software firms tend to be more specialized in exports are India and Israel (China and Kenya are the lowest in this regard). These findings are interesting because they show that there is no simple relationship between software export activity and the level of economic development in countries.

In the preceding sections we examined diversification of firms in the development and marketing of software in a number of directions—between applications and operating systems, between different business models, between open source and proprietary software, and between domestic sales and exports. We have shown that there is a lot of comingling of these various activities, though there remain some interesting differences, particularly in the export orientation of open source and proprietary software. One of the basic conclusions from this analysis is that open source software is surprisingly very much market oriented. Firms make money from open source by combining a variety of business models, including the provision of support services. This revenue is a leading source of the financing for their ongoing software innovation. At the same time, however, part of the financing of open source software development comes from external corporate funding, and we examine this important element in the next section of the chapter.

Corporate Funding for Open Source Development

It is the conventional wisdom among many observers, analysts, and advocates of open source software that its development of is driven by a widely dispersed pool of voluntary contributors. But the fact is that corporations increasingly invest large amounts of money to finance open source development, both in terms of direct finance to other companies and through paying their employees to engage in such activity. There are many examples of corporations hiring open source developers and champions, making equity investments in corporations doing open source development, encouraging their employees to volunteer for open source projects, and even releasing proprietary code to the open source community.[22] In chapter 3 we provided a number of examples of how proprietary software corporations engage with and support the open source community.

---

22. For example, in July 2009 Microsoft announced the release of 20,000 lines of device driver code to the Linux kernel community, and of Microsoft Live Services Plug-in to integrate their Live@edu services with the (open source) Moodle course management system. See Gutierrez (2009).

There are at least two reasons why companies provide such financing. The first is to encourage and influence the direction of open source innovation in the hope that they can exploit the knowledge in their own software development programs. This is akin to what economists call "pure knowledge spillovers." The second reason for supporting open source activity is the hope that the results can be embodied, typically after some customization, in the computer hardware produced by the company. The ability of the firm to benefit in this way depends on the license under which the open source is developed. If produced under the more restrictive GPL license, the code cannot be used in a product (even in modified form) unless the source code is made available. The company underwriting open source development can more effectively exploit it if the open source is under a less restrictive license, such as the BSD. For this reason we would expect external companies to be more willing to provide such finance to software firms that operate under less restrictive licenses.

To our knowledge, there is no evidence in the literature on open source about how and to whom corporate funding of open source is distributed. Our survey of developers provides a window onto this phenomenon. In particular, the survey has information on which software firms receive "external funding from a large computer corporation" and how the recipient companies assess the importance of that funding to their activities. We summarize this information in table 4.8.

Table 4.8 shows that external corporate funding is not an isolated occurrence. Overall, 15.3 percent of firms developing some open source receive corporate funding, and nearly two-thirds of these firms report that this funding is "highly important" for encouraging their open source activity. While the survey does not provide information on the level of such funding, the many examples of alliances and other contractual arrangements between open source and proprietary software companies suggest that such funding is substantial. To take one leading example, IBM announced plans in 2001 to spend $300 million over three years to fund a variety of technical, research, and marketing initiatives to boost Linux development and use, and added a further commitment of $100 million in 2005.[23]

---

23. See "IBM Puts Cash behind Linux Push," http://news.bbc.co.uk/2/hi/technology/4276287.stm (accessed August 20, 2009). Some put the IBM commitment as high as $1 billion, but whatever the exact figure is, there is no doubt about IBM's financial support for Linux development and use, and this applies to other leading software companies as well (see Shankland 2002).

Table 4.8
Corporate funding for open source software (percentage of respondents)

	OS firms with corporate funding	Corporate funding ranked "high importance"
Aggregate	15.3	63.0
	(1.6)	(5.4)
Size		
Small	12.4	59.5
	(1.9)	(8.1)
Medium	19.3	68.4
	(2.8)	(7.5)
Large	18.8	50.0
	(6.9)	(20.4)
Ownership		
Domestic	12.2	66.1
	(2.3)	(6.3)
Foreign subsidiary	36.2	56.0
	(5.8)	(9.9)
Business model		
OS, separate software	12.3	66.7
	(2.5)	(10.3)
OS, customized software	18.7	61.5
	(3.3)	(9.5)
OS, bundled software	17.8	68.8
	(4.0)	(11.6)
OS, support services	14.1	55.6
	(3.1)	(11.7)
OS license		
BSD license	31.1	19.7
	(2.0)	(1.7)
Other licenses	13.3	8.4
	(1.4)	(1.1)

Note: Multinomial standard errors are in parentheses. These are computed as $\sqrt{p(1-p)/n}$, where p is the reported proportion and n is the relevant sample size.

The table indicates three important features of this financing.[24] The first is that small firms are somewhat less likely to get such financing than their larger counterparts.[25] However, company ownership is an important determinant of corporate funding. Foreign subsidiaries are three times more likely than domestic firms to receive such funding. It is striking how common corporate funding for open source is, with 36 percent of foreign subsidiaries in our survey receiving it.[26] The second feature is that the likelihood of external financing depends on the business model of the software company. Firms that specialize in customized software and software for bundling with other firms' hardware are more likely to get funding than those focused on separate (packaged) software and support services. This is what we would expect if the computer corporations that are underwriting this development are doing so, at least in part, in order to incorporate the new developments into their own hardware. Finally, the table shows that companies operating (predominantly) under the BSD open source license are more than twice as likely to receive corporate funding than those operating under the more restrictive GPL or other licenses. This also holds if we restrict the analysis to recipients who rank the funding as highly important to their operations (second column in the table). This finding makes sense, since the less restrictive BSD license allows the funding corporation greater latitude in commercializing the resulting open source innovations.[27]

Conclusion

In this chapter we have provided a detailed examination of the development and marketing of software by firms. This investigation is made possible by the new and unique survey of software companies we conducted, covering nearly 2,000 firms in 15 countries. The data provide many new insights into the diversification behavior of

---

24. Because the descriptive evidence in table 4.8 does not hold other factors constant, we also used multivariate regression analysis to pin down the effects of firm characteristics more sharply. The results (not reported) confirm these results, even more strongly than is suggested by the figures in the table.

25. While we suspect that the donor firms are typically larger than the companies receiving support, the survey has no information about the size of the donor firms.

26. The survey question was designed to elicit information about external funding by a "large computer corporation," but it is possible that respondents in foreign subsidiaries may have included financing from their parent companies. So this ownership effect may be overstated.

27. For more discussion of open source licenses, see chapter 3.

software firms, and in particular, the ways they comingle open source and proprietary software.

We would like to highlight three empirical conclusions that emerge from the analysis:

• First, and most important, software companies extensively comingle open source and proprietary software development, much more than the conventional wisdom would suggest. Firms that do a particular *open source* activity frequently also do that activity under the *proprietary* license form. To take two leading examples, the same firms frequently develop and market both open and proprietary software for bundling in computer hardware, and they develop software for operating systems under both license forms. This comingling behavior strongly points to the existence of development and marketing cost synergies linking open source and proprietary software. Yet this comingling is not found everywhere—for example, firms do not tend to combine development of open source and proprietary applications software.

• Second, software companies extensively diversify in other dimensions. The most striking examples are found in the ways firms combine different business models to earn revenue, both for open source and proprietary software activities. Moreover this diversification occurs in settings where firms have the most to gain. Three examples illustrate this point. The first is that large firms diversify more than smaller ones, as they are more likely to be able to exploit the cost synergies without sacrificing economies of scale. The second example is that companies frequently combine development of separate software and software designed to be bundled in hardware, exploiting multiple marketing opportunities for the same (or similar) software. Finally, companies tend to combine development of (proprietary) software for bundling in hardware by other firms with the provision of support services which are complementary.

• The third empirical conclusion we want to highlight concerns software export activity. Even though open source and proprietary software are similar in many respects and are extensively comingled, they differ substantially in their export orientation. While export activity is widespread among software firms, and is not limited to proprietary software, the evidence shows that companies developing proprietary software are more likely to export, and more intensive in their export activity, than open source firms. This reflects the greater fixed costs of setting up the necessary distribution and marketing networks for open source. Of course, this may evolve over time, and it could be that this difference in export potential may shrink. Still this finding should be taken into account in the policy debates over promoting open source, particularly in developing economies favoring an export-driven growth strategy.

In closing, we want to emphasize that the central theme in this chapter—the extensive similarity between, and cohabitation of, open source and proprietary software—has important policy implications. This view emphasizes that the fundamental tension that underlies innovation policy also characterizes the software industry (both open source and proprietary). Open source software offers no free lunch, no easy way to avoid the tension between ensuring both an efficient distribution of software and the incentives for continued innovation in this sector. This perspective in turn shapes our analysis of the choices governments face and the policies they should adopt and those to avoid. In the next chapter we will argue that in their role as a buyer of software, governments should evaluate alternatives on the basis of their individual quality and costs much more than on the type of licenses under which they are distributed, and in their role as regulator, governments should adopt policies that promote effective competition between open source and proprietary software. We will argue that this is the way governments can best advance software innovation and economic welfare.

Appendix 4.1: Econometric Analysis of Open Source Development and Comingling

In the text we showed that there is widespread participation by firms in open source development and extensive comingling of open source and proprietary software. To pin down the factors that influence these decisions, we turn to econometric analysis. We estimate two regressions. The first is a Probit regression of whether a company engages in developing any open source software. The dependent variable is defined as one if the firm does open source and zero if it does not. The second is an Ordered Probit regression of the degree of specialization in open source software (higher specialization is equivalent to lower diversification). Specialization is measured by the percentage of developer hours allocated to open source, in four discrete intervals: less than 25 percent, 25 to 50 percent, 50 to 75 percent, and greater than

75 percent. The dependent variable is defined as one for the interval in which the firm falls and zero for the other intervals. In this regression we include only firms doing some open source development.

For both regressions we use the following set of explanatory variables: the size of the firm, ownership (domestic or foreign subsidiary), and the business models adopted by the firm. In addition we allow for differences among countries by including a set of country fixed effects (dummy variables). In these regressions we use a more detailed classification of business models than the one used in table 4.2. In that table we classified firms into one of four (mutually exclusive) business models, based on the main activity they report in the survey. In the survey, however, we asked firms whether they were active in each of five different software areas: separate software, customized software, own bundled software, other bundled software, and support services. We use this information by defining a dummy variable for each of these software activities and allowing firms to be in more than one of them.

The results are reported in table A4.1. We discuss the two regressions in parallel to highlight how the different factors affect both the decision to engage in open source and the degree of specialization. Rather than go through all the details, we summarize the key findings.

The first is that both the propensity to engage in open source development and the degree of specialization vary across countries. The chi-square tests strongly reject the hypothesis that there are no country differences in these regressions (p-value is less than 0.001). However, inspection of the individual country coefficients (not shown) reveals that this finding reflects a few notable stand outs rather than pervasive differences. In the decision to develop open source, only three countries stand out as different from the rest: Kenya, Singapore, and South Africa. Software developers in Kenya have a significantly higher probability of engaging in open source than those in other countries, while the opposite is true for Singapore and South Africa.[28] For the degree of specialization in open source, the only significant cases are Thailand and Turkey, both of which exhibit more focus on open source. These findings show that open source development is *not* a phenomenon particularly associated with, or concentrated in, developing countries.

The second finding is that large firms are significantly more likely to engage in open source activity than either small- or medium-sized

28. For both regressions, if we include dummy variables for the two or three countries mentioned, we cannot reject the hypothesis that the fixed effects for the other countries are jointly zero.

Table A4.1
Mixing open source and proprietary software development: Econometric estimates

Variable	Develop any open source (1)	Degree of specialization (2)
Medium-sized firm[a]	−0.045	0.007
	(0.071)	(0.093)
Large firm	0.354**	−0.452**
	(0.152)	(0.190)
Foreign subsidiary[b]	−0.006	0.248*
	(0.105)	(0.133)
Separate software	−0.114*	−0.049
	(.067)	(.091)
Customized software	0.244**	−0.113
	(0.066)	(0.086)
Own bundled software	0.415**	−0.093
	(0.079)	(0.104)
Other bundled software	0.309**	0.082
	(0.066)	(0.087)
Support services	0.183**	−0.039
	(0.085)	(0.119)
Test: size dummies (p-value)	0.033	0.047
Test: software business model dummies (p-value)	<0.001	0.627
Test: country dummies (p-value)	<0.001	<0.001
Pseudo-R^2	0.087	0.034
Number of observations	1894	750

Note: * and ** denote statistical significance at the 10 and 5 percent levels, respectively. The coefficients in column 1 are from a Probit regression; column 2 is from an Ordered Probit regression.
a. The reference size category is small firms.
b. The reference ownership category is domestic firms.

companies, as shown by the positive coefficient on large firms in column 1. However, large firms are less specialized in open source than the smaller firms that do undertake such development, as shown by the negative coefficient on large firms in column 2. These results are what we would expect if there is a fixed "entry" cost of engaging in open source development. It is more likely that large firms will be able to cover the entry cost and thus to do some open source, without the need to specialize in order to do so.

The third finding is that firm ownership does not affect the probability that the firm develops open source. There is no difference between domestic firms and foreign subsidiaries in that decision (the coefficient on the foreign subsidiary variable is not statistically significant). However, we find that among firms doing some open source, foreign firms are significantly more specialized in that development activity than domestic firms (this is shown by the significant, positive coefficient on the foreign subsidiary variable in the second column).

The decision to develop open source is also affected by the set of software business models the firm adopts. In particular, companies that work on customized software, bundled software and (to a lesser extent) support services are significantly more likely to engage in some open source than pure software developers. However, companies that develop separate software are less likely to be engaged in open source. These facts suggest that there may be some kind of cost savings or other (e.g., marketing) advantages—"synergies" for short—that make it attractive to combine open source with particular business models. We investigate this idea in more detail in the chapter. However, the choice of business models has no statistically significant impact on the degree of specialization in open source. Thus the synergies at work appear to be associated with the fixed costs of combining business activities, affecting the "entry decision," rather than the variable costs which would affect the level (specialization) in those activities.

Appendix 4.2: Econometric Analysis of Open Source and Proprietary Software Exporting Activity

In the text we showed that the export orientation of open source and proprietary software are related to the developer firm's characteristics. To get a sharper view on how these factors affect export behavior, we estimate two sets of multivariate regressions (table A4.2). The first is a Probit regression that explains whether a company engages in exporting as a function of firm size, ownership, software business models, and country fixed effects (columns 1 to 3 in the table). The second is an Ordered Probit regression that relates the percentage of sales derived from exports (measured in quartile intervals) against these same variables (columns 4 to 6 in the table).[29]

We turn first to the factors affecting whether a company exports. The results confirm that the likelihood a company exports is strongly

---

29. We also estimated ordinary least square regressions using export intensity measured as a continuous variable. The quartile specification performs better because the export intensity figures constructed from the survey data are bunched rather than smoothly distributed from zero to 100 percent.

Table A4.2
Export activity in open source and proprietary software: Econometric estimates

Variable	Probability of exporting			Export intensity		
	(1)	(2)	(3)	(4)	(5)	(6)
Medium-sized firm[a]	0.363**	0.354**	0.358**	−0.154*	−0.044	−0.092
	(0.070)	(0.071)	(0.070)	(0.087)	(0.093)	(0.092)
Large firm	0.711**	0.723**	0.716**	0.027	0.410**	0.358**
	(0.155)	(0.158)	(0.158)	(0.167)	(0.179)	(0.180)
Foreign subsidiary[b]	0.498**	0.510**	0.493**	0.403**	0.390**	0.466**
	(0.102)	(0.103)	(0.102)	(0.109)	(0.115)	(0.115)
Only open source[c]	−0.200*			0.222		
	(0.105)			(0.139)		
Proprietary and open source	0.180**			−0.084		
	(0.071)			(0.093)		
Separate software		0.481**			−1.559**	
		(0.082)			(0.104)	
Own bundled		0.153**			−0.804**	
		(0.067)			(0.094)	
Other bundled		0.214**			−0.496**	
		(0.072)			(0.100)	
Support services		−0.122*			0.142	
		(0.072)			(0.098)	
PS, separate software			0.359**			−1.301**
			(0.076)			(0.123)
PS, own bundled			0.078			−0.448**
			(0.073)			(0.102)
PS, other bundled			0.155**			−0.301**
			(0.080)			(0.114)
PS, support services			−0.146**			0.208**
			(0.070)			(0.096)
OS, separate software			0.099			−0.218*
			(0.086)			(0.123)
OS, own bundled			0.076			−0.820**
			(0.104)			(0.150)
OS, other bundled			0.083			−0.076
			(0.116)			(0.166)
OS, support services			−0.020			0.306**
			(0.084)			(0.115)
Test: software focus dummies (p-value)	0.002			0.12		
Test: business model dummies (p-value)		<0.001			<0.001	

Table A4.2
(continued)

Variable	Probability of exporting			Export intensity		
	(1)	(2)	(3)	(4)	(5)	(6)
Test: proprietary activity dummies (p-value)			<0.001			<0.001
Test: open source activity dummies (p-value)			0.34			<0.001
Test: country dummies (p-value)	<0.001	<0.001	<0.001	<0.001	<0.001	<0.001
Pseudo-R^2	0.093	0.111	0.105	0.051	0.228	0.199
Number of observations	1,894	1,894	1,894	851	851	851

Note: * and ** denote statistical significance at the 10 and 5 percent levels, respectively. OS and PS refer to open source and proprietary software, respectively.
a. The reference size category is small firms.
b. The reference ownership category is domestic firms.
c. The reference software category is firms developing only proprietary.

related to firm size and is higher for foreign subsidiaries than for domestic firms (this holds for each of the specification in columns 1 to 3). The software licensing mode of the firm also affects the decision to export. In column 1 we distinguish companies by including dummy variables for those that develop only open source and both open source and proprietary (the reference category is only proprietary). Companies that develop only open source software are *less likely to export* than those that develop only proprietary software, while firms that develop both types of software are the most likely to export. We can easily reject the hypothesis that the license type does not affect the firm's decision to export (p-value is less than .001). Column 2 examines how the export decision varies with the specific software business models the firm adopts (the survey asks each company to identify all of the relevant business models). Exporting is most strongly associated with firms that develop separate (packaged) software, followed next by software for bundling in either their own or other firms' hardware (the coefficients on these dummy variables are positive and statistically highly significant). Firms that provide software support services are significantly less likely to export.

Taken together, these results show that both software license type and the business strategies of software firms affect the decision of firms to engage in exports. But is the effect of the business models the same for open source and proprietary software? To answer this, in column 3 we combine these elements by introducing dummies for the various software models separately for open source and proprietary. The results are striking: it is *only proprietary software* models that increase the likelihood of export activity. In particular, exporting is more likely for firms that develop separate software and software for bundling in other firms' hardware, but support services again are less likely to be exported. Moreover the choice of business models for open source activity have no statistically significant impact on whether a company exports; none of the estimated coefficients on the associated dummy variables is statistically significant.

Interestingly the results are quite different when we examine the determinants of export intensity (columns 4 to 6). As before, we find that large firms and foreign subsidiaries tend to be more specialized in exports. However, export intensity is not statistically different for firms that develop only open source software, as compared with others (column 4). Moreover it is lower for firms that develop separate (packaged) software and software for bundling in hardware (column 5). In short, these software business models increase the likelihood of exporting in the first place, but are associated with less specialization in exports among those firms. This conclusion also holds when we disaggregate activities by software license type, in column 6.

In short, this evidence shows that it is more difficult for an open source firm to find export outlets, but when it has found one, the firm is able to exploit it as intensely as would a proprietary software firm. To put this point another way, the evidence suggests that the fixed setup costs of exporting (but not the marginal costs) are higher for open source software than for proprietary software.

Finally, in all of these regressions we find that there are differences across countries both in the propensity to export and in export intensity (the individual coefficients are omitted, for brevity). The countries in which firms are most likely to export are India, Israel, Kenya, and Singapore. The countries in which exporting software firms tend to be more specialized in exports are India and Israel (China and Kenya are the lowest in this regard). These findings suggest there is no simple relationship between software export activity and the level of economic development in countries.

5 The Demand Side: Assessing Trade-offs and Making Choices

In chapter 4 we examined how open source and proprietary software are licensed, developed, and sold. The most striking fact that emerged from our analysis is that there is no sharp divide between the open source and proprietary worlds for software developer companies. The preeminent characteristic of the supply side is the pervasive diversification by software developers. Firms typically are active in more than one business activity, and they frequently develop both open source and proprietary software within each activity.

In this chapter we turn to a discussion of the demand side of the software market. By the "demand side," we mean the way in which software users assess the alternative offerings available in the market and how make their choices among them. We will explain how economic analysis can shed light on the way in which licensing and mode of development influence the cost of using software, and its quality, and thus the choices users make. We want to understand the trade-offs that users face in making their choices between open source and proprietary software, how these trade-offs are influenced by the characteristics of users, and how they vary across countries. We will also explore how users mix between open source and proprietary software and will show how this behavior is related to user characteristics.

We develop three main themes in the chapter. The first is that there is no such thing as "*the* cost of software." Each piece of software involves a variety of different costs for a user. Some costs are explicitly monetary, such as the initial purchase price of the software, but other costs of adoption, such as learning or interoperability, are more disguised, though none the less real for that. Not only are costs multidimensional, but the mix of costs are different for open source and proprietary software. Some costs (e.g., the initial price of the software) are lower for open source but others are higher. In other words, in their adoption decisions, users face trade-offs and their choices will depend on how much importance they attach to the different types of costs, which determines the relevant "total cost of operation" of the various software options consumers face.

The second theme is that consumers are heterogeneous in terms of how they assess the different components of cost. For small firms that are cash-constrained, for example, the initial purchase price of software may be particularly important, but far less so for larger companies. Other components—such as learning costs—may be the dominant consideration for applications software for technically less sophisticated users. Using the detailed survey evidence, we will show that consumers vary widely in how they assess these cost trade-offs, and this leads them to make different choices between open source and proprietary software.

Not only do consumers make different choices, but they also can and do mix-and-match open source and proprietary programs. This is the third theme of the chapter. From a technical point of view, nothing prevents the use of the open source Open Office on top of proprietary operating systems such as Windows or MacOS, the use of IBM's proprietary WebSphere Portal software on top of Linux, or even the use of a proprietary add-on such as Flash Player to the open source browser Firefox, which is itself running on top of a proprietary operating system. There is no need for users to make a choice between belonging to the open source world or to the proprietary software world. As we will see in this chapter, users typically have a foot in both.[1] Consumers mix software because the cost trade-offs that open source and proprietary software offer depend on the software application. For some applications, price may be the dominant factor (e.g., operating systems), for others learning costs may be more important. In the chapter we will show that users do not specialize in either open source or proprietary software. They mix extensively, and this holds in all fifteen countries we study. Moreover we will show that the pattern of mixing we observe depends on user characteristics in ways that are consistent with economic principles. For example, users who attach more impor-

---

1. We recognize that this statement is controversial for those who believe that "free software" is a fundamental value in and of itself. As one source starkly puts it, "The Free Software Foundation follows the rule that we cannot install any proprietary program on our computers except temporarily for the specific purpose of writing a free replacement for that very program. Aside from that, we feel there is no possible excuse for installing a proprietary program" (see http://www.gnu.org/philosophy/categories.html#semi -freeSoftware, accessed April 20, 2005).

tance to nonprice elements of the total cost of operation are less likely to adopt open source software.

We begin the chapter with an analysis of how users assess the cost trade-offs that open source and proprietary software offer. The discussion is organized around the concept of the "total cost of operation," which recognizes the multidimensionality of software costs. We first examine the extent to which software consumers undertake any formal assessment of the total cost of operation before making their purchasing decisions. We then turn to a detailed examination of how open source and proprietary software differ in the various components of cost, and how these trade-offs vary for different types of users. Finally, we show how consumers mix-and-match open source and proprietary software and show that this mixing is related to their assessment of the cost trade-offs they face. Before turning to the core material, we take a brief detour to describe the methodology and scope of the survey data that underpins the empirical analysis in this chapter.

The User Survey Methodology

The empirical analysis is based on a new, cross-country survey of software users. We developed an extensive survey questionnaire that was translated into the language of each of the fifteen countries covered (and then back-translated into English to confirm accuracy), and administered by telephone by a professional survey company (Lieberman Research Worldwide).[2] The countries in the survey are Brazil, Chile, China, France, Greece, India, Israel, Kenya, Mexico, Poland, Russia, South Africa, Singapore, Thailand, and Turkey. These countries span a wide range in terms of the levels of economic development. According to the World Bank categories (WDR 2004), two of the countries are lower income (India and Kenya), six are lower middle income (Brazil, China, Russia, South Africa, Thailand and Turkey), three are upper middle income group (Chile, Mexico, and Poland), and four in the upper income category (France, Greece, Israel, and Singapore).

The sample design was the same in each country. Within each country, the survey company constructed a nationally representative random sample of business within the target industries and government agencies to be surveyed. Individual, private users were not surveyed.

---

2. The complete questionnaire is provided in an online appendix. We thank Daniel Garcia-Swartz at Law and Economics Consulting Group (LECG) for his many contributions to the development of the survey and his help in organizing its implementation.

Table 5.1
Composition of the user sample

	Percentage of sample
By size	
Small (<25 employees)	39.8
Medium (25–250)	38.2
Large (>250)	22.0
By ownership	
Government agency	19.5
Domestic company	70.5
Foreign subsidiary	10.0
By industry	
Services	30.2
High-tech manufacturing	23.2
Low-tech manufacturing	22.1
Wholesale and retail trade	24.5

The list of companies was compiled from the registry of firms (hence self-employed workers were excluded), and the survey company contacted the person responsible for making the decisions regarding technology for the company.[3] If the respondent was unable or unwilling to respond, another user was added to the list until the quota was met. The sampling was stratified in several dimensions: (1) 125 corporate users and 30 government users, (2) among corporate users, a minimum quota of 20 was applied to each of the four broad industry groupings (services, high-tech manufacturing, low-tech manufacturing, and wholesale and retail trade), (3) among the government agency users a quota of 10 was ensured for each of federal, state, and municipal governments. The survey company extensively checked the data for outliers, and in some instances, contacted respondents to check the accuracy of responses.

Table 5.1 summarizes the composition of the user sample. In total we have 2,342 responses, spread almost equally across the fifteen countries. The sample covers the range of sizes, with 39.8 percent being small firms (less than 25 employees), 38.2 percent medium-sized firms (between 25 and 250 employees), and 22.0 percent large firms (more than 250 employees). Company users account for 80.5 percent of

---

3. Among survey respondents, 67.0 percent were in charge of all IT-related matters, 19.6 percent were the chief information officer (19.6 percent), and 13.4 percent were some other form of senior IT executive.

respondents; the remaining 19.5 percent are government agencies. Of the company respondents, 87.6 percent are domestic companies while the remaining 12.4 percent are subsidiaries of foreign corporations. The firms in the user survey are fairly evenly spread across four broad industry categories. The composition of the user sample is very similar across the fifteen countries.

Investing in Cost Assessment for Open Source and Proprietary Software

The Multidimensionality of the Costs of Using Software

While the price of software certainly matters to users, it is only one part of the overall calculation of users in deciding what software to adopt. There have been many debates about the relative costs of owning each type of software, and the discussion is often framed in terms of the "total cost of ownership" (TCO), which is defined as the total cost of providing a functionality using one program. The proper accounting of cost should include total costs of procurement, management and support, associated hardware costs, and, when one is thinking of changing software solutions, migration costs. Despite claims by parties on both sides of the software debate, very little is known about the relative TCO of open source and proprietary software. Our large-scale survey of software users in different countries provides an opportunity to quantify the importance of some of the key costs and to understand how they vary across different types of users and countries.

The terms of open source licenses do not constrain the price at which the software can be sold, but the mode of distribution limits the price that sellers can charge in the marketplace: if they charge too high a price, it is easy to buy a copy, duplicate it, and resell the software at a lower price, although compiling and preparing a version of the software that is ready to be utilized is not always simple. Some firms try to increase the value of their offerings by bundling the software with services. For instance, as noted, Red Hat sells its Linux distribution bundled with services and a subscription service that provides for free upgrades during the year.[4] Of course, sellers of proprietary software are also subject to competitive pressure, both from proprietary and

---

4. It is also subject to competition by programmers who recompile its software. See Shankland (2005).

open source firms that sell similar products or from potential imitators, but this pressure is less strong and less direct. As a consequence open source software is likely to be less expensive than proprietary alternatives, but price is only one component of the total cost of ownership.

To begin, we want to emphasize a key point, one that is often underappreciated: There is no simple ranking of open source and proprietary software, either in terms of the full costs of adoption or in terms of the quality of the software: users are heterogeneous and open source and commercial software offer different combinations of costs and quality. Moreover the importance users attach to different characteristics depends on the particular task for which the software is needed. These observations have two important implications. First, there is no reason to expect different users to make the same choices in terms of open source and proprietary software, and every reason to allow them the flexibility to make that choice freely. As we will see later, users appreciate the need for this freedom to choose, and strongly favor policy regimes that allow it. Second, since every user will have a variety of tasks for which software is needed, we should expect to observe users to mix between open source and proprietary software. In the empirical work that follows, we will show that this is exactly what we see in the data.

Our survey of software users provides the first systematic, cross-country information on the cost trade-offs and the adoption choices of open source and proprietary software. We study five distinct dimensions of the total cost of ownership along which these competing software forms differ: the initial price of the software, switching costs (adapting and learning to use new software), interoperability costs (ensuring that different pieces of software and hardware can communicate with each other), the availability and cost of support services, and access to and cost of future software upgrades. Before turning to the evidence in the survey, we will first discuss the economic factors firms need to take into account in deciding whether to invest in a formal evaluation of software costs.

The Economics of Doing TCO Analysis

We view the decision about whether to invest in TCO analysis as an economic one, driven by the associated costs and benefits. Regarding costs, it is no easy task to conduct such an analysis, especially making an assessment of the costs required to address problems of switching and interoperability. It requires technical and financial expertise to identify and assess the comparative cost-effectiveness of alternative software solutions. Users will certainly differ in terms of their own software expertise, or their access to affordable market intermediaries for this purpose. Users without such expertise may simply find such an analysis too costly to make doing it worthwhile. This is more likely to be the case for smaller users and those in low-tech industries. On the benefits side, there are two main considerations. The first is the scale of the firm, or more precisely, the scale of the software investment under consideration. The larger the software requirement, the greater will be the potential savings from making a more informed software adoption decision. On this account we would again expect larger firms to be more likely to make the investment in a TCO assessment. But there is a second, less obvious factor, created by public policy, that can affect the willingness of users to undertake TCO analysis—government incentives for software adoption. These incentives can take the form of direct subsidies, tax credits, government procurement policies, and even strong "moral suasion." Whenever government uses these instruments to favor the adoption of one type of software over another, it changes the private incentives for users to incur the costs of a TCO analysis to make the decision on the basis of the underlying cost (and quality) effectiveness. This would be the case regardless of which way government policy tilts, either in favor of open source or proprietary software (or particular vendors of either).

To illustrate this important point, consider the following scenario strictly for argument's sake. Suppose that there is a subsidy given for the adoption of proprietary software but not for open source software. Suppose further that the user thinks that open source is the less costly alternative (which is certainly likely to be true, in the absence of a careful examination of the less visible costs of switching, interoperability and support services). Now consider what happens when the subsidy to proprietary software becomes larger. The potential gains from doing a TCO analysis will be greater if that cost assessment ends up shifting the user from his original open source choice to the proprietary solution. This is because the proprietary software is even less expensive to the user because of the increased subsidy. Of course, TCO analysis will not necessarily result in this outcome—there is some probability that it shows that open source is still cheaper in TCO terms—but the basic point remains valid because the *expected gains* from such an analysis will be larger. This line of argument implies that higher subsidies for proprietary software should increase the likelihood the user does a TCO analysis, while greater subsidies for open source have the opposite effect.

In appendix 5.1 we develop a simple economic model of the choice by a user to undertake a TCO analysis that formalizes this line of reasoning. The basic idea behind the model is that a user has only imperfect information about the total cost of ownership of the open source and proprietary software alternatives. By investing money (and time) in a TCO analysis, the user can learn the true comparative costs of each type of software. Thus the user faces a trade-off between incurring a sunk cost of doing a TCO analysis and the expected benefit of getting more information about the true costs of open source and proprietary software before making the adoption decision. A cost-minimizing user does the TCO analysis when the benefit of the information gain exceeds the sunk cost of doing so. Since both the costs and benefits can vary across users, a point we return to at some length later, we expect different users to make different decisions. Factors that reduce the cost, or raise the expected benefits of a TCO analysis, will increase the likelihood that a user undertakes it. As pointed out above, the main factors we would expect to play a role (of those we can measure in the survey) are the size of the user, whether the user is in a high-tech industry and government software incentives.

Who Uses TCO Analysis?
With these economic principles in mind, we now examine how widespread the use of TCO analysis is among different types of software customers. In the survey we asked users whether they usually conduct a TCO analysis before they make software adoption decisions. Table 5.2 presents the raw responses broken down by user size, ownership and industry. In the overall sample, 59.5 percent of users report that they use TCO analysis. This is good news, but at the same time it is a concern that 40.5 percent of users apparently make no systematic assessment of the cost of software. It is difficult enough to make a cost-efficient choice, even with a TCO analysis. Without it, there is a real danger that users may be swayed by other considerations that have little relation to cost-effectiveness and quality—for instance, ideology for or against open source or blind continuation of existing practice. Of course, for some firms it may not be efficient to conduct a TCO analysis. It only makes economic sense to do it if the expected benefits exceed the cost of such analysis.

Table 5.2
Adoption of TCO analysis, by user characteristics and country (percentage of users adopting)

Panel A		Panel B	
Aggregate sample	59.5	Brazil	71.0
	(1.0)		(3.1)
By size		Chile	54.2
Small	50.3		(3.9)
	(1.6)	China	76.7
Medium	61.2		(3.5)
	(1.6)	France	59.6
Large	72.0		(3.9)
	(2.0)	Greece	89.7
By ownership			(2.3)
Government agency	57.2	India	53.8
	(1.2)		(4.0)
Domestic company	59.6	Israel	66.9
	(1.2)		(3.8)
Foreign subsidiary	62.8	Kenya	21.0
	(3.2)		(3.3)
By industry		Mexico	83.3
Services	61.3		(3.0)
	(2.0)	Poland	52.2
High-tech manufacturing	62.8		(4.0)
	(2.3)	Russia	42.3
Low-tech manufacturing	56.5		(4.0)
	(2.4)	South Africa	58.1
Trade	59.2		(4.0)
	(2.3)	Singapore	30.3
			(3.7)
		Thailand	43.9
			(4.0)
		Turkey	89.0
			(2.5)

Note: Binomial standard errors are in parentheses. These are computed as $\sqrt{p(1-p)/n}$, where p is the reported proportion and n is the sample size.

Four facts stand out from the table, all of which hold up when we do statistical analysis to control for other factors (see below). The first is that the decision to use TCO analysis is strongly related to the size of the user. Small users are much less likely to use it than medium-sized users (50.3 percent and 61.2 percent, respectively), and the latter in turn are less likely than large users (61.2 percent versus 72.0 percent). Part of the reason may be scale—for small users, the benefits of TCO analysis may not justify incurring the fixed cost of doing so. But we think this is at best only a partial explanation because, if it were the dominant factor, we would not expect to find many (or any) small firms doing it, and half of these firms do adopt it. Inexperience or lack of technical expertise may also be a factor. In the context of the economic principles we discussed (and the formal model in the appendix), lack of technical software sophistication raises the effective cost of doing a TCO analysis and thus makes it less attractive. Unfortunately, the survey does not provide any information that allows us to investigate this hypothesis.

The second finding from the table is that companies in low-tech manufacturing are less likely to use it than those in other industries. This again suggests that lack of technical expertise or experience may be a relevant consideration when users decide whether to undertake a TCO analysis before making software adoption decisions.

The third interesting finding is that government agencies appear less likely to use TCO analysis than companies. The differences are modest—government agencies are about 5 percent less likely to use TCO analysis than domestic companies and about 10 percent less likely than foreign subsidiaries. But in the econometric analysis, where we control for other factors that may influence the choices, we will find that the differences are actually larger and statistically significant.[5] The fact that government agencies do not rely as much as private firms on TCO analysis is perhaps not surprising, given that public agencies typically lack the monetary incentives to "get the decision right." Moreover, as in most bureaucracies, there may be a strong disinclination in public agencies to take risks associated with changing the existing software policy or experience, even when the cost-effectiveness calculations may warrant it.

---

5. The reason the econometric difference is larger is that government agencies in our survey are larger than companies, on average, and size is positively related to TCO use. Thus, in the simple tabular comparisons, the size effect obscures the fact that government agencies are less likely to use TCO analysis, but this is taken into account in the regression analysis.

Finally, the table shows that there are very large differences across countries (and many of these differences are statistically significant, despite the large standard errors associated with them). The use of TCO analysis varies from a low of just 21.0 percent of users in Kenya to a high of 89.7 percent in Greece. We will investigate what might account for these wide variations below.

Of course, these simple comparisons do not control for the other factors that affect the use of TCO analysis—for example, part of the difference between government agencies and companies may reflect differences in their size. In order to pin down the sources of these differences in the table more sharply, we estimate a multivariate regression model which relates the likelihood that TCO analysis is employed against a set of explanatory variables. These variables include the size of the user, ownership type, industry sector, and country (dummy variables—also known as fixed effects—are used to capture the different groups).

The results of this analysis generally confirm what we learned from the simple descriptive statistics in table 5.2.[6] We still find that the adoption of TCO analysis varies significantly across countries, even after we control for all of the other factors (the null hypothesis that there are no differences is rejected with a probability smaller than .001).[7] Based on the estimated parameters (country fixed effects) from this regression analysis, we find that the use of TCO analysis is least common in India, Kenya, Russia, Singapore, and Thailand. With the obvious exception of Singapore--which is among the wealthiest of our sample countries—these are in the lower income groups of countries. Users in Kenya are the standout—they have the lowest likelihood of adopting TCO analysis among all countries by a wide margin. The econometric analysis also confirms the findings in the simple comparisons presented in table 5.2: first, the use of TCO analysis is strongly and positively related to the size of the user; second, it varies across ownership types (being significantly lower for government agencies than for domestic and foreign companies); and third, it is significantly less common in low tech manufacturing than in the other sectors (there are no differences among the other sectors in this regard). We

---

6. For the interested reader the parameter estimates from this regression are provided as table A.5.1 in appendix 5.1.

7. For the less technical reader, the p-value represents the level of statistical significance for the test. A p-value of 0.05, for example, means that the test result can be stated with a 95 percent level of confidence (equivalently, 5 percent level of significance).

decisively reject both the null hypotheses that there are no differences across size categories (p-value < 0.001), industries (p-value $= 0.020$), and ownership types (p-value $= 0.002$).

What might account for the cross-country differences in the use of TCO analysis, once we have already accounted for variations due to the size, ownership, and industry of users? There are two main explanations: the *cost hypothesis* and *the incentives hypothesis*. The cost hypothesis is a supply side explanation—the costs of conducting a TCO analysis may significantly differ across countries. It is no easy task to conduct such an analysis, as it requires technical and financial expertise to identify and assess the comparative cost-effectiveness of alternative software solutions. In countries where users often lack the necessary expertise or easy and affordable access to market intermediaries for this purpose, many users may simply find TCO analysis too costly to make it worthwhile.

The second explanation is a demand-side argument: the willingness of users to invest in TCO analysis is affected by public policy, in particular by government incentives for software adoption. These incentives can take the form of direct subsidies, tax credits, government procurement policies, and even strong "moral suasion." Whenever government uses these instruments to favor the adoption of one type of software over another, it alters the private incentive to incur the costs of a TCO analysis to make the decision on the basis of cost (and quality) effectiveness. This would be the case regardless of which way government policy tilts, either in favor of open source or proprietary software (and particular vendors of either).

With the available data and the small number of countries, it is not possible to test these hypotheses with any degree of confidence. The cost hypothesis is especially challenging because we have no evidence in the survey on the average level of technical expertise or other determinants of the costs of TCO analysis.[8] The user survey does provide some evidence on the extent to which users receive government incentives to adopt either open source or proprietary software. We will discuss the survey information on government incentives in more detail in chapter 6 on public policy. For the present discussion, we take the proportion of software users who report receiving some form of government incentive and ask whether it is correlated with the estimated

---

8. We tried using proxy variables for potential technical expertise, such as the number of Internet users (or portals) per capita, but these were not significantly correlated with the use of TCO analysis at the country level.

coefficients on the country dummy variables from the regression that explains the use of TCO analysis.[9] Controlling for other factors, these coefficients measure the differences across countries in TCO usage. The results give some support to the incentives hypothesis. When we use the proportion of users receiving open source incentives, the correlation coefficient is negative (-0.41), as predicted, and close to statistical significance at the 95 percent level of confidence. The proportion receiving proprietary software incentives is also negatively correlated with TCO usage (-0.20), contrary to our prediction, but is not statistically different from zero. Of course, because the sample of countries is small, the result should be interpreted with care. But it at least suggests that government policy to promote a particular type of software might have an unfortunate, unintended consequence of reducing the use of TCO analysis and thereby undermining cost-effective adoption decisions.

The evidence in this section is consistent with the idea that users make "rational" decisions about investing to conduct a TCO assessment. Doing so involves both costs and benefits, and rational behavior implies that users for whom costs are higher and benefits are lower are less likely to conduct such assessments. This is what we find in the data. Small users, government agencies, and consumers in low-tech manufacturing sectors are the least likely to do a TCO analysis before purchasing software. As these users probably have less technical sophistication about software, they are likely to face higher costs of conducting such assessments. Moreover small users and government agencies are likely to derive lower benefits from such assessments; small scale reduces the payoff and government agencies are not profit oriented and thus are less likely to value the reduction in TCO in the same way as private-sector users. For the same reasons large users and those in high-tech sectors are likely to have lower costs and higher benefits, and thus find such investment more attractive. Of course, the fact that users behave rationally in deciding whether to do TCO analysis does not imply that their decisions are "socially optimal" and that there is no role for government policy. We take up this question in chapter 6,

---

9. Unfortunately, we do not have any information on the size of the incentives involved. There is a lot of variation across countries in the proportion receiving incentives (for more detailed discussion, see chapter 6). For proprietary software, the proportion ranges from a low of 0.6 percent in Russia to a high of 45.2 percent in Thailand; for open source, it runs from zero in Russia and South Africa to a maximum of 14.8 percent in Kenya. It is interesting that the extent of government subsidy for proprietary software is also very high in Singapore, which we showed earlier has one of the lowest rates of TCO analysis in the sample of countries.

Table 5.3
Ranking and cost components in TCO analysis (percentage of respondents)

	Users of TCO analysis: TCO for proprietary		Users of TCO analysis: TCO for open source		Non-users of TCO analysis
	Top rank	Cost	Top rank	Cost	Top rank
Initial software	50.5	37.3	36.6	27.6	53.4
	(1.4)	(1.3)	(2.2)	(2.1)	(1.3)
Support services	18.1	19.8	20.1	22.0	14.4
	(1.1)	(1.1)	(1.8)	(1.9)	(1.1)
Switching (learning)	9.0	13.9	14.0	16.7	10.8
	(0.8)	(1.0)	(1.6)	(1.7)	(1.0)
Interoperability	11.6	13.7	17.4	18.6	10.9
	(0.9)	(0.9)	(1.7)	(1.8)	(1.0)
Upgrades	10.9	15.3	11.8	15.1	10.5
	(0.8)	(1.0)	(1.5)	(1.7)	(0.9)

Notes: Binomial standard errors are in parentheses. These are computed as $\sqrt{p(1-p)/n}$, where p is the reported proportion and n is the sample size.

where we discuss appropriate public policies regarding software development and adoption.

In the next section we turn to a careful examination of what the data reveal about the users' assessments of the costs of open source and proprietary software. In particular, what are the cost trade-offs offered by these two types of software as they are perceived by users, and how do these trade-offs depend on the characteristics of the users?

Identifying the Cost Trade-offs for Open Source and Proprietary Software

What Does TCO Analysis by Users Reveal?
We begin, in table 5.3, with a summary description of the way in which users estimate the relative importance of the different components of the costs of adopting open source and proprietary software. In this table we are pooling all the data and thus ignoring any differences across either countries or types of users. The survey is structured so that users only answer the specific TCO questions for the type or types of software that they actually use. Thus we do not have any information on the way in which firms that use only proprietary software view the cost of open source software (and vice versa). Recall that 40.5 percent of firms say they do not conduct any TCO analysis before they adopt software. In the survey these firms were asked to rank

the five cost components in terms of their overall importance if the firm were to conduct a TCO analysis, but without specific reference to open source or proprietary software.

The first and third columns show the proportion of those users (who employ TCO analysis) who rank the cost component in the row as the most important factor for proprietary and open source software, respectively. The initial cost (price) of the software is the top-ranked element for *both* proprietary *and* open source software. That this is true for open source is striking, and it illustrates that users often buy open source programs in forms that make their installation more user friendly. Moreover it points to important heterogeneity among users. If the initial cost of software were the largest part of cost for all users, as it is in the aggregate, we would have 100 percent in the first row and zero in all other rows. The fact that this number is only 50 percent for proprietary and 37 percent for open source software shows that there is quite a bit of variation among customers on the importance of the different elements of costs.[10] We will shortly return to discuss this important feature—the heterogeneity of users—in more detail. The other noteworthy fact is that users much more often rank switching costs and interoperability as the primary factor for open source than for proprietary software.

We can also assess the relative importance of the different cost factors in terms of the average percentage of TCO accounted for by each cost component, as is done in columns 2 and 4 of the table. A similar picture emerges: the initial cost (price) of the software is the leading component, accounting for 37 percent of the TCO for proprietary software and 28 percent for open source software. For proprietary software, support services are second, followed by roughly equal roles for switching costs; problems related to interoperability and the availability and cost of upgrades account for a slightly lower percentage for proprietary software. These factors play a relatively larger role in TCO for open source.

A simple *t*-test of the equality of means enables us to test whether the average cost shares for proprietary and open source software, given in columns 2 and 4 of the table, are equal to each other. The probability value (i.e., the critical level at which the test is statistically

---

10. A more detailed analysis of the survey responses shows that the 50 percent figure is not just due to half the users reporting zero percent and the other half 100 percent. The responses are much more evenly dispersed.

significant) is smaller than 1 percent for the initial cost of software, for switching cost for interoperability and for support services. But it is not significant for upgrades (p-value = 0.76). In short, there are statistically very significant differences between open source and proprietary software for all of the cost components except upgrades.

As discussed above, users are heterogeneous in terms of their assessments of the different components in the TCO. We can view this issue from a slightly different perspective. Suppose it is the case that some users attach more importance to certain cost elements—for instance, users with less technical expertise in IT may have more of a problem with switching costs or interoperability than other users who are more experienced. We will refer to this as "heterogeneity among users." In this case we would expect such users to attach greater weight to the switching cost and interoperability cost components *both* in their assessment of open source *and* proprietary software. To put the point more generally, if there is heterogeneity among users, we should expect to see *positive correlation* between the importance a user attaches to a given cost component in her TCO assessment of open source software and the corresponding component in proprietary software. The evidence confirms this prediction. For users that use both types of software, the correlation coefficient between the cost shares of these two types, as reported by the users, is both positive and large for each of the five cost components in the TCO.[11]

There is one more interesting point that emerges from the table. This relates to whether users who do not employ TCO analysis view the cost trade-offs in open source and proprietary software differently from those who have experience with such analysis. The answer is given by comparing the rankings of cost components in the last column of the table with those in columns 1 and 3. What we see is that users who do not do TCO analysis appear to overestimate the importance of the initial cost of software but underestimate the importance of costs associated with interoperability and support services. This empirical finding suggests that TCO analysis can be helpful in bringing out more informed, cost-effective choices.[12]

---

11. The correlation coefficients are 0.46 for the initial software cost, 0.47 for support services, 0.39 for switching costs, 0.54 for interoperability, and 0.55 for upgrades. All of these coefficients are statistically highly significant.

12. A possible alternative interpretation is that the better informed users do not conduct TCO analyses. But we are skeptical of this interpretation because our earlier regression analysis showed that small firms and those in low-tech manufacturing that *are less likely* to employ TCO analyses.

The numbers reported in table 5.3 are simple averages of the survey responses. While they point to clear conclusions about the trade-offs between open source and proprietary software, averages can sometimes be misleading. For example, it is possible that technically sophisticated users, who find it easier to switch between different types of software, might rank the switching cost component of proprietary software higher than open source, while other, less experienced users might report the opposite ranking. The simple averages we discussed in this section would not reveal such differences of opinion. To be more confident about our conclusions, we need to check whether these findings are confirmed in different parts of the distribution of responses.[13] We examine this question in the next section.

More on the Differences between TCO for Open Source and Proprietary Software

Before conducting the formal tests, we start with a simple visual inspection of the distributions of answers we got in the survey because that tells the basic story. In figures 5.1 through 5.5 we depict the cumulative distributions for open source and proprietary software for each cost component. The horizontal axis in each graph represents the percentage of the total cost of ownership that is accounted for by a specific cost element. The vertical axis represents the percentage of respondents in the survey. Each curve shows the proportion of respondents who say that the cost component accounts for less than a specified percent of TCO as indicated on the horizontal axis.[14] For example, the proprietary software curve in figure 5.1 shows that 20 percent of users report that the initial cost of proprietary software accounts for less than about 20 percent of total costs, 40 percent say it is less than 60 percent, and so on. The open source curve in figure 5.1 has the same interpretation. It is apparent that the curve for open source lies everywhere above the curve for proprietary software. That is, for any specified percentage of

---

13. Even if our findings about the cost trade-offs hold over the whole distribution, this does not mean that every user views the cost trade-offs in the same way. For example, we find that switching costs are relatively more important for open source software than for proprietary software over the whole distribution. Yet some users in the survey report that switching costs account for a higher proportion of TCO for proprietary software. This could easily be the case, especially for users that currently rely heavily on open source or on a different type of proprietary software.

14. The curves are not smooth because survey respondents almost always answer in terms of multiples of 5 percent, even though the survey did ask them to do so.

Figure 5.1
Initial cost for open source and proprietary software

total costs, a higher proportion of users say they are below that thresh-
old for open source than for proprietary software. In this case we say
that the distribution of the cost component for open source "stochastically dominates" the one for proprietary software. Loosely speaking,
the cost component is less important for open source *over the whole
range of the distribution*.[15]

The graphs reveal that there is a clear ranking between open source
and proprietary software in the different components of the total cost
of ownership. We turn first to the initial cost of software, depicted in
figure 5.1. As explained above, this graph shows that the curve for
open source software once again stochastically dominates the one
for proprietary software, as is seen by the fact that the open source
curve always lies above the curve for proprietary software. What
this means is that the initial cost of software accounts for a *smaller percentage* of total costs for open source over the whole distribution of
responses. This is not surprising, as it simply reflects the fact that open
source programs are typically less expensive than their proprietary
counterparts.

---

15. A distribution function $F(x)$ (first-order) stochastically dominates another distribution $G(x)$ if $F(x) < G(x)$ for every value of the variable x. This means that for every value
of x, the probability that the outcome is higher than x is greater for distribution F than for
G.

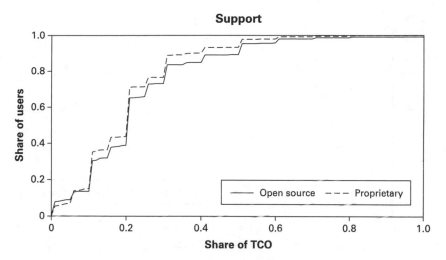

Figure 5.2
Cost of support services for open source and proprietary software

Consider next the case of software support services, which is depicted in figure 5.2. Here we observe that the curve for open source lies below the one for proprietary software for almost all of the distribution. This means that support services account for a *larger proportion* of total costs for open source than for proprietary software. This conclusion reflects the fact that open source is typically less user friendly than proprietary software and that it is normally not accompanied by extensive support services. The evidence is less clear-cut at low levels of the distribution where respondents do not rank support services as a significant cost element, as indicated by the fact that the open source and proprietary curves reverse position for cost proportions below about 10 percent.

Now consider the cases of switching costs and interoperability costs, shown in figures 5.3 and 5.4. The ordering of open source and proprietary software are very similar in these two cases. In both we see that the open source curve lies below the curve for proprietary software, which tells us that switching and interoperability costs account for a *larger proportion* of total costs for open source than for proprietary software, and that this holds over the entire distribution of responses.

Finally, figure 5.5 shows that there is virtually no difference between the open source and proprietary curves for the cost of upgrades

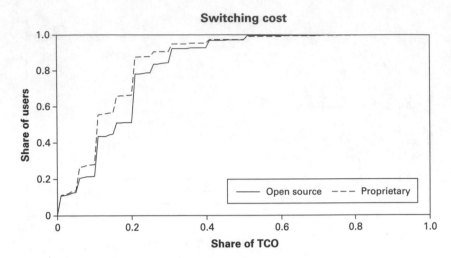

Figure 5.3
Switching costs for open source and proprietary software

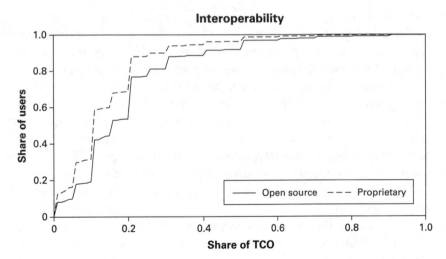

Figure 5.4
Interoperability costs for open source and proprietary software

Figure 5.5
Cost of upgrades for open source and proprietary software

anywhere on the distribution—the curves very nearly lie on top of each other.[16] This tells us that users do not see any real difference between open source and proprietary software in terms of the availability or cost of upgrades. This result is noteworthy because it suggests either that proprietary software exposes the consumer to less risk of later "holdup" than is commonly believed or that, if such holdup risk does exist, there are also very real costs associated with the frequency of upgrades or the lack of well-documented upgrades in open source.

Taken together, these graphs tell us a lot about the different cost structures of open source and proprietary software. They confirm our earlier finding (based on simple averages) that the initial cost of software is less daunting to users, while switching, interoperability and support service costs are relatively more important, for open source software. In the next section we back up this evidence with formal statistical tests on whether these cost share curves characterizing open source and proprietary software are really different from each other.

---

16. We examined the TCO distributions for each of the fifteen surveyed countries to see whether the patterns are similar to the ones we get using all the data. For every cost component and country, the stochastic dominance ranking is the same as when we pool the country data, but in some cases the ranking is weaker (the curves are more similar to each other). This is not surprising since the sample size for each country is only 1/15 as large as the overall sample, so the proportions are much noisier estimates.

Formal Tests on the TCO Distributions

In this section we undertake a formal statistical test of the hypothesis that there is no difference between the open source and proprietary software in terms of the importance users attach to each of the five cost components: the initial software price, switching costs, interoperability costs, access and cost of support services, and the availability and cost of future upgrades.[17] Essentially this test summarizes whether each of the curves depicted in figures 5.1 through 5.5 are the same for open source and proprietary software. If we reject the hypothesis that the curves for open source and proprietary software are the same, we will conclude that the cost structures of the two types of software differ.

Table 5.4 reports the test statistics. To implement the test, we need to group the cost shares reported in the survey—in figures 5.1 through 5.5 this corresponds to dividing up the horizontal axis into intervals. We use two alternatives: cost shares measured in 5 percent intervals (0–5, 5–10, etc.) and 10 percent intervals (0–10, 10–20, etc.). Most survey respondents answer in terms of these intervals (very few use more refined gradations).

Turning to the table, we decisively reject the null hypothesis that the distributions of TCO are the same for open source and proprietary software for the initial cost of software, switching costs and interoperability costs. This conclusion holds both when we use 10 percent intervals on the cost shares and the more narrowly defined 5 percent intervals. The chi-square test statistics are greater than the critical values of 31.4 for the 5 percent intervals and 18.3 for the 10 percent intervals. The conclusion for support services depends on which intervals we use, however. We reject the equality of the cost shares for open source and proprietary with the 10 percent intervals, but not otherwise. This simply reflects the fact that the curves for support services cross at the low end of the distribution (see figure 5.2), which gets picked up only when we use the 5 percent cost share intervals. Finally, we do not reject the null hypothesis that the distributions are the same for upgrades.

These formal tests confirm what the plots of the raw data revealed. Open source and proprietary software present users with a different composition of costs. The key trade-offs are between the importance of the costs of the initial software, switching, interoperability, and sup-

---

17. The methodology is described in the notes to table 5.4.

Table 5.4
Equality tests on TCO distributions for open source and proprietary software

	10% Cost share intervals		5% Cost share intervals	
	Chi-square statistic	Test of equality	Chi-square statistic	Test of equality
Initial software cost	73.5	Reject	85.4	Reject
Switching cost	36.5	Reject	47.6	Reject
Interoperability	44.1	Reject	49.0	Reject
Support services	19.5	Reject	24.4	Do not reject
Upgrades	4.4	Do not reject	10.9	Do not reject

Note: The critical values of the chi-square test at the 5 percent level of significance are: 18.3 for the 10 percent cost share intervals (df = 10) and 31.4 for the 5 percent cost share intervals (df = 20). The methodology is as follows: Let $p(m,s)$ denote the observed proportion of users who say that the share of a given cost component (e.g., switching costs) lies in the interval m for software type s (where s denotes either open source or proprietary), and let $\pi(m,s)$ denote the true theoretic proportion. Assuming that survey responses are independent of one other, the observed proportions have a multinomial distribution defined by $\pi(m,s)$ and sample size $n(s)$. For large samples, the terms $n(s)(p(m,s) - \pi(m,s))$ have a normal distribution with zero mean, so the statistic $\sum_{s=1}^{2} \sum_{m=1}^{M} n(s)\{(p(m,s) - \pi(m,s))/(\pi(m,s))\}^2$ has a chi-square distribution. To test the null hypothesis that the true proportions are equal for open source (s) and proprietary software (s′), we write H_0: $\pi(m,s) = \pi(m,s')$ for each interval m. Under H_0 the constrained estimates of the theoretic proportions for each interval m, say $P(m)$, are weighted averages of the observed proportions for open source and proprietary software, with sample size as weights. Then the test statistic $\sum_{s=1}^{2} \sum_{m=1}^{M} n(s)\{(p(m,s) - P(m))/(P(m))\}^2$ has a chi-square distribution with M degrees of freedom (equal to the number of proportions if the null hypothesis is not true, which is $2M$, minus the number under the null hypothesis, M). For more details, see Pakes and Simpson (1989).

port services. Interestingly there is no evidence that users see any difference in the importance of upgrade costs. This is noteworthy because it contradicts a widely held belief that using proprietary software runs the risk of being exposed to later "hold-up" in the form of high-priced upgrades. The fact that we do not see this expressed in the survey evidence suggests that competitive incentives mitigate this risk: proprietary software firms build and protect their reputations and exploiting users by such "holdup" will undermine this reputation and be counterproductive. Of course, this also applies to firms selling open source software bundled with other features. In addition users are not without a related risk when they use open source software. But here it is not so much the risk of high prices for subsequent upgrades, but rather the risk that there will not be upgrades available to the less sophisticated user who is not in a position to undertake them herself.

This evidence confirms that the differences between the composition of the total cost of operation between open source and proprietary software hold not just in terms of the means, but also over the whole distributions. The next task is to understand what factors shape users' assessments of the various cost components. We would like to able to identify which types of users care more about price of initial software, switching costs and the other elements that make up the total cost of operation.

TCO Assessments and User Characteristics
Although the composition of the total cost of operation is less different between open source and proprietary software than is probably commonly believed, differences do exist. Users face different cost trade-offs in choosing between these software alternatives. Furthermore there is a lot of variation across users in their own assessments of these relative costs. In this section we use the survey information to examine the determinants of this "user heterogeneity." In particular, we employ econometric analysis to identify in more detail how these trade-offs depend on key characteristics of software users—size, ownership, and industry, and how they vary across countries.

As we discussed earlier, we measure these trade-offs by looking at the share of TCO accounted for by each component, and doing this separately for open source and proprietary software. Of course, these cost shares add up to 100 percent. So when we investigate these data econometrically (using individual user data), it is only meaningful to talk about the cost shares relative to a reference point—that is, we need to normalize by one of the cost shares. It does not matter which we choose as the reference point, provided that we keep it in mind when we interpret the results. We choose the share accounted for by the initial cost of software as the reference point. For example, if switching costs account for 30 percent of the TCO and the initial cost of the software accounts for 20 percent, then we will use 10 percent ($= 30 - 20$) as the relative share of switching costs for this user. Comparisons using relative shares have a simple interpretation: for example, if the relative share of switching costs for open source is larger than the corresponding share for proprietary, it means that switching costs are more important relative to the initial cost of software for open source than for proprietary software. All of the analysis in this section is conducted in terms of these relative shares.

Table 5.5
Cost trade-offs in open source and proprietary software and user characteristics

Cost component	Country	Size	Ownership	Industry	Adjusted R^2
Proprietary software					
Switching cost	Yes (<0.001)	No (0.25)	No (0.84)	No (0.81)	0.063
Interoperability	Yes (<0.001)	Yes (0.12)	No (0.76)	No (0.87)	0.090
Support services	Yes (<0.001)	Yes (0.04)	No (0.76)	No (0.19)	0.068
Upgrades	Yes (<0.001)	No (0.072)	No (0.59)	No (0.43)	0.053
Open source software					
Switching cost	Yes (<0.001)	Yes (0.009)	No (0.081)	No (0.39)	0.153
Interoperability	Yes (<0.001)	Yes (0.008)	No (0.27)	No (0.47)	0.096
Support services	Yes (<0.001)	Yes (0.004)	Yes (0.016)	No (0.32)	0.136
Upgrades	Yes (<0.001)	No (0.096)	Yes (0.049)	No (0.74)	0.086

Note: Yes/No indicates whether the coefficients on the dummy variables for the column element are jointly statistically significant at the 5 percent level of significance or better. The p-value of the test is shown in parentheses. There are 1,298 observations in the proprietary software regressions, and 465 in the open source regressions.

To analyze the impact of user characteristics, we estimate regression models that relate the relative shares of each of the four dimensions of TCO (apart from price)—switching costs, interoperability, support services, and upgrades—to a set of explanatory variables. These include dummy variables that capture the effects of different user sizes, ownership type, and sectors, as well as a set of dummy variables for different countries (Brazil is the reference country, so all country differences are measured relative to it). For brevity, we do not present the full set of results here (for the interested reader, they are provided in table A.5.2 in appendix 5.3). Instead, table 5.5 summarizes which factors are statistically significant determinants of each cost component and which are not. For instance, the "no" in the first line of the table shows that the (relative) TCO share of switching costs is not affected by the size of the firm for proprietary software (at the 95 percent level of confidence). In contrast, looking at the bottom half of the table, the "yes" in the first line shows that user size does affect this share for open source software.

A number of interesting findings emerge from this table. The first and most striking fact is that there are strong differences across countries in the way users assess the cost trade-offs for both open source and proprietary software. We strongly reject the hypothesis that the cost shares are the same across countries, controlling for the other factors in the regression analysis. This conclusion holds for each of four cost dimensions and for both open source and proprietary software. We examine the country differences in more detail later in this section.

The second finding from the table is that the size of the user has a significant effect on the user's assessment of the importance of some components but not others. Size matters for support services both in proprietary and open source. In both cases the estimated coefficients (table A.5.1 in appendix 5.2) show that the cost of support services (*relative to the initial cost of software*) is less important for small users than for medium-sized and large users. This difference is even larger for open source than for proprietary software. This last point suggests that the source of the problem is at least partly that access and cost of support services are more problematic for small firms, not just that the initial cost of software is more important for small users. The table also shows that the size of the user affects the importance of switching costs for open source software, but not for proprietary. The estimated regression coefficients show that switching costs are relatively less important for small users as compared to medium-sized and large users.

The third, perhaps surprising, result is that the ownership and industry of the user do not affect the importance of most cost components relative to the initial cost of software. The only exceptions to this are that ownership matters for support services and upgrades in open source software. Inspection of the individual regression coefficients reveals that government agencies assess these cost factors to be more important than do domestic companies and foreign-owned subsidiaries. One plausible explanation for this result is the technical expertise needed to exploit ongoing improvements in open source software (which is typically less "user friendly") may be less strong in government agencies, and budgets too small to allow them to go to the market for such help.

A Closer Look at Country Differences
Before closing this discussion, we take a closer look at the variations across countries which, as we noted, are statistically significant for each cost component in open source and proprietary software. There

are two questions we want to ask: first, are the differences across countries systematic—that is, do similar patterns hold for the different cost components in each nation? To put it another way, if switching costs (relative to initial cost of software) are more important in, say Kenya, is this also true for its assessment of support services? If the answer is yes—and we will show that it is—then we want to ask how one can explain the observed cross-country differences.

To examine whether the cross-country differences are systematic, we compute the correlation coefficients between the four cost components for open source and proprietary software (more formally, we compute the correlations between the coefficients on dummy variables for each country and cost element). A correlation coefficient of zero—say, between switching costs and interoperability—would mean that there is no relationship between whether a particular country ranks both switching costs and interoperability as important (or unimportant). A correlation coefficient of one (the maximum value) means that there is a perfect association between these two rankings. The closer the correlation coefficient is to one, the more systematic are the country differences in these rankings of the different components of costs.[18]

Rather than go through all of the correlations here, we simply summarize the key finding from this exercise (table A.5.3 in appendix 5.2 presents the full matrix of correlation coefficients, for the interested reader). The main result is that all of the correlation coefficients are large and positive. The smallest correlation we obtain is 0.54, between switching costs and upgrades for open source. The maximum correlation is 0.98, between switching costs and interoperability for proprietary software. This evidence confirms that countries differ in a systematic way in terms of how users rate the importance of switching costs, interoperability, support services and upgrades (relative to the initial cost of software). This in turn suggests that there are underlying, country-level factors that are, at least in part, determining these differences. The next task is to try to understand what these factors are.

We consider four possible explanations. The first is the level of economic development. Given the small number of countries in our survey, we use the World Bank income categories: lower, middle (this

---

18. The correlation coefficients can also be negative (up to minus one), which would indicate that countries that attach a lot of importance to one cost component tend to place little weight on another. However, all of the correlations in the data are positive. Remember each cost component is measured relative to the share of costs associated with the initial cost of software.

includes the World Bank's lower and upper middle groups) and upper income. Our hypothesis is the initial cost of software is likely to be more important for users in lower income countries, and thus we expect that the *relative cost share of the other components* will be smaller in those countries.

The second factor is the level of software infrastructure and technical expertise possessed by, or available to, software users. Our hypothesis is that higher levels of expertise and infrastructure would reduce the cost of the complementary services needed to integrate software, such as switching costs, interoperability, and support services. At the country level there are only rough, proxy measures for software expertise and infrastructure. We measure software infrastructure by the number of internet portals per capita. We use two variables to capture the size and quality of the potential pool of technical expertise: the number of Internet users per portal for the size of the pool and the literacy rate for the educational quality of the pool. Our hypothesis is that more extensive infrastructure, and larger and better educated pools of expertise, should reduce the relative TCO shares of switching costs, interoperability and support services, and upgrades.

Finally, we consider two additional factors that might reduce the burden of the initial cost of software, and thus raise the relative cost share of the other four cost components. The first is the software piracy rate in each country in the year 2005 (as reported by the IDC 2008). While the survey data exclude self-employed (individual) users who might be more likely to use pirated proprietary software, it is possible that some of the survey users also do so. To that extent, the cost share of the initial software will be "too low" and thus the relative cost shares of the other TCO components will be larger.

The second factor is government incentives for software adoption. Countries differ in the extent to which they offer such incentives. When these incentives are more pervasive, we would expect the burden of the initial cost of software for the user to be smaller. The survey has information on whether users receive incentives, but it has no information on the magnitude of the adoption incentives. In this regression analysis, we use the proportion of users in the country that receive subsidies for open source or proprietary software, as reported in the survey.

To test these hypotheses, we estimate econometric models that relate the country-specific effect—namely the coefficients on the country dummy variables from the TCO regressions—to the four variables discussed above.[19] Table 5.6 presents the results. In the first column, the incentive measure we use is the proportion of users who receive incentives in any form—tax credits, direct subsidies, government procurement policy, or more informal means. In the second column, we use a narrower measure of incentives—the proportion of users who rank the monetary forms (tax credits or subsidies) as most important. Before turning to the specific coefficients and what they say about our hypotheses, it is worth noting that the regressions account for a considerable part of the observed variation across countries (this is given by the R^2 values reported at the end of the table). Despite its simplicity and the small sample size, the regression model accounts for 30 and 67 percent of the cross-country variation.

In the table, the estimated coefficients that have a statistically significant impact (at the 95 percent level of confidence) are designated by an asterisk.[20] The estimated coefficients on the dummy variables for low- and middle-income countries (high income is the reference group) are negative and statistically significant, which confirms the first hypothesis. They show that the relative importance of complementary cost components—those involving switching, interoperability, support services and upgrades (relative to initial cost of software)—grows as we move up the income scale. To put it another way, we find that the initial cost of software is relatively more important in lower than in middle-income countries, and at the same time, more important in middle-income than in high-income countries.

The evidence in table 5.6 also supports the hypothesis about the role of technical expertise in reducing the relative importance of complementary cost components. This is shown by three coefficients. The first is the negative coefficient on the number of Internet portals per capita ("software infrastructure"), which indicates that higher levels of infrastructure are associated with lower shares of the complementary cost

---

19. There are eight equations, one for the relative share of each of the four cost components, both for open source and proprietary software. Because there are only fourteen countries (Brazil is the reference country), we estimate these equations as a system using generalized least squares, with the coefficients of each variable constrained to be the same in the different equations (i.e., for open source and proprietary software, and for the different cost components). We can relax some of these constraints but the results do not change materially. We cannot allow for all coefficients to vary across equations, however, due to the small sample at the country level.

20. For the less technical reader, statistical significance is tested by comparing the ratio of the estimated coefficient and its standard error, which is given in parentheses below the coefficient. If this ratio is greater than 1.96, we can say that the true coefficient is not zero, with a 95 percent level of confidence.

Table 5.6
Cost trade-offs in open source and proprietary software: Explaining the differences across countries

Variable		
Low-income dummy	−36.9*	−36.0*
	(8.8)	(8.6)
Middle-income dummy	−16.0*	−17.4*
	(3.2)	(3.1)
Internet portals/capita	−77.2*	−83.3*
	(21.7)	(21.0)
Internet users/portal $\times 10^3$	20.4*	20.0*
	(5.1)	(5.0)
Literacy rate	−0.57*	−0.50*
	(0.22)	(0.22)
Software piracy rate	0.07	0.10
	(0.077)	(0.075)
Percentage with some incentive	−0.30*	
	(0.12)	
Percentage with monetary incentive		−0.59*
		(0.17)
R^2 for equation:		
Switching, PS	0.30	0.32
Switching, OS	0.60	0.61
Interoperability, PS	0.49	0.59
Interoperability, OS	0.66	0.67
Support services, PS	0.16	0.23
Support services, OS	0.37	0.37
Upgrades, PS	0.49	0.59
Upgrades, OS	0.61	0.64
Number of observations	102	102

Notes: High income is the baseline income category. An asterisk denotes statistical significance at the 5 percent level. PS and OS denote proprietary and open source software, respectively.

components in TCO. The second is the positive sign on the number of internet users per portal, which shows that the complementary cost components are more important in countries where the population contains a larger proportion of users of services as opposed to "computer savvy" creators of services, for which the number of portals serve as a rough proxy. And finally, greater literacy is associated with a lower burden from these components. However, the third hypothesis is not supported by the results. While the positive sign on the software piracy rate variable is as predicted, it is not statistically different from zero.

We expected incentives for software adoption to reduce the burden for the user to purchase the software, making the other cost components loom larger for the user (relative to the initial cost of software). Surprisingly, the regression results suggest the opposite—in countries with more pervasive incentives, the other (nonprice) cost components are less, not more, important. One possible explanation for this anomalous result is that countries where the initial cost of software is particularly burdensome to users may be those countries that introduce incentives for software adoption. Unfortunately, we have no way to test this conjecture with the available data.

The evidence in this section shows that economic factors—most important, income levels and the level of technical expertise (computer literacy)—can at least partly explain differences across countries in the cost structures of open source and proprietary software, as users perceive them. Before concluding this lengthy discussion, we want to emphasize the limitations of our analysis on the use of TCO. While our survey information on TCO reveals important and new findings about how users view the costs of open source and proprietary software, it is important to bear in mind that our survey measures are an incomplete metric. In many cases the cost of software is a small part of the total cost of running a system, and the comparison of total cost of ownership will depend on the allocation of internal costs of the firm, in particular labor costs.[21] The management accounting literature has stressed the fact that this is a very difficult task and is subject to a high degree of inexactitude. Furthermore the TCO measure does not capture any differences in the functional value, or quality, of different software, and this aspect would also need to be included in a full assessment. We now briefly discuss this issue of quality before turning to our examination of how users actually mix open source and proprietary software.

Quality

Beyond an assessment of the total cost of ownership, software quality is important in any adoption decision.[22] For the lay person, "higher

---

21. For instance, the cost of one hour of a skilled IT professional in India is estimated at USD 30 (see Kumar 2003). Even a USD 1,000 difference in the cost of server software would be wiped out by thirty-five hours of difference of work time, over the lifetime of the server.

22. It is not easy to separate the cost and quality component of software. For instance, the fact that end users are more efficient with program A than with program B can be interpreted as a difference of quality (program A provides better tools) or a difference in cost (it is less costly to obtain a certain final product with A than with B).

quality software" means a superior product that would be recognized by all users as such (even if not everyone buys it, as that will also depend on its price). But economics distinguishes between two types of "quality" differences: vertical differentiation and horizontal differentiation. Vertical differentiation is roughly the same as the lay meaning—all consumers would rank it as better (putting aside the question of whether it is worth the price charged). An automotive example is the BMW versus the Yugo. Few if any would dispute the ranking. However, there are many products where consumers have a different ranking, in part because they are looking for different features to match their specific needs or just due to different "tastes." Trying to rank BMW and Mercedes Benz, or a Yugo and a stripped-down pickup truck, illustrates this idea.

Where does software fit in this scheme? There may be pure cases of vertical quality differences (e.g., a program that is functionally identical to another but more efficient). But the vast majority of cases surely involves horizontal differences. Open source software (at least that which is not provided commercially) is typically less user friendly and thus attracts more technically sophisticated users. As we emphasized earlier in the chapter, it is not sufficiently recognized in many of these discussions that customers are heterogeneous, that as a consequence "quality" is not one-dimensional, and that the willingness to pay for different features of software varies across customers. The fact that different customers see different trade-offs between quality and cost makes it possible to have coexistence between two programs even if one of them was generally accepted as being of better technical quality than the other.

With this understanding in mind, we turn to some evidence on how users view the importance of "quality." Table 5.7 shows the reasons, *as reported by software developer firms*, why their customers hesitate to adopt open source software. Taking the sample as a whole (first row in the table), the most important consideration for software adoption is quality—it gets the top rank from 39 percent of respondents, followed closely by switching costs and support services. The importance of switching costs and support services is consistent with what users themselves report, as we discussed earlier and illustrated in table 5.3. The new information here is the critical role of software quality. Unfortunately, it was not possible to survey firms on the separate vertical and horizontal aspects of "quality."

There are some interesting differences in the relative importance of software quality across different user groups. The rows in table 5.7

Table 5.7
Obstacles to open source adoption, by customer type: Perspective of software developers
(percentage with top rank)

	Switching	Support services	Quality
Aggregate	33.4	27.2	39.4
	(1.1)	(1.0)	(1.1)
Corporate sales > 75%	30.8	29.0	40.1
	(3.5)	(3.5)	(3.7)
Government sales > 75%	36.4	27.3	36.3
	(8.4)	(7.8)	(8.4)
Individual sales > 75%	36.8	31.6	31.6
	(10.8)	(10.4)	(10.4)
Operating system sales > 75%	37.4	30.8	31.8
	(4.7)	(4.5)	(4.5)
Application sales > 75%	31.8	26.8	41.4
	(2.4)	(2.2)	(2.5)

Note: Binomial standard errors are in parentheses. These are computed as $\sqrt{p(1-p)/n}$, where p is the reported proportion and n is the sample size.

show the ranking of obstacles to user adoption of open source software, as assessed by software developers that focus on different types of customers (as measured by the percentage of revenues coming from customer groups). For instance, among firms for which corporate sales account for more than 75 percent of revenues, 30.8 percent say that switching costs is the most important obstacle to their customers adopting open source software, 29.0 percent say that support services are the leading obstacle, and 40.1 percent report that software quality is the dominant consideration. What we see is that the ranking of the different obstacles depends on the type of customers. Quality is most frequently top-ranked by developers with primarily corporate customers. For those with primarily government or individual customers, there are no significant differences between the primacy of quality and switching costs. Interestingly the ranking also depends on the type of software—specifically, software for operating systems and applications. Switching costs appear most important for customers of operating system software, while quality is top-ranked for applications. This last difference is what we might expect if users of applications software are less technically sophisticated than users of operating system software, since they would be less able to navigate around the deficiencies and modify the open source software.

Because quality is so important to users, we want to understand whether there are systematic differences, one way or the other, between the quality of open source and proprietary software. Two lines of arguments are often made. First, authors make comparisons between some open source software and some proprietary software in the hope that the accumulation of such evidence will lead to an answer; this approach does not lead to clear-cut conclusions.[23]

Second, a number of authors have suggested that the mode of development of open source software leads to better quality. A complete review would take us too far astray, but the arguments center on the following points.[24] Because open source software is developed by users, proponents say that it should be more attuned to their needs, although this argument is presumably only relevant for rather technical software. On the security front, many people have the opportunity to scrutinize open source software, and if they did so, most bugs, including security bugs, could be corrected. However, the fact that the code source is accessible is no guarantee that it will be scrutinized, and in any case, a proprietary firm can pay debuggers (see Anderson 2002; Obsanjo 2002; Viega 2000). Other arguments center on the relative innovativeness of proprietary and open source software, and on the "finish" of the programs, in particular the quality of the documentation.

Many of the preceding arguments can be better understood in light of the discussion of chapter 2. Innovation will depend on the incentives of innovators. Open source projects leave their contributors a smaller share of the increase in social welfare generated by improvements in the programs. On the other hand, they make it easier for programmers who spot an improvement that they would find useful to propose a change in the program itself, rather than trying to implement it through an add-on program. This may not provide sufficient incentive for very large and risky investments in, say, the development of a radically new user interface, but it can provide incentives for some of the technical innovations in the core of the program,

---

23. In many cases the methodology of these studies is not public. In the economic literature we can point to the discussion by Jennifer Kuan (2001) who finds that the correction of bugs is faster in open source software than in proprietary software, but her sample is quite limited and she cannot measure whether the number of bugs with which the software is released is different. Alexandre Gaudeul (2003) studies programs developed around the TeX typesetting engines and finds that proprietary software leads open source software in developing new interfaces. For a discussion of the security of open source and proprietary software, see Ross Anderson (2005).

24. Of course, not all of the following arguments apply to all open source projects. Our discussion is more oriented to the large projects than to the numerous, small projects.

which would be difficult to exploit commercially. Similarly, improving documentation and help systems yields relatively small benefits to an expert user, whereas proprietary software can compensate people monetarily for this work.[25]

To this point in the chapter, we have emphasized that the costs of adopting software are multifaceted. Some costs are monetary, such as the initial purchase price, but other costs of adoption, such as learning or interoperability, are less visible and yet can be very important for some users. Our evidence demonstrates that the structure of costs is different for open source and proprietary software, though perhaps less than conventional wisdom might suggest. Users face trade-offs in making their adoption decisions, and their choices will depend on how much importance they give to the different types of costs. It is critical to recognize that consumers are heterogeneous in terms of how they assess the different types of software cost. This arises because of cash constraints, the level of technical sophistication of the consumer, and other factors. Our survey evidence reveals this heterogeneity and shows that the differences are related to a variety of characteristics of users.

In short, the total costs of ownership for open source and proprietary software vary across consumers. Not only that, but this comparison may vary with the different applications a given consumer may have. Thus we would expect consumers to make different choices and to mix-and-match open source and proprietary programs as appropriate to their needs. In the remainder of this chapter, we examine this cohabitation of open source and proprietary software in detail. We focus in particular on the extent to which users mix the two types of software and how their decisions to do this are related to their assessments of the various cost components that make up the total cost of ownership, which we studied earlier.

Mixing by Consumers: The Cohabitation of Open Source and Proprietary Software

The Choice of Whether to Mix
In the previous sections we have shown that consumers vary in terms of how they assess the total cost of ownership of open source and

---

25. A solution to this conundrum is the independent sales of help manuals, as the book publisher O'Reilly does. This partly solves the problem by using commercial software techniques to provide part of the services.

Table 5.8
Use of proprietary and open source software, by country (percentage of respondents)

	Users operating with:		
	Only proprietary	Only open source	Both proprietary and open source
Aggregate	67.3	5.9	26.8
Country			
Brazil	51.0	12.9	36.1
Chile	73.5	1.9	24.6
China	79.2	6.9	13.9
France	66.0	8.8	25.2
Greece	72.3	0.0	27.7
India	62.7	2.5	34.8
Israel	79.6	3.2	17.2
Kenya	47.7	12.3	40.0
Mexico	65.4	8.3	26.3
Poland	67.5	6.4	27.1
Russia	46.1	12.8	41.1
South Africa	80.0	1.9	18.1
Singapore	87.7	1.9	10.4
Thailand	74.2	9.0	16.8
Turkey	56.1	0.0	43.9

proprietary software. Consumers attach different degrees of importance to the various components of TCO, reflecting their particular user characteristics. In addition they have a variety of software needs and the available open source and proprietary options to meet them will vary. For both reasons we would expect users to mix their purchases of open source and proprietary software rather than buy from one or the other exclusively. In this section we exploit our new survey data to examine how consumers mix. The survey of users provides very useful data on the use of software by firms in the fifteen countries. They enable us to evaluate the extent to which different forms of software are used—in particular, the mixing of open source and proprietary software—and by implication, to assess the relative strengths of the different types of software as reflected in market demand. We summarize the key findings in this section.

We begin with some descriptive information about variations across countries. Table 5.8 shows the use of proprietary and open source software in the fifteen countries in which the survey was conducted. A high percentage of respondents report using only proprietary software, but there are sizable variations across countries, and these are not related to stage of economic development in any simple way. In all countries, very few respondents use only open source software. But the countries with the highest percentage that exclusively adopt open source are low- or lower middle-income countries–Brazil (12.9 percent), Kenya (12.3 percent), and Russia (12.8 percent). What is also noteworthy is how common it is for users to mix open source and proprietary software, as shown in the last column of the table. But here too there are large differences across countries. Mixing appears to be generally more extensive in the low- or lower middle-income countries, such as Brazil, India, Kenya, Russia, and Turkey, though there are also lower income countries with low levels of mixing (China, South Africa, and Thailand).[26] The rankings of countries in terms of the patterns of their software use are confirmed when we use regression analysis to control for the effects of size, ownership type, and sector.

Table 5.9 shows that the use of open source, and the mixing of open source and proprietary software, depends on the characteristics of the user. The first thing to notice is that small firms are much less likely than medium-sized and large firms to use some open source software. This is consistent with the often-expressed view that it is more technically demanding to use than proprietary software, an interpretation also suggested by the fact that firms in high-tech manufacturing are more likely to use some open source software than those in low-tech manufacturing and trade. The second observation is that small firms are much less likely than large firms to mix open source and proprietary software, though 19.3 percent of even small firms do mix.[27]

---

26. The survey also provides more detailed information on the use of open source software, breaking it up into operating systems and applications, and within each of those categories into use in workstations and in servers. We will not discuss the results using this information, but instead we just summarize the main features that emerge. First, in the overall sample, open source is adopted by a larger proportion of users for operating systems than for applications. This holds for all countries in the survey. Second, within operating systems, open source is more widely used in servers than in workstations, and this conclusion holds in all but one of the countries in the survey (Kenya is the exception). This pattern is consistent with the idea that open source is less user friendly than proprietary software and requires greater technical expertise to adapt and use it. But this is not likely to be the whole explanation, since we find a more mixed pattern for open source used in applications. Here, about half the countries use open source more frequently in servers, the rest in workstations, and this breakdown does not relate in any simple way to the level of economic development.

27. One possible explanation for why small firms mix less often is due to scale. Suppose, for example, that firms decided between open source and proprietary software, for any given software "task," by the toss of a coin (more generally, with any fixed probability). With fewer tasks (hence fewer random tosses), the probability of observing mixing will

Table 5.9
Use of proprietary and open source software, by user characteristics (percentage of respondents)

	Only proprietary	Only open source	Both proprietary and open source
Aggregate	67.3	5.9	26.8
	(1.0)	(1.9)	(0.9)
Size			
Small	74.7	6.0	19.3
	(1.4)	(1.9)	(1.3)
Medium	66.9	7.3	25.8
	(1.6)	(2.1)	(1.5)
Large	53.8	3.6	42.6
	(2.2)	(1.5)	(2.2)
Ownership			
Government agency	60.3	6.6	33.1
	(2.3)	(2.0)	(2.2)
Domestic company	69.0	6.0	25.0
	(1.1)	(1.9)	(1.1)
Foreign subsidiary	69.7	3.8	26.5
	(3.0)	(1.5)	(2.9)
Industry			
Services	52.8	4.8	42.4
	(4.5)	(1.7)	(4.4)
High-tech manufacturing	62.4	7.3	30.3
	(2.3)	(2.1)	(2.2)
Low-tech manufacturing	75.1	4.5	20.4
	(2.1)	(1.7)	(2.0)
Trade	74.0	5.6	20.4
	(2.0)	(1.8)	(1.9)

Note: Binomial standard errors are in parentheses. These are computed as $\sqrt{p(1-p)/n}$, where p is the reported proportion and n is the sample size.

While there is no difference between domestic and foreign firms, government agencies are significantly less likely than firms to use proprietary software exclusively. This difference may reflect more severe budget constraints for government agencies, if it is the case that open source is less costly to use, taking into account the total cost of ownership. The difference may also reflect the fact that some governments

---

be lower for small firms. But this story is at best a partial explanation because it cannot explain two observed facts: first, why small- and medium-sized firms are so similar in the extent to which they rely exclusively on open source (column 2 in the table) and, second, why the big difference in mixing is not between small- and medium-sized firms but between those two and large firms.

Table 5.10
Decision to mix open source and proprietary software: Impact of user and country characteristics

Variable	Operating systems	Applications
Test: size dummies (p-value)	<0.001	<0.001
Test: ownership dummies (p-value)	0.25	0.49
Test: industry dummies (p-value)	<0.001	<0.001
Test: country dummies (p-value)	<0.001	<0.001
Pseudo-R^2	0.099	0.099
Number of observations	2,186	1,947

Note: Test statistics are taken from multinomial logit regressions using three categories: only proprietary (the reference group), open source, and both.

have proactive policies in favor of the use of open source software in government agencies. But it is also worth pointing out that earlier in the chapter we showed that government agencies are also far less likely than firms to employ TCO analysis in making their software adoption decisions.

These simple comparisons do not control for the other factors that affect the decision to mix open source and proprietary software—for example, part of the difference between government agencies and companies may reflect differences in their size. To pin down the sources of these differences more sharply, we estimate a (multinomial logit) regression model that relates the choice between the three mutually exclusive choices—using only proprietary, only open source, or mixing the two—to a set of dummy variables that capture the groupings of user size, ownership type, industry, and country fixed effects. The survey data allow us to do this separately for operating systems and applications software. Table 5.10 summarizes the statistical tests of whether user characteristics affect the software adoption choice (the individual coefficients are not reported, for brevity). The results confirm the basic descriptive findings in table 5.9. The adoption choice is significantly related to the size of the user (smaller firms are less likely to mix) and to the sector (low-tech manufacturing and wholesale and retail trades are less likely to use any open source than high-tech manufacturing and services). However, the decision to mix is not related to ownership—there is no difference in this regard between domestic firms, foreign subsidiaries, and government agencies. In addition we find that the propensity to use open source varies significantly across countries.

The Choice of How Much to Mix

Thus far we have looked only at *the choice of whether to mix*, but the survey provides information that allows us to go further to investigate the *choice of how much to mix*. In particular, we asked survey respondents about the extent to which they use open source software in their operating systems and in software applications, separately. We have information on whether the proportion of open source operating system software among all of its operating system software is less than 25 percent, between 25 and 75 percent, or above 75 percent, and we have similar information for applications software.[28] As before with the choice of whether to mix, here we want to examine how user size, ownership, industry, and country affect the decision about how much to mix. But there is another important ingredient we can add to this analysis. In the previous sections we showed that the users' assessments of the composition of TCO differed somewhat for open source and proprietary software. In particular, we found that the relative importance of the complementary cost components (i.e., components of TCO other than the initial cost of software) is different for open source and proprietary software and for different types of users. It is natural to ask whether these different assessments have any effect on the choices users make between open source and proprietary software.

To examine this, we use the individual data on users to estimate an empirical model that relates the degree of mixing between open source and proprietary software to the TCO assessments. (Because the survey responses are in ordered [successively higher] intervals, we use Ordered Probit regressions for this purpose.) Since the focus is on the user's choice between the two types of software, for the explanatory variables we use the cost share of each component for open source minus the cost share for proprietary software. For example, if switching costs account for 30 percent of open source TCO and 20 percent of proprietary TCO (relative to the initial cost), the measure for that user would be $30 - 20 = 10$ percent. Essentially this measures the importance of the cost component for open source relative to proprietary software.[29]

---

28. The original survey data is broken down into quartiles, but we combine the 25–50 and 50–75 percent groups for the econometric analysis.

29. Since the shares of the five cost components add up to 100 percent, we have to exclude one from the regression, so everything is measured relative to it. We use the initial cost of software as the reference point. In effect, this means we are using the share of cost components minus the share of the initial cost of software in open source minus the same for proprietary software.

Table 5.11
TCO assessments and the software adoption decision: Ordered Probit regressions

Variable	Operating systems		Applications	
	(1)	(2)	(3)	(4)
Switching OS-PS	−0.019*	−0.017*	−0.016*	−0.016*
	(0.005)	(0.006)	(0.006)	(0.006)
Support services OS-PS	−0.011*	−0.011*	−0.009*	−0.010*
	(0.004)	(0.005)	(0.004)	(0.005)
Interoperability OS-PS	−0.020*	−0.019*	−0.009*	−0.006
	(0.005)	(0.006)	(0.0048)	(0.005)
Upgrades OS-PS	−0.002	−0.002	−0.006	−0.004
	(0.006)	(0.007)	(0.006)	(0.006)
Test: size dummies (p-value)		0.066		0.11
Test: ownership dummies (p-value)		0.22		0.92
Test: industry dummies (p-value)		0.43		0.74
Test: country dummies (p-value)		0.19		0.27
Pseudo-R^2	0.038	0.073	0.019	0.109
Number of observations	329	326	332	330

Notes: * denotes statistical significance at the 5 percent level. PS and OS denote proprietary and open source software, respectively. Switching OS-PS is defined by the share of switching costs in TCO for OS minus the share of the initial cost of software, minus the same calculation for PS. The other variables are defined analogously.

Table 5.11 summarizes the econometric results.[30] Columns 1 and 3 present the results for a stripped down model in which we include only the TCO assessments but none of the other user characteristics. The coefficients on the four complementary cost share variables are negative and statistically significant for three of them. This means that when open source software involves larger cost shares (relative to proprietary) for switching, support services, and interoperability, users adopt the less open source. This conclusion holds both for operating systems and software applications.[31] However, the cost disadvantage

30. The survey covers 2,432 users, but the number of observations is much smaller in these regressions. This is because we can only include users who conduct TCO analyses (and hence answer the TCO survey questions) for both open source and proprietary software.
31. It is also rather striking that the estimated coefficients on these three variables are similar in magnitude. In the regressions in the table we use the *difference* between the cost shares in open source and proprietary TCO for each of the four cost components. This is a constrained version of a more general specification that includes both shares, where the coefficient on the proprietary share is equal in magnitude but opposite in sign to the share on open source. We tested whether these four restrictions hold in the data, and do not reject them—the p-value for the test is 0.35 for operating systems and 0.87 for applications.

with respect to upgrades does not have any significant impact on the extent to which open source software is used. This suggests that upgrade costs are not a big factor in the choice between the two types of software. However, remember that there is very little difference between open source and proprietary software in the distribution of this cost share in the first place, hence not much information with which to pin down the effect econometrically.

In columns 2 and 4 we add a full set of dummy variables to account for the different categories of size, ownership, industry and country of the user. When we do this, the coefficients on the TCO variables do not change much, which is reassuring. It is also worth noting that once we account for the TCO assessments of open source and proprietary software, there is essentially no residual impact of user size, ownership, industry, or country. The estimated coefficients on the dummy variables for these factors are not statistically significant (only the size of the user enters with some, marginally significant, role). To put this point another way, the user's characteristics affect the extent of mixing behavior only through their impact on her assessment of the cost components for open source and proprietary software.

In this section we analyzed the patterns of open source and proprietary software use in the fifteen countries covered by our survey. The data show that the use of open source software is widespread—the proportion of users who adopt some open source varies from a low of 20 percent (in South Africa) to a high of 54 percent (in Russia). There is some tendency for open source use to be more common in low- and middle-income countries, but there are exceptions at both ends of the income spectrum.

At the same time very few consumers rely exclusively on open source. Of those that use open source, the vast majority adopt a mixture of open source and proprietary software to meet their needs, and this is true for low-, middle-, and high-income countries. The extent of mixing varies with certain user characteristics, being greater in larger firms and in the high-tech manufacturing and trade sectors.

Moreover the software adoption decisions users make depend on how they evaluate the different cost structures that open source and proprietary software offer. Users who give more importance to switching costs, interoperability, and support services are more likely to use proprietary software. Users who by contrast put more weight on the initial cost of software lean more toward open source.

Conclusion

In this chapter we have provided an in-depth examination of the assessments by software users of the costs of open source and proprietary software and studied their demand for both of these types of software. This examination is made possible by the new and unique survey of users we conducted, covering more than 2,000 users in fifteen countries. The data provides many new insights into the structure of demand for software, and in particular, how it relates to a number of user characteristics and to their perceptions of the various costs involved in adopting software.

Three main empirical conclusions emerge from the analysis, which we now summarize:

• First, open source and proprietary software pose different cost trade-offs to users. With open source, the initial cost of the software is a smaller component of the total cost of operation than with proprietary software; on the other side, open source involves a relatively greater burden due to switching costs, interoperability, and support services. While there are differences in the details, this characterization holds for all of the countries we surveyed, and this is striking given that they cover a wide range of economic development.

• Second, users are highly heterogeneous not only in terms of their software needs but also the weight they attach to different types of costs. As a consequence the choices users make as between open source and proprietary software will depend on the characteristics of the users and the weights they attach to different components of cost.

• Finally, not only do users choose different types of software, but they also extensively mix the two types of software, and this mixing behavior is found in all the countries we study. Moreover the extent to which open source is used and the degree of mixing between open source and proprietary software both depend on user characteristics in ways that are consistent with economic principles.

Despite the real differences between open source and proprietary software, they do not live in two totally different worlds. Our detailed survey data on software development and usage have allowed us to document the extensive cohabitation between these worlds. As we showed in this and the previous chapter, many software developer firms sell proprietary software while contributing to open source development, and software users extensively mix and match the two types of software. The problem is not to choose between one and the other form of software, but to identify the proper mix. And the challenge for public policy is to set a regulatory framework that facilitates the competitive interplay between open source and proprietary software in ways that promote efficiency and innovation. We take up these critical issues in the next chapter on government policy.

Appendix 5.1: An Economic Model of the Decision to Invest in TCO Analysis

In this appendix we present a simple model of the decision by a user to undertake TCO analysis in making software adoption decisions. The basic idea behind the model is that each user faces a trade-off between incurring the cost of doing a TCO analysis and the benefit of getting more information about the true comparative costs of open source and proprietary software before deciding which software to buy. The user does the analysis when the expected benefit of the information gain exceeds the cost of the analysis. Since both the costs and benefits can vary across users, a point we return to later, we expect different users to make different decisions.

Assume that the total cost of operation (hereafter, cost) of two types of software can take two values c_H and c_L, with $c_L < c_H$. Let π^O denote the probability that open source software is expensive—namely that its cost is c_H—and π^P be the probability that proprietary software is expensive. We assume that, a priori, users believe that the expected cost of open source software is lower than that of proprietary software. Formally this is expressed as

$$\pi^O c_H + (1 - \pi^O)c_L < \pi^P c_H + (1 - \pi^P)c_L, \tag{A.1}$$

which is equivalent to $\pi^O < \pi^P$.

Now suppose that by spending an amount F, a user can learn the true costs of both type of software (F is the sunk cost of doing a TCO analysis). If she does not spend F, the user will choose the open source software and her expected cost will be $\pi^O c_H + (1 - \pi^O)c_L$. If she conducts TCO analysis, the total expected cost for the user will be $c_H \pi^O \pi^P + c_L (1 - \pi^O \pi^P) + F$. Note here that her cost of purchasing software will be c_H only when both open source and proprietary software are expensive (with cost c_H). Otherwise, she chooses the less expensive option.

Therefore the user will conduct TCO analysis if, and only if,

$$c_H \pi^O \pi^P + c_L(1 - \pi^O \pi^P) + F < \pi^O c_H + (1 - \pi^O)c_L.$$

This is equivalent to the condition

$$F < (c_H - c_L)\pi^O(1 - \pi^P). \tag{A.2}$$

Equation (A.2) says that the user undertakes TCO analysis when the expected benefits exceed the sunk cost of doing so. The expected benefits are the savings $c_H - c_L$, which occur when open source software is expensive and proprietary software is cheap, and this happens with probability equal to $\pi^O(1 - \pi^P)$. Any factor that reduces the cost of a TCO analysis increases the likelihood that she will undertake it—for instance, greater technical expertise of the user, which may be associated with larger users and with those in high-tech industries. Similarly factors that increase the expected benefits make it more likely that the user does such analysis. A leading example is the scale of the software requirement. On this account we would expect larger firms to be more likely to undertake TCO analysis.[32]

In practice, governments provide various incentives for software adoption (see chapter 6). We can easily extend the model to allow for subsidies. Let s^P be the subsidy for proprietary software and s^O be the subsidy for open source software. We make three assumptions:

1. Even with the subsidies, if the choice is made on the basis of a priori information (i.e., without TCO analysis), the user purchases open source software, which implies that

$$\pi^O c_H + (1 - \pi^O)c_L - s^O < \pi^P c_H + (1 - \pi^P)c_L - s^P.$$

2. The subsidy for proprietary software is larger than the subsidy for open source: $s^O \leq s^P$. While we do not have any survey information about the magnitude of the subsidies, in practice, monetary subsidies are likely only to apply to the cost of the initial software (it would be hard for governments to compensate for switching, interoperability, and related costs). As we demonstrate in this chapter, the initial cost is a substantially larger proportion of the TCO for proprietary software and thus the subsidy is likely to be larger for proprietary.[33]

---

32. This assumes, reasonably, that the sunk cost of TCO analysis increases less than proportionally with the scale of the software purchase.

33. In order to reverse this ranking, the *monetary* subsidy rate would have to be much larger for open source software, but we have no evidence to support this assumption.

3. The subsidies do not reverse the relative costs—even with the subsidies, the user prefers to buy the software at cost c_L rather than c_H. Formally, $c_L - s^O < c_H - s^P$. This assumption implies that the user will buy low-cost, open source software rather than high-cost, proprietary software despite the higher subsidy for the latter: $c_L - s^P < c_H - s^O$.

Under these assumptions, if the user conducts a TCO analysis, she will purchase proprietary software whenever its cost (ignoring subsidy) is equal to or less than the cost of open source software. Her total cost will be

$$(c_H - s^P)\pi^O\pi^P + (c_L - s^O)\pi^P(1 - \pi^O) + (c_L - s^P)(1 - \pi^P) + F. \qquad (A.3)$$

Note that when the cost of the two types of software is the same, the user buys the proprietary software whose subsidy is larger. Therefore she only buys open source software when its cost is low and the cost of proprietary software is high. She will choose to do a TCO analysis when

$$(c_H - s^P)\pi^O\pi^P + (c_L - s^O)\pi^P(1 - \pi^O) + (c_L - s^P)(1 - \pi^P) + F$$

$$< \pi^O c_H + (1 - \pi^O)c_L - s^O$$

which is the same as

$$F < (c_H - c_L)\pi^O(1 - \pi^P) + (s^P - s^O)(1 + \pi^O\pi^P - \pi^P). \qquad (A.4)$$

The new element here is the last set of terms involving the subsidies. The key point is that subsidies for software adoption affect the benefits from undertaking a TCO analysis and thus the willingness of the user to do a TCO analysis. But there is an asymmetry: subsidies to proprietary software increase the incentive to do TCO, while subsidies to open source reduce it (in this model, it is only the difference between the two subsidies that matters).

Appendix 5.2: Who Does TCO Analysis: Econometric Estimates

In this appendix we use multivariate regression analysis to examine the factors that determine whether a user invests in a TCO analysis before making software adoption decisions. Table A.5.1 presents the parameter estimates from a Probit regression that relates whether the TCO analysis is undertaken against a set of user characteristics,

Table A.5.1
Determinants of the use of TCO analysis: Econometric estimates

Variable	
Medium-sized firm[a]	0.328*
	(0.067)
Large firm	0.523*
	(0.093)
Foreign subsidiary[b]	0.373*
	(0.120)
Domestic firms	0.303*
	(0.091)
High-tech manufacturing[c]	0.001
	(0.087)
Low-tech manufacturing	−0.248*
	(0.089)
Wholesale/retail trade	−0.119
	(0.087)
Test: firm size dummies (p-value)	<0.001
Test: ownership dummies (p-value)	0.002
Test: industry sector dummies (p-value)	0.020
Test: country dummies (p-value)	<0.001
Pseudo-R^2	0.144
Number of observations	1,894

Notes: * denotes statistical significance at the 5 percent level.
a. The reference size category is small firms.
b. The reference ownership category is government agencies.
c. The reference industry sector is services.

including firm size, ownership and industry sector, plus a full set of country fixed effects.

The coefficients on the dummy variables for medium and large firms (small firms are the reference group) are both statistically significant and show that the likelihood of doing TCO analysis increases with firm size. This conclusion holds both when we compare medium to small firms (given by the coefficient on medium-sized firms), and in the comparison between large and medium-sized firms. The chi-square test decisively rejects the joint hypothesis that firm size does not matter, with a p-value of less than 0.001 percent (i.e., at confidence levels higher than 99.9 percent).

We also find that ownership affects the decision to do a TCO analysis. Both domestic firms and foreign subsidiaries are significantly more likely to do it than government agencies (the reference category), as shown by the positive coefficients on these two ownership variables. While the point estimates differ, there is no statistically significant difference between domestic and foreign firms in this regard. In short, it is private ownership that affects this decision to do TCO analysis, which strongly suggests that the profit (cost reduction) incentive is the key driver. Again, the chi-square test confirms the joint significance of the ownership dummies, with a p-value of 0.002.

Turning next to the effect of industry sector, we see that the chi-square test confirms that the likelihood of TCO analysis varies across sectors (the test is significant at the 2 percent level). However, inspection of the individual coefficients shows that this result is driven by low-tech manufacturing. Firms in that sector are significantly less likely to do a TCO analysis (in part because users may be less sophisticated in terms of software), but there is no difference among the other three sectors.

Finally, we decisively reject the hypothesis that there are no country differences (the p-value is less than 0.001). Inspection of the individual coefficients on the country dummies (not shown) reveals that the countries with significantly lower use of TCO analysis (all less than Brazil, the reference country), listed in order from the lowest, are Kenya, Singapore, Russia, India, Thailand, Chile, Poland, South Africa, and France. There are two countries that stand out as using TCO substantially more than others, Turkey and Greece. It is clear from this ordering that the use of TCO is not related systematically to the country's level of economic development.

Appendix 5.3: Cost Structure of Open Source and Proprietary Software: Econometric Estimates

In this appendix we present econometric analysis of how user characteristics affect the cost structure of open source and proprietary software, as revealed by users' TCO assessments. To measure the cost structure, we use the cost share of each of the four cost components of TCO relative to the share for the initial cost of software—the cost components are switching costs, interoperability, support services and upgrades. The explanatory factors we use are dummy variables that capture the effects of different user sizes, ownership type, and sectors, as well as a set of dummy variables for different countries (Brazil is the reference country, so all country differences are measured relative to it). We conduct this analysis separately for each of the four cost components for open source and proprietary software. Table A.5.2 reports the estimated coefficients from ordinary least squares regressions.

We organize the results in terms of the different user characteristics. Turning first to the cross-country variation, the chi-square test statistic shows that there are significant differences across countries in the way users assess the cost trade-offs. For each of the four cost components, in both proprietary and open source software, we decisively reject the hypothesis that there are no country differences (the p-value is less than 0.001). From the individual coefficients on the country dummies (not shown), we can identify the top and bottom three countries in terms of the burden of each cost component (relative to the initial cost of software). These are given below:

Proprietary software:

Switching costs—Top: Brazil, South Africa, Turkey. Bottom: Poland, Greece, Thailand.

Interoperability—Top: Kenya, India, Turkey. Bottom: Poland, Thailand, Greece.

Support services—Top: Brazil, Thailand, Kenya. Bottom: Poland, Chile, Greece.

Upgrades—Top: Kenya, India, South Africa. Bottom: Poland, Brazil, Greece.

Open source software:

Switching costs—Top: Brazil, Kenya, Turkey. Bottom: Poland, Thailand, Chile.

Interoperability—Top: Brazil, Kenya, Turkey. Bottom: Poland, Thailand, Mexico.

Support services—Top: Brazil, France, Kenya. Bottom: Poland, Mexico, Chile.

Upgrades—Top: Brazil, France, Singapore. Bottom: Poland, Brazil, Greece.

Two conclusions emerge from this evidence. The first is that there is considerable consistency in the positioning of countries in terms of how they view the burden of different cost components, both for open source and proprietary software. At the end of this appendix we examine this feature in more detail. The second conclusion is that these

Table A.5.2
Determinants of cost structure for open source and proprietary software: Econometric estimates

| | Relative cost share of: | | | | | | | |
| | Proprietary software | | | | Open source software | | | |
Variable	Switch (1)	Interop (2)	Support (3)	Upgrade (4)	Switch (5)	Interop (6)	Support (7)	Upgrade (8)
Medium-sized firm[a]	2.39	3.50	3.65	1.91	12.41*	13.62*	14.22*	-3.22
	(2.47)	(2.54)	(2.53)	(2.51)	(4.20)	(4.73)	(4.56)	(3.82)
Large firm	3.21*	4.06*	5.07*	4.42*	8.93*	10.90*	11.26*	7.03*
	(1.94)	(2.00)	(1.99)	(1.98)	(3.62)	(4.08)	(3.92)	(3.52)
Foreign subsidiary[b]	-1.55	-2.43	-1.98	-2.65	-12.44*	-6.73	-17.48*	-12.91*
	(3.31)	(3.41)	(3.40)	(3.37)	(5.57)	(6.28)	(6.04)	(5.42)
Domestic firm	0.01	-0.73	-0.01	0.072	-4.24	1.69	-7.29*	-3.22
	(2.56)	(2.64)	(2.63)	(2.61)	(3.93)	(4.42)	(4.26)	(3.82)
Hi-tech manufacturing[c]	-0.57	1.33	0.076	1.25	-2.65	-6.19	0.41	0.23
	(2.38)	(2.45)	(2.44)	(2.43)	(3.70)	(4.17)	(4.01)	(3.61)
Low-tech manufacturing	-2.30	-0.62	-3.41	-3.01	1.33	-0.46	1.56	-0.77
	(2.48)	(2.55)	(2.54)	(2.52)	(4.55)	(5.13)	(4.94)	(4.43)
Wholesale/retail trade	-0.29	1.01	2.27	-1.02	4.98	-1.22	8.19*	4.10
	(2.39)	(2.46)	(2.46)	(2.43)	(4.29)	(4.84)	(4.65)	(4.18)
Test: firm size dummies (p-value)	0.25	0.12	0.040	0.096	0.009	0.008	0.004	0.096
Test: ownership dummies (p-value)	0.84	0.76	0.76	0.59	0.081	0.27	0.016	0.049
Test: industry dummies (p-value)	0.81	0.87	0.19	0.43	0.39	0.47	0.32	0.74
Test: country dummies (p-value)	<0.001	<0.001	<0.001	<0.001	<0.001	<0.001	<0.001	<0.001
Adjusted R^2	0.063	0.090	0.068	0.053	0.112	0.096	0.136	0.086
Number of observations	1,298	1,298	1,298	1,298	465	465	465	465

Notes: * denotes statistical significance at the 5 percent level. All estimated coefficients are from ordinary least squares regressions.
a. The reference size category is small firms. b. The reference ownership category is government agencies. c. The reference industry is services.

assessments are correlated, though imperfectly, with the level of economic development. The countries where the cost components (relative to the initial cost of software) are the most burdensome are typically among the less developed countries in our survey. Since we would also expect the initial cost of software to be more of a problem in those countries (unless pirated), this finding suggests that these other costs are genuinely more problematic in those countries. This may be due to their having less technical expertise to deal with the challenges of switching, interoperability, and support services.

The second main finding from the table is that the size of the user has a significant effect on the user's assessment of the importance of some components, particularly for open source. Size matters for support services both in proprietary and open source. In both cases, the estimated coefficients (rows 1 and 2) show that the cost of support services (*relative to the initial cost of software*) is less important for small users than for medium-sized and large users. This difference is even larger for open source than for proprietary software. We also see that switching costs are relatively less important for small users of open source software, as compared to medium-sized and large users. This does not apply, however, to proprietary software.

While size is important, the test statistics show that the ownership and industry of the user do not have a significant impact (jointly) on the burden of most cost components. The p-values of these tests are typically well above the conventional 5 percent level. The two exceptions are that ownership matters for support services and upgrades in open source software. The estimated coefficients in rows 3 and 4 show that both domestic and foreign firms view these (nonprice) components as less important than for government agencies (the reference group). Private firms may typically have more expertise in dealing with these costs of open source, and thus view them as less burdensome.

Finally, we use the estimated country fixed effects (coefficients on the country dummy variables) from the regressions above to examine whether countries that give more importance to one cost element also give more to another. That is, we want to analyze the correlations between the rankings a given country gives different cost elements. The correlation matrix of these estimated parameters is given in table A.5.3. Each correlation coefficient in this matrix summarizes the closeness of the relationship between the average country rankings of two cost components (net of the effects of size, ownership, and sector).

Table A.5.3
Cross-country correlations between the cost structures of open source and proprietary software

	Proprietary software				Open source software			
	Switching	Inter-operability	Support services	Upgrades	Switching	Inter-operability	Support services	Upgrades
PS switching costs	1.00							
PS interoperability	0.98	1.00						
PS support services	0.84	0.77	1.00					
PS upgrades	0.93	0.90	0.91	1.00				
OS switching costs	0.71	0.69	0.60	0.54	1.00			
OS interoperability	0.79	0.80	0.91	0.65	0.95	1.00		
OS support services	0.63	0.62	0.64	0.55	0.87	0.91	1.00	
OS upgrades	0.69	0.72	0.55	0.60	0.87	0.86	0.89	1.00

Recall that the importance of each cost component is measured by the proportion of TCO accounted for by that type of cost minus the proportion due to the initial cost of software. The main finding is that all of the correlation coefficients are positive and large, which indicates that countries that rank non-price components of TCO high tend to do so for all such components. It is noteworthy that this conclusion holds both for proprietary and open source software. For both types of software, the correlation is especially high between switching costs and interoperability.

6   Assessing Government Policies toward Software

Both in developed and developing countries there are vocal calls for public support for open source software. Many governments have adopted such initiatives. According to one tabulation, in 2008 there were 182 different initiatives in force worldwide, and many more proposed.[1] These take a wide variety of forms, including R&D support, subsidies, preferences in government procurement, and even outright mandates for public institutions to adopt open source. They span the globe: of the 182 initiatives adopted in 2008, 95 were in Europe, 47 in Asia, 20 in Latin America, but only 9 in North America.

We can illustrate this movement toward open source support with a few concrete examples. Under the Malaysian Public Sector Open Source Software Masterplan, as of 2004, all government procurement must show a strong preference for open source software.[2] In 2008, Argentina proposed a bill to make open source mandatory throughout all government institutions, as Brazil had done in 2005 (Kingston 2005; Marson 2005). Similar proposals have been made in a number of other countries. Since 2003, Singapore has offered tax breaks to companies using GNU/Linux operating systems rather than proprietary ones in order to encourage the development of the local software sector (UNCTAD 2003). The government of Thailand actively promotes the adoption of the Linux operating system in government agencies, schools, and universities through its Software Industry Promotion Agency, and Indonesia has a similar program to encourage the use of open source IGOS, which stands for "Indonesia, go open source!" (Marson 2005; CNET Asia 2006).

This chapter is co-authored with Jacques Crémer.
1. A good summary of policy initiatives in favor of open source software, both at the federal and lower levels of government worldwide, can be found in Lewis (2008).
2. http://opensource.mampu.gov.my/index.php (accessed September 8, 2009).

In 2004 a brochure published with the help of the United Nations Development Program stated, in a way that is representative of many claims in support of such initiatives:

> At the national level, FOSS (free and open source software) aids in the development of local capacity/industry, reduces imports, conserves foreign exchange, increases the security of the national ICT infrastructure (this is distinct from application level security), reduces copyright infringement and brings localized ICT tools to help develop local knowledge communities .... FOSS provides many socio-economic benefits. The most commonly cited are fostering the ICT industry through increased competition, lowering the ICT application cost and Total Cost of Ownership, increasing access to powerful yet localized ICT applications, increasing security of ICT applications and providing vendor independence .... Yet for all these clear benefits, many nations find that without a national FOSS policy, the uptake of FOSS in the country is far too slow for their needs. There are a number of reasons why FOSS requires policy intervention, including limited marketing of FOSS, lack of attention to its many non-commercial benefits and the need to overcome entrenched legacy systems. (Wong, 2004)

The American humorist, Will Rogers, once said, "It isn't what we don't know that gives us trouble, it's what we know that ain't so." As the previous two chapters should have made clear, many of the asserted facts used in the preceding quote to justify government support for open source software do not stand up to closer examination. For example, in chapter 5 we show that there is no evidence that open source software has a lower total cost of ownership. It has a different *cost structure* than proprietary software, which is attractive to some types of users but not to others. Indeed even the idea of there being a single TCO, one that is common across the population of heterogeneous users, does not stand up to scrutiny.

However, the fact that there are bad reasons for governments to give preferential treatment to open source software does not mean that there are no good reasons, grounded in "real" facts. What is important is to have a policy environment that promotes innovation and efficient use of software in general, and open source in particular. To accomplish this end, governments need to formulate public policies based on systematic evidence and solid economic reasoning. In this chapter we build on the empirical analysis of the software sector presented in earlier chapters to examine the extent to which government intervention is warranted on economic grounds, and to discuss the broad form of government policies that should be adopted with regard to the software sector.

Governments have two main channels through which they can influence the development and use of open source software: first, as large-scale buyers of software and, second, as regulators who set the rules of the competitive game between open source and proprietary software, including the provision of incentives and the policy toward standards that affect software compatibility. In this chapter we focus on two main questions:

• Should governments favor open source software in their procurement policies?
• Should they provide special incentives for firms who develop or use open source software?

In both their procurement and regulatory roles, we will come to the conclusion that government should adopt a neutral attitude that favors neither proprietary nor open source software. We argue that market failures are not large enough to suggest that either mode of software development is seriously disadvantaged by the normal play of competition. While the installed base of proprietary software is certainly larger, the analysis in chapters 4 and 5 shows that there is already extensive comingling of the two types of software both by users and software developer firms. This fact suggests that network effects do not pose a serious enough threat to effective competition that would justify government intervention, provided that an appropriate regulatory framework is in place. We argue that the primary focus of such regulation should be promoting "open standards" and a vigilant competition policy to prevent any abuse of network effects. These twin policy instruments will go a long way toward ensuring effective competition between, and comingling of, open source and proprietary software. Of course, just as parents should not treat their children identically, even if they do not favor one over the other, this does not imply that the treatment of the two categories of software should be absolutely identical. They have different characteristics, and we will explain how, and where, public policy can sensibly respond to these differences.

We begin our analysis by presenting new survey evidence on how developers and users view alternative regulatory regimes for software. The evidence shows a dominant preference among all categories of developers and users for a regime that allows them the freedom to choose, rather than one that restricts their choices to either open source or proprietary software. We then take up a series of arguments often made to justify proactive government support of open source, as reflected in the introduction to this chapter. We use economic analysis and empirical evidence to assess whether, and under what conditions, any of these arguments are valid. In this analysis we deal with possible imperfections both on the demand side of the market (e.g., users lacking information about open source) and the supply side (e.g., the argument that open source uses more local resources and less foreign exchange). We then turn to a discussion of the two key roles of government in shaping the software market: procurement and regulation of standards. Finally, we provide new survey information on the extent to which governments provide incentives of various forms for open source and proprietary software development, and discuss whether there is a good economic justification for them.

What Regulatory Regime Do Developers and Users Prefer?

Many observers who call for government intervention in the market for software do so because they believe that the market has coordinated on the "wrong" solution. The quotation from the United Nations in the introduction to this chapter suggests such "coordination failure" too, by asserting "the need to overcome entrenched legacy systems." As we discussed in chapter 3, the presence of network effects can create the possibility that users choose to buy a particular type of software because others do, or have done so in the past. Because the installed base can strongly affect the trajectory of purchases in the future, it is possible, at least in theory, that all users (and software developers) might be better off if they switched *en masse* to another solution. But if this were the case, we should expect users and developers to be aware of this fact and, if asked, to register regret at having to purchase an inferior good in order to flow with the crowd.

Our survey provides us with the first available data on the regulatory framework that software developers and users in different countries prefer. We asked software developers and users to rank five alternative regimes: only open source allowed, open source when available, only proprietary allowed, proprietary when available and complete freedom to choose. For simplicity, we aggregate these into three categories: open source, proprietary, complete freedom to choose (the conclusions are similar if we use the full breakdown). As table 6.1 shows, both users and developers overwhelmingly favor the unrestricted (freedom to choose) regulatory regime. Turning first to panel

Table 6.1
Regulatory regime preferred by software developers and users (percentage of firms giving top rank)

	Open source	Proprietary	Complete freedom to choose
Panel A: software developers			
Aggregate	15.8	31.6	52.6
	(0.8)	(1.1)	(1.1)
Developers of only proprietary	12.1	36.3	51.6
	(0.9)	(1.3)	(1.3)
Developers of only open source	25.6	24.0	50.4
	(1.8)	(1.7)	(2.0)
Developers of both	18.8	25.0	56.2
	(1.4)	(1.5)	(1.7)
Panel B: software users			
Aggregate	18.0	30.9	51.1
	(0.8)	(1.0)	(1.0)
Users of only proprietary	13.8	36.7	49.5
	(0.9)	(1.2)	(1.3)
Users of only open source	38.1	15.8	46.1
	(4.1)	(3.1)	(4.2)
Users of both	23.9	19.8	56.3
	(1.7)	(1.6)	(2.0)

Note: Multinomial standard errors are in parentheses. These are computed as $\sqrt{p(1-p)/n}$, where p is the reported proportion and n is the sample size.

A in the table, we see that 53 percent of software developers prefer a regime which leaves complete freedom to choose between proprietary and open source software. Of those who prefer some kind of targeted regime, two thirds of them (32 percent of all respondents) prefer a regime which favors proprietary software and one third (16 percent of all respondents) prefer a regime that favors open source. This majority preference for "freedom to choose" holds not only for firms that currently develop both proprietary and open source software but also for firms that currently develop only one type of software.

Panel B in the table confirms that the picture is very similar for software users, where 51.1 percent prefer the complete freedom to choose over any kind of restricted regime. As with developers, the dominant preference is for a neutral regime for all three types of users—those who currently use only open source (this only constitutes 5.9 percent of users), only proprietary, and both types of software.

Of course, the regulatory regime that developers and users prefer might be expected to depend on their characteristics. For example, large software development firms and users, who are more likely to find diversification an attractive strategy, might have stronger preferences for regimes that ensure freedom to choose. In fact the reported preferences are remarkably similar across the spectrum of software firms and users, though there are a few interesting exceptions, as we summarize here. The most important conclusion from these tables is that *all categories of developers and users* register a dominant (plurality) preference for "complete freedom to choose." This is true for developers in each size, ownership and business model group. While there is some variation in the strength of preferences across these groups, econometric analysis shows that these variations are not statistically significant. The only factor that has a statistically significant effect on their preferences is the firm's current development focus. Unsurprisingly, software firms that develop both open source and proprietary software (as opposed to only one of them) are especially likely to prefer "complete freedom to choose."

For users, two additional noteworthy conclusions emerge. The first conclusion we want to highlight is that smaller firms are *more* attracted to a regime of "complete freedom to choose" than large firms. This finding might seem initially surprising, since small firms are less likely to diversify and thus one might have expected them to benefit less from such freedom. But the evidence shows that this is not the case.[3] Moreover the finding has an important policy implication for governments that are interested in promoting a supportive environment for entrepreneurship and small firms. The second noteworthy finding is that the majority preference for "complete freedom to choose" is registered not only by domestic firms, but even by government agencies (51.6 and 52.0 percent, respectively). Later in this chapter we will return to the issue of government regulation of software use by its own agencies.

While all categories of developers and users tend to prefer a regime that allows them complete freedom to choose the software most appropriate to their needs—and to comingle them, as we have seen—there

---

3. If we restrict our attention to firms that are not in favor of freedom to choose, they are more likely than large firms to prefer a regulatory regime that favors open source software. Among firms that do not prefer complete freedom to choose, 67 percent of small firms and 61 percent of large firms prefer a regulatory regime that favors open source. But, as in table 6.2, there is variation in this regard across countries.

Table 6.2
Preferred regulatory regime (users), by country (percentage of firms giving top rank)

	Open source	Proprietary	Complete freedom to choose
Brazil	24	15	61
Chile	4	24	72
China	21	26	53
France	16	14	69
Greece	4	27	69
India	19	51	30
Israel	23	31	46
Kenya	41	15	43
Mexico	19	32	49
Poland	12	38	50
Russia	13	16	71
South Africa	13	35	52
Singapore	13	39	48
Thailand	24	64	13
Turkey	22	38	39

is considerable variation across countries. Table 6.2 summarizes user preferences in the survey countries (the conclusions are similar for developers, but the table is omitted for brevity). In eight of the fifteen survey countries, there is a strict majority preference for freedom to choose, and it is the dominant preference (a plurality of users register it) in all but two countries, India and Thailand, which prefer a proprietary software regime (a policy that restricts use to only proprietary or proprietary when available). The proportion of users who prefer an open source regime (a policy that restricts use to only open source or open source when available) varies from a low of only 4 percent in Chile and Greece to a high of 41 percent in Kenya. It is clear from table 6.2 that there is no relationship between the level of economic development and the preference for particular regulatory regimes.

Of course, we fully recognize that the extensive survey evidence presented in this section is not by itself sufficient to make the case for a neutral government policy that gives developers and users complete freedom to choose. There is the risk of "coordination failure" among these responses. The fact that the majority of respondents *individually* prefer a particular regime does not ensure that such a regime would be efficient. Nonetheless, the pervasive preference by developers and users for an unrestricted regulatory regime certainly provides, at a minimum, a prima facie basis for thinking that government policy should be neutral between open source and proprietary software. In the remainder of this chapter we explain why we feel they are right on this account. Given these preferences, any argument that governments should favor one or the other type of software would have to explain why users and developers have the "wrong" preferences. We turn next to an economic evaluation of the various arguments that are often made in favor of nonneutral policies.

Should Governments Support Open Source Software?

Economists generally agree that in market economies, governments should intervene not only to provide for public goods (e.g., national defense or education), and perhaps to redistribute income, but also in order to correct market imperfections. For instance, the market does not attach a price to the environmental cost of polluting activities. As a consequence firms and consumers facing this distorted market would pollute more than is socially optimal, and governments intervene through regulations and taxes to correct this "market failure."

As we discussed in chapter 2, the software market has a number of potential market imperfections, suggesting that there may be scope for government remedies. However, we are well advised to keep in mind that government intervention is far from perfect in practice: like everyone else, public officials make mistakes and are subject to political and lobbying pressures that can lead to policy choices motivated more by personal than public interest. Thus, in any specific situation, policy analysis must weigh the costs of "market imperfections" against the costs of "government imperfection." Disagreement about the advisability of policy interventions is often due to differing assessments of these costs, but it is important that any such assessments be grounded in evidence, not wishful thinking.

We now turn to a review the types of public policies that can be implemented to correct market imperfections in the software market, and more specifically, those affecting the choice between open source and proprietary software. We do this in two steps. First, we review the policies that can be used to correct "demand side" imperfections—namely reasons why the choice by users between open source and proprietary software might be distorted, as compared to what would be socially optimal. In the second step, we discuss "supply side" imperfections that affect the provision of new software. This analysis will provide us with the background that we need for analyzing some specific policies.

Correcting Demand Side Imperfections in the Software Market

We begin with a discussion of the demand side because it is the only one for which formal policy analysis has been conducted in the economic literature.[4] We first present a simplified and nontechnical version of the model developed by Schmidt and Schnitzer (2003) that has become the canonical model to study the consequences of government support for the use of open source software (for the interested reader, appendix 6.1 provides a more technical description of the model). After the analytical framework is described, we show how it has been used to address some policy issues.

To give the underlying intuition behind the argument that we will develop, we start with a simple observation. As explained in chapter 2, providing one more customer with a copy of a program is very inexpensive; in many cases it is only the cost of uploading the additional copy. However, when the program is sold by a profit-maximizing firm, its price will be substantially above this marginal cost because firms need to recoup the large fixed cost they have had to incur to develop the software. This creates an economic inefficiency, as some users who would have been willing to compensate the producer of the software for the extra cost of providing them with a copy will choose not to acquire it. For example, if distributing an extra unit of the program cost $2 and it is sold at a price of $200 by the producer who needs to recoup the fixed cost of production, there could be many consumers willing to pay, let us say, $100 who will not buy it. From a social welfare point of view, the inefficiency stems from the fact that a potential increase in welfare of $98 (= $100 − $2) is not realized. This inefficiency is a manifestation of the basic trade-off in the economics of innovation between static and dynamic efficiency, which we discussed in chapter 2. To provide incentives for innovation, the firm needs to cover the associated fixed costs by marking up price above marginal cost, but to promote efficient use of an existing innovation, price should be set equal to marginal cost.

---

4. There is an analytical literature exploring the supply of open source software, including the reasons for and consequences of voluntary contributions of code and the implications for economic growth. Leading examples include Lerner and Tirole (2003), von Hippel and von Krough (2003), Belenzon and Schankerman (2008), and Saint-Paul (2001). But, for the most part, these papers do not do normative (welfare) policy analysis.

This applies to proprietary software, but what about open source? It is true that the production of open source is not free from a social perspective, even if it done by "volunteers." Not only are private firms active in developing and/or funding open source software, but the time and other costs incurred by individuals who contribute to open source projects also constitute real social resources that need to be somehow compensated. However, as we have seen in the previous paragraph, economic theory tells us that in an ideal world these "fixed costs," which are independent of the utilization of the software, should not be reflected in the price. Therefore open source software, which is priced at (or near) zero, is appropriately priced from a social perspective when we restrict our attention to the efficient *distribution* of the software (as opposed to ensuring incentives for *development* of the software). As a consequence consumers are choosing between open source, which is "well priced," and proprietary software, which is "over priced." This distortion in pricing creates a distortion in the choices made by users. The formal model developed below examines how this works, and what policy conclusion emerges from it.

Consider a market in which both an open source and a proprietary program are offered. To make things simple, we assume that both programs are produced at a marginal cost of zero and that the open source program is sold at a price of zero.[5] (Of course, as we discussed in chapter 5, in reality open source users incur other forms of costs; these could easily be included in the analysis without changing the main insights). The programs are of the same quality, but different consumers have different taste for one or the other. Each consumer is characterized by a "taste" parameter, which we denote by t, that takes values between 0 and 1. The benefit the user attaches to one program or the other depends on her taste parameter t: the smaller is t, the more she likes the open source program; the larger is t, the more she likes the proprietary program. A natural way to interpret this taste parameter, here is as a summary index of the various costs the user incurs in adopting that type of program, apart from the initial cost of obtaining the software (e.g., the costs of switching, interoperability, support services, or upgrades).

We represent this situation in the left panel of figure 6.1, which depicts the value the user attaches to the open source program. When

---

5. As we discussed in chapter 4, many open source programs are sponsored by firms who generate income by selling complementary programs or services. For a model that studies the consequences of this fact, see Lambardi (2009).

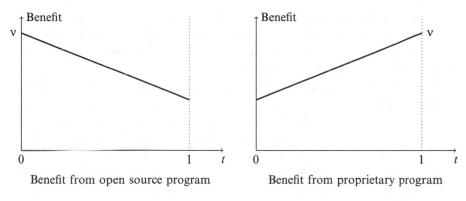

Figure 6.1
User benefits from open source and proprietary software

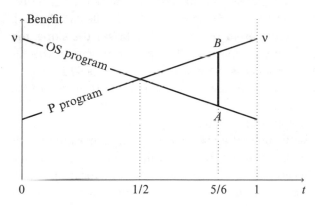

Figure 6.2
Comparing benefits from open source and proprietary software

her type t is equal to 0, she values it at v; the larger her t, the less she values the open source software, so users with a taste parameter equal to 1 value it the least. Assume for a moment that the proprietary program is given away for free. Then the value it has for the different users, which is represented in the right panel of figure 6.1, is the mirror image of the value that they attach to the open source program. For the hypothetical user, this value is v and this value decreases as t declines.

In figure 6.2 we combine the two previous graphs to enable us to compare the values derived from the two programs by the different users. The users whose taste parameter t is less than $\frac{1}{2}$ attach a higher value to the open source program than to the proprietary program; given the choice between the two (at the same price), they would choose the former. The preferences are reversed when t is greater than $\frac{1}{2}$. These assumptions of very strong symmetry between both programs are made in order to help focus the analysis on the main difference between them: the mode of distribution.

The distance between the two lines in figure 6.2 represent how much more the users are willing to pay to have access to their favorite programs. For instance, the length of the segment $\overline{AB}$ represents how much more the consumer whose taste parameter is 5/6 would be willing to pay for the proprietary program than for the open source program. If the price difference between these two programs were equal to this difference, the consumer would be indifferent between acquiring one or the other.

Depending on the applications, users can be more or less attached to their favorite program: an increase in the slope of the two lines represent how much more a change in the taste parameter affects the value that users attaches to the different programs. The larger the slope, the larger is the difference between the value that a user attaches to his favorite program and the smaller is the value that he attaches to his least favorite program: as the slope increases, the length of $\overline{AB}$ in figure 6.2 increases.

Of course, the developer of a proprietary program does not give away its program. The value that a user derives from using the proprietary program will be equal to its intrinsic value *minus* the price she pays to acquire it. This adjustment simply shifts the line for proprietary software in figure 6.2 down by the amount p. No adjustment is needed for open source software, on the assumption that it is available to the user for free.

We put these elements together in figure 6.3, where we analyze the choice users make between the two programs when the developer of the proprietary software charges a price equal to p. For all taste parameters smaller than $\bar{t}$, the straight line that plots the benefits to the users for the open source program is above the line that plots the benefits for the proprietary program: thus, users with $t < \bar{t}$ will choose the open source program. On the other hand, users with taste parameters $t > \bar{t}$ will choose the proprietary program. The allocation of the users between the two programs is represented by the arrows below the horizontal axis.

If the price of the proprietary software were zero, the figure would be symmetrical and $\bar{t}$ would be equal to $\frac{1}{2}$: the users would split themselves half and half between the two programs. On the other hand,

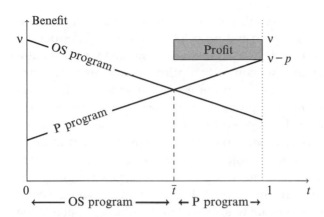

Figure 6.3
Choosing between open source and proprietary software

when the price p is positive, the "P program" line shifts downward and $\bar{t}$ increases: fewer users purchase the proprietary program and more purchase the open source program. Therefore the developer of the proprietary software faces a trade-off between increasing his profit per unit sold, which is equal to the price, and increasing the number of these units. This is represented graphically on the figure by the gray rectangle: the profit is proportional to the price, which is equal to the distance between v and $v - p$, multiplied by the proportion of users who choose this program, which is equal to the distance between $\bar{t}$ and 1 on the horizontal axis.[6]

In appendix 6.1 we show that this leads the developer to choose a price that is proportional to the slope of the benefit lines: the more the users are attached to their preferred program, the higher the price the developer can charge without losing too many clients. This increase in price decreases the number of buyers. In the special case we consider, where the allocation of taste parameters is uniform, these two effects cancel each other out and the proprietary software firm sets the optimal price $\bar{t}$ at $\frac{3}{4}$. At this price 25 percent of consumers buy the proprietary program and the other 75 buy open source. However, recall that the socially efficient allocation would have the market split equally between open source and proprietary software. Thus the market generates *overuse* of open source software.

---

6. We are assuming that the taste parameter is uniformly distributed between zero and one. This means that tastes are not bunched at any particular point. This assumption is not needed for the model to generate the main policy conclusion we focus on here.

Schmidt and Schnitzer use this model to highlight this inefficiency in the relative use of open source and proprietary software. Consider the user with taste parameter $t = 2/3$. If the two programs were sold at a price equal to marginal cost, namely at a price equal to zero, this consumer would choose to buy the proprietary software. However, because he must pay for the proprietary software, he chooses open source software and ends up using the program he likes less, despite the fact that the costs of production are the same. To put it in other terms, because the proprietary software developer is extracting profits by charging a higher price than the open source community, its product is not utilized enough. This implies that policies that would extend the use of open source software will, at least in the simple version of the model, *decrease* social welfare.[7]

To summarize the essential elements: in this model, each consumer buys either an open source or proprietary program. Consumers have different tastes for the two types of programs, which can be interpreted as the switching and other costs associated with using that software (other than the initial purchase price). The consumers for whom these other costs are relatively low (a "taste for open source") adopt open source, which is available at a price of zero, while users for whom these other costs are high prefer to pay the price for proprietary software. The division of consumers depends on the price set by the producer of proprietary software. If the price of both proprietary and open source software were equal to the marginal cost of production (here assumed to be zero), the model generates an equal division of the market. This is the socially efficient allocation of consumers in this framework. But because proprietary software is priced above marginal

---

7. This conclusion will be familiar to economists (and probably counterintuitive to non-economists). A standard argument in economics is that to correct the underproduction by a firm with market power using the price system requires a subsidy, rather than a tax, which would only exacerbate the problem. The benchmark used in this analysis is how prices should be set to ensure socially efficient use of software: prices set at marginal costs. This is what economists call the "first-best" solution, as it maximizes welfare. However, this is only so if it is assumed that the fixed costs of developing software (both proprietary and open source) are compensated by government transfers to the firms or other agents who incur them. In practice, this is unrealistic, and in such cases socially efficient pricing that ensures development of software would require prices above the marginal costs (economists refer to this as the "second-best" solution). A full analysis of optimal pricing is beyond the scope of this discussion. The key point we want to emphasize is that the often-heard argument that there is underuse of open source that justifies a subsidy is not supported by economic principles (an exception might arise because of informational imperfections, which we discuss later).

cost, the equilibrium involves greater use of open source than this efficient outcome would dictate.

The conclusion that governments should try to extend the use of proprietary software might seem paradoxical, perhaps even unwarranted and unfair. After all, in the model it is proprietary software that is, from a social welfare point of view, mispriced, with a price above the marginal cost of production. Yet we are drawing the policy conclusion that government should, in some sense, reward it for this mispricing by facilitating its use: for example, it may be that government policy should encourage the use of Microsoft Office because it is sold at a positive price, whereas Open Office is distributed at no cost. As we have already mentioned, and will discuss in more detail below, part of the unease stems from the fact that the model does not include important aspects of reality arising from the supply side that might counterbalance these effects.

Supply Side Arguments

While most of the formal economic literature focuses on the demand side of the market, many of the arguments put forth by proponents of government intervention in favor of open source software rely on supply side arguments. It is often claimed that the development process for open source software is more efficient, and that some form of market imperfection hinders its development. It is these arguments that we will review now. We pay special attention to developing countries, since many authors have argued that open source software is especially well adapted to these countries. In this section, we review the reasoning behind the advocacy of proactive governments in favor of open source software. In later sections, we will discuss specific ways in which governments can intervene and the advisability of such policies.

Local Content Argument   One of the main supply side arguments used by advocates of government support for open source is that it is stimulates greater use of local resources than proprietary software. The argument runs as follows: even if the total cost of ownership of open source and proprietary software were similar, open source software requires more complementary support services (in fact, there is only weak evidence for this fact in our data on the cost components of TCO analysis; see table 5.3 in chapter 5). The use of labor for support services contributes to local employment and skill acquisition in the software sector. On this account, proponents argue, open source development should be promoted. In addition proprietary software is typically imported, and it is better to generate local information technology employment rather than draw on foreign firms. It is also argued that such additional skilled programmers make a net contribution to future economic growth.

This type of reasoning is well illustrated by the following statement of the Chief Information Officer of South Africa's State Information and Technology Agency:

Adopting open source software would boost the local software industry.... Most companies that supply open source software applications are local companies. Money spent on open source software would most likely be kept within the South African economy, as opposed to money spent on proprietary software that goes to foreign companies.[8]

Similar sentiments are found in pronouncements by the Malaysian Minister of Energy, Communications and Multimedia, who stated at the 2003 World Summit of the Information Society:

As an option to reduce dependency, the idea of using open source software needs to be explored and evaluated. Besides cost competitiveness, the use of open source software can also complement efforts in capacity building and development of local content in line with our commitment to cultural diversity.[9]

These views are not limited to policy makers in developing countries. Similar arguments have been expressed by the United Nations, the German Foreign Minister, and representatives of other industrialized countries.[10]

These arguments rely on the assumption that the prices for labor and foreign exchange are not set properly. When prices of these inputs are market based, they adjust so as to reflect the social cost of the resources in the absence of serious externalities. Given two goods of equal qual-

---

8. See Yarney (2003). This quotation is drawn from Lerner and Herman (2005). At the same time (and perhaps as a consequence of such statements) the South African government accepted a donation of Microsoft in February 2009 that will provide free proprietary software for all of South Africa's 32,000 government schools (http://www.bridges .org/commentaries/115 (accessed July 28, 2009).

9. http://www.itu.int/wsis/geneva/coverage/statements/malaysia/my.html (accessed July 28, 2009).

10. In 2003 the United Nations Conference on Trade and Development (UNCTAD) called on poor countries to adopt open source software. See UNCTAD (2003). The statement of the German Foreign Minister is available at Steinmeier (2009).

ity, it is not only privately but also socially advantageous to choose the cheapest. For our purposes this implies that there is no justification for preferring one type of software over another on the basis of the amount or mix of inputs that go into producing them, including the extent of "local content." This applies to labor and foreign exchange, as to other inputs, and it applies both to decisions by private firms and governments.

A simple example may help illustrate this important, but often neglected, point. Consider two alternative software projects of equal quality. The proprietary project has a total cost of $500,000. The open source project costs $480,000 up front but uses four more developers than the proprietary project. If the market wage of a developer is $15K, then the total cost of the open source project is $540,000. If the government ignores the $60,000 required to pay the four extra developers—on the basis of the argument that these funds support local employment—the open source project looks like the cheaper option. That line of reasoning, however, ignores the value of the production of the four developers in the next-best alternative employment. If labor markets are working properly, this "opportunity cost" is given by their wages of $60,000. Properly accounting for the value of the extra human capital used in the open source project makes it more, not less, expensive than proprietary software, by $40,000. Choosing the open source project would be justified only if its up-front cost was less than $440,000. If quality is the same, not only profit-maximizing firms but also governments should choose the least expensive project after taking account of the opportunity cost of any additional developer time.

In reality, of course, there are imperfections in labor markets, persistent unemployment being their clearest manifestation. In the example above, if the four extra developers needed for the open source project were otherwise going to be unemployed for a year, then choosing the open source project might make sense. However, unemployment among skilled workers indicates problems with matching the right person with the right job, the volatile nature of demand for information technology and other labor market distortions. A policy preference for more labor-intensive software is a blunt and indirect instrument for addressing these problems. It is hard to imagine that additional demand for developers stemming from government software purchases will somehow overcome these labor market imperfections. Indeed experience has shown that distortions in the economy should be corrected as directly as possible rather than through indirect means whose side effects are extremely difficult to predict.

Furthermore a strong case can be made that developers' skills are a relatively scarce resource both in emerging and developed economies. There is clear evidence of the high demand for these skills, as registered in the relative wages we observe. In a sample of nine countries for which we have information, the average ratio of the salary of a "software engineer/developer/programmer" to the average wage in the country is 5.85, with a low of 1.20 in Singapore and a high of 16.91 in Thailand.[11] The wages of developers in these economies has been bid up because their services are in high demand, not because they are sitting around waiting for something to do. Their talents should be directed to high-value endeavors, not to make-work projects.

The argument in favor of open source software, based on the fact that much proprietary software is imported, relies on similar reasoning. If the exchange rate is set correctly, it represents the relative value of domestic and foreign goods. Returning to our example above, suppose that the proprietary software is imported at a cost of $500,000. The open source software requires imports of goods and services valued at $480,000 and four local developers. Thus the open source project requires $20,000 less in imports. But, if the local annual wage is 30,000 pesos and the exchange rate is two pesos per dollar, then the time of the four developers for a year is valued at $60,000 at the current exchange rate. It is socially inefficient to use $60,000 of developer time in order to save $20,000 in imported inputs. Favoring local production distorts the markets in an inefficient fashion in the same way as an import tariff.

Common Input (Platform) Argument   For a long time governments have subsidized the development of software tools that they felt would not be commercially viable but would be useful to a large community. For instance, the development in the early 1980s of the widely used scientific typesetting software TeX, by Donald Knuth was supported by both the National Science Foundation and the Office of Naval Research (see Knuth 1984). Of course, such software is a public good, akin to a scientific discovery, and traditional economic theory tells us that it

---

11. The countries covered are Brazil, Greece, India, Israel, Mexico, Poland, Russia, Singapore, and Thailand. The data come from the Economist Intelligence Unit and http://www.payscale.com/salary-survey (accessed June 1, 2006).

should be supported with public funds. However, the implementation of such support is complex and risky, and the aim of this section is to examine how government can organize it.

To do this, we build on the analysis of Camara and Fonseca (2007) and Camara et al. (2008), who examine the development of open source projects in developing countries. They argue that there is room for targeted government subsidies towards "low-shared conceptualization, high-modularity" open source projects. This term refers to projects with a high degree of innovation, usually with no proprietary counterpart, a relatively simple software kernel, and a high degree of innovation at the periphery. In simple economic parlance, these are programs that generate strong externalities. Camara and Fonseca illustrate their more general analysis with a case study from Brazil. Since 2000 the Brazilian government has been funding a large-scale open source geographical information system (GIS) project, TerraLib, which is an open source library for GIS and associated applications. The project was developed by two research groups, at the cost of more than 50 person-years of training, and "aims to offer functionalities for spatio-temporal data handling that are not available in any commercial or open source GIS software." Eventually the program was put into a format so that it could be used by other parties. The Brazilian government has guaranteed its long-term support, and INPE, the Brazilian National Institute for Space Research, "provides capacity building for developers, and supports service companies that use the software." By mid-2007 approximately ten service providers used TerraLib in commercial applications, constituting 10 percent of the Brazilian market.

There are strong theoretical arguments for such a policy: there are clear economies of scale in having the basic software developed only once, and distributing such a program at marginal cost (which is close to zero) is what classical economic theory would recommend. However, the practical implementation of such policies is much more difficult. In the absence of price signals, it is difficult for governments to do the appropriate cost–benefit analysis before subsidizing such projects, and the risk of undue political influence is large. In the best case, some firms might want the government to subsidize their products, even when the cost to society is higher than the benefits. In the worst case, firms lobby so that they are put in charge of developing a product that has very little use to anyone.

In any case, such a policy is not necessarily a subsidy in favor of open source software if the infrastructure is not restricted in its subsequent use. As in the Brazilian case the "periphery" can be composed of proprietary as well as open source programs, and it is the sponsors of these peripheral programs who are the ultimate beneficiaries of the subsidies.[12] To ensure that the firms in the periphery could indeed use the program, TerraLib has been released under the LPGL license, which allows the creation of proprietary applications.

A similar argument arises with respect to the appropriate software license for such "common inputs (platforms)." There are many possible alternative licenses that could be used, both proprietary and open source. However, open source licenses may have the benefit of familiarity for users and lower transaction costs. This line of argument has been made for the use of open source licenses for software developed with the collaborative support of several governments. For instance, Steven Chu, the US Energy Secretary, has argued that cooperation between developed and industrializing countries is indispensable for improving the technology to design more energy-efficient buildings. He advocated that this be done through open source software so that the "intellectual property is co-owned, co-developed, free to be used by each country" (see Mackenzie 2009).

While it may seem natural that these "common inputs" software should be distributed under an open source license, proprietary licenses could also be adopted. Governments could own the copyright (or patent), and license the program under commercial terms with special dispensation given to users whom it deems worthwhile—in particular, national users. However, if the costs of implementing such a licensing policy are high enough, it may make sense to use an open source license. Even in this case there is a legitimate debate on which type of open source license should be used. TerraLib is distributed under the LPGL license: as a consequence it can be used in conjunction with proprietary programs, but any change to the program itself falls in the public domain. One can imagine that a BSD-type license would be more suitable for some programs, especially when substantial private incentives for development are needed and when the dangers of "forking" are limited.[13]

---

12. The issues here are similar to those that arise in discussions of government support to R&D and of the terms under which it should be licensed to private firms. There is a large economic literature on the topic. For a good example, see Jaffe and Lerner (2001).

13. The TeX code was simply put in the public domain so that anyone can use the code as she sees fit. However, the name TeX cannot be used for a modified version of the program.

Twin Roles of Government: Procurement and Standards

In the last section we reviewed some of the arguments put forward in favor of government support for open source software. In this section and the next, we review some of the policies through which governments can implement this support and, more generally, influence the software industry. We will find it convenient to group these policies in two categories: procurement and regulation. First, governments are very large purchasers of software, when we aggregate the purchases of all its departments and its agencies, so their procurement rules can have industry-wide implications. We study these rules in the next section. In addition to their procurement role, however, governments can powerfully influence the development trajectory and use of software through the laws and regulations they adopt. We study this important aspect of policy in a subsequent section. In both cases we focus primarily on aspects that influence the balance between open source and proprietary software, rather than arguments for general support to information technology. Before doing so, in this section we present survey evidence on the importance of the government as a purchaser of software, and then discuss two different strategies government can adopt in its procurement role.

Government as Purchaser of Software

Most observers would agree that the government sector is an important purchaser of software. Our survey of software developers allows us to examine this supposition with hard evidence, and to establish whether the importance of government software procurement is similar for open source and proprietary, and between firms of different types. Table 6.3 summarizes the survey data on the percentage of revenues for software firms (combining open source and proprietary software) that originate from different types of consumer accounts.

While corporate sales are the dominant source of revenue—accounting for 60 percent in the overall sample—governments account for 21 percent, about equally divided among the federal, local, and municipal governments. Government purchases are a less important source of revenue for small companies, but for all three size categories, government is a significant client. The separate revenue breakdowns for open source and proprietary software are very similar to each other (not shown, for brevity). One noteworthy point is that the client mix is not significantly different for domestic firms and foreign subsidiaries,

Table 6.3
Sources of revenue for software firms (percentage of total revenues)

| | Corporate | Government | | | | Individuals |
		Subtotal	Federal	State	Municipal	
Aggregate	61.3	20.8	6.2	7.0	7.6	17.9
	(1.1)		(0.6)	(0.6)	(0.6)	(0.9)
Size						
Small	63.4	18.2	5.2	5.9	7.1	18.4
	(1.4)		(0.6)	(0.7)	(0.7)	(1.1)
Medium	57.8	24.9	7.9	8.7	8.3	17.3
	(2.0)		(1.1)	(1.1)	(1.1)	(1.5)
Large	58.3	26.8	8.0	10.1	8.7	14.9
	(5.3)		(2.9)	(3.2)	(2.7)	(3.8)
Ownership						
Domestic	60.9	20.7	6.3	6.7	7.7	18.4
	(1.2)		(0.6)	(0.6)	(0.6)	(0.9)
Foreign	64.4	22.1	5.6	9.5	7.0	13.5
Subsidiary	(3.3)		(1.6)	(2.0)	(1.8)	(2.4)

Note: Multinomial standard errors are in parentheses. These are computed as $\sqrt{p(1-p)/n}$, where p is the reported proportion and n is the sample size.

and this holds both for open source and proprietary software. There seems to be no national bias as far as government software purchases are concerned, at least when we average across the countries in our survey.

Finally, inspection of the individual country results (not reported, for brevity) confirms that the public sector is an important software client in almost all of the countries in our survey, but its role varies considerably. The three countries where the government accounts for least are (in percent) Turkey (5.7), India (8.1), and Singapore (9.5); the top countries are Thailand (39.3), Israel (37.2), and Kenya (35.2). Clearly, the government's software procurement impact is not related in any simple way to the level of economic development.

Because governments are large consumers of software, whether or not they intend to do so, their procurement policies materially influence the sector. In the next sections we identify the issues at stake and analyze how economics can help shape appropriate policies.

Two Procurement Strategies for Government
Government is the largest single buyer, but there are also many smaller corporate and individual consumers in the software market. As a start-

Table 6.4
Adaptive play

	Others	
Big player	A	B
A	**(9, 8)**	(11, 5)
B	(8, 4)	(10, 6)

ing point, we need to review how "big players" like the government can use their power. To do this, we follow the game theory literature in distinguishing between two basic types of strategies big players can adopt: *adaptation* and *leadership strategies*.

When a big player uses an adaptation strategy, it makes its decisions so as to maximize its own payoff (whatever form that takes), assuming that its decision will not affect those of the other smaller players. Of course, its choices affect the other players, but the big player does not take this into account when designing its own strategy—it simply adapts to the environment; the other players do the same thing. An example of an adaptive strategy is when the government makes its procurement decisions strictly on the basis of a TCO analysis, without consideration for how that decision might shape the decisions of smaller consumers. In game theory adaptation strategies are referred to as "Nash strategies," and we will do so here.

We can illustrate this mutual dependence with a simple software example with two players, one "big" and the other not. Each must choose between two programs, A and B. The game is represented in table 6.4.

In each cell of the table, the first number represents the benefit of the "big player" and the second the benefit of the other players. For instance, if the big player chooses program A, while the others choose program B, the benefit of the big player is 11 and the benefit of the others is 5. Given the (admittedly arbitrary) numbers that we have chosen for our example, the outcome ("Nash equilibrium") when the big player adapts to the behavior of the others is (A, A). If the big player deviated by choosing program B, its benefit would decrease from 9 to 8, while if the others deviated from A to B, their benefit would decrease from 8 to 5. It is easy to see that no other cell has the same property.

We next describe the leadership strategy. In this case the big player takes into account its influence on the other players. When the big

Table 6.5
Leadership play

	Others	
Big player	A	B
A	(9, 8)	(11, 5)
B	(8, 4)	**(10, 6)**

player acts in this way, it computes the way its behavior will affect the strategy of the others in making its own decision. This is referred to as a "Stackelberg strategy." In the numerical example given above, this kind of behavior yields an outcome where all the players choose software B as in table 6.5.

Given that the big player has committed itself to software B, the others are better off also choosing B (they take the big player's strategy as given). This yields a benefit of 10 for the big player. If it had committed itself to choosing A, the others would also have chosen software A, and its benefit would have been only 9.

Economists often interpret the difference between these two types of strategies as a matter of which player "moves first." In the case of adaptation strategies, we say that the players choose their strategies simultaneously, while in the case of leadership strategies the "big player" is the one who plays first. Note that this is largely metaphorical—governments and other users typically buy software at the same time. The real distinction here is that the leadership strategy occurs when one of the players can pre-commit to a particular behavior, which we normally associate with a big player.

Of course, "the" government does not typically make purchases—procurement is done through its agencies. But the government is a leader with respect to its agencies: it sets the rules that govern their procurement (objectives and trade-offs between cost, quality, security, etc.), and in this capacity it can instruct them to use either an adaptation or a leadership strategy.

If the agency has the same preferences and capacities as the central government, the fact that the policy implementation is delegated to the agency creates no difficulty. However, in general, preferences and capacities are not the same, and this can change the preferred strategy. To illustrate this, let us modify the numerical example above by assuming that the "big player" is the agency. Suppose that the government is what economists call "benevolent," in that its objective is to

Table 6.6
Is leadership a desirable policy?

	Other players	
Agency	A	B
A	**(9, 8, 17)**	(11, 5, 16)
B	(8, 4, 12)	(10, 6, 16)

maximize the benefits of society, given here by the sum of the benefits of the government agency and other consumers.

Table 6.6 represents the game. The benefit of the government is represented by a third number (underlined) in each cell. If the government instructs the agency to use an adaptation strategy, it will do so taking into account only its own payoff. Following our earlier analysis, this leads to the (A, A) outcome. By contrast, if the government instructs the agency to use a leadership strategy, the (B, B) outcome will occur. In this example, the government is better off instructing its agencies *not* to use their potential power to commit.

In reality the situation is much more complicated, but it is generally true that the government sets the long-term objectives that are embedded in formal policy statements. As a first (and sometimes loose) approximation, we can think that these policies are chosen in a more or less open way, after public debate, and reflect the values of societies as a whole. On the other hand, the decision taken by the agencies will be done faster, with more awareness of deadlines and ease of administration, and it is likely to be subject to more lobbying activities.

As the example above shows, when the preferences of the agency and the government are not perfectly aligned, it can make sense to restrict the behavior of the agency to respond to the environment and not to try to shape it. However, in other circumstances it may be preferable for agencies to adopt a leadership strategy. An example of a leadership strategy would be for a government agency to announce, and commit to, a preferred programming language for its purchases of customized software. This is a way of ensuring interoperability and may make sense where that is considered to be a critical feature. This is the approach adopted by the US Department of Defense for the Ada programming language.[14] At the same time it may be preferable for a

---

14. For more information, see http://en.wikipedia.org/wiki/Ada_(programming_language).

government agency to act as a Nash/adaptive player when it chooses standards for transmitting information to outside parties, where intra-agency interoperability is not an important requirement. There is no hard–and-fast rule about this choice between adaptation and leadership strategies; governments need to make this assessment on a case-by-case basis.

In the next sections we use this simple analytical framework to examine the two key roles of government: software procurement and the choice of standards.

Government as Software Purchaser: TCO Analysis and Beyond

As we showed in chapter 5, there are strong indications that governments are not doing an adequate job rationalizing their purchasing decisions. Governments, which are very large buyers, are less likely to do a TCO analysis before adopting software than even medium-sized firms. This may not be so surprising—the public sector is less subject to competitive pressure or effective internal incentives than private sector firms, and thus less likely to base their decision making on efficiency criteria, and public accounting and management systems may not be designed in a way that encourages efficient allocation of expenditures. Still it surely ought to be a source of concern.

In what follows we discuss some aspects of the purchasing policies of governments. We begin with a quintessential example of adaptive strategies: how should government agencies evaluate the different software options in the market in their adoption decisions? We then turn to examples of leadership strategies, where the government takes advantage of its size and power of commitment to compensate for imperfections in the software markets.

Governments Should Use TCO Analysis

While weak efficiency incentives and monitoring may play a role, part of the reason government agencies do less TCO analysis than most large firms may be due to their not having access to a proper methodology for choosing between different programs. What is needed is a set of formal guidelines for government agencies to assess the full range of cost and benefits of different software choices. While there is undoubtedly going to be variation across agencies in detail and implementation, to ensure coherence and consistency of these rules, the central government needs to take a more active role in developing the evaluation framework. Independent consultants can help agencies evaluate specific software products, but it is important to have a general framework specially adapted to the public sector of each country.

This is not the place to develop such an evaluation framework in any detail, but we would like to discuss some aspects. From an economic perspective the best approach is to identify the key performance characteristics of the software (speed, durability, adaptability, etc.), attach a monetary value to each of these features, add them up to get an estimate of total value, and then adopt the software with the largest difference between this value and the full cost of the software (in practice, measuring the quality of the software in monetary terms can be very difficult, and a "point" system might provide a reasonable second best alternative.) The cost dimension should be measured by the TCO, as discussed at length in chapter 5. Perhaps more than for the other dimensions of software evaluation, there is a need to have widely accepted ("standard") TCO evaluation frameworks to enable public institutions in both developed and emerging economies to assess the full costs of the software more effectively before adoption.[15] Especially for large projects any evaluation of costs will be fraught with uncertainty, and some analysis of the impact of alternative (uncertain) scenarios should be included in the evaluation.

While certainly challenging, this task is not insuperable. Even if imperfect, a rigorous methodology, based on explicit criteria, would go a long way toward addressing the weaknesses of public decision making, in particular, the biases introduced by public accounting and management practices.[16] Such a methodology would compel decision makers to make the reasons for their choices between different programs more explicit. It would also help alleviate the widespread dissatisfaction among software vendors about the ways in which public purchasing is conducted, with proprietary software firms complaining that the use of open source software is often politically motivated, and

---

15. The Danish government has commissioned development of a TCO model to facilitate such assessments, with the intention of making it available to all public institutions.

16. For instance, the article "Administration centrale: 225 chantiers ouverts," which describes the use of open software in French public administration states "... le libre évite de passer un appel d'offres public, processus coûteux" (... free (software) escapes the requirement of a formal public procurement process, which is costly). Notice that this is very bad managerial practice, which favors projects whose immediate costs are low as opposed to those who deliver lower costs over the long range, in order to go around formal procedures which are considered too onerous. See Caillerez (2005).

open source proponents complaining that the greater marketing clout of proprietary firms biases evaluations.[17]

The cost analysis should be based on the best offers obtained directly from different suppliers. Vendors adjust their price both to competition and to the "willingness to pay" of customers. This customization of price to the reality of the particular market is a normal part of business; economists refer to it as price discrimination. It is a well-known principle of economic theory that in industries with large fixed costs such as the software industry, such price discrimination is both privately and socially beneficial under very general conditions.[18] In the case of software, price-discriminating behavior by software firms will normally induce lower software prices in poorer countries.[19] In the absence of such price discrimination, one would expect open source software, available at a low up-front cost, to be comparatively more attractive to developing countries than to developed countries. In the presence of price discrimination, this comparative attractiveness will depend on how aggressively proprietary software firms differentiate prices across regions.

When government agencies purchase customized software, the total cost of ownership can be influenced by the form of the software license.[20] An open source license (e.g., GPL) guarantees that the agency will be able to benefit from subsequent improvements made by the

17. We would assume that the difference of marketing clout between open source and proprietary software has certainly decreased in recent years, as suppliers of open source software are more and more professionally run firms, some of them very large.

18. For discussion of this important result, see Tirole (1988, ch. 3).

19. This phenomenon is illustrated by Mr. Jumrud Sawangsamud, president of the Association of Thailand Computer Industry. When discussing the budget PC program, which is aimed at providing Thai households with low cost computers, he explained: "We talked to Microsoft and let them know people in the remote areas could not afford an expensive system. Microsoft offered us a lower priced version of the operating system which was localized for the Thai language." This quotation is taken from the Thai case study we conducted as part of this research project, which is available on line as part of the supplementary materials for this book.

20. This sensitivity to the consequences of different types of licenses is compatible with neutrality between open source and proprietary software. For instance, the US Office of Management and Budget (OMB) issued a memorandum on software acquisition on July 1, 2004, that reminded senior procurement offices that acquisition should be vendor and technology neutral and stressed that this policy applied "to acquisitions of all software, whether it is proprietary or Open Source Software." It also stated "These differences in licensing may affect the use, the security, and the total cost of ownership of the software and must be considered when an agency is planning a software acquisition." See Evans and Burton (2004).

open source community, including perhaps other governments. On the other hand, a developer might accept a lower price for its proprietary software if it owns the copyright or patent and expects to be able to sell the program to other customers (other government entities, domestic or foreign). Other considerations might also be relevant, such as the risk of lock-in and the future bargaining power of the developer (though the evidence in chapter 5 indicates that users do not assess these risks very differently for open source and proprietary software).[21]

Making purchasing decisions on a neutral evaluation procedure based on explicit criteria, and at the same time imposing open specification standards (see below), will put important competitive pressure on both open source and proprietary software providers. And opening the competition to as many suppliers as possible enhances the bargaining position of governments.

Compensating for Imperfection in the Software Market: Favoring Open Source Software?

As we argued in the previous section, in making its software decisions, it is often sensible for government to take the behavior of the rest of the society as given—adopting an "adaptive strategy"—rather than aim to shape it. This is essentially what government does when it employs a TCO analysis for making its software purchasing decisions.

However, as we discussed in chapter 2, it is possible for society to become "locked in" to inferior software for historical reasons. Because of network effects and switching costs, consumers may find it attractive to stay with the dominant software, and this can entrench market power. In such cases, although each customer finds it individually rational to continue using the leading software rather than a challenger, users would be collectively better off if they could coordinate on a shift. It might appear that a possible solution to this "coordination failure" is

---

21. This seems to be the lesson drawn from the following episode reported by Jean-Marie Lapeyre, head of the Copernic Program, on the effort by the French Tax Administration (Direction Générale des Impôts) to modernize its IT infrastructure: "The ILIAD system was built around two technologies: a Unix server, which is AIX 4.2, by IBM, and another technology, Oracle Forms version 3. One day in 2000, Mr. IBM, came in and said, 'We do not support version 4.2 of AIX anymore. You have to switch to 4.3.' We said 'OK' and planned a migration. But then Mr. Oracle said, 'Version 3 of Oracle Forms is not supported on AIX 4.3. You have to switch to Oracle Forms version 6.' We had very little choice in the matter. We had to pay for the migrations at a separate cost of €15 million. And the service was worse!" This quotation is taken from the French case study we conducted as part of this research project, which is available online as part of the supplementary materials for this book.

for government to announce a changeover to the new software. If government purchases are large enough to affect network externalities, or if it can enforce the change by selection of standards, this would induce customers to switch, with a gain in social welfare.[22]

In later sections we will discuss the role of government procurement and standard setting as ways to shape the environment. In this section we examine other types of government policy that can affect the software market, and open source in particular.

There are three main types of policies that can be used to intervene in favor of open source software: public provision of information about open source, subsidies, and mandated adoption of open source software (e.g., by government agencies). Economists have made some progress in analyzing whether policies to promote open source software are likely to increase or reduce economic welfare. In this section we discuss a few key papers, to bring out what we consider to be the main lessons for policy (this is not intended as a exhaustive literature review). While these papers are certainly not the last word on the subject, they provide a cautionary lesson about jumping to any quick conclusion about the advisability of such policy measures. Of course, all models are simplifications that abstract from some relevant features of reality, and the policy lessons they deliver always have to be interpreted in light of those limitations. Nonetheless, the models are useful because they help systematize, and discipline, our thinking about these important issues. At the end of this section we highlight some of main limitation of the models, after we have discussed the insights they provide.

The model by Schmidt and Schnitzer (2003), which we discussed in a preceding section, shows that there is overuse of open source software because of distorted pricing (proprietary prices are above marginal production cost). However, in recent work Comino and Manenti (2005) have emphasized that informational imperfections can cut the other way and lead to underutilization of open source. Some consumers may simply be unaware of the availability of open source programs that can meet their needs, and at least some of these uniformed users might choose open source if they knew about it. Comino and Manenti study three alternative policies to address this problem: direct government provision of information to consumers, subsidies for open source use, and government mandates of open source adoption. In each case

----

22. A discussion of these issues by four authors with different perspectives can be found in Hahn (2002).

they study how the policy is likely to affect economic welfare. The evaluation of these policies is quite complex, especially in the presence of network externalities, so we will only summarize their policy conclusion and the underlying economic intuition.

We begin with information provision. The main policy conclusion reached by Comino and Manenti is that a policy of information provision generally *increases* economic welfare (by which we mean consumer and producer surplus). They extend the framework of Schmidt and Schnitzer, introducing imperfect information on the part of consumers by assuming that a certain proportion of users are unaware of the open source alternative. By making these users aware, the policy generates two forms of welfare gains. The first is that some of these users (depending on their "tastes") end up adopting open source, which generates more benefit for them than the proprietary option they would have selected in the absence of the information. In addition, when consumers have this information, price competition is intensified (consumers know of the alternative to proprietary software). This lowers the price of proprietary software and again increases welfare. Comino and Manenti find that the policy conclusion that information provision improves economic welfare is quite general, but it can be reversed in two circumstances: first, when network externalities are very strong (and thus migration of consumers away from proprietary software raises costs substantially) and, second, when the cost to the government of providing information is too high, compared to the number of consumers reached.[23]

The second form of policy intervention is direct subsidies (or tax credits). Later in this chapter, we provide evidence from our surveys of fifteen countries that shows that governments provide a variety of incentives for both open source and proprietary software development and use (including direct subsidies and tax credits). But are such incentives justified in terms of economic principles? Are they likely to increase economic welfare? In their study Comino and Manenti also

---

23. A similar conclusion is reached by Gutsche (2005). His analysis is narrower in that it focuses on consumer welfare alone, but it is more general because he takes into account both network effects and consumer switching costs. This extension is important because the survey evidence in chapter 5 shows that switching costs are an important component of the total cost of ownership for software users, and are particularly prominent for open source software. In addition he takes into account the fact that in many countries the profits of proprietary software firms accrue to foreigners, which reduces the domestic benefits. But even with these extensions, Gutche concludes that "we do not find much support for interventions in favor of OSS on the whole."

analyze the welfare effects of a policy of directly subsidizing open source software. They reach the stark conclusion that this policy always *reduces* economic welfare. The basic trade-off involved is between the underutilization of open source created by the informational imperfection as against the overuse of open source induced by its being priced too low relative to the socially optimal level. Their particular model produces a clear result—there is net overuse—so an open source subsidy only makes things worse. But, in general, the result could go either way, so we cannot state with certainty that open source subsidies are ill advised. The key message here is that there is a trade-off, and governments need to evaluate it carefully before adopting subsidies.

Finally, we turn to policies that mandate adoption of open source software. This type of government policy has also been examined by Comino and Manenti (2005), who extend the Schmidt–Schnitzer model to study the welfare consequences of a government requirement that a specified proportion of users adopt open source software, even when their individual preferences would be to purchase proprietary software. In this they are thinking of agencies, schools, universities, and publicly owned firms, over whose procurement government has some measure of control. They assume that these entities have exactly the same (distribution of) tastes as the rest of the population. This assumption can be defended on the ground that the government does not have the means to know the value of the taste parameter for each of these users, so it cannot make the policy contingent on that parameter. In this setting Camino and Manenti show that the policy of mandating adoption of open source unambiguously decreases social welfare. This result is not particularly surprising under these assumptions, since open source software is already overused due to underpricing, and the mandate exacerbates the distortion.

In their original paper Schmidt and Schnitzer (2003) also studied a government policy of mandated use for public entities. They modify the setting of their model by allowing for a group of "devoted" consumers who always use proprietary software, whatever its price, and a group that always uses open source. These authors study the welfare effects of having the government force some of the consumers devoted to proprietary software to buy open source. Not surprisingly, this policy also reduces social welfare: the policy is similar to that studied by Camino and Manenti, but targets the mandate for open source on users who are, on average, even more averse to using it. These two analyses illustrate the potential costs of a government policy that would require agencies to use open source software more than they would think it desirable on the basis of their own TCO analyses.

The important policy lesson we draw from our review of these academic studies is that a policy of providing information to consumers is more likely to improve economic welfare than direct subsidies to open source, and that government-mandated uses of open source software are likely to be damaging. Yet it seems that governments have generally taken the opposite approach, focusing more on incentives and mandates than on information provision to improve consumer choice and facilitate more effective competition between the two modes of software.

Of course, the academic literature in this area is still young and underdeveloped. Despite considerable advances, the modeling efforts have not yet incorporated some important, but challenging, dimensions of the problem. Some features the models omit may weaken the specific policy conclusions, others may strengthen it. There are four main limitations of the models that should be acknowledged:

• First, they are static models and thus do not capture the complex dynamics of learning effects on the part of both users and developers. While such learning effects are present in both open source and proprietary, there is a presumption that other things being equal, open source generates greater, and more rapid, knowledge spillovers precisely because the code is open. Models that do not incorporate this feature are likely to understate the case for policies that favor open source.

• The second limitation involves their treatment of network effects in software. These models make no allowance for vendor behavior that can weaken network advantages that one form of software may initially have—in particular, firms with a smaller installed base (network disadvantage) can reduce price to enlarge its demand.[24] When this is allowed, the competitive advantage due to network effects can be substantially reduced. This is likely to weaken the case for open source support, since part of their justification is "kick-starting" markets with network effects and overcoming the legacy costs of the existing installed base.

---

24. As we discussed in chapter 2, the recent work by Chen, Dorazelski, and Harrington (2009) shows that allowing for price competition can, under certain circumstances, dramatically change the dynamics and long run equilibrium in markets with network effects. In particular, the risk of persistent dominance is mitigated by competitive pricing behavior by the firm(s) with the smaller installed base.

• Third, the existing models treat consumers as choosing either an open source or proprietary program, and software firms as offering one or the other. Yet our analysis in chapters 4 and 5 shows that software users and developer firms typically comingle the two types of software, reflecting the synergies that often exist between them.

• Finally, it is important to keep in mind that there are "government imperfections" as well as market imperfections. Even when there is the potential for a government policy to improve welfare, this does not ensure that it will. Taking serious account of the welfare costs of policy errors (e.g., choosing the wrong standard) is also urgently needed.

Whether these various considerations will tilt the balance in favor of, or against, government intervention on behalf of open source remains to be seen. Nonetheless, we are skeptical of policies justified by the "co-ordination failure" argument—that network externalities and switching costs led society to be "locked in" to an inferior outcome over the long run. There is very little concrete evidence for the loss of welfare due to such "coordination failures" in software. A better way to guard against abuse of any entrenched network positions may be for government to maintain a vigilant competition policy in this sector and to set standards that facilitate interoperability among different types of software, and thus intensify competition among them. We take up the important issue of standards in the next section.

Government Policy and Open Standards: Ensuring Competition and Efficient Comingling

Governments are not only some of the largest single purchasers of software and have the same concerns as all large buyers of obtaining the best possible combination of quality and price. They must also ensure interoperability across a wide variety of government departments, between different (federal and subfederal) levels of government and sometimes with agencies in other governments. In addition they have the special concern of ensuring public access to government information services. This may imply something as simple as making sure that laws and regulations are made available on the Web in a way that can be read by the whole population, or something much more complicated like the possibility for firms to participate in online procurement without the cost of buying expensive special software. Of course, private users also want the information they provide to be easily accessible and widely distributed. But for governments, the obligation is stronger: they have a fundamental responsibility of ensuring access to information to all the citizens in their countries.

This obligation to provide access to information can be fulfilled by a Nash strategy: the government uses the software and associated technology that are the most likely to reach the greatest number of citizens at the lowest total cost of ownership. But it can also be fulfilled as part of a Stackelberg strategy that tries to encourage society as a whole to use a particular type of information technology. This applies, in particular, to the types of standards governments use in their internal and external communications, and more specifically to their promotion of "open standards." While such standards can be, and are, used by proprietary software, they are linked in the mind of many proponents to open source software (see Wheeler 2006). In this section we use economic analysis to examine the appropriate role of government in promoting standards. We begin with a short general discussion of standards. After defining them and explaining how the "adaptation" and "leadership" strategies can be used in their choice, we turn to an analysis of "open standards."

Communications between computers are mediated through the use of standards. For instance, many computers (depending on the operating system) know that files whose extension is .htm or .html are intended to be read through a browser, and the browser "knows" that it should interpret the file according to the HTML "standard." From an economic perspective, although not in strict computer usage, this naming convention is also a standard. A simple HTML file would read, for instance, as illustrated in the text box. The fact that <p> opens a paragraph while </p> closes it is part of the standard, and all the browsers must be programmed to "know" that.

```
<!DOCTYPTE html>
<body>
<p>Hello World!</p>
</body>
</html>
```

Clearly, the use of standards gives rise to the type of network externalities that we discussed in chapter 2: users prefer to utilize standards that have many other users. For many applications there are competing standards. For example, there are many different standards for encoding audio files, and some devices cannot play certain of these files. This limits the transmission of files between music-playing devices and lowers the network externalities that can be enjoyed by the users. It does not necessarily follow that there should be only one standard: different standards may be better adapted to different uses, and society faces a trade-off between taking advantage of network externalities and allowing for standards well adapted to these different uses.

Governments can decide to use a "Nash strategy" and simply choose the standards that have been adopted by the rest of society. For instance, many documents published by government agencies are encoded in the PDF format because most computers are able to interpret PDF files. Much more sophisticated analysis is needed in some circumstances, for instance, when deciding which standards to use for communicating data between government agencies. This is well illustrated by a recent speech by the then European Union Commissioner for Competition Policy, Nellie Kroes:

As purchasers, we need to be smart when we buy technology. We need to be aware of the long-term costs of lock-in: you are often locked-in to subsequent generations of that technology. There can also be spillover effects where you get locked in to other products and services provided by that vendor .... That is just bad purchasing. (Kroes 2008)

And she went on to explain how this could influence the practice of the Commission when purchasing technology:

For all future IT developments and procurement procedures, the Commission shall promote the use of products that support open, well-documented standards. Interoperability is a critical issue for the Commission, and usage of well-established open standards is a key factor to achieve and endorse it.

In these statements, Commissioner Kroes is using the same type of reasoning that any large buyer of technology would use: how do I ensure that my decisions are wise in the long run? This is standard Nash-type reasoning. On the other hand, some commentators argue that governments should take advantage of their size and play a "Stackelberg strategy" in which they try to influence the standards adopted by society as a whole. They can use a number of techniques to do this: for example, favoring one specific standard by ordering communications between government agencies to use this standard or, more aggressively, announcing that communications to and from government agencies use specific standards. We also find traces of this strategy in Commissioner Kroes's speech:

No citizen or company should be forced or encouraged to choose a closed technology over an open one, through a government having made that choice first.

What is the source of this concern? She is clearly worried about the possibility that the government might choose the wrong "Stackelberg strategy" and lock users into suboptimal standards.

These quotations are representative of the important recent debate about the use of "open standards," which is, at least according to some commentators, linked to the issue of choice between open source and proprietary software. In what follows we begin by discussing the definition of "open standards"—which turns out be quite a difficult task—and then move to discuss the links to the debate over open source.

Open Standards
In chapter 5 we showed that switching and software interoperability costs are important elements of the total cost of ownership for consumers, especially for open source users. At the same time both users and developers register strong preferences for a regulatory regime that allows them the freedom to choose between open source and proprietary software. In order to ensure that this freedom is meaningful, enabling both users and developers to comingle as they find most appropriate, governments need to maintain open standards. They are the key to lowering switching and interoperability costs, and thereby intensifying competition between open source and proprietary software.

Over the last few years the definition of open standards used by most authors has changed. In 2005 Wikipedia defined them as follows: "[They] are publicly available specifications for achieving a specific task."[25] According to this definition, a standard was open as soon as its description was available for use by anyone. By 2009, the definition became more restrictive:

The term "open" is usually restricted to royalty-free technologies while the term "standard" is sometimes restricted to technologies approved by formalized committees that are open to participation by all interested parties and operate on a consensus basis.

Notice the two main requirements in this newer definition: open standards should be royalty free, and they should be managed by a

---

25. See   http://en.wikipedia.org/w/index.php?title=Open_standard&oldid=12349364 (accessed April 20, 2009).

Standard Setting Organization (SSO) where decisions are taken under some form of consensus rules.[26]

This book is not the place to do a complete analysis of this problem, but we need to examine some aspects that affect the use of open source software. In order to clarify discussion, we adopt the distinction between "open specification" formats, which are publicly available, and "open standards," which are maintained by a standards body.[27] We will use the new term "open specification standards" to designate standards whose use is open to everyone under "reasonable" conditions, as distinct from open standards, which must be royalty free and maintained by a standard setting organization.

It is important to understand that open standards can be, and are, respected both by proprietary and open source products.[28] Therefore, by itself, a commitment to open standards provides no basis for a preference for one type of software. For example, the Internet and the World Wide Web were the result of the efforts of government and academic institutions, for-profit companies and individuals who developed the standards (e.g., IP, TCP, DNS, PPP, HTTP, HTML, XML, SMTP, and POP) on which the Internet is based. This was done through standard-setting organizations such as the IETF and W3C. Many implementations of these technologies were developed both in open source and proprietary software and are distributed under a wide variety of open source and proprietary licenses.

On the other hand, some standards embed proprietary technology, and the owners of the technology demand compensation. In principle, one could imagine open source software that would be compatible with the payment of licenses to such owners. For example, each user could be responsible for paying them. In practice, however, the fact that software is easily copied would make enforcement of this requirement very difficult. As a consequence standards that embed proprietary technology are typically only implemented in proprietary software.

Users are concerned about making a commitment to a standard that requires licensing of technology for its implementation. The fear is

---

26. This is consistent, for example, with the definition used by the European Commission in its "European Interoperability Framework for Pan-European eGovernment Services," http://ec.europa.eu/idabc/servlets/Doc?id=19529 (accessed July 6, 2009).

27. http://www.ibm.com/developerworks/blogs/page/BillHiggins?entry=the _openness_matrix (accessed February 17, 2009).

28. Wheeler (2006) argues that every successful open standard has one implementation in an open source program.

that once the standard is widely used, the owner of the relevant intellectual property can try to exploit the lock-in of users by raising its licensing fee. To circumvent this problem, SSOs often require their participants to divulge any intellectual property they own that they believe bear on the standard, and to commit to not overcharging for the use of the intellectual property. This last requirement is usually referred to as a commitment to RAND (reasonable and nondiscriminatory) or FRAND (fair, reasonable and nondiscriminatory) licensing terms.[29]

The most important features of standards are that they can be used by anyone and are subject, at most, to RAND license fees for any intellectual property they contain. In principle, the use of open specification standards could ensure that the general public will have access to the information provided by the government and that different government agencies can communicate with each other. But for this to happen, the standard must be implemented in software that users can afford in practice. Insofar as possible, government agencies should choose standards that are widely used and that can be implemented in

---

29. The dangers involved are well-illustrated by the effort by Rambus, a semiconductor designer, to control computer memory technology. As with software, an important feature of the computer memory industry is that both computer makers and consumers benefit greatly if the memory products made by different companies are interchangeable. This requires that memory chips be designed consistent with industry "standards"—technical specifications ensuring that any memory chips, meeting the standards, will work as expected in any computer design. At the same time this creates the strong danger of "holdup," since any company with a patent that covers technology required by such a standard can insist on royalties from the entire industry. For this reason the standard setting body, JEDEC, like many such associations, requires their members to (1) disclose any pending patent applications that bear on the elements of standards under discussion and (2) license any patents that end up covering the standard to everyone in the industry at "reasonable" royalty rates. Of course, defining what constitutes a "reasonable" royalty and enforcing a reasonable royalty policy are tricky undertakings. This difficulty makes the disclosure obligation all the more important, so people working on drafting standards have a clear understanding of the extent to which products designed to conform to the standard are going to be subject to royalty claims.

In the early 1990s, when the standards for SDRAM chips were being discussed at JEDEC, Rambus was a member of the organization. The JEDEC committee working on standards for DRAM knew that one patent from the 1990 application had been issued. But Rambus did not disclose to the committee that it had additional applications pending. Worse, unbeknown to the other members of JEDEC, Rambus was crafting yet more applications (still retaining the original priority date) in which it attempted to cover the features of the JEDEC SDRAM standard as that standard was being discussed at committee meetings, attended by Rambus representatives. Ultimately Rambus initiated an aggressive litigation campaign against fellow industry members that continues to this day.

For a more detailed discussion of the Rambus case, the reader is referred to Jaffe and Lerner (2007 paperback edition).

reasonably priced software (this way they participate in the creation of network externalities). A reasonable price might be zero when the information is to be accessible to everyone (as in the case of tax documents), but it could be higher when firms require access to specialized information. Looking to the future, governments need to ensure that the specifications of the standard remain open in the long run and are modernized as technology improves.

However, open source advocates emphasize that any type of licensing of technology creates major difficulties for open source software—the fact that licensing terms are reasonable has nothing to do with the issue. For example, the Open Source Initiative has developed "Open Standards Requirements for Software."[30] The objective of these "requirements," which they believe should be part of any formal definition of open standards, is to ensure that any such standard "not prohibit conforming implementations in open source software." This implies that "all patents essential to implementation of the standard must [either] be licensed under royalty-free terms for unrestricted use, or be covered by a promise of nonassertion when practiced by open source software."[31]

There is little doubt that standards that do not meet a rather strict definition of openness, including no fees, create difficult issues for open source software. But public policy regarding the intellectual property in standards has another concern: innovation in standards is important, and firms that are investing in the development of new technologies should expect to be rewarded. A policy that favored standards with no licensing fees, simply in order to level the playing field for open source software, would undoubtedly be detrimental to innovation.

In practice, both patent policy and the functioning of standard-setting organizations are very imperfect, and some of their failings are certainly more costly to open source software. To take just one example, it is likely that weak patents (whose validity is unlikely to be upheld by courts, if tested) create more difficulties for open source software than for proprietary software, where the developer can at least threaten to defend against their enforcement. How the system should

---

30. http://opensource.org/osr (accessed August 19, 2009).
31. A more explicit attack on the term RAND licensing can be found on the Free Software Foundation site: "That term white-washes a class of patent licenses that are normally neither reasonable nor non-discriminatory ... these licenses ... discriminate against the free software community, and that makes them unreasonable." http://www.gnu.org/philosophy/words-to-avoid.html (accessed August 19, 2009).

be reformed to limit these distortions raises a host of very difficult issues that are far from resolved. We will focus on only one of them: should the government try to compensate for these distortions by requiring that every standard used by its agencies is "open" in the sense which the Open Source Initiative gives to the term?

Adopting such a policy would be an example of a Stackelberg (leadership) strategy: the government is exploiting its size and ability to commit to a policy in order to change the nature of the market. We have the same reluctance to endorse Stackelberg strategies for government policy toward standards as we have for using government procurement to compensate for imperfections in the software market. The design and evaluation of such policies requires very sophisticated analysis of the consequences of such actions, which is especially difficult in the technologically dynamic settings under consideration. Furthermore the politics of standards setting are complicated and perilous— endless discussions can arise over the fact that this or that SSO is really driven by consensus.[32] We do not believe that government procurement policy or standard-setting efforts should introduce industrial policy through stealth, and there is a real danger of this occurring. Nonetheless, we fully recognize that the issue is very complex and requires further analysis. Easy answers are not on the horizon.

Government Incentives and Promotion of Open Source

The government influences the development of the software industry in many ways—most important, as purchaser of software, as regulator, and through the provision of incentives. We have discussed the arguments for and against proactive government intervention in the development and use of software through procurement and regulation.[33] In this final analysis we present evidence on the provision of software incentives by governments.

How Common are Software Incentives?

Governments intervene in the development and adoption of software through various incentives. Our surveys of developers and users

---

32. For an example of the type of discussions to which this can lead, see David Wheeler (2008).

33. Governments also influence the development of the software industry through their choice of intellectual property policy. This problem was briefly explored in chapter 3, and we will not revisit it here.

Table 6.7
Incentives for software development and adoption (percentage of developers/users receiving incentives)

	Developers: proprietary	Developers: open source	Users: proprietary	Users: open source
Aggregate	12.2	7.4	12.2	8.9
	(0.8)	(0.8)	(0.7)	(0.6)
Size				
Small	9.7	5.7	8.1	6.9
	(0.9)	(0.9)	(0.9)	(0.9)
Medium	16.3	10.0	17.7	12.0
	(1.5)	(1.6)	(2.2)	(1.9)
Large	15.9	7.7	10.0	6.8
	(4.0)	(3.7)	(2.0)	(0.6)
Ownership				
Domestic	11.8	6.5	7.8	5.3
	(0.8)	(0.9)	(1.2)	(1.0)
Foreign	14.9	13.2	13.8	7.0
	(2.6)	(3.1)	(4.1)	(3.0)
Government			27.2	19.3
			(3.3)	(2.9)
Sector				
Services			32.8	22.0
			(4.3)	(3.8)
High-tech manufacturing			8.4	9.1
			(1.4)	(1.4)
Low-tech manufacturing			8.5	4.8
			(1.4)	(1.1)
Wholesale/retail trade			10.6	3.3
			(1.5)	(0.9)

Note: Multinomial standard errors are in parentheses. These are computed as $\sqrt{p(1 - p)/n}$, where p is the reported proportion and n is the sample size.

provide detailed information on the extent and form of government incentives for proprietary and open source software development and adoption. The survey questions ask specifically about software-related incentives, distinguishing them from general investment incentives.

Although the public debate seems more focused on government policies to promote the development and adoption of open source software, the survey evidence indicates that both proprietary and open source software benefit from incentives of various forms. Table 6.7 shows that, averaging across the fifteen countries in our survey, 12.2 percent of firms developing proprietary software say that they receive some form of incentives, as compared with 7.4 percent for open source developers. These figures are not statistically different from each other, so we can say that the frequency of incentives is similar for the two types of software, at least when we average across all countries in the sample. The frequency of incentives for software adoption (given in the last two columns of the table) is nearly identical to those for software development.

The likelihood that firms and users receive incentives depends on their characteristics. This could be due to provisions in government policies that target specific types of firms or users, or to different take-up rates among potential recipients. With the available information we cannot distinguish between these hypotheses. In any event, we find that small firms and users are less likely to receive incentives for proprietary (but not open source) software development and adoption than larger entities. Regarding ownership, there is no statistically significant difference between domestic firms and foreign subsidiaries, but we find that government agencies are more than three times as likely as private firms to receive some form of incentives for software adoption.

Incentives for software development or adoption can take a variety of forms, including monetary incentives such as direct subsidies and tax credits. But they can also be more indirect, such as when governments attach specific software conditions to procurement decisions, regulatory policy and even informal pressure and "moral suasion." Our survey provides information on the relative importance of these different forms of incentives for proprietary and open source. As table 6.8 shows, the sources of developer incentives are broadly similar for proprietary and open source software, the main difference being that indirect subsidies through procurement are more important (and tax credits less important) for open source than for proprietary software. Nearly a third of developers rank procurement conditions as the leading form of incentives. For users, the dominant forms of incentives for proprietary software are direct subsidies and tax breaks. For open source, the ordering of these two is reversed, with tax credits being more important than direct subsidies. For both types of software, informal and regulatory channels are much less important as incentives for software users than they are for developers, with only 13 percent giving them top rank for open source and 2 percent for proprietary.

As the survey does not provide any information about the magnitude of these incentives, we cannot evaluate whether the current

Table 6.8
Form of incentives for proprietary and open source software adoption (percentage of firms giving top rank)

	Developers: proprietary	Developers: open source	Users: proprietary	Users: open source
Direct subsidy	34.7	30.4	43.2	20.6
	(2.2)	(5.1)	(3.0)	(4.9)
Tax credit	37.6	29.1	25.3	41.2
	(3.3)	(5.1)	(2.7)	(6.0)
Procurement contract conditions	22.1	32.9	28.8	25.0
	(2.8)	(5.3)	(2.8)	(5.3)
Regulation and informal	5.6	7.6	2.7	13.2
	(1.6)	(3.0)	(1.0)	(4.1)

Note: Multinomial standard errors are in parentheses. These are computed as $\sqrt{p(1-p)/n}$, where p is the reported proportion and n is the sample size.

incentive regime is neutral between the two types of software. But it is worth asking what would constitute a neutral subsidy scheme. To do this, we draw on the detailed survey evidence on the composition of the total cost of ownership, which we presented in chapter 5. Even if the subsidy rates were the same for open source and proprietary software, such incentives would not be neutral. The initial price of software is only one component of the total cost of ownership, though a larger proportion for proprietary software. Subsidies to the other cost elements, such as switching and interoperability costs, are harder to implement because of difficulties in monitoring the true expense incurred by the user. This implies that a uniform rate of subsidy for both types of software would, in practice, favor proprietary software where price is a larger component of the TCO. Designing a truly "neutral" subsidy policy would involve setting different rates if it is only applied to the purchase price of the software. The information on the cost structure of open source and proprietary software, presented in chapter 5, might be helpful in calibrating appropriate, neutral subsidy rates if policy makers choose to support software in general in this way.

Conclusion

In this chapter we provided an economic analysis of some key aspects of government policy in the software sector. In particular, we focused on a variety of arguments made by proponents of open source for why government policy should promote it. We hope to have shown how economic principles can help to assess the validity of these arguments and to formulate good public policy. In addition, drawing on our unique surveys in fifteen countries, we provided new evidence on the regulatory regimes preferred by software developers and users, and on the extent to which governments provide incentives of various forms for the development and adoption of open source and proprietary software.

We would like to highlight four main conclusions that emerge from the analysis:

• First, our survey evidence shows clearly that the dominant preference among software developers and users is for a regulatory regime that allows them complete freedom to choose between open source and proprietary software, rather than one that either requires or favors one or the other. This finding holds in each of the fifteen countries we surveyed, and for software firms and users with different characteristics. The pervasive preference for an unrestricted regulatory regime certainly provides, at a minimum, a prima facie basis for thinking that government policy should be neutral between open source and proprietary software. The heavy burden of proof should be on those who advocate policies that favor preferential treatment of either form of software.

• Second, in their role as a large buyer of software, government can influence the choices of private-sector consumers through both network and demonstration (information) effects. Whether they should exercise such leadership strategies in their procurement policies is far from clear, however, and we argue that this depends very much on the specific context. In cases where an adaptive strategy is warranted, governments should base their purchases on evaluations of the total cost of ownership of the software alternatives in the market, on the basis of their individual quality and costs rather than the type of licenses under which they are distributed. What is needed is a set of formal guidelines for government agencies to assess the full range of cost and benefits of different software choices. To ensure coherence and consistency of these rules, the central government needs to take a more active role in developing the evaluation framework.

• Third, in its regulatory role, governments should adopt policies that promote effective competition between open source and proprietary software. Foremost among these are an aggressive competition policy to prevent abuse of network dominance and a policy to encourage the maximum degree of openness in standards to intensify competition between different forms of software, but cognizant too of the need to preserve economic incentives for innovation in standards.

• Finally, our survey evidence shows that governments currently provide a range of incentives, both formal and informal, for the development and use of both open source and proprietary software. But we argue that the economic justification for such incentives is generally weak. There is a stronger case for a proactive role for government in providing information to consumers about open source to correct informational imperfections in the market. There is also some argument for government sponsorship of selected demonstration projects involving open source, and perhaps also proprietary software, but it is critical that these not become a source of ongoing subsidy or industrial policy by stealth.

Governments face many challenging and important issues regarding the use and development of information technology in general and software in particular. They need to improve the procedures governing government procurement in information technology; to formulate evidence-based policies about whether, and how, to promote the use and development of software; to organize and finance the use of modern information and communication technologies in education; to ensure a healthy competition interaction between open source and proprietary software; and much more. In all these areas more research is needed to assist decision makers with the difficult choices they have to make. We hope that some of the energy that has, in recent years, been directed at the rather polarized debate between open source and proprietary software will be redirected more constructively toward these issues.

Appendix 6.1: Model for Policy Analysis

For the interested reader, in this appendix we summarize the technical version of the Schmidt–Schnitzer model, which we use in the text for policy analysis. The authors develop a Hotelling model in which both an open source and a proprietary program are offered. This is a model of horizontal product differentiation, in which users differ in their preferences between open source and proprietary software for some specific task, but there is no intrinsic quality difference between the two types of software (i.e., no vertical differentiation).

To make things simple, in this model we assume that both programs are produced at a marginal cost of zero, and that the open source program is sold at a price of zero. The developer of the proprietary program chooses its price p to maximize its profit.

Each consumer is characterized by a "taste" parameter, t, that describes her preferences between open source and proprietary software. This parameter takes values between zero and one. She obtains benefits equal to $v - \alpha t$ if she buys the open source software at a zero price, and $v - \alpha(1 - t) - p$ if she buys the proprietary software.[34] Higher values of t correspond to a stronger preference for proprietary software, relative to open source. In the software context it is natural to interpret this taste parameter as a summary index of the various costs the user incurs in adopting that type of program, apart from the initial cost of obtaining the software (e.g., the costs of switching, interoperability, support services or upgrades). The parameter α describes the intensity of the consumer's preference for one type of software.

The consumer chooses to buy the program that yields the greatest benefits (net of price). Thus, she buys proprietary software if

$$v - \alpha(1 - t) - p \geq v - \alpha t \Leftrightarrow t \geq \frac{\alpha - p}{2\alpha},$$

and open source software otherwise. Note that if $p = 0$, all the consumers with taste parameter $t > 1/2$ choose proprietary software, while the others prefer the open source software. If we assume that the parameter t is uniformly distributed on the interval $[0, 1]$, then $(\alpha - p)/2\alpha$ is the proportion of consumers who acquire the open source software and $1 - (\alpha - p)/2\alpha$ is the proportion of consumers who purchase the proprietary software. Letting N denote the total number of consumers, the demand for the proprietary software is

$$N \times \left(1 - \frac{\alpha - p}{2\alpha}\right),$$

which generates profit equal to

---

34. We assume that v is large enough to ensure that, if there were no proprietary software available, all consumers would choose to use the open source program rather than none. The consumer with the least taste for open source software is the consumer for whom $t = 1$. Therefore this assumption translates into the restriction $v - \alpha > 0$. This ensures that when proprietary and open source software compete with each other, all consumers purchase at least one of them: "the market is covered."

$$N \times \left(1 - \frac{\alpha - p}{2\alpha}\right) \times p.$$

The developer chooses the price p to maximize this profit. It is easy to confirm that this yields a price of $\alpha/2$. The firm's profit is

$$N \times \left(1 - \frac{\alpha - \alpha/2}{2\alpha}\right) \times \frac{\alpha}{2} = \frac{3\alpha}{8}N.$$

The consumers who buy the proprietary software are those consumers for which

$$t \geq \frac{\alpha - \alpha/2}{2\alpha} = \frac{3}{4}.$$

Thus the proprietary software is sold to one-fourth of the consumers and open source software to the other three-fourths. Recall that the efficient allocation would involve an equal division of the market between open source and proprietary software. Thus the market generates overuse of open source, which occurs because it is available for free.[35]

An increase in the parameter α corresponds to increase in the attachment of consumers to their preferred software. When α is higher, a rise in the price of proprietary software discourages fewer of its consumers. This induces the developer to raise the price, and due to the specific formulation of the model, it does that in such a way that the number of programs that it sells stays constant (e.g., this would not be the case if the distribution of t were not uniform). Because the price increases and its sales do not change, the profit of the developer increases.

Schmidt and Schnitzer use this model to highlight the resulting inefficiency in the relative use of open source and proprietary software. Consider the consumer for whom $t = 2/3$. If the two programs were sold at a price equal to marginal cost, namely at zero, this consumer

---

35. A slightly more sophisticated version of the model can allow one program to be intrinsically better than the other. A consumer of taste parameter t then obtains benefits of $v_{OS} - \alpha t$ if he buys the open source software, and $v_P - \alpha(1 - t) - p$ if he buys the proprietary software, where v_{OS} can be either larger or smaller than v_P. In this case the efficient allocation is for consumers with $t \geq 1/2 + \Delta v/(2\alpha)$ to purchase the proprietary software, where $\Delta v \equiv v_{OS} - v_P$. However, the profit maximizing proprietary developer will charge a price of $\alpha/2 - \Delta v/2$ and it is only consumers with $t \geq 3/4 + \Delta v/(4\alpha)$ who purchase its product. As in the simple version of the model, there is underconsumption of proprietary software. (This reasoning holds only if $\Delta v < \alpha$; if this were not the case, no consumers would purchase proprietary software, even at zero price.) The economic conclusions drawn from the analysis are the same in this more sophisticated model.

would choose to buy proprietary software. However, because she must pay for the proprietary software, she chooses to buy the open source software and ends up using the program she likes less, despite the fact that the costs of production are the same. To put this point another way, because the proprietary software developer is extracting profits by charging a higher price than the open source "community," its product is not utilized enough. This implies that policies that would extend the use of open source software will, at least in this simple static model, *decrease* social welfare. It is policies that extend the use of proprietary software that increase social welfare. But as we discuss in the text, there are other considerations—including imperfect information by the consumer about open source—that can have a countervailing effect.

7 The Takeaways

Over the course of this book we have examined the way in which open source software works and how it interacts with proprietary software. Our goal in doing so has been to better shed light on how these programs affect firms, the economy, and society.

We were motivated in large part by the fact that policy discussions around open source have frequently been characterized by more heat than light. While the questions at the heart of the debate—Can open source software stimulate economic development? What policies should government pursue?—are fundamentally economic questions, the discussion is frequently framed in nearly theological tones. Advocates of open source passionately assert its benefits, while more skeptical voices make equally passionate counterclaims. Rigorous economic analysis, which might help sort out these competing claims, has been largely missing from the debate.

We began this book by describing the way in which software in general is developed, sold, and licensed, and the economic characteristics of the sector. We then discussed the differences between open source and proprietary software, and examined their respective strengths. We showed that the two types of software are developed and commercialized in ways that are more similar than is commonly described. We then turned to policies that governments might follow, both as purchasers of software and as regulators of the economy. We find that, in both roles, they should typically adopt a policy of neutrality with respect to both types of software: as purchasers of software, they should simply decide on a case-by-case basis that software is better adapted for the task at hand; as regulators, they should support the developers and the users with a transparent and stable policy framework, whatever the type of software they choose to work with.

As we have emphasized throughout, our analysis highlights the complexity of drawing "fast-and-easy" conclusions. This paucity of easy conclusions reflects the difficulty of conclusively answering these questions empirically. Software usage in general, and open source software more in particular, is difficult to track, and the economic impacts of software utilization are hard to measure. As economists, we are certainly not qualified to determine whether proprietary or open source software is inherently better from a technical standpoint. Moreover, even with the best data, it would still be very hard to infer whether the choice of a certain type of software leads to beneficial outcomes such as a vibrant industry developing or employing that type of software or whether both outcomes are driven by some third factor.

Beyond these measurement issues there is a deeper challenge: these relationships are really complex! There is lots of uncertainty surrounding the relative merits of the proprietary and open source approaches. Given the results of our surveys, which indicate that users and developers take advantage of both proprietary and open source software, we are skeptical of even technical experts making any broad claims of superiority of one kind or the other. Even assessing the relative viability of the open source and proprietary software business models, an issue with a large component of economics to it, is a hazardous exercise. These difficulties are compounded by the special nature of the software industry, which combines strong network effects in which the decision of one firm can affect many others, relatively high switching costs and rapid technological progress.

But, as we argue repeatedly, despite these challenges there are many things that can be said with confidence about open source. There is much truth in what advocates for this software claim, and in the arguments of its critics. But in many respects the dichotomy between open and proprietary software that many authors—whether enthusiasts or critics of open source—claim is profoundly misleading. There is little economic reason to see these two systems as alternatives being in isolation from each other.

These claims are borne out by our survey, which shows that open source and proprietary software are at the same time more complementary and more similar than is often portrayed. Most users of software choose a mixture of open source and proprietary software, and many firms develop both types. For instance, over the whole sample of fifteen countries in our surveys, only 15 percent of the firms that develop at least some open source software devote more than 75 percent of their developers' time to open source.

In our view, it is far better to consider the world of software developers and users as a complex ecosystem, such as a rainforest jungle or (if we are of a more sanguine view) a stretch of prairie. While many kinds of birds dwell in the habitat, from birds of prey to songbirds, they typically each have their own nest, with their own set of food sources, predators, and partners. To view a falcon and a warbler as simply substitutes for each other—as somehow playing an identical role in the ecosystem because they are both birds—would be a grievous error. In a similar way, to see open source and proprietary software as two identical substitutes is misleading.

In light of these insights, we highlight some critical takeaways. In this final chapter we look at some of the implications of these discussions. We will consider the meaning of these shifts for three audiences: policy makers, corporate managers, and academics.

Implications for Government Officials

There is no right answer. Despite the well-understood imperfections of the software market, we find no reason to believe that market mechanisms inherently favor either type of software. Under these conditions, and given the serious hazards of governments trying to pick winners, it is appropriate to let competition (controlled, of course, by competition law) and the decentralized choices of diverse economic agents do their jobs.

More specifically, government officials need not—and should not—favor either open source or proprietary software. Rather, they should maintain a neutral stance toward the way in which software is licensed, developed, and procured. There are many reasons for encouraging competition between open and proprietary software. Open source and proprietary software differ on many dimensions, including such criteria as functionality, cost, quality, and product evolution. These considerations are each likely to require careful assessment. To consider the last-mentioned criteria, for instance, open source software gives the user access to the underlying software code—thus there is no danger that the software will be "snatched away" because of the change of a corporate strategy. But the development of future versions of open source programs will be a function of its ability to attract the interest of individual and corporate contributors. When encouraging the development of a local computer industry, government officials should let firms weigh these complex considerations and choose the model of software development that they find most appropriate. Recommending that governments should encourage competition, however, is not the same thing as arguing that they should not be involved in regulating the software industry.

When funding the development of software, whether for their own use or as a more general R&D effort, government officials need to apply a different calculus as opposed to private entities. In particular, the same issues, such as cost and quality, should be weighted, but government officials must also take into account the benefits to society. This implies that different countries may make different choices. For instance, a small country might want to take advantage of further improvements by others to its software and would be more inclined to fund open source projects with licenses that limit commercial utilization, such as the General Public License. In a large country with a dynamic software industry, government officials may wish to make it easier for commercial firms to benefit from publicly funded research and development. (Indeed our survey findings suggest that countries in the real world do make different choices.)

A foundation of shared standards is essential. Our advocacy of neutrality between open source and proprietary software is consistent with, and in some sense underpinned by, a very strong commitment to what we call open specification standards: that is, standards whose specifications can be used and implemented by all those who desire to do so. Governments should use open specification standards to facilitate communications with and from the users of public services, as well as with their suppliers. Open specifications can be, and often are, put to use both in proprietary and open source software.

Implications for Corporate Managers

Be sensitive to the lack of a "right" answer. There is no reason to expect different firms to make the same choices in terms of open source and proprietary software. There is no simple ranking of open source and proprietary software, either in terms of the full costs of adoption or the quality of the software. The basic reason is that open source and commercial software pose different trade-offs in terms of costs and quality, and companies are heterogeneous. These users do not all attach the same weights to the different dimensions of cost and quality. Moreover the trade-offs regarding the various dimensions of cost and quality, and the weights that users attach to them, are likely to depend on the particular task for which software is needed, so the same user could make different choices about which software to use.

When considering the costs and benefits of open source and proprietary software, approach the received wisdom with caution. Our survey of firms regarding the costs of different types of software suggests that some of the commonly accepted patterns about the differences in costs and benefits between these two types of software do not hold. For instance, the relative differences in the cost components are not as sharply different as we would have assumed. Therefore it is important to do a precise analysis adapted to each specific case.

The appropriate mixture between open and proprietary software will vary with the company's circumstances. Our survey suggested a number of patterns that drive firms to engage in open source development. For instance, not surprisingly, larger firms were much more likely to engage in some open source activity than either small- or medium-sized companies but less likely to specialize in open source. Similarly companies that work on customized software, bundled software, and (to a lesser extent) support services are significantly more likely to engage in some open source than pure software developers. Synergies are likely to make it attractive to combine open source with some business models than others.

The appropriate mixture between open and proprietary software will vary with the stage of development of the nation in which the company is based. Our survey showed that the relative importance of the initial cost of the software and what we term complementary costs—those involving the costs of switching, assuring interoperability, support and upgrades—vary with the level of national economic development. We find that the initial cost of software is relatively more important in less wealthy countries than in middle-income countries, and at the same time more important in middle-income than in high-income countries. Meanwhile the complementary costs grow in importance in wealthier nations.

Remember not to confuse vertical and horizontal differentiation. As we highlighted in chapter 5, there are really two kinds of quality differences: vertical differentiation, where one product clearly dominates the other (the BMW vs. the Yugo, in our example) and horizontal differentiation, where different consumers with different needs would choose different options (the Yugo and the pickup truck). The vast majority of instances in software involve horizontal differences, where different customers will make different choices. As a result coexistence between open source and proprietary software is the rule rather than the exception. Managers must make choices with a keen eye to their target audience and awareness that no one product is unlikely to satisfy all users.

Mixing is the rule, not the exception. We observe that users extensively mix the two types of software, and that this pattern held in all the countries we studied. Moreover the extent to which open source is used and the degree of mixing between open source and proprietary software both depend on user characteristics, in ways that are consistent with economic principles. Companies should see the use of open source and proprietary software not as an either-or decision, as it is so often depicted in the literature, but as a continuum.

Implications for Researchers

Beware of simply "transporting" economic frameworks from elsewhere. Michael Boskin, chairman of the first President Bush's Council of Economics Advisors, was reputed (perhaps apocryphally) to have said, "Potato chips, semiconductor chips, what is the difference? They are all chips" (Cannon 2001). But the economics of high-technology industries—and software specifically—are very different from those of more traditional industries. As we have highlighted, the presence of a whole host of factors—from switching costs to network effects to information gaps—means that the simple frameworks of supply and demand and the reliance of the market's "invisible hand" to set things right may not apply. As a result researchers must approach the study of the economics of software—and the choice between open and proprietary programs—with a degree of care and caution.

Much more research is needed to assist policymakers with the difficult choices they have to make. We hope that some of the energy that has been directed at the rather polarized debate between open source and proprietary software in recent years will be redirected more constructively toward these issues. In particular, several topics are critical: governments need to decide whether or not to promote a domestic software industry, they need to organize and finance the use of modern information and communication technologies in education, they need to design intellectual property regimes that respond to software innovations, and they need to improve the rationality of government procurement in information technologies. In all these areas careful research can shed light and suggest approaches that are and are not likely to work. These insights are especially likely to be useful in developing countries, where these tasks need to be completed with limited human and financial resources.

Research into the open source phenomenon must focus more on the dynamics of choices within software-producing and using firms. Much of the initial wave of open source research focused on the incentives and choices of individual developers. As we highlighted in our history of open source, while individual developers played key roles in the development of open source, the corporate presence has become ever more important. Moreover the choices that firms face regarding open source software are not easy ones. Among other issues, corporations face the challenge of integrating new software in the supply chains of their customers, of hiring and training information technology professionals, and of determining the advisability of using the most advanced technologies. Economics and management research can certainly provide useful guidance into these questions.

The issues posed by and lessons learned from the experiences of firms with open source extend far beyond software. In recent years we have seen numerous efforts to engage in what we have termed "technology sharing" across a variety of high-technology industries. Examples include patent pools, standards-setting organizations with reasonable and non-discriminatory (RAND) licensing rules and umbrella cross-licensing arrangements between firms. In many instances the motivations of firms for participating in these collaborative efforts, often while still competing in the sale of competing products, resemble those of software firms participating in open source initiatives. The experiences of firms balancing between open source and proprietary software development should have many lessons for knowledge-sharing organizations elsewhere in high-technology industries.

Final Thoughts

We began this chapter by acknowledging what we didn't know about the choices between open source and proprietary software, as well the challenges that limit empirical work in this area. But while not minimizing these difficulties, a more optimistic conclusion is in order.

In particular, in this book we have sought to blend evidence from large-sample analyses, case studies, and our own surveys with formal theorizing and more general economic reasoning. Taken together, the chapters suggest to us that quite a bit *can* be understood about the choice between open source and proprietary software. In particular, our analysis highlights how so much of the discussion—whether by advocates for or critics of open source software—is misleading, as it understates the extent to which these two forms of software can, should and will exist alongside and interact with each other in the long term.

It is our hope that this discussion will stimulate others, from both the academic and practitioner communities, to explore these complex and economically important dynamics in a reasoned and balanced manner.

Glossary

The terms in italics found in the definition are terms that are defined in the glossary (or for which a very closely related term is defined).

Apache is an open source *Web server*, first developed in 1995, and since 1996 the most widely used Web server.

Application programming interface (API) is a set of definitions of the ways in which one program will accept instructions from other programs and will provide them with information.

Application software is a computer program that is directly accessed by a user to perform certain tasks, in contrast to, for instance, system software that provides services to other programs.

Average cost is equal to total cost incurred in production divided by the quantity produced: if 150 tons are produced at a cost of $900, the average cost is $6/ton.

BASIC is a programming language, characterized by limited direct access to the hardware. It was created in 1964 by John George Kemeny and Thomas Eugene Kurtz at Dartmouth College. Their aim was to provide computer access to nonscience students. BASIC is widely used, especially under the form of its descendant Visual BASIC.

Berkeley Software Distribution (BSD) Unix is a version of the UNIX operating system developed and distributed by the Computer Systems Research Group of the University of California, Berkeley, from 1977 to 1995.

BSD license is an open source software license that imposes few restrictions on the use of the software. Most important, it allows integration of the code in proprietary software. It was first used in 1980 for the *Berkeley Source Distribution UNIX* (BSD UNIX) and has a certain number of variants.

Bundled software is software that is supplied either as part of a package with other programs or with hardware.

C is a general purpose computer programming language characterized by extensive direct access to the memory of the computer. It was created in 1972 by Dennis Ritchie at the Bell Telephone Laboratories. It is widely used for developing system software and application software that can be used on different platforms.

C++ is a computer program developed starting in 1979 by Bjarne Stroustrup at Bell Labs as an *object-oriented* evolution of C. It is widely used for many different types of applications.

CAD (computer-aided design) is the practice of using specialized software to design products, which can range from electronic circuits to airplanes. CAD software is often used as part of an integrated set of applications that includes *CAM* software.

CAM (computer-aided manufacturing) is the practice of using specialized software to aid in the prototyping and manufacturing of products. CAM software is usually used as part of an integrated set of applications that includes *CAD* software.

Compiler is a program whose main purpose is to translate *source code*, which is written in a programming language understandable to humans, into machine language that a computer's processor uses.

Coordination failure refers to situations where several economic agents, each following their own interests, do not coordinate in a way that leads to an optimal allocation.

Correlation is a measure of the strength of the linear relationship between two random variables. It takes values between −1 and +1, where a value of zero indicates that the variables are independent of each other and −1 or 1 indicates that they are proportional to the other. When the correlation is positive (resp. negative), an increase (resp. a decrease) in one variable is correlated with an increase (resp. a decrease) with the other.

Cost synergy refers to the case where the total cost of producing output in two distinct activities (or entities) is lower when they are combined, rather than done separately. Examples (in our context) include combining software development of different types within one firm, or combining the development and marketing of software by a single firm.

Critical value refers to the numerical value of a statistical test beyond which the *null hypothesis* of the test can be rejected.

Database is a collection of information that is organized so that it can easily be accessed, managed, updated, and analyzed.

Database Management System (DBMS) is a program that helps manage and access a *database*.

Development costs are the costs incurred by an economic entity before the launch of a new product. It is sometimes used in a more restricted meaning that includes only the costs of R&D and engineering.

Device driver is a computer program that allows other computer programs to interact with a hardware device, such as a printer, a scanner, or a screen.

Domain Name System (DNS) is the system by which the Internet translates a "domain name" such as mitpress.com into IP addresses, which are numerical addresses that the computers actually use to find each other.

Econometrics is the application of statistical methods to test economic hypotheses.

Economies of scale refers to cases where the total cost of production increases more slowly than the level of production, so the unit cost is declining as the scale of product ion rises. There are diseconomies of scale in the opposite case, when the unit cost increases with scale.

Economies of scope refers to cases where the total cost of producing a set of products (or services) together is smaller than the combined cost of producing each separately.

Embedded system is a combination of hardware and software with a specific function, as can be found in cars, medical equipment, toys, phones, and so on. (See *general purpose computer*.)

Entry cost is the cost an existing firm incurs to enter a new market or the cost of establishing a new firm to enter a specific market.

Fair, Reasonable, and Nondiscriminatory terms (FRAND) refer to the obligations that are often imposed by *Standard Setting Organizations* on their members that participate in the standard setting process. These obligations are: they must license any intellectual property that they own and that is necessary for implementing the standard at terms that (1) do not impose burdensome or illegal conditions on the licensees (Fair), (2) that are compatible with the relative value of the intellectual property in the overall license (Reasonable), and (3) treat all licensees in the same way (Nondiscriminatory).

Fixed costs are business expenses that do not vary with the level of activity in a business.

Foreign subsidiary is an economic firm operating in a country that is owned and controlled by another firm located (headquartered) in a different country.

Forking occurs when different developers create a new version of an existing software program, and when this new version competes with the original version.

FORTRAN is a general purpose programming language originally developed in 1957 by John Backus of IBM for numeric and scientific computing, and is still widely used.

General purpose computer is a computer designed to perform a wide variety of tasks. (See *embedded system*.)

General Public License (GPL) is a widely used open source license. It requires any work derived from software licensed under the GPL, and any work that integrates elements of its code, to also be distributed under the same license. This is refereed as the "copyleft" feature of the license. It was originally designed by Richard Stallman in 1989. (Stallman stresses the fact that the GPL defines "free" software rather than "open source" software.)

GNU is a project of a Unix-like computer *operating system* composed entirely of free software, initiated in 1984 by Richard Stallman. Its "kernel" is not finished, but the project has produced other components, such as compilers and other utilities that are in wide use. These components play an important part in Linux systems.

Google Apps is a service offered by Google for businesses that bundles specialized versions of several of its Web applications to provide functionalities similar to that of traditional office suites and collaboration tools.

Gross domestic product (GDP) measures the value of final goods and services produced in a country in a given period of time, generally a year.

Horizontal product differentiation refers to cases where different products cater to different tastes, as opposed to being of different intrinsic quality levels. Specifically, it applies when different consumers would choose different goods or different varieties of the same good when they are sold at the same price. This would apply to different flavors of ice cream, but not to different classes of airline travel. (See *vertical differentiation*.)

Human capital is the economic value of the accumulated knowledge and skills of a person or of a group of people.

Hyper text markup language (HTML)   is a standard for describing Web pages.

Hypertext transfer protocol (HTTP)   is the protocol by which a browser asks a server to provide it with the information it requires.

Installed base   is the number of units of software or hardware that have been purchased in the past and are currently in use.

Integrated circuit (IC),   sometimes called a chip or microchip, is an integrated miniaturized electronic circuit, containing many components such as *transistors*. They are used in nearly all modern electronic equipment, including computers. They were invented by Jack Kilby of Texas Instruments and Robert Noyce of Fairchild Semiconductor in 1958.

Integrated development environment (IDE)   is a set of tightly integrated tools, with similar visual interface, that assist programmers. They usually include a *compiler*, a debugger that helps find mistakes in the program, a text editor, and a number of other tools.

Internet Protocol (IP)   is one of the core protocols of the Internet. It describes the structure of the "packets" in which a sender must divide the information that it desires to send as well as the "administrative" information, such as the address of the recipient, that the packets must contain.

Interoperability   refers to the capability of different information technology components, applications, or networks to exchange and use information.

Invisible hand   is a metaphor coined by Adam Smith in *The Wealth of* Nations (1776) to describe the coordination of economic agents through the functioning of the market, in particular the competitive price system.

ISO (International Organization for Standardization),   founded in 1947, is a worldwide standard setting organization composed of one standards body from each of over 150 countries. It approves commercial, industrial, and technical standards with "global relevance."

Java   is a programming language developed by James Gosling at Sun Microsystems in 1995. It is expressly designed for use on the Internet. It is close to C++ but does not allow as direct an access to the hardware.

Killer application   is software that is very exceptional in its use and popularity. It sometimes refers to a program that is so successful that it increases substantially the market share of the hardware or operating system on which it runs.

Knowledge spillovers   refer to the informal (noncommercial) acquisition of information and knowledge by economic agents, where the value of the information is not paid for by the acquirer. They can arise from direct interaction with other economic agents, or from indirect sources.

Linux   is an open source *UNIX*-like *operating system*, originally written in 1991 by Linus Torvalds. Linux, which comes in many different distributions, is primarily used in servers but can be installed on a wide variety of hardware from supercomputers to mobile phone.

Lock-in   is the situation in which a customer cannot change supplier without incurring a substantial cost.

Lotus Notes   is a business email, calendaring, and contact management program that also includes collaboration tools and allows mobile and offsite access. It was first developed by the Lotus Development Corporation and Iris Associates in 1989 and since 1995 is developed and sold by IBM.

Marginal (or incremental) cost   is the increase in the total cost caused by the production of an extra unit.

Market demand   is the schedule (in mathematical terms, a function) that expresses the total amount of the good that will be purchased in a given time period at each possible price of the good.

Market failure   exists when the market leads to an allocation of resources that is not socially efficient. Socially efficient allocation or optimal allocation is an allocation where there exists no other that could make all the agents in the economy better off (or at least no worse off).

Market share   is the percentage of the total sales of a product, or specified group of products, that is accounted for by a particular firm.

Marketing synergy   refers to cases where the total cost of marketing a group of products or services is lower when they are combined rather than marketed separately. Examples (in our context) include combining the marketing of different types of software within one firm (e.g., customized and *bundled software*) or marketing both open source and proprietary software of a given type.

Microsoft Word   is Microsoft's word processing software, first released in 1983. There currently exist both a Microsoft Word and a Mac OS X version.

Minix   is a *UNIX*-like open source *operating system*, created by Professor Andrew Tanenbaum, of Vrije Universiteit in Amsterdam, as an educational tool in 1987. Its design inspired the design of Linux.

Mozilla Firefox   is an open source Web browser that has been developed since 2004 by the Mozilla Corporation. It find its origins in the *Netscape* browser, which itself begun life as MOSAIC in 1994. It is the second most popular browser in terms of current use worldwide, after Microsoft's Internet Explorer, with a market share estimated between 20 and 25 percent.

Mozilla Public License (MPL)   is an open source software license, similar to the GPL license in that modifications of the code must be distributed under the MPL license, but allowing for the creation of software that mixes code covered by the license and code that is not.

Multivariate regression analysis   refers to any econometric technique that studies how an outcome variable is simultaneously affected by more than one explanatory variable. Such techniques are designed to isolate the separate effects of each explanatory factor.

MySQL   is a widely used open source database management software that was first released in 1996. It is owned and developed by the Swedish company MySQL, which was purchased by Sun Microsystems in 2008. (In January 2010, Oracle finalized the acquisition of Sun.)

Nash equilibrium   is the outcome of a game in which every player chooses an action or *strategy* that makes him or her as well off as possible given the strategies of the other players.

Nash strategy   is the action (more precisely, an action conditional on the actions of others) that maximizes the benefit to the player.

Netscape Communications was a US computer company, founded in 1994. Its main product was the Netscape browser, which was the dominant Web browser for a few years. After its fortunes declined, it transferred the source code of its browser to the Open Source project *Mozilla* in 1998 and in the same year was acquired by AOL.

Network effect (externality) refers to cases where the value of the good for an individual user is larger when there are more consumers of the good. These often occur when connectivity is an important characteristic of usage, as in computer software or telephone networks.

Null hypothesis is a term used in statistics and *econometrics* to describe the hypothesis of interest that is to be tested against the available data.

Object code is a sequence of instructions that a computer can understand but that is difficult for a human to read or modify. It is generally obtained by compiling *source code*.

Object-oriented programming (OOP) is a paradigm that sees a program as organized around "objects," which are individual entities that interact with each other to carry out a task. It has become the dominant programming paradigm since the 1990s.

Office suite is a collection of programs, such as a Word processor or a spreadsheet program for use by clerical and knowledge workers, that are distributed together, have a consistent user interface, and can interact with each other. By far the most widespread Office suite is Microsoft Office.

OpenOffice.org (OOo) Writer is an open source word processing program, and a component of the OpenOffice.org software package. It can be used on a large variety of platforms, including Mac OS X, Microsoft Windows, and Linux. It has been an *open source software* since 2000 and is a "descendant" of the proprietary Star Writer program.

Open source software is computer software that is distributed with its source code and that permits users to change the software and to redistribute it in modified or unmodified forms, subject to a variety of license terms.

Operating system is the program that handles the operation of the hardware in a computer, acts as an interface between the hardware and applications, and performs a wide variety of other services depending on the operating system. Microsoft Windows and Linux are two leading examples.

Opportunity cost of using a resource for a specific purpose is the value that it would have generated in the next best alternative use. It is the core concept of 'cost' in economics, and does not depend on that resource having any explicit price.

Outlier is an observation that "does not fit" with the rest of the data. This can be due to chance but is often indicative of measurement or reporting error.

Patent thicket refers to an overlapping set of patent rights that requires those who seek to commercialize a new technology using the patented inputs to obtain licenses from multiple patentees. The expression is usually used to highlight the density of patent rights and the potentially onerous nature of obtaining the proper licenses.

Permissive license is an open source software license that puts few restrictions on the reuse of the software, in particular as part of proprietary software.

Personal computer (PC) is any computer whose size, capabilities, and price make it suitable for individuals, whether in a private or work setting.

Personal digital assistant (PDA)   is any small mobile handheld device that provides services such as calendars and task management for personal or business use. Many personal digital assistants, such as the iPhone, are also mobile phones, and referred to as *smart phones.*

PHP   is a programming language that is very widely used in the production of dynamic Web pages, that is Web pages that are created "on the fly" when requested by a user. It was first developed in 1995 by then IT consultant Rasmus Ledford.

Physical capital   refers to the inputs used in production (or consumption) that yield productive services over an extended period of time. Such capital can be either produced (as with machines or houses) or given by nature (as with land or other natural resources).

PLUS (Professional Liability Underwriting Society)   defines itself as "a nonprofit organization established in 1986 to support and enrich the careers of people involved in the field of professional liability underwriting."

Point-to-Point Protocol (PPP)   is a protocol used by devices, such as telephones, to establish a connection before communicating.

Post Office Protocol (POP)   is an Internet standard protocol used by local email clients (e.g., Outlook) to retrieve email of which they are the recipient from a server, of which the email is stored while waiting to be delivered.

Programming tool   is any program or application used by programmers in the development of new software code.

Proprietary software   refers to any software developed by a firm or individual who maintains property rights over it. Such software can be distributed under any form of license chosen by the owner.

Public domain software   refers to software that is not protected by either copyright or patents, and thus can be used, copied, and changed without restriction by any party. In some cases the name of the software is copyrighted, and any modified version can only be distributed under a different name.

RAND   is an abbreviation for Reasonable and Nondiscriminatory, a phrase used to describe intellectual property licensing terms where the price is "reasonable" and the same for all licensees.

Regression analysis   is an alternative way to refer to a *multivariate regression analysis.*

SCO Group, Inc.   is a software company better known in recent years for claiming that Linux contained code on which it had intellectual property rights, filing suit against IBM for $1 billion, and demanding that end-users of *Linux* pay license fees.

Sendmail   is an open source application used for sending email, first developed by Eric Allman in the beginning of the 1980s. It provides services such as authentication of sender, queuing mails that cannot be delivered, or fighting the transfer of spam through an organization server. A commercial company called *SendMail, Inc.* sells hardware and applications to help large firms and governments manage their email infrastructure.

Server   generally refers to a computer that provides services, such as storing files or information, to other computers. It can also refer to a computer that is concurrently providing services to several end-users.

Shareware   refers to proprietary software that can be acquired without paying, for a limited period of time on a trial basis.

Simple Mail Transfer Protocol (SMTP)   is an Internet standard for communications between email sending software (e.g., Outlook) and SMTP servers (whose job is to make the emails available to their recipients).

Smart phone   is a mobile phone offering advanced capabilities, often also acting like a *PDA*.

Software bug   is an error in a computer program.

Software kernel   is the central and most basic component of computer operating systems. Its main responsibilities are to provide to the rest of the operating system and applications access to the hardware, especially to memory, processors, and input/output devices.

Source code   is a sequence of instructions written in a programming language so that it can be understood by humans (as opposed to computers) and be directly modified. It must be *compiled* into *object code* to be understood by a computer.

SourceForge   is the largest single Internet site that provides resources for the management of open source projects and the coordination of the effort of the developers.

Stackelberg leadership model   is a game in which (1) a "leader" chooses its action first so as to maximize its benefit given the (subsequent) *Nash strategy* of the other players, and (2) the other players choose their (Nash) actions after observing the action of the leader.

Standards Setting Organizations (SSOs)   are the groups that define standards. The members of SSOs are generally interested industry players.

Subsidy   is any financial assistance given to a business or individual, typically by a government for some specific purpose or action.

Sunk cost   is any business expense that cannot be retrieved if the activity for which it is used is shut down.

SUSE Linux Enterprise Desktop (SLED)   is a Linux distribution targeted at the business market. It has been distributed since the mid-1990s by the German company SUSE, which was purchased by Novell in 1994.

Switching costs   refer to any cost incurred by a customer who changes its purchase from one product to another. In the software context, these typically involve learning and adaptation costs, and exist even if the two products are functionally equivalent.

Synergy   refers to any opportunity for advantageous (cost-reducing or profit-enhancing) cooperation between different entities. Examples include production or marketing cost synergies where different activities are done together at lower total cost than if done separately (also known as *economies of scope*).

System software   is software used to control computers and provide tools for applications. It includes *operating* systems but also such programs as *device drivers* and *compilers*.

Third-degree price discrimination   is the practice of offering different prices for the same good or service to consumers in different locations or with different characteristics. An example would be senior discount in movie theaters. This is different from first-degree price discrimination where the seller can offer a different price for each consumer.

Total cost of ownership or operation (TCO)   is a measure of the total cost of owning and operating a piece of software (in our context), including both the initial monetary cost of purchasing it and any associated costs of implementing it.

Tradable good is any product or service that can be sold in another location distinct from where it was produced (even if the transportation costs are high). Many services are nontradable, including person-to-person software support services.

Transaction cost is any cost associated with the process of market or nonmarket exchange, as distinct from the cost of production. Leading examples include the time and money cost of bargaining and licensing.

Transistor is a semiconductor device that is the building block of electronic devices. An *integrated circuit* can contain billions of transistors. Modern development of the transistor started in 1947 at Bell Labs.

Transmission Control Protocol (TCP) is one of the core protocols of the Internet. It describes the way in which an originating computer and a receiving computer should communicate to manage the flow of information between them. An example is the description of the methods by which the receiving computer can check if there is lost data and how it can ask that it be resent.

t-**Test** is a statistical test usually used to determine whether a parameter is equal to a specified value (e.g., zero).

Unbundled software is software that is not *bundled*.

Uniform distribution is a probability distribution defined over a bounded interval such that the probability of every event in that interval is the same.

UNIX is an operating system written at Bell Labs in 1969 by Ken Thomson and Dennis Ritchie. It was designed from the start to be portable, and to allow for many users. There are many versions of UNIX available, used mostly in *servers* and workstations.

Usenet is an Internet discussion system, first established in 1980, that allows groups of users to exchange news and opinions.

User interface (UI) is the elements included in a computer or other device (e.g., cell phone) with which people interact, including the display screen, keyboard, and mouse.

User-written software is software written by end-users to meet their specific needs, for instance, spreadsheet templates, word processor macros, or scripts for animation.

Utility is a small program designed to do a single task that helps manage either the hardware or the software on a computer. Operating systems typically contain many utilities.

Vertical product differentiation refers to cases where different products are perceived by all users as being of different intrinsic quality levels, as opposed to as catering to different tastes. Specifically, it applies when different consumers would rank the goods (or varieties of the same good) the same way if they were sold at the same price (this does not mean that all consumers buy the same product). This would apply to different classes of airline travel, but not to different flavors of ice cream. (See *horizontal product differentiation*.)

Web server is a program that serves as an interface between Web users and websites. It provides tools for websites to respond to Web users who request content. The term can also be used to refer to hardware on which a Web server program is running.

Windowing systems are systems that provide resources for applications that display windows on a computer screen.

Word processor   is a program used for the production (e.g., composition, editing, and formatting) of any sort of textual material.

Workstation   is a powerful computer designed for technical or scientific applications, typically by one user at a time.

Ximian   was an open source company created in 1999 by Miguel de Icaza and Nat Friedman to produce a range of integrated application software for business. It was bought by Novell in 2003.

XML (extensible markup language)   is a standard to describe how information is structured in a document of any type, in a database, in a graphics or audio file, and so on. Its first version was published in 1998, and it has become in very wide use since.

References

Note: All Web files were accessed on September 21, 2009.

Anderson, Ross. 2005. Open and closed systems are equivalent (that is, in an ideal world). In *Perspectives on Free and Open Source Software*. Cambridge: MIT Press, 127–42. http://www.cl.cam.ac.uk/~rja14/Papers/toulousebook.pdf.

Anderson, Ross. 2002. Security in open versus closed systems: The dance of Boltzmann, Coase and Moore. http://www.cl.cam.ac.uk/~rja14/Papers/toulouse.pdf.

Arrow, Kenneth. 1962. Economic welfare and the allocation of resources for invention. In Richard Nelson, ed., *The Rate and Direction of Inventive Activity: Economic and Social Factors*. Princeton: Princeton University Press for National Bureau of Economic Research, 609–26.

Bartel, Ann, Casey Ichniowski, and Kathryn Shaw. 2007. How does information technology affect productivity? Plant-level comparisons of product innovation, process improvement, and worker skills. *Quarterly Journal of Economics* 122: 1721–58.

Belenzon, Sharon, and Mark Schankerman. 2008. Motivation and sorting in open source software innovation. *Centre for Economic Policy Research*. Discussion paper 7012.

Bessen, James E., and Robert M. Hunt. 2003. An empirical look at software patents. SSRN working paper. http://ssrn.com/abstract=461701.

Boston Consulting Group. 2003. Boston Consulting Group/OSDN Hacker Survey. http://www.linuxtoday.com/news_story.php3?ltsn=2002-02-01-013-26-PR-DV.

Bok, Derek. 2003. *Universities in the Marketplace: The Commercialization of Higher Education*. Princeton: Princeton University Press.

Bloom, Nicholas, Luis Garicano, Raffaella Sadun, and John Van Reenen. 2009. The distinct effects of information technology and communication technology on firm organization. NBER working paper 14975. http://www.nber.org/papers/w14975.

Bresnahan, Timothy, Erik Brynjolfsson, and Lorin Hitt. 2002. Information technology, workplace organization, and the demand for skilled labor: Firm-level evidence. *Quarterly Journal of Economics* 117: 339–76.

Caillaud, Bernard. 2003. La propriété intellectuelle sur les logiciels. *Propriété Intellectuelle*. Conseil D'Analyse Economique, Rapport 41: 113–71.

Caillerez, Pascal. 2005. Administration centrale: 225 chantiers ouverts. http://www.01net.com/editorial/263192/e-administration/administration-centrale-225-chantiers-ouverts/.

Camara, Gilberto, et al. 2008. TerraLib: An open source GIS library for large-scale environmental and socio-economic applications. In Brent Hall and Michael Leahy, eds., *Open Source Approaches in Spatial Data Handling*. Berlin: Springer, 247–70. http://www.terralib .org/docs/papers/TerraLib-OSBook-versionJanuary2008.pdf.

Camara, Gilberto, and Frederico Fonseca. 2007. Information policies and open source software in developing countries. *Journal of the American Society for Information Science and Technology* 58: 121–32.

Campbell-Kelly, M., and Daniel Garcia-Swartz. 2008. Pragmatism not ideology: IBM's love affair with open source software. SSRN working paper. http://ssrn.com/abstract =1081613.

Cannon, Carl. 2001. Letter from Washington: The bill comes due. *Forbes ASAP*, September 1.

Chen, Jiawei, Ulrich Doraszelski, and Joseph Harrington. 2009. Avoiding market dominance: Product compatibility in markets with network effects. *Rand Journal of Economics* 49: 455–85.

Chesbrough, Henry, Wim Vanhaverbeke, and Joel West, eds. 2006. *Open Innovation: Researching a New Paradigm*. Oxford: Oxford University Press.

CNET Asia. 2006. Indonesian government launches IGOS release 3. http://www.asia .cnet.com/reviews/blog/toekongit/0,39056105,61962859,00.htm.

Comino, Stefano, and Fabio Manenti. 2005. Government policies supporting open source software for the mass market. *Review of Industrial Organization* 26: 217–40.

Desphande, Amit, and Dirk Riehle. 2008. The total growth of open source. In Barbara Russo, Ernesto Damiani, Scott Hissam, Bjorn Lundell, and Giancarlo Succi, eds., In *Proceedings of the Fourth Conference on Open Source Systems*. New York: Springer Verlag/IFIP International Federation for Information Processing, 197–209.

Dessein, Wouter. 2005. Information and control in ventures and alliances. *Journal of Finance* 60: 2513–50.

Evans, Karen, and Robert Burton. 2004. Software acquisition. http://www.whitehouse .gov/omb/memoranda_fy04_m04-16/.

Farrell, Joseph, and Carl Shapiro. 2008. How strong are weak patents? *American Economic Review* 98: 1347–69.

Gaudeul, Alexandre. 2003. The (La)TeX project: A case study of open-source software. http://www.tug.org/TUGboat/Articles/tb24-1/gaudeul.pdf.

Ghosh, Rishib. 1999. Cooking pot markets: An economic model for the trade in free goods and services on the Internet. http://dxm.org/fm/cookingpot/.

Graham, Stuart, and David Mowery. 2003. Intellectual property protection in the software industry. In Wesley Cohen and Steven Merrill, eds., *Patents in the Knowledge-Based Economy: Proceedings of the Science, Technology and Economic Policy Board*. Washington: National Academies Press.

Gutierrez, Horacio. 2009. Collaboration, competition and IP in the real world. http://microsoftontheissues.com/cs/blogs/mscorp/archive/2009/07/22/collaboration -competition-and-ip-in-the-real-world.aspx.

Gutsche, Joerg. 2005. Competition between open source and proprietary software, and the scope for public policy. In Marco Scotto and Giancarlo Succi, eds., *Proceedings of the First International Conference on Open Source Systems*, 196–99. http://oss2005.case.unibz .it/Papers/1.pdf.

Hahn, Robert, and Scott Wallsten. 2003. A review of Bessen and Hunt's "Analysis of Software Patents." Unpublished working paper. American Enterprise Institute–Brookings Joint Center for Regulatory Studies, Washington, DC.

Hahn, Robert. 2002. Government policy toward open source software. Unpublished working paper. American Enterprise Institute–Brookings Joint Center for Regulatory Studies, Washington, DC.

Hammerly, Jim, Tom Paquin, and Susan Walton. 1999. Freeing the source: The story of Mozilla. In Chris DiBona, Sam Ockman, and Mark Stone, eds., *Open Sources: Voices from the Open Source Revolution*. Cambridge, MA: O'Reilly, 197–206.

Hann, Il-Horn, Jeff Roberts, Sandra Slaughter, and Roy Fielding. 2004. An empirical analysis of economic returns to open source participation. Unpublished working paper. Carnegie-Mellon University.

Haruvy, Ernan E., Fang Wu, and Sujoy Chakravarty. 2003. Incentives for developers' contributions and product performance metrics in open source development: An empirical investigation. Unpublished working paper. University of Texas at Dallas.

Heller, Michael, and Rebecca Eisenberg. 1998. Can patents deter innovation? The anticommons in biomedical research. *Science* 280: 698–701.

Jaffe, Adam, and Josh Lerner. 2001. Reinventing public R&D: Patent law and technology transfer from federal laboratories. *Rand Journal of Economics* 32: 167–98.

Jaffe, Adam, and Josh Lerner. 2007. *Innovation and Its Discontents: How Our Broken Patent System Is Endangering Innovation and Progress, and What to Do about It*. Princeton: Princeton University Press. Paperback edition.

Jorgenson, Dale, and Kevin Stiroh. 2000. U.S. economic growth at the industry level. *American Economic Review* 90: 161–67.

Jorgenson, Dale, Mun Ho, and Kevin Stiroh. 2008. A retrospective look at the U.S. productivity growth resurgence. *Journal of Economic Perspectives* 22: 3–24.

Kingston, Steve. 2005. Brazil adopts open-source software. BBC News. http://www.news .bbc.co. uk/2/hi/business/4602325.stm.

Kirkpatrick, David, and Christopher Tkaczyk. 2004. Inside Sam's $100 billion growth machine. Sam Palmisano has two huge goals: to get this giant growing again and return IBM to greatness. *Fortune*, June 14: 80–96.

Knuth, Donald. 1984. *The TeXbook*. Reading, MA: Addison Wesley.

Krishnamurthy, Sandeep. 2009. CASE: Mozilla vs. Godzilla: The launch of the Mozilla Firefox Browser. *Journal of Interactive Marketing*. http://faculty.washington.edu/sandeep/ d/firefoxjim.pdf.

Kroes, Neelie. 2008. Being open about standards. OpenForum Europe–Breakfast seminar. http://europa.eu/rapid/pressReleasesAction.do?reference=SPEECH/08/317.

Kuan, Jennifer. 2001. Open software as consumer integration in production. Haas Business School, University of California at Berkeley. http://papers.ssrn.com/sol3/papers .cfm?abstract_id=259648.

Kumar, Shalabh. 2003. How sustainable is the cost advantage of offshore outsourcing? http://www.nasscom.org/download/Cost_Advantage.pdf.

Lach, Saul, and Mark Schankerman. 2008. Incentives and invention in universities. *Rand Journal of Economics* 39 (2): 403–33.

Lakhani, Karim, and Eric von Hippel. 2003. How open source software works: "Free" user-to-user assistance. *Research Policy* 32: 923–43.

Lambardi, German. 2009. Software innovation and the OS threat. Unpublished working paper. Toulouse School of Economics.

Lerner, Josh, and Kerry Herman. 2005. South Africa and FOSS: A mixed environment. Global Open Source and Economic Development Study. Unpublished working paper. Harvard University.

Lerner, Josh, and Jean Tirole. 2002. Some simple economics of open source. *Journal of Industrial Economics* 50: 197–234.

Lerner, Josh, and Jean Tirole. 2005. The scope of open source licensing. *Journal of Law, Economics, and Organization* 21: 20–56.

Lewis, James Andrew. 2008. Government open source policies. Center for Strategic and International Studies. http://csis.org/publication/government-open-source-policies.

Lyons, Daniel. 2005. Has open source become a marketing slogan? *Forbes.* http://www .forbes.com/technology/2005/08/26/open-linux-proprietarycz_dl_0826open.html.

Mackenzie, Kate. 2009. Steven Chu: Open source software can reduce need for coal plants. http://blogs.ft.com/energy-source/2009/05/28/stephen-chu-open-source-software-can-reduce-need-for-coal-plants/.

Marson, Ingrid. 2005a. Brazil to mandate open source use. ZDNet UK. http://www.news .Zdnet.co.uk/software/1,1000000121,39196592,00.html.

Marson, Ingrid. 2005b. Linux Thais up more support. ZDNet UK. http://news.Zdnet .co.uk/software/linuxunix/0,39020390,39187561,00.htm.

Murray, Fiona, and Scott Stern. 2007. Do formal intellectual property rights hinder the free flow of scientific knowledge? *Journal of Economic Behavior and Organization* 63 (4): 648–87.

Nadeau, Tom. 1999. Learning from Linux. http://www.os2hq.com/archives/linmemo1 .html.

Noel, Michael, and Mark Schankerman. 2006. Strategic patenting and software innovation. Discussion paper 5701. Centre for Economic Policy Research, London.

Obsanjo, Dare. 2002. The myth of open source security revisited. http://www.developer .com/open/article.php/983621.

Raymond, Eric. 1999. The magic cauldron. http://www.linuxtoday.com/news_story .php3?ltsn=1999-06-24-004-05-NW-CY.

Roberts, Mark, and James Tybout. 1997. The decision to export in Colombia: An empirical model of entry with sunk costs. *American Economic Review* 87(4): 545–64.

Saint-Paul, Gilles. 2001. Growth effects of non-proprietary innovation. Discussion paper 3069. Centre for Economic Policy Research, London.

Schmidt, Klaus M., and Monika Schnitzer. 2003. Public subsidies for open source? Some economic policy issues of the software market. *Harvard Journal of Law and Technology* 16: 473–505. http://opensource.mit.edu/papers/schmidtschnitzer.pdf.

Schwarz, Michael, and Yuri Takhteyev. 2008. Half a century of public software institutions: Open source as a solution to hold up problems. Unpublished working paper. http://www.takhteyev.org/papers/Schwarz-Takhteyev-2008.pdf.

Shankland, Stephen. 2002. IBM: Linux investment nearly recouped. http://news.cnet .com/IBM-Linux-investment-nearly-recouped/2100-1001_3-825723.html.

Shankland, Stephen. 2005. Programmers bypass Red Hat Linux fees. http://news.zdnet .com/2100-3513_22-141969.html.

Shapiro, Carl, and Hal Varian. 1998. *Information Rules.* Cambridge: Harvard Business School Press.

Shapiro, Carl, and Hal Varian. 2004. Linux adoption in the public sector: An economic analysis. Unpublished working paper. University of California. http://www.sims .berkeley.edu/~hal/Papers/2004/linux-adoption-in-the-public-sector.pdf.

Solow, Robert. 1987. We'd better watch out. *New York Review of Books,* July 12: 16.

Steinmeier, Frank-Walter. 2009. About Linux. http://www.linuxtag.org/2009/en/about/ schirmherrschaft.html.

Thursby, Jerry, and Marie Thursby. 2003. Has licensing changed academic research? Issues of productivity, faculty incentives, and public policy. Unpublished working paper. Emory University and Georgia Institute of Technology.

Torvalds, Linus. 1999. Interview with Linus Torvalds: What motivates free software developers? http://firstmonday.org/issues/issue3_3/torvalds/index.html.

Tirole, Jean. 1988. *The Theory of Industrial Organization.* Cambridge: MIT Press.

UNCTAD. 2003. E-commerce and development report 2003, ch. 4, p. 116. http://www .unctad.org/en/docs//ecdr2003Ch4_en.pdf.

Viega, John. 2000. The myth of open source security. http://www.developer.com/tech/ article.php/626641.

Von Hippel, Eric, and Georg von Krough. 2003. Open source software and the private-collective innovation model: Issues for organizational science. *Organization Science* 14 (2): 209–23.

Wheeler, David. 2006. Open standards, open source. http://www.dwheeler.com/essays/ openstandards-open-source.html.

Wheeler, David. 2008. Is OpenDocument an open standard? Yes! http://www.dwheeler .com/essays/opendocument-open.html.

Wong, Kenneth. 2004. Free/open source software: Government policy. http://www.iosn
.net/government/foss-government-primer/foss-govt-policy.pdf.

Yarney, John. 2003. South Africa, Nigeria move on Linux adoption. InfoWorld, http://
www.infoworld.com/article/03/07/08/HNafrolinux_1.html.

Yuhanna, Noel, Mike Gilpin, and Catherine Salzinger. 2008. Open source databases remain a viable choice for business applications. Forrester Research. http://www.forrester
.com/Research/Document/Excerpt/0,7211,46061,00.html.

Index

THE CONSUMER'S
GOOD CHEMICAL GUIDE

THE CONSUMER'S GOOD CHEMICAL GUIDE

A jargon-free guide to the chemicals of everyday life

JOHN EMSLEY

Science Writer in Residence
Imperial College of Science, Technology & Medicine, London

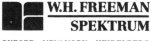

W.H. FREEMAN
SPEKTRUM

OXFORD · NEW YORK · HEIDELBERG

W.H. Freeman and Company Limited
20 Beaumont Street, Oxford, OX1 2NQ
41 Madison Avenue, New York, NY 10010

British Library Cataloguing-in-Publication Data
A catalogue record for this book is available from the British Library.

Library of Congress Cataloging-in-Publication Data

Emsley, John.
The consumer's good chemical guide; a jargon-free guide to
the chemicals of everyday life / by John Emsley.
p. cm.
Includes bibliographical references and index.
ISBN 0-7167-4505-4:
1. Toxicology—Popular works, 2. Medical misconceptions.
I. Title.
RA1213.E47 1994   615.9—dc20   94—8286   CIP

Set by KEYWORD Publishing Services, London
Printed by The Maple-Vail Book Manufacturing Group

ACKNOWLEDGEMENTS

There are many people who helped me with information and advice during the writing of this book, and to whom I am most grateful. They are Dr Tom Addiscott, Dr John Baldwin, Dr Ian Campbell, Dr Dick Challand, Dr Bernard Dixon, Dr Peter Fell, Dr Keith Goulding, Dr Christopher Kenyon, Dr Robyn Marsack, Dr Gregory Place, Dr Ray Richards, Mr John Russell, Dr Marshall Smalley and Dr Charles Sell. For any scientific errors that still remain I take full responsibility.

My thanks also to those who helped me with their encouragement and support: my wife Joan; my children Julian and Helen; and my friends Tom Wilkie, Steven and Rosemary Ley, and Marcus and Karen Chown.

Last but not least I should like to thank my publisher Michael Rodgers, and editor Jane Gregory.

CONTENTS

INTRODUCTION

The Consumer's Good Chemical Guide is mainly a book about chemicals that are popularly regarded as anything but good; indeed many people think most of them should be banned. If you are of that opinion I hope I can persuade you to change your mind. In this book I will discuss some of the chemicals which I believe cause a lot of unnecessary alarm, but which no longer deserve to be thought of as dangerous. Many chemicals seem to come into this category, but I have chosen to discuss those which I feel cause most worry. There may be some chemicals that you are worried about which are missing from this book, but they may well be missing because they really are dangerous, like CFCs, lead or radon.

Those chemicals I have chosen to cover are those which I feel have been particularly subjected to a lot of misinformation. Sugar, artificial sweeteners, painkillers, cholesterol, animal fats, PVC, dioxins, nitrates and carbon dioxide come into this category. I have also put in two chapters on things which are entirely chemical, but you probably never think of them as such: perfume and alcohol. In the perfume chapter I will show you how my fellow chemists are trying to make the world a better place, and at the same time saving wildlife. In the chapter on alcohol I will show how a little understanding of the chemistry of this chemical can improve the quality of your life, and maybe even prolong it.

Although this book is all about chemicals, I have tried to keep it free of chemical jargon and chemical formulas. However, for those readers who want to know more about the chemistry of the materials involved, there is an appendix at the end where you can find this information.

To a large measure almost all the positive associations of the word 'chemical' have now been lost under a barrage of bad publicity, and it is increasingly difficult even for a scientist to use the word in a neutral way, simply to mean a chemical element or chemical compound. Many readers will know that to describe a product as 'free of chemicals' in meaningless, but many people take these words to mean 'free of additives'. Where possible I will try and use less emotive words like substance, compound or molecule. Yet the negative implications of 'chemical' are difficult to shake off, and phrases like 'chemical disaster' and 'chemical warfare' only serve to reinforce its poor image. Even the words 'chemical industry' now seem menacing to some people, and you may think that they deserve to be thought of in this way because of the dreadful mistakes the chemical industry has made in the past.

If we go along with the current climate of opinion, and disapprove of all things 'chemical' and blame chemists for the ills of the world, then we are in danger of undermining an area of science that can solve many of the problems we face: finding cures for cancer, Alzheimer's and AIDS; developing renewable sources of energy; replacing depleted natural resources of fossil fuels and minerals; and even lifting the threat of pollution, most of which, you may be surprised to learn, is not caused by the chemicals industry.

Here, then, is my guidebook to some parts of chemistry that impinge on all our lives. You may find some of it rather surprising, and I hope that it will change the way you see substances that are often branded as 'chemicals'. At the end of the book is a Bibliography which suggests other books that you might want to consult for further reading, and lists the sources that I have consulted during the writing of *The Consumer's Good Chemical Guide*.

Weights, volumes, areas, temperature and energy

The measurements for these quantities in *The Consumer's Good Chemical Guide* are in the metric system, which is standard throughout Europe and Australia, mainly used in the UK, but little used in North America. For the non-scientist the relative quantities may be unfamiliar. Here are the more commonly used measurements.

Weights
A tonne is 1000 kilograms (kg); a kilogram is 1000 grams (g); a gram is 1000 milligrams (mg); and a microgram is one millionth of a gram.
An Imperial ton of 2240 pounds equals 1016 kg, while a US ton of 2000 pounds equals 907 kg.
An ounce is 28 g, and a pound is 453 g. A milligram is 0.000035 ounce.

Volumes
A cubic metre (m^3) is 1000 litres (l); a litre is 1000 millilitres (ml).
The Imperial pint is equal to 568 ml, while a US pint is 473 ml.
An Imperial gallon equals 4.55 l, while a US gallon equals 3.79 l.
A cubic yard equals 0.765 m^3.

Lengths and areas
A kilometre (km) is 1000 metres (m); a metre is 100 centimetres (cm) or 1000 millimetres (mm). A hectare is 100 metres square, i.e. 10 000 m^2.
A foot equals 30.5 cm; a yard equals 0.914 m.
An acre equals 0.404 hectare.

Temperature
On the Celsius scale (°C) water freezes at 0 °C and boils at 100 °C. Body heat is 37 °C.
On the Fahrenheit scale (°F) water freezes at 32°F and boils at 212°F. Body heat is 98.6°F.

Energy
A calorie is the energy required to raise the temperature of one gram of water by one degree Celsius. A Calorie is 1000 calories, and this is the commonly used unit of energy when talking about food. It is more correctly referred to as a kilocalorie (kcal).

CHAPTER ONE

Perfume

Chanel N° 5; the chemistry of smell; making fragrant molecules; human scents; aphrodisiacs; aromatherapy

MOST of this book is about chemicals that are commonly regarded as threatening. I hope I will be able to persuade you that some of them are not—that they are good rather than bad. But to begin with I want to talk about a group of chemicals towards which you may already have very positive feelings: the fragrance chemicals. Indeed, you may not even think of them as chemicals at all; nevertheless, they are just as chemical as the other materials I will be dealing with in later chapters. Not only do fragrance chemicals give a great deal of innocent pleasure, but their synthetic versions have even been responsible for reducing the large-scale slaughter of some equally innocent animals.

The fragrances in a bottle of perfume are just chemicals with attractive aromas. Some may have originally come from exotic tropical plants, and some from exotic wild animals, but today most of them come from the mundane world of the chemistry laboratory. Perhaps we expect the fragrances that we encounter in detergents, fabric softeners and toilet cleaners to be produced by chemists, since these are merely added to mask the smell of soap or detergent. Similarly you might not be surprised to discover that cleaning aids and air fresheners for use in kitchens, living rooms and bathrooms use equally synthetic chemicals. But as far as the chemist is concerned, there is no difference between their use in such everyday products and their use in expensive perfumes.

Nevertheless, there is a difference. The melodies of the fabric softener and the air freshener are the pop songs of fragrance chemistry, whereas the symphonies of perfume are a much richer harmony, among which there may even be a few discordant notes, deliberately introduced to contrast with the harmonic ones. This is certainly true of even the world's most famous perfume, *Chanel N° 5*.

Chanel N° 5

The screen icon Marilyn Monroe was once asked what she wore in bed, and she scandalised cinema audiences in the 1950s by replying: "Only *Chanel N° 5*". When she made that remark, the perfume she referred to had been on the market for 30 years, and 40 years later it is still selling well. In the 1990s it now has to compete with over 400 other perfumes for women, and every year there are more and more of them. *Chanel N° 5* has a special place in the history of chemistry, because it made a synthetic ingredient acceptable for the first time, although most of its components were still derived from natural products. It was launched in 1921 by the Paris designer Gabrielle 'Coco' Chanel, and was created for her by Ernest Beaux to complement her collection of clothes, whose themes were elegance and simplicity. Even the bottle she chose for *Chanel N° 5* was part of this image. Little did she realise that she had launched a perfume that would immortalise her name.

Chanel N° 5 was a landmark in fragrance chemistry for two reasons. Firstly Ernest Beaux, *le grand nez*[1] who 'composed' it, chose an oil derived from the flowers of the ylang-ylang tree which grows in Philippines, to provide the middle note of the perfume. Secondly he used a purely artificial fragrance material, called **2-methylundecanal**,[2] for the top note. This compound is one of a class of molecules

---

[1] *Le grand nez* literally means 'the big nose' and refers to those men and women who design a new perfume.

[2] Where the name of a substance is given in **bold** type, it means that there is more information about its chemistry in the Appendix.

called aldehydes, which generally have a pleasant smell, and several are now used to provide the top notes of perfumes.

The top note is the most volatile part of a perfume, and the one we detect first. The middle notes take a little longer to register, and these are often derived from flowers that give off a heavy, almost over-powering aroma, such as jasmin, tuberose, lily of the valley, lilac, carnation, rose and ylang-ylang. The base notes of a perfume are the least volatile—we may not even notice them to begin with—and yet they are the most tantalising and the most erotic. The base note is there to stir emotions and suggest experiences such as the mysterious East, a wood at night, and sexual encounters. Base notes smell of rare woods, damp earth, oriental spices, moss, and leather. The base notes also carry the most intimate messages of a perfume, and they even hint of baser smells such as sweat, urine and excrement. Base notes also serve an important chemical function in 'fixing' the top and middle notes by slowing their evaporation, so that together they give a more balanced fragrance over the lifetime of the perfume.

In a mixture of molecules the most volatile tend to evaporate first and the least volatile last. The wearer of the perfume wants a blend of top, middle and low notes to be released steadily and in the same proportions, otherwise their scent would change over the course of the day. The skill of the perfumers is to use the laws of chemistry to achieve this, and it can be done by carefully choosing base notes that will delay evaporation of the top notes. This is possible thanks to a curious chemical property of certain mixtures of liquids in which, given the right formulation, the volatility of each component changes so that they evaporate together and in a constant ratio.

The secret of *Chanel N° 5* is not only its chemical components but also the proportions in which these are blended. The ingredients are listed overleaf, and their relative proportions are known, but before modern methods of analysis came into use the original formula of Ernest Beaux was a trade secret.

The chemistry of smell

It is perfectly natural to want to attract other people, whether to enjoy an interesting or intimate conversation with them, or maybe to flirt.

The fragrances which make up *Chanel N° 5*

Top notes   *major:* aldehyde
                   minor: bergamot (a citrus fruit), lemon, and neroli.
                             Neroli oil comes from the bitter orange tree which grows mainly in
                             North Africa. It has a spicy, bitter-sweet odour.

Middle notes   *major:* ylang-ylang
                   minor: jasmin, rose, lily of the valley, and orris.
                             Orris oil comes from the root of the iris pallida, which grows around
                             Florence in Italy. It has a warm-woody, violet-like smell.

Base notes   *major:* vetiver
                   minor: sandalwood, cedarwood, vanilla, amber, civet and musk.
                             Vetiver oil is extracted from a tropical grass and has a heavy smell
                             of earth and wood. Natural civet and musk are strong-smelling
                             secretions of animals and smell of urine and dung, but their
                             synthetic counterparts smell sweetish. The use of animal products
                             in perfumery is now insignificant.

How do we communicate these desires to those around us? Body language is one way, smell is another. Both rely very much on our 'chemistry', but using the sense of smell is a way of broadcasting this message that is *purely* chemical. The sense of smell is thought to be weak in humans compared to in other animals, and certainly smell is the least understood of the senses. It is known to be a molecular interaction which occurs in our nose. There we have sensors which can briefly trap and examine molecules that are carried on the air we breathe. If they fit the right receptors they will trigger recognition, and this will register in our brain. Clearly there are several types of receptor, and what combinations of these are activated will define the way we perceive a particular smell.

In the upper nasal tract are our olfactory nerves which consist of cilia, tiny hairlike tendrils that are too fine to be seen, but which carry an estimated five million receptor cells in the two square centimetres of the lining of the nose. The cilia are in effect bare nerve endings leading directly to the brain. Molecules are caught briefly by the fluid on the cilia, and in a fraction of a second they can move to a cavity on the surface of the receptor and be registered. How this is done is still not clear.

When they trigger a receptor, it sends its signal to the olfactory part of the brain, which in evolutionary terms is one of the oldest. From this the message passes to other parts of the brain, and in particular to the primitive limbic system which is the controlling point for mood and emotion. Part of the limbic system is the hippocampus, which is particularly important in forming long-term memory. This may explain why smells are sometimes such powerful reminders of events long ago.

Not all molecules that are volatile have a characteristic smell: the most notable exceptions are water and the gases of the air, which our noses have evolved to ignore. It is rarely of evolutionary benefit for living things to expend their energy in making or detecting molecules, unless they serve some purpose such as a sex-attractant or a warning. The smells that humans react to most strongly are those associated with food that is going bad, when invading bacteria give off the molecules **dimethyl sulfide, methyl mercaptan** and **ammonia**. Happily we rarely come across these smells from food, although we may smell them as 'bad breath' caused by bacteria in the mouth. In today's world we are much more likely to encounter fragrances specially designed to please. The addition of such chemicals to ordinary household products is now common practice, and more recently it has become part of the air conditioning of shops and hotel rooms.

When you go into a flower shop, the smell which pervades your nostrils is partly due to the blooms on sale, but also due to a commercial product that simulates how we expect such a shop to smell. High class dress shops use aromas with leathery notes to create an illusion of quality. Dr Alan Hirsch from the Smell and Taste Research Foundation in Chicago observed people shopping for sports shoes, some in a room with no smell and others in a room with a floral smell. He found that there was a marked preference for the shoes in the perfumed room.

The basic smells

By a process of trial and error, fragrance chemists have deduced a few general guidelines about what makes a molecule smell the way it does. As yet there is no exact *science* of smell, but this has not prevented chemists from adopting empirical guidelines and successfully designing hundreds of new fragrant molecules, simply by studying the structures of known examples and then copying them but with slight variations.

All hues and colours can be produced by the combination of three primary colours: red, blue and yellow in the case of paint; red, blue and green in the case of light. Colours are based on activating specific colour detectors at the back of our eyes. Taste too can be reduced to four basic flavours—sweet, sour, bitter and salt—based on four kinds of taste receptors on our tongue. Similarly there have been attempts to define a set of basic smells, and likewise we expect there to be just a few types of receptors on the cilia. The link between smell and chemical makeup is very clear because whole groups of chemically similar molecules have the same kind of smell, and this applies to groups such as alcohols, amines, aldehydes, thiols, acids and esters.

One way of classifying fragrances is according to their traditional sources. The basic categories with the largest number of fragrances notes are:

floral, consisting of oils from flowers like rose, jasmin, lilac, lily of the valley and tuberose;

green, which includes eucalyptus, pine, citrus, lavender, rosemary, camphor and basil;

animal, which consist of musk, civet, ambergris and castoreum;

spicy-wood, with extracts of oak-moss, sandalwood, myrrh, cedar, cinnamon and clove.

An early attempt to define the basic smells of perfumery had as few as five: mint, ether, floral, naphthalic (e.g. mothballs) and anise (e.g. liquorice). A later approach defined seven basic odours: camphor-like (e.g. **camphor** itself), ethereal (e.g. pears), floral (e.g. roses), minty (e.g. peppermint), musky (e.g. musk itself), pungent (e.g. vinegar) and putrid (e.g. rotten eggs).

The most sophisticated system so far devised has 14 groups, and is shown in the illustration opposite which places them in order of volatility: citrus (e.g. lemon), lavender, herbal (e.g. mint), aldehyde, green (e.g. hyacinth), fruit (e.g. peach), floral (e.g. jasmin), spice (e.g. clove), wood (e.g. sandalwood), leather (e.g. birch tar), animal (e.g. civet), musk, amber (e.g. incense) and vanillic (e.g. vanilla itself).

One day, when we know more about the receptors in our cilia, we will be able to classify all molecules according to which receptors they fit. It may also be that a particular molecule will trigger more than one type of receptor. We already know enough about receptors to realise

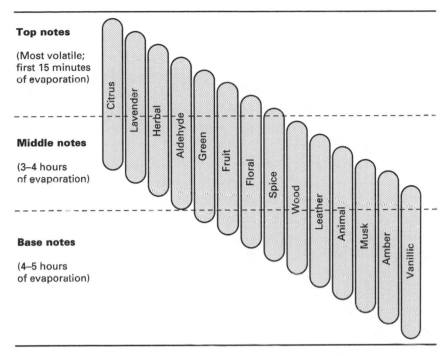

The scale of notes of a perfume. As a perfume evaporates the top notes come off first, and the base notes come off last. The perfume components shown are the 'lignes de force' of the Quest International system of fragrance classification.

that if we want to register an amber smell we need a certain shape of molecule. Chemists can study those which have the desired smell, and then make molecules that are very similar. The method sometimes works, but more often than not it fails to produce just the right fragrance combination. The difficulty with all odours is in separating the basic smell from an individual's reaction to it, which may be rooted in past experiences.

The result of research by fragrance chemists is often a new compound with its own unique aroma and nuances, and in this way they have been able to make smells that have no counterpart in nature. Such synthetic fragrances are now added to products to give them 'April freshness' or a 'summer breeze'. The skill in making these lies not so much in their smell as in their stability. Natural fragrances are complex mixtures and are often not very stable. Synthetic ones are much simpler and much more stable. They can be added to household detergents and fabric softeners because they will survive the chemical reactions of the washing process, and end up clinging to the washed clothes. This is quite a remarkable achievement because laundry products are designed to wash away unwanted materials, and they also contain highly reactive bleaches to destroy odours and stains.

Some of these artificial fragrances also find their way into fine perfumes. The problem then is to keep the price high for one kind of product, the bottle of scent, while taking advantage of its low cost to encourage its use in a large range of everyday consumer products.[3]

The price of a bottle of perfume is partly inflated by expensive packaging and advertising, but mainly determined by the degree of exclusiveness which the perfume house is trying to create for that particular fragrance. Nor should we forget that we are basically dealing with works of art, skilfully blended by a *grand nez*. The price we pay can also be justified if we feel that smelling right is important in our successful dealings with other people, be it in business or in bed. I will return to this latter topic later in this chapter when I look at aphrodisiacs.

The development of perfume

Perfumers can be seen at work on the wall paintings of Egyptian tombs of four thousand years ago, and it was clearly a well established temple industry even then. The name perfume derives from the Latin *per fumum* meaning 'through smoke', because it was common practice to send prayers to heaven by the burning of sweet-smelling incense such as frankincense and myrrh. The Law of Moses has instructions for the preparation of incense that includes myrrh and cedarwood. Incense has been burnt in places of worship for over three thousand years.

---

[3] The promoters of the respective industries have managed this with great dexterity, and there is an amazing difference in selling price between the same molecules in different packages. This is where chemistry gives way to the subtler science of economics.

Perfumes at Christmas

'Entering the house, they saw the child with Mary his mother, and bowed to the ground in homage to him; then they opened their treasures and offered him gifts: gold, frankincense, and myrrh.'

[ST. MATTHEW, CHAPTER 2, VERSE 11].

Perfume is a traditional Christmas gift, and sales of perfumes reach a peak each year in December. Frankincense and myrrh are still used by perfumers: *Timeless* by Avon and *Prélude* by Balenciaga contain frankincense; *Le Jardin* by Max Factor and *Fidji* by Guy Laroche contain myrrh. Frankincense and myrrh are resins that ooze from wounds cut into the bark of certain Middle East trees. They are not single compounds but a collection of many substances. Plants make these chemicals, and others like them such as pine rosin and galbanum, to protect their injuries against the ravages of bacteria and fungi, which would make them rot. This is partly the reason why they made good preservatives for perfumes, and explains why myrrh was also used by embalmers and in mummification.

The word frankincense comes from the Old French *franc encens*, meaning 'pure incense', but it is better known to perfumers as olibanum. It comes from boswellia trees which grow in Somalia and Saudi Arabia. Cutting the trunk of the trees causes a white juice to flow, which hardens on exposure to the air forming tear-like drops up to an inch long. These drops are harvested after 14 days. The oil that is extracted from this resin has a balsam-like, spicy note with hints of lemon.

The word myrrh comes from the Arabic *murr*, meaning bitter, and this material is a red-brown gum which exudes from thorny commiphora trees. It is still harvested in Somalia and some tears of myrrh can weight up to 250 grams (half a pound). It has a pleasant aromatic odour and was used by the ancient world in incenses, perfumes, cosmetics and medicines. It still finds use in some toothpastes, mouthwashes and tonics, and in a few perfumes.

From the fall of Rome in 410 AD until the Renaissance a thousand years later, the art of chemistry was mainly the province of the Arabs and Persians, and so was the art of perfumery. The prophet and founder of Islam, Mohammed, was a believer in the value of perfume as one of his oft-quoted sayings shows: "Three things are dear to me on Earth—women, perfume and prayer." He also made the observant remark: "Perfume is the food that nourishes my thoughts", the truth of which we are now beginning to appreciate.

The perfume industry as we know it developed in the Middle Ages and was centred at Grasse in Provence, Southern France, where the climate and soil were ideal for growing plants such as rose, jasmin, lavender, tuberose and violet, from which the fragrant essences were extracted. The traditional way of extracting oils was to place the flowers between layers of animal fat which absorbed the fragrant oil—a process known as *enfleurage*. This perfumed grease was known as a *concrete* and sometimes used as a haircream, or the fragrance oil was extracted from the fat with alcohol, to give a product known as an *absolute*.

This method was superseded by steam distillation, whereby the plant material was extracted with super-heated steam which carried off the oils. When the steam was condensed the oily layer could then be run off. A later development, introduced about 200 years ago, was solvent extraction, and the fragrance companies of Grasse specialised in this method. It involved the raw plant material being stirred in a volatile solvent, which in the nineteenth century was often **benzene**. Benzene has fallen out of use for of safety reasons, and the solvent is now more likely to be an **alkane**, and even **butane**, which is normally a gas but can be used as a solvent by working with it under pressure. After filtering the extract, the solvent is boiled off to leave behind the fragrance oil. Other solvents which have been used are **methanol**, which is a simple alcohol, and **toluene**, which is a safer alternative to benzene. Recently liquid **carbon dioxide** gas has been used as the extractant (see also Chapter 9).

The table opposite shows where some of the more common fragrances originated. Jasmin absolute is one of the most popular ones, and it has a heady, almost narcotic, smell which is ideal for middle notes of a perfume. The bitter orange tree is a particular source of fragrance oils, yielding orange from the fruit peel, neroli from the flowers and petitgrain from the leaves and twigs. Some of the oils in the table may seem out of place as components of a perfume, but pepper oil, for example, is an extract with an oriental, spicy note that is sometimes added to male fragrances.

Perfume has always been a fit offering for gods, emperors, kings, queens, and courtesans. While it was in short supply its use was

The original sources of essence oils extracted from plants

Plant material	Essence oil extracted
Blossom	rose, jasmin, tuberose
Stems and leaves	geranium, peppermint
Grasses	tarragon, sage, thyme
Roots	orris, angelica
Mosses	oak moss
Wood	sandalwood, rosewood, cedarwood
Needles	spruce, Scotch pine, cypress
Resins	myrrh, olibanum, galbanum*
Seeds	cardamom, pepper
Fruits	anise, nutmeg, coriander
Fruit peel	orange, lemon, bergamot

*Galbanum is one of the eight ingredients which God told Moses to include in incense; it comes from the resin of a Persian tree. It has such a powerful smell that if a single drop were to be dissolved in a swimming pool of water you would still be able to smell it. Its aroma is described as an earthy green pepper smell.

limited to the rich and the rulers, and this remained the case until chemistry came along. An individual plant produces very little fragrance. It takes over five tons of rose blossom to produce a kilogram of rose oil. It takes eight million jasmin blossoms to produce a kilogram of jasmin fragrance. It is not surprising that the price of each of these natural oils is several thousand dollars per kilogram.

In ages past, perfume was costly because it was rare. When Madame de Pompadour (1721–1764), the mistress of King Louis XV of France, spent the equivalent of $250 000 on perfumes, her perfumers had about 200 fragrances to choose from. Today there are over 25 000 fragrances available. Blending them into a commercial product is the art of *le grand nez*, someone who can recognise nearly 2000 different smells. It is not surprising that their skills are compared to those of great artists. A successful composition can earn a fortune.

Masculine and feminine fragrances.*

Perfume has been a part of civilized living for centuries, for both men and women, and there are differences in the fragrances which appeal to the sexes. Here is a list of the various ways into which they are divided, although some are liked by both men and women, such as chypre.

(*continued*)

Masculine and feminine fragrances.* (continued)

The classification is based on the idea that there is an overriding 'concept' which provides the theme to a perfume. The terms are generally self-explanatory, except for *chypre*, which refers to the heady scents associated with the Eastern Mediterranean, and *fougère* which means fern-like. Each 'concept' has several 'interpretations' allowing variations on the basic theme. These 'interpretations' are again self-explanatory, with *green* referring to the odour of fresh grass and leaves, *aldehydic* being the synthetic fragrances based on the chemicals called aldehydes, and *ambery* associated with the heavy and intense smell of blossoms.

Concept	Interpretation	Popular fragrances
Feminine fragrances		
Floral	Green	Chanel N° 19, Calvin Klein
	Fruity	Eau de Givenchy
	Fresh	Anaïs Anaïs, Le Jardin
	Floral	Quelque Fleurs, Fidji, Charlie, Chloé, Giorgio
	Aldehydic	Chanel N° 5, Je Reviens
	Ambery	Blue Grass, Poison, Charles of the Ritz
Oriental	Ambery	Obsession, Samsara, Shalimar
	Spicy	Coco Chanel, Opium, White Diamonds
Chypre	Fruity	Femme
	Floral–Animal	Miss Dior, Intimate, Timeless
	Floral	Ysatis, Ma Griffe
	Fresh	4711
	Green	Armani
Masculine fragrances		
Lavender	Fresh	English Lavender
	Spicy	Acqua di Selva, V by Victor
Fougère	Fresh	Drakkar Noir, Eternity for Men, Jazz
	Floral	Dunhill, Paco Rabanne pour homme
	Woody	Sandalwood, Kouros
	Ambery	Blue Stratos, Brut, Imperial Leather
Oriental	Spicy	Égoïste, Old Spice
	Ambery	Balenciaga pour homme, Relax
Chypre	Woody	Giorgio for men

	Leathery	Macassar, Aramis, Denim
	Conifery	Men
	Fresh	Aqua Velva Ice Blue
	Green	Fahrenheit
Citrus	Floral	Eau Sauvage
	Fantasy	English Leather, Onyx, Tabac Original
	Fresh	Drakkar

*Taken from the system known as the H&R Genealogies as given in *The H&R Book of Perfume* published by Glöss Verlag, Hamburg.

Modern perfumery really began this century, and looking back it is possible to see certain periods that were particularly important. These occurred as we emerged from the two World Wars, when the perfumes appeared which we now regard as landmarks. *Chypre*, launched in 1917, was eventually to give its name to a whole range of perfumes that sought to capture the heady scents of the Eastern Mediterranean. *Chypre* itself was taken off the market after a few years because it was created from components that were too limited in supply, and its manufacturers could not cope with the huge demand it generated. Its top notes were bergamot, lemon, neroli and orange; its middle notes were rose, jasmin, carnation, orris and lilac; and its base notes were oakmoss, patchouli, labdanum, styrax, civet and musk.

The table below gives other key perfumes that were typical of their generation and of which there were to be many copies. Also listed are the main fragrance for the top, middle and base notes, although of course there are several other fragrances present in smaller amounts. Once the success of *Chanel N° 5* was assured then the synthetic fragrance chemicals industry was able to contribute more and more.

Molecules with a wonderful fresh smell, a so-called 'green' note, were discovered by chemists in the 1930s; one such was called leaf alcohol, whose chemical name is **cis-3-hexenol**. This group of chemicals led to *Ma Griffe*, by Carven, introduced in 1944. Soon to follow was *Miss Dior* from Christian Dior, which combined a classic chypre with a green top note. Dior launched it to accompany his New Look fashions in the late 1940s. *L'Air du Temps* was also a success when it was introduced in 1947 by Nina Ricci, and this relied heavily

on synthetic floral fragrances. It was the first 'linear' perfume, in other
words it kept the same smell to the last drop. The perfume which
made the biggest impression at this time was *Femme* by Rochas. Its key
fragrances were peach and plum top notes, a jasmin middle note, and
oakmoss and vanilla as the base notes.

The 1960s saw the introduction of fragrances designed for the
'liberated woman', and these often relied on methyl dihydrojasmo-
nate, the man-made version of jasmin, but with a lighter, fresher
odour. The 1960s also saw the launching of *Brut* by Fabergé, the
first successful male fragrance to be marketed as such, rather than as
an aftershave or a 'toiletry'. *Brut* contained a synthetic musk. The next
decade also saw a great deal of perfume innovation when the 'lifestyle'
perfumes of *Chloé* (Lagerfeld), *Charlie* (Revlon), *Opium* (St Laurent)
and *Anaïs Anaïs* (Cacharel) appeared.

If plants can produce enough fragrant oils for our needs then we
can grow and harvest them as a cash crop. The oils they yield are of
course mixtures of molecules, and sometimes this natural blend is
preferred to a blend of the pure chemical essences. It is possible to
detect a slight difference between the natural blend and one made by
combining synthetic ingredients. Even so the use of plant extracts has

---

The key notes of trend-setting perfumes

Perfume	Decade	Top note	Middle note	Base note
Quelque Fleurs	1900s	green note	rose, jasmin	sandalwood, oakmoss
Chypre	1910s	bergamot	rose, jasmin	oakmoss
Shalimar	1910s	lemon	patchouli*	opopanax
Chanel N° 5	1920s	aldehyde	jasmin, rose	vetiver
Soir de Paris	1930s	violet	linden blossom	vetiver, styrax
Ma Griffe	1940s	gardenia	jasmin, rose	styrax, oakmoss
Femme	1940s	peach, plum	jasmin	oakmoss, vanilla
Miss Dior	1950s	aldehydes, accord	jasmin	patchouli*, amber
Fidji	1960s	galbanum, hyacinth	carnation, orris	vetiver, musk
Charlie	1970s	citrus oil	jasmin, tuberose	cedarwood, sandalwood
Chloé	1970s	coconut	tuberose	musk
Opium	1970s	aldehydes	carnation	benzoin, tolu balsam,
Anaïs Anaïs	1970s	leafy green	jasmin	cedarwood, vanilla
Poison	1980s	pimento, plum	rose, tuberose, ylang-ylang	heliotrope, vanilla

*patchouli comes from the leaves of an Indonesian shrub, and has an intense woody, sweet, balsam-
like odour with spicy undertones.

declined dramatically in favour of the industrial production of aroma chemicals, and it is not difficult to see why. In Morocco, the world's largest jasmin growing area, a flower picker could pick up to 15 000 blossoms a day, working early in the morning when the oil content of the jasmin flowers is at its highest. Even so this number of blossoms is only enough to produce about 1.5 grams of jasmin absolute. World-wide demand for some fragrances like jasmin is now of the order of thousands of tonnes per year.

Making fragrant molecules

Chemists have made and recorded the properties of several million organic molecules, and many of these have a smell. However, most molecules were not made with their aroma in mind, and although reporting the smell of a compound was important to nineteenth century chemists, sadly the practice fell out of favour because it revealed nothing about the chemistry of the substance.[4] Yet for perfumers the smell is everything. The industry is still linked to natural fragrances because Nature can still come up with some inter-esting fragrance molecules, and these can provide leads to new variants that chemists can produce easily and cheaply. The two historical sources of fragrances are plants and animals.

Perfumes from plants

Once chemists identify the components of natural fragrances, they can then make modifications to them, hopefully to produce more exotic fragrances. In this way lemongrass oil can be turned to **ionone** which smells more like violets, and **eugenol** from cloves can be turned into **vanillin**, the key component of vanilla. **Limonene** from orange oil is converted to **carvone**, the major flavour component of spearmint.

Jasmin absolute contains over 200 components, and chemists have identified most of them. The main ones which play a part in the aroma, and which are named after the plant, are **cis-jasmone** and **methyl cis-jasmonate**. There are several other components which

---

[4] Modern health and safety guidelines advise against inhaling any untested vapour, but in any case chemists long ago ceased to report the smell of a new chemical as a way of identifying it.

contribute to the smell, such as benzyl acetate, benzyl alcohol, benzyl benzoate, cis-3-hexenyl benzoate, methyl N-acetylanthranilate, cresol, linalool, eugenol and indole. A blend of all these in the right proportions will give a good imitation of the natural product. To make an *exact* copy of jasmin absolute would in theory be possible, but it would probably cost more than the natural material because it could be difficult to make some of the molecules that are present in tiny amounts. In any case, some components have still to be identified, and it would also be rather pointless to go to the trouble of putting these in the synthetic blend if they contribute nothing to the scent.

Jasmin oil relies on a relatively few per cent of its ingredients to give it its characteristic aroma, and of the ones listed above, cis-jasmone and methyl cis-jasmonate are the main fragrance molecules. But even identifying an aroma component does not automatically mean that chemists can make them cheaper than the natural variety. However, there are ways around this problem. Cis-jasmone itself consists of a ring of five carbon atoms to which is attached a chain of another five atoms. Half way along this chain is a so-called double bond, which means that two hydrogen atoms on adjacent carbon atoms are missing. It is possible to make this molecule in the laboratory, but it requires extra steps to get the double bond in place, and to get the right molecular geometry around it. Without the double bond the compound can be made much more easily and is called dihydrojasmone—and the chemists who first made it found that it smelt the same. The double bond was not crucial to the smell.[5]

Other molecules have jasmin-type odours, and the price varies considerably. Natural jasmin extract can cost over $5000 per kilogram, chemically identical jasmone costs about $500, while dihydrojasmone costs less than $50 per kilogram. And if you want the cheapest jasmin smell of all you can get it for as little as $5 per kilogram if you use a completely synthetic aldehyde which doesn't even pretend to have any affiliation with the natural source. The scale on which these substances are manufactured reflects their price: natural jasmin production is only a few tens of tonnes per year, while over 10 000 tonnes of the lowest priced versions are made.

[5] But it can be used to show whether the jasmin oil is purely natural or adulterated with the synthetic material

The first natural aroma substance to be manufactured artificially was cinnamon in 1856, and this was made by a chemist named Luigi Chiozza. Its chief component is **cinnamic aldehyde**. In 1882 the perfumer Paul Parquet created *Fougère Royale* (royal fern) using **coumarin**, which was first made in the laboratory in 1868. Coumarin has the odour of freshly cut grass, and its addition to other fragrances produced a smell best described as fern. In 1876 vanillin, the fragrant molecule of the vanilla pod, was made in the laboratory by Professor Ferdinand Tiemann of Berlin and Dr Wilhelm Haarmann from Holzminden. They went on to become a leading manufacturer of fragrances. Cinnamon and vanillin are better known as flavours, although they are used in perfumes. Vanillin is also present in jasmin and other natural scents, and indeed it is added to the synthetic varieties as a fixative.

It was only in 1893 that the first truly synthetic fragrance molecule was patented, again by Dr Haarmann. This was ionone, which has the aroma of violets, and smells even better than the real thing. The big breakthrough in synthesis came with the discovery of the fragrant aldehydes in the early years of this century, such as **alpha-amyl-cinnamaldehyde** which has a wonderful jasmin-like fragrance, even though it is not a component of the natural material. **Hydrocinnamaldehyde** is a related chemical that gives off the heavy scent of hyacinths.

In 1885 **quinoline** compounds were first made in the laboratory, and these had the smell of leather. A natural quinoline was used in *Chypre*, and thereafter in many perfumes for both men and women: *Aramis* (by Aramis) and *Macassar* (by Rochas) are chypres for men, and they have strong animal notes although of purely chemical origin. *Diva* (by Ungaro) and *Ysatis* (by de Givenchy) are similar chypres for women.

The middle notes of perfumes were originally derived from flower oils such as rose, lily and violet. A rose fragrance can be achieved with **geraniol, citronellol** and **2-phenylethanol**, all cheap to make and just as nice to smell. Molecules which are derived from methyl anthanilate successfully mimic the heady, sweet notes of tropical blooms. The biggest success of the chemists has been to find molecules that smell of lilies of the valley or lilacs, both of which resisted the attempts of perfumers to extract their natural oils commercially.

But the chemists don't always have it their own way. According to Dr Horst Surburg of the German fragrance manufacturer Haarmann & Reimer, there are some scents that still cannot be made at acceptable prices compared to those extracted from plants. Equally frustrating is that natural fragrances may contain a molecule in tiny amounts that is critical to the smell. This used to pose a problem, but identifying such a component is now easy thanks to the advances in chemical analysis, even when there is as little as a hundredth of a milligram, about as much as a drop of mist.

You get what you pay for

What do we get when we buy a bottle of perfume? In terms of chemicals, the short answer is not very much. We never buy a pure fragrance chemical, or even a neat blend of several of them; they are always dissolved and diluted with alcohol as a solvent. Fragrances have to be diluted this way because the amounts we need to use are so small that even a tiny drop of undiluted perfume would be far too strong.

There is a great deal of difference in the price of a bottle of scent, depending on whether it is labelled 'perfume', 'parfum de toilette', or 'splash Cologne'. This reflects the concentration of the solution you are buying. There are three factors involved in pricing: first, the quality of the perfume essence; second, the amount of this you are getting; and third, the quality of the solvent alcohol. This list is a rough guide to perfumery terms:

	Concentration of fragrance essence	Strength of alcohol (alcohol:water)
Perfume	15%	95%:5%
Parfum de toilette	8%	90%:10%
Eau de toilette	4%	80%:20%
Eau-de-Cologne	3%	70%:30%
Splash Cologne	1%	70%:30%

Perfumes may in fact contain more than 15% of the fragrance chemicals and some have double this amount; the same is true of the other grades. What this list shows is the minimum amount of perfume that you can expect. The alcohol too varies, and here it is the extent to which it has been purified of its water content that is the primary concern. The highest grade of alcohol is not 100% as you might expect, but about 95% since there is always a small residue of water which no amount of distillation can remove. Although the 'eau' of eau de toilette and eau-de-Cologne refers to 'waters', these are still basically alcoholic solutions although they hold a significant amount of water. These are the forms in which most perfume is bought, and indeed some fragrances are only sold as eau de toilette or eau-de-Cologne.

For some people, notably Muslims, the alcohol content poses a dilemma. Mohammed, who loved perfumes, also forbade the drinking of alcohol, and although perfumes are not drunk, the alcohol is breathed in. The answer is to find another solvent, and the leading manufacturers of fragrances are now producing non-alcoholic versions.

The scents of animals

When it comes to taking raw materials for perfumes from animals, our attitudes have changed, especially when the animal concerned has to be slaughtered to provide that little bit of its body that the perfumers need. The purists may still claim to prefer natural musk to synthetic musk, but their exquisite sensitivity brings them no credit in modern eyes. The base notes of modern perfumes, the animal notes of old, must be the product of chemical synthesis. Anything else is now unacceptable.

Only four odorants come from animals: musk from the male musk deer; civet from both sexes of the civet cat;[6] castorcum from the beaver; and **ambergris** from the sperm whale.

Musk. A few plants smell vaguely of musk, such as the roots of the angelica plant, which is cultivated in Central Europe, and ambrette seeds, which come from the tropical plant *Hibiscus abelmoschus*, which are grown for this purpose. Real musk comes from the musk deer *Moschus moschiferus* which lives at altitudes of about 1500 metres in the Himalayas, China and Mongolia. This delightful little animal stands about half a metre high (20 inches) and has attractive striped markings of shades of brown on its coat. It also has a gland the size of a golf-ball at the

---

[6] Civet is not really a distinct class of aroma, and perfumers rank it alongside musk.

base of its anus, from which it secretes an aroma during the rutting season. A musk doe finds the smell irresistible. For centuries human hunters found it equally attractive, and even today musk deer are killed simply for this gland.[7]

In 1864 the English perfumer Eugene Rimmel, a *grand nez* of his day, reported that when hunters removed the sac from a slaughtered deer they covered their mouth and nose with linen rags to counteract the smell, which they believed was so strong that it could cause a rush of blood to the head and result in a brain hemorrhage. Even when they had gathered their harvest of musk they had difficulty in getting it back to Europe, since the fastest ships of their day, the tea clippers, refused to transport it because of its objectionable smell. At the height of the musk trade in 1900 about 1400 kg (about 3000 lbs) of musk was being collected every year, representing the slaughter of about 50 000 animals. The gland was worth three times its weight in gold by 1978, when supplies were running low, and the price peaked at $24 per gram ($675 per ounce), making a musk deer worth about $700. Real musk is still regarded as a human aphrodisiac in parts of Asia, and this is now the only market for the genuine article—but more of this topic later.

Musk has a woody, animal scent with strong hints of sexual secretions and excrement. The amount in a bottle of perfume was tiny, sometimes as little as a milligram, but that was all that was required. In some perfumes, those which relied on musk, it was of course higher. Today the amount is not limited by price, but by the effect that is desired. It would make a perfume unacceptable to many people to know it contained even a trace of natural musk, nor need it contain any, because chemists can make a perfectly acceptable artificial musk. The first such musk molecule was discovered in 1888 when the German chemist Adolf Baur made the tertiary-butyl derivative of **trinitrotoluene** (TNT) and found it smelled of musk. It became known as *Musk Baur,* and although it was a cheap alternative, it did not compare to the real thing. Even so, it led to further research of ringing the changes by attaching other atoms to TNT, and some variants were used commercially.[8]

---

[7] Today this trade is regulated by international treaty, but over 300 kg of natural musk is still collected every year, requiring the deaths of several thousand animals.

[8] Manufacture of this type of fragrance is now obsolescent on the grounds of safety.

The real musk still tantalised chemists, even when a German called Walbaum isolated the key odour component as white crystals in 1906 and named it **muscone**. It took until 1926 for another chemist, Leopold Ruzicka of Switzerland, to work out its molecular structure, and give it its correct chemical name of 3-methylcyclopentadecanone. Meanwhile other synthetic musks were appearing and Wallace Carothers, the inventor of nylon, found that by heating certain polyesters he could convert them easily to a chemical very much like muscone. His synthetic musk oil was a thousand times cheaper than the real thing, and is still used.

The main chemical components of real musk are muscone, cholesterol, **androstenone** and dehydroepiandrosterone,[9] plus traces of other more pungent molecules. Perfectly acceptable varieties of synthetic musk are now produced, and are sold under the trade names Galaxolide, Tonalid and Traseolide. Together these total about 10 000 tonnes per year.

Civet. Unlike the poor musk deer, the civet cat did not have to die to yield up its treasure, a white fluid which it excretes into an anal sac. The civet, *Viverra civetta*, is an African cat and it can even be bred in captivity—there are civet farms in Ethiopia. Under the stress of a confined existence the cats will actually produce more civet. In its raw state civet has a very strong, slightly fecal smell, but diluted down it has a floral–musky odour and has been used in perfumes for over two thousand years. Cleopatra was reputed to be very fond of it. The chief aroma constituent is **civetone**, and this chemical is now made by the fragrance industry.

Castoreum. This is an oily substance obtained from the anal gland of the beaver, *Castor fiber*, which lives wild in Canada, and is raised on farms in Russia. The secretion is found in the glandular sac between the hind legs. It has a warm, sensual, leather-like smell, but in the raw state is rather offensive and needs to be diluted to be appreciated, when it acquires a pleasantly sweet aroma. It is used in perfumes such as fougères,

---

[9] Androstenone and dehyroepiandrosterone are male sex hormones.

chypres and orientals, but it requires great skill to accommodate its dominating aroma.

Ambergris.   Once upon a time beachcombers could find wealth by coming across a large ball of ambergris on the sea shore. This pale grey material is produced in the intestine of sperm whales, although why it forms is not certain. Lumps the size of footballs could be found floating on the sea or washed up on beaches. It was highly prized by perfumers, and was also taken as a tonic and aphrodisiac. Ambergris floats on the sea because it is composed of terpenes and steroids, which are like hydrocarbon waxes. In the last century it was also harvested from slaughtered whales. Ambergris gives off a lingering, sweet, dry odour, reminiscent of wood, moss and seaweed.

The key component of ambergris is ambreine, which undergoes natural changes to a variety of chemical derivatives of which the one called ambergris is the key odour component. The ambergris used by modern perfumers is of synthetic origin and is sold under the trade names of Ambrox, Ambrosan and Amberlyn. These are the same chemical but produced in different ways, and from different starting materials. Most come from sclareol, which is present in clary sage. Recently, a whole new range of ambergris fragrances has been discovered, based on a very different chemical called **2–cyclohexyl-1,3–dioxan**. This bears little resemblance to the natural ambergris molecule but it has several variants which combine an amber smell with flora, woody, lily or earthy nuances.

Some day synthetic fragrances will replace all those derived from animals, and to all intents and purposes that is already the case in the developed world, thanks to the skill of chemists. Synthetic fragrances are the preferred choice, sometimes because they have unique aromas of their own, or because they are better than the naturally extracted originals and are more reliable in quality, last longer and are cheaper.

The World's largest producer of fragrance and flavour chemicals is International Flavors and Fragrances (IFF) of Union Beach, New Jersey, USA. The second largest is Givaudan-Roure, of Dübendorf, near Zurich, Switzerland, formed by a merger between Givaudan and Roure-Bertrand-Dupont. Givaudan was a company set up by the brothers Leon and Xavier Givaudan, both of whom were experimental chemists, and were based in Grasse, France. The third largest producer in the world is Quest International of Ashford, Kent, in the UK.

Human scents

Napoleon was clearly aroused by Josephine, and part of her attraction was her own personal odour. "Don't wash. I am coming home!" was the famous message he sent from his army headquarters.

According to Michael Stoddart, who is Professor of Zoology at the University of Tasmania, Australia, and author of *The Scented Ape*, there remains a biological link between the nose and the pituitary gland which controls our sex organs. Neither male nor female human sexual behaviour is triggered by specific odour chemicals—as far as we are aware—whereas many animals are known to be sexually activated by them. There is some evidence that humans respond to molecules which others are releasing, even if they cannot smell them. These molecules may even bring us attentions we do not seek.

A young woman who used a hormone treatment called cyproterone acetate to remove facial hair found herself the object of her pet rottweiler's affections. According to a report in the medical journal the *Lancet* the dog would not leave her alone and tried to mount her on several occasions, much to her embarrassment. Thinking she had an over-sexed dog she even had it castrated in an attempt to control it, but that had no effect. Little did she know that her hormone pills were acting as a powerful canine sex-attractant.

In December 1992 in Littledean, a village in Gloucestershire, England, a pig named Doris fell instantly in love with a young man delivering newspapers, and pursued him down the village street. He took refuge in a public telephone kiosk from where he telephoned the local police for help. They rode to his rescue and captured the besotted 200 pound sow. Although the young man did not realise it, he was sending Doris a message she could not ignore. He was releasing a chemical called androstenone of which she was acutely aware.

Androstenone is the sex-attractant of the wild boar. Pig farmers can buy spray cans of this substance which acts as a strong aphrodisiac for their animals. Its odour is described as musky and a bit like that of urine. The related molecule alpha-androstenol is a musky-smelling steroid found in the testes and saliva of the boar, and it will stimulate a wild sow. The truffle, an edible fungus, also produces it, which is why a sow can sniff out this delicacy even though it may be growing as much as a metre underground. There are even some sex-shops that sell it as a supposed human sex-attractant, but its efficacy is doubtful.

Androstenone is produced by glands in our armpits, and men produce much more of it than women. Humans have sebaceous glands all over their bodies, but they are concentrated particularly in the hairy parts and give off an oily liquid, especially when we sweat. This liquid contains 12 steroid-like odorants, of which androstenone is the most abundant. It seems unlikely that androstenone is a human sex-attractant because not everyone can smell it, and in a concentrated form some women are reported to find its faint aroma slightly off-putting, although there is anecdotal evidence that they may respond to it without knowing.

When one of several chairs in a doctor's waiting room was sprayed with androstenone it was observed that women were more likely to choose that chair to sit on, rather than one of the others. In another experiment in the late 1970s Tom Clark of Guy's Hospital Medical School in London sprayed unreserved seats in a theatre with androstenone and observed that these were taken in preference to unsprayed seats. Androstenone can be detected at one part per billion, and women can be ten times more sensitive to picking up its smell than men. Ovulating women can even detect the smell at one part per trillion. One theory is that humans may react to this molecule because it is the smell we associate with close human bonding, and that we learn this association when we feed at our mother's breast, because this is the area of a woman's body which also gives off androstenone.

Nowhere is the importance of chemistry more apparent than in the sexual communication between living things. For insects, there are pheromone molecules which convey messages about food trails or act as alarm signals, but the best known are the sex pheromones, the molecules that convey the presence of a female to a male and bring him winging to her. This behaviour is built in to the insect's genes. When an animal is ready to reproduce then it needs to broadcast this information, and what better way than to release a few molecules into the environment, molecules that will be picked up by the receptors of potential mates and which at the same time switch them on sexually. Insects can be caught by traps baited with sex-attractants.

Few of the smells that humans produce are attractive. Some of the worst-smelling are the sulfur compounds which are the result of bacterial action on our body's waste products. Our sebaceous glands start working at puberty and discharge an odourless oil which bacteria can work on and convert to fatty acids which smell unpleasant. Bacteria can do the same to butter, hence the similarity between the smells of stale sweat and rancid butter.

The strongest smelling molecules from human skin are excreted by the apocrine glands, which are located in the armpits, the scalp, and around the sex organs and anus. The chemical responsible for the offensive odour of human armpits was discovered in 1991 by Dr George Preti of the Monell Chemical Senses Center in the USA. It is a substance called **3-methyl-2-hexenoic acid** (MHA) and was extracted from the sweat of male volunteers who wore absorbent pads under their arms for 24 hours. Dr Preti actually identified almost 40 molecules, and then made samples of each of these in the laboratory. As soon as he made MHA the smell of armpits was obvious. The chemical is formed by bacteria whose enzymes attack a protein from the apocrine glands, of which men have many more than women. The protein contains chemically bound derivatives of MHA which the enzymes release. Most deodorants work by blocking the glands which release the protein, but a new deodorant has been patented which works in a different way: by attacking the bacteria and stopping the release of MHA.

Having eliminated unpleasant body odours by daily showering and using deodorants, we no longer need to seek refuge in perfume to mask smells as did previous generations. Now we can enjoy perfumes for their own sake. Nevertheless a good perfume is more than just a nice smell, and our knowledge of what the deeper notes of perfume are saying may incline us to believe that there is a strong link between perfumes and sex. They may even be regarded as mild aphrodisiacs.

Aphrodisiacs

Perfumes may not be true aphrodisiacs, but they come very close, and they have always been the stock in trade of the professional purveyors of sex.[10] Throughout history prostitutes have been highly perfumed, and some were even more subtle. Parisian courtesans of the last century were reputed to wear a bag of musk between their breasts. Aphrodisiacs are generally regarded as something to be taken by mouth rather than merely sniffed. It may be true that chemicals may make us smell much more alluring that we would otherwise be, but it is not true that they can improve our physical performance. Until we realise this then other species will be driven to extinction—and no amount of chemistry can prevent it.

When an Indian bull rhino mates with a female, the sex act lasts an hour and during this time he can ejaculate a dozen times or more. Little wonder then that the rhino is regarded as a potent sex symbol, and Chinese doctors prescribe rhino horn as a natural medicine for impotence as well as such ailments as fever, arthritis and lumbago. A couple of grams of rhino horn shavings cost about $30, making a complete horn worth several thousand dollars. Indian rhino horn commands a premium price many times that of the African rhino.

Rhino horn is sold in many parts of the East as an aphrodisiac even though it has been shown scientifically to be useless for this purpose. Drinking rhino horn tea, the traditional way of taking this love potion, gives you the same boost as making tea from your own nail parings. Rhino horn is keratin, the same chemical that pigs grow as trotters, cows grow as hoofs, and humans grow as fingernails. International groups such as the World Wide Fund for Nature are now attempting to stamp out the sale of rhino horn because in Africa there are fewer than 5000 rhinos left, and in India the numbers are down to 2000.

Love potions have been sought since the dawn of time, and there are scores of natural products that have the reputation for increasing our sexual appetite. Alcohol and marijuana are regarded as mild aphrodisiacs, but that is because they make us less inhibited. Some foods have this reputation as aphrodisiacs because of a resemblance to human sex organs: bananas, asparagus and the stinkhorn mushroom

[10] Aphrodisiacs are named after the Greek Goddess of love, Aphrodite.

have the shape of an erect penis; mussels, figs and oysters look like female genitals.

Casanova, the 18th century lover, certainly thought food could be an aphrodisiac—he ate 50 oysters in an evening. There may even be a scientific explanation for his predilection for these molluscs. A key trace element in our diet is zinc, which is essential for growth and is a constituent of many key enzymes of the body, especially those which synthesise protein. Zinc is very important for the maintenance of the sex glands, and in the hormones that govern our sex-drive. Semen has a high level of zinc, and this continually needs to be replenished. One food rich in zinc is oysters, so Casanova was doing himself no harm in eating lots of them: a pound of oysters provided him with 120 mg of zinc.

There are scores of other foods that are reputed to have aphrodisiac properties: among them are chocolate, oats, sunflower seeds, nuts, avocados, carrots, celery, mangos and fish. Garlic is claimed to be an aphrodisiac in France, but in Greece it is thought of as a passion-killer. None of these foods contains any chemical that has been proved to be effective, but some, like chocolate, contain **phenylethylamine** which is thought to be linked to sexual arousal in the brain, and it has similarities to natural chemicals that act as stimulants, such as amphetamines.

Some of these foods provide us with essential nutrients: for example carrots are rich in vitamin A, and this is important for converting cholesterol into the male hormone testosterone. If he does not get enough vitamin A a man becomes sterile, but he is rarely in danger of not taking in enough of this vitamin in a normal diet. Indeed he is more likely to take in too much and provoke a toxic response. The aphrodisiac properties of food are imaginary, and the Sexual Research Institute at Hamburg University failed to find any 'active' ingredient in over 200 supposed aphrodisiacs. If popular aphrodisiacs work it is really because they act on our imagination.

Very few true sex stimulants are known to science. There are some spices that seem to have an effect, such as chili peppers, but this probably is because they contain irritating chemicals that cause a tingling sensation in our bowels or bladder in the same way that they burn our mouth and tongue when we eat them. The chemicals **yohimbine** and cantharides cause an erection in men as the outward sign that they are having an effect on the body. Whether this means they are aphrodisiacs is a debatable point, since they do not stimulate the desire for sex, only the ability to engage in sexual activity. Yohimbine is a crystalline compound that comes from the bark of the yohimbé tree (*Corynanthe yohimbé*) which grows in central Africa. People there have used it for centuries to stimulate their sexual powers. It dilates the blood vessels of the sex organs, leading to an erection in men and increased sensitivity in the genitals of women. Scientific research on rats and humans has proved that the effect is real. As little as 10 mg of yohimbine is enough, and too much is dangerous. A man who injected himself with 1800 mg collapsed in a coma and only just survived.[11]

Spanish fly, the ground-up powder from the brilliant green beetle *Lytta vesicatoria*, is the source of cantharides, but there are risks because this chemical can also kill. In one case in the 1940s a young man working with a London firm of medical suppliers laced some coconut ice with it and gave it to his girlfriend. After two days of agony she died, her intestines eaten away by this corrosive irritant. A small dose of Spanish fly does produce a strong erection in men, the effect being due to its irritant effect on the urethra, the tube that runs from the bladder to the tip of the penis.

Arsenic is a deadly poison, but in small doses it gained a reputation as a tonic and was especially popular with Victorian businessmen. Even Charles Dickens resorted to it. It probably got the reputation as an aphrodisiac because it was used in medicine to treat tuberculosis. In the final stages of this wasting disease male patients become notoriously sexually aroused, and this became associated with Dr Fowler's Fever Cure, which many of them were given as treatment. The famous fever cure was a solution of potassium arsenate, a few drops of which were taken in a glass of water. In many parts of Britain it became common practice for pharmacists to dispense doses of the tonic over the counter. It may have had some effect because a small dose of arsenic will boost the body's metabolism, making people feel more alive, and so more sexually alert. The arsenic factor may also explain why certain foods with high arsenic content also gained the reputation of being aphrodisiacs, such as plaice and shell fish.

[11] The fatal dose is 3000 mg.

Aromatherapy

Perfumes may not be aphrodisiacs but they can have strong psychological benefits, and this is the philosophy behind aromatherapy. Because so few of the fragrant molecules are actually trapped by the invisible hair-like cilia in our nostrils, it is unlikely that they can have an effect on our bodily processes, but they may have an effect on our emotions, in just the same way that music, colour and the spoken word can affect us deeply. Extracts of the sebaceous gland have been tested at stress clinics and found to have a calming effect, and the reason appears to be that we associate them with the time we felt most secure in our lives—when we were being suckled as a baby.

Research at the Toho University School of Medicine in Tokyo indicates that smell can have a profoundly moving effect. Electrodes attached to a person's scalp were used to monitor changes in brain waves as the person was exposed to different aromas. Jasmin, for example, acted as a stimulant, just as aromatherapists claim, while lavender calmed brain activity down: this fragrance is recommended as a sedative. The researchers also found that the aromatherapists correctly predicted the stimulant or sedative readings of various smells—except that of rose oil. Aromatherapists speak of rose as a sedative, whereas according to the brain-wave measurements it is a stimulant. Green notes such as mint and rosemary improve concentration; citrus notes make us feel more alert; lavender relaxes us; rose, jasmin and ylang-ylang make us think of love; while musk and sandalwood are decidedly warm and sensual.

The Fragrances Foundation in New York, headed by Annette Green, is researching and promoting smell and drawing up lists of behavioural fragrances. Mood perfumes are set to become part of everyday living. Peppermint is said to increase production and reduce accidents in factories, while vanilla comforts patients in hospital, and floral scents make people spend more time, and money, in shopping malls.

We have every reason to believe that the golden age of fragrances is only just beginning. Research in chemistry will continue to turn up yet more wonderful smells, and perhaps psychologists and medics will be able to use them as the most gentle of mood-modifying chemicals. The philosophy of perfumers and aromatherapists may one day turn into a science of chemistry and mind. Even the major perfume houses are starting to market products with emphasis on mood. For example *Wings* (Giorgio Beverly Hills) claims to make you feel 'uplifted', *Champagne* (YSL) to make you feel happy, and *Tuscany Per Donna* (Aramis) to make you feel seductive. They might be right.

CHAPTER TWO

Sweetness and Light

Sugar; honey; sugar as a chemical resource; bulk sweeteners; artificial sweeteners; what makes a molecule taste sweet?

I N the previous chapter we looked at fragrance chemicals, which we are happy to use to improve the quality of our lives, and in the knowledge that they no longer involve the needless slaughter of wild animals. Advances in chemistry have brought this about, but advances in other areas of chemistry have not led to similar acclaim. One such area is the production of chemicals that are put into foods. Indeed the very idea of *eating* chemicals seems wrong, and yet we do it every day.

Of course I could point out that every mouthful of food we swallow is merely a collection of molecules, but this can be countered by pointing out that food molecules come from other living things and are part of a natural food chain. When people speak of something as 'chemical' they often mean it as a criticism of something unnatural, originating as it does in a chemical laboratory. Sometimes this approval of things natural and condemnation of things chemical is turned on its head, and this is what has happened with the sweet-tasting components of our food. Sugar, which is entirely natural, is seen as a threat, while artificial sweeteners are booming, although they too are considered a health hazard by some people. When we look a little closer, however, we find that there is little to worry about in either case. The dangers of sugar are much exaggerated, and it has much to offer the world.

We like sweet-tasting foods, and we have specific sweetness detectors on our tongue that register this pleasant sensation. So what exactly is sweetness? And why do relatively few natural substances have this property? The answers to these questions are to be found in chemistry. If we take the molecule's eye view of sweetness we can perhaps understand better the controversies that surround both white sugar and artificial sweeteners.

Food chemists divide sweeteners into two kinds: bulk sweeteners and intense sweeteners. Sugar is the best known bulk sweetener; it is sweet but we require a lot of it to achieve the degree of sweetness we want. Bulk sweeteners may also give us something we don't want, and that is excess Calories.[1] Intense sweeteners avoid this problem, but some people believe they may be dangerous in a different way because they threaten our health. To put it rather simply: eat too much sugar and you end up overweight, with tooth decay and possibly heart disease; eat too much **cyclamate**[2] or **saccharin** and you might end up with cancer. Either way it seems we have to pay a heavy price for indulging a craving for sweet foods. Or do we?

Sugar

The sugarcane plant is native to Polynesia. It was taken from there first to China, and then to India, where it was refined into sugar in about 700 BC. Slowly the cultivation of sugarcane spread westward through Persia to Egypt, and was to be found around the warmer parts of the Mediterranean by the early Middle Ages, around 800 AD. Muslims were particularly active in growing it and appreciated the sweet-tasting sherberts made from it. These they drank in place of alcohol which had been forbidden by The Prophet.

---

[1] A calorie is the energy needed to raise the temperature of a gram of water by one degree Celsius. It takes about 50 000 calories to boil a pint of water. Food chemists and dieticians talk in terms of the kilocalorie, which is 1000 ordinary calories, and they would say that it takes about 50 kilocalories to boil a pint of water. Sometimes kilocalorie is written as Calorie with a capital C, and this is the common unit for the energy value of food.

[2] Where the name of a substance is given in **bold** type, it means that there is more information about its chemistry in the Appendix.

The first sugar reached England in 1319 AD, but it was an expensive novelty to begin with and used only in medicines. It had to be imported and cost ten times as much as locally produced honey. Nevertheless there was a demand for it for special occasions, and in Shakespeare's *The Winter's Tale*, which was perfomed in 1611, the Clown asks: 'What am I to buy for our sheep-shearing feast? Three pound of sugar, five pound of currants; rice—what will this sister of mine do with rice?. . .' Sugar continued to be expensive for people living in northern Europe throughout the Middle Ages and right up to the seventeenth century, when cheaper imports from the Caribbean began to arrive.

Sugarcane is a jointed reed standing 2–3 metres tall (6–9 feet), and a plant will grow for up to ten years in deep, rich and well-watered soil. It will not survive frost. Sugarcane shoots were transported by Columbus to the New World on his second voyage in 1494, and there it thrived. The climate of the West Indies was ideal, but even so it took two hundred years before it was being exported back to the Old World.

Cutting sugarcane is hard work and the notorious slave-trade developed to provide planters with cheap labour to harvest this twice-a-year crop and to work the vats in the sugar mills, where temperatures regularly reached 50 Celsius (over 120 Fahrenheit). Sugar is easy to extract from the crushed cane because it dissolves readily in hot water. On cooling the solution the first crystals to appear are pure and white, while subsequent crops of crystals become progressively darker. This brown sugar is referred to by a variety of names, the most common being demerara. Finally a black tarry liquid, molasses, remains which is still about a third sugar: the remaining two thirds are other carbohydrates, various acids, salts and amino acids. Molasses are fermented today to produce chemicals such as **ethanol**, **acetone**, **glycerol** and **citric acid**. It can also be turned into rum or used to grow baker's yeast.

The impetus for change in the sugarcane industry came as a result of the Napoleonic Wars and the blockade of France by the British Navy, which cut off supplies of sugar from the French colony of Dominica (Haiti). Napoleon set his scientists to seek alternative sources and they took up the researches of Andrew Marggraf, a chemist at the Berlin Academy. Marggraf had discovered that sugar could be extracted from root crops such as parsnips, but he was particularly impressed by the amount that came from the sea beet, a cousin of the beetroot. Selective breeding of sea beet to maximise its sugar content began about 1800, and within ten years a high-yielding variety was developed and the beet industry was born. The French Government encouraged farmers to grow sugar beet so that the country would never again be dependent on imported sugar from the West Indies. Sugar-beet was ideal for the cooler climes of Europe, and today it is a major crop around the world. Indeed, it outstripped sugar-cane as the main source of sugar over a hundred years ago.

White sugar is just one of a group of sugars. To put it more exactly: **sucrose** (which is another name for sugar) is a simple carbohydrate. Or, to put it in chemical terms: saccharose (which is the technical name for sugar) is a di-saccharide. There are many saccharides.[3] This group of compounds ranges from the simplest so-called mono-saccharides, such as **glucose**, up to the large poly-saccharides, such as starch and **cellulose**, in which there are long chains of hundreds of saccharide units strung together.

Glucose is the most abundant monosaccharide and is the first product of photosynthesis in plants. It is present in many fruits and vegetables, and is the main source of energy for both plants and animals. Other monosaccharides are **fructose** which is also found in fruits, and **galactose** which is produced by animals.

When two of these simple sugars join together we get a disaccharide, and sugar itself is the combination of glucose and fructose. Maltose, the saccharide of malted barley, is also two units, both of them glucose. Lactose, the saccharide of milk, is glucose plus galactose. Other common saccharides are fucose, which is a component of mucous, and **xylose**, which is found in plant gums. The most abundant carbohydrates in plants are the polysaccharides starch and cellulose. Both consist of many glucose units, but these are connected together slightly differently, with the result that we can digest starch by breaking it down into glucose, but we can not digest cellulose. Consequently starch is a rich source of food energy, while cellulose

---

[3] The technical term saccharides derives from a Medieval Latin term which in turn came from the Greek *sakkharon*, meaning sweet.

passes through us unchanged, and is better known as dietary fibre (see Chapter 4).

Glucose is also known as 'blood sugar' because it accounts for 0.1% of our blood. Our body tries to keep the level of this constant. The glucose derived from our food, by the action of enzymes in our stomach, can pass directly into our blood stream and be taken to where its energy is needed. As it is used, it breaks down into simpler molecules and eventually ends up as carbon dioxide and water,[4] a process which releases a great deal of energy for our body, either as heat or muscular action. When the level of glucose in our blood rises after a meal we turn the excess into another polysaccharide called glycogen, which we store in our muscles and liver. There it waits until the glucose level in our blood falls again, and it can then be turned back into glucose and used as required.

The average adult has about 350 grams (three quarters of a pound) of glycogen stored in their tissue at any one time—and this has energy to supply us with about 1400 Calories, enough to keep us going for a day. If we eat more food than we need, and the glycogen reserve is already full, then our body starts to turn glucose into fat, which it can store more economically and of which we have a bigger reserve— enough to keep us alive for a month. We will come back to the problem of running down this energy store in Chapter 4.

Sugar is also easily digested, and provides half its weight as glucose. The other half, fructose, is an equally good source of energy, although it is absorbed more slowly. Fructose actually tastes sweeter than sugar, but it was the fructose part of sugar that some suspected of causing ill health.

Earlier generations viewed sugar as a wholesome food, valued for its purity, and much used in the home for baking cakes and apple pies, or for making toffee and jam. Sugar is nice, but there has always been a price to pay. Dietitians, dentists and doctors warned their patients about eating too much sugar. Dietitians told their obese patients to give up sugar as part of a weight-reducing diet. Being overweight can have serious effects on our health, leading to less activity, high blood pressure and heart disease. Dentists knew that sugar caused tooth

---

[4] The overall reaction is chemically the same as burning it in air and thereby reacting it with oxygen.

decay, which it does by penetrating the film of plaque which covers our teeth. Plaque bacteria, and in particular *Streptococcus mutans*, break down the sugar and form acids like lactic acid which then attacks the **calcium phosphate** that makes up the enamel surface of the tooth. A cavity forms, which might eventually etch its way to the pulp part of the tooth, causing pain and allowing infection to spread deep into the tooth and even down to the root, where it results in an abscess.

Doctors once warned patients with diabetes to avoid sugar at all costs since they lacked the insulin necessary to utilise glucose and release its energy. Before insulin was available on prescription, a person with diabetes was advised to eat a high-fat, low-carbohydrate diet, since their body could digest fat but not carbohydrate.[5] A diet comprising at least two-thirds fat was the target to aim for. Many ate special diabetic food if they wanted a sweet-tasting treat, and these were made with bulk sweeteners like **sorbitol**, a simple sugar made from glucose. However, a person with diabetes who can produce some insulin, but not enough, does not have to avoid sugar assiduously; indeed this would be almost impossible since a lot of ordinary foods contain a little sugar. The modern approach to diabetes, which for many people can be managed by controlling the diet, is not to rely on sugar substitutes: such people are advised to watch what they eat, and of course to avoid eating foods made with lots of sugar. Dietary advice for diabetes is now high-fibre and low-fat, and to eat some bread and potatoes, food that earlier sufferers were once warned against. Of course not all diabetes can be managed by diet, and many diabetics have to rely on injections of insulin.

A whole new range of diseases for which sugar was to blame began to emerge in the 1960s. The public became aware of these with the publication in 1972 of the catchily titled book *Pure, White and Deadly*, written by Professor John Yudkin, a nutritionist at Queen Elizabeth College, London.[6] Yudkin's book blamed sugar for causing diabetes and ulcers and promoting heart disease. He claimed that sugar was not

---

[5] Strictly speaking people with diabetes can digest carbohydrate, but to stimulate cells to take up glucose and use it requires insulin.

[6] The book *Dietetics, Coronary Thrombosis and the Saccharine Disease* by T.L. Cleave, G.D. Campbell and N.S. Painter appeared in 1969, and was the first to warn of the dangers of sugar.

like other carbohydrates: 'recent research shows that it also has unique effects in the body, different from those of other carbohydrates.' Moreover, and more startling, was Yudkin's assertion that 'if only a small fraction of what is already known about the effects of sugar were to be revealed in relation to any other material used as a food additive, that material would promptly be banned.' He could not explain exactly how sugar caused these various diseases, but he speculated that it might do it in several ways, such as by swelling organs in the body, or by causing the over-production of hormones like insulin, or maybe by boosting the population of microbes in our intestines.

He wrote off sugar as merely 'empty calories', the implication being that it provided nothing but energy, and indeed sugar has none of the other components we need for a balanced diet, such as protein, vitamins and minerals. We need these to repair our body and keep it functioning effectively. The term 'empty calories' could equally be applied to all carbohydrates, including glucose, fructose, lactose and starch. Yet carbohydrates are not used by the body solely to generate energy: some are needed to build essential structures within the body, and some end up attached to proteins or to cell membranes, where they play an important role in the process whereby one living cell recognises another. To label sugar and its components as merely empty calories was rather unfair. Even so, the amount of sugar in the average person's diet was far in excess of the body's need for cellular building blocks, and of course most sugar is used as energy or turned into fat. The problems of sugar were really the problems of being overweight, and this was often to blame for most of the accusations being made against sugar.[7]

As the years went by the list of ailments which appeared to be linked to sugar grew to include not only heart disease, but also appendicitis, gallstones and hernias, until by 1983 the Royal College of Physicians in London felt constrained to recommend that the national intake of sugar be reduced by half. By this time sugar was even accused of causing breast cancer and varicose veins. In 1986 a more rigorous study of all the charges against sugar was

---

[7] Later the blame was to pass to fats in the diet, and this aspect we will consider in Chapter 5.

carried out by the US Food and Drugs Administration (FDA). This body reported that it could find no evidence for singling out sugar as the primary cause of ill health. Nor was this conclusion surprising, because the glucose and fructose of sugar are no different to that of other foods.

However, the years of bad publicity had had their effect. People stopped putting sugar in coffee and tea, yet surprisingly the amount of sugar consumed did not change significantly. People ate it in other ways, such as in biscuits, snacks and confectionery. The average person in the West still eats around 100 grams (4 ounces) of refined sugar a day; in some countries, such as Australia, sugar consumption is a third higher than the average, while in others, like Japan, it is a third lower.

So how should we think of sugar? Should we do all we can to avoid it? In fact it would be almost impossible to cut out sugar completely from our diet, because that would mean eating no fruit or vegetables. In all respects, both chemically and nutritionally, sugar molecules are the same whether they come from sun-dried raisins or from a sugar refinery. Apples have 2% sucrose, 2% glucose and 5% fructose; oranges have 5%, 2% and 2% respectively; bananas have 7%, 2% and 1%; and grapes have no sucrose but 8% each of glucose and fructose. The total amount of these sugars in grapes rises to 64% when they have been dried to make raisins or currants. Dried dates are 73% sugars. Half of the sugar we eat is refined sugar; the other half is naturally present in foods. Together they provide us with about 20% of our daily energy requirement.

A lot of refined sugar is eaten in cakes, biscuits, fruit pies and confectionery, which are obviously sweet to the taste, but a lot is eaten in other foods which we do not think of as predominantly sweet, such as savoury snacks, bread, pickles, sauces and convenience foods. Some people may have stopped adding sugar to tea and coffee, but they may take more than they suspect in fruit-flavoured drinks, mixers and colas, where it is used as a balance to the acidity.

As a natural resource, sugar is pure, white and *heavenly*. Refined sugar has some wonderful advantages: its chemical purity means we do not need to worry about contaminants; it is easily digested and provides energy in abundance; and it is stable and acts as its own preservative. Sugar will last for years if it is kept cool and dry. Any country whose agriculture fluctuates between feast and famine would be well advised to store sugar as insurance against the lean years.

The simple equation linking weight and energy explains why this is so. Bare survival requires us to take in 1000 Calories of energy every day, which we can get from about 280 grams (10 ounces) of sugar. If this were the only source of energy in our diet, a normal person would need 102 kilograms (228 pounds) a year to stay alive. A million tons of sugar would provide enough *energy* to keep about ten million people alive for a year. Fats and oils, which weight-for-weight provide over twice the energy, might seem better foods to store, but they are susceptible to attack by oxygen in the air and go rancid, although this can be delayed by adding antioxidants.

Of course more than sugar is needed to sustain life, and a famine diet still has to include some essential **amino acids** from proteins, plus vitamins and minerals, without which the body cannot make new cells nor keep existing cells functioning. A diet to get you through a famine must include at least some of these, and this is why skimmed milk powder, which is rich in protein and minerals, is also considered a good stand-by food —although not for everyone. Adults in some ethnic groups cannot digest the lactose in milk. Dried egg would be an alternative source of easily stored protein.

Meanwhile in the overfed economies of the West, people fight the twin scourges of sugar and artificial sweeteners. To help them in their struggles, products in supermarkets are labelled 'no added sugar' or 'contains no artificial sweetener', although the former might well contain natural sugar and the latter almost certainly contain the refined variety. Some people even try to do without sweet-tasting foods altogether, in the mistaken belief that if something tastes sweet it must be dangerous to health. The only exception they make is honey, which of course is beyond criticism, and is often labelled 'pure'[8] and 'natural'.

---

[8] The phrase 'pure honey' refers not to the chemical composition, but to the source of the honey, and means that it is not a blend of honey but is from a particular apiary or local area. It does not mean the same as the 'pure sugar', which does refer to its chemical composition.

Honey

Many who oppose sugar advocate honey as a healthier alternative, but a closer look at this food shows that they are deluding themselves. Honey is basically just a collection of sugars.

Honey is as old as history. There is a reference to honey bees in ancient Egypt 5000 years ago, and honey is mentioned several times in the Old Testament of the Bible, where its sweetness was proverbial. Today over a million tonnes of honey are produced worldwide, the main exporting countries being Russia, China, the USA and Mexico. A colony of bees can produce up to 70 kg of honey (about 150 lbs) in a season. Honey is gathered by billions of bees plundering the nectar from trillions of flowers. Nectar is mainly a sugar solution, and when this is taken back to the hive it breaks down into glucose and fructose.

Honey is a collection of saccharide chemicals and water. Glucose and fructose together make up about 70%, sucrose and maltose about 10%, and water accounts for the remaining 20%. There are tiny amounts of many other components, and these provide the characteristic aroma and flavour. Over twenty other saccharides have been identified in honey. There is also gluconic acid, and minute traces of proteins and minerals, but there is so little of these that they do not make honey a good dietary source for anything but carbohydrates. If sugar is to be derided as 'pure, white and deadly' by those who oppose it, then logically they should refer to honey as 'impure, golden and deadly'.

Honey is regarded by many as a health food, and spoken of as if it had almost magical qualities. Unlike pure sugar, honey has a comforting smell and a taste all its own, and these come from 120 aroma chemicals that are present. Food chemists have identified most of them, but about 40 still remain to be classified. Some of these chemicals come from the flowers from which the bees have gathered the nectar, and it is possible to identify lavender honey or heather honey if the bee hives have been next to a large area of these plants. One flavour molecule dominates and gives honey its characteristic smell, and that is ethyl phenylacetate.

In effect honey is mainly **invert sugar**—and so is golden syrup. The resemblance is more that just superficial. Invert sugar is the name given to ordinary sugar when it has reacted chemically with water and split into glucose and fructose—which is what happens to nectar in the hive. Add a drop of the flavouring ethyl phenylacetate to invert sugar, and you would be hard pressed to tell it from honey.

All the sugars in honey can be broken down to alcohol by fermenting them with yeast, and this makes mead, which was a drink of the rich for hundreds of years, especially in northern climes where grapes could not be grown. Mead continued to be made on a large scale in Russia even in the last century, and it is still produced as a novelty drink in England today.

Sugar as a chemical resource

Sugar makes a superb agricultural crop, quite apart from its use as a human food. Sugar-cane and sugar-beet can be grown as sources of renewable energy, and sugar can be used as a resource for the chemicals industry. The world produces about 120 million tonnes of sugar per year, and could produce much more in both tropical and temperate regions. Brazil was the first country to grow sugar-cane on a large scale to make fuel for transport, in this case to make alcohol which today powers millions of cars. We will return to this aspect of sugar in the next chapter.

Sugar can also be used as a chemical in other ways, not by breaking it down to simpler compounds like alcohol, but by using the sucrose molecule itself and adding other groups of atoms to it. The company Procter & Gamble turns sugar into a fat substitute which they call Olestra. Other chemical companies are using sugar to make detergents, pesticides and even an anti-cancer agent. Attaching eight **acetate** groups to sucrose creates one of the most bitter compounds known, sucrose octa-acetate, and this can be used to give a liquid a nasty taste so that people are warned against drinking it.

Except where they are destined for human consumption, few of these sugar-based products have achieved commercial success because they compete with oil-based chemicals, which are much cheaper. But if there ever comes a time when fossil fuels run out, we could turn to carbohydrates like sugar to make the hydrocarbons we now get from oil. Hydrocarbons are the starting point for most of the industrial chemicals used to make plastics, resins, fibres, solvents, dyes, paints, drugs and adhesives.

We could get hydrocarbon petrochemicals from sugar by two routes. One way would be to ferment the sugar to alcohol, and then take this one step further by heating to a high temperature to convert the alcohol to the more useful gas ethylene. This is the starting point for materials such as plastics and resins (see Chapter 6). Another way would be to ferment sugar with the micro-organism *Bacillus acidi levolactiti* which produces lactic acid. When this chemical is heated in water under very high pressure it forms **acrylic acid** from which acrylates can be made. These are used in paints, metal coatings, fibres and polishes.

Other micro-organisms can work on sugar to yield such products as **acetone**, **butanol** and **2,3-butanediol**, all of which have a role in the chemical industry. Sucrose is already used to manufacture other consumables apart from alcohol, and the amino acids, L–glutamic acid and L–lysine come from the sucrose of molasses. L-Glutamic acid is best known as its sodium salt, the flavour enhancer monosodium glutamate (MSG). Other industrial processes now in use convert sugar to glucose, and ferment that to make the vitamins B_2 and C. Glucose can also be fermented by the moulds *Martierella* or *Rhizopus* to make γ**-linolenic acid**, which commands a high price as evening primrose oil.

The most environmentally friendly product made from sugar is the biodegradable plastic polyhydroxybutyrate (PHB). The chemical company Zeneca produces this from sugar and markets it under the name of Biopol, which has won environmental awards in the USA and Germany. The German hair care company Wella sells its Sanara brand of shampoo in bottles made of Biopol, and they reported increases sales when these were introduced. Biopol is biodegradable because PHB makes an ideal food for other microorganisms, which dispose of the plastic by digesting it. In so doing they return it to the air as carbon dioxide.

PHB can be modified by adding another hydroxy-acid such as 3-hydroxypentanoic acid, and in this way the texture of the polymer can be tailored to make it suitable for plastic envelopes or carrier bags. However, PHB is expensive, and a container made of Biopol is several times more expensive than the same container made of PVC or polythene. But its cost can be justified for some uses, and 5000 tonnes a year are manufactured. PHB will not solve the problem of plastic litter because it is too expensive to be used for throw-away packaging. Its main use is likely to be for surgical sutures and supports within the body where it can slowly dissolve during healing, or for medical and personal hygiene products that we flush away to the sewers.

Bulk sweeteners

Bulk sweeteners, as their name implies, need to be used in relatively large amounts to give you the desired level of sweetness. Glucose, **sorbitol** and **xylitol** are bulk sweeteners, and sugar is *the* bulk sweetener—others are generally less sweet. Sweetness is measured by making a 10% solution of the compound in water and then asking a panel of people to taste it. It is then diluted, tasted again, diluted, tasted again, and so on until they can no longer taste it. This way you can compare sweetness, but it is still rather subjective. The values in the table below are only a rough guide, and sugar is used as the standard against which the others are judged. The values fall in a narrow range, and you should bear this in mind when we consider artificial sweeteners later in this chapter, some of which are over a thousand times sweeter than sugar.

Golden syrup can be made from sugar either by the action of enzymes or acid, and it is only one type of liquid bulk sweetener. Others can be made by doing the same to starch from corn, potatoes or wheat, and the glucose syrups they produce are used when a liquid

---

Sweetness factors compared to the sweetness of sugar

Fructose	120%
Xylitol	100%
Erythritol	75%
Glucose	70%
Galactose	60%
Maltose	50%
Sorbitol	50%
Lactose	40%

sweetener is required for ice cream, chewing gum, chewy sweets or candy. We could even turn **cellulose** (fibre) into a sweet-tasting nutritious syrup, but the process is more difficult and not economical at the moment. If there were ever a severe worldwide famine, chemists could increase the food supply by turning sawdust and paper into life-saving 'empty calories' of glucose.

It is possible to turn sugar into other sweet-tasting saccharides apart from glucose and fructose. There are enzymes that will take sucrose and rearrange the molecule to a form known as isomaltose, which is also sweet but nowhere near as sweet as sugar itself. The saccharide which comes nearest to meeting the requirements of a bulk sweetener that is as sweet as sugar is xylitol.

Xylitol

Xylitol was first made over a century ago in Germany by Emil Fischer and his associates. It has a sweetness rating about the same as sugar itself, and it has as many calories, but it cannot be digested by the bacteria that cause tooth decay. Xylitol penetrates the plaque on our teeth but no acid forms. It may even help fight the bacteria by loosening their grip on the tooth enamel.

The inability of xylitol to cause tooth decay was demonstrated in a large-scale test on 11 and 12-year old children in a rural community in northern Finland, and was carried out by the Ylivieska Health Care Centre from 1982 to 1984. Those who chewed xylitol gum three times a day, taking in about 10 g of xylitol, had half the number of dental cavities as a group who were not given the gum. When the children were examined again in 1987 those who had chewed xylitol gum still had 50% fewer cavities.

If you put a xylitol sweet in your mouth you may even recognise it in a rather unusual way, by a brief sensation of coolness on the tip of your tongue. You are not imagining things: you are experiencing the chemistry of xylitol. When this simple sugar dissolves in water it absorbs heat and the solution gets cooler. The same happens on your tongue. Xylitol is slowly gaining a market as a sweetener for chewing gum, for sweets that you suck, like mints and fruit gums, and for pharmaceutical tablets that are to be kept in the mouth such as throat lozenges, decongestants, and pastilles used to heal mouth ulcers.

The old name for xylitol is birch-sugar, and most of it still comes from Finland where there are whole forests of birch trees. Xylitol is made by treating birch wood with water, but the processes of extraction are relatively costly. This is why xylitol is not a cheap substitute for sugar if a formulation requires a lot, but it makes an ideal coating for things like chewing gum and medicinal products.

Of course xylitol was not without its critics, and they were alarmed when investigations in the 1970s showed that it caused various disorders in rats. However, these effects were only observed when the rats were fed abnormally large amounts of xylitol, and this sweetener was never at risk of not being accepted by the licensing authorities because it occurs naturally in several fruits and vegetables. Strawberries and raspberries are particularly rich in xylitol, and so is cauliflower. Both yellow plums and greengages contain almost 1% of xylitol.

It is not economical to extract xylitol from any of these sources, but it can be got from wood. Wood consists of three main components: cellulose, which is used to make paper; lignin, which consists of polyphenols and has few uses; and hemi-cellulose, which is like cellulose but is a polymer of other saccharides, and is mainly xylose from which xylitol is made. Hemi-cellulose rich in xylose is also part of other plants such as corn cobs, cotton seed, sugar-cane bagasse, straw and nut shells. The xylose can comprise up to a quarter of the dry weight of these materials. Xylose is easier to extract than cellulose, although the process to turn it into xylitol requires several stages; the end product is pure crystals of xylitol.

Xylitol may solve the problem of tooth decay, but it still has the calorific value of a carbohydrate-like sugar. There are some bulk sweeteners which get round this problem, and **erythritol** is one. This is found in fruits, fermented foods and soyabean sauce. It has 75% the sweetness of sugar, but no calories, nor does it cause tooth decay. Erythritol is rather like xylitol but with one fewer carbon atom. It was discovered in 1874, and it can be made from glucose by fermenting with the right yeasts, but the yields are low and the processes are not yet commercial. Currently the Japanese Nikken Chemical Company of Tokyo are investigating a fermentation process which will convert glucose into erythritol with almost 50% yields and with few side-products.

Artificial sweeteners

The alternatives to bulk sweeteners are intense sweeteners, of which a few milligrams will give the same response on the tongue as a gram of sugar. Not all of these are artificial, although the most successful ones are. Because such molecules are the product of the chemical laboratory, they are automatically viewed with suspicion by some. Even so, millions of us willingly consume them every day.

The term 'artificial sweetener' has been much abused and carries such tones of disapproval that those in the industry prefer to use the phrase 'non-nutritive sweetener', which may be technically correct but has little else to recommend it. Intense sweeteners are big money earners with sales exceeding $1 billion per year. The table below lists several of them, divided into the truly artificial ones and those that come from plant material.

Sweetness factors (compared to sucrose taken as 1)	
artificial sweeteners	
cyclamate	30
aspartame	180
acesulfame	200
saccharin	300
sucralose	600
alitame	2000
plant-extract sweeteners	
steviosin	300
hernandulcin	1000
neohesperidine	1800
thaumatin	2000

The first artificial sweetener

Before we look more closely at modern day intense sweeteners, it will be instructive to look at an earlier one, *sapa*, which should definitely have carried a health warning. *Sapa* was the artificial sweetener of Ancient Rome, and a part of civilised living at the time of Christ. It has a strange story to tell which shows the extent to which the demand for sweetness will often override other considerations.

Honey alone was never capable of satisfying the demand for sweet-tasting food, and in Imperial Rome sugar was little more than a rare novelty from the East. *Sapa*, on the other hand was easy to make, it found a ready outlet in the sweetening and preserving of wine, and was especially popular with cooks for making sauces. Roman cooks were very fond of *sapa*, and it is mentioned in 85 recipes of the Roman Empire's best-seller, *The Apician Cookbook*. *Sapa* was like honey, an intensely sweet syrup, but the dangers of using it were great indeed.

Wine producers also used *sapa* to improve the quality of wines and extend their life. The Greeks discovered this useful little ruse, and although Greek wines were much admired they also had a reputation for causing miscarriages. Pure *sapa* was eaten neat by Roman prostitutes deliberately to produce abortions, and for another reason: it gave them an attractive pale complexion.

The Romans suspected *sapa* was deleterious to their health, but they continued to use it. It was reputed to make people tired and listless, anaemic, constipated and infertile. It did all this because it was made from lead. Pliny the Elder, who lived from 23 AD to 79 AD, described how *sapa* was prepared by boiling down grape juice, wine lees, or sour wine in pans until most of the water and alcohol had gone. If you want good *sapa* he wrote, then it was essential to use a lead pan.

All can be explained with a little bit of chemistry. Wine contains natural organic acids, such as tartaric and citric acid, and if wine picks up spores of the bacterium *Acetobacter*, which are quite common, then it will become more acidic as the alcohol is converted to **acetic acid**. Eventually it becomes sour wine, *vin egar*, i.e. vinegar. The Romans did not waste wine that was going off, but made *sapa* from it. Lead-lined pans were essential for this purpose since the lead was attacked and dissolved by these various acids which reacted to form lead salts, mainly **lead acetate**. The lead compounds were responsible for the sweet taste, and modern analysts have demonstrated that *sapa* would have had 1000 parts per million of lead (0.1%). Beautiful white crystals of lead salts could be grown from *sapa*, and these tasted very sweet. When their chemical nature was realised in the 18th century they were called sugar of lead.

Sapa did all that it was reputed to do. It sweetened food, it preserved wine by killing bacteria, it caused abortions because of the lead, and it produced pale complexions because a feature of chronic lead poisoning is anaemia. What the Romans did not realise, however, were other side effects of a high lead intake, which are constipation, stomach pains, muscular weakness and headaches. The reputed infertility of the upper classes is now thought to have been due to *sapa*. This artificial sweetener passed into history along with the Roman Empire, but not the trick of putting lead into wine. Even in the last century vintners were still adding lead to port wine, and the traditional trick of the trade was to put a pellet of lead shot in every bottle.

Saccharin

In the years when sugar was cheap and plentiful there was no demand for artificial sweeteners. When the first modern sweetener was stumbled upon in the last century there was already a need building up, and one which kept up a demand for it. Doctors who told their patients to eat less sugar no longer condemned them to a life without sweetness. They could tell them to choose saccharin to flavour their drinks and desserts instead.

Saccharin was discovered by Ira Remsen and Constantin Fahlberg at the Johns Hopkins University in the USA in 1879. They were researching sulfur–nitrogen compounds and made a new derivative of benzene. In those days it was common practice to record the taste of all new substances and the intense sweetness of the new compound was reported. Its taste led to the name saccharin.

Saccharin is over 300 times sweeter than sugar, and a tiny tablet of saccharin is as sweet as a spoonful of sugar but without its 20 Calories. It does not taste quite as nice as sugar, and some people say it has a metallic aftertaste. Its safety had been debated endlessly, and saccharin is probably the most investigated ingredient in the food industry.

During the last century there were almost no tests for health and safety before marketing a new food additive, and manufacturers were quick to realise the potential of saccharin. Even so, tests were soon demanded when they started to use it as a cheap substitute for sugar. Testing in those days consisted of the blunt but effective method of feeding 5 grams of saccharin a day for six months to volunteers. They came to no harm and public fears were allayed.

Some people continued to oppose it even so. Controversy raged and the then US President Theodore Roosevelt set up a review board, which concluded that saccharin was safe below 0.3 g per day. Saccharin became part of the regular diet of diabetics and the occasional diet of slimmers. When sugar rationing was introduced in both World Wars, saccharin was used by millions of people. Manufacturers of fruit drinks found that a blend of saccharin and sugar gave a better, less syrupy product than sweetening with sugar alone. In this way saccharin became an unsuspected part of many people's diet. In the 1950s, when the modern vogue for slimness began, saccharin became popular in its own right, and its use was not challenged again until another artificial sweetener, **cyclamate**, was banned in the USA in the 1970s.

Saccharin was suspected of causing bladder cancer because of its similarity to cyclamate. The two were often used in combination. When saccharin was tested on rats, a few male rats, but only slightly more than expected, developed bladder cancer when fed extremely high doses of saccharin (up to 3% of their diet) throughout their lives. One observer said it was equivalent to drinking 800 cans of diet cola per day. The evidence is difficult to translate into human terms. Saccharin had been around since great grandmother's day and if it had been causing bladder cancer this had gone unnoticed. Saccharin was not banned, and since then many other studies have failed to find any link between saccharin use and human cancers. Saccharin passes unchanged through the body and does not react with DNA, which is what has to happen with a cancer-triggering chemical. Saccharin is still approved for use in 90 countries around the world. It cannot promote dental caries and there is the suggestion that it may even help prevent this condition because it inhibits the micro-organisms in plaque by interfering with their cellular membrane.

Cyclamate

Cyclamate is also a sulfur–nitrogen compound, and again it was pure chance that led to its discovery as a sweetener in 1937. When Michael Sveda of the chemical company E.I. DuPont de Nemours put his cigarette down on the edge of his laboratory bench, it picked up a few grains of the material he had just made. When he next put it to his lips he was struck by an intense sweet taste, and cyclamate had been discovered. This was to be an even bigger money-spinner than saccharin, because it had three advantages: it was patentable; it did not have a bitter aftertaste; and you needed more of it to get the same level of sweetness because it has only a tenth of the sweetness of saccharin. However, you still needed only one thirtieth of the amount of sugar. By the mid–1960s cyclamate dominated the US market for artificial sweeteners.

The warning bell for cyclamate had sounded in 1957 when a research team in England found that mice exposed to saccharin developed bladder cancer. They had observed this after they had implanted a pellet directly into the animals' bladders, a somewhat unusual method of testing. This evidence was not accepted by the FDA as indicative of a risk to humans, but the seeds of doubt had been sown. A later study showed that the same thing happened with a mixture of cyclamate and saccharin. A lifetime study was undertaken in which rats were fed high dietary doses of cyclamate, saccharin and cyclohexamine. This last chemical is the compound that cyclamate turns into inside the body, and was also suspect. The study found an increased number of bladder tumours in male rats. A media blitz against cyclamate was unleashed and the FDA banned it. Cyclamate had fallen foul of the 'Delaney clause' of the US 1958 Food Additives Amendment which said: 'no additive shall be deemed to be safe if it is found to induce cancer when ingested by man or animal.' The Canadian and UK governments also outlawed cyclamate, but other countries were unimpressed by the tests because of the abnormally high amounts fed to the animals, and cyclamate is still popular in many countries around the world. Then in 1984 the FDA and the National Academy of Science announced that cyclamate was not carcinogenic after all. But by then it was too late to reinstate it as the leading sweetener in the world's largest market.

Acesulfan

Acesulfam is the latest of the sulfur–nitrogen sweeteners. It is about 200 times sweeter than sugar, and was discovered in 1967 by Karl Claus of the German chemical company Hoechst, again quite by chance. Claus licked his finger to pick up a piece of paper in the lab and got a pleasant surprise since it had picked up a trace of the new compound he was working on.

Aware of the fate of the other sulfur–nitrogen sweeteners, Hoechst tested acesulfam very thoroughly before they put it on the market. Acesulfam, which is sometimes called **acesulfam-K** (K is the chemical symbol for potassium, and acesulfam is a potassium salt), goes by the trade name of Sunett and it is used in soft drinks, desserts and puddings, as well as being sold as individual tablets for sweetening tea and coffee. It is approved in over 50 countries, including the USA, and there are over 2000 products throughout the world that contain it, including toothpastes, mouthwashes and pharmaceuticals. This sweetener has a synergistic effect with the next one we are going to look at, **aspartame**, which means that each boosts the sweetness of the other. Used in combination, much less of either is required to achieve the same intensity of taste.

Aspartame

Most people will probably know aspartame by its brand name of NutraSweet, and products such as Canderel or Equal. Sales of this around the world now exceed $1 billion, and in the US this artificial sweetener outsells all others. It was discovered in 1965 by James Schlatter working for the US firm G.D. Searle & Co. of Stokie, Illinois. Schlatter was making compounds for testing as anti–ulcer drugs, and had joined two protein amino acids together, **aspartic acid** and **phenylalanine**. He discovered that the product tasted sweet, but the company found it even sweeter when eventually they sold out to the chemical giant Monsanto for $2.7 billion in 1986. Today there are manufacturing plants in the USA, Japan, Brazil and France.

While it was protected under patent, Searle was able to charge a very high price for NutraSweet, about $100 per kilogram, and people were prepared to pay the price because so little aspartame was required. It is 200 times sweeter than sugar so that only a few milligrams were needed to flavour a cup of tea or coffee. Not only that, but it tasted as good as sugar, and some even preferred its 'clean' taste to that of sugar.

Like all artificial sweeteners, however, it had its critics. The FDA approved aspartame in 1974, then had second thoughts in 1975 and demanded more stringent tests. They finally cleared it for general use in

1981 provided it carried a warning that it contained phenylalanine. Now at first sight this seems rather strange because phenylalanine is an *essential* amino acid—in other words we cannot live without it. Nevertheless the warning was necessary for those people who suffer from a condition called phenylketonuria. They are sensitive to excess phenylalanine because they lack the enzyme which disposes of it when there is too much of it in the body. About one person in 15 000 is affected by phenylketonuria, and they need professional advice from a hospital dietitian. They must monitor what they eat and avoid foods that have a lot of phenylalanine, like steak, eggs, cheese, yoghurt and chocolate. Knowing that NutraSweet also contains phenylalanine means that they should avoid this artificial sweetener.

Aspartame is digested in the human body, as we might expect from its being a tiny protein fragment. It breaks down into aspartic acid, phenylalanine and **methanol**. The first two are amino acids which our body may use as building blocks in making its own protein. The amount of aspartic acid and phenylalanine we get from aspartame is tiny compared to the amount in a normal diet where they come from foods such as meat, milk and fish. The methanol has to be disposed of—as we shall see in Chapter 3, this is an undesirable molecule to have in our body—but again the amount we get from aspartame poses no risk. A glass of fruit juice, beer or wine will give us just as much.

Attacks on aspartame came from several quarters. Some claimed it raised the level of phenylalanine in the brain, which might affect those suffering from high blood pressure and Parkinson's disease. In 1984 the US public interest group, Common Cause, complained that the testing of aspartame by the FDA had been seriously flawed. In the UK, the national newspaper the *Guardian* carried several articles in 1983, the year when NutraSweet was launched in the UK, that questioned the safety of aspartame. They reported the claims by Professor Richard Wurtman of the Massachusetts Institute of Technology that aspartame interferes with the body's chemical messengers, increasing the desire for food, affecting blood pressure, making us more sensitive to pain, and causing insomnia.

The anti-aspartame campaigners kept up their attacks throughout the 1980s with claims that it even caused eye damage and mental illness (that came at a meeting of the American Association for the Advancement of Science in 1988). In Britain the *Guardian* again attacked NutraSweet in July 1990, making more serious allegations in which they implied that the manufacturers had faked laboratory tests submitted to the FDA when they applied for approval of aspartame as a sweetener. NutraSweet sued the *Guardian* for libel and malicious falsehood and won substantial damages.

The anti-aspartame campaigners did not have it all their own way, and there were even reports by a group at the University of Illinois in Chicago that the sweetener protected against tooth decay. Research at the University of Leeds, England, showed that it helped dieters by reducing their appetite slightly. Such reports generally failed to get a public airing beyond specialist science journals and trade magazines.

The makers of NutraSweet were confident that they had a winner, and knew that on chemical grounds it was just like a tiny piece of meat as far as the body was concerned. It now dominates the diet drinks and desserts market. For 99.994% of the population NutraSweet can be of real benefit. The unlucky 0.006% who suffer from phenylketonuria must use other artificial sweeteners. Despite all the attacks, NutraSweet has survived and it is used in 5000 products in almost every country of the world.

The patent for aspartame expired in 1992 and other companies can now challenge NutraSweet, whose production is about 10 000 tonnes a year and growing. With healthy competition the price should fall for what is after all a relatively cheap chemical. The present makers will no doubt dominate the market since they have exclusive rights to the brand name NutraSweet, which they have carefully fostered.

There are still two important features of an ideal sweetener that aspartame lacks: stability to heat and stability in solution. You cannot bake with the raw powder and this is a major drawback, although 'encapsulating' aspartame to protect it is seen as one way round this problem. Its stability in solution is less of a problem, even though a few per cent of the aspartame in a drink decomposes each month to a compound with no taste, and it decomposes more quickly if heated. It is reasonably stable in acid drinks like colas, or lime and lemon drinks, and at low pH 4 it has a shelf-life of six months or more.[9]

[9] The measure of acidity is the pH scale which ranges from 0 (very acidic) through 7 (neutral) to 14 (very alkaline). The acids we encounter in our everyday life range from weakly acid rain water, which has pH 5, to tomato juice pH 4, vinegar pH 3, lemon juice pH 2, and stomach acid pH 1.

Aspartame is made from two amino acids. Other combinations of amino acids are also very sweet, such as alanine and aminomalonine, and when this combination was discovered in 1985 it was claimed to be more stable than aspartame in water. Pfizer, the pharmaceutical company, has a sweetener which is a combination of aspartic acid and alanine under the name of alitame. It is 12 times sweeter than aspartame and much more stable. Normally small changes to a sweet-tasting molecule lead to large changes in taste, and tinkering with one of the amino acids of aspartame itself might have been expected to kill the sweet taste. Yet alitame still tastes as sweet even when one of its component amino acids is attached to the molecule back-to-front.

Sucralose

Sucralose is an artificial sweetener that will withstand heating, and it is water-soluble and stable in acids. Indeed, it comes near to being the perfect sweetener. It was discovered accidentally in 1976 at Queen Elizabeth College, London, by a graduate researcher Shashikant Phadnis who was reacting ordinary sugar with a reagent that attached chlorine atoms to the molecule. When he was rung up by Tate & Lyle, the sugar company he was collaborating with, and asked if they could have some samples of the material he was making for testing, Phadnis misheard them and thought they wanted it for *tasting*, and so tried it himself. The result was sucralose.

Sucralose has three chlorine atoms attached to a sugar molecule, and this multiplies the sweetness factor by about 600. Replacing more than three can give even more intense sweeteners, but these are difficult to make. Testing so far has shown this chlorinated sugar to be safe, but there is a snag. Most sucralose is taken in by mouth and passes through the body unchanged, but a tiny amount is split into its two components, *chloro*glucose and *chloro*fructose, and these are intrinsically dangerous and toxic, although not at the levels at which Sucralose would be used. The danger was enough to cause the FDA in 1992 to question the wisdom of using Sucralose, and to ask for more tests. Nevertheless, it has already been approved for use in Canada, Russia and Australia.

Although most intense sweeteners in common use are artificial ones, there are some that are derived from natural sources. These are given in the Box below.

Natural intense sweeteners

Thaumatin

This is a very large protein-like molecule extracted from the West African fruit ketemfe (*Thaumatococcus danielli*) and is 3000 times sweeter than sugar. Like aspartame it is compounded of amino acids, but instead of only two units it has hundreds of these joined end-to-end. It tastes so sweet because it can trigger many receptors on our tongue at once, but this also means it has the drawback of clinging to the tongue and the sweet sensation lingers too long. This may be used to advantage in some things such as chewing gum or bitter medicines, and it is also used in toothpastes, mouthwashes, jam and soy sauce. Animals love thaumatin and dogs and cats can be persuaded to eat canned pet foods, and pigs to put on more weight, if their food is flavoured with it. Thaumatin is sold under the trade name of Talin.

Stevioside

This is a mixture of saccharide molecules which come from a plant of the chrysanthemum family called *Stevia rebaudiana*, which was originally grown in Paraguay and used for centuries by the natives there to sweeten their food and drink. It is 300 times as sweet as sugar. It can be separated into various components called rebaudisodes which make up to 3% of the plant leaves, and these are even sweeter, but they have a lingering bitter aftertaste. Stevioside has the advantage that it is stable to heat. It has been used in South American and Japan for many years and it does not cause tooth decay.

Glycyrrhizin

This comes from the liquorice root and is more than 50 times sweeter than sugar. It also has several medicinal properties, and research has shown that it is an anti-ulcer, anti-inflammatory, and anti-spasmodic agent. There are even claims by its supporters that it is an anti-viral agent and good for the heart.

(continued)

Natural intense sweeteners (*continued*)

Neohesperidine

This is derived from a naturally occurring chemical found in orange peel. At concentrations less than 4 parts per million (ppm) it is not perceived as sweet, but it enhances fruit flavours and suppresses bitter tastes. At higher concentrations, above 5 ppm, it registers as several hundred times sweeter than sucrose. It enhances the sweetness of other sweeteners and allows the amount of these to be reduced. Neohesperidine lingers for a long time on the tongue and has a liquorice aftertaste. It has been approved for use in Europe, and is used in chewing gums and in some speciality Belgian beers.

What makes a molecule taste sweet?

Most of us would consider flavours to be the special preserve of cooks and chefs, and to look upon their blending as an art, not a science. Yet flavour is part of food chemistry, and, just as with fragrances, there is an industry whose job it is to extract long-established flavours, analyse them, and then to make them by chemical means. Some chemists also research into new flavours, hoping to discover and prepare entirely different tastes for our delight. The chemistry of taste may still be in its infancy, but great strides have been made in the past few years in understanding at least one area of taste, and that is sweetness. Chemists now know enough about the nature, or rather the 'structure', of sweetness to be able to predict which molecules will produce this sensation on our tongue.

So what is the secret of sweetness? The answer does not lie, as you might expect, with the chemical behaviour of a molecule, and if you search for a common feature among those materials which taste sweet you will find none. We can see this if we compare sweeteners like lead acetate, sucrose, aspartame and saccharin which are all chemically very different. Yet surprisingly the answer to sweetness lies with their molecular structure, or at least to a triangular part of it.

Just how subtle taste can be is demonstrated by the amino acid phenylalanine, which in its right-hand form tastes slightly sweet.[10] When you make the left-hand form of phenylalanine, you find it

[10] Left and right-handed molecules are discussed in Chapter 5.

tastes bitter. These two molecules are exactly the same chemically, with the same atoms and groups joined by exactly the same chemical bonds. The difference is merely that they are mirror images of each other, and this is enough to alter radically their taste. Our own experience of putting on shoes the wrong way round tells us that an apparently small difference can have disproportionate consequences when we mis-match left- and right-hand objects, and so it is with receptors on our tongue. Just as a key only needs a small modification for it not to turn a lock, so a molecule with the wrong sized sweetness key will not turn on the sensors in our taste buds.

In the 1960s Robert Shallenberger and Terry Acree suggested that molecules could activate the sweet buds on our tongue if the hydrogen atoms they contained were positioned at exactly the right angle to lock on to atoms in the receptor. Lemont Kier of Massachusetts College of Pharmacy at Boston identified three parts of a sweet molecule that determined the shape to fit the receptor, and this became known as the triangle-of-sweetness theory. Support for this suggestion was forthcoming when molecules were constructed with the shape he predicted, and were shown to be sweet.

The triangle of sweetness. If a molecule is to taste sweet then it must trigger the sweetness receptors on the tongue. To do this it requires three features: an oxygen or nitrogen atom carrying a hydrogen (OH or NH) at location A; an oxygen or nitrogen atom at location B; and a water repelling group, such as a hydrocarbon, at location C. The numbers along the sides of the triangle are the ideal distances between these three centres expressed in picometres (10^{-12} metres).

At one corner of the triangle of sweetness there has to be a hydrogen atom that will lock on to oxygen or nitrogen on the receptor. In so doing it forms what is called a hydrogen bond. This is a weak interaction between molecules and relies on the attraction between a hydrogen atom (which is positively charged) in one molecule, and an oxygen or nitrogen atom (which is negatively charged) in another molecule. At the second corner of the triangle of sweetness there has to be an oxygen or nitrogen which will similarly attract a hydrogen on the receptor, again forming a hydrogen bond. At the third corner there are hydrogens that do not want to engage in hydrogen bonding, and these are hydrogens attached to carbon atoms. Get all these components in just the right positions and you can almost guarantee the molecule will taste sweet. The triangle of sweetness fitting a receptor is rather like an electric plug fitting a socket; when molecule and receptor connect a current flows to the brain and we sense sweetness.

Even though we can design a molecule which will be sweet, there are other factors that may make it unsuitable for commercial use. Most of the artificial sweeteners discovered so far decompose when heated, which is a big disadvantage because it excludes their use in cooking. Strangely, the first ever sweetener, *sapa*, did not suffer from this defect, which explains why it was so popular with the chefs of the Roman Empire. Sugar is still the only chemical that retains, and even improves, its sweetness on heating. What the world needs now is an artificial sweetener we can cook with, so that we can enjoy reduced-calorie cakes, biscuits, fruit pies, tarts and candies. Sugar makes up at least a third of these, and in some cases they are almost pure sugar.

The perfect sweetener has yet to be discovered or designed, although we can suggest its specifications: it should be hundreds of times sweeter than sugar yet with the same 'rounded' flavour and taste profile, in other words quick to register on our receptors and just as quick to de-register. Nor do we want any aftertaste like the metallic bitterness that some people experience with saccharin. Our model sweetener must of course be non-toxic (a child might eat a whole packet at once), and it must not cause dental caries. Either it has to pass straight through our gut or, if it is absorbed, it has to be digested like other components of our food. The manufacturers' requirements should not be overlooked either. They want it to be cheap to make and easy to purify, and to have a long shelf-life. It should be soluble in water and alcohol, unaffected by acids, and stable when heated at least to normal cooking temperatures. Find such a molecule and your fortune is made.

We know that the perfect sweetener will not solve the problems of the overweight people in Western societies, and if past campaigns against artificial sweeteners is anything to go by, there will always be someone ready to accuse it of being a health risk. The irony of low-calorie sweeteners is that they have not led to a decrease in the numbers of overweight people, but this clearly is a social problem and not one that can be solved by making better sweeteners. Indeed, sweeteners may even be counterproductive if they encourage people to eat more of so-called 'diet' foods. These people are using the skills of the chemists to indulge their longing for sweet-tasting foods.

The ever-increasing sales of convenience foods keeps the sugar producers in business despite the apparent decline in the sales of sugar, jam, golden syrup and all the products our mothers bought to bake the traditional home-made treats of cakes and pastries. Artificial sweeteners can only help people if they use them to *replace* some of the sugar in their diet, and thereby keep their weight under control. Sweetness, whether natural or artificial, bulk or intense, is not something to fear. A little chemistry and a little care, and you can enjoy this pleasant sensation for the rest of your life, which may even be longer and healthier, thanks to artificial sweeteners. These chemicals can promise nothing more.

CHAPTER THREE

Alcohol

Alcohol and body chemistry; the production and chemistry of alcoholic drinks; fraudulent drinks; the risks and benefits of drinking alcohol; industrial alcohol.

WHEN sugars ferment under the action of yeasts they generally produce alcohol. Unlike sugar, for which chemists can make artificial alternatives as we saw in Chapter 2, there is no substitute for alcohol. In this chapter we will take a chemist's eye view of this molecule—how it forms, what effects it has on us, how it offers us an alternative fuel, and how we can learn to live with it and not die from it. We all have alcohol naturally in our body in small amounts, and it has no effect because there is so little of it. When we suddenly increase the amount, by drinking a lot of it, then we experience some rather unusual effects—elation to begin with, but deflation a few hours later. Were alcohol to be discovered today its sale to the public would never be permitted because of the potentially lethal side-effects.

There are many people in the world for whom alcohol is taboo, such as Muslims and Mormons. Muslims are forbidden it supposedly because of Mohammed's displeasure when he discovered his troops were drunk on the eve of battle. A Muslim can only drink alcohol if it is prescribed by a doctor. Mormons and other Christian sects can find plenty of reasons for not consuming alcohol: it is addictive; it causes illness; it ruins lives; it leads to violent behaviour in young people; and it is a major cause of death on the roads. Alcohol has another, although less socially destructive, drawback: weight for weight it provides almost as much energy as fat: 7 Calories per gram compared to 9 Calories per gram for fats.

There are also those who suspect alcoholic drinks of harbouring other unwanted chemicals, and they claim that brewers, vintners and distillers use additives to improve the colour, the clarity and the keeping quality of their drink. And they do. More worrying still are reports of fraudulent drinks, made from cheap supplies of industrial alcohol to which other chemicals have been added to provide flavour and colour. If they are made with methyl alcohol, such drinks can kill. And they do.

Yet for every person who opposes the demon drink there is an ardent supporter of alcohol, and they too have good reasons for their opinions. Alcohol is enjoyable and relaxing; it makes social and sexual contacts easier because it releases us from our inhibitions; and there is evidence that those who drink alcohol suffer less from coronary heart disease, and have fewer colds. We may also endorse alcohol not as a drink but as a renewable and sustainable source of fuel for transport, and as a feedstock for the chemicals industry. It can be made easily and cheaply, it can be stored and transported safely, and it burns cleanly leaving little environmental pollution.

It is rare to find such a collection of emotions, warnings, hazards and benefits surrounding a simple molecule. So what is special about this chemical? Can we balance its advantages against its disadvantages? Can we prevent addiction to it? Can we detect phoney drinks? The answer to these questions is to be found in a closer look at its chemistry.

Alcohol is also called ethyl alcohol or **ethanol**,[1] which is the correct chemical name for this molecule.[2] There are two ways in which alcohol is produced on a large scale: by the fermentation of sugars, or by the chemical reaction of water and **ethylene**. The former is agriculturally derived alcohol; the latter is often referred to as industrial alcohol. Although they are chemically identical, agriculturally derived alcohol is classed as drinkable, while industrial alcohol is made undrinkable by adding unpleasant chemicals. It is then popularly referred to as methylated spirits or meths for short.

[1] A reminder that when the name of a substance appears in **bold** type, it means that there is more about its chemistry in the Appendix.

[2] The name alcohol comes from the Arabic *al kohl*, but its origin is not clear.

The alcohol which is made by the fermentation of agricultural products is produced by the activity of fungi called yeasts. These grow by feeding on sugars such as glucose, and as they do this they make alcohol, which for them is an unwanted by-product. Alcohol is a small part of the cycling of carbon through the environment, a subject we shall return to in Chapter 9. We could follow an individual carbon atom through this cycle and the scenario might go as follows. The carbon begins as carbon dioxide in the atmosphere, which is absorbed by a leaf of barley and turned into carbohydrate. After the barley has been harvested, and malted to break the carbohydrate down into simple sugars, it is then digested by yeasts whose enzymes turn it into alcohol. It may then be drunk. Inside the drinker the alcohol is processed and its energy extracted, thereby turning it back into carbon dioxide. This is breathed out and returned to the atmosphere. There are two halves of such a cycle, production and consumption, and since the latter affects us intimately when we drink alcohol I will begin with the chemistry of this.

Alcohol and body chemistry

We can analyse the contents of an alcoholic brew and find that it contains lots of things apart from alcohol and water. For instance a litre (about two of the traditional pints) of the world-famous Irish drink, Guinness, in addition to providing you with 370 Calories of energy, contains the following:

alcohol	30 g	thiamine (vitamin B_1)	0.04 mg
carbohydrate	30 g	riboflavin (vitamin B_2)	0.4 mg
protein	3 g	pyridoxine (vitamin B_6)	0.6 mg
phosphorus	557 mg	nicotinic acid (niacin)	6 mg
iron	0.3 mg	biotin	0.01 mg
sodium	25 mg	folic acid	0.07 mg
potassium	300 mg		
calcium	54 mg		
magnesium	133 mg		

Clearly Guinness is also a good source of some essential minerals, and if we drink it regularly it will provide a significant fraction of our daily requirements of the B vitamins. The surprise of drinks like Guinness is the large amount of potassium compared to sodium, and this is true of all beers. Most foods have much more sodium than potassium.[3]

Despite these dietary components an alcoholic drink is not regarded as a food, a medicine, or a tonic, although in earlier times alcohol was advertised as all of these. Today we treat it mainly as a relaxant. Our body treats it as a poison. There are many ethical questions that alcohol raises which a knowledge of its chemistry cannot answer, but it can answer two key questions. Why does drinking make us feel good for a while, and then a few hours later make us feel so bad? Why do many people have to take special care because their tolerance of alcohol is low, such as women, native Americans and Japanese?

Alcohol does not occur as part of the complex chemistry going on inside the cells of the human body, but a little alcohol is produced naturally within our intestines by bacteria and yeasts which have enzymes that can turn carbohydrate into alcohol, and this alcohol gets into our bloodstream. Our liver has an enzyme called alcohol dehydrogenase (ADH) with which to get rid of this unwanted chemical, and it converts the alcohol to **acetaldehyde**. This molecule is then turned into **acetic acid** by another enzyme, and the acetic acid is used in the so-called Krebs cycle of chemical reactions, by which its energy is extracted and it emerges as carbon dioxide.

The liver can deal with large amounts of alcohol, but it needs time to do so. If a person takes in too much alcohol at one session they may even die, and a lethal dose can be as little as 400 ml, the amount of alcohol in a litre bottle of spirits. A normal liver can only process 12 ml (10 grams) of alcohol per hour. A glass of wine, which is about 12% alcohol, may provide this amount, as will half a pint of beer which is around 4% alcohol, and so will a tot, or shot, of spirits which is generally 40% alcohol. These measures are only rough guides because the amount of alcohol in wine, beer and spirits can vary within quite wide margins. The quantity commonly referred to by those who give advice about drinking is the 'unit', which is generally that quantity of a drink which will deliver 10 grams of alcohol. It is not a precise amount, only a guide, since it varies widely even among drinks of apparently the same type.

---

[3] We often redress the balance when drinking by eating salted snacks.

The effects of alcohol

Units	Number of drinks			Alcohol level in blood (mg per 100 ml)	Effects on the average man*
	beer	wine	spirits		
2	1 pint	2 glasses	2 singles	30	feeling of well-being
3	1.5 pints	3 glasses	3 singles	50	lack of inhibitions
5	2.5 pints	5 glasses	5 singles	80	unfit to drive
6	3 pints	1 bottle**	6 singles	100	unsteady on feet
10	5 pints	1 litre	10 singles	150	slurring of speech
12	6 pints	2 bottles	$\frac{1}{2}$ bottle***	200	drowsy and confused
18	9 pints	3 bottles	$\frac{3}{4}$ bottle	300	drunken stupor
24	12 pints	4 bottles	1 bottle	400	dead drunk, maybe dying

*For a woman the same effects may be experienced with about two thirds the amount of alcohol that a man needs, assuming they are the same weight.
**Wines are traditionally sold in 700 ml bottles.
***Spirits are often sold in bottles of 700 ml, and this is what is meant by a bottle here, not the 1 litre bottle which is becoming more common.

The effects of drinking alcohol can be seen in the table above. This table cannot take into account all factors which determine the effect that alcohol will have, because this depends on a person's weight, the condition of their liver, and whether the alcohol is taken with a meal.

When we drink alcohol it starts to be absorbed the minute it enters our mouth, but most is absorbed from the stomach and the gut. Ten per cent of the alcohol we take in is lost from our body without being digested. It is exhaled on our breath, sweated through our pores, or passed out in our urine. The other 90% is processed by the liver. The two chemicals which most affect our body when we drink are alcohol itself and acetaldehyde, and these affect different organs in different ways.

Brain and central nervous system: alcohol makes us feel happier, more at ease with people, and less inhibited about what we say and do. Technically alcohol is referred to as a depressant, but this does not mean that it makes us depressed. It means that it slows down the activity of the central nervous system, so that messages take longer to travel along nerve fibres. We become more relaxed and overconfident of our abilities, but also slower to react, and our speech becomes slurred. Alcohol has this effect on the brain because it replaces water molecules around nerve cells, and this interferes with the movement of electrically charged atoms which are responsible for transmitting information along a nerve fibre. Alcohol also slows the movement of chemical messenger molecules which carry information from cell to cell.

Ears: these are the organs which give us our sense of balance. Alcohol changes the density of the tissue and fluid in the ear, and the more alcohol we take the bigger are the changes, until we lose our normal sense of balance. The result is that we sway and stagger, trying to compensate for the feeling that we are about to fall over.

Skin: here it is the acetaldehyde which has an effect, dilating the blood vessels and making us feel hot. The dilation of blood vessels in the scalp and around the brain results eventually in a bad headache. Alcohol raises our pulse and blood pressure which increase the sensation of warmth. We can achieve the same effect if we take a shot of spirits on a cold day, but the comforting idea that people dying from exposure in the snow can be saved by a drink of brandy (carried by a St Bernard dog, of course), is a popular myth. In fact the alcohol would only serve to increase the loss of heat from their body.

Stomach: Men digest alcohol quicker than women because they have more ADH in their stomach, and this is the enzyme that converts alcohol to acetaldehyde. Consequently men can tolerate more alcohol than women, because drink-for-drink, less alcohol gets into a man's blood stream from his stomach. Native American Indians and Japanese people have the same lower level of ADH as women. The male and female kidney disposes of alcohol at the same rate, so that is not the reason for the difference between the sexes. Tests in the US showed that when both men and women were given the same amount of alcohol by injection into their bloodstream there were no sex-related differences in behaviour.[4]

---

[4] Even so, alcohol generally has a greater effect on women than on men because of the difference in body weight.

Liver: this is the main organ for removing alcohol, but as we have seen it does this only slowly. Indeed, people have been known to fail a breathalyser test 24 hours after their last drink. Alcohol also stimulates the breakdown of glycogen to glucose in the liver, so depleting the body's immediate store of energy. Although alcohol is high in Calories it does not satisfy your desire for food—indeed, it seems to stimulate it.

Kidneys: if you drink 250 ml of wine (about 2 glasses) you will lose at least 500 ml of water from your body as urine during the next two hours. Normally our kidneys will reabsorb and reuse water, and are prompted to do so by a hormone called vasopressin, which is released by the pituitary gland at the base of the brain. Alcohol reduces the amount of vasopressin, and so the kidneys fail to get the message to recycle water, which then passes to the bladder and out of the body. The result is dehydration unless this fluid loss is replaced.

Sex: alcohol can make us feel sexy and more easily aroused by lowering our inhibitions. It can prolong our performance in bed by slowing down the nervous system. Too much alcohol for a man can so relax his muscles that it interferes with his erection (the infamous 'brewers droop').

All these effects are the results of an immediate toxic reaction to alcohol. There are also long term effects of taking alcohol over many years, such as impaired brain function and memory. Excess alcohol can lead to acute inflammation of the stomach, especially if drunk on an empty stomach, and this is aggravated by the acetaldehyde formed, which is why for men one effect of alcohol can be a stomach ulcer.

The morning after, and how to avoid it

The body turns alcohol first to acetaldehyde, then to acetic acid, and finally to carbon dioxide. Acetaldehyde is the most likely cause of our hangover, because this is known to cause headaches and nausea. These unpleasant side effects can even be intensified, and this is one way to keep people off alcohol (see the Box on p. 68). Once alcohol is absorbed by our body we have its effects to contend with, and later those of its by-product acetaldehyde. As the alcohol disappears we sober up, but as the acetaldehyde forms we begin to experience the effects of this as a hangover. Sobering up is possible in theory by boosting the amount of ADH. Achieving this is another matter, but you cannot sober up by any of the popular remedies of sweating in a sauna, vigorous exercise, drinking black coffee or putting your head under the cold tap.

The morning after a bout of heavy drinking is simply the slow process of waiting for the acetaldehyde to disappear, but there are a few tips for coping with hangovers. No successful hangover cure has yet been marketed, and we know why this is unlikely to work for chemical reasons, unless it can speed up the removal of the excess acetaldehyde from the body. The following suggestions may relieve the worst excesses of a hangover:

- Have a glass of milk before you start drinking so you are not drinking on an empty stomach.

- Stick to one type of alcoholic drink, and occasionally have a soft drink.

- Drink a pint of water before going to bed.

- For breakfast eat something sweet, such as honey or jam. This is because these foods contain a lot of fructose, as we saw in Chapter 2, and this is the sugar that generates nicotinamide adenine dinucleotide (NAD) which is involved in the processing of alcohol. Extra sugar will also prevent depletion of the body's glycogen store.

- Avoid dark-coloured drinks such as port, sherry and red wines. However, the link between colour and hangover is not always a good guide. Whisky sometimes gets its dark rich colour from added **caramel**, and so does rum. But the reds of wines come from chemicals in the skins of grapes, and these may be partly responsible for a hangover.

The traditional remedy for a hangover is to resort to the hair of the dog that bit you and have another drink. This will only be of relief if you are addicted to alcohol, so that the unpleasant effects of your hangover are mainly withdrawal symptoms. Otherwise it is rather foolish advice.

People who are addicted to alcohol and really want to break their addiction can seek treatment and be helped to stop drinking. To prevent them succumbing to temptation and starting again, they can be prescribed a compound called **Antabuse** (see the Box below). This ensures that they will think twice before drinking any alcohol because the effects are so unpleasant. Antabuse works by blocking the enzyme which converts acetaldehyde to acetic acid, thereby removing it. A build-up of acetaldehyde produces a condition known as acetaldehydemia which can be extremely unpleasant. Even a little alcohol taken by someone on antabuse produces enough acetaldehyde for their body to react badly to it. They feel very ill because they are in effect experiencing a severe hangover, the symptoms of which are nausea, vomiting, laboured breathing, flushing, chest pains and throbbing headache. The experience is so dreadful that they will usually avoid alcohol while they remain on antabuse, although it has been found that some people can become tolerant to the drug and its effect is diminished. However, most people who take antabuse find it effective; but they must also be alert to the fact that some common household products contain alcohol, such as **vanilla** extract (35% alcohol), cough medicines (up to 25% alcohol), and mouthwashes (e.g. Listerine is 25% alcohol).

The Antabuse story

The effects of antabuse came to light in Denmark during World War II at a company called Medicinalco, where the policy was for employees to test any new drug that they discovered on themselves before it was prescribed for general use. And this is what Dr Jens Hald did while he was working on a drug against intestinal parasites such as worms. The chemical he took was called disulfiram, which had been used successfully to treat the parasitic skin disease scabies. Hald tested disulfiram on rabbits infected with parasites and it appeared to cure them. He then began to take the drug himself, and so did the company's medical research director, Dr Erik Jacobsen. They took a disulfiram pill every day for several weeks.

Most days they were fine, but on some days they went down with a bout of severe sickness, generally immediately after lunch. Curiously both men were only affected occasionally, and neither could link it to any particular cause—that is until one evening when Hald had a large drink of cognac with a friend. Immediately he became very ill while his friend was fine. He then realised that previous attacks coincided with meals at which he had drunk alcohol. When he told Jacobsen he too confirmed Hald's suspicion that it was disulfiram and alcohol that caused the vomiting and flushing. Tests on fellow workers confirmed that this was so. The immediate result was that disulfiram was dropped as a possible treatment for worms.

But that was not the end of the story. A few years later, in October 1947, Jacobsen was asked to stand in for another speaker at a public meeting and he told the disulfiram story as an amusing aside. This part of his talk was highlighted in a Copenhagen newspaper, the *Berlingske Tidende*, by a journalist who was at the meeting. The result was that alcoholics began writing to Jacobsen asking for some of his disulfiram pills. Clinical tests on alcoholics followed and a regime devised whereby Antabuse, the trade name Jacobsen gave the drug, could be used to help people to break their addiction to alcohol.

The production and chemistry of alcoholic drinks

Alcoholic drinks come in a large number of guises, but the main ones are beers, wines and spirits. What distinguishes the last of these from the other two is the chemical process of distillation which concentrates and purifies the alcohol. Concentrating alcohol this way led to a whole new range of drinks, but removing alcohol altogether requires more sophisticated chemistry. At the end of this chapter I will explain how this is done.

Grapes, barley, corn, sugarcane, fruit, potatoes and rice are all used to make alcoholic drinks. When the crop is harvested, and the sugars of the carbohydrate component are released, they may be fermented into alcohol by acting as food for a yeast. Yeast uses simple sugars in much the same way we do—as a source of energy—but unlike humans, who generate their energy with the help of oxygen from the air, the yeast generates its energy anaerobically, in other words without oxygen, and the product is alcohol.

Any source of sugary solution can be fermented, and in many countries there are drinks produced from a wide variety of fruit sugars. For example in the UK there is a large industry fermenting apple juice to make cider, and pear juice to make perry. There is even a cottage industry of homemade wine using soft fruit and wayside berries, such as blackberries and elderberries. Such fermented juice can be improved by adding ordinary sugar and the final strength of the drink may be as high as 13% alcohol.

All naturally fermented drinks contain hundreds of chemicals which come from the cereals, grapes or fruit. Other chemicals are also put into our drink, and additives commonly used by brewers and vintners are: **sorbic acid** and potassium sorbate, **sodium alginate**, ammonium caramel, sodium sulfite caramel, **silicon dioxide**, **propane-1,2-diol alginate**, and **sulfur dioxide**. All of these additives sound very chemical, but all have passed stringent health and safety tests. In fact some of them have been used for decades, and some, such as sulfur dioxide, have been used for thousands of years. As health risks they are insignificant compared to the risks from the alcohol itself.

Sorbic acid and potassium sorbate occur naturally in many fruits, and they are good at killing wild yeasts and other fungi. Sodium alginate enhances the texture of the drink by removing unwanted proteins. It is a long molecule made up of carbohydrate units joined together to form a chain, and is extracted from seaweed. Alginates are used to impart a smooth taste to many foods, such as ice cream. Ammonium and sodium sulfite caramels are forms of caramel and impart a rich golden or brown colour. Ammonium caramel is used mainly in beers, and sodium sulfite caramel in whisky and brandy. Silicon dioxide is a natural mineral that occurs in many forms, of which sand is the most common. It can be used in combination with isinglass, a natural gelatin, or as its sodium salt, sodium silicate, to clarify wine and beer by causing proteins, which may make these drinks cloudy, to cluster together and settle out. Propane-1,2-diol alginate is probably the most commonly used beer additive in the world; it produces a good frothy head. Sulfur dioxide is used in wines to destroy invading micro-organisms that might spoil the fermentation by producing other by-products.

In his well researched book *Name Your Poison* Ted Parratt discusses everything that is added to drinks, and makes the point that unlike foods, which must list all their ingredients, drinks need list only their alcohol content. All the drinker can do is trust the integrity of brewers, vintners and distillers. This is expecting rather a lot, in view of their behaviour down the ages, but with today's international news coverage the producers know how costly the wrong kind of publicity can be.

Wine

Wine can be made simply by crushing grapes, squeezing out the juice and allowing it to ferment with the wild yeasts that are naturally present. This can be a hit-and-miss affair, and does not always produce the desired result. It is better to add the right yeast to the grape juice, but even doing this still does not always stop millions of litres of wine going to waste because rogue yeasts have outpaced the starter yeast which the vintner added. Some rogue yeasts even produce toxins which can kill the commercial starter yeasts. Not all wild yeasts are bad: some were discovered to impart a new flavour to the wine, and so are cultured and added to the crushed grape. Winemakers jealously guard their strains of yeast. The preferred yeast for wine is *Saccharomyces ellipsoideus*, and unwanted bacteria are kept down by using sulfur dioxide, which is added as its solution in water or as sodium sulfite which dissolves in water and forms sulfur dioxide. In earlier times 'sulfiting' was done simply by burning sulfur near the vat of grape juice.

There are thousands of wines which divide first into red, white and rosé, then into region. White wines are made from grape juice which has been separated from the grape skins. Red wine is fermented with the skins and their colour chemicals are extracted into the alcohol solution. This also extracts **tannins** and other compounds which add flavour and help the wine to keep better. The red dye compounds from the skins can be extracted quicker by heating to 50 Celsius. Rosé wines are produced from a blend of white and red grapes.

The amount of alcohol in wines can vary between 5 and 13%, which is about the maximum concentration that a yeast can survive. Most have about 10–12%. If the content exceeds 13%, then the product must include added alcohol, and these are called fortified wines of which the best known are sherry, vermouth and port with about 15% alcohol. These also have added sugar (vermouths have added herbs as well), and they are left to stand in casks from whose wood they also extract more chemicals.

The world's major wine producers, in order of output starting with the largest, are: Italy, France, Spain, Argentina, the USA and Romania. Grape cultivation needs an average annual temperature of 10–12 °C and must not fall below 15 °C during the months April to October (September to March in the southern hemisphere). Traditionally the northern limit for grape cultivation is latitude 50°, which should exclude all of the British Isles, but there are a few vineyards in Southern England. Cultivation also depends on altitude, soil, and weather.

Vines bloom and form fruit, but until August these remain green and hard, with a high acid and a low sugar content. Throughout September things change rapidly as the fruit ripens, and the sugar content, which is mainly glucose, rises to over 200 grams per litre of grape juice. Ideally grapes should be picked at their peak glucose level because this is the sugar the yeast thrives on best.

The bunches of grapes are gently squeezed between rollers, so as not to crush the seeds or break the stems. These are then separated out with a stemming machine. The crushed grapes are pressed to release their juice which is called the 'must'. The harder the pressing the more juice is obtained, but the top quality juice comes off first. The average yield of must from a tonne of grapes is 750 litres. The must can be pasteurised to kill rogue yeasts by heating to near boiling (87 °C for two minutes) and then pure wine yeast has to be added. If the must has undesirable odours these can be removed by filtering the liquid through activated charcoal filters.

Fermentation takes about three weeks and is traditionally carried out in large oak vats, but more likely nowadays it is done in stainless steel or in glass-lined or plastic-lined tanks. White wines ferment best at about 12 °C, while red wines need to be at 20 °C or over. Fermentation slows down and eventually stops as the concentration of alcohol reaches 12–13%. Sediment (called 'lees') collects at the bottom of the vat along with crystals of **tartrate**. The wine is decanted into large vats or tanks that have been treated with sulphur dioxide, and is left to settle again. Fresh, sterilised grape juice may be added at this stage to sweeten ('round-off') the wine.

The wine is then left for up to nine months before being bottled. Ageing continues in the bottle with the great Burgundy and Bordeaux wines taking between four and eight years to develop their full potential. After about ten years most wines begin to lose some of their quality, but really great wines may endure for 20 years or more.

Wine consists of hundreds of chemicals apart from water and alcohol. There are other alcohols, **aldehydes**, **acids** and **esters**. There are phenolic compounds such as tannins, amino acids, minerals and aromatic substances. Sparkling wines contain carbon dioxide gas under pressure, and this is generated in a second fermentation by adding sugar and a pure yeast culture. These bottles are kept clamped tight and left for three to five years while pressure builds up, and this may eventually exceed four times atmospheric pressure. The residual yeast is removed by freezing the neck of the inclined bottle and removing the sediment as an ice plug. This is a time-consuming procedure, and a more general way is to carry out the second fermentation in steel pressure tanks and bottle the wine under pressure.

Beer

All that was needed to discover wine was to crush the grapes to release the juice, and the wild yeast spores on the skins would do the fermenting. On the other hand brewing beer is such a complex process that John Postgate in his book *Microbes and Man* says that it is a wonder that it was ever discovered. Yet the first written accounts of beer date from the Egypt of the 1st Dynasty, around 3000 BC.

There is evidence that beer was first brewed in Babylon about a thousand years earlier than this. The clue was traces of the chemical **calcium oxalate** on the inside of a jar. Archaeologists Rudolph Michel and Patrick McGovern, of the University of Pennsylvania, and Virginia Badler, of the University of Toronto, came across the jar while excavating a site at Goden Tepe in Iran. Calcium oxalate is the main component of 'beer-stone' which precipitates from beers in storage tanks. The only other foods rich in oxalate are rhubarb and spinach, neither of which are likely to have been the source of this calcium oxalate.

In fact what the ancient Babylonians were brewing was ale, not beer. Beer requires hops to be added to make it bitter.[5] It is rather remarkable that ale was first brewed 6000 years ago, when we understand the chemistry involved. Ale is produced from fermented barley, yet the starch in cereal grains cannot be fermented by yeasts, which need simple sugars to work on. The first step in brewing ale is to steep the barley in water for a day or two and then leave it in a warm, damp room for a few more days so that it will germinate. This process is called malting. The grain sprouts develop enzymes which break down the starch into simple sugars. The malted barley is next heated to stop the sprouting and steeped in water to soak out the sugars and other plant chemicals on which the yeast can grow. The resulting solution is sieved and is the malt 'wort'.

To make beer the wort is then boiled with hops, which imparts flavour and releases preservative chemicals that prevent the growth of bacteria which might spoil the beer. Finally the yeast *Saccharomyces cerevisiae*[6] is put in, and the whole lot is allowed to ferment for a week or so. As the yeast multiplies it produces not only alcohol but also a whole cocktail of organic molecules which give the beer its flavour. When the fermentation is over, the brew is processed to remove sediment, clarified, and packaged for distribution. Beers for export are often pasteurised. The skill of the brewer is in getting it all right. Brewing so-called real ale, in which there is still active yeast, is still regarded as more of an art than a science.

There are hundreds of brands of beer, although only a few types, which divide roughly into top fermented beers, such as the traditional mild, bitter, pale ale and stout, and the bottom fermented beers, such as pilsner and lager. Ale is made by fermenting malted barley wort with a top-floating yeast which cannot ferment all the malt sugars and which works best above 10 °C. Real ale is then allowed to settle and mature in the cask with the yeast still alive. Extra hops may be added. Real ale does not travel well and has a short life-span. Keg ale is filtered, pasteurised to kill the yeast, and pressurised with carbon

[5] The name beer comes from the Old English word 'beor', which was used in earlier times to indicate an inferior sort of mead.

[6] Most brewers of beer use this yeast, of which there are over 300 strains.

dioxide. It stores well and travels well. Stout is a very dark, bitter, top-fermented beer made from concentrated boiled wort. Porter is a sweet stout, popular with earlier generations but now out of favour and rarely brewed.

Lager is made from less strongly malted barley and is fermented with a yeast (*Saccharomyces carlsbergensis*) which works at the bottom of the wort, and which can ferment all the malt sugars. This yeast will continue to ferment down to 0 °C. Lagers also store well. Fewer hops are added so it is less bitter than beer. Real lager is that produced according to the purity law of Duke Wilhelm IV of Bavaria which was enacted in 1516. This stipulated that only malt, water, hops and yeast could be used. So-called 'lite' beers and lagers have been allowed to ferment until all the sugars are turned to alcohol. Their name is misleading because they are only slightly less calorific than normal beers and lagers.

In chemical terms fermentation is a successful method of synthesising ethanol, and could be the basis of a renewable fuel economy as we shall see. Because fermentation is so successful it has been virtually unchanged since it was first discovered. But that does not mean it can not be made even more efficient, and it may change if genetic engineering can produce a better yeast. Imagine a yeast that could ferment starch directly and tolerate higher concentrations of alcohol before it dies (say 20%).[7] It might even be designed to multiply faster than, or even kill, invading organisms. A yeast that could do all this, and brew a beer that tasted good, would finally turn brewing from an art to a science. Some progress has been made towards this perfect yeast. The world's largest supplier of starter yeasts, the Canadian company L'Allemand of Montreal, has genetically engineered a yeast which has the ability to produce a toxin that can kill rogue yeasts from the wild.

Spirits

To make drinks with a high level of alcohol it is necessary to use a still. Distillation was discovered by the ancient Romans over 2000 years

---

[7] Some yeasts that home-brewers can buy are reputed to produce a concentration of 20% alcohol after about three weeks fermentation of sugar.

ago, and brought to a fine art by the monks of the Middle Ages. Distilling wine drives off the alcohol, and when the vapours, the 'spirits', are cooled and collected you have a product which is mainly alcohol. In fact **methanol** distills off first because this boils at 65 °C, and should be discarded, then the alcohol comes off, boiling at 78 °C. The vapour that condenses from a still also contains a lot of water, but a second and maybe a third distillation will reduce this until we collect almost pure alcohol. Distillation alone cannot remove the last traces of water because water and alcohol form a so-called azeotropic mixture, which means they distill over together once a certain composition is reached. This composition is about 95% ethanol, 5% water. To get absolutely pure alcohol, ways other than distillation are needed to remove the water, but such alcohol is never required for making drinks.

Distillation produces a liquor that burns the mouth and throat, but diluted with pure water to around 40% alcohol it becomes drinkable. A litre bottle of spirits of normal strength consists of 400 ml of alcohol and 600 ml of distilled water, plus traces of essential extras. Many drinks are based on spirits that have been mixed with other things, and the Box opposite lists the contents of some of the better known ones.

In theory spirits are an alcoholic beverage that will do all that beers and wines will do, but freed of impurities. Spirits also act as their own preservative since nothing can live in them, and so no micro-organisms can oxidise their alcohol to acetic acid.

Through the centuries distilled alcohol has been a part of the medical pharmacopeia. The first distilled alcohol was known as *aqua vita* or water of life, and was valued for its restorative properties. Spirits were also used by surgeons as an early form of anaesthetic and to clean wounds. Alcohol was used to wipe the skin before injections because it is a good antiseptic when pure. For the same reason it is also a good preservative.

What distinguishes the different kinds of spirits are the tiny amounts of other volatiles which distill over with the alcohol, and in this way we have brandy (which comes from wine), whisky (which like beer is made from fermented barley), rum (from fermented molasses) and bourbon (from fermented maize). Vodka is made from fermented grain or potatoes, and is the purest drink of all because it is passed through a charcoal filter to remove everything except the alcohol. This is why it is almost tasteless.

Exotic drinks (liqueurs and cordials)

Liqueurs, also known as cordials, have 20–35% alcohol, are sweetened with sugar, glucose or caramel (up to 500 g per litre) and flavoured with various fruit essences, spices and herbs. Manufacturers are under no legal obligation to reveal what they use. Indeed, part of the mystique of speciality drinks is the 'secret recipe', and when most of these were first introduced their secrets were safe. Modern chemical analysis can now reveal exactly what has been used in their concoction. Some are artificially coloured. Here are the main ingredients of the more popular varieties.

Name of drink	Spirit base	Other ingredients apart from sweeteners
Advocaat	gin	egg yolk
Benedictine	Cognac brandy	honey, herbs
Campari	brandy & wine	bitters★
Cherry brandy	brandy	cherry essence
Cointreau	brandy	orange essence
Crème de Menthe	brandy	mint extract
Drambuie	whisky	honey
Malibu	rum	coconut essence
Martini	wine & spirit	mixed herbs extract
Ouzo	raw spirit★★	aniseed
Pernod	raw spirit★★	aniseed and herb extract
Pimm's No. 1	gin & wine	herb extract
Southern Comfort	bourbon	peach essence
Tia Maria	rum	coffee extract

★mainly extract of wormwood
★★can be any distilled alcohol produced by fermentation

Gin is made from fermented grain alcohol, and is flavoured by a second and even third distillation from a blend of herbs, fruits and berries. These so-called botanicals are a secret blend of up to ten fruits, herbs and spices which must include juniper, this being the essential component which identifies a drink as gin. Other botanicals may be coriander, angelica, orris root, almonds, cassia bark, liquorice, orange and lemon peel, cardamom, cinnamon, and nutmeg. After the botanicals have been steeped in the spirit it is distilled a final time. (In some distilleries the spirit is distilled through the botanicals suspended above it.) The first fraction which distills over is discarded. The middle fraction of distillate is collected, diluted to between 47% and 37%, and bottled and labelled as London gin, a term that is protected by international regulations.[8] Distillers guard the blend of their botanicals, although there is really nothing to be secret about, because chemical analysis of the product will reveal all.

Scotch whisky producers on the other hand are very open about how they make their product, safe in the knowledge that all attempts to produce it synthetically have failed, despite the fact that chemists have identified the hundreds of molecules that are present. The flavours of Scotch are introduced at all stages in its production, and even include **phenols** from the peat smoke used to dry the malt. Though most malt is now dried by gas heating, a little peat smoke is always added. Some malt is still dried over peat fires, especially for the whisky that is produced on the island of Islay. The mashing stage which extracts the sugars from the malted barley also extracts other flavours, and the fermentation with yeast produces yet more volatile substances. Many of these are related to alcohol itself, such as methanol, **propanol** and **butanol**, but only in small amounts. None of these adds to the flavour, but they convert easily to aldehydes and these do have flavour, and then to carboxylic acids, which are even stronger and sharper tasting. Most flavour of all comes from esters, which are often fruity to taste when pure, and they are produced by the chemical reaction of alcohols and acids. (In some cases just one substance may provide most of the taste, such as **2-ethyl-3-methyl-butanoic acid**, which is what gives rum its characteristic flavour, but for most spirits there are several molecules which provide the aroma and flavour.)

---

[8] Gin can be made simply by adding flavours and essences to distilled spirits, thereby reducing the cost of a final distillation. Such gin cannot be called London gin.

The final stage in the life of a whisky is its stay in a bonded warehouse for at least three years, although this may be up to 12 years or more. Ageing not only leaches out more chemicals from the wood of the cask, but is an expensive process since 2% of the whisky evaporates through the walls of the cask each year. The leached chemicals are aldehydes or acids that are derived from benzene compounds such as the aldehyde vanilla, but there are also wood sugars, **steroids**, tannins and even minerals. All are there in minute traces, but all add to the whisky's complex taste, and make it impossible to forge.

According to Dr John Piggott, senior lecturer in the Department of Bioscience and Biotechnology at the University of Strathclyde in Scotland, the flavour of Scotch is a mystery: 'If you blend all the identified flavour components of whisky together it doesn't make whisky. The secret still eludes us.' Most Scotch is a blend of whiskies, from different distilleries. Even the expensive, so-called single-malt whiskies are generally blends, but of whiskies from different casks in the same distillery. There are some single-cask whiskies, but these are only for the dedicated connoisseurs.

Fraudulent drink

Chemical analysis shows there to be some rather surprising natural chemicals in drink, such as dimethyl sulphide, the chemical responsible for bad breath, and hydrogen cyanide (also known as Prussic acid or hydrocyanic acid). This almond-flavoured chemical is there only in a few parts per million, and too little to affect us. Another component in much larger amounts is methanol, and this can be worrying. It is possible to end up literally blind drunk on illicit spirits with high levels of methanol. Our body turns this into **formaldehyde** and **formic acid**, which attack the retina of the eye. The low level of methanol in wines and spirits is quite harmless.

Chemists are now able to isolate and identify almost all the chemicals in a drink, some of which are present only as parts per billion. In theory with this knowledge it should be possible to combine these chemicals to make synthetic versions, and this is constantly being tried by drinks forgers. Some drinks are easier to forge than others, but it has also become correspondingly easier for analytical chemists to prove that a drink is not what it appears.

While it is acceptable to produce alcohol for industry from agricultural surpluses such as grain and molasses, it is not acceptable to turn the alcohol from industrial plants into drinks. To prevent this happening such alcohol can be 'denatured', and this is done by adding a small amount of a bitter-tasting agents such as sucrose octa-acetate or **Bitrex**, which makes them too unpleasant to drink.[9]

There is no chemical difference between alcohol produced naturally and that made industrially. Fraudsters have been tempted to turn industrial alcohol into wines and spirits, or to boost the level of alcohol in other drinks by adding the industrial variety. Such rogue liquors are easily detected. The tell-tale marker which traps them is radioactivity, or rather the lack of it. The carbon dioxide of the atmosphere which is picked up by grape and grain is composed of three varieties (called isotopes) of carbon. These differ in the number of particles in the nucleus of the atom. The most abundant is carbon-12, which has six protons and six neutrons, and constitutes 98.90% of carbon, while carbon-13 with an extra neutron constitutes 1.10%. There is also present the naturally occurring carbon-14 with two extra neutrons, of which there is a minute trace. Carbon 12 and 13 are stable atoms, but carbon-14 is radioactive and decays with a half-life (see pp 136–137) of 5730 years.

Fossil fuels, which have lain underground for millions of years, have no radioactive carbon-14 left. Consequently alcohol made industrially from ethylene, which is produced from oil, can be distinguished from that made by fermenting carbohydrates. If forensic chemists suspect a drink has been made or doctored with industrial material they simply measure the radioactivity of the alcohol. Too low and it must be phoney.

The non-radioactive isotopes, carbon-12 and carbon-13, can also help in more subtle forms of analysis, together with the hydrogen isotopes, hydrogen-1 and hydrogen-2.[10] Normal hydrogen is

---

[9] Industrial alcohol used to be contaminated with high levels of methanol (hence its common name of 'meths'). The level of methanol is not such as to constitute a health hazard, and there are down-and-outs prepared to drink meths as a cheap substitute for gin.

[10] Hydrogen-2 is also known as deuterium.

99.985% hydrogen-1 and 0.015% hydrogen-2. Together these isotopes can reveal whether a drink has been doctored in any way at all.
The technique, developed at the University of Nantes in France, is so
sophisticated that it can identify the country and region of a wine.
The method analyses the proportion of the different isotopes of
hydrogen and carbon in a sample, and this can be done extremely
accurately by a technique called mass spectrometry. The ratio of the
isotopes in any sample of alcohol varies according to the type of vine
and the environment in which it grows.

The alcohol produced from fermented grape sugars is different from
that which comes from the sugars of malted barley, or from fruit such
as apples. Using this technique, the researchers were able to show that
17 out of 23 samples of Holland gin contained alcohol from fermented beet sugar instead of from grain. When they did a survey of
Beaujolais wines they discovered that some had up to half their
alcohol derived from added sugar. The isotope technique can even
tell whether the carbon dioxide in a sparkling wine is 'natural', in
other words comes entirely from the fermentation, or whether industrial carbon dioxide has been used to supplement the natural gas in
order to perk up the wine.

Other methods of chemical analysis can also reveal suspect drinks by
identifying compounds which should *not* be present. The spirit which
often turns out to be less than it seems is brandy. Every year hundreds
of suspect bottles are tested in Germany and almost all turn out not to
have been made by the traditional method of distilling wine. Many
contain evidence of being made from rotting fruit, a fact that chemists
can easily prove by showing the presence of **allyl alcohol** or **acrolein**
which are only produced by decaying fruit. Some 'brandy' is pepped
up with added esters taken off the shelf of chemical stores, such as
ethyl heptanoate. A lot of 'brandy' is diluted with cheap wine.[11]

Other cheats try to forge the more sophisticated drinks such as
whisky and gin. Exactly what these contain is known, but it is not
necessary to add all the components found in the true spirits to
produce a passable imitation of the aroma and taste. However, it is
the absence of some of the components that is convincing proof that
the drinks are phoney.

[11] Cognac is the brandy to choose if you want the real thing, and it must have been
made in France and only from wines of the Charente.

It is possible to make wine by blending fruit flavourings, artificial colours and alcohol, but things can sometimes go wrong as they did in Italy in 1986, when 19 people died from drinking cheap wine made with methanol. In Bombay, India, in 1992 during New Year celebrations 85 people died through drinking cheap bootleg liquor, again made from methanol. In the Austrian wine scandal of 1986 the fraudsters did not try to make artificial wine, but to up-grade the quality of low-grade wine by adding the anti-freeze **diethylene glycol**. This had the effect of making the wine sweeter and smoother to the palate. Happily so little of this chemical was needed to boost the quality that no-one died.

The risks and benefits of drinking alcohol

The health risks that a heavy drinker faces are broken bones, obesity, addiction, ulcers, cirrhosis of the liver, brain damage, a particularly nasty form of heart disease called cardiomyopathy, and possibly even cancer of the oesophagus. A more immediate risk may be death, if he or she drives while drunk—and the death may not necessarily be only their own. The upper legal limit for regarding someone as drunk was once based on an alcohol level of 0.15%, equivalent to 150 mg in 100 ml of blood. While this may not incapacitate a person for some activities, such as playing darts, it is far too high for anyone who is driving a vehicle. There are good reasons for believing that even 50 mg is too high a level for safe driving, although some countries permit up to 80 mg.

Alcohol can do serious harm to the human body. The effects on the liver are complex and still not clearly understood. They stem from changes in the levels of co-factors, which are chemicals that are necessary to the action of enzymes. The outcome is that the oxidation of fatty acids is impaired in the mitochondria, the structures in the cells that produce energy, and more fats are synthesised. These fats accumulate in the liver to produce what is known as fatty liver, a symptom of alcoholism. Cirrhosis of the liver is a condition exacerbated by long term abuse of alcohol. It was once thought to be caused by it, but this seems unlikely. Cirrhosis was seen as a toxic response in which normal tissue is replaced by collagen (fibrous tissue). As a consequence the liver functions less efficiently.

Alcoholism is believed to affect about 20 people in 10 000. This condition may be partly inherited according to studies by Ernest Noble of the University of California, Los Angeles, and Kenneth Blum of the University of Texas. They discovered that a certain receptor in the brain was much more common among alcoholics than in the general population. This receptor responds to dopamine, the chemical messenger in the brain that triggers pleasurable feelings. Women are also more likely to develop alcoholism than men, and a study on 1033 pairs of identical female twins has provided further proof of a genetic factor. Kenneth Kendler at Virginia Commonwealth University in Richmond reported in the *Journal of the American Medical Association* that the numbers of twins both becoming alcoholics were much higher than expected, which led him to suspect that hereditary factors may account for this condition in up to 60% of cases.

Alcohol can be regarded as a form of food. A unit of alcohol (10 grams) provides us with about 70 Calories of energy. The recommended maximum intake for a man is 21 units of alcohol a week, and this will provide about 1400 Calories of his energy intake. For a woman the recommended amount is 14 units of alcohol, which will provide around 1000 Calories. While these are not excessive amounts they nevertheless must be taken into account when planning a diet. Alcohol accounts for about 10% of the food intake of adults in the USA and Europe. It was once considered such a convenient way of providing energy that it used to be added to intravenous drips as a supplement.

As a food, alcohol has some disadvantages. It cannot supply energy in the same way as carbohydrates, so it does little to help us work or exercise, but it can supply excess Calories that lead to weight gain, and can be a very expensive form of food. A pint of beer will provide between 140 and 210 Calories depending on whether it is mild, bitter, keg, lager or stout. Draught mild has the fewest Calories (140) while stouts like Guinness have the most (210). The Calorie content of wines and ciders depends also on the sugars they contain, and that can be judged on whether they are labelled sweet, medium, or dry. Four fluid ounces of wine (a normal glass) will be about 110

Calories if it is sweet, but 75 if it is dry. It makes no difference whether the wine is red or white. A glass of sherry is about 50 ml and provides between 55 (dry) and 65 (sweet) Calories. A single measure of spirits or liqueurs is about 25 ml (a sixth of a gill) and provides between 50 and 75 Calories. Whisky and gin are about 50, while liqueurs like cherry brandy and Cointreau are nearer 75.

Alcoholic drinks like beer and wine also provide other dietary nutrients such as minerals and vitamins, but spirits and other distilled drinks lack these. A pint of beer contains about 50 mg of calcium and 0.1 mg of iron, while a glass of wine has only about 10 mg of calcium but up to 1 mg of iron. Cider has almost 3 mg of iron per pint. Beer is also a source of the B vitamins, although wines have less of them. These vitamins come from the yeast. No alcoholic drink provides vitamins A, C or D.

The benefits of alcohol are varied. Some are well known, such as a nightcap of a glass of beer, or a shot of whisky, to help us get off to sleep. However, it may not be a good night's sleep, because alcohol appears to deprive us of a key type of sleep, the early sleep in which we dream. Continued loss of this essential sleep may be the reason why very heavy drinkers eventually suffer the hallucinations traditionally known as the 'DTs' (*delirium tremens*), although these are more likely to strike as part of the symptoms of alcohol withdrawal.

Moderate drinkers, those who take two or three units of alcohol a day, suffer less coronary heart disease and have lower cholesterol levels. Drink may be beneficial for the heart but only in moderation. Men who drink more than the equivalent of six pints of beer a day (12 units) are twice as likely to suffer a sudden heart attack as non-drinkers, according to Professor Gerry Shaper of the Royal Free Hospital in London who carried out an eight-year study of over 7500 middle-aged men. Each year about 25 died this way, and two thirds of these were heavy drinkers.

Studies of the life-style of French farmers supports drinking as beneficial, as revealed in the leading medical journal the *Lancet* in 1992. Dr Serge Renaud of the National Institute of Health and Medical Research in Lyons, France, believes that French farmers are less prone to coronary heart disease, despite a diet rich in animal fats, because of their relatively high consumption of alcohol in the form of red wine. Two glasses a day is the recommended amount.

Red wine is not a medicine, and it will not cure or relieve heart problems that are already present. If there is any value in drinking red wine, it lies in its ability to prevent heart disease. This message of the benefits of red wine increased sales by over 44% in the USA when it was announced in 1992. A group at Kaiser Permanent Medical Center in Oakland, California, claimed that drinkers of white wine were also less likely to suffer coronary heart disease. Whether it is the alcohol itself or phenolic compounds in the wine that are responsible is a matter of debate. The antioxidant behaviour of the phenolics may slow down plaque formation from low-density lipoproteins, the 'bad' form of cholesterol, which we will be discussing in the next chapter.

Not only do drinkers appear to have lower cholesterol levels, and have less coronary heart disease, but they also get fewer colds. That was the conclusion of the final research project carried out by the now-defunct Common Cold Unit at Salisbury, England. Not every common cold virus we catch leads to a cold. Between four and ten viruses infect us every year, but only half of these end up as a bad cold—for the rest we either have existing antibodies against the virus, or we can shake it off easily. If we are under stress this may reduce our immunity. Nor can you stop a cold with the popular cure of hot whisky and lemon—all this does is to make the misery a bit more bearable. However it works its magic, alcohol certainly seems to reward many of its moderate users: those who drink two units of alcohol a day catch half the number of colds that non-drinkers suffer. This does not apply to smokers though; smoking cancels out the protection against colds which comes with drinking.

The medicinal benefits of wine drinking have a long history, and in his quirky books *Wine is the Best Medicine* and *Your Good Health!* the late Dr Eduard Maury set out a careful list of the right wines to treat various ailments from indigestion to arthritis. He advocated a bottle of wine a day (700 ml) for the average 70 kg person, which is about twice the number of units recommended for a male. Some of the supposed benefits of wine are already popular folklore, for example Dr Maury recommends champagne for indigestion, high blood pressure, and as a tonic during convalescence. Less well known are his rather whimsical recommendations of drinking Vouvray for constipation,

Médoc for diarrhoea and arthritis; and Bordeaux or Riesling for obesity.

Low-alcohol drinks

If you are not convinced that there are any benefits to be gained by drinking alcohol, or if you are driving, then you can choose a non-alcoholic wine or lager. Low-alcohol beer can be made simply by stopping the fermentation of the wort when the level of alcohol is still under 1.2%, which is the legal limit for a beer to be so classified. Another way is to ferment the wort with a yeast that cannot digest maltose. Wine yeasts would never normally encounter maltose, as there is none in wine must, and so adding such a yeast to wort will result in an alcoholic content of around 0.5%.

For a beer to be called alcohol-free it must have less than 50 ppm of alcohol (0.05%). This can only be achieved by removing as much alcohol as possible after normal fermentation. Distilling wine or beer is the way to make spirits, and it is also the way to lower the alcohol content of the wine or beer. Distilling beer and wine also changes their flavour, so to prevent this the alcohol is distilled off with much gentler heating by lowering the pressure. In this way the level of alcohol can be reduced to well below 1%. Distillation also removes other components of the beer, and these have to be put back later.[12] The other components which can be lost during removal of the alcohol are the flavoursome esters which the yeasts produce, and again these can be added later.

Removing alcohol may seem a rather thankless task for the producers of beer and wines, since the customer is reluctant to pay the full price for a drink that lacks the key ingredient and the one which they wrongly assume makes drink so expensive to produce. The sophisticated process to remove alcohol explains why such drinks are no cheaper than their normal counterparts. It is a myth that alcohol is what makes drinks expensive. Alcohol is cheap and easy to make, as home-brewers and wine-makers know. It is only expensive to buy in countries where it is heavily taxed.

---

[12] In fact to have more quality control over their products, brewers are increasingly using extracts of malt for colouring beer, and extracts of hops for flavouring them.

Industrial alcohol (ethanol)

A conflict of interests surrounds alcohol (ethanol). Some people regard it as essentially an agricultural product and deserving of special consideration, while others produce it for use as a chemical and they see it merely as an industrial chemical like any other. This conflict leads to political questions of priority and pricing, but one day there may only be agricultural alcohol available. Alcohol production from fermented crops is a natural renewable resource, and it gets our approval for being environmentally friendly, but the real cost is higher than when it is made synthetically in an industrial plant. But whichever way alcohol is produced, chemically it is exactly the same molecule.

To make ethanol industrially, by the reaction of water and ethylene at 300 °C requires a pressure of about 60 times atmospheric pressure, with the presence of phosphoric acid as a catalyst. The rate of conversion of ethylene to ethanol is low, about 5%, and the ethanol has to be separated out and the reaction mixture put through the process again and again.

Alcohol was once a feedstock for the chemicals industry in its own right, and was used to make acetaldehyde, from which acetic acid and acetic anhydride were then manufactured. These were used to make paints, fibres (like rayon and acetate), plastic film (like cellophane), and aspirin. The acetic anhydride to make these products can now be made more efficiently in other ways than starting with ethanol. Alcohol is still used as an industrial solvent, and of course as the solvent for perfumes (see Chapter 1). Alcohol is also used to manufacture various flavours, detergents and disinfectants.

The Brazilians looked to ethanol as their way to overcome the oil crisis of 1973. Alcohol makes a useful liquid fuel, and although weight for weight it does not release as much energy as petrol when it burns, it still releases a lot.[13] In Brazil there are over one million cars which run on neat ethanol, and another million which use an ethanol/petrol mixture in the ratio of 20%/80%. For a time in the 1980s it looked as though all cars produced in Brazil would eventually run only on alcohol, but the price of crude oil on the world markets fell, and

---

[13] A gram of ethanol releases 7 Calories, and a gram of petrol releases 9 Calories—exactly the same amounts of energy as alcohol and fats release in our diet.

once again petrol became the more economic fuel. During the 1980s, home-produced ethanol saved the Brazilian economy over \$20 billion, and generated employment for over a million people.

The Brazilians began to turn their surplus molasses into ethanol as long ago as the 1920s, and it was added to petrol to the extent of 5%. At the time many other countries did the same, since it was thought to produce a cleaner burning petrol, although in those days this was seen as primarily of benefit to the engine rather than to the environment. Brazil had a supply of molasses that could be turned into ethanol very easily, and molasses was a surplus by-product of their sugar industry. By 1987 they were producing 25 million tonnes of cane sugar a year, of which 7 million tonnes were used as food and the rest was fermented to make almost 12 billion litres of ethanol. This replaced over a quarter of the petrol from imported oil.

Some remarkable advances were made in sugarcane production. Year by year more and more land was turned over to growing this crop until it exceeded 4 million hectares, although this was only 8% of their cultivated land. In addition crop yields went up almost 20% from 65 tonnes per hectare to 77 tonnes per hectare, and the amount of alcohol produced from this increased by nearly 40% from 2700 litres per hectare to 3700 litres per hectare. This improved productivity came about through better industrial methods of converting the sugar of the sugarcane to alcohol, and by better distillation techniques.

Not only was Brazil producing over 12 billion litres of ethanol by 1988, it was also gaining a modest amount of electricity by burning the sugarcane residues, called bagasse. This was used mainly as heating fuel in the ethanol refineries, but an excess was going to generate electricity. One very noticeable change of all this activity was to the quality of the air of São Paulo (15 million inhabitants), where most cars run on ethanol. This city was no longer afflicted with the kind of smog that afflicts Mexico City (17 million inhabitants) where cars burn only petrol, and where smog and ozone levels pollute the air due to the effects of sunlight on unburnt hydrocarbons from the exhausts of cars.

Another unexpected benefit of the ethanol economy was that the sugarcane needs relatively little input in terms of nitrogen fertilizers—about 80 kg per hectare—although we will discover other unsuspected sources of nitrogen in Chapter 8. You might think that the

Brazilian experiment is an ecological success story, and you would be right. You might applaud it as an environmental success story too, but it is no longer an *economic* success story. That was true only when the price of oil was high. When it fell below $20 a barrel in the late 1980s the Brazilian experiment began to falter, and whereas in the mid-1980s they had talked of producing only ethanol-burning cars in Brazil by the end of the century, by 1993 they were talking of returning once again to the manufacture of petrol-burning cars.

The Brazilian chemical industry was also geared to using ethanol as a feedstock and turning it to ethylene (this is the reverse of the chemical reaction that is more generally used to turn ethylene into ethanol). Other chemicals that are produced from ethanol include acetaldehyde, acetic acid, diethyl ether, ethyl acetate, butanol, **octanol** and **ethyl chloride**. Relatively little ethanol went into the manufacture of these, about 400 million litres a year, but this list of chemicals shows what can be produced from a renewable resource if the need arises.

Sugarcane is not the only carbohydrate-producing plant from which ethanol for industry is currently being made, and in the USA over 3.5 billion litres of ethanol a year are produced by fermenting starch of surplus corn. This looks set to rise to over 7 billion litres by the year 2000, and much of it will end up in reformulated blends of gasoline for use in cities where pollution is a problem.

In a future world which has used up its accessible fossil reserves, we might be dependent on carbohydrates for all our energy and chemicals. Our lifestyle by then might be so closely tied in with the production of alcohol from crops that drinking it may seem merely an antisocial waste of a key natural resource. But for the time being: cheers!

CHAPTER FOUR

Cholesterol, Fats and Fibre

Cholesterol; oils and fats; fibre; hidden fibre (resistant starch); the chemistry of successful dieting

M OST people eventually die of heart disease, and many of them are carried off in the prime of life. The causes of coronary heart disease still remain unclear and a bewildering number of suggestions have been advanced to explain it, many based on epidemiological studies of the health records of large numbers of people. A list of over two hundred factors that have been implicated in heart disease was published by P. N. Hopkins and R. R. Williams in the journal *Atherosclerosis* in 1981. Among the non-dietary contributory factors were: being a man; living in a city; snoring; baldness; lack of exercise; an aggressive personality; being rich; being poor; stress at work; and being Jewish.

We have little control over most of these, and so perhaps it is not surprising that attention has focused on dietary contributory factors that have been suggested as the causes of heart disease. Among those which Hopkins and Williams list were some that were thought to be dangerous in excess—such as sugar, coffee, saturated fats, chlorinated water, alcohol and milk—and some that were thought to put a person at risk if they did not get enough, including zinc, fish oils, garlic, unsaturated fats, alcohol (again) and milk (again). Clearly none of these is the primary cause of heart disease, but many of them might be indirectly linked to it. Plainly some of them are way off target, even though they have the support of epidemiological studies.

Protecting the most important organ of our body throughout our life has become the concern of many, and they have been encouraged to believe that this can be done by eating healthy foods, and especially those low in cholesterol, low in animals fats and high in fibre. In this chapter we will look a little closer at the chemistry of these foods, which are given a high profile by food advisers and advertisers, and discover how realistic the claims are.

Cholesterol[1] is now regarded by many people as the number one enemy in the fight against coronary heart disease, and they believe that if they can reduce their cholesterol intake they can reduce the risk of dying this way. Enemy number two is animal fats, and there has been a long campaign to persuade people that these should be avoided and replaced by vegetable oils, which are said to be much healthier on the grounds that they are higher in polyunsaturates and monounsaturates, and lower in saturates.[2] Current food lore is that in addition to avoiding cholesterol and animal fats, we should be taking in more of the great cure-all, fibre. Eat enough of this each day and we can protect ourselves against heart disease. The advice here is to switch from foods such as white bread and rice to their brown counterparts which still retain their natural fibre.

The overall message is that you can protect your heart by knowing about cholesterol, fats and fibre. These three are in fact closely linked: fats in the diet increase the amount of cholesterol in the blood stream, whereas fibre, and especially soluble fibre, will reduce it. However, the *science* behind this simple message is not quite so simple, and the next few pages may reveal a few unexpected truths. Most of the cholesterol in our blood stream is made by the body itself; lard contains more unsaturated fats than saturated fats; and white bread and rice have a lot more fibre than hitherto suspected.

Cholesterol

We all have quite a lot of cholesterol in our blood, and it is there for the excellent reason that it is an essential chemical for the efficient

[1] A reminder that when the name of a substance appears in **bold** type, it means that there is more about its chemistry in the Appendix.

[2] Saturated, unsaturated and polyunsaturated are explained later in the chapter.

running of the human body. Only a small amount of this cholesterol comes directly from the food we eat: most of it is made by our own body. Nevertheless, it is not a good thing to have too much. Unfortunately, some individuals have very high cholesterol levels, and the cause is hereditary; about 25 people in 10 000 carry this trait. This is a worrying condition which requires constant monitoring and medical attention to correct it. For such people the battle against cholesterol is never-ending because they are prone to heart disease. The rest of us are lucky by comparison, but that is little comfort to many people who now fear that they too are at risk unless they can reduce the amount of cholesterol in their blood. If you find your blood cholesterol level is too high you can generally reduce it by following the advice of a trained dietitian, which generally means eating less fat and more fibre, and especially soluble fibre. Alcohol may also help reduce cholesterol as we saw in Chapter 3, although this is more likely to be a self-prescribed treatment.

Cholesterol is not a life-threatening toxin, but a medium-sized molecule that is really a building block for important parts of the body. In particular it is an essential component of cell membranes. Cholesterol also stabilises a cell against temperature changes. It is a major part of the membranes of the nervous system, the brain, the spinal cord and the peripheral nerves. In particular it is incorporated into the myelin sheath that insulates the nerves from the surrounding tissue. Cholesterol is also the forerunner of important hormones such as the female sex hormone, oestradiol, and the male sex hormone, testosterone, and of vitamin D, which we need in order to utilise calcium and form bone. Nearly all body tissues are capable of making cholesterol, but the liver and intestines make the most. We require cholesterol to produce the bile we need to digest the fats in our food, and the name itself comes from the Greek words for 'bile solids'.

Essential though cholesterol is, there can be too much of it, and too much causes a build-up of deposits in the arteries, constricts them, and may even block them, with dire consequences.[3] The causes which are now seen as contributing to higher-than-normal cholesterol levels are:

---

[3] Worse still, if a piece of this deposit breaks free it could stop the flow of blood to the heart muscle.

hereditary factors, which are the most important; then high blood pressure, stress, smoking, obesity and dietary cholesterol.

We can do nothing about the first of these since it is written in the genes we inherited from our parents. It is also difficult to change the pressures of work, but we can give up smoking and we can change our diet and lose weight, and maybe reduce the level of blood cholesterol at the same time. Dieting as a course of action is relatively easy to undertake and perhaps this is why it has received most attention, although the focus of that attention has tended to be directed at cholesterol. This is perhaps not surprising in view of the known danger of heart disease suffered by those with naturally high levels of cholesterol in their blood. In their case the high blood cholesterol level can be brought down with medical treatment using potent pharmaceutical drugs, but for most people a change of diet may be all that is required. The drug treatment works in that it prolongs the life of the high risk group, and there is a growing tendency to believe that it will do the same for the rest of us. Regular cholesterol monitoring is possible, even using a home test kit. The simple message that most people have now picked up is that cholesterol is bad news and that foods with high levels of this should be avoided.

Only a little of the cholesterol in our blood comes from our food. The eating of oils and fats has much more effect in boosting it. Our bodies produce bile acids in order to digest these food molecules, and bile acids are made from cholesterol. The more fat we eat, the more bile acid we need. The more bile acid we use, the more cholesterol we make, and the more of this gets in our intestines. When it has done its job it can be reabsorbed by the body and reused.

Food manufacturers have responded to the public's heightened awareness of cholesterol as a dangerous chemical, and today you can even see 'no cholesterol' or 'low cholesterol' on some product labels on supermarket shelves. The public has got the message, but is it a helpful one? Cholesterol itself does not cause heart attacks or high blood pressure. We make four times as much cholesterol a day as we could possibly absorb from our food, even assuming we were to eat a lot of dairy foods such as eggs and cream which contain relatively high amounts.

Cholesterol is so important that together our cells, intestines, and especially our liver make about a gram of it every day. The average adult has 150 grams (5 ounces) in their body, enough to fill a wine glass. Very little of this has come from the cholesterol in their food, and if a person is a vegan vegetarian and eats no animal products, they take in none at all. Their own bodies have to produce all the cholesterol they need. Those who eat meat, fish or dairy products generally consume about half a gram of cholesterol a day, and their body can absorb a little of this. How much depends upon other components of their diet, such as soluble fibre which scavenges cholesterol.

In theory the ideal level of cholesterol in the blood is 200 milligrams per 100 millilitres of blood, and this is the target to aim for in the USA. In Europe the magic number is 5.2, with the cholesterol being measured in the chemical units of millimoles per litre of blood. These numbers are just different ways of expressing the same amount.[4] Because cholesterol is chiefly a hydrocarbon-type molecule, it is insoluble in water, yet it has to be transported by the blood. To do this it combines with lipoproteins, tiny globules which are a combination of fatty acids and proteins. The low density lipoproteins (LDLs) are where most of the cholesterol in our blood is to be found, and this explains why LDL is regarded as threatening because it deposits as plaque and clogs up our arteries, and may even trigger the formation of a blood clot. There is also another type of lipoprotein called high density lipoprotein (HDL), but this is considered less harmful—indeed some claim it acts as a protective factor. HDL is thought to be responsible for removing cholesterol and transporting it safely to the liver.

Given a balanced diet, our bodies regulate the production, use and removal of cholesterol, and it stays at around the 200 mg (or 5.2 mmole) level. There are several factors that may push it above this figure, such as a fatty diet, smoking, stress, and drinking too much coffee.[5] There are some foods which can reduce our cholesterol, such as garlic, alcohol, oats and baked beans. These last two contain a lot of soluble fibre, and a diet which includes them regularly will reduce your blood cholesterol level by about 10%.

---

[4] A millimole of cholesterol is 386 milligrams. This weight is based on the chemical formula of cholesterol.

[5] Not all coffee does this, only coffee which has been kept hot for a long time.

People with naturally high levels may have cholesterol in excess of 300 mg (or 8 mmole), and some even exceed 800 mg (20 mmole). The cause is a hereditary defect in those receptors of the liver that remove cholesterol from the blood. In addition to controlling their diet such people need drug therapy, and there are two kinds of drug they can be prescribed. One type binds the cholesterol in our intestines and prevents it from being absorbed. This type is a more effective form of scavenger than soluble fibre, and requires the patient to take an ounce or two of the prescription a day. To compensate for this loss of cholesterol, the body then uses more cholesterol to make bile and so the level in the blood falls. A modified form of wood cellulose has also been discovered to lower cholesterol by up to 33% within two weeks. The material HPMC (short for hydroxypropylmethylcellulose) is manufactured by Dow Chemical as a thickening agent for cheesecake and desserts, but health and safety tests revealed quite by accident that it dramatically lowers cholesterol levels, and especially LDL levels, by as much as 50%.

The other treatment aimed at reducing cholesterol uses drugs and actually interferes with the way cells produce this chemical; in other words the drugs turn off the supply at source. These pharmaceuticals now have worldwide sales in excess of $1 billion annually, and they are one of the fastest growing drugs. The anti-cholesterol drugs most commonly used are **lovastatin** and **mevastatin** which are derived from a natural substance found in fungi. They work by deactivating an enzyme that is needed to produce **mevalonic acid**, the molecule from which cholesterol is made, and it will reduce cholesterol levels by up to 50%.[6]

Only the few people with naturally high levels of cholesterol really require such a drug; the rest of us can keep ourselves at the normal level with very little effort, just by eating less fat and more fibre. A common course of action is to target high cholesterol foods and cut out dairy products such as butter and eggs, although the effect this has on the level of cholesterol in the blood is minimal. In fact four ounces of chicken contains more cholesterol than an ounce of butter. The table below gives the cholesterol level in several foods. Eating those

---

[6] It is slightly toxic towards the liver.

Cholesterol content of some foods

Food	Amount of cholesterol (grams per 100 g)	Food	Amount of cholesterol (grams per 100 g)
Brain (offal)	3.10	Cheddar cheese	0.07
Egg yolk	1.26	Fish	0.05
Kidney	0.70	Bread	0
Caviar	0.50	Vegetables	0
Butter	0.23	Fruit	0
Chicken	0.07	Margarine	0

high in cholesterol should not worry us, because only a small fraction of the cholesterol we eat ends up in our blood stream.

Fat intake is much more important in determining cholesterol levels because it stimulates bile production which in turn stimulates cholesterol production. Not only that, but the fat that is absorbed by the gut is then the raw material for more cholesterol to be made in the liver. Cooks and chefs of the future may well design meals which combine high cholesterol foods with foods high in soluble fibre.[7]

Reducing cholesterol in the diet is not without its risks, however, as an epidemiological survey in 1992 discovered. Fifty thousand Swedish men and women over 45 who lived in Värmland were studied over a period of 20 years by Dr Gunnar Lindber of the Centre for Public Health Research at Karlsttad. The results were not quite as reassuring as people had hoped: the group of men with low blood cholesterol did not have a much lower death rate than the group with high cholesterol levels. Admittedly they were less likely to die of heart disease, but they made up for this by being more likely to commit suicide or to die prematurely in accidents. Curiously these effects were not found in women.

For the rest of us the best advice, if we suspect our cholesterol level is too high and is putting us at risk, is to eat less fat and more fibre. This advice is also the same as that of many weight-reducing diets, and since being overweight is now thought to put a greater strain on the heart than cholesterol, the advice is still good, although for the wrong reasons. At the end of this chapter I will show how a little chemistry

---

[7] For example caviar is very high in cholesterol, so what better way to deal with this than to serve this delicacy with baked beans? Stranger things have happened!

can enable you to lose weight quickly and effectively, albeit using the world's most boring diet.

Oils and fats

If we have a diet that has a high level of fat then we are more likely to suffer heart disease, but the connection between them is not a simple cause-and-effect relationship. This can be illustrated by comparing heart disease deaths in countries where fats make up about a third of calorie intake. This includes some of the most prosperous, such as Switzerland, where the death rate from heart disease is low at 30 deaths per 10 000 people per year, while in Germany it is 40, Sweden 60, UK 70, and the USA 80. The French also have a high fat diet, yet they have the second lowest death rate from heart failure of only 20 per 10 000. The Japanese are lower with about 10 per 10 000, but they eat much less fat.

Faced with such a spread of results there clearly must be other factors at work. Some nutritionists, backed up by epidemiological evidence, say that it is the *type* of fat which is the key. According to them it is animal, or saturated, fats which are to blame. These are the real villains, whereas vegetable oils, which are unsaturated, are fine. They found statistical support for their ideas and this showed that there was a slight increase in heart disease among those who ate a lot of dairy products. The evidence fell far short of scientific proof, but it convinced those who wanted to be convinced, and gave them an excuse to preach to the rest of us. Their simple message went forth: animal fats are saturated and so are bad, vegetable oils are polyunsaturated and so are good. Perhaps not surprisingly the facts about fat are much more sophisticated than these simplistic slogans, which show a lack of understanding of their chemistry.

Saturated and unsaturated fats

Even if you already know about saturated fats, it may come as a surprise to learn that butter and cream contain a lot of *unsaturated* fat. It is highly misleading to talk as though all animal fat was saturated, and therefore a health risk, whereas vegetable fats are unsaturated, and therefore good for the heart. Indeed some confectionery contains coconut oil which is almost entirely *saturated* fat. Puzzled?

The words saturated, unsaturated and polyunsaturated are used to describe fats, yet many people have no clear idea of what these chemical terms really mean. Although the phrase 'saturated fat' sounds to be more fattening than 'unsaturated fat', these terms have nothing at all to do with the quantity of fat or its calorie content. Our normal idea of something being saturated is of a sponge saturated with water, but this mental picture is misleading when we talk of saturated fat. Saturation is an old-fashioned chemical term, which is related to the bonds between atoms. The chemical explanation of saturated and unsaturated oils and fats is given in the Box below.

What is meant by saturated and unsaturated oils and fats?

From a chemist's point of view, oils and fats belong in the same class of chemical compounds, the **triglycerides**, which are derivatives of **glycerol**. You might know this compound by its older name of glycerine. It is a triple alcohol (it has three alcohol groups), and if a long-chain fatty acid is attached to each of these alcohol groups then we have a triglyceride. This may be a liquid (an oil) or a solid (a fat). The fatty acids consist of a line of carbon atoms, and it is these carbons which are described as saturated or unsaturated.[8]

Single bonds between atoms are called saturated, whereas double bonds are said to be unsaturated. If we have a chain of carbon atoms each carrying two hydrogen atoms then the chain is depicted in the following way: $-CH_2-CH_2-CH_2-CH_2-$ etc. This is called a saturated chain. However, if adjacent carbon atoms are joined by a double bond ($=$), with a hydrogen missing on each carbon, then the chain is said to be unsaturated and is shown thus $-CH_2-CH=CH-CH_2-$ etc. We can saturate such a chain by reacting it with hydrogen gas.

When there is one double bond in the chain we have a mono-unsaturated material—the name comes from the Greek word *monos* meaning

---

[8] A saturated carbon atom forms four chemical bonds linking it to four surrounding atoms. If it is bonding to only three surrounding atoms (which means a double bond to one of them) then it is described as unsaturated.

single. If there is more than one double bond in the chain we have a poly-unsaturated fat, from the Greek word *polus*, meaning many.

Generally each of the three long-chain fatty acids in a triglyceride is different. In animal fats most of them are saturated and the triglycerides are solids; in vegetable fats most may be unsaturated, and these triglycerides are liquids. Each type of fat has its advantages, and in terms of food storage, solids are better than liquids because they resist attack by oxygen and so do not go rancid. If we want to reduce the risk of this happening, we can add the missing hydrogens to unsaturated fats and produce 'hydrogenated vegetable oils' or 'partially hydrogenated vegetable oils'. The French chemists of the last century discovered margarine this way. There is nothing sinister in doing this—all that is happening is that a triglyceride of vegetable origin with perhaps two of its long-chains unsaturated is being turned into a triglyceride that has only one chain unsaturated. It then resembles a fat of animal origin.

No fat is entirely saturated or unsaturated, whether it be of animal origin or not. Certain types of fat contain so-called 'essential fatty acids' which are vital to various body functions and which we cannot manufacture. These are the polyunsaturated fats such as **linoleic acid**. We have to get our supply of these from what we eat, so a totally fat-free diet would be bad for us.

Some of the information in the table below may surprise you. It shows that in general vegetable oils have more unsaturated fats than saturated fats, but not all vegetable oil is polyunsaturated and not all

Saturated and unsaturated components of oils and fats (triglycerides)

Triglyceride	Saturated (%)	Unsaturated (%)		
		Total	Mono-unsaturated	Polyunsaturated
Rapeseed oil	6	94	64	30
Sunflower oil	11	89	20	69
Olive oil	14	86	77	9
Lard	41	59	47	12
Palm-kernel oil	51	49	39	10
Beef dripping	52	48	44	4
Butter fat	66	34	30	4
Coconut oil	92	8	6	2

animal fat is saturated—far from it. It reveals that lard is mainly an *unsaturated* fat while palm-kernel oil is mainly *saturated*—just the opposite of what you might expect. Coconut oil is really in trouble, but how often has the message to avoid animal fats ever warned you against eating sweets and candy made from coconuts?

In proportion to their weight, humans have at least ten times as many fat cells in their bodies as most other mammals. In the developed world the tendency is to eat a diet with a lot of fat, and it makes up about 40% of our food on average. We must have some fat because it is a natural source of the fat-soluble vitamins A, D, E and K, and we also need essential polyunsaturated fatty acids such as linoleic acid for growth and tissue repair. The current trend is to reduce the fat-content of our diets to a more healthy 30%, of which only a third should be saturated. For a normal person, taking in about 2200 Calories of food energy per day, their fat intake should contribute 700 Calories, which is equivalent to 80 grams or three ounces of fat or oil. Most of this will be part of other foods, and many common items contain a lot of fat. The next table lists a few examples of foods that have more fat than people imagine. It also gives their Calorie content, which again might be rather surprising. Few people would guess that half an avocado pear will provide 20 grams of fat, and a snack-size packet of nuts will provide 15 grams. A fried egg has 8 grams, but then a boiled egg has 6 grams anyway. Eating a lot of fat provides Calories we do not need, and this encourages the body to make and store fat of its own.

Foods containing more fat than is generally realised

Food	Portion weight	Fat content (%)	Calories
Cashew nuts (20 nuts)	40 g	45 g	220
Cheddar cheese	40 g	35 g	170
Chevda (e.g. Bombay mix)	100 g	32 g	490
Croissant*	50 g	20 g	180
Candied popcorn	100 g	20 g	480
Digestive biscuit (two)	30 g	20 g	150
Individual fruit pie	110 g	15 g	410
Avocado pear (half)	130 g	25 g	200
Pilau rice	200 g	11 g	420

*A doughnut is about the same

If animal fats are so bad for us it seems strange that mammals evolved to store a large part of their surplus energy in the saturated form. Even so, less than half is of this type. Humans store mainly unsaturated fat: the body fat of an average adult is about 40% saturated, 60% unsaturated, just as in lard. Of the unsaturated fat all but a few per cent is mono-unsaturated. These ratios will vary a little depending on the individual and on their diet, but clearly we store a lot of our fat as saturated fat because there is some advantage in doing so, perhaps because such fats are more stable to the damage that oxygen can cause. Unsaturated fats are susceptible to chemical reaction with oxygen, and this is why cooking oils require antioxidants, whereas cooking fats have a longer shelf-life and keep without the need of protective chemicals. One curious epidemiological observation uncovered in the saturated versus unsaturated controversy was that people who ate more saturated fats had fewer cancers.[9]

So what should we do about fats? The answer is first to cut down all fats if we are overweight, and then to worry about the saturated-to-unsaturated content of what we eat. This change need be no more difficult than simply changing from butter to margarine and from red meat to white fish. It would not hurt in any case to change to a low-fat spread, and that will generally be made from something like sunflower oil. But don't expect these simple changes to do much in the way of keeping you out of a cardiac unit in hospital, or making you live to be a hundred. If you want to lead a longer, healthier life then you need to do more than make a token gesture of changing from 'unhealthy' saturated animal fats to 'healthy' polyunsaturated vegetable oils. There is no substitute for losing weight if that is your real problem.

Fibre

'Today Americans and Europeans are bombarded with high-powered advertisements by health-food advocates, food faddists, food manufacturers, phar-

---

[9] A reason for this might be that the chemical attack of oxygen on the double bond of an unsaturated fat could form a free radical, a type of compound that is known to trigger cancer.

maceutical manufacturers, and lesser-known charlatans, who offer us what we want to hear about the fibre cure-all, at prices we're willing to pay.'

ROBERT ORY, *Grandma Called it Roughage*

Fibre is the indigestible component of our food, and it has undoubted benefits in preventing constipation (more politely called irregularity) and piles (more politely called haemorrhoids). These afflictions are very common and are exacerbated by today's sedentary lifestyle. Fibre is good because it bulks out stools and keeps them soft and moist so they are easier to pass. Even if fibre only made defecating less of a strain it would be worth making sure our diet contained enough of it, but fibre is reputed to be able to prevent the two big 'Cs': cancer, particularly of the colon, and coronary heart disease. The theory is that it prevents cancer of the colon by removing waste products that may harbour carcinogens, and prevents coronary heart disease by removing cholesterol.

Whole books have been written about fibre and fibre-based diets, and as you might expect they carry a lot of anecdotal evidence in support of eating more fibre. If you worry about high blood pressure and heart trouble then you could do worse than taking in more fibre, and soluble fibre at that, in the knowledge that it is completely harmless, and might do you some good. It is a natural cure for constipation and may prevent some of the problems that are attendant upon this condition.

The man who rediscovered fibre

Hippocrates, the Greek physician who lived around 400 BC, recommended wholemeal bread for its beneficial effects on the bowels. His advice was sound because wholemeal flour contains a lot of fibre. The current craze for fibre can be traced to the late Dr Denis Burkitt, who gave his name to a form of cancer, Burkitt's lymphoma, which affects lymphoid tissue, and which is prevalent in tropical countries. It was while he was working in Africa in the 1960s and 1970s that Dr Burkitt noticed that native Africans rarely suffered from cancer of the colon or rectum, and this he attributed to the ease with which food passed through their bodies, which in turn reflected the large amount of fibre in their diet. Indeed, many of the ailments that he had come across while practising in London, such as piles, diverticular disease, hiatus hernia, appendicitis, atherosclerosis, circulatory disorders and even varicose veins were unknown among rural Africans whose diet of coarsely ground grains, beans and peas was high in fibre. Dr Burkitt then put forward his theory that Westerners who wished to avoid these ailments should likewise take in much more fibre with their food.

What goes into our bodies also has to come out again. We never tire of talking about the food we eat, but social etiquette forbids us talking about the other end of the process—expelling the waste products. Happily we come into the world endowed with a superb system of waste disposal. In some ways it is even more sophisticated than the intake system in which everything enters the same channel. All we have to do with food is find it, chew it and swallow it—after that our body chemistry takes over.

Because atoms can neither be created nor destroyed in chemical processes, those we take in as food have to be got rid of somehow. We dispose of them as gases, liquids and solids. Carbon, the main component of our food after water, can be breathed out as odourless carbon dioxide, and every breath removes this to the extent of about 17 litres of the gas per hour. We also get rid of a little sulfur this way if we have eaten onions or garlic, which have a high sulfur level, and then our breath smells unpleasant because of these volatile sulfur compounds. In addition we can expel carbon as methane gas, again accompanied by sulfur compounds, in other unmentionable ways.

Soluble waste materials, along with the surplus water from the food and drink we consume, exits via our urine. We get rid of water and some waste molecules when we sweat, and again some of these waste molecules, such as butyric acid, are a bit malodorous. But it is the excretion of solid waste that causes us the most worry. It can also cause us the greatest pain if it becomes dehydrated so that we retain it too long and have difficulty ejecting it. This leads to haemorrhoids, which are swollen veins around the anus that can bleed and become infected. One way to prevent this is to eat a lot more fibre.

So what is fibre? The simple answer is indigestible material in our food, of which the main chemical type is a form of carbohydrate called **cellulose**. We produce enzymes in our saliva, stomach and pancreas to break down our food into its basic units. We have various enzymes to digest proteins, fats and normal carbohydrates, but they are powerless against fibre. Although most fibre has no food value, it still serves a useful purpose by providing bulk for our intestines to work on. Some, like lignin and cellulose, passes through virtually unchanged, while some may be partly fermented by the bacteria which live in our lower intestine.

Somewhat surprisingly cellulose is made from glucose, the same as sugar and starch, but in this form of fibre the glucose units have been linked together chemically in such a way that the enzymes in our bodies cannot attack. There may be up to ten thousand glucose units in a cellulose chain. Plants turn glucose into cellulose, and from it they construct their roots, stalks and leaves. They also make other indigestible carbohydrates for the shells and husks which protect their seeds. Cows, sheep and goats can digest cellulose, which is why they feed happily on grass, and they do this by having two stomachs. In one of these stomachs live microbes which can digest cellulose by using enzymes to break it down into glucose units. Single stomach animals like pigs, hens and humans have neither the enzymes nor the microbes with those enzymes to enable them to live off cellulose.

Cellulose is not the only carbohydrate we refer to as fibre, although it is the main one. There are other kinds of indigestible saccharides, such as the pentosans and pectins, which are found in soft fruits and natural gums, and lignin, which is a woody material. All these chemicals count as fibre and they serve various purposes within a plant, with some plants producing a lot of one kind. They differ chemically in their behaviour in water, which is why some are used in food. The least soluble and most abundant is cellulose, although this too has a great capacity to attract water. We make use of this property with paper products such as kitchen towels, nappies and handkerchiefs, all of which are virtually pure cellulose. Some forms of fibre are extremely good at binding to water, and these are referred to as soluble fibre.

Some dietary advisors maintain that soluble fibre clings best to bile acids and ensures that they are excreted, so that the cholesterol is not reabsorbed into the blood stream. Bile acids pass from the gall bladder and mix with food to help break up the fat and oil globules so that enzymes can better digest them. When the bile has served its purpose it is reabsorbed by the gut and stored until another fatty meal comes along. When soluble fibre prevents the bile acids being reabsorbed the liver has to use cholesterol to make more, and the amount in the body falls.

Some foods have a lot of soluble fibre, such as oats and natural gums like gum arabic which is widely used and comes from the stems of *Acacia Senegal* and related species of trees which are native to Sudan, West Africa and Nigeria. It consists of a carbohydrate polymer built from **galactose** and glucoronic acid to which are attached sugars such as **arabinose**. Other forms of soluble cellulose come from seaweed (the alginates and carrageenan), and yet others from beans (for example, guar gum). The bacterium *Xanthomonas campestris* produces xanthan gum, which like cellulose is built of glucose chains with other saccharide units attached. Foods which include these gums will lower the blood cholesterol level.

Gums are often used in food to provide the right texture ('mouthfeel'), rather than being there merely as soluble fibre. Cellulose can also be used for this purpose if it is made water soluble, and that can be done by turning it into methylcellulose. Next time you see this word on the side of a packet of cake mix, or a bottle of salad dressing, remember that it may look rather chemical, but what you are about to eat is perfectly safe and it will provide you with a little extra fibre. It has probably been made from wood cellulose which is chosen because it has no flavour of its own.

Fibre in foods

Food	Fibre (%)	Soluble fibre (%)
Wheat bran	44	3
Oat bran	28	14
All-Bran	27	2
Dried apricots	24	5
Baked beans*	15	6
Rolled oats	14	8
Cornflakes	12	7
Raspberries	7	4
Sweet corn	6	2
Apple	2	1
Brown rice	2	1
White rice	1	see the text

*Canned with tomato sauce. Beans by themselves are usually about 25% fibre

---

Methylcellulose behaves like so-called soluble fibre, the type that has great affinity with water and which when dissolved in water leads to very viscous solutions.

So what foods should we eat to take in more fibre? Plant foods contain fibre; animal products do not. Some foods, such as bran, oats, apricots and beans, have a great deal of fibre. Ideally we should take in 32 grams of fibre a day (just over an ounce). This does not seem much, but most people in the West take less than half this. The table on the previous page lists a few foods that are commonly cited as being high in fibre. Not all are.

Baked beans and porridge, once derided as staple foods of the very poor, are very good ways of taking in fibre and soluble fibre.[10] Today bran-based and oat-based breakfast cereals like All-Bran and muesli are popular, and brown bread and brown rice are much praised by food advisors. Books about fibre-based diets appeared in the 1980s and sold in millions. A lot of their advice about food was basically sound. A lot was written in ignorance.

White versus brown

The general recommendations for a healthier diet could be summed up thus: change your eating habits from white foods to brown. Some people now believe that brown bread, brown rice and brown sugar are much better than the white varieties. A few people even prefer eggs with brown shells, if they still buy them at all. Although they are an excellent food for all ages, eggs are now avoided by many merely because of the cholesterol they contain.

Ironically, our parents' and grandparents' general guide to healthy eating was to avoid colour. White was right. White was a symbol of purity. The 19th century had seen many food scandals, as producers and shopkeepers adulterated food with everything from sawdust to powdered bone. White foods were thought to be the hardest to cheat on, and they were among the most nutritious; milk, sugar, lard, flour, bread, salt and even white shell eggs were thought to be best. Sugar and salt are among the purest of all because these are crystallised from water, a process which chemists use to remove impurities.

---

[10] Baked beans are navy beans, which are grown in the USA.

Brown eggs: Let us begin with the easiest myth to dispel: brown eggs are better than white. It is often popularly imagined that battery hens, which are fed only on cereals, lay eggs with paler yolks and white shells because they lack some vital nutrients which free-range hens get from the seeds, grass, insects and grubs they eat. Diet does affect the eggs that a hen lays, but only marginally, and brown eggs with deep yellow yolks also come from battery hens. We may object to any animal being raised in unnatural conditions merely to provide humans with cheaper food and farmers with higher profits, but that is another issue, and little to do with the chemistry of eggs. The colour of a bird's egg depends upon the species, and so it is with hens. It has no nutritional significance. Brown or white, battery or free-range, eggs are just eggs.

Brown bread: Bread is baked from three types of flour: white, brown and wholemeal. Wholemeal bread has to be made from the whole wheat grain, so that it contains the maximum amount of fibre. In white flour the outer third of the grain is removed as bran, and along with it goes most of the fibre. Brown bread is intermediate between these two extremes, with about 15% of the bran being removed. Some bread can have extra fibre added, and some can be baked with malted flour when it is described as granary bread.

A slice of bread, be it white, brown or wholemeal, provides about the same amount of energy, protein, fat, carbohydrate, iron and B vitamins. They differ in the amounts of calcium and fibre they provide: a slice of white bread has 40 mg of calcium and 1.5 g of fibre; a slice of brown bread has 35 mg of calcium and 2 g of fibre; and a slice of wholemeal bread has 20 mg of calcium and 2.5 g of fibre. The calcium of white bread should make it the preferred choice for children and pregnant women. For the rest of us it is the fibre which may influence our choice. If we aim at 32 g of fibre a day then switching from white to wholemeal bread will go a little way towards this total, depending on how much bread we eat. But even here the superiority of brown over white is partly an illusion, as we shall see when we talk about hidden fibre (see p. 108).

Brown sugar: If you like your warm drinks sweet, then brown sugar gives a richer taste in coffee but spoils the more delicate flavour of tea. If we have to choose between brown or white sugar, then taste alone is our only guide, because in all other respects they are the same. As we saw in Chapter 2, the brown component in sugar is the sort of chemical that forms when we heat sugar and caramelise it. Sometimes sugar and molasses are simply mixed to give the various kinds of brown sugars that are called by a variety of names, such as demerara, which is nice in coffee, or dark Muscovado, which has a stronger taste and is ideal for spicy cakes and gingerbread. All are virtually pure carbohydrate, all provide the same amount of energy per spoonful, and the only difference is the taste which in brown sugar comes from traces of many chemicals, such as complex saccharides, salts, organic acids and amino acids.

Brown rice: Brown rice is to ordinary rice what brown bread is to white: richer in fibre. The brown variety also provides a little more protein, calcium, vitamins and fat, but that was not the reason for encouraging people to make the switch. Brown rice needs cooking for longer and is harder to chew, but some believe this is a price worth paying in the battle for more fibre.[11] Closer inspection shows that it is not really worth the effort. Brown rice certainly has almost twice as much fibre as white rice, but that is still not a lot. Boiled brown rice is 1.5 per cent fibre, while white rice is only 0.8 per cent. A normal portion of brown rice will provide you with 2.5 grams of fibre, and white rice with only 1.3 grams. However, white rice has more fibre than these figures suggest, as we shall now see.

Hidden fibre (resistant starch)

Those who advocate a change to brown rice did not realise that when white rice is cooked something rather wonderful happens: the amount of fibre actually increases. The same is true of products

---

[11] It is probably worth the struggle if this is your only source of B vitamins, of which brown rice has a lot and white rice very little.

Cooked foods high in resistant starch (hidden fibre)

Food	Resistant starch*
Boiled white rice	78%
Kelloggs' cornflakes	64%
Spaghetti	38%
Boiled potatoes	33%
White bread	29%
Peas	21%

*Resistant starch as a percentage of the total fibre content

made from white flour. Removing the outer layer of the wheat or rice does remove most of the plant fibre. What is not appreciated is that this is compensated for in another way, with hidden fibre or, as it is more correctly called, resistant starch, which forms on cooking. It is called this because it resists digestion by the enzymes of the stomach and intestines and passes out of the body with its energy store intact.

A dish of a supermarket own-brand of cornflakes will provide you with half a gram of dietary fibre. On the other hand, if you choose Kelloggs, the world's best selling proprietary brand, you will get twice as much fibre. Yet both are made from the same type of flour; the only difference is in the way they are cooked. The traditional high temperature method used by Kelloggs converts some of the carbohydrate into resistant starch. This hidden fibre was discovered in 1982 by food chemists at Cambridge, England, and now it has turned up in all sorts of cooked foods such as potatoes, pasta, peas, beans, and especially rice. Scientists believe that it can be considered as a form of dietary fibre, and may even be a superior form, as we shall see. Some foods contain remarkably high levels of resistant starch, and the table above shows those foods in which it accounts for a fifth or more of the fibre they contain. All-Bran for breakfast can provide a third of our daily fibre needs, but so can an evening meal of white rice and peas.

Resistant starch explains some other mysteries of cooked food. It was known in the last century that when some foods were re-heated their nutritional value went down. What was hard to explain was why this happened to mashed potato, but not to carrots. The answer came to light when a team led by Hans Englyst, of the Dunn Centre, Cambridge, was able to show that this effect could be explained by the formation of resistant starch from ordinary starch.

Colin Berry, head of nutrition and food safety at the Flour Milling and Baking Research Association in the UK, has researched resistant starch and looked at ways in which this could be deliberately increased. His work has shown that it needs three things for its formation: there has to be starch present in the food; it needs a high cooking temperature; and the food has to have a high moisture content. When these conditions come together they allow some of the starch molecules to bind so closely that our digestive enzymes cannot attack them. Once resistant starch has formed it cannot be changed back into digestible starch. Indeed, reheating food will only serve to make more of it.

For years, official tests for dietary fibre ignored resistant starch, and so the tables of fibre content tended to be on the low side. Recently the published fibre level in many foods has increased, much to the embarrassment of some dietary advisors, because it has increased most among the foods which they said should be avoided. Colin Berry claims that it is now possible to have foods with high levels of resistant starch that could actually be better for us than the brown counterpart, even though officially they contain no dietary fibre at all. Rats fed a diet rich in resistant starch for the whole of their natural lives were found to have fewer bowel cancers than rats fed conventional high fibre foods. The resistant starch in rice might also explain why the Japanese suffer much less from diseases of the bowel, such as cancer and diverticular disease, than we would predict from their preference for white rice.

The chemistry of successful dieting

Dieting is surrounded by a mystique that needs to be swept away. A little knowledge and you can learn how to do it effectively, effortlessly and cheaply. You will also learn that you can cheat yourself, but not the laws of chemistry.

Dieting is probably the most popular, but least enjoyed, activity in developed societies. It is nevertheless fascinating because it is easy to do, it provides hours of innocent agony and is a good topic of conversation—and yet we are not really expected by our friends to do it successfully. There are hundreds of books devoted to dieting.

These advise us how to lose weight, but they require us to monitor what we eat very carefully, and some seem to regard food almost as if it were medicine, to be measured carefully and its calories counted for each meal.

At the other extreme are the proponents of another popular hobby—eating too much. There are even more volumes devoted to this pastime. Cookery books can also be aimed at dieters but the best-sellers appeal to the *bon viveurs*, and those who are entertaining friends. They present food in terms of tasty dishes, menus for dinner parties and even exotic banquets. Cookery books may make concessions to the latest health fad but generally their authors seem unperturbed by recipes that require lots of butter, olive oil or cooking fat. They cater for the vast majority of people who still enjoy classical dishes, produced with no thought as to their salt, sugar, fat or calories. Many people have spent most of their lives eating the 'wrong' foods,[12] and clearly it did most of them little harm, although a better diet might have kept a few more of their friends alive for longer and themselves healthier.

The best dietary advice is that which keeps your weight at the right level. Body fat is very noticeable. If you have too much body fat then lose it. But how is this to be done? A bit of chemistry will show you how.

When we diet and take in fewer calories, we make our body draw upon its own store of fat. The best target to aim for is reducing our intake of fat, because triglycerides have more calories than any other type of food. Both fats and oils are equal in terms of calories, and it makes no difference whether it is butter, cream, margarine, olive oil, dripping, polyunsatured spreads or lard. You must cut down on triglycerides if you want to lose weight and stay slim.

The difficulty with diets is sticking to them: a crash diet lasting two weeks tests the limits of most people's endurance. The chemistry of dieting is straightforward, and understanding it may help you to do it successfully. Once you understand the chemistry of food in terms of

[12] Though not all their life, especially if they lived through the 1940s. Britons in the Second World War from 1939–1945, and for a while after, were forced to eat a high fibre diet when all bread was a standard National Loaf. This was deliberately milled to remove less bran, and was unrationed until the world famine of 1947. After that white bread returned.

the energy it provides, you have no-one to blame but yourself if you stay fat. By fat I mean obese, a condition which afflicts growing numbers of people in the West, with over 10% of the population now coming into this category. Obesity is defined by dietitians as a body mass index of 30 or above (see the Box below).

The average man needs about 2500 Calories[13] per day, and the average woman needs 1900 Calories. Exactly how much depends on circumstances. A retired person doing very little may require 200 Calories a day less, whereas people doing strenuous work or sport may need an extra 200 Calories or more. To make the sums easy I will assume the average amount for a man and a woman is 2200 Calories. I will keep the other figures as round numbers as well.

Body mass index

The weight of a person varies with their height and build, and these depend to a certain extent on their sex. To take this into account a system of calculation has been devised called the Body Mass Index (BMI) which can be calculated for each person regardless of whether they are male or female. The BMI of a person is defined as their weight in kilograms divided by the square of their height in metres, so that the average person with a weight of 70 kg and height of 1.80 m will have a BMI of $70/(1.80)^2$ which comes to 22 to the nearest whole number. In the more familiar units of pounds, feet and inches a slightly different formula is required. Divide the weight in pounds by the square of the height in inches, and then multiply this by 700. For example, if a person's weight is 155 pounds and their height is 5 feet 9 inches (i.e. 69 inches in total) then their BMI is $[155/(69)^2] \times 700$ which gives 23.

If your BMI is within the range 20 and 25 you have nothing to worry about as far as your weight is concerned. If your BMI is between 25 and 30 you are too fat and should consider losing some weight, and if it is over 30 you are officially classed as obese. You ought to go on a weight-reducing diet. If your BMI is above 40 you are very obese.

If you reduce your intake of energy to 1000 Calories a day you draw the other 1200 that you need from your own body's reserves.

---

[13] A Calorie is 1000 calories. A chemist would refer to a Calorie as a kilocalorie.

Since your body is not aware you are dieting it supplies the missing calories from its glycogen carbohydrate store in the liver, which it can draw upon straight away. When this reserve is depleted, the body draws upon its fat reserves. Many people fondly imagine that dieting is a direct attack on their flabby bits and are puzzled when these do not immediately start to shrink. Many people also expect their body to shed the fatty tissue which they think appears least attractive, which is around the stomach, hips and thighs. Would that it would.

What does a cut of 1200 Calories mean? You would have to burn up 300 grams (11 ounces) of carbohydrate to provide 1200 Calories. Alternatively your body could consume 140 grams (5 ounces) of its fat. Two weeks on 1000 Calories a day must mean a loss of at least 2 kilograms (4 pounds) if you lost only fat. In fact our body loses carbohydrate, fat and protein, at the rate of about 250 grams (8 ounces) a day. Loss of water from the disappearing tissue will make our weight loss much more than this. A rough guide is that a pound of water is lost for each pound of fat, so that a strict 1000 Calorie diet for two weeks could see your weight drop by an average of a pound a day if you are a man, and slightly less if you are a woman.

There is nothing magical about dieting. You must release energy within your body to keep you warm and active, and that energy must come from fuel provided either by your food or by your own reserves. Obey the rule of a 1000 Calorie diet and you must lose weight—you cannot defeat the laws of chemistry. Hospital dietitians and doctors know that their obese patients are being less than honest when they don't lose weight, while claiming that they are sticking to a 1000 Calorie diet.

Once you have lost weight then the difficult part begins if you are not to put the weight back. Return to your old ways of eating and you could be back to your old weight within another two weeks. Again, chemistry can come to your aid to prevent this happening. You can turn to the substitutes which food chemists have devised to replace high calorie foods. Change to diet drinks, diet soups and diet desserts; buy low-fat snacks, spreads, pickles and dressings; choose calorie-controlled complete meals; and use artificial sweeteners. If you do then you can easily cut 500 Calories a day from your energy intake without any effort. You can also afford to reward yourself with occasional treats like hot buttered toast, a slice of cake, fried egg and bacon, or a pizza. You won't put on weight if you indulge yourself once or twice a week. You cannot put on weight by eating a jam doughnut or a slice of cheesecake occasionally. You only do so if you eat such a treat every day.

Now that you understand the chemistry and energy count, all you need is the will-power. One tip though—don't weigh yourself every day or you will become disheartened when some days you see your weight has gone up despite the diet. The water in our bodies is not something we can control, yet it weighs a lot because we are 60% water. The human body goes through a daily cycle of water retention and loss which reaches its minimum at about midday. The only way to cope with this fluctuation is to weigh yourself once a week on the same day, and at the same time of day.

The other problem with diets is that most humans are rather lazy, and most of us do not have the time to fiddle around weighing bits of food and counting calories. Those who propose a diet plan generally assume that they must make it as varied as possible so that people stick to it. I believe this is the wrong policy to adopt. If the will to lose weight is not there, then no amount of low calorie titbits will keep people on a diet. Those who have to deal with people who are addicted to something realise that they can do nothing until the person really *wants* to be cured. I believe the same goes for dieting. Until you really want to lose weight then diets are a waste of time. But once you have crossed that barrier the rest is easy: you don't need an interesting weight-reducing diet, you need a *boring* diet. Anything less could well tempt you back to eating for pleasure. The other advantage of a boring diet is that you have nothing much to remember, so you know immediately when you have broken it. There can be no trade-off in this diet. Either stick to it and chemistry will *guarantee* you lose weight—or forget it.

Think of the benefits of a boring diet. You save yourself the mental agony of what to choose, because it is the same set of meals every day for two weeks. As an example I give below a diet you you will find easy to remember because the main foods also begin with the letter B. B for boring. For the first three days you may lose weight rapidly as you use up your body's glycogen store (and that will disappear at the rate of about a pound a day), then things will slow down as you start to use your body fat (and that will disappear at about half a pound a day). If you can keep the diet going for an extra two weeks you will lose several more pounds of fat, and then people will really begin to notice. If eventually you find yourself returning to your old ways, then a three-day crash diet will deplete the carbohydrate store before your body has time to start making fat. Again use the boring diet. Once learnt it is easy to remember, but then you have no excuse for not knowing how to lose weight.

The boring diet

A bowl of All-Bran for breakfast, a corned beef or salt beef sandwich[14] and an orange for lunch, baked beans on toast for dinner, and a pint of half-fat milk taken throughout the day. Spread your sandwich with low-fat margarine. Tea, coffee or diet drinks with artificial sweeteners can be drunk any time you want. You can also use an artificial sweetener on your All-Bran. The beauty of this diet is that you can forget the details just remember the Bs: bran, beef, bread and beans. The chemical details are given in the table below (again I am using round numbers to make it easy). A side plate of salad greens and tomato, but with no dressing except salt and vinegar, is also

The boring diet that's guaranteed to work

Meal		Amount	Calories
Breakfast	All-Bran	50 grams (2 ounces)	120
Midday	Corned beef, etc.	30 grams (1 slice)	70
	Bread	2 slices (medium)	200
	Low fat spread	10 grams ($\frac{1}{3}$ ounce)	40
	Orange*	1 medium	40
Evening	Baked beans in sauce	225 grams (8 ounces)	130
	Toast	2 slices (medium)	200
Throughout the day			
	Half-fat milk	400 mls ($\frac{2}{3}$ pint)	200
		Total:	1000

*An apple plus a 100 mg vitamin C tablet will do just as well.

[14] Other protein fillings will do equally well, and you can substitute chicken breast, boiled ham, boiled egg, or canned tuna provided it is in brine.

allowed. The diet is well balanced nutritionally in terms of protein, vitamins and minerals. All it lacks is calories.

The human body is not the fragile flower some would have us believe. People have survived for days trapped without water beneath ruined buildings, have drifted for weeks without food on boats at sea, lived for months in besieged cities with only a few ounces of bread a day, survived a year of starvation in drought-plagued Africa, and even suffered a decade of malnutrition in concentration camps. Having survived and recovered from their ordeal, they have gone on to live their allotted span of three score years and ten.

Of course food is vital to life, although it can not keep us forever young. There are times in our lives when what we eat is very important—when we are growing up, when we are pregnant, when we are ill, and when we are growing old. For some people, such as diabetics, their diet must be a life-long concern and there are trained dietitians to help. The rest of us can *enjoy* our food, although the sign of a bad diet will be if we end up grossly overweight. Because the pleasure of eating usually wins over our plans to be perfectly fit, we need to watch ourselves, but not obsessively, and we should take advantage of the diet aids that the food chemists have devised.

Several consumer organisations have taken up the theme that we can enjoy a healthier and longer life through better eating. Some people go further and allege that everything from allergies to cancer is due to eating the wrong type of food. Curiously these messages seem to have most impact in those countries where, for the first time in history, most of the inhabitants live out their natural lives and die of the diseases of old age.[15] Can everyone now live longer than the Biblical three-score-years-and-ten, maybe even to four-score years and ten? The best advice is to avoid being overweight. This is much more important than what we eat.

The rapidly growing legions of the elderly consist of people who spent their formative years in eating foods that are now considered unhealthy. When they were young, in the first half of this century, the prevailing philosophy for good eating was to consume lots of cream,

---

[15] This of course has been brought about by the advances of medical science and public hygiene in eradicating infectious diseases.

milk, and meat, and to avoid so-called starchy foods like bread, pasta and potatoes. In those days poverty and malnutrition, caused by wars and economic depression, were only too real. The poor ate a diet that was largely cheap carbohydrate ('starch'), whereas the rich were better fed and healthier. They ate more dairy products and meat. The inferences to be drawn by comparing the health and longevity of two groups were obvious, but the reasoning, we now realise, was faulty.

You might wonder if one day current food fads will fade in their turn, and the message to cut down on foods rich in cholesterol and animal fats and to eat more fibre will no longer be heeded. This advice is well meaning, and has the support of doctors—but so did the earlier advice. In fact we *should* eat more fibre and less fat, as this chapter has shown. In the final analysis it may matter little what sort of fibre we take more of, or what kind of fat we cut out, and trying to avoid foods with a lot of cholesterol may turn out to be a waste of time.

The chemistry of food has come a long way in the second half of this century, and so has the food industry. Chemists in the industry have been at the forefront of research in this area. Both food chemists and the food industry are regularly criticised by those who campaign for a healthier diet, and I think these criticisms have been a little too harsh. The food chemist, the nutritionist, and the qualified dietitian are all marching in step towards a healthier world. Food chemists are professionals whose first loyalty, one assumes, is to their science. Of course they are not infallible, and the food firms that employ many of them are not run as charitable organisations but for profit, and we must always bear that in mind. In the final analysis though, we are not what we eat, but what we weigh.

CHAPTER FIVE

Painkillers and painful decisions

Thalidomide; painkillers; arthritis and non-steroid anti-inflammatory drugs; opiates; toxicity; risk

THERE are in Nature plants which produce chemicals that relieve pain. However, they did not evolve to provide relief from human suffering, and even though we can extract painkillers from some of them, it is perhaps not surprising to find that these chemicals have side-effects. Indeed, were they to be tested using today's standards for safety in medicines they would fail, and be banned for use on humans. Yet some of these ancient painkillers are still the most effective we have. They are given to relieve the intense pain of accident victims, or of those who have undergone surgery. They are used to make life bearable for people in the last stages of painful diseases such as cancer. The drugs in question are the opiates **morphine**, **diamorphine** (better known as heroin), **codeine** and **hydromorphone**.[1]

Merely to deaden pain is simply to treat the symptoms without dealing with the underlying cause of that pain. For this reason we are perhaps less willing to take risks with painkillers. We accept that healing treatments involve some degree of risk in the form of adverse side-effects, and these we are prepared to live with in the hope of securing long-term benefits to our health. On the other hand, ending the pain of a headache or an inflamed muscle is purely a short-term

---

[1] A reminder that when the name of a substance appears in **bold** type, it means that there is more about its chemistry in the Appendix.

gain, lasting a few hours at most, and if we take something to ease that pain we want it to be free of risk.

If a person demands *absolutely* no risk at all, then they are demanding too much, and would be best advised to seek relief in treatments that do not involve taking a pharmaceutical compound. They should opt for something like homeopathic medicine or aromatherapy. If these work, then they probably do so by relieving psychological stress, which might well be the origin of the pain. Most people who want relief from pain turn to over-the-counter[2] drugs such as **aspirin** or **paracetamol** when they have an ache in their head, back, joints or muscles. Many old people also take these general purpose painkillers as prescribed by their doctor, and they take them every day to deaden the pain of arthritis. All these painkillers carry a risk, and naturally this has led to attacks on them, not least by those who offer alternatives or who see them as 'chemical' cures as opposed to 'natural' cures.

Should a warning signal flash through our mind every time we swallow a headache pill? Perhaps it should, because there are few times in life when you are taking into your body such a large amount of a potent chemical. The chemists of the pharmaceuticals industry may have transformed the quality of life for billions of people, but they have sometimes made terrible mistakes. The thalidomide tragedy of deformed babies is one of which we are often reminded. I shall begin this chapter with the thalidomide story and tell how this drug is still being used. I will then go on to explain the chemists' fight to control pain, and finally end the chapter with a discussion of the vexed question of how much risk we should be prepared to accept when taking painkilling drugs.

Thalidomide

A woman who is expecting a baby can enjoy her condition for much of the nine months of pregnancy, although many experience morning sickness during the early months. While this may be perfectly natural it is inconvenient, and can sometimes be very unpleasant. At one time

---

[2] Pharmaceuticals that are available for self-medication are generally known as over-the-counter drugs.

there was little a doctor could do but give reassurance, although this was not much help if the woman was also trying to lead a normal life and do a full-time job.

Then suddenly there was thalidomide. In 1958 this drug was launched in Germany in a blaze of publicity by the company Chemie Grünenthal, who even felt it was safe enough to be sold without prescription under the brand name Contergan. Within a few years it was available in over 40 countries. The liquid form of thalidomide quickly gained a reputation in Germany as the babysitter's friend because it was superb at calming young children and sending them to sleep. Chemie Grünenthal were so confident that Contergan was safe that it was advertised with a picture of a child taking a bottle from a shelf with the claim: 'completely harmless, even for infants'.

There were some side-effects—a few patients complained that thalidomide made them constipated and slightly dizzy—but these kinds of reports are to be expected for any drug, and mean very little. In the UK, thalidomide was called Distaval and was prescribed as an anti-depressant, and it was also sometimes given to control morning sickness. It was much safer than the other anti-depressants that were available, such as the barbiturates, and accidental overdoses were not lethal—indeed, an adult could take as much as 350 grams (12 ounces) of thalidomide without its being fatal. It seemed the perfect sedative, and it stopped the morning sickness.

Doctors and patients were unaware of a dreadful side-effect of this drug—it was a teratogenic compound. This is the technical term for a substance which causes a developing foetus to become deformed. A woman who was prescribed thalidomide in her first weeks of pregnancy was at risk of giving birth to a limbless child. A typical thalidomide baby could have an arm missing, and just a tiny hand protruding from its shoulder.

The first inkling that something was wrong came in 1961 when a young doctor, William McBride, who worked at the Crown Street Women's Hospital in Sydney, Australia, first noticed an unusually high number of babies being born with tiny arms and legs, a deformity that was not unknown but was normally extremely rare. When he made enquiries of the mothers, he discovered that they had all taken thalidomide during pregnancy. McBride wrote to the medical journal the *Lancet*, pointing out this coincidence. His suspicions proved to be well founded, and when they were followed up the link with thalidomide became evident. As a result the drug was withdrawn in most countries.

The publicity and sympathy for the victims of thalidomide, and the large financial settlement which they were given, highlight the risks that are attendant on all new pharmaceuticals. Yet Chemie Grünenthal had a superb product in thalidomide, and what they did not realise was that while half the molecules in thalidomide were safe, the other half were anything but. The two forms of thalidomide are identical except for one minor detail: they come as left- and right-handed pairs.

Gloves, cars, screws and molecules have one thing in common: they can all be made in two versions—left-handed and right-handed. We never think twice about gloves coming in pairs, and we know that cars built for Australia, Britain and Japan have the driver's seat on the right side, while for most of the rest of the world the driver's seat is on the left side. Screws are less obviously of two kinds, and most people would not know, just by looking at it, whether a screw had a left- or right-handed thread. Molecules are like screws in that we would not instinctively know by looking at one that it had within its structure the ability to be right- or left-handed. Not all molecules are like this; it is a feature which generally comes with size and complexity.

Chemists talk of such pairs of molecules in terms of one being the mirror image of the other. They label them not as left or right, but as S (from the Latin *sinister*) or R (*rectus*).[3] R-thalidomide was fine, but the S-thalidomide could interfere with the development of the foetus and deform it. In the form in which it was manufactured, thalidomide consisted of both R and S molecules in equal numbers, and back in the 1950s it would have been impossible to separate them on a commercial scale, even if they had known that this was necessary.

Today chemists can do this separation relatively easily, and now they *must* do it, because all new pharmaceuticals have to be tested separately as both their R and S versions. If this had been a stipulation back in the 1950s then doctors would still be prescribing R-thalido-

---

[3] An alternative system which is still widely used has the letters D (from the Latin *dexter* for right) and L (*laevo*, left).

mide as the remarkable multi-purpose drug that it is. In those days, however, chemists had neither the skill to separate left- and right-handed molecules easily, nor did they have chemical reactions that could make the one without the other. Advances in chemical research over the past 40 years have brought such achievements about, but this has still not been done for thalidomide, presumably because the cost would never justify the commercial risk involved in trying to reintroduce a drug with such a negative public image.

Yet thalidomide is still being manufactured in Brazil, using the original recipe, and is given to treat leprosy. Provided it is not taken by a pregnant woman there is no risk. Thalidomide is remarkable at dealing with the adverse effects which can follow any treatment that involves destroying bacteria in large numbers, which is what happens in leprosy. It is possible to prescribe thalidomide in some countries such as the UK, and this is done to treat patients where such conditions apply. Thalidomide is still being investigated because it has the potential to deal with inflammatory conditions by suppressing the immune system. This has alerted researchers to the possibility that it might also alleviate AIDS, rheumatoid arthritis, and even prevent the rejection of organ transplants. Were this to be proved it might one day justify the manufacture of the *R*-form.

Painkillers

There are natural painkillers within our brain called enkephalins. These consist of five amino acid units joined together as a short peptide chain, and they are powerful painkillers produced in response to traumas and with effects similar to morphine. They are derived from longer peptides called endorphins, which are made up of 80 or so amino acid units.[4] Endorphins come to the aid of the brain when the body has to cope with intense pain experienced over a long period, but they can not be produced to relieve such pain immediately, and this is why we seek quicker-acting painkillers.

There are basically two kinds of painkilling drugs: those which operate at the site of the pain and stop the damaged tissue sending

[4] The name endorphin is derived from the phrase 'endogenous morphine', meaning morphine produced from within.

signals to the brain, and those which act in the brain and prevent the incoming signals from registering as pain. The latter, which act on the central nervous system, are more likely to have side-effects such as affecting a person's mood, and some are addictive. The former, which act peripherally, may have side-effects as well, but sometimes they may even be beneficial in actually treating the cause of the pain itself.

Before chemistry and the pharmaceutical industry developed, the only source of painkilling chemicals was plants. Hippocrates, the ancient Greek pioneer of medical science, had recourse to some such remedies; for instance, he recommended an infusion of willow bark to ease the pain of childbirth. If this bark was that of the white willow then we know that this advice would have been of some use, because this tree produces salicin which on boiling in water is converted to **salicylic acid** which is a painkiller. This chemical is called after the willow, whose scientific name is *Salix*. Although salicylic acid deadens some pain it can also cause pain, because it irritates the stomach lining to the extent of causing bleeding.

Today there are four commonly used, over-the-counter painkillers: aspirin, paracetamol, codeine and **ibuprofen**. They are taken in their millions every day, and some countries favour one type over another. For example Britons prefer paracetamol-based tablets, while the second most popular is aspirin, the painkiller that helped launch the modern drugs industry a century ago. Aspirin is still the number one in the USA. Codeine has been around a long time and is also still popular, but is now only sold combined with other painkillers for reasons we shall see. The newest over-the-counter painkiller is ibuprofen which is slowly gaining in popularity.

Aspirin

It was to be another 2000 years before Hippocrates' advice about willow bark was taken further. In the eighteenth century the Reverend Edmund Stone, an English parson living in the Cotswolds, was trying to find a local plant whose bark might have the same effect as cinchona bark that was imported from Peru. This Peruvian bark contains **quinine**, which is a natural chemical that was known to ward off fevers, and especially malaria. Parson Stone experimented with the bark from the white willow, and gave an infusion of this to 50 people who had fever and found they were much improved. He reported his findings to the Royal Society of London in 1763.

In the 1820s an Italian chemist, Raffaele Piria, isolated the chemical salicin from willow bark, and from it he made salicylic acid. It was later discovered that this acid could also be extracted from the wild flower meadow-sweet (*Spiraea ulmaria*).[5] It is from this plant that aspirin gets its name (a+spiraea), and the word was coined by the firm Bayer for the derivative, acetylsalicylic acid. This had first been made around 1850 by a Frenchman, Charles Frederic Gerhardt, but although it was known to be a painkiller it burnt the mouth and stomach of those who tried it, and it tasted unpleasant. It later transpired that these side-effects were caused by impurities in the product.

In 1893 Felix Hoffmann and Henrich Dreser, chemists working for Bayer, found a way of purifying acetylsalicylic acid and obtained it as a white powder. It was worth taking the trouble because by doing so they produced one of the most successful proprietary drugs ever made, and one considered safe enough to be sold direct to the public. Americans swallow 50 million aspirin tablets a day, which is almost two billion a year. Aspirin is not risk-free and would not be passed for use under modern testing methods. It causes stomach inflammation in some people, and it slowly reverts back to salicylic acid which is even worse. For this reason old aspirin tablets should never be taken.

Aspirin is regarded as more than just a painkiller. At various times in the 100 years since it was first marketed it has been the standard treatment for virus infections (such as fevers, colds and 'flu) and for arthritis (once commonly referred to as rheumatism). It is a cure for none of these, it just makes them more bearable by reducing the aches and pains they cause. Aspirin is still bought and taken for these complaints under a variety of trade names, such as Anacin, Anadin, Aspro, Disprin, Ecotrin, Excedrin, etc., and of course as its best known version, Alka Seltzer. Nor is this plethora of names limited only to aspirin: it has become an integral part of the drug industry (see the Box).

---

[5] Salicylic acid itself is a simple organic molecule made industrially from phenol and carbon dioxide.

What's in a name?

It has been said that most human illness is psychological in origin, and so perhaps we should not find it so surprising that psychology plays an important part in the effect of pharmaceuticals. We all know about placebos, the capsules of glucose or some such, which are given in double blind tests, and which we suspect doctors sometimes give to their more troublesome patients who are simply seeking attention. In fact it would be unethical for a doctor to do so. What doctors may opt to do instead is to prescribe the same medication under a different name. Most pharmaceuticals have many names.

Every drug has at least two official names: the chemist's systematic name, which may run to several lines of text, and the agreed *generic* name which is approved by international agreement. The chemical name, with its curious italics, brackets, Greek prefixes, symbols or numbers, is unreadable and easy to get wrong, especially by those who are not familiar with them. The generic name is usually simple, short and memorable. Thus we have N-acetyl-*para*-aminophenol as the chemical name, and paracetamol as the generic name.

In addition there are the trade names, of which dozens are in use for this one drug alone. We may be persuaded by heavy advertising always to buy Panadol, Tylenol, or whatever name it is given in the place in which we live; and in just one country, the UK, doctors can give paracetamol as Alvedon, Catadol, Disprol, Paldesic, Panaleve, Salzone, and Tylex. Some of these are mixtures with other compounds.

Doctors can prescribe a drug under its trade name or generic name, when it will be cheaper. But is the cheaper alternative really costing us dear in the long term? Companies who make generic drugs generally do no research. On the other hand the big pharmaceutical companies need their higher prices to fund the huge costs of research into new drugs. Sadly, they need to spend even more on promoting, protecting and improving their existing drugs, than on research. What the research-based pharmaceutical companies require are longer patent rights, starting from the date the drug is finally cleared for use, rather than from the date of its discovery. Until such times they need the support which a well-known brand name can provide. That's what's in a name.

Tablets of Alka Seltzer also contain **citric acid** and **sodium bicarbonate** as well as aspirin. The bicarb reacts with the aspirin to form its sodium salt, thereby making it soluble in water and quicker acting. It also reacts with the citric acid to generate bubbles of carbon dioxide. The citric acid gives the final drink a pleasant citrus-like flavour.

Soluble forms of aspirin can be made by converting the acetyl-salicylic acid, which is not very soluble in water, into its sodium or calcium salt, which is soluble. When dissolved in water these give a clear liquid which some find reassuring to drink and easier to take than swallowing a tablet. However, once aspirin is in the stomach the acid conditions there immediately turn it back to the insoluble form, although this is now as very fine crystals. These are slightly less irritating to the lining of the stomach than particles of a large tablet. Yet even they may be too irritating for some patients, in which case a doctor can prescribe a clinical form of aspirin, called enteric aspirin, in which the tablets have a coating that resists the acid of the stomach but dissolves once the tablet passes into the small intestine where the conditions are alkaline.

Although aspirin has been used for a long time it is not without its more serious risks. For some young children aspirin can be fatal, and if they are given it to treat the symptoms of a viral infection, such as 'flu or chicken pox, they can develop Reye's syndrome. For this reason children under the age of 12 should never be prescribed it, and in the USA aspirin packs must carry the warning: 'Children and teenagers should not use this medicine for chicken pox or 'flu symptoms before a doctor is consulted about Reye's syndrome, a rare but serious illness'.

Despite its disadvantages, aspirin is still a remarkable drug and much more than just a painkiller. It is said to ward off heart disease and prevent thrombosis, and it has even been mooted as a possible treatment of cancer, cataracts and senile dementia. It is used in the treatment of people who have suffered a heart attack. If you suffer no stomach pain with aspirin then you might be well advised to take a small aspirin tablet (100 mg) each day. Aspirin inhibits the formation of those chemicals which cause blood platelets to aggregate together, which is what starts a blood clot. This may also be why it might help in senile dementia, because it keeps up the flow of blood to the brain. Aspirin is also thought to be able to destroy free radicals, those super-active natural chemicals that are formed within the body and which are thought to initiate cancer. Aspirin can also prevent cataracts because it counters the proteins that make the lens of the eye opaque.

Aspirin is normally sold as 300 mg tablets and can safely be taken at a rate of two or three every four to six hours to a maximum dose of a dozen tablets or about 4 g per day. A single dose of 10 g (30 tablets) is life-threatening for an adult because it makes the blood too acidic. The body tries to cope by rapid breathing to dispel CO_2 and thereby reduce acidity, and by boosting the action of the kidneys, which leads to dehydration. If the acidity cannot be corrected by natural means, tissue damage occurs and eventually death.

How does aspirin work? It interferes with an enzyme that makes **prostaglandins**. We need these chemicals to regulate digestion, kidney function, blood circulation and reproduction. Prostaglandins also generate pain signals. They are released in many injuries and diseases, and it is because of them that we suffer inflammation, pain and fever. This was discovered in 1969 when John Vane and a group of workers at the Royal College of Surgeons in London, England, proved that aspirin prevented the synthesis of prostaglandins in damaged tissue. Vane shared the 1982 Nobel Prize in Physiology or Medicine with Sune Bergström and Bengt Samuelsson of the Karolinska Institute, who had also studied the role of prostaglandins.

There is a whole sequence of chemical reactions which lead to the appearance of prostaglandins, and the first is the liberation of the polyunsaturated fatty acid called **arachidonic acid** from a cell membrane. This acid reacts with oxygen to form chemicals such as cyclic prostaglandin endoperoxides that trigger inflammation. Aspirin blocks the enzyme which controls this reaction and so prevents the chain of events which starts with a broken cell membrane and leads to painful prostaglandins being produced.

Arthritis and the non-steroid anti-inflammatory drugs

Some drugs relieve inflammation, such as steroids like cortisone, but are not painkillers, and some relieve pain, such as morphine, but are not anti-inflammatory, and these latter types we will deal with later in the chapter. There are some drugs which do both, and these are the non-steroid anti-inflammatory drugs (NSAIDs). Aspirin is one such drug, and it used to be the first line of defence in the treatment of arthritis.

Rheumatoid arthritis occurs when the body mounts an immunological attack on itself, in this case on the connective tissue between the joints. It can deform the body and is a crippling illness. There can be periods of remission and most patients improve with care and exercise. Osteoarthritis is less damaging in that it does not deform the body and is generally considered to be part of growing old. It affects the joints of the hips and knees, and is made worse if the victim is overweight. According to the Arthritis Foundation in Atlanta, about 75 people per 10 000 in the USA are afflicted with rheumatoid arthritis, and it is twice as common in women as in men. Osteoarthritis affects nearly 600 per 10 000, which is over 16 million Americans. Again, two thirds are women.

Osteoarthritis is caused by wear and tear of the cartilage which surrounds the bone at the joints. Cartilage has no blood supply to bring in the chemicals it needs, but it is 70% water and it uses this to do the job instead. As joints move this water is squeezed out of the cartilage, carrying unwanted wastes with it, and then within fractions of a second the joint relaxes the pressure and water seeps quickly back bringing in fresh nutrients.

Clearly, the more exercise we do the better our joints will be, but as old age creeps on not only do we exercise less, but our cartilage also begins to age and, like a rubber seal between two metal joints, it weakens and begins to leak. As it breaks down it begins to produce arachidonic acid which then leads to the production of prostaglandins which cause inflammation. This in turn makes a person less likely to move the joint, so the condition intensifies in a vicious circle.

As the cartilage fails, the bone beneath tries to compensate by growing harder, as the joint now has bone grinding against bone. The harder bone, however, is more likely to crack if we fall or bang it hard. These cracks then grow more hard bone to compensate and the joints start to deform. Scientists may one day find a chemical that will lubricate the joints, or even stimulate the body to repair its own worn-out cartilage. Until that day we have to rely on drugs that limit the damage and the pain.

There was a period after the Second World War when steroids were the recommended treatment for arthritis. These check the disease but can have serious side-effects, and this led to the search for non-steroid drugs to do the job. Several have been discovered, but these were not a cure for arthritis—they merely suppressed the symptoms and made the condition easier to live with. Recent pharmaceutical advances have gone some way toward a cure, and doctors can now prescribe drugs such as penicillamine, hydroxychloroquine (which is also used to treat malaria), sulfasalazine, and even ones containing gold. If you suffer from severe arthritis and you are given **auranofin** (the trade name is Ridaura) then you are taking a molecule which contains an atom of gold at its heart. This drug is effective in suppressing rheumatoid arthritis. It can be taken by mouth, rather than being injected as this type of drug generally is, and it has fewer side-effects.

Meanwhile most people who suffer from arthritis are helped with the so-called non-steroid anti-inflammatory drugs (NSAIDs). The sales of these in the USA amount to around $2 billion per year. In Western countries there is a potential market of around 50 million older people who can easily afford treatment, which may explain why drug companies are prepared to invest so much in the search for a cure for arthritis.

There are several NSAIDs now available to doctors, so that if a patient cannot tolerate one of them there are alternatives that can be prescribed. Doctors will usually start with ibuprofen or paracetamol (see below), and if these provoke an adverse reaction then they have a repertoire of about 25 others to try until they find one that can be tolerated. It really does help for there to be alternative NSAIDs, and doctors prescribe the newer NSAIDs because these are slightly better than the older varieties, which are in any case out of patent and earning no royalties for the companies that discovered them. In fact 25 seems somewhat excessive, but there are still more awaiting approval. NSAIDs differ generally in their acidity and their ability to penetrate to various parts of the body. What suits one person will form ulcers in another, but why this is so remains a mystery. Two of them are even sold as over-the-counter drugs and are also prescribed for arthritis sufferers, and millions of people take them as general painkillers.

Paracetamol

Paracetamol, like aspirin, is a chemical derivative of phenol. It too is sold under many names, such as Tylenol in the USA and Panadol in the UK. It has two advantages over aspirin: it is absorbed through the lining of the stomach and so acts within about ten minutes, whereas most aspirin is absorbed through the gut and may take an hour or more to start working. Nor does paracetamol inflame the stomach lining. The pain-killing properties of paracetamol came to light when **acetanilide**, a derivative of benzene, was mistakenly added to a patient's medicine and proved to be an excellent pain-killer. Acetanilide is rather toxic, and the body detoxifies it by converting it to paracetamol. Clearly the benefits of acetanilide could better be obtained by prescribing paracetamol directly. Like aspirin, paracetamol works by blocking the enzyme needed for making prostaglandins.

Paracetamol is also a drug we can misuse. Two paracetamol tablets will give temporary relief from muscular pain or a headache, but 22 tablets will make that relief permanent—in Heaven. Yet two 500 mg tablets can safely be taken four times a day by an adult, week after week, month after month, year after year, provided the patient is of average build and weight and in reasonable health. Small and under-weight people have been known to die of paracetamol poisoning having taken only ten tablets in a 24-hour period.[6]

Others at risk of paracetamol poisoning are would-be suicides, alcoholics with already damaged livers, and people suffering the condition known as bulimia nervosa. Bulimia nervosa generally afflicts young women who feel a compulsive urge alternately to starve themselves and then to over-eat. Some take paracetamol to make themselves vomit.

Those who attempt to commit suicide with paracetamol often succeed, even though they change their mind, or are found in time. They can be pumped out, put on an artificial support system and given blood transfusions, but this often cannot save them. Paracetamol has damaged their liver beyond repair and the

---

[6] Some people may inadvertently take dangerously high doses of paracetamol if they have a cold and take a combination of tablets, cough linctus and 'night time' medicines, all of which might contain paracetamol.

temporary recovery will only last a few days. They will die after about a week. Around the world paracetamol kills over two thousand people each year.

Although paracetamol is good at blocking pain receptors, our body treats it as a toxin to be disposed of as quickly as possible, and this is why its toxicity appears so puzzling. Our body has two ways of removing paracetemol—the most common route is to use enzymes to add a sulfate group to the molecule. This makes it very soluble in water so that it can be filtered out by our kidneys. Alternatively our body's enzymes can use glucuronic acid, a derivative of glucose, to add a carbohydrate to the paracetamol, and this too will help its removal. While the amount of paracetamol in our body is low, as it is with the recommended dosage, then these enzymes can cope quite easily.

When we take too much paracetamol the body tries its best to remove it with sulfate or glucuronic acid, but when these cannot cope it relies on oxidation. This is risky because it converts it to a deadly poison which then has to be quickly removed by the liver, which uses **glutathione** to do the job. However, glutathione is not easily replaced by the liver and is soon used up. The poisonous compound then attacks and destroys the liver itself. Ten hours of assault by the poison and the liver is beyond repair.

All this can be prevented with an injection of a compound called **N-acetylcysteine** which can act just as well as the liver's own glutathione. Accidental overdosing on paracetamol is not dangerous provided you get an injection quickly. It could even be made impossible by adding methionine to tablets of the painkiller. This simple sulfur-containing amino acid increases the amount of glutathione in the liver naturally. There are now plans to market a safe form of paracetamol with methionine.

Ibuprofen

This NSAID was discovered by a group of chemists at the drug company Boots, in Nottingham, England, who were trying to improve upon aspirin. The idea was to retain its painkilling and anti-inflammatory action while reducing the irritation to the stomach. At first they found that changes to the molecule would indeed make it more potent as a drug, but its toxicity increased as well. Sometimes they found compounds that had ten times the painkilling ability of aspirin, but there was always some drawback. For example, one variant caused people to come out in a rash.

After making hundreds of versions they eventually hit upon ibuprofen. It was over 20 times better than aspirin as a painkiller, and it controlled inflammation and reduced fever. The first clinical trial took place in 1966, and doses of 200, 400 or 600 mg showed no adverse side effects. Ibuprofen was so successful that it became an over-the-counter drug in the UK in 1983—Boots sold it under the trade name Nurofen. It also went on sale in the USA as Nuprin, Motrin and Advil. A daily dose of three 400 mg tablets is the accepted rate of prescription, but twice this amount can be given under certain circumstances.

Of course ibuprofen did not agree with everyone, and perhaps it was inevitable that an alarm bell was to be sounded. Scientists at Johns Hopkins University Medical School in Baltimore published a paper in *Annals of Internal Medicine* in 1990 which claimed that 12 women on ibuprofen suffered kidney failure when taking the drug. In fact they were all suffering chronic kidney disease before treatment with ibuprofen started. Was ibuprofen to blame for worsening their condition? According to Boots such patients probably should not have been put on the drug anyway, and the same is true of people with peptic ulcers. The number of women involved was actually quite small compared to the millions who had obtained relief with ibuprofen and who had come to no harm. The media sensed a scare story but quickly lost interest once the facts were explained.

Not all drugs escape the media's attentions so lightly. Another NSAID, Opren, was superb at relieving the symptoms of arthritis sufferers, and they watched in dismay as a media campaign in the UK led to its withdrawal. Again, a few unexplained deaths of some very frail people who were given Opren set off the alarm. We will return to the Opren affair later, because it illustrates the choices we as a society sometimes have to make.

Opiates

The opiates[7] are the most powerful of all painkillers. The opium poppy, *Papaver somniferum*, is the source of these, and codeine, morphine, diamorphine and hydromorphone are the best known derivatives. All are effective painkillers, with side effects that include constipation, and two also cause addiction. Diamorphine and morphine carry this risk, and may take as little as a week to become established.[8] Hydromorphone may also come into this category.

However, it is the painkilling features of the opiates on which we want to concentrate. One of the great triumphs of modern chemistry has been the discovery of new molecules that relieve pain, but few discovered so far can compare with the opiates. The raw material can be collected by making cuts in the unripe poppy seed capsules, from which a milky juice exudes which dries and can be scraped off. This is the traditional form of opium. For the pharmaceutical industry the opium is harvested mechanically. Its main component is morphine, a complex organic molecule which acts on the central nervous system by blocking the so-called opioid receptors which register the sensation of pain. If you take some opiates, such as morphine or diamorphine (heroin), even though you are not in pain, then you experience their well-known narcotic effects.

Morphine works because it is chemically like the body's own painkillers. However, these take many hours to build up in the brain, whereas morphine can be injected and works within seconds, ending even the most unbearable pain. Sadly, it is addictive. Modifying the molecule slightly, by replacing one of its hydrogen atoms with a methyl group, got over this problem. The new compound was called codeine, which has lost its power to produce addictions but it is much less effective. However it is safe enough to be included in many over-the-counter painkillers.

[7] The word opium comes from the Greek *opion* meaning poppy juice.

[8] **Methadone** can be used to help people break with heroin; this takes about 30 days of regular use to produce addiction. Methadone is most active as the left-handed molecule (see page 121).

Morphine can be changed into an even quicker-acting painkiller by replacing two of its hydrogen atoms with acetyl groups. This is diamorphine, derived from the name diacetylmorphine, and it can now penetrate the brain more easily than morphine. When it gets there it is quickly reconverted into morphine by losing its acetyl groups. Diamorphine has the power to relieve terminal cancer patients of their pain, and is prescribed in Europe for these people in their last few months of life. To them it matters little that it is even more addictive than morphine, and its narcotic effect may even make them feel better—for a while. In the USA the opiate hydromorphone has been approved for use, and can be prescribed to relieve the suffering of cancer patients. It is the most potent opiate painkiller of all, as the table below shows.

The potency of the opiate painkillers

Opiate	Potency*	Solubility**
Codeine	60 mg	20%
Morphine	20 mg	5%
Diamorphine	10 mg	50%
Hydromorphone	2 mg	25%

*This is the maximum safe single dose. The smaller the dose the more potent is the molecule.
**This is the solubility in water of the phosphate salt of codeine and the hydrochloride salts of the others. The more soluble the drug, the easier it is to administer, and therefore the more effective it is.

In 1992 a new painkilling molecule was reported that was even stronger than morphine. It is produced by an Ecuador tree frog *Epipedobates tricolor*. John Daly at the National Institutes of Health at Bethesda, Maryland, extracted it from the frogs in tiny amounts and called it **epibatidine**. It turned out to be 200 times as effective as morphine in standard pain tests on rats. Not only that, but the molecule is also relatively simple and is an organochlorine compound. Whether epibatidine will open a new era of non-toxic, low-dose, non-addictive, over-the-counter painkillers remains to be seen. Before an epibatidine-type molecule is used it will have had to undergo a battery of tests to ensure it is effective, and that the risk to life of those who take it is as low as possible. As we shall see, the chances are that it will fail such a test.

Toxicity

We know that it may only take one molecule to attack the DNA in a cell, and to cause that DNA to mutate. This mutant cell can eventually multiply into millions until it kills us of cancer. Although this is true, it is not the whole truth. Every one of the billions of cells in our body has its DNA damaged by radioactivity or by chemicals, by which I mean natural background radiation and by natural chemicals. Evolution produced the living cell and created a wonderful thing, endowing it with ways of checking itself, so that when it finds itself with broken or mutant DNA, it can remove it or repair it. We may of course expose ourselves to more radiation or dangerous chemicals than our defences can cope with, and end up with a damaged cell that escapes detection, or one that our repair system cannot cope with. Then we are in real danger, but that is such an unlikely event for most of us that we can ignore it for most of our life.

Oxygen gas, which we think of as so essential to keeping us alive, is in fact far more dangerous than many 'chemicals', and yet we take in massive amounts of oxygen each day. Oxygen will attack anything given a little help, and it can attack various parts of cells, because it forms dangerous chemicals called free radicals. These are molecules with a loose electron and they can react with anything. But we do not need to worry about oxygen behaving like this, because our bodies have lots of antioxidants on hand to destroy such free radicals. Likewise we also have a superb defence system to protect us against the toxins and unwanted chemicals that we take in with our food quite naturally.

The plants and animals that we eat were not designed to be safe for us to dine on; in a way we had to design ourselves around them. Of course there are some natural poisons so dangerous that they kill us if we eat a tiny amount, and there are lots of substances in our diet which are toxic, but which we encounter only in amounts too small to be lethal. We still need to detoxify them, and our body does this by modifying them slightly to make them more soluble in water (as we saw with paracetamol). In this way our kidneys can filter them out and get rid of them.

The same action is taken against all threatening molecules, and explains why we do not get cancer even when we take in chemicals that can be shown to cause cancer in laboratory rats. We can prove that a chemical causes cancer by exposing a rat to it in huge doses. We can be exposed to the same chemical, but in much lower doses of course, day after day, all our lives and yet it never causes cancer, because day after day our defences cope easily with it. It may also be that unlike the rat's genes, our genes have in-built protection anyway. This is much more likely to be the case than perhaps we realise.

We could ask the same question about the human response to medicines: why should one person be cured by a dose of a drug while another person suffers side-effects, and maybe even not tolerate the drug at all? The answer to this idiosyncrasy lies in our genes, and in how these have equipped us to detoxify chemicals. One way to detoxify is to modify an alien molecule by adding an acetyl group of atoms to it, and so make it more soluble in water. (You can see the effect of acetyl groups by comparing the solubilities of morphine and its acetylated counterpart, diamorphine, in the table on page 134.) The enzyme which enables us to do this acetylating naturally is caused by a single difference in one chromosome.

Asian people are generally fast at acetylating, Americans and Europeans less so. A poor ability to do this may put some people at risk. Earlier this century workers in the dye industry were exposed to benzidine and *ortho*-toluidine, both of which can cause bladder cancer. Those who were good acetylators were less at risk than their poor-acetylating colleagues. Of the 23 men who died of this condition in Britain, 22 were found to be slow acetylators, and so their bodies were exposed to higher levels of these chemicals for longer.

Another important property of a painkilling drug is its duration in the body. How long will its effect last? It is important that it should last a long time. The dose of a drug that you are prescribed can vary from less than 10 mg, about the size of a pinhead, to 1000 mg, the size of an Alka Seltzer tablet. The reason is partly related to how long it takes your body to get rid of what it regards as an alien chemical— even though it is there to help. It may take days to remove the last molecule of a substance from the body even though the drug's effectiveness has long since worn off, so that the time for complete removal from the body is no real help in deciding the dose.

When comparing the retention of a drug in the body, scientists refer to its half-life. This is the time it takes for the body to remove half the given dose. If something has a half-life of ten hours, then after ten hours the amount will be half the original dose, after another ten hours it will be halved again (in other words down to a quarter of the original), in another ten hours it will be halved yet again (now an eighth of the original), and so on. We should still be able to detect a trace of the original drug even after 100 hours, when the amount would be about a thousandth (0.1%) of the original.

Even when we are talking about a system as complicated as an individual's body chemistry, we can still use the concept of half-life, although it will of course vary from person to person. For example, it will depend on how well their liver and kidneys are working, but the list in the table below gives the usual half-lives of some chemicals in the average healthy human body.

The half-life of chemicals in the human body

Drug	Half-life
Aspirin	15 minutes*
Caffeine	5 hours
Cocaine	45 minutes
Valium	18 hours
Morphine	3 hours
Nicotine	2 hours
Streptomycin	5 hours

*Fifteen minutes seems too short, but aspirin works by being converted to another chemical which has a much longer half-life.

About half of all chemicals tested are carcinogenic, but this does not mean that they automatically cause cancer. Every mouthful of food we eat contains some arsenic and arsenic is a known carcinogen, but we happily survive this daily onslaught because our body can cope with arsenic and may actually need a small amount of it. Because a substance causes cancer when fed in large doses to animals, it does not mean that it will cause cancer when given in low doses to humans. We have to swamp the natural defences of a laboratory mouse day after day before we can show whether it can trigger off a cancer in the poor animal.[9] But if you carry out such tests, and a cancer results, then in the USA the chemical is banned by the Food and Drug

---

[9] Such mice are specially bred to be particularly prone to get cancer anyway.

Administration (FDA), who are regarded as the world authority on safety.

The FDA came into being as a result of a drug disaster, and it justified its existence 20 years later when its lengthy procedures happily prevented the thalidomide tragedy from happening in the USA. This success, though, was more by accident than design. The case which brought the FDA into existence was the first antibacterial drug, **sulfanilamide**. In December 1932 a chemist called Gerhard Domagk, working for the German chemical conglomerate IC Farben, patented an azo-dye called Prontosil. Safety tests were carried out on rabbits and cats and they were not harmed by it, but tests on infected mice revealed something rather unusual. Twelve mice which had been injected with streptococci bacteria that would normally kill them within two days recovered when given Prontosil. Tests at a local hospital confirmed its efficacy, and Domagk even used his new compound to cure his daughter of an infection.

What Prontosil did was to produce sulfanilamide in the body, and this is the key chemical that was effective, not the dye itself. Prontosil could not be patented as a therapeutic agent because the sulfanilamides had been recognised as having antibacterial activity in 1919. We now know how sulfanilamide works: it blocks an enzyme that the bacteria need to make folic acid, which is essential for them just as it is for humans. But whereas we take in all the folic acid we need from our food, bacteria have to make all theirs themselves. Giving a dose of sulfanilamide to a human who was infected with bacteria would stop these spreading, and hold them in check until the body's defences could produce its own antibodies to kill the bacteria.

Sulfanilamide was launched in 1936, and for the first time doctors could prescribe a successful treatment for conditions such as bacterial pneumonia in children. In Britain it was known as M&B after the firm May & Baker which produced it, and it was given in tablet form.[10] Tablets are difficult for children to take and a liquid is much easier to swallow, but there was a problem with sulfanilamide. It was not very soluble in the normal solvents used to administer medicines, which in those days were either water or alcohol. It was soluble in another kind

---

[10] I was given M&B when I had pneumonia as a child, so I can testify to its effectiveness.

of alcohol, **ethylene glycol**, a liquid normally used as antifreeze, and that was how it was supplied for use as a so-called 'elixir'.

In 1937 doctors began to report to the American Medical Association that some patients unexpectedly died when they were treated with sulfanilamide. Supplies of the drug were recalled but 107 people died, mostly children, before all the samples were traced. Tests by a Dr Francis Kelsey showed that the cause was not the drug but the solvent. The tragedy of the elixir of sulfanilamide led to the 1938 Food, Drug and Cosmetic Act, and this stated that henceforth the FDA must approve all products before they are put on the market.

Drug companies of course carry out very stringent tests before they hand a new drug over to the FDA for approval. Even so, about a quarter still fall at the first fence, the so-called phase 1 trials which involve up to 100 patients. Another quarter will fail the phase 2 trials, which involve several hundred people. And a third quarter will fail the phase 3 trials which involve thousands of volunteers. Only about one drug in four emerges on to the market.

It is interesting at this point to ask how well-established drugs would have fared under the FDA regime of testing. The first ever scientifically designed drug was salvarsan, which was discovered in 1909 by Paul Ehrlich as a cure for syphilis.[11] This disease results from sexual contact in which one partner passes on to the other a spirochaete, which is a corkscrew-shaped bacterium called *Treponema pallidum*. Ehrlich reasoned that it should be possible to find a poison which would kill the micro-organism circulating in a victim's blood stream without affecting the person. He thought an arsenic compound might be capable of doing this, and he started to make so-called arsenicals, testing them on rabbits infected with the disease. When he tested his 606th compound it worked, and salvarsan and hailed as a great triumph. The scourge of syphilis was lifted.[12]

The success of salvarsan proved what chemistry could do. And yet today it would not even have been submitted for testing because of

[11] The compound was actually prepared by Alfred Bertheim.
[12] Salvarsan was eventually superseded by penicillin. It is now held in reserve in case an antibiotic resistant strain of syphilis emerges. If this were to happen it is most unlikely that the syphilis bacterium would ever mutate in a way that would allow it to resist arsenic.

the arsenic it contains. And if salvarsan were submitted because of its effectiveness it would not to secure FDA approval because arsenic compounds are carcinogenic, and so it would fail the Delaney clause in the 1958 amendment to the US Food, Drug and Cosmetic Act. In effect, this simply states that no chemical which can be shown to cause cancer in human or animal can be approved for general use.

Other drugs that would fail today are the opiates, because they are addictive, and aspirin, because it causes internal bleeding. Needless to say, natural remedies, such as dried plants or seeds, which are sold as alternative medicines would never pass the tests demanded of chemically derived drugs. For a start they contain thousands of compounds, some of which are bound to be carcinogenic.

The biggest breakthrough in modern drugs came with penicillin, which is a fairly simple molecule. Thalidomide was discovered too soon, and that worked to its disadvantage; penicillin was discovered too soon and that worked to its advantage. It is produced by a mould, and it is deadly to certain bacteria. Had it not been for the exigencies of the Second World War, penicillin would never have been approved for human use since it would never have got past the testing stage—it has the disadvantage of killing guinea pigs (see the Box below). But penicillin was used and with remarkable results, saving millions of lives.

Since penicillin was such a success no one demanded that it be banned, even when its adverse side effects were noted. A few people are allergic to it, often violently so. Some have died from it. The millions of lives saved by penicillin have more than paid for these deaths, and yet the fear of being the unlucky one who has to pay that price has led some people to refuse to take any treatment that involves a chemical drug. It has been estimated that as many as 25% of all prescribed medicines are never taken by patients.

Guinea pigs

You may be pleased to know that these days guinea pigs are rarely used as guinea pigs. These unhappy creatures may have a lot in common with humans, in respect of their physiology and their inability to make vitamin C, but they tend to die rather easily. Dioxins kill them, and so does penicillin. It was their sensitivity to the former compounds that resulted in the dioxins being called the most dangerous chemicals known, as we shall see in Chapter 7. As little as a *millionth* of a gram is enough for a guinea pig. Guinea pigs are not much use when it comes to testing chemicals for their toxicity. Rats make better guinea pigs, and they have an in-built advantage: they cannot vomit. If you can persuade or force a rat to eat something which you suspect of being very toxic then you can be sure that the animal's body can not just spew it back at you. It has to digest it.

Hazard identification, by giving chemicals to animals, is the first step to determining their safety. If it does not kill them, then the next stage is to find out how much of a chemical can be tolerated. The final stages of testing may be the notorious LD_{50} trials, short for Lethal Dose 50%. The name refers to the amount necessary to kill 50% of a group of animals such as mice or rats (this test is now being phased out). If the chemical being tested has no cancer forming capabilities and low toxicity, in other words a high LD_{50} value, then it can proceed to tests on larger animals, and then on primates such as monkeys, before it finally goes for testing on humans.

Risk

If you want a treatment for a medical condition that is entirely without risk or side effects, then you must avoid all pharmaceutical preparations and surgery. Alternative medicine can offer you treatment that is almost risk-free, such as homeopathy, drinking or bathing in spa waters, aromatherapy or faith healing. However, these may not always be effective. How much risk you are prepared to accept depends on the severity of the disease your body is fighting. Sometimes the odds are so much in your favour that the fear is irrational, and yet the fear may be so great that it provokes a response out of all proportion to the danger, and people would prefer to suffer rather than take the prescribed treatment. Strangest of all is that the most opposition to a drug generally comes from those who have never been exposed to it. Which brings me back to the case of an NSAID that highlights the degree of risk we are talking about.

The real Opren scandal

Among the NSAIDs that emerged as a result of research by pharmaceutical companies was a painkiller that was given the name **Opren**. This worked better than aspirin and did not have the side-effects of causing internal bleeding. However, it did have side-effects of its own: of those treated with it a few people reported being very sensitive to sunburn, and a few old people died unexpectedly. Opren was blamed, and after a media scare the drug was taken off the market in the UK. Hundreds of thousands of people who were taking Opren were put on to other, less effective painkillers.

Of course the reason for withdrawing Opren was that it was less than perfect, and taking it did involve a degree of risk. What that risk was can be discussed numerically. If 25 000 people are operated on for arthritis, about 400 of them will die from the effects of that surgery, or from post-operative complications. If those 25 000 were to be prescribed Opren, so that they could live with their arthritis, then only *one* would die from side-effects of the drug. In gambling terms your odds of dying as a result of surgery are about 60 to 1, whereas with Opren treatment it was about 25 000 to 1. If you were to bet on which treatment would be most likely to be phased out you would have lost you money. Surgery continues, Opren was banned.

The statistics of life and death

We can imagine a drug with zero risk. It would target only the infecting organism or faulty cell, killing the former and repairing the latter. All healthy cells would be unaffected, and the amount of the drug that was surplus to requirements would simply be excreted by our body. In addition we would want the product to be safe enough to be sold over-the-counter, and to know that a child could take an accidental overdose and still be all right. One substance which meets these safety requirements is water, which explains why homeopathic medicines operate with zero risk. Water is the only active ingredient in such medication.

Most people opt for conventional medical treatment and have to live with the risk that attends all chemicals used as medicines. Many over-the-counter medicines are toxic when an overdose is taken, and some can have this effect on individuals even with a normal dose.

Many drugs have unpleasant side effects, such as the chemotherapy drugs used to fight cancer, and the risks are high. But what level of risk are we prepared to accept? By risk I refer, of course, to the risk of dying. This attends us every day of our life, and we generally accept the risk of a car accident, or climbing a ladder, and some of us even look for high risk adventures in leisure and sporting activities, such as climbing a mountain, hang gliding or underwater exploration.

These are clearly much more risky than taking medicine, and yet we will accept these risks provided we feel we are in control. We may even pass this control over to someone we trust, such as a pilot, or a surgeon. We are much less inclined to trust the tablets which a doctor prescribes, and we have become very suspicious of the chemists in white coats who make them. This puzzles chemists like me, and while we can quote statistics to show how safe our products really are, such messages do not seem to get through. The reason may be that our arguments appeal only to our rational brain, whereas our emotional brain is where the fear springs from.

However, there is a chance that if I can persuade you with logic, your emotions may follow. Suppose you need minor surgery for a condition that is not life-threatening, and the operation requires you to be given an anaesthetic. Once upon a time the risk of dying from the anaesthetic was as high as 60 in 10 000, but today it is less than 1 in 10 000. Would you go ahead? You probably would, even though it is difficult to place such a risk in the context of other rare events. But there is one event we all share—being born. The chance of your baby dying at birth, even in the most advanced countries of the world, is about 120 in 10 000. The chances of a woman dying while giving birth is 1 in 10 000, and this is also about the risk of having triplets. You can get a feel for a risk with such odds by asking yourself how many times you have personally known a woman who has died in labour, or who has given birth to a set of triplets. Like most people, you may know of neither.

These, then, are the baseline statistics of *risk*. The subject is dealt with in the award-winning paperback *Living with Risk* published by the British Medical Association Board of Science, which covers all aspects of risk such as smoking, alcohol, diet, occupation, sport, transport, and disease. Logically we should be prepared to accept odds of 1 in 10 000 against a medical treatment causing us to die.

The book reveals that we live with similar odds in other areas of life. For example, in the UK each year 1 in 10 000 of us will die in a car accident or a skiing accident, and 10 in 10 000 will die as a result of an accident at home. Many people are afraid of being struck by lightning, even though the chances of dying this way are about one in ten million (0.001 in 10 000). Which all goes to show how powerful our emotional brain really is. Yet of those who fear a bolt from the blue, how many are smokers? Of 10 000 smokers, 2000 will eventually die as a consequence of their addiction to nicotine.

According to statistics given in *Living with Risk*, people who work in the chemicals industry are safer at work than if they stay at home for the day. That may sound wrong, because every year we read of explosions and fires at chemical plants and the people there are working with some of the most dangerous materials known. Nevertheless it is true. Workers who use chemicals in industry and in agriculture are more likely to die from the beer they drink after work than from the chemicals to which they are exposed. Again that sounds wrong, but again it is true. People in restaurants, shops, offices and at home are exposed to solvents in cleaning fluids, pesticide residues, atmospheric pollution and lots of other chemicals. But they are more likely to be electrocuted than to die by inhaling such chemicals. Again you might think I am simply turning statistics on their head to shock you. I am— but only because these things are true.

Why then do we demand better odds on drugs than 1 in 10 000? For over-the-counter drugs the risks are probably less than one in a million, and we need give risk only a millisecond's thought as we take them. For more serious illnesses the chances must of course be greater. Anything which brings relief to human suffering will have side-effects for a few and be fatal for one or two. We must accept that this is so because there is no way we can change the chemistry of existing drugs, or the human body, to produce zero risk.

As our expectation of living a long life has increased, so we tend to forget the medical and pharmaceutical advances that make it possible. The healthier and longer our life, the more obsessed we have become that it should be even healthier and even longer. Books, magazines, newspapers and television are full of news and advice about things that will help us achieve this, but our biggest asset is the human body itself. It is much better equipped than we realise to protect us against all sorts of threats, since it has evolved to deal with many of them. Every cell of our body probably undergoes some malfunction every week of our life, and each time a wonderful battery of natural chemicals rushes to repair it. So long as we do not abuse it and so long as we protect it from infectious diseases, then it will serve us well.

Our fear of the side-effects of drugs is irrational, and this has undermined our faith in them, predisposing us to go along with campaigns to reject new drugs at the first sign of any risk. Yet if we are to make progress against the illnesses which cut life short we must continue to support research in this area. There are still many conditions which make life miserable for young and old. If we want a cure for acne, arthritis or AIDS we must go on. The answer to these afflictions can only come from the test tube, whether it is discovering new drugs or extracting hitherto unsuspected drugs from natural sources, and developing safer variants of them. We can even find a cure for cancer—but only if we are prepared to take the risk.

CHAPTER SIX

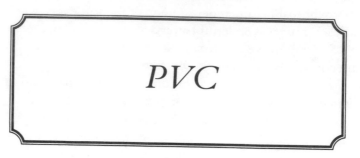

*In praise of plastics; the manufacture of PVC; the additives
and hazards of PVC; the environmental audit*

THE plastic we have learned to avoid is **PVC**, which is the abbreviation for **poly(vinyl chloride)**.[1] There appear to be three
good reasons for this: PVC is made from a liquid which causes
cancer; when it is used as packaging it contaminates our food; and
when it burns it forms dioxins. All these things are true, yet the risks
they pose to our health are so minuscule that they can be ignored.
Which is why PVC is still used to make bottles for mineral waters, and
containers for blood. It may come as a surprise to learn that PVC is the
plastic chosen for catheters, the very fine tubes that are inserted by
doctors and surgeons into the human body, even into premature
babies. Nor need special care be taken to sort out PVC from other
domestic waste before this is burnt in municipal incinerators, because
it will produce no more in the way of dangerous dioxins than other
materials that are burnt.

Not everyone sees the widespread use and benefits of PVC as tacit
approval by society that this plastic is safe. Some environmentalist
groups, such as Greenpeace, would like to see PVC banned altogether because it is an organochlorine compound.[2] As a result of

[1] A reminder that when the name of a substance appears in **bold** type, it means that
there is more about its chemistry in the Appendix.
[2] An organochlorine compound is defined as one that has a carbon-to-chlorine bond
in its molecule.

their alarms you can sometimes see the words 'not made from PVC' printed on a product, as if those that were made from PVC should carry a health warning. However, it is going to be very difficult to replace PVC because this plastic offers many benefits. It is a superb electrical insulator, it is flexible, it is tough, it is scratch-resistant, it does not crack, and it does not catch fire easily. PVC products last for decades and they are cheap to make.

Because PVC resists corrosion and weathering it is used for electrical wiring, water pipes, water butts, window frames, mud flaps, floor covering, fences and garden furniture. It recycles well and some of these outdoor products are indeed made from recycled PVC. Another benefit of this plastic's wide use is the employment it gives to the 70 000 people around the world who make it. Or should we really think of them as victims of an industry which puts them at risk by exposing them to undesirable chemicals? Indeed if what is said about PVC is true then we may all be at risk. However, before I discuss the health and environmental aspects of its use, I would like to set it in the context of other plastics.

In praise of plastics

PVC is a plastic, although it is more correct to call it a polymer.[3] Chemists were once greatly admired for the new materials they kept discovering, not least of which were a series of wonderful plastics. These replaced the older materials that were derived from animal and vegetable sources, such as leather, latex, cotton, ivory and wood, materials we would now call biopolymers, signifying that they are derived from living things. Nature finds such polymers indispensable, of course, but for our purposes they needed to be modified before they were suitable for such things as footwear, rubber, clothes, combs and books. But there were limits to these natural polymers, not only to what the materials themselves could do, but also to the amount which Nature could provide.

[3] Plastics and resins are the older words that came into use before we understood what these materials really were. The modern equivalents are polymers and cross-linked polymers.

Biopolymers have admirable qualities such as lightness, toughness and durability. Nature in its bounty evolved many natural polymers, such as strong wood, insulating wool and waterproof skin, but it tended not to give priority to features such as electrical insulation, high temperature stability, transparency and colour, all of which are regarded as important in manufactured products. Some polymers made from natural products have these properties: for example rubber is an insulator, it can be coloured, and early electrical wiring was sheathed with it, but a major drawback is that rubber oxidises slowly in air and after a few years becomes brittle and develops cracks.

Nevertheless many biopolymers are very good and perform very well, including fur, leather, lambswool, silk, mahogany, ebony and ivory.[4] The Industrial Revolution changed manufacturing methods and brought newer and cheaper products to an expanding population. To begin with the new industries simply produced more of the known materials more efficiently, but the vagaries of weather and disease could seriously interfere with supplies from distant countries, not to mention the other socially disruptive activities that humans are prone to indulge in: financial speculation, politics and war. These, and the growing pressure of an expanding population, encouraged industry to use the alternative materials that chemists discovered. To begin with, such products were welcomed by everyone.

By the second half of the nineteenth century the demand for ivory had grown to such an extent that 100 000 elephants were being slaughtered every year for their tusks. These consist of the peptide biopolymer keratin, and ivory was ideal for making combs, piano keys, buttons, cutlery handles, and billiard balls. These could also be made from the first synthetic plastic, which was **cellulose nitrate**. Alexander Parkes discovered this and it was put on display in the Great Exhibition in London in 1862. It was not completely synthetic because it was made from wood cellulose, but he modified this chemically rather than merely processing it. Cellulose nitrate, or Parkesine as it was called, was used to make many of the items that had previously been made from ivory. In the US an inventor John Wesley Hyatt was also experimenting with cellulose nitrate for billiard

---

[4] The dilemma is that these could be the materials of the future, because they come from renewable resources.

balls, but these were far from ideal. Sometimes they exploded when they collided violently, and one burst into flames when it came into contact with a lighted cigar. Cellulose nitrate is highly flammable and products made from it were always potentially dangerous.

All was not lost, because in 1869 Hyatt showed that cellulose nitrate could be turned into a better plastic by mixing it with **camphor**, and heating it under pressure. He called the product celluloid, and the first things he made from it were false teeth. He set up the Celluloid Manufacturing Company of Newark, New Jersey, in 1872 to produce a range of household goods, and these found a ready market. The firm continued in business for over 75 years until the factory closed in 1949.

The next big breakthrough, this time in artificial fibres, was also a modification of cellulose. When this is converted chemically into its acetate derivative, **cellulose acetate**, it can be drawn into fibres and woven to form artificial silk. This was first marketed about a century ago, and at a time when the natural fibre could no longer keep pace with demand. Cellulose acetate polymer, derived from wood pulp, is still made on a large scale today and called by a variety of trade names as well as the generic names of rayon, viscose, acetate and art silk.[5] This polymer is ideal for soft furnishing, carpets, linings and blouses, but it does crease easily. Another useful form of cellulose acetate was Cellophane, again a product that was greeted with enthusiasm when chemists finally mastered its production in the 1930s.[6]

Research chemists are still working to improve cellulose acetate, and a recent development has been a manufacturing method which keeps the long chain cellulose polymers of the wood intact, rather than breaking them down as happens with the older processes. The improved rayon is achieved through the use of a new type of solvent, which is also recycled in a process that reclaims 99% of it each time it goes through the process. The new rayon is produced by the chemical company Courtaulds and is called Tencel, and has features that rival the purely synthetic fibres such as **nylon**. It is not only very strong and soft to the touch, but it also takes dyes very well.

---

[5] The 'art' stands for artificial, although many think this is another form of real silk.

[6] Cellophane is still manufactured, but it is now in competition with polypropylene which is stronger.

Biopolymers are based on compounds of carbon that are made naturally by plants and animals. Synthetic polymers are also based on carbon compounds, and when they were first discovered the source from which they came was coal, a fossil fuel resource which seemed inexhaustible and of which there are still reserves of a trillion (10^{12}) tonnes. Supplies were also less prone to disruption. Chemicals from coal led to the first truly synthetic polymer, **Bakelite**, which was first made in the USA in 1909 and took its name from its discover Leo Baekeland. It was much safer than celluloid, and tougher, and it replaced this plastic in many of its applications. Bakelite was a thermo-setting resin[7] made from **phenol** and **formaldehyde**. It was stiff, light, reasonably strong, had insulating properties and could be moulded easily. It was the ideal plastic for electrical appliances, and it was Bakelite which made possible the generation and distribution of electricity, and made electrical appliances safer for use in the home.

Bakelite was not without its drawbacks. It came only in dull colours, and though it was a good electrical insulator it was a rigid plastic and useless for electrical wiring. Nevertheless, it made synthetic plastics acceptable and so paved the way for others that were to be discovered in the years between the two World Wars. This was the time when the chemical nature of polymers was finally explained by the German chemist, Hermann Staudinger. He referred to them as macromolecules (meaning large molecules) rather than polymers, and his theory was that they were built from smaller units that had joined together to form long chains. He was to be proved right.

By the end of the 1930s several purely synthetic polymers were in commercial production. Some caught the public imagination imme-diately. Stockings made from nylon, the polymer which had been discovered by the chemist Wallace Carothers in 1935, almost caused riots among shoppers when they went on sale in New York in 1939.[8] Other polymers that had been discovered about this time were **poly-ethylene** (polythene), **polystyrene**, **poly(methyl methacrylate)** (Perspex), and poly(vinyl chloride) (PVC). All were to be developed further during the Second World War. With the end of the war in

---

[7] Such a material is originally soft, but on heating it changes permanently to a hard rigid form.

[8] Carothers did not live to see the success of his polymer. He had committed suicide in 1937.

1945, the chemicals industry that was producing these plastics found a public eager to buy products made from them. Within a few years they were to become part of everyday living, and their names entered the language. By 1990 the yearly output of synthetic polymers reached 80 million tonnes a year, and all are derived from oil or natural gas.

Perhaps we have become so used to plastics that we no longer notice or appreciate the benefits they bring. Plastics do not rust, corrode, or break easily, and they can be permanently coloured. In many applications they are better than metals, and this has become particularly important in aircraft and car components where their lightness also improves fuel efficiency. Polymers can be turned into packaging, such as transparent film, rigid containers or unbreakable bottles, and again their lightness saves on transport costs. They have revolutionised building and furnishings, because unlike wood they do not rot, unlike wool they do not stain or wear, and unlike iron they do not rust or need painting. The modern electrical and electronics industries would be unthinkable without plastics. In hospitals they are used for disposable syringes, intravenous blood tubing and bags, all of which can be destroyed by incineration after use.

There are various classes of polymer depending on the type of molecule from which they are constructed. PVC belongs to the ethylene family, which has a backbone chain made entirely of carbon atoms, each with two hydrogen atoms attached. **Ethylene** gas, whose two carbon atoms are joined by a double bond, gives rise to the simplest polymer, polyethylene, which consists of chains of $-CH_2-$ units. It forms this by using one of its double bonds to link to another ethylene molecule, which then links to another ethylene molecule, and so on *ad infinitum*, or at least until there are no more molecules to be linked up.

In this way very long chains of carbon atoms are produced, and these have the wonderful properties that we associate with polymers. Derivatives of ethylene, in which there are atoms other than hydrogen attached to the carbon chain, also undergo the same type of reaction to give some very interesting varieties of polymers. These are listed in the table (next page). Among this list are the world's leading polymers: PVC, polyethylene and polystyrene. PVC consists of chains of carbon atoms with every other carbon atom carrying a chlorine, like beads on

Ethylene based polymers

Monomer*	Polymer	Uses
acrylonitrile	polyacrylonitrile (PAN), Orlon, Dralon, Courtelle	Knitwear, high impact plastics
ethylene	polyethylene, polythene	Kitchen utensils, containers, plastic bags, wire insulation, toys, etc.
methyl methacrylate	poly(methyl methacrylate), Perspex, Plexiglas, Lucite	Transparent objects, transparent panels, illuminated signs
styrene	polystyrene	Foam, lightweight cartons, insulation, etc.
tetrafluoroethylene	poly(tetrafluoroethylene) (PTFE), Teflon	Insulation, non-stick surface coatings
vinyl acetate	poly(vinyl acetate) (PVA)	Paints
vinyl chloride	poly(vinyl choride) (PVC)	Rainwear, window frames, pipes, adhesives, cling film (plastic wrap), bottles, flooring, insulation, furniture, car components, etc.

*These names are the older chemical names. There are also systematic chemical names for these compounds: for example, vinyl chloride is more correctly known as chloroethene (see the Appendix).

a necklace. PVC is used to make hundreds of products, and in some situations it offers just the right combination of properties. For instance, it is ideal for the colour-coded, flexible, long-life plastic coating for electrical wires. It also has another benefit: it is one of the cheapest polymers to make.

The manufacture of PVC

There are three steps in making PVC: first, the production of the monomer, vinyl chloride; then the polymerisation of this to form the polymer; and finally the blending and tailoring of the polymer to give the product we know as PVC. At all stages there are risks to be considered. In the first step **chlorine** gas is reacted with ethylene gas. Both these chemicals are hazardous: chlorine is toxic and ethylene is flammable. The product of their reaction is ethylene dichloride and then vinyl chloride, which is also hazardous and has caused cancer.

Ethylene comes from natural gas or oil, and is made by heating **ethane**, **propane** or **butane**, or it can be produced from naphtha

The production of PVC. This shows the main stages in converting salt and natural gas into hundreds of manufactured articles that are made from this plastic. Each stage consists of several steps, including reclaiming unused material and recycling it through the system again. In addition there are by-products of the various processes such as caustic soda, hydrocarbons such as propylene, and hydrochloric acid.

which comes from oil. **Methane** and hydrogen are given off as by-products during the process, but these gases can be burned to provide energy on site. Propylene is also produced, and this is valuable enough to be reclaimed. Chemists are familiar with these materials, and though they are flammable they are neither toxic nor cancer forming. It is the chlorine and vinyl chloride about which there has been most concern.

Chlorine

Because chlorine is needed to make it, PVC now finds itself at a disadvantage. Chlorine gas is produced from sodium chloride (common salt), and the manufacture of PVC accounts for about 30% of the chlorine that is produced industrially. Chlorine is a highly corrosive and lethal gas that was used in the First World War, to kill thousands of troops.[9] Today it is used to make bleach and purify water supplies. Of course chlorine is dangerous to handle, and there have been industrial accidents involving it in which people have died. Official figures show that chlorine has killed a total of 81 people throughout the world since 1960, which is about three per year on average. At the time of writing, the last fatal accident in Europe was at Málaga in Spain in 1974, where the gas was being used to purify water supplies.

Most chlorine is produced at the site where it is to be used. Some has to be shipped to where it is needed, and indeed millions of tonnes of *liquid* chlorine are moved by road, rail and sea each year. It is stored and transported as a liquid under pressure because in this form it takes up much less room. When it is destined for industrial use it is transported in steel containers in quantities of up to 50 tons. For non-industrial uses, such as water sterilisation, it is delivered in 50 kg containers. All this chlorine on the move sounds very frightening, and there are occasional accidents, but none of these has yet compared with the spectacular fireballs that have engulfed motorists when petrol tankers have crashed and exploded on motorways. Hopefully

[9] It was eventually superseded by much more toxic vapours, such as mustard gas and lewisite.

the margins of safety surrounding chlorine are stringent enough to ensure that a major spill will never happen.

Official records are reassuring, and show that the precautions and regulations which govern chlorine are capable of reducing the number of accidents to a minimum and of dealing effectively with those that do occur. In the 40 years from 1950 to 1990 there were 90 major incidents involving road and rail tankers transporting chlorine. In these a total of 22 containers were ruptured and 36 tonnes of chlorine escaped. Luckily no one died. There were also 32 accidents involving small containers of chlorine of which 25 were broken with the loss of 10 tonnes of chlorine. Four people died, all in the one incident in Málaga mentioned earlier.

Where does chlorine come from and how is it made? There are unlimited supplies of salt in the sea, but more accessible are the large . deposits which are the remains of dried-up prehistoric seas, and which are to be found in many countries. When salt is dissolved in water it forms a solution known as brine, and if a current of electricity is passed through such a solution in a special cell, it releases the elements of sodium chloride: chlorine gas bubbles off in one part of the cell while sodium metal is produced in the other.[10] The sodium then reacts with water to form sodium hydroxide (**caustic soda**), at the same time releasing hydrogen gas. Both of these products also have their own commercial uses.

The equipment used to generate chlorine gas involves the liquid metal mercury, and this causes environmental problems because its compounds are toxic. Over the years there have been several escapes of mercury, sometimes with disastrous consequences, such as that which happened in the 1950s in Japan at Minamata Bay. There the mercury contaminated fish and so entered the food chain, and as a result local people were poisoned. Some died, others suffered brain damage. Today, a mercury disaster is looming in Brazil where miners use it to extract gold from the sediment of rivers. For every ounce of gold produced, several ounces of mercury are lost.

In theory there should be no loss of mercury in the process to generate chlorine, but in older plants there was substantial loss of this toxic metal to the environment where it polluted water and

[10] See the Appendix under chlorine for a description of a chlorine cell.

soil. This was rightly seen as unacceptable, and such have been the improvements in cutting the loss of mercury, that in some plants it may be as little as a quarter of a gram for each *tonne* of chlorine produced. However carefully the process is carried out, there is always some loss of mercury, and this is why this method of manufacturing chlorine is on the decline. For example, manufacturers of chlorine gas around the North Sea are pledged to phase out the mercury process by the year 2010.

Chemists have devised two other ways for making chlorine, and neither involves mercury. In the so-called diaphragm process there are two compartments in the cell, one producing chlorine and one producing caustic soda and hydrogen, and the brine in the two compartments is kept separate by an **asbestos** diaphragm which still allows electric current to flow. Asbestos is used because this is porous and resistant to the corrosive action of both chlorine and caustic soda. You may think that this has merely swopped one hazard for another—mercury for asbestos—but there is no loss of asbestos during the process, and when the diaphragm needs replacing it can be disposed of by burying it safely on site.

The 'cleanest' technology for producing chlorine is the membrane process. Here the two compartments are kept separate by a membrane made from a polymer material which is highly resistant to chemical attack. The method is more expensive to run because it leads to a more dilute solution of the caustic soda which has to be concentrated to make it saleable. To do this the excess water has to be removed by steam heating, which takes a lot of energy, and even then the final product is contaminated with brine.

Vinyl chloride

When ethylene and chlorine gases react they form a liquid, **ethylene dichloride**. This was once widely used as a dry-cleaning solvent, but has been phased out on health grounds because long-term exposure to its vapour was damaging to the kidneys. Ethylene dichloride is then turned into vinyl chloride by heating, which causes it to lose hydrogen chloride gas. Things are bit more complicated than this, and side reactions also occur which lead to various other organochlorine compounds, including minute traces of dioxins. Some of the by-products are worth collecting because they have a commercial market, although this is declining as the damand for organochlorines declines. Those that are not wanted can be burned to reclaim their hydrogen chloride, which can be recycled and reacted with more ethylene to make another batch of ethylene dichloride.

Vinyl chloride is a gas which boils at −14 °C. It is harmless compared to chlorine, but it is not without its drawbacks. Vinyl chloride was even tested as a general anaesthetic in the 1940s, and until the 1960s it was regarded as perfectly safe, provided it was treated with respect because it is potentially a flammable gas. The first inkling that all was not well came from those working with it. They reported a numbness in the tips of their fingers. Was vinyl chloride to blame? Tests were carried out on rats which were exposed to high concentrations of the gas. These tests did not reveal the cause of the numb fingers, but they did reveal something far more worrying—a rare form of liver cancer called angiosarcoma. More tests were ordered and the results were confirmed. A study among the health records of all who had worked with vinyl chloride in the USA found cases of people with this type of cancer.

Government health agencies, trade unions and managers in the industry were alarmed, and cooperated to bring about major changes. Leaks and losses of vinyl chloride gas in plants were reduced to the absolute minimum; workers exposed to it were to be protected; any residual traces of vinyl chloride in the product PVC were to be removed as far as possible. These changes are now part of national and international law wherever PVC is made. Today there are no cases of numb fingers caused by exposure to excess vinyl chloride, but there are still a few new cases of angiosarcoma being reported. The reason for this is that it takes about 25 years before someone heavily exposed to vinyl chloride contracts the disease, so that people exposed in the 1960s and early 1970s may still develop angiosarcoma. It will be a few years yet before we have seen the last of this rare industrial illness.

The first case reported was in 1964 at a plant in the USA. Of the 1800 people who worked at that plant, only ten have so far contracted the disease. By 1988 there were 200 known cases of the disease worldwide. Levels of vinyl chloride to which workers are exposed today are kept below 1 part per million (ppm) of the air wherever possible. In the cancer tests on rats they breathed air in which there was 30 000 ppm for 20 hours a week for a year.

Might cases of angiosarcoma yet appear among the general public? This is almost certainly not going to happen. Angiosarcoma is a very rare complaint, and no member of the public has ever been identified as contracting this disease because of exposure to vinyl chloride. Of course when polymerisation of vinyl chloride takes place there is always a little of this material trapped in the final PVC. Improvements in technique and chemical know-how can keep this to a minimum, but they cannot exclude it totally. Incomplete polymerisation during manufacture once left a significant amount of vinyl chloride in the finished PVC. Today's regulations demand that if the PVC is destined for food containers then the level of vinyl chloride must not exceed 1 ppm, and most of this evaporates during subsequent processing of the plastic. For general purposes 5–10 ppm of vinyl chloride is the limit, but again much lower levels are to be found in the final product.

Even so, you may wonder if the tiny trace of vinyl chloride could escape from articles made of PVC and affect those working with it, or even consumers who are using products made from it. Could some of us get cancer because of it? The short answer is no. The most likely way in which you would be exposed to the vinyl chloride residues in PVC is by breathing the dust if you work with it in industry. PVC dust can irritate the lungs just as any dust does, but there is no evidence that it causes cancer, and in any case the working environment for PVC dust is set at the same low level as for all such dusts. Nor does heating PVC cause it to revert to vinyl chloride. The general public is at no risk at all from this chemical. You can stop worrying about catching cancer from contact with PVC—it never happens.

What about people who live in towns where PVC is manufactured? They are not protected by special safety gear like those working in an industrial plant. Are they at risk from vinyl chloride? Investigators in Sweden and Norway compared the health of those living in communities where there were PVC plants with the health of people living in towns where there were no PVC-based industries. They found no difference in the incidence of disease. This is reassuring, and shows that the regulations now in force are working. These regulations are designed to prevent any obnoxious material escaping from such plants into the environment. Of course tiny amounts of all the materials used in making PVC do escape—that is unavoidable—but detecting these is rather a tribute to the skills of public analysts and their monitoring equipment. We shall return to this aspect of analytical chemistry in Chapter 8.

Under pressure vinyl chloride becomes a liquid, and it is in this state that it is used to make PVC. The process is carried out inside high pressure chambers. The reaction is usually performed with the vinyl chloride dispersed in water, as a suspension or an emulsion. The reaction in water is done at temperatures of 50–70 °C, and the water controls the process by removing the heat that is given off during the polymerisation. The PVC appears as tiny particles, and when these have grown to the right size the reaction is stopped and any vinyl chloride that has not polymerised is distilled off and recycled. The PVC is separated and dried in a stream of hot air.

The additives and hazards of PVC

Are there any health hazards to the public in using PVC? Again the simple answer is no. Yet people are worried about PVC and it continues to receive adverse publicity. One worry is the trace of vinyl chloride, which we have seen is now so low it can do no harm. The second worry concerns incineration of PVC waste and whether this releases dioxins. There is also a small emission of dioxins from the plants which make PVC. The third worry is the other components which are put into PVC to make it a suitable plastic for the job intended. Are these additives safe?

Let us look at the more dangerous toxin first, dioxins. The disposal of PVC could give rise to dioxins if it were burned. These chemicals are given off when household waste is incinerated, and for a time it looked as though the main source of dioxins might be the PVC waste. PVC has all the right elements for making dioxins, but the amount of dioxins given off from burning PVC is tiny. This was graphically demonstrated in Homsund, Sweden, when a wooden warehouse caught fire. Inside it were stored 200 tonnes of PVC and 500 tonnes of plastic carpets, all of which were consumed in the conflagration, which produced a cloud of smoke. Due to some rather unusual weather conditions at the time—the temperature outside was -30 °C—the cloud of smoke from the fire was trapped by atmospheric inversion and most of it came down on to fresh snow within a radius of about a mile of the warehouse[11]. Samples were taken and analysed for dioxins. As we might have expected they were detected, but in surprisingly tiny amounts. The investigators calculated that only 3 milligrams had been produced in the fire, and most of that had probably come from the wooden building itself. We shall return to this in Chapter 8 when I will discuss dioxins in more detail.

So is there nothing really to worry about burning PVC? Well, not quite. It is common practice to reclaim copper and steel wire by burning off the PVC coating. This is a dangerous thing to do especially when copper wire is involved. This metal has the chemical property of catalysing the formation of dioxins from PVC fumes. A better method is to strip the PVC off mechanically and recycle it separately.

Public concern about PVC did not arise from the vinyl chloride residues or from the dangers of dioxins. The alarm came over the

---

The modifiers (additives) used in PVC

Modifier	Average (%) in PVC when used*
Common modifiers	
Plasticisers	30
Fillers	30
Processing aids	5
Colours	2
Heat stabilisers	2
Lubricants	0.5
Specialist modifiers	
Fire retardants	4
Antistatics	1
Flow modifiers	1
Foaming agents	1
Biostabilisers	1

*Not all additives are used in all types of PVC—these are averages of quite wide-ranging values. For example, plasticisers may be as little as 10% or as much as 50%.

---

[11] In this unusual weather pattern there is a layer of warm air trapped below a layer of heavy cold air.

additives which PVC contained. The simple polymer produced from vinyl chloride has to be blended with up to ten other materials to create the texture, colour and stability of PVC we desire. These additives may account for a large part of the finished product, as the table opposite shows. Indeed, in some cases they account for most of it.

Plasticisers are the key to the versatility of PVC, which by itself is a rigid material. They are needed to make it flexible, and how flexible it is depends on how much plasticiser is added. The compounds used for this purpose include natural oils and other polymers, but the best plasticisers are **adipates** and **phthalates**. Half the weight of the finished product may be plasticiser, and for very flexible PVC, like the transparent film used to wrap food, the plasticiser has sometimes proved a problem. When it is in contact with fatty foods, such as certain types of cheese, the plasticiser can migrate from the plastic film to the product. The realisation that this was happening led to a public outcry, and although such film was very useful in the kitchen in keeping food clean and fresh, many people stopped using it because they feared that the plasticisers were capable of causing cancer.

The other additives in PVC are designed to make it hard or soft, insulating or conducting, transparent or opaque, or to colour it. Some of these additives may slowly work their way to the surface and be lost during the lifetime of the article. In theory all the additives are safe for the application for which the plastic is intended, and where the PVC comes in contact with food, or human tissue, the additives employed have passed recognised safety tests. Lead compounds cannot be used as additives for food containers, but they are allowed for insulation on underground cables. Phthalates cannot be used in fridges, but they are permitted for carpet edging. So what are additives designed to do? Could some of them really be health hazards?

Plasticisers To make PVC flexible we need to add chemicals that will allow the chains of polymer to move past one another smoothly. Up to half the weight of the plastic may be plasticiser, and this may become a problem if the plasticiser migrates from the PVC to something that is in contact with. Phthalates, adipates and organophosphates are used as plasticisers. **DEHP**, short for di(2-ethylhexyl) phthalate, accounts for more than half of all plasticisers put into PVC. Another common plasticiser is **DEHA**, short for di(2-ethylhexyl) adipate. DEHP is used in PVC which comes into contact with food, and it is the only one permitted for medical uses such as blood storage bags, catheters and other devices. DEHA is approved for use in cling-film and food containers. Both DEHP and DEHA are non-toxic, and you would probably survive even if you ate two kilograms of either. Their long term safety was put in doubt in the 1980s when it was shown that mice and rats fed DEHP had high incidences of cancer. Whether these compounds cause cancer in humans is not known (see the Box, below) but since people only come into contact with minute amounts their use probably carries no risk.

The American National Cancer Research Institute carried out tests with rats and mice, giving them an amount of DEHP which was the equivalent of two coffee mugs full every day for life for a human. Not surprisingly, given these massive doses, the rats developed cancer. The International Agency for Research on Cancer said there was a risk, but the European Union Scientific Committee on Food says they can still be used, and has set an acceptable maximum daily intake of 25 mg/kg for DEHP and 30 mg/kg for DEHA. This corresponds to an intake of 1750 mg (DEHP) and 2100 mg (DEHA) per day for an average adult weighing 70 kg. Nothing approaching this amount would ever migrate from a piece of PVC.

Cancer testing

If we suspect that a chemical will trigger cancer, how do we test it? Clearly we must test it on animals, but the more these resemble humans, the harder and costlier it will be to carry out the test. Indeed, even to expose primates like monkeys and chimpanzees to such tests is almost unthinkable, let alone human volunteers, however willing they may be. Testing rats and mice is more acceptable since we normally think of these animals as rodents and vermin, although of course those reared for testing are rather special creatures.

In 1984 David Haseman and Hans Zeisel discussed the validity of testing mice and basing predictions about the effects on human beings from the results. In one piece of research 88 chemicals suspected of causing cancer were tested on both rats and mice. Of these, 17 compounds caused cancers in both animals, 14 in mice but not rats, and 12 in rats but not mice. Six compounds that were known to start cancers in both groups of rodents were then tested on monkeys, but only one of them was found to cause cancer in these animals.

It may be true that what causes cancer in humans also causes cancers in rodents, but the reverse does not necessarily apply. When next you hear of some food component, or environmental contaminant, causing higher-than-expected cancers in mice and rats, do not automatically assume that it will do so in humans. The chances are it probably won't.

Heat stabilisers   PVC would decompose when heated if it were not for heat stabilisers. These are metal salts or metal soaps.[12] Tin, calcium, barium and zinc salts are the metal compounds most commonly used. Lead salts are also used for such things as electrical cables, pipes and window frames. Tin salts stabilise the clear rigid PVC of bottles. Could these metals taint the contents? The answer is no, because the amounts which migrate from the surface of the plastic are insignificant. Lead-stabilised PVC water pipes are in use and are acceptable in Europe, although the USA has now gone over to tin-stabilised pipes. Once the lead-containing pipes have been installed they are thoroughly flushed to remove the lead additives at the surface, after which they perform well within acceptable limits.

There is growing concern that no heavy-metal compounds should come into contact with food, toys and medical devices, and we can expect to see such stabilisers phased out. Another reason for phasing them out is that they contribute to the burden of heavy metals in the environment, especially when they are disposed of. The metals will be released extremely slowly if the PVC is disposed into a landfill site, but very rapidly if the plastic is incinerated. PVC is highly resistant to biodegradation, and so far there is no evidence that heavy metal stabilisers are released from discarded PVC. On the other hand flue-dust and slag from incinerators is assumed to be toxic waste and treated as such. It is taken to special landfill sites.

There are some heat stabilisers which do not use metals. They are made from unsaturated natural oils such as soya bean oil, sunflower oil

---

[12] These are the salts of fatty acids.

and linseed oil. When this type of PVC is incinerated, the organic stabilisers simply end up as carbon dioxide. Nevertheless some of these organic stabilisers can not be used by themselves, and there has to be some metal soap put with them. For example the PVC for medical applications, which uses mainly organic stabilisers, has to have a combination of zinc and copper soaps as well.

Lubricants   These are added to PVC to control its rate of flow when it is molten, and to prevent it sticking to metal surfaces, especially to machinery. Lubricants, which are organic waxes or organic acids, never amount to more than 1% of the polymer, and sometimes only 0.1% is needed.

Processing aids and impact modifiers   These may make up 10% of the finished PVC, and they consist of other polymers. Their purpose is to make the plastic more workable or make the final article stronger. If the final product is to be used for food containers or medical applications, then processing aids and modifiers which are used have to meet approved specifications.

Fillers   These may contribute up to half the weight of a PVC plastic article. They are there because they are cheaper than the PVC they are displacing, and so they increase profits. Powdered chalk or limestone are the commonest fillers, and they pose no health or safety risks, either when the polymer is in use or when the PVC is disposed of.

Colourants   These are either organic dyes or inorganic pigments, and care has to be taken if the intended use of the PVC is for food containers or medical equipment. Traditional pigments such as lead or cadmium compounds may seem to be safely locked away within the structure of the plastic, but they are intrinsically toxic and they can be released, for example if a child chews a piece of plastic and swallows it. Such colourants are no longer acceptable in either toys or paints, and not only because of the risk to children. Workers who manufacture or dispose of such materials are also at risk of exposure, and these colourants are now controlled by various regulations. Organic dyestuffs may appear less of a threat, but again these must be tested for safety because in some applications, such as high temperature processing of materials, they may give off vapours which are more toxic than the fumes of metal-based pigments.

Flame retardants   PVC is less flammable than most polymers, but it can be made even safer by adding a few per cent of a metal oxide such as **antimony oxide**. A little added molybdenum oxide also reduces the amount of smoke given off when the plastic burns. Here there is an environmental price to pay for these safety benefits, because these metals are toxic, but the benefits of flame retardants still outweigh their disadvantages. Rigid plastic objects, however, need no flame retardants.

Other additives   So-called blowing agents are needed to produce a foam texture in PVC by creating gases like carbon dioxide or nitrogen which expand the molten plastic with lots of fine bubbles. Other specialist additives are biostabilisers, antistatic agents and viscosity modifiers. As with all the major additives they have to be tested for toxicological safety and environmental compatibility before they can be used.

The environmental audit

Making PVC depletes natural resources, manufacturing it produces dangerous chemicals, and disposing of it adds to the environmental burden. The same is true of every synthetic plastic, indeed it is true of almost all manufactured materials that humans have used throughout recorded history, including such traditional products as iron, lead and glass. People have always been aware of the threat these activities posed to their local environment, but nowadays the global environment has to be taken into account. Today it strikes people as folly that our grandparents regarded the Earth as an exploitable resource. Minerals were mined regardless of their location, the desolation it caused, and the disruption to the habitats of other species. Solid waste was piled up in slag heaps, liquid waste was pumped into rivers or dumped in the sea, and toxic fumes were vented to the air. Domestic rubbish was tipped into natural or man-made holes in the landscape and covered with soil. Out of sight, out of mind was the general attitude, and Nature was left to look after itself. Indeed, industrial waste seemed a necessary evil that came with flourishing industry, full employment, fat profits and cheaper products. The ends justified the means.

Thankfully attitudes have changed, and the 1960s saw the start of a public debate about pollution and the environment which has continued to the present day. Talk gave way to action as people sought ways to reduce the mountains of waste that everyday modern living seemed to be generating. In fact industry, mining and agriculture are still the major producers of waste, but for most people it is the waste they generate themselves that they feel they should do something about. Packaging, and particularly plastic packaging, falls into this category, and yet plastics make up less than 10% of all refuse, and PVC only about 1% of all waste. Paper, glass and metal still account for most of what we throw away.

Against this background, how then do we assess the environmental cost of something like PVC? Ideally we should carry out a cradle-to-grave analysis for both the synthetic plastic and the traditional materials it replaces. One day this will be done, and already there are techniques being developed to carry it out under such titles as Lifecycle Analysis and Ecoprofiling. These methods of analysis divide the problem into conservation, which deals with the production and distribution of a product in terms of renewable and non-renewable resources, and pollution, which covers the environmental costs after the article has ended its useful life. The longer its working life and the safer it is, the better. We might expect PVC to come out badly in such an audit because it is the least loved of any plastic. We lack the data as yet to do a full environmental audit for PVC, or any biopolymer for that matter, but we can do a partial audit.

Despite strict controls and guidelines that have made PVC safe for food packaging and medical use, people still remember the time when it was considered dangerous. Some people consider it an environmental hazard, and it finds itself grouped with other organochlorines such as **DDT**, **PCB**s, **CFC**s, dangerous solvents and dioxins. In fact PVC poses little threat to the environment, and is no worse than other synthetic polymers and biopolymers; and there are uses which demand PVC for reasons of safety and economy.

Many materials carry a high environmental price, very high indeed if they threaten a species with extinction by destroying its natural habitat. Even crops such as those used for fibres and paper, which we think of as benign and of which we may approve, still require the using up of natural resources: they require fertilizers to maximise growth; fossil fuels for harvesting and transportation; and energy and chemicals for processing into the final products. PVC cannot be accused of depleting natural resources to any greater extent than traditional materials. To make PVC requires rock salt, of which supplies are virtually unlimited, and hydrocarbons, which are ultimately of limited extent but are at present very abundant. Biopolymers get their carbon from the carbon dioxide of the air and in this respect they score over PVC. In theory PVC could also be made from renewable sources—salt can be extracted from seawater, and ethylene from crops—and one day it may have to be so made, if we are to continue to enjoy the benefits of this versatile plastic. Then it will cost more to produce, but so will all plastics.

Pollution The part of the environmental audit where PVC appears to build up a large deficit is the release of pollutants, and accidental losses of dangerous chemicals. As we saw earlier in this chapter these 'costs' are now under control and well within budget. PVC is no more environmentally damaging than other plastics. Ideally a PVC plant would take in natural gas, electricity, salt and water, and the only product to emerge would be the polymer and the by-product caustic soda. All waste gases, liquids and solids would be cleaned up and recycled on site. In the next century all chemical plants will be like this, and some have already been built. Admittedly their products would be more expensive but that is a price we should be prepared to pay, and we must keep up the pressure for industry to invest in the necessary technology for site monitoring. The threat to achieving this goal comes from emerging nations, where firms may be able to run a large environmental deficit because of lax regulations, lack of investment, and local people giving priority to jobs over safety and the environment.

Mercury and asbestos are used in the manufacture of chlorine, and these also need to be taken into account on the debit side of the environmental audit. Loss of mercury has been a serious problem in the past, but an environmental target has been set that chlorine plants should lose no more than 2 grams of mercury per tonne of chlorine produced. Some plants can operate with losses as low as 0.25 grams per tonne, and in a typical plant producing 100 000 tonnes of chlorine a year the loss of mercury could be only about a tonne in 40 years. In any case it has been agreed that mercury cells will be phased out by the year 2010. They will be replaced by diaphragm cells which use no mercury. These have asbestos as part of their construction, which is also a debit factor in an environmental audit.

Some chlorine-containing compounds are a threat to the ozone layer. To be so, however, they have to be unreactive towards the lower atmosphere so that they can reach the upper atmosphere and release their chlorine atoms there among the protective ozone which they will help to destroy. The gas vinyl chloride and the volatile liquid ethylene dichloride, both of which are involved in PVC production, are too reactive to survive the journey to the upper atmosphere. They react rapidly with oxygen in the lower atmosphere and are washed out in rain. Minute traces may reach the ozone layer, but these are insignificant compared to the amount of CFCs in the atmosphere. On this environmental score the manufacture of PVC poses no threat to the atmosphere.

Energy and fossil fuels The chief part of any environmental audit is energy, and most of this comes from fossil fuels. Current methods of power generation based on fossil fuels may be convenient, but many are very inefficient, especially when the waste steam is allowed to escape unused. Other sources such as hydro-electric power are more acceptable, but constructing a dam takes a lot of concrete and energy so even water power is not really 'free'. The chemical industry in general uses only 9% of fossil fuel output, of which plastics account for 5%, and PVC less than 0.5%. The first method of manufacturing vinyl chloride used coal as the hydrocarbon source, in this case to make acetylene gas which was reacted with hydrogen chloride. Some plants in Germany still use this method of making vinyl chloride. Coal reserves are barely touched by PVC manufacture.

Globally we make about 18 million tonnes of PVC a year, which requires 8 million tonnes of fossil hydrocarbons. The industry also uses these as fuel for heat and transport. We need to add together the hydrocarbons used at all stages of PVC production, from the raw materials mentioned above right through to the final product delivered to the consumer. This must include not only the ethylene used to make PVC, but also the energy used to make the ethylene and to generate the electricity to extract chlorine from salt. We also need to take into account other energy that is used in a manufacturing plant for heating and driving equipment, and in the offices and storage depots. PVC has also to be made into various products, all of which takes more heat and power in more factories. And even when the product is finished it still has to be transported to distribution points and thence to shops where the customer can buy it.

In some cases a product made of PVC will last a long time, and longer than alternative materials, so that during its lifetime it could actually save resources. For example, a PVC water pipe will not corrode or burst when frozen, and so will prevent water loss and damage to property. However, it will crack if struck violently, whereas a metal pipe may be able to withstand such a blow. If a PVC component is lighter, and part of a vehicle, it will require less energy to move it. Generally an object made of PVC is about half the weight of one made of metal, so that a car having such a component will use slightly less petrol during its lifetime.

The energy required to produce steel is 32 megajoules per kilogram[13] (MJ/kg), for cardboard it is 56 MJ/kg, and for aluminium is 146 MJ/kg. How do plastics compare with these materials? The energy consumption involved in the production of PVC and other common polymers is as follows: for PVC it is 68 MJ/kg; for polyethylene, polypropylene and polystyrene it is about 100 MJ/kg; for **PET**, the plastic used to make carbonated drinks bottles, it is 123 MJ/kg. The reason why PVC is more economical is mainly because it weighs more, on account of the chlorine it contains.

Having produced the PVC we need more energy to turn it into things, but the energy to do this is generally much less than that to prepare the plastic itself. For example, moulded articles take 10 MJ/kg and sheeting 12 MJ/kg. But energy inputs can be misleading. Sometimes PVC can appear much cheaper, but is not necessarily so,

---

[13] A megajoule is a million joules, and megajoule per kilogram is roughly 100 000 kilocalories per pound.

and in other circumstances it appears dearer even though other cost factors may make it the cheaper alternative in the long run. For example, to make one thousand 250 ml containers from PVC requires 450 MJ; to make them from glass needs 1800 MJ. This shows PVC in a good light, but if the glass container is used several times then this last figure falls considerably. In some cases PVC compares badly at first glance, for example sewer pipes made of clay cost less than half the price of PVC, but PVC pipes are less labour and capital intensive because they can be installed in longer lengths and using lightweight machinery.

Incineration   The dangers of fire represent a debit item for plastics when compared to metals and glass. Both natural and synthetic polymers alike are seriously compromised in this respect, and both may contaminate the environment when they burn. Some catch fire dangerously easily, and all produce toxic gases such as carbon monoxide. PVC is among the safest in terms of flammability: paper will ignite at 130 °C, whereas polypropylene requires 260 °C, polyethylene 350 °C, polystyrene 490 °C, PVC 450 °C, and Teflon 580 °C.

When most plastics are ignited they will continue to burn as long as there is oxygen. Most PVC will not burn by itself,[14] unless the air contains 50% oxygen. In ordinary air, which has 21% oxygen, PVC will only burn if it is kept in contact with materials that are already burning. Even then it tends to give out much less heat. Unlike some plastics it does not drip molten material, but it does produce smoke and toxic fumes and it is these which have led to some disquiet. All burning materials produce carbon dioxide and carbon monoxide. Burning PVC produces hydrogen chloride, which is about as toxic as carbon monoxide. On the other hand, burning wool, leather and wood produce the very toxic gases acrolein and hydrogen cyanide.

The risk of producing dioxins is more worrying, but we have seen that PVC does not produce these to any greater extent than say burning wood, or any material which burns to form a hot plasma of carbon, hydrogen, oxygen and chlorine atoms. Such a plasma will

[14] Some flexible PVC with a high plasticiser content will continue to burn once it is ignited.

form dioxins if it cools slowly, and this will be helped by dust particles that are present and which act as a catalytic surface.

Recyling   Recycling is also part of the environmental audit. PVC manufacturers recycle their own PVC scrap as a matter of course. Low grade scrap ends up as car mud-flaps or as composition soles for footwear. The building industry uses a lot of PVC in pipes, guttering, flooring, facades, windows, shutters, blinds and ducting. All this could be recovered and recycled eventually, and this is beginning to happen. However, PVC waste is still gathered up along with all the other waste and buried in land-fill sites or burnt. That which is buried will slowly degrade over a period of thousands of years, but the residues will not leach anything that is dangerous into the ground water. The modifiers it contains will also degrade.

Packaging is often seen by the public as unnecessary waste, and many concerned people are willing to take the time and trouble to sort such waste for recycling. A mixture of plastics can be shredded and mechanically sorted according to the different densities of the various plastics. PVC and PET, which is also used to make bottles, are almost identical in this respect, but if a mixture of the two is passed through a hammer mill then the PVC is fragmented more than the PET, and the mixture can be separated by sieving. The PVC stream will contain small amounts of PET (about 0.5%), but this acts as an inert filler.[15]

To help sort waste plastics they are stamped with identification codes, but separating them by hand is slow, costly and prone to error. Automatic sorting can be faster, cheaper and foolproof. A method has been developed at the Sandia National Laboratories in Albuquerque, New Mexico, which relies on an infrared ray being reflected from a piece of plastic and then analysed by computer. This can distinguish the six most commonly used plastics: PET, PVC, polystyrene, polypropylene and the two types of polyethylene, the low density form used in making plastic bags and the high density form used to make things like containers.

---

[15] However the 0.5% PVC in the PET stream renders this plastic useless.

To summarise: our environmental audit would suggest that PVC is no worse than other plastics or natural materials, and in some ways it scores well: it is cheap; not very flammable; can be recycled; and many of its uses help save lives. In other ways it loses out: it depletes fossil reserves; and some dangerous materials, such as dioxins, are formed during its manufacture and in its incineration—but as we shall see in the next chapter, the amounts are insignificant compared to other sources of dioxin. On balance, if PVC were to be phased out and replaced by another material that was of biological origin, this would certainly be to the detriment of human society, but a slight benefit for the environment. I still think the former far outweighs the latter.

PVC is the most versatile plastic there is. It can be turned into anything from a park bench to a length of tubing so fine and gentle that it can be threaded into an artery of a sick baby. PVC can be as transparent as crystal, or as black as coal. It can be any colour and any shape, it does not rot, splinter or shatter, and it can automatically be sorted out of waste plastic and recycled. In the next century we could see PVC descending through a cascade of uses, starting perhaps with clear plastic bottles, which could be recycled as coloured containers, which in their turn could be turned into garden fencing, office flooring or sewer pipes. Finally, when its quality was too poor for recycling, it could be incinerated to provide heat energy and its ashes buried. We are still a long way from such careful stewardship of the Earth's resources, but we can help our children to plan for such a day.

At the start of this chapter I said that PVC was accused of causing cancer, contaminating our food and polluting the environment with dioxins. You will now know why I said that all these were true, and I hope you will now understand why I also said we need not worry about them. As far as I am aware, no member of the public has ever been harmed in any of these ways by PVC, and many people owe their lives to it. It is time we learned to live in peace with a rather wonderful plastic.

CHAPTER SEVEN

Dioxins, The World's Deadliest Toxins?

Chlorinated phenols; tracking down dioxins; dioxins at large; hidden dangers; the verdict

IN the previous chapter I said that one of the fears about PVC concerned the emission of **dioxins**,[1] because these could be formed as this plastic was burnt in incinerators. We now realise that these fears about PVC were exaggerated, but the threat from dioxins is still taken very seriously, whatever their origin. Every time dioxins are mentioned in the media they are described by environmentalists as the deadliest chemicals ever made, and to prove the point people are told that less than a millionth of a gram is enough to kill a guinea pig. They may also be told that dioxins cause cancer and birth defects. It is therefore not surprising that people worry when dioxins are shown to be present in parks and swimming pools, or when they turn up in paper and food; and when dioxins are found in mother's milk, and in our own bodies, we begin to protest and campaign that whatever is producing them must be stopped.

As a consequence of some alarms about dioxins, people have fled their homes in panic, such is the fear that they provoke. And yet no member of the public has ever died of dioxin poisoning, despite the fact that for 40 years the chemicals industry inadvertently produced large amounts of dioxins as impurities in other products. During this

---

[1] A reminder that when the name of a substance appears in **bold** type, it means that there is more about its chemistry in the Appendix.

time there were some major industrial accidents and explosions that released dioxins, yet the number of workers who died from exposure to them was probably only four. How can a chemical be so deadly and yet this death toll be so low?

The amount of dioxins in the environment increased markedly when the chemicals industry started to make organochlorine compounds on a large scale early this century, and especially when chlorinated weedkillers came into general use. It was always known that dioxins were trace impurities in such weedkillers, but they were not regarded as particularly dangerous, and this seemed to be borne out by the apparently safe application of these garden chemicals for over 30 years. The occasional worker in industry and agriculture was sometimes adversely affected, but that is only to be expected considering the risks involved in dealing with large amounts. The risk to the public was regarded as negligible, and seemed worth taking as part of the price of more efficient farming in the years after the Second World War.

Dioxins are organochlorine compounds, and today they stand condemned by some environmental groups on this fact alone. Greenpeace, for example, has declared war on all organochlorines, and they refer to chlorine as 'the Devil's element', with some justification; some of their major struggles have been fought over organochlorine compounds such as the insecticide **DDT**, and the aerosol gases, the **CFC**s. To a chemist like me it seems a little unscientific to vilify a common chemical element, or to rail against a chemical bond, in this case the carbon-to-chlorine bond, the possession of which determines whether a material is an organochlorine compound.

Living things make organochlorines. The red algae that live in the sea produce chloroform and carbon tetrachloride in vast amounts, seemingly unaware that these are environmental pollutants and health hazards, and that they are now banned for use as anaesthetics or solvents. Hundreds of other plants and microbes also make organochlorine molecules, and these have also been detected in the gas clouds of volcanic eruptions. Nor are all synthetic organochlorines bad. Some bring enormous benefits, such as the versatile plastic PVC (as we saw in Chapter 6). The effective healing drug aureomycin is also an organochlorine chemical.

Ironically it was chemists themselves who put dioxins at the top of the agenda of public debate, not because they produced them, but because they found ways of measuring them in incredibly tiny amounts. Advances in chemical analysis made it possible to detect one dioxin molecule in a million billion molecules of water, which is like finding a needle in a haystack the size of a mountain. While this was a triumph of the chemists' skill, it opened a Pandora's box, because it suddenly made people aware that dioxins were everywhere. They were seeping into water courses from landfill sites where the chemicals industry had dumped its unwanted wastes; they were polluting the countryside around Seveso in Italy where they had been scattered in an explosion at a chemical works in 1976; they were in the soil of Vietnam where millions of litres of dioxin-contaminated defoliant had been sprayed. Then people discovered that dioxins were in their food, in the air they breathe, in the water they bathe in, in the paper tissue they used to wipe their nose, and in the disposable nappies (diapers) they were putting on their babies. Even mother's milk was discovered to harbour them. They were there in our own bodies. How had it all happened? Where was it all coming from? What had the chemicals industry been doing?

In fact dioxins have been part of the environment since dinosaurs walked the Earth. There is a natural background level of these chemicals which are formed whenever things burn. The first bush fire or forest fire polluted the planet with them and these natural sources have been producing them ever since. What the chemicals industry had done was add a lot more, and they may even have doubled the amount in the environment over a relatively short period of time. Although this source of the pollution is under control we still cannot relax our guard, because other things are still producing dioxins. However, this was not realised for a long time.

Chlorinated phenols

Let me begin the dioxin story by going back to where it apparently started—with a chemical called **phenol**. This used to be known as carbolic acid, and comes as crystals that are slightly soluble in water. Phenol came to public notice as the first surgical antiseptic, pioneered by Joseph Lister at Glasgow University, Scotland, in 1865. He showed that if phenol was used in operating theatres to sterilise equipment and dressings there was less infection of wounds, and patients stood a much better chance of survival. By the time of his death, 47 years later, Lister's method of antiseptic surgery was accepted throughout the world.

As a result of Lister's success, phenol became a popular household antiseptic and was put as an additive in so-called carbolic soap. Despite its benefits at the time, this soap is now banned, and you will discover why if you look up phenol up in the latest edition of Sax's *Dangerous Properties of Industrial Materials*, where you will find frightening phrases like 'spillage on the skin can result in death within 30 minutes', 'kidney damage', 'toxic fumes' and 'co-carcinogen'. Clearly phenol is totally unsuitable for general use, but the benefits 130 years ago plainly outweighed the disadvantages. However, it was not long before phenol was turned into something much safer: chlorinated phenol. Chlorine gas reacts with phenol to add one, two, or three chlorine atoms to the molecule. The two-chlorine derivative is called **2,4-dichlorophenol**, and the three-chlorine derivative is called **2,4,6-trichlorophenol**. These chemicals are less soluble in water than phenol itself, but what does dissolve is a much more potent antiseptic, so far less is needed to do the job.

For the first half of this century a bottle of antiseptic chlorophenols was to be found in the medicine cabinet of most homes, and the solution was used for bathing cuts, cleaning grazes, rinsing the mouth, and gargling to cure sore throats. Little did our grandparents realise that they were doing all this with a solution that probably contained dioxins. The manufacture of chlorinated phenols became an even more flourishing part of the chemicals industry when other remarkable properties of these compounds were discovered.

Chemists can ring all sorts of changes with phenol and chlorine. There are in fact 19 different chlorophenols, and other groups of atoms can also be added to these molecules. One product in particular, with the name **2,4-dichlorophenoxyacetic acid**, or **2,4-D** for short, had a curious effect on plants: it acted like a growth hormone, but one that was out of control. Plants that absorbed 2,4-D died, and it made a particularly effective weedkiller against broad-leaf weeds. A tiny drop of this herbicide was all that was needed. Yet it did not kill grass or crereals, so that it became a superb selective weedkiller for lawns and grain crops. In some circumstances 2,4-D was used to trick plants into flowering, which was how visitors to Hawaii could be guaranteed a greeting of pineapple flowers all the year round.

But was 2,4-D safe? Tests on animals showed that it was, and for rats the toxicity measured as the LD_{50} factor[2] was about 0.5 gram per kilogram of body weight. Scaled up to human terms this would mean that 35 grams would be a likely fatal dose for the average person who weighs 70 kg (155 pounds). Because it required only 100 grams of 2,4-D to treat a hectare of land (about two and a half acres), and because the solution in which it was applied was very dilute (about 100 parts per million), it would have required the drinking of 350 litres (90 gallons) to take in a fatal dose. Moreover 2,4-D was ideal for weeding public places such as play areas, paths and parks because it could be sprayed from a back-pack. It was cheap, effective, more selective than other weedkillers, and much safer than the sodium arsenate and sodium chlorate that had been popular weedkillers up to the 1950s. Sodium arsenate had featured in many domestic murders because it is a deadly poison, and sodium chlorate had featured in accidental fires and explosions, because it is a powerful oxidant.

But 2,4-D did not kill every broad-leaf plant, and not the woody creepers and brambles that choke woodland paths and encroach on railway lines. The answer to those was to add another chlorine to the molecule to produce **2,4,5-trichlorophenoxyacetic acid (2,4,5-T)**, and this herbicide came on to the market in 1948. It appeared to be safer than 2,4-D, even though we now know that it must have contained larger quantities of dioxin. Rats did not die when they were fed a diet rich in 2,4,5-T for months, at what would have been the equivalent of a human eating 2 grams a day, but they suffered severe damage to their liver and kidneys as we might expect.

2,4,5-T contained more dioxin than 2,4-D because it was made in a different way. With 2,4-D you start with phenol and add chlorines, but with 2,4,5-T you start with chlorinated benzene and convert it to a phenol. A subsequent chemical reaction converts it to 2,4,5-T, and this step is carried out at 140 °C. The process has to be very carefully watched because if the temperature

---

[2] The LD_{50} is explained in the Box on page 141.

rises above 140 °C a side-reaction takes place and this produces dioxin.

The makers of 2,4,5-T were always aware of this possibility and took great care to see it did not happen. They were not aware then, as we are today, of the dangers of dioxin, but they knew that any product contaminated with it was unpleasant to handle because it caused a skin complaint called chloracne. The victim's face became covered with blackheads and cysts, particularly around the eyes and ears.[3] Chloracne generally clears up within a few months, but some people continue to be affected by it for many years. The German dermatologist K.H. Schulze first realised the link between chloracne and dioxin when he had a patient with the disease who was a chemist, and who had made a 20 gram sample of pure dioxin in the laboratory.

Apart from the chloracne, which developed when workers were exposed to large amounts, dioxin did not appear to be toxic to animals in the tiny amounts in which it was present in 2,4,5-T. There were about 10 parts per million (ppm) of dioxin in the product and this was deemed to be acceptable. Had they been manufacturing 2,4,5-T under today's more stringent laws, then the amount of dioxins permitted would have been set at least ten thousand times less than this at 1 part per billion (ppb), although ideally the herbicide should contain none at all.

Back in the 1950s the benefits of 2,4,5-T were all that mattered. It killed the tough weeds that 2,4-D did not kill. Indeed, it was so successful in killing woody plants that it was deployed in the Vietnam War. For about seven years, from 1962 to 1969, a 50:50 mixture of 2,4-D and 2,4,5-T called Agent Orange was sprayed from the air to destroy the dense foliage of trees that provided cover for the Viet Cong troops. During those years 50 000 tonnes of the herbicide were sprayed on the jungle. Agent Orange was contaminated with 2 parts per million of dioxins, and as it rained down on the forests it carried with it a total of 100 kilograms in all. The first inkling that something other than defoliation was happening came with reports that deformed babies were being born in higher numbers than

---

[3] Other chlorinated compounds, such as the poly(chlorinated biphenyls) (PCBs), can also cause chloracne.

expected in zones that were heavily sprayed. Nor was this just Viet Cong propaganda. We now know now that dioxins are teratogens, compounds known to cause birth defects.

The US Government put restrictions on the domestic and agricultural use of 2,4,5-T in 1970. The public were still not alarmed, but those in the industry knew by then that things could go seriously wrong with the manufacture of 2,4,5-T, although they were still unaware when this happened that the dioxins which were produced were so dangerous. However, before we look at the social and environmental issues surrounding dioxin we need to look more closely at the chemical itself.

Tracking down dioxins

From a chemist's point of view it seems rather ironic that the dioxin scares were based on improvements in chemical analysis. As analysis got better, the fear got worse. The alarms were magnified by the confusion over the term dioxin. Let me explain: the word 'dioxin' is used not only for one particular chemical, but also for a whole group of very similar chemicals. Over the years this has led to confusion. We can see the problem if we consider the following statements, both of which are true: (i) dioxins are among the deadliest molecules ever made; and (ii) dioxins can be completely non-toxic. In fact dioxins are a group of chemicals each having two benzene rings joined together through one or two oxygen atoms. Those with two linking oxygens are called dibenzo-dioxins (DD for short), and those linked through one oxygen are called dibenzo-furans (DF for short). Often they occur together, and the general term dioxins is used for the whole set.

Both DD and DF can have up to eight chlorine atoms attached to the molecule. There are 75 ways of arranging between one and eight chlorines on the dibenzo-dioxin molecule, so there are 75 separate compounds in this group of DD dioxins. There are 135 ways of arranging between one and eight chlorines on the dibenzo-furan molecule, so again there are 135 separable compounds in this group of DF dioxins. Of the 75 dibenzo-dioxins only seven are toxic, and of the 135 dibenzo-furans only ten are toxic. Out of a total of 210 dioxin-type molecules only 17 or 8% are poisonous; the other 92% are relatively harmless.

The most dangerous of all are 2,3,7,8-tetrachlorodibenzodioxin, abbreviated to 2,3,7,8-TCDD, and often referred to just as **TCDD** and 2,3,7,8-tetrachlorodibenzofuran or **TCDF**. The second most toxic are 1,2,3,7,8-PCDD and 2,3,4,7,8-PCDF, both of which have half the potency of TCDD.[4] The other 14 toxic derivatives have at most only about a tenth of the potency, many have only a thousandth, and the rest we can regard as essentially non-toxic. The total toxicity of a sample of dioxins is given by adding together all the toxic components, taking into consideration their relative amounts and toxicities. TCDD and TCDF get a toxic rating of 1, others 0.5, yet others 0.01, and some even 0.001. These are combined to get the so-called toxic equivalent, or TEQ.

TCDD is *the* dioxin. There is no doubt that this is a deadly poison, and just how deadly can be seen from the table opposite, which shows the LD_{50} for several animals.

To put these toxic doses into perspective, and to compare them to other poisonous chemicals, we should note that for humans the LD_{50} for botulinus toxin is 0.01 milligrams per kilogram, while for nicotine it is about 1000 mg per kg. As the table opposite shows, the fatal dose of TCDD for hamsters is about 5 mg per kg bodyweight, but a guinea pig needs only one *micro*gram, which is a millionth of a gram. It was this figure which led to TCDD being commonly referred to as 'the most toxic synthetic chemical known', which is probably correct—at least for guinea pigs—but as we saw on pp 140–1 these poor animals are rather sensitive to poisons. Although the LD_{50} figure for humans will probably never be known, we might at first glance expect it to be like those for our primate cousins, the monkeys. However, experience suggests that it is much higher than this and maybe even much higher than the LD_{50} of the hamster.

TCDD has several effects on animals apart from killing them. It will damage the thymus, spleen and testicles, enlarge the liver, build up fatty deposits, cause cancer and lead to birth defects. Research at the University of Wisconsin has shown that TCDD does not affect

[4] The initial letter T in these abbreviations stands for tetra, meaning four, and P stands for penta, meaning five.

The toxicity of TCDD

Animal	LD_{50}*
Guinea pig	0.001
Monkey	0.070
Rat	0.200
Dog	3.0
Hamster	5.0

*milligrams per kilogram body weight.

sexually mature male laboratory animals, but if it is given to pregnant rats then their male offspring showed reduced sexual drive and had smaller sexual organs. Other research shows that TCDD affects the immune system. The toxic response of an animal to TCDD can vary widely, as the LD_{50} shows, and this is true of other symptoms—for example humans break out in spots when exposed to it, but rodents never do.

What alarms people most about TCDD is the threat of cancer. When the US Environmental Protection Agency ordered tests on laboratory animals it discovered that TCDD was the most potent cancer-causing chemical it had ever encountered. Was the same true with regard to its causing cancer in humans? Happily the answer appears to be no, judging from the fate of those who have been accidentally exposed to large amounts of it in Europe and the USA. The numbers involved have thankfully been relatively small. The circumstances under which they were exposed to TCDD were very varied, but this has meant that there is very little evidence linking the extent of exposure to the incidence of disease. Nevertheless, some conclusions can be drawn, the main one being that TCDD appears to increase the risk of some rare forms of cancer, but only very slightly. It may even *protect* women against breast cancer.

Surveys have been carried out on workers in chemical plants which made products that were contaminated with TCDD. Some people had been exposed to dioxins for over 20 years of continuous employment at companies where 2,4,5-trichlorophenol was produced. The number who had eventually died was more or less the number expected from natural causes, although the incidence of cancer was indeed slightly higher than expected when compared with the general population, but only by one or two, and with no particular type of cancer being prevalent. One study was based on 1500 workers who had been employed at a chemical plant in Hamburg where there had once been an accident in the 1950s. Of those who had worked there for at least three months, a few more than statistically expected had died of cancer, but again we are talking of single figures.

An American study carried out by Marilyn Fingerhut and colleagues at the National Institute for Occupational Safety and Health in Cincinnati examined the health records of over 5000 male workers at dozens of chemical companies where products were produced that were contaminated with TCDD. Men who were exposed to very little dioxin did not have significantly increased levels of any kind of cancer, but among those who were heavily exposed there were a few extra cases of soft tissue sarcoma.

Another large study involved over 18 000 workers from ten countries who had either worked on the production of trichlorophenol or had sprayed 2,4,5-T as a herbicide. There was a doubling of deaths from cancer of the soft tissue, which sounds rather worrying until you realise that the investigators found that four people had died of this condition over a period of 20 years, instead of the expected two. We will look more closely at the long term analysis of those affected in some dioxin disasters later in this chapter.

TCDD may be a carcinogen for laboratory animals but not for humans to any extent, and clearly our defences can generally repair the DNA damage it causes. If TCDD has a role to play it is not so much as an initiator of cancer, but as a factor in its later development. Even then it is not easy to understand what this might be. TCDD is also an anti-cancer agent: animal studies revealed a slight increase in liver cancer, but a remarkable *decrease* in breast and uterus cancers to animals fed this dioxin.

Chemical analysis

The aspect of dioxins that has clouded the issue, and indeed led many campaigners astray, has been their remarkable sensitivity to chemical analysis. This lay behind many of the false alarms. There could have been no environmental dioxin scare in the 1950s because chemical analysis at the time could only have detected them at levels of parts per thousand. By the mid-1960s accuracy had improved a

thousandfold and chemists could detect parts per million. By the mid-
1970s another thousandfold increase made it parts per billion, and by
the mid-1980s yet another thousandfold jump made it an unbelieva-
ble parts per trillion.[6] Today it is even possible to identify the components in a mixture of dioxins. Previously chemists thought there
was only one dioxin being produced in the manufacture of 2,4,5-T,
and that was the deadly TCDD. Now we know that there are others
as well. The peak that recorded 'dioxin' on an analyser chart 20 years
ago might well have been a composite of 20 dioxins or more, many of
which were not toxic at all, and yet which were being recorded as
though they were TCDD and assumed to be equally dangerous.

Professor Christoffer Rappe of the University of Umeå, Sweden,
has made a close study of how to analyse dioxins and is the world
authority on the subject. Several methods are available, but the best is
the so-called capillary gas chromatography method which separates
the component dioxins, and high resolution mass spectroscopy which
can identify them individually. Extreme skill is required for measuring
amounts as small as a billion millionth of a gram, and even today there
are only a few laboratories that can do it reliably.

Analytical results for dioxins are displayed as a chart on which there
are clusters of many signals as we might expect, and in theory all 210
dioxins might be present. It is possible to identify the dioxin of each
signal by injecting a sample of that particular dioxin, such as 2,3,7,8-
TCDD, which has been tagged in some way, say by having its atoms
as the carbon isotope carbon-13 instead of the normal carbon-12
isotope. All the toxic dioxins are now available as labelled versions
using atoms of carbon-13, carbon-14 (radioactive), chlorine-37 and
hydrogen-3 (which is also radioactive). By having a heavier version of
an atom in a molecule we can identify it by mass spectrometry which
measures its molecular weight. These days we no longer expect to
hear of analysts merely finding 'dioxins' in something, and so worrying us needlessly. Now we expect them to say how much of these

---

[6] In weight terms these quantities are as follows: one part per thousand is one gram in a
kilogram. One part per million is a gram in a tonne. One part per billion is a gram in a
thousand tonnes, and one part per trillion is a gram in a hundred thousand tonnes. Even
this last amount does not represent the limit of modern chemical analysis, which can
detect dioxins in so-called femtogram quantities, which is equivalent to a gram in a
million tonnes.

dioxins are the poisonous TCDD and TCDF, and what is the overall TEQ (p180).

Analytical chemists were the ones who finally set the dioxins in their global and historical context. In 1991 they found dioxins in soil collected 150 years ago, long before the organochlorines from the chemicals industry had been let loose on the world. There in the carefully preserved samples of yesteryear were the dreaded TCDD and TCDF, along with many of the rest. The total amount of dioxins in the 1840s soil samples was tiny, on average about 30 picograms per gram of soil (30 parts per trillion), but they were undeniably there. The soil samples were taken from Rothamsted, a rural area in the south of England, but as this country was already heavily industrialised in the 1840s the dioxins could still have come from human activity, such as the burning of coal, although we know now that this type of combustion produces relatively little.

Other samples that predate the industrial age also contain dioxins, and they have been found in sediments in Japan that were laid down over 8000 years ago. Clearly dioxins have been released into the environment throughout history. When any wood burns dioxins are formed, and when forests burn a lot of dioxins are formed—enough to contaminate the whole planet. Wood is still gathered and burned as fuel by people in the Third World, and forests fires are started by lightning strikes or other accidents. How much wood gets burnt is not certain, but it could be as high as 5 billion tonnes per year, and if we assume that one ton of wood produces a milligram of dioxins (this is the amount generally produced by incinerating organic waste) then this source may release 55 *tonnes* of dioxins into the environment every year. The planetary burden of dioxins has risen in this century, partly because of the chemicals industry, and partly because of the increased combustion of all kinds of fuel. The level in Rothamsted soil in the early 1980s was around 90 picograms per gram—three times the level of the previous century.

These days samples for analysis are regularly taken from inside chemical plants and tested for dioxins. Monitoring is done not only on batches of chemicals, and on the products made from them, but also on waste effluents and emissions, and on soils and sediments both inside the plants and in the surrounding areas. Workers and locals are checked, and so is wildlife. Some chemical works that use chlorine gas in their processes now do environmental audits, and are able to say exactly how much dioxin they produce each year and how much escapes. The amounts are tiny. Whereas a manufacturer of 2,4,5-T in the 1960s might have sent out 1000 grams of TCDD each year mixed with their products, today a chemical firm would be worried if it lost only 10 grams a year.

Analysis for traces of dioxins is one thing, but experimenting with these chemical compounds in the laboratory is another. Because TCDD is so toxic there have been few chemists willing to research the chemistry of this key dioxin, but a few brave souls have investigated it. From their researches we know that it is a very stable molecule, but it will react with some chemicals. Ultraviolet light will knock off its chlorines, and if it is heated above 750 °C it rapidly decomposes.

The natural process that destroys most dioxins in the environment is probably the action of sunlight, although there are some microbes that can digest them. Dioxins are slightly volatile, and when they enter the atmosphere they are then at the mercy of ultraviolet rays from the Sun. Dioxins are resistant to breakdown in animals, and tend to collect in fatty tissue. There is some evidence from rats and dogs that they are capable of converting them to simpler molecules that are then easily lost. There is also evidence that enzymes that are present in sewage can remove dioxins.

Dioxins at large

The first industrial accident involving dioxins occurred in 1949 in Nitro, West Virginia, at a Monsanto plant which was making 2,4,5-T. Over 120 workers were severely affected by it and developed chloracne. Those who were exposed to dioxin were monitored for 30 years by the University of Cincinnati's Institute of Environmental Health, and were found to live longer than average, and to have fewer cancers and other chronic diseases than normal.

The second accident happened on 17 November 1953 at the BASF plant in Ludwigshafen, Germany, where trichlorophenol was being made. The temperature of the reaction went out of control and an explosion occurred which released dioxins over the site and the immediate neighbourhood. Of the 250 workers who were exposed to dioxin, about half suffered chloracne. Attempts were made to clean up the site by washing with detergents, and when this had little effect, they resorted to burning contaminated material and blow-torching surfaces. When this failed to remove it all they demolished the entire building. The medical histories of the workers who were affected by the accident were investigated 25 years later, by which time eight had died of cancer, five more than statistically expected. By 1990 the number who had died was 78, of whom 23 had cancers of various kinds. Again this was higher than would normally be expected for a group of this size among the general population.

The third accident was in 1963 at the Philips plant at Duphar in the Netherlands. Of the 50 people put to work to clean up the site, 16 went down with chloracne, and not long afterwards four of them died. These are the only people who may have died as a result of direct contact with dioxins. The plant was sealed for ten years before being dismantled brick by brick. The rubble was embedded in concrete blocks and sunk in the Atlantic Ocean.

The fourth industrial accident occurred in 1968 in the research laboratory of Coalite Chemicals in the UK. The chemical reaction making 2,4,5-T went out of control and the vessel holding it exploded, killing one man. The building was not seriously damaged and continued in use until people began to go down with chloracne. Eventually about 80 people were affected. The company then dismantled the whole plant and buried it down an old mine shaft. A new laboratory was constructed, equipped with built-in safety features, and when another accident occurred in 1974 these played a major part in containing it.

Then in 1976 came the disaster that brought dioxins to the attention of the world.

Seveso, Italy, 1976

At 7.30am on Saturday 10 July 1976, a cloud of gas and dust escaped when a reaction vessel overheated in the Icmesa chemical plant, about 13 miles north of Milan. The accident was caused by a sequence of failures, both mechanical and human. The pressure inside a reaction vessel making chlorophenols shot up, and a safety valve came into

ICMESA Factory

0   1   mile

Milan

Seveso

A

Cesano
Moderno

C

B

Bovisio
Masciago

Rome

ITALY

Monza

35

A4

Milan

The Seveso accident. The diagram shows the fall-out zones of dioxin contamination following the release of material from the Icmesa factory on 10 July 1976. The degree of exposure was calculated according to the amount of dioxin in the soil. Zone A, nearest the factory, had the highest levels, and 724 people lived in this area. Zone B, with lesser amounts, extended in a narrow band for about 4 km (2.5 miles), and 4800 people lived in this area. In Zone C, which showed a small amount of contamination, there were about 31 000 residents. [Source: *Journal of the American Medical Assocation*.]

operation. The solvent in which the reaction was occurring was **ethylene glycol** which boils at 197 °C, whereas normally the reaction is done in methanol which boils at a lower, safer 65 °C. The disaster might still have been averted if the safety valve had released escaping materials to a catch-pot, which is what usually happens in such situations. Instead a cloud of gas and fine dust shot into the atmosphere, and this settled on the nearby suburb of Seveso with its population of 17 000. Among the dust was an estimated 3 kilograms of TCDD.

The need to evacuate the area was paramount, but the carrying out of that evacuation was less than efficient. Attempts were made by those at the chemical plant to alert the community, but key local officials were away on holiday for the weekend. When they were contacted they did not appreciate the gravity of the situation, and for about a week no action was taken. Meanwhile, pets in the town sickened and died, and the hands and faces of the children who played with the 'snow' began to break out in chloracne.

Squabbles between the company and local officials wasted valuable time, but eventually 250 people were evacuated. Of these 180 had by now contracted severe chloracne. There were 150 pregnant women who had been exposed to dioxin, and 30 of them decided to have abortions for fear that the children they were carrying would be born badly defective. It turned out that 29 of the foetuses were perfectly normal, and one had Down's syndrome, which is not caused by TCDD but is a defect that occurs at the moment of conception. Of the 100 women who came to term, only two babies had birth defects, which is well within the number normally expected, and both were corrected by surgery.

Eventually 600 people were told to leave the Seveso area that was most affected, and 2000 more were given blood tests. Despite the heavy exposure to dioxins, no-one died, demonstrating that compared to animals, humans are not particularly sensitive to TCDD. The Seveso affair rumbled on, sometimes with bizarre results. For example, contaminated waste from the area 'disappeared' only to turn up years later in a disused abattoir in the village of Anguilcourt-le-Sart in France. In 1983 five senior managers of Icmesa were brought to trial and given prison sentences of up to five years, while the parent company, Hoffmann-La Roche, paid out £80 million in compensation. Analysis at the plant revealed that the reactor which had gone out of control had actually been shut down for the week-end, but it was later realised that the process itself was capable of heating up spontaneously.

In 1988 a more detailed report on Seveso came out, and this focused on the 15 291 births that had occurred in the area since the accident in 1976. Among the Seveso babies born after 1976 there were 742 with defects, which is about 5%, and the number to be expected statistically for such a population as a whole.[7] The 26 women living nearest the plant at the time of the disaster and who were most exposed to TCDD gave birth to perfectly normal babies. Food grown near the Icmesa factory was analysed a year after the accident and no TCDD was detected in the flesh of apples, pears or peaches, but it was detected at 100 parts per trillion in their peel, suggesting that the source was dust and not uptake by plant roots.

The University of Milan's Institute of Occupational Health (IOH) has monitored the Seveso disaster. Medical records covering the ten years following the accident were analysed carefully, but there were no dramatic rises in cancer cases, even in the most heavily contaminated areas of the town, just one or two more cases than might have been expected for a population of around 35 000. Among women there were more cases of cancer of the gall bladder, but fewer cancers of the stomach, colon, breast and uterus. Men had a higher incidence of hematologic and liver cancers, but fewer cases of stomach, colon and larynx cancers.

In 1993 Pier Alberto Bertazzi of the IOH published a more detailed analysis of the hospital records covering the years following the disaster, and compared the incidence of various cancers in 37 000 people who were exposed to dioxin and 182 000 who were not. In the exposed group there were slightly more cases of some rare types of cancer, but the numbers were in single figures. There were no extra cases of cancer among the 724 people who suffered the greatest degree of exposure to dioxins. The extra cases of cancer came from the 4800 people who were in the 'moderately contaminated' area and the 32 000 people in the 'least-contaminated' area.

---

[7] The majority of these were simple birthmarks.

Love Canal, New York, 1978

Love Canal is near Niagara Falls in New York State. It was a community of about a thousand homes, some of which were built on top of an old chemical waste tip, seepage from which was leaking dioxins and other materials into the canal. Luckily the solubility of dioxins in water is very low, and a cubic metre of water (1000 litres) will dissolve only 0.2 milligrams (giving a solution concentration of 0.2 ppb). Exactly which dioxin derivatives were in the canal could not be determined at the time; it was known only that they were 'dioxins'.

Those living nearest to the canal itself were convinced that their health was being affected in many ways. Some even blamed dioxins for causing their asthma and piles, while others thought that chemicals were more of a threat to the next generation, as evidenced by miscarriages, deformed babies, and puny children. There were fears that the pollution was causing cancer and brain damage, the latter being evidenced by cases of epilepsy and unexpected suicides.

Action was needed. The New York State Commissioner of Health showed the way, and published a report with the alarming title *Love Canal: Public Health Time-bomb*. It exploded immediately. Over 230 families living nearest to the canal demanded to be rehoused. Studies were initiated, and those residents who said they were affected filled in a questionnaire. The Environmental Protection Agency (EPA) got involved, and worried about possible genetic effects and damage to the central nervous system caused by the chemicals. When in 1980 they reported that there was a real danger, President Carter declared Love Canal an emergency area and the remaining 700 or so families were evacuated. The canal was dredged and the contaminated sediment sealed in drums and taken away. It was a triumph for community action groups, and in 1990 Lois Marie Gibbs, a local housewife and environmental activist, was awarded $60 000 for her work by the Goldman Environmental Foundation of San Francisco.

Further research continued, but somewhat perversely the new scientific and medical evidence did not support the claims that the leak of dioxins was causing health problems. The Center for Disease Control (CDC) had been naturally alarmed by all that had happened and carried out its own survey, comparing Love Canal residents with a similar group chosen from a community far removed from the area.

The CDC analysis was conducted on a so-called double-blind basis, which eliminated subconscious factors that might influence the results. The survey found that the illnesses afflicting the residents of Love Canal were not unusual, but were to be expected in a normal community of that size.[8]

Times Beach, Missouri, 1983

In 1971 a chemical plant in Verona, Missouri, that produced 2,4,5-T hired a company to clean out sludge and other oily waste from the plant. The company found a second use for all this, and spread it on horse arenas throughout the state, where it compacted the dust and loose earth into a hard surface. This treatment also had an added bonus: as well as keeping down the dust, it also kept down the flies. The sludge was contaminated with dioxins to which horses are particularly sensitive, and they began to sicken. Over 50 died. In 1974 the CDC investigated and found the cause to be the arena soils which contained 33 ppm of dioxins.

That appeared to be the end of the mystery, but the waste had also been sprayed on the dusty roads of Times Beach, and that was another time bomb that would explode eight years later. When the nearby Meramec River flooded in December 1982, it washed dioxin-contaminated dirt into homes and shops. A team of EPA officials, dressed in protective clothing, arrived to take samples and assess the danger. The locals fled. In the end the US Government bought the whole town for $33 million and evacuated it. Most of the alarmed residents were happy to quit and to be tested for dioxins. They were reassured to find the levels in their blood were no higher than in the rest of the population, and probably never had been. A closer investigation of the incidence of cancers and birth defects in the people of Times Beach found them to be no more common than elsewhere.

[8] According to the *New York Times* of 26 July 1990 the homes at Love Canal have been refurbished and new residents have moved in. In 1994 a Federal court in New York State ruled that the chemical company which dumped the waste chemicals at Love Canal in the 1940s and 50s was not liable for punitive damages.

Agent Orange

For over seven years the US Air Force sprayed Agent Orange on the jungles of Vietnam. The 50 000 tonnes (about 40 million litres) they used during that time contained about a tenth of a tonne of dioxin as contaminant. Could this have affected the men who carried out the operation, and those on the ground? Veterans of the campaign who had been involved with Agent Orange were tested many years later and found to have only 5 parts per trillion of dioxins in their blood, but those who loaded the herbicide on to the aircraft had higher levels. Ex-soldiers had on average only slightly more dioxin in their bodies than the general public, for whom the normal range is 2–20 parts per trillion.

Nevertheless, veterans suspected that dioxins might be causing various illnesses and they began to agitate for compensation, although some of the effects they attributed to dioxins, such as baldness and impotence, had never before been linked to these chemicals. A major law suit was started in 1984 and this cost the chemical companies who had manufactured Agent Orange $180 million in an out-of-court settlement. Closer analysis failed to reveal an unusual pattern of disease, and though the CDC tried very hard to find a correlation between Vietnam service and health problems, they were not able to pin any condition down to dioxin exposure. The difficulty was in knowing which of the three million US troops who served in Vietnam had been exposed to Agent Orange, and the extent of individual exposure.

Part of the problem was again due to chemical analysis, because for many years it was very difficult to measure the amount of TCDD in someone's body. Up until 1986 a person had to donate 20 g of fatty tissue for analysis, and this had to be removed in hospital. Then a method of measuring the level of TCDD in blood serum was developed, so that a patient needed to give only a pint of blood, whereupon veterans came forward in large numbers for testing. About a quarter of a million men were examined and 27 000 were admitted to hospitals for illnesses thought to be related to dioxins. The only reliable sign of exposure to dioxins like TCDD is chloracne. Only five Vietnam veterans had fallen victim to this disease and qualified for disability payments. The men whose job it had been to load aircraft with Agent Orange and to clean up afterwards were deemed to have been most exposed, and they have been selected for monitoring until the year 2002. So far this study has shown that the half-life of TCDD in the human body is about seven years, and much longer than presumed.

In 1993 the report entitled *Veterans & Agent Orange: health effects of herbicides used in Vietnam* was published. This was a review of the 6400 scientific papers published on Agent Orange and had been carried out by the Institute of Medicine (IOM), part of the US National Academy of Sciences complex. It said that five medical conditions show a statistical association with the herbicide: soft tissue sarcoma; non-Hodgkin's lymphoma; Hodgkin's disease; chloracne; and porphyria cutanea tarda, which is another type of skin disorder in which blisters form. Whether these were caused by traces of TCDD, or by the herbicides themselves in Agent Orange (2,4-D or 2,4,5-T) was not determined. The IOM concluded that Agent Orange could not be linked to leukemia, bone cancer or birth defects, and was probably not implicated in cases of skin cancer, gastrointestinal cancers, bladder cancer or brain tumor.

Hidden dangers

Bleached paper

Chlorine was once commonly used to bleach wood pulp to make clean white paper. While it did this very well, it also reacted with molecules in the defoaming agents that were used, and formed dioxins. The paper industry also used pentachlorophenol as a fungicide to prevent darkening of the wood pulp by fungi, and this was also contaminated with dioxins. Both these sources of contamination have since been eliminated, but back in 1985, when investigators analysed the effluent and sludge from paper mills, they discovered dioxins. Not only that, but paper was also found to have measurable amounts of dioxin, and this naturally triggered public alarm because some types of paper, such as toilet paper and handkerchiefs, come into intimate contact with the human body.

In 1988 the EPA in conjunction with the American Paper Institute began a survey of over one hundred US plants that used chlorine to bleach wood pulp. They discovered that the pulp from which paper is made had between 3 and 6 parts per trillion (ppt) of dioxins, the sludge had 17 ppt and the wastewater from the mills had 0.024 ppt. This dioxin was coming from the wood pulp itself, which contains molecular components that will react with chlorine to form dioxins. For all the years that chlorine had been used to bleach wood pulp there must have been dioxins in paper and paper products, but the amounts had been well below the limits of detection, and only the advances in chemical analysis of the 1980s put bleached paper in the frame.

Women were worried about dioxin contamination of the materials used to make tampons, and this led to publications such as *The Sanitary Protection Scandal* from the Women's Environmental Network. Parents too were alarmed; they were using disposable nappies (diapers) on their babies, and the milk their children drank often came in paper cartons. There is no evidence that a child was ever affected. It has been estimated that six nappy changes a day would only expose a baby to 0.01 picograms (trillionths of a gram) of dioxins, whereas it would get about 100 picogrammes from its mother's milk.

The pulp industry began to look for alternatives to chlorine, and many mills now employ bleaches such as ozone, hydrogen peroxide or chlorine dioxide. Chlorine dioxide sounds as though it might also behave like chlorine itself, but this compound is an oxygenating chemical not a chlorinating chemical. The levels of dioxins in effluents and products decreases markedly when chlorine dioxide is used in place of chlorine, and this is likely to be the bleaching agent of choice when the hundreds of pulp and paper mills in the US change their processes to meet the EPA draft regulations that were published in November 1993. When these come into force in 1998 the aim will be to cut the discharge of TCDD from these mills from an estimated 350 grams of dioxins per year at present to 30 grams per year.

Dioxins in food

Lots of foods contain small amounts of dioxins. Even human milk has them, and breast milk generally has more than cow's milk. We are exposed to dioxins from the moment we are born, and we all have detectable amounts in our bodies. Most of the dioxins which humans take in come from our diet, and the main sources are meat and dairy products. Farm animals absorb dioxins from the grass and plants they eat. The dioxins are there as surface contaminants. The World Health Organisation (WHO) defines a Tolerable Daily Intake of dioxins of 10 picogrammes of dioxin per kilogram body weight per day, which is 700 picogrammes for the average human. The actual intake is about 100 picogrammes.

Other species pick up much more dioxins than humans, and fish appear to be able to concentrate them into their bodies. Catches of bottom-feeding fish like carp from Saginaw Bay, USA, have been found to have up to 700 parts per trillion of TCDD in their flesh. Most other fish have levels of around 10 ppt. Herring and salmon from the Baltic Sea in Northern Europe also have detectable amounts of TCDD, even though there are no industrial sources of dioxins in the region. Probably all meat and fish have detectable amounts of TCDD at a level of a few parts per trillion, and this we must assume is the natural background level of dioxins in everything on this planet.

Combustion

In 1977 it was discovered that burning wood produces some dioxins. Clearly anything that is burnt which is a mixture of carbon, oxygen, hydrogen and chlorine has the potential to release dioxins, even though the chemical reaction which forms them rarely occurs. Whenever we burn wood or straw, or cremate bodies, we produce some dioxins as part of the natural chemical processes that flame promotes. Timber that has been treated with chlorophenols to preserve it will of course evolve more dioxins than burning ordinary untreated wood, but now that such wood preservatives are no longer used, this problem will diminish. Every time you strike a match or have a bonfire you produce dioxins. Forest fires contaminate the whole planet with them. These we can regard as natural sources, but there are still other ways that dioxins are formed by burning, and attention has focused on one particular source, the incineration of municipal waste in cities.

Dioxin levels are highest in cities. They have been detected in car exhausts and spent motor oils, especially from vehicles which use leaded petrol. The dioxins arise because of the need to add organochlorines to the petrol to help remove the lead from the engine. When all cars ran on leaded petrol they may well have been adding thousands of grams of dioxins to the environment every year. As the use of leaded petrol has declined, so has the amount of dioxins from cars.

A much larger source of dioxin in cities has been municipal incinerators which have become the favoured method of disposing of domestic waste in many countries. In 1977 dioxins were discovered in the fly ash and flue gas of municipal incinerators in Holland and Switzerland. In Europe there are now more than 500 municipal incinerators and in Denmark and Switzerland almost all waste is disposed of this way. A modern incinerator burns about 750 000 tonnes of waste a year, generating electricity and providing low cost heat for homes and offices. Such an incinerator saves the burning of 300 000 tonnes of fossil fuel.

Modern incinerators have been greatly improved and tight standards are set for their emissions. Flue gases can be passed through carbon filters which reduces the amount of dioxin released to the environment to trillionths of a gram of dioxin per cubic metre of gas emitted. An incinerator may in fact destroy more dioxin in the waste being burnt than it produces in the furnace. According to Professor K. Nilsson, of Lund University in Sweden, if the same amount of waste were to burn in an uncontrolled landfill fire then there would be a far higher emission of dioxins. But even from an efficient incinerator some dioxin escapes, a milligram for every tonne of waste burned. This does not seem a lot, but would be 750 grams per year for a large incinerator. Environmental pressure groups have alerted those who live near incinerators to the risks, and there is often much opposition to new incinerators being built. Yet the amount of dioxin that residents would be exposed to each day would be only a thousandth of the tolerable daily intake.

Hazardous waste incinerators seem more threatening in that they are there to dispose of bulk chemicals, many of which are organochlorines, such as **polychlorinated biphenyls** (**PCB**s). These were manufactured all over the world in hundreds of thousands of tonnes per year from the 1950s to the late 1970s, and were used in electrical transformers since they were very stable and acted as insulating fluid. Other uses included hydraulic fluids, lubricants, inks, plasticisers and adhesives. Companies that specialise in incinerating chemical waste have come in for criticism, and although their plants are generally located in remote areas there have been vigorous campaigns by farmers and local residents to get them closed down. These incinerators do emit dioxins, but the amounts are relatively small because the through-put of such plants is measured in tens of thousands of tonnes per year rather than the millions of tonnes in municipal incinerators. Hazardous waste incinerators add very little dioxin to the global burden.

Nevertheless, combustion is still the main source of dioxins from human activity. For example, in 1988 the emissions of dioxins in Sweden, where environmental monitoring is well advanced, were judged to be:

Emissions of dioxins, Sweden 1988

Source	Emission* (g per year)
Incineration	110
Iron and steel industry	100
Paper industry	35
Hazardous waste	6
Motor vehicles	5

*Upper limit for all dioxins, but calculated in terms of their TEQ (see p. 180).

Although we now realise that dioxins are not the threat they once appeared to be, there is no point in allowing any to escape to the environment if it can be prevented. We must keep improving incinerators, and replace older ones as quickly as possible. Cutting emission of dioxins is more of an engineering problem than a chemical one. Many combustible materials are likely to produce a trace of dioxins given the right conditions. Such conditions may pertain in the waste gases from any burning organic material, when the speed at which these cool and the presence of solid particles may allow tiny amounts of dioxin to form. Combustion research has shown that it is not so much the air supply or the temperature of incineration that leads to dioxins being formed, but the time taken for the burning process. If this is optimised then the amount of dioxins is minimised. As a final precaution we can clean up the flue gases before they are vented to the atmosphere.

The verdict

What are we to make of all this? Throughout the 1980s environmentalists became concerned as they discovered how toxic and hazardous dioxins were, and especially when they discovered that these were present in several commonly used chemicals and household products. Thanks to these pressure groups, industry was made aware that they had to do more than just prevent accidents in their plants. Today we can look back at what has been done and realise that although dioxins still represent a risk, they are not as threatening as they first appeared. The natural environment has always had a background level of these chemicals, and we humans have them naturally within our bodies. It would appear that we have learned to live with a certain amount of dioxins. We may even have evolved to be immune to low levels of dioxins, and this may be why the expected upsurge in cancer cases resulting from industrial accidents has not materialised, even though tests on animals suggested that dioxins were highly carcinogenic.

Why then have so few people died of dioxin poisoning? Some claim there have been no deaths at all, but there is evidence that a few men who were heavily exposed to TCDD in industrial incidents, and who died a few months later, were directly affected by it. They were very unlucky. Although TCDD is deadly to animals, most humans who have been exposed to large amounts, and enough to give them chloracne, have not had their general health seriously impaired. People do react idiosyncratically to dioxins—some people break out in chloracne when exposed to tiny doses, while others can cope with much larger amounts without a single spot appearing. This was one of the more puzzling findings following the Seveso accident.

The early industrial accidents that involved dioxins were not sufficiently alarming to cause companies to invest effort or money to ensure that dioxins, and especially TCDD and TCDF, were eliminated from their products. This lack of foresight by the chemicals industry was a costly mistake. It allowed those who fought to eliminate dioxins to occupy the moral high ground, from which they have continued to direct a vigorous campaign against dioxins, even extending this to all organochlorines.

In 1993 the environmental pressure group Greenpeace issued a report called *Dioxin Factories* in which it accused PVC manufacturers in Europe of producing 'huge amounts' of dioxins. The report calculated that enough dioxins were being produced from this one area alone to supply every living soul on the planet with more than the maximum annual dose as laid down by the World Health Organisation. Now this is true, but it needs putting in context. What is the tolerable daily intake of dioxins?

To answer this question the Chlorine Institute Inc. of Washington DC, the Environmental Protection Agency and the Food and Drug Administration co-sponsored a conference in October 1990 at the Banbury Center, Cold Spring Harbor, Long Island, New York, to which they invited 38 scientists from all over the world, and especially those from environmental, biological and medical research institutes. The object of the conference was to reach an agreed figure for the tolerable daily intake of dioxins, which in some countries was as high as 10 picograms per kilogram of body weight, and in others as low as 0.0062 picograms, for example in the USA. No agreement was reached, although it was agreed that the higher limits were too high and the lower limits too low. The upper limit appears to be around 5 picograms per kilogram of body weight per day. Some countries permit less than this, such as Germany with 1 picogram, and some allow more, such as Canada with 10 picograms. The World Health Organisation also fixes the tolerable daily intake at 10 picograms.

The USA puts the tolerable daily intake of dioxins as 0.0062 picograms per kilogram of body weight, which is 0.434 picograms for the average 70 kg person. This is rather an unrealistically low limit considering the average person probably takes in between 1 and 3 picograms per kilogram body weight per day.[9] Just how tiny a picogram is can be seen by taking a gram of dioxin and expressing this in terms of an allowable daily intake. A gram would be enough to give every one of the world's 5.5 billion people their tolerable daily intake

---

[9] The average person probably has around 5000 picograms of dioxins in their body. Or put another way, this is 0.005 millionths of a gram.

for every day for a year. (For those in the USA it would supply their tolerable daily intake for over a hundred years.) It is more than likely that the 0.0062 pg per kg body weight per day, which the EPA and FDA recommend, was being exceeded when humans first walked the Earth over a million years ago. It was certainly exceeded the day they first started cooking. We can now see that the claim in *Dioxin Factories* would be correct if the chemicals industry emitted only a single gram of dioxins.

There are genuine concerns about dioxins, and especially about the potent ones like TCDD. The main sources of dioxins in the environment are given in the table below. In the USA the National Council for Air and Stream Improvement estimated in 1991 that the release of dioxins were as follows: general fuel combustion (for heating, industry and power generation) 26%; municipal incinerators, 26%; hospital incinerators, 16%; motor vehicles 7%; fuel-wood combustion, 7%; forest fires 7%; municipal sewage, 4%; pulp bleaching, 1%; other sources, 6%.

The major sources of dioxins

Industrial
Chemical industry   Pulp and paper industry
Smelting and refining of metals   Manufacture of flame retardants
Leakage from waste disposal sites   Recycling scrap metal
Warehouse fires   Hazardous waste incineration

Urban combustion
Municipal waste incineration   Accidental fires in buildings
Hospital waste incineration   Cremation
Combustion of sewage sludge   Car exhausts

Domestic fires
General heating   Wood burning stoves
Bonfires   Cigarette smoking
Accidental fires in homes

Environmental
Forest fires   Wood burning stoves
Use of sewage sludge as fertiliser*

---

*The dioxins in sewage sludge may come from a variety of sources.

Not included in the above table are the dioxins found in the solvents used in dry-cleaning establishments. These solvents can be organochlorine compounds which might lead you to expect that they would be contaminated with traces of dioxins when they are manufactured. This is not so—they come dioxin-free. In fact the dioxins are found only in the used solvents and they are picked up from the clothes being cleaned. These are dioxins from car exhausts, crematoria, incinerators, bonfires, and all the other domestic and urban sources mentioned in the table opposite.

The manufacture of chlorophenols and chlorobenzenes was once the main source of dioxins, but these have now largely been phased out in the West, although in some Third World countries such as India their production is just starting up. At various times they were used as wood preservatives, pesticides and weedkillers, and the annual production of chlorophenols was probably in excess of 150 000 tonnes a year. How much of the toxic dioxins they inadvertently produced is now impossible to know.[10]

Conclusions

Given enough time all dioxins spread throughout the environment because they are slightly volatile. Consequently every mouthful of food we eat contains some dioxin, including TCDD. Dioxins are almost insoluble in water but they are slightly soluble in organic matter such as fats and oils. Levels in fruit, vegetables and eggs are extremely low, and in milk are very low. In meat, fats and oils they are slightly higher, and in fish and fish oils higher still, but all the amounts are still tiny. In the human body dioxins collect in fatty tissue, and this is also the reason why human milk contains dioxins in its cream.

Although they were unaware of it, humans began to experience dioxins at first hand when they first used fire. Indeed, we may well have built up a certain degree of tolerance to dioxins because humans have been in close contact with them for so long. Hundreds of thousands of years of cooking and keeping warm with wood fires has produced a human tolerance to these chemicals which is far higher than in other species. Wood has all the elements necessary

---

[10] Based on the Agent Orange contamination figure of 2 ppm, the annual industrial production of dioxins would have been about 300 kg, making a total of 7.5 tonnes over a period of 25 years.

for dioxin formation, including up to 0.2% of chlorine as chloride. Burn wood and a measurable amount of dioxins will be produced, and they form remarkably easily, as research was to demonstrate in the following experiment. Benzene and ferric chloride were absorbed on to a silicate material and heated at 150 °C when detectable amounts of dioxins were generated. This sounds like a rather odd chemical reaction, but it mimics a primitive wood fire on solid earth. The surprising thing was that dioxins were generated at relatively low heat. Here we are talking about a range of dioxins, not just TCDD, and this is how it is with wood fires.

In 1985 Hermann Poiger of the Swiss Federal Institute of Technology was so sure that dioxins were fairly harmless to humans that he ate some in order to chart their progress through his own body. He found they concentrated in his fatty issue and had a half-life in his body of five years. Of course, he took only a tiny dose.

In 1981 the amount of dioxins released to the global environment by human activity was estimated to be about 1500 kg from the chemicals industry, about 13 kg from combustion (fuels and incinerators), 0.2 kg from motor vehicles, and a mere 0.002 kg from cigarette smoke. Since then the levels of dioxins have been falling in the West as the major industrial polluter, the chemicals industry, has controlled the making of the chlorophenols, 2,4,5-T, 2,4-D and PCBs, and in some countries their manufacture has ceased altogether.

Less well publicised is that Nature itself makes chemicals like these. The soil fungus *Penicillium* produces 2,4-dichlorophenol. Grasshoppers make 2,5-dichlorophenol, and the Lone Star tick (*Amblyomma americanium*) uses 2,6-dichlorophenol as its sex attractant. Nature has ways of getting rid of chlorophenols, which are broken down in soils by the white rot fungus *Phanerochaete chrysosporium* which can even digest DDT, PCBs and pentachlorophenol. PCBs are also destroyed by the soil bacterium *Pseudomonas*.

So what is the position today with regard to dioxins? Should we still feel threatened by them? The answer is 'yes' if we are talking about TCDD itself and the other highly toxic dioxins. We must remain alert to any concentration of these compounds contaminating the environment as they did as Seveso. The answer is 'no' if we are talking about the general background levels of dioxins of the kind which we encounter when we light a cigarette, have a bonfire in the garden, drink a glass of milk, or pass an incinerator. Among these dioxins there is some TCDD and TCDF, but as this chapter has revealed, most of them will be the harmless kind and so none of these activities puts us at risk.

Professor Christoffer Rappe, the world's leading researcher into dioxins, has been quoted as saying: 'More people make their living from dioxins than ever suffer from them.' He did not mean just the manufacturing chemists, or the toxicologists and analysts. He was referring to people such as medics and lawyers who have to deal with people who think they have been affected by exposure to dioxins and wish to take legal action. Nor must we overlook those who made political capital out of dioxins. In Holland the Green Party used the news that cow's milk was contaminated with dioxins to score impressive gains in elections.

In 1991 Michael Gough of the Center for Risk Management, Washington DC, reported on the human health effects of dioxins in a paper in the journal *The Science of the Total Environment*. His findings were rather reassuring, and he concluded: 'no human illness, other than the skin disease chloracne, which has occurred only in highly exposed people, has been convincingly associated with dioxins.'

To end this chapter I would like to quote Professor W. Gribble of the University of Hawaii at Manoa, Honolulu. In response to the oft-repeated claim by environmental campaigners that organochlorines do not occur in Nature, he wrote a 40-page review in the October 1992 edition of the *Journal of Natural Products* in which he discussed hundreds of known examples of organochlorines which are made by living things. He also concluded of dioxins: 'There is no scientific evidence that dioxin (TCDD) causes any serious health effects in humans apart from the skin disease chloracne and some reversible liver dysfunction. Nevertheless the extraordinary toxicity of some polychlorinated dioxins (PCDDs) and related compounds, such as the polychlorinated dibenzofurans (PCDFs) in some animals is reason enough for the continued study of these compounds, especially since it is now recognized that PCDDs and PCDFs are in fact, natural products.'

As far as our animal friends are concerned we should continue to research the dioxins, but as far as humans are concerned the dioxin scare is over.

CHAPTER EIGHT

Nitrate

*The nitrogen cycle in Nature; food; fertilisers; nitrate in
natural waters; nitrate in the diet; nitrate and human health;
conclusions*

IN the previous chapter we considered the dioxins, toxic chemicals
that we unknowingly dissipated into the environment. Thankfully
they are less hazardous to humans than tests on animals would indicate. In this chapter I want to talk about another chemical which
worries people, yet one that we manufacture on a massive scale,
and deliberately spread far and wide. This chemical is the fertiliser
nitrate,[1] which many people believe damages the land, pollutes
rivers, contaminates water supplies, and threatens human health.
Nitrate has been guilty of all these charges at some time or other.
Some blamed overproduction by industry and overuse by farmers,
because it appeared that as nitrate use went up, so did the level of
nitrate in rivers and drinking water. The visible evidence of excess
nitrate in natural waters was the growth of weeds and slimy algae; the
less obvious effects were said to be sick babies and cancer.

Some groups see nitrate as a threat from the moment it is produced
in a chemical plant, to the time it ends up in our stomach, and all
stages in between. Others would like to see an end to inorganic nitrate
fertiliser production, and a return to organic manures to replenish

---

[1] A reminder that when the name of a substance appears in **bold** type, it means that
there is more about its chemistry in the Appendix.

farm land, claiming that we could break this chain of pollution and so save lives. In fact the opposite would happen—if we were now to stop making nitrate fertilisers *millions* of people would starve to death. Nor is the link between fertiliser production and environmental pollution as simple as some people assume. Indeed, there may be hardly any connection between them.

Little that is said about nitrate is true, much is distorted, and explanations of how it affects our health are based more on fear than on fact. We need nitrate to grow enough food to feed the people of the world. The effect of inorganic nitrates on food production is well illustrated by looking at the history of Britain. By 1900 the British Empire was the greatest the world has ever known, but in the two World Wars in the first half of this century it discovered its Achilles' heel: the heart of the Empire was an overcrowded island of 50 million people which had to import most of its food. This vulnerability was not lost on the enemy whose submarines sent ship after ship of food to the bottom of the Atlantic. 'Dig for victory!' was the call to which millions responded, but despite all the digging, and the drafting of young women to work on farms, Britain still grew less than a third of the food it needed.

Fifty years after the Second World War, and with a few more million mouths to feed, the farmers of that overcrowded island grow twice as much of their staple crops, and on less agricultural land. Indeed, the British Isles could be self-sufficient in food if it so wished, but people now put land to other uses. Fields that once grew wheat and potatoes are planted with trees; meadows on which cows and sheep grazed have become theme parks and golf courses; and farmers whose land once bloomed yellow with oilseed rape are now paid to let it lie fallow.

Such is the abundance of food grown in developed countries that some farmers are returning to the methods of a bygone age, or 'organic' farming as they prefer to call it. They plant crops in strict rotation, and they fertilise with manure and compost generated on the farm. If all farmers were to do this, countries like the British Isles would again have to import food on a massive scale. The bounty of modern agriculture is only possible because of chemical fertilisers, and in particular nitrate. To understand why this is so we need to understand the environmental chemistry of **nitrogen**.

The nitrogen cycle in Nature

Nitrogen is essential to life because it is one of the five elements which make up DNA; the others are hydrogen, oxygen, carbon and phosphorus. Apart from its role in DNA, nitrogen also has a part to play in hundreds of other molecules, and especially in **amino acids** which are the building blocks of protein. The average human being weighs 70 kg (155 pounds) and contains about 1.8 kg (4 pounds) of nitrogen, mainly in the form of protein.

We could trace the route by which an individual nitrogen atom in DNA or protein started its journey from the nitrogen gas of the air and passed through a series of different forms in plants and animals before it ended up as part of our body. We could also trace its journey back again. When material of which it is part breaks down, the nitrogen atom may be recycled within out body, or it may be excreted in our urine as amino acids, **ammonia**, **urea** or other chemicals. But what is one animal's waste is another organism's food, and this discarded nitrogen can be used by bacteria or plants as their sources of nitrogen. A particular atom of nitrogen may circulate round the food supply many times before it meets an organism that turns it back to nitrogen gas and expels it to the air. Then the cycle is complete. The term 'nitrogen cycle' refers to the movement of nitrogen through the environment, and the illustration opposite shows the main paths around which it revolves.

The atmosphere is 79% nitrogen gas, N_2, but this is useless as a fertiliser resource for plants because it is a very unreactive molecule, and though it will dissolve in water to a limited extent, it still does not undergo chemical reactions. Generally high temperatures are needed to get N_2 to react with oxygen. **Nitric oxide** (NO) and **nitrogen dioxide** (NO_2) are produced naturally by lightning and by combustion of fuels, and these can be washed to earth.[2] To be of use they have to be turned into nitrate (NO_3^-) or ammonia (NH_3) which plants can use as nutrients.

Reaction of nitrogen with hydrogen to form ammonia is rather subtle when carried out in Nature. There are micro-organisms that can take nitrogen gas and add hydrogen atoms to it at outdoor

---

[2] These are often referred to as NO_x, where the x stands for one or two oxygen atoms. But the main one is NO_2.

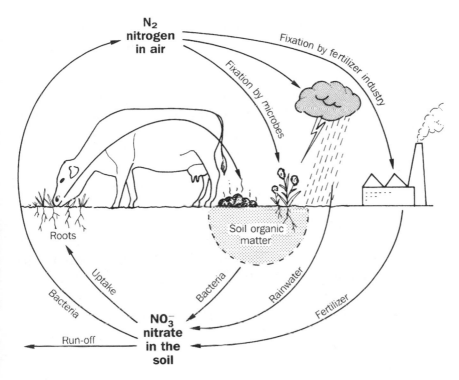

The nitrogen cycle in nature. The main 'reservoirs' of nitrogen are nitrogen gas in the atmosphere and nitrate in the soil. In addition to these inorganic forms there are thousands of organic nitrogen compounds which are part of living things.

temperatures, and the most important ones are the so-called nitrogen-fixing bacteria. Some can do this with apparent ease, such as the free-living *Clostridium pasteurianum*, which is anaerobic—in other words it can live without oxygen from the air—and *Azotobacter vinelandii* which is aerobic, in other words it needs air. The most important nitrogen-fixing bacteria are those which live in symbiotic relationships with plants, such as *Rhizobium* which lives in nodules on the roots of legumes such as peas and beans. The plants provide the bacteria with carbohydrates while the bacteria provide the plants with ammonia. These bacteria are the first step in the nitrogen cycle on land, and there are others that begin the food chain of the sea, such as *Cyanobacteria* and *Rhodospirillum* which fix nitrogen gas dissolved in sea water.

In addition to the bacteria which turn N_2 into ammonia, there are others called nitrifying bacteria which can take the process one step further: *Nitrosomonas* can convert ammonia to **nitrite** (NO_2^-), and *Nitrobacter* turns nitrite to nitrate (NO_3^-). This may be absorbed by the roots of plants, which in turn may be eaten by animals. Animals can return a lot of the nitrogen to the soil as urine or dung, and it may go round the biological cycle again. Alternatively it may be absorbed by bacteria which use nitrate (and *nitrite*[3]) as a source of oxygen, thereby converting it to N_2 and returning it once more to the atmosphere. The bacteria that do this are called denitrifying bacteria, some of which can also produce nitrous oxide gas, N_2O, which likewise returns the nitrogen to the atmosphere.

The nitrogen cycle in Nature is now dominated by human activity. Nature and humans together fix about 275 million tonnes of nitrogen annually in various ways:

Natural fixation of nitrogen (175 million tonnes annually):
agricultural crops	80
wood and forests	40
marine plants	35
lightning	10
other	10

Nitrogen fixation due to human activity (100 million tonnes annually):
fertilisers	70
combustion	20
other	10

The amount fixed by plants grown for human consumption is the single largest contributor, and this is achieved by crops such as legumes (peas, beans, etc.) and rice. If this is seen as part of the nitrogen fixed by human endeavour, then we are responsible for fixing 180 million tonnes a year, far exceeding Nature's 95 million tonnes. The most important part of the nitrogen cycle is that in the soil. An instructive way of thinking about this is to consider all the nitrogen compounds

[3] The name nitrite is very like nitrate, and yet in chemical terms they behave very differently. We need to keep this in mind for later in the chapter. To avoid confusion *nitrite* will be in italics.

in the soil as a nitrogen reservoir, which is added to and taken from each year. The total pool is a mixture of many forms, from simple nitrate ions dissolved in the water of the soil, to complex proteins and molecules in the cells of microbes and all the many other creatures living there.

We add to this reservoir when we fertilise the land, and both inorganic ('artificial') fertilisers and organic (manure and compost) fertilisers provide nitrogen compounds. We tap this reservoir when we grow and harvest crops, because plants use their roots to absorb nitrate from the water of the soil.

Food

We get a lot of the amino acids we need by consuming the protein of other living organisms, such as the flesh of animals, or by raiding the protein stores of plants, such as their seeds. The world relies on a small number of crops that we have cosseted for generations. The top four are wheat (annual production about 400 million tonnes), maize (350), rice (350), and potatoes (300). Others in the big league, with 100 million tonnes or more, are barley, sweet potato, cassava and soya-bean; and sugarcane and sugar beet together yield 120 million tonnes of sugar a year.

Some of these crops are excellent sources of protein. One such is the soyabean, which has been popular in China for thousands of years, and is now among the top four crops grown in some Western countries such as the USA. Soya flour, which is very high in protein, is increasingly used in bread and other products. The components of a soya bean are protein (42%), carbohydrate (29%), and vegetable oil (21%). Soya flour is 50% protein, and this is much higher than lean beef (20%), wheat (14%), eggs (13%) or milk (4%).

A well fertilised hectare[4] of soyabeans will yield 500 kg of protein, ten times as much as we could get from cattle grazing on the same area of grass. Most of the nitrogen that passes through an animal in the course of its life is returned to the land, and this tends to be distributed rather unevenly, so contributing to the problems of leaching, as we

---

[4] A hectare is the area of a square 100 metres by 100 metres, i.e. 10 000 square metres. In Imperial units this is about 2.47 acres (an acre is 4840 square yards).

shall see. Protein is about 15% nitrogen, so a crop of soya beans will remove 75 kg of nitrogen per hectare from the land, whereas cattle taken to slaughter will remove only 6 kg. We can see why the former is not a sustainable crop without a large input of nitrogen fertiliser, but a herd of cattle can be—at least in theory.

The value of most crops lies in the vegetable oil or carbohydrate they produce, neither of which contains nitrogen; but without access to nitrogen such crops would not grow. All plants need nitrogen to be able to carry out photosynthesis, which is the process that converts carbon dioxide from the air to carbohydrate. This reaction requires sunlight and takes place in leaves. In order to intercept sunlight efficiently, a hectare of crop needs to maintain a green canopy of three hectares of leaf area. Cereals need about 90 kg of nitrogen to form such an amount of leaf.

This, then, is why farmers apply nitrate fertiliser at the start of the growing season. It would be little use applying it in late summer, and if they were foolish enough to do so they would lose most of it in the rains of the following winter. The nitrogen of the leaves eventually ends up in other parts of the plant, such as stems, roots and storage organs, which may be tubers or grains. The proportion of nitrogen that is removed at harvest time will vary from as much as 75% in the case of cereals, to as little as 35% for sugar beet. What is left behind generally adds to the organic reservoir in the soil, the so-called humus.

The most important source of nitrate in soil is the humus. A few percent of the nitrogen in this is converted to nitrate each year, and this is taken up by plants in the spring and early summer when it is needed for growth. A lot of the nitrogen from humus is released too late in the year to be of use to plants, and it may be leached from the soil by rain in the autumn and winter. The reservoir of nitrogen compounds in soil is very large, and only a small part is accessible to crops. It is possible to tap this reservoir and grow crops without fertilisers year after year, although with slowly diminishing returns.

If we did nothing to refill the nitrogen reservoir in the soil, but simply grew crops and harvested them, we would find yields falling as the humus store was used up. Eventually the land would sustain only the amount of vegetation that could be supported by the nitrogen that Nature provides each year. Under such conditions the Earth might just be able to feed the current population of 5.5 billion people if we cultivated as much land as possible. Today about 1.5 billion hectares (10% of the global total) are cultivated, but a further 2 billion hectares, mainly in South America and Africa, could be brought into production. Yet even this would not be enough because the human population would continue to expand, so we would have to cultivate yet more land. The alternative is to farm existing land more intensively. This is only possible if we replenish the nitrogen pool in other ways, and the best way to do this is to fertilise the soil with inorganic nitrates. Yet nitrate fertilisers are said by some to be a major environmental threat, despite the fact that millions of us are already dependent on them for the food we eat.

The Earth and its organic nitrogen resources were outstripped by our expanding population many decades ago. The gap has to be filled with inorganic fertilisers. The Worldwatch Institute reported in *State of the World 1990* that the Earth's food output would plummet by 40% if the use of these fertilisers were to be discontinued. In other words about 2 billion people are now alive, and are kept alive, by the nitrate which comes from fertiliser factories.

Fertilisers

'And he gave it for his opinion, that whoever could make two ears of corn or two blades of grass to grow upon a spot of ground where only one grew before, would deserve better of mankind, and do more essential service to his country than the whole race of politicians put together.'

So wrote Jonathan Swift in *Gulliver's Travels*, published in 1726. Two hundred and fifty years later we have done just this over large parts of the globe. Indeed, farmers can now grow not two, but four and even six ears of corn where only one grew before. The miracle has been achieved partly by breeding better strains of corn, but mainly by applying fertilisers, and especially nitrogen fertilisers, to the soil. The value of fertilisers can be illustrated by looking at the world's longest running agricultural research station.

The 150-year experiment

About 25 miles north-west of London is the Rothamsted agricultural research centre. It was set up in 1843 by John Lawes and Henry

Gilbert. Lawes manufactured fertiliser phosphates and Gilbert was a professionally trained chemist. From its inception Rothamsted's brief was to examine the effects of artificial and natural fertilisers, and this it has continued to do; but it has also become a major centre of fundamental research into all aspects of agriculture, from recycling waste within peasant economies to genetic studies on ways to give plants an inbuilt resistance to predators.

What fascinate most visitors to Rothamsted are the so-called Classical Experiments, which are plots of wheat, grass, and other crops that have been grown on the same strips of ground year after year for over a century, with the same amounts of inorganic and/or organic fertilisers added to each plot every year. Rothamsted even has a herd of cows which are fed in the traditional manner so that their manure can be used as organic fertiliser. They also have a plot of land which has been growing winter wheat for 150 years with no input of fertiliser at all. Every year the soil is sown with wheat, the crop is allowed to grow with nothing being added to the soil, and then it is harvested. Nothing else is done to the land until the next season when it is ploughed and sown again.

When you compare the yields of crops from these experiments, you can see the benefit of fertilising the land. The yields of wheat and potatoes per hectare, averaged over many years, are given in the table below.

The Classical Rothamsted fertiliser field tests

Fertilisers	Crop yields*	
	Wheat	Potatoes
none	1.2	8.2
NPK** (1:1:1)	5.5	20.4
farmyard manure	5.8	32.9
NPK** (5:1:1)	6.8	35.6
farmyard manure + N	7.7	37.8

*Tonnes per hectare   **N = nitrogen, P = phosphorus, K = potassium

What first strikes us about these figures is that the unfertilised strip of land can still produce an average crop of 1.2 tonnes of wheat. It will even yield 2 tonnes per hectare in a good year, although only 0.5 tonne in a poor year. A neighbouring plot to which nitrogen fertiliser has been added every year has never produced less than 2 tonnes even in a bad year.

In the late 1960s new varieties of wheat were introduced at Rothamsted, and these could better use the nitrogen in the soil. On the fertilised plots yields went up to 7 tonnes, while it stayed at around 1 tonne on the unfertilised soils.

Growing a crop and taking it to market means that we are removing nutrients from the land, and so it is with the Rothamsted unfertilised plot. The wheat cropped from this plot removes about 12 kg of nitrogen, 5.5 kg of phosphorus and 7 kg of potassium; most nitrogen and phosphorus are in the grain, and most potassium is in the straw. Where do these nutrients come from? Indeed, what sustains the fertility of this soil? The wheat needs nitrogen, phosphorus, sulfur, potassium, sodium and a few other essential minerals. It must get these from its roots, which absorb them from the water in the soil.

In the Middle Ages, when crop yields began to fall, a field was left to lie fallow for a year. This had the effect of allowing weathering to break down soil particles and release phosphate and potassium, and also to add more nitrogen by way of rain water, natural fixation and bacterial release from humus. The immediate beneficiaries of this bounty are the microbes in the soil, of which there are vast amounts, and these act as the real reservoir of nutrients which they release when they die and decay. It is this organic reserve from which plants derive their nutrients in undisturbed soil. Ploughing, sowing, harvesting and removing crops upsets this natural balance. With no replenishment the nitrogen reservoir dries up, and yields fall until the vegetation is sustained only by rainfall and bacterial fixation, and we reach the minimum of the Classical Experiment.

The table on the next page shows how much fertiliser is used worldwide, and the figures include phosphorus and potassium as well as nitrogen. The amounts of these fertilisers manufactured each year are roughly 70 million tonnes of nitrogen (mainly as nitrate), 35 million tonnes of phosphorus (as phosphate), and 30 million tonnes of potassium (as the chloride). Nitrogen is the key nutrient because it is the one most likely to be in short supply. It needs replenishing yearly, and if we do so the effects are dramatic. In Europe, for example, the amount of nitrogen used in fertilisers has increased from less than four million tonnes to nearly ten million tonnes in the last 25 years. As the

Changes in the use of fertilisers throughout the world, and major crops produced, from the early 1950s to the early 1980s

	North America	South America	Europe	Asia	Africa	Russia
Fertilisers*						
1950s	6	0.3	9	2	0.5	2
1980s	24	4	32	29	4	19
Crops**						
1950s	149	26	294	768	20	141
1980s	504	94	623	1402	53	373

*Millions of tonnes per year. Averages have been taken for the early 1950s and early 1980s.
**Millions of tonnes per year. These are the totals for the major staple foods: wheat, rice, potatoes, barley and maize.

amount has gone up so have crop yields, and wheat production has doubled from 2.5 tonnes per hectare to 5 tonnes. Maize yields went up to 6.5 tonnes.

The amount of fertiliser used per head of population varies widely. For example in Europe and North America it is around 30 kg per person per year, while in Africa it is less than 5 kg. Wherever modern fertilisers are used crop yields have gone up, sometimes increasing threefold, as the table shows. Of course not all the increase is due to fertilisers, and in developing countries there has been an increase in the land brought into cultivation, as well as an increase in yields from new varieties of crops.

Inorganic fertilisers have affected farming in four ways:

1. They have permitted naturally infertile soils to be brought up to a level of nutrition that will support the growing of staple crops. For example, in Australia cereals are now grown on 16 million hectares compared to 6 million thirty years ago.

2. They have eliminated the need to replenish the nitrogen in the soil by older methods such as leaving the land fallow for a year, or by planting legumes or clover which can fix nitrogen in their roots, and then ploughing these back in. The sequence of the traditional Norfolk system of annual crop rotation is: wheat → root vegetables → barley → clover → and then back to wheat. This system alternated human and animal crops, and worked very well. We still

need to rotate crops, but today the reason is pest control rather than to maintain soil fertility.

3. Fertilisers increase yields on farmed land, thereby allowing other land to be used for different purposes, such as forestry or recreation, and some may even be left undisturbed as a haven for wildlife. Of course intensive farming also frees land for less desirable uses such as sprawling suburbs, supermarket car parks, and six-lane motorways.

4. Fertilisers influence which crops are grown because they affect their profitability. Farmers will tend to cultivate those crops which respond best to fertilisers. The cost of fertilisers finally ends up in the price of the crop, but how much it contributes is difficult to calculate because of the many fixed costs in farming. Happily, inorganic fertilisers are cheap, although some see this as a disadvantage, encouraging profligate use and causing pollution.

Organic or inorganic nitrogen?

There are some who think that inorganic fertilisers are alien to the environment, and they advocate 'organic' farming with 'organic' fertilisers as the natural way to replenish the land. Organic farming is a luxury that only advanced economies can afford because it is highly inefficient. Organic farming means less produce and higher prices, but some city dwellers are prepared to pay a premium for such food in the belief that it is somehow healthier. They may even imagine that the protein it contains is made up of 'organic' nitrogen, produced from 'organic' nitrate, which is provided by the 'organic' fertilisers which organic farmers spread on their land. A little chemical knowledge shows that this is not so: there is only one kind of nitrate.

Nitrate is a simple negatively charged molecule consisting of a nitrogen atom surrounded by three oxygen atoms, and its formula is NO_3^-. Organic nitrate is also NO_3^-. Nitrates are salts of **nitric acid**, HNO_3, which is used in the chemistry laboratory and in the chemicals industry. The acid is made by reacting ammonia with oxygen, and it is then converted to salts, such as **ammonium nitrate**. Today 70 million tonnes a year of this are made industrially. This is the material referred to as inorganic nitrate, of which 90% is used as fertiliser and about 10% is used in explosives.

There are some natural nitrate minerals. Chile nitre, for example, is naturally occurring sodium nitrate, and was once mined on a large scale for the fertiliser and explosives industries. It is still mined for the relatively high level of iodine that it contains. Another long-known nitrate is saltpetre, which is potassium nitrate. This has been used for centuries as a component of gunpowder, and for centuries it came from organic sources, scraped from the walls of latrines and leached from cesspits, where it is produced by bacteria working on the nitrogen compounds in human excreta. No use was found for it until the discovery of gunpowder, after which it had a major impact on world history. In the Napoleonic Wars in the early 1800s the British Navy stopped supplies of nitrate reaching France from the teeming cities of India and the Far East. The French had then to use all kinds of rotting human and animal wastes to produce saltpetre.

For the wars of the 20th century, the demand for nitrate for explosives was far in excess of domestic production on this scale. The First World War might have ended with a quick victory for the British Empire if the navy blockade of Germany had been effective in cutting off supplies of nitrate, but it was to no avail, and that terrible war was to last four years and end in stalemate. The Germans no longer needed to import nitrate because their chemicals industry had found a way of using nitrogen from the air to make nitric acid and nitrates. They had discovered a chemical method of fixing N_2 gas, and on a scale that would one day rival that of Nature. The Haber process, named after its developer Fritz Haber (1868–1934), turns N_2 into ammonia. This can then be oxidised to nitric acid and nitrates. In 1918 Haber was awarded a Nobel Prize for his chemical achievements.

Jonathan Swift may be rejoicing in Heaven at the abundance of modern farming with nitrate fertilisers, but here on Earth we wonder if we are doing the right thing. More and more we hear the warnings of environmentalists that we should give up our inorganic fertilisers and return to the methods that farmers used when Swift was alive. Their advice is to use organic fertilisers, which they see as sustainable fertilisers—in other words, producing them requires no fossil fuels or mined resources.

At first glance there seems to be advantages in using animal manure, including human sewage, and compost made from municipal waste. The Rothamsted results in the table on p. 212 showed that farmyard manure is just as good as inorganic fertiliser, and what is more it appears to come free—provided you have farm animals to excrete it and pasture on which they can feed. Natural sources of potassium such as composted vegetation, and the traditional phosphate source, bone meal, are also part of Nature's bounty. Inorganic fertilisers on the other hand cost money because they come from chemical plants, and producing them requires energy and raw materials. Closer analysis, however, reveals that organic fertilisers are not free either: it is just that the costs are hidden. Animals that provide the manure have also to be reared and fed, and the food or grass they eat is also grown on farm land that cannot be cropped indefinitely without it too losing its fertility.

Plants are capable of absorbing nitrogen only as nitrate or ammonia, which they then convert to nitrate. Ammonium nitrate makes an ideal fertiliser, and whether it comes from the chemicals industry, or from manure, it makes no difference to the roots of a plant. Indeed, plants prefer the artificial variety because it is generally applied in spring and at just the right time to maximise their growth.

Despite what the advocates of organic fertilisers may believe, both types of fertiliser, organic and inorganic, supply the same essential nutrients. They differ in that they supply differing amounts and at different times. Organic ones have the advantage of recycling waste, and they release their nutrients over a period of months or even years as they decompose slowly in the soil. There are certain disadvantages to set against these benefits: the nutrient content of organic fertiliser is difficult to judge and may be low for certain elements. Moreover, the slow release may mean that it gives up its nitrate at a time when plants do not require it, so there is a higher risk of its nitrate being leached from the soil by winter rain.

The nitrogen in animal feed mainly returns to the land, but the nitrogen in human food rarely does so. Most exits down sewers and eventually ends up discharged into rivers and is carried to the sea. This seems a waste of a hard-won resource, and so more and more slurry from city sewage works is being taken to fertilise farm land— in other words, to go through the cycle again. It cannot replenish the reservoir by itself, and in some cases the sewage may be polluted with heavy metals from industry, making it unsuitable as a fertiliser for food crops.

A way round this problem is to limit its use to permanent woodlands, and to crops that are processed before they are used for human consumption. City dwellers produce sewage sludge all year round, whereas plants really need it only during the growing season. Like farmers who store animal slurry, we could store human slurry for spreading during these seasons, but the cost would be prohibitive. In any event there is the expense of transporting tankers of human slurry or trucks of compost over long distances.

These considerations apart, the benefits of organic fertiliser are still enough to outweigh the disadvantages. The problem with organic fertilisers is that there can never be enough of them to supply all the nitrogen that is needed for new crops, and there is no escaping that simple fact of environmental chemistry. No matter what we do, we cannot defeat the net transfer of nitrogen from countryside to city, for which no amount of manure, be it animal or human, can compensate.

Organic farming also benefits from another source of nitrogen fertiliser, albeit an inorganic one: the dissolved nitrogen oxides in rainwater. You might be surprised to learn that most of the nitrogen in rainwater is not there as a result of lightning, but comes from car exhausts and industrial pollution. Today's rainwater brings down more fixed nitrogen than it used to, principally because of air pollution. This bounty of nitrogen also falls on organic farms, and they may get as much as 50 kg of nitrogen per hectare from rainwater.

Inorganic fertilisers have the advantages of being easy to make, store and transport. Inorganic fertilisers can be put on the land at the time they are needed, thereby preventing wastage and nitrate run-off. They are cheap, but this is a mixed blessing in that it may encourage the misuse of land. If you look back to the table on p. 212 you will see that, in terms of crop yield, the blend which is richer in nitrogen gives the best result, and modern farming methods can improve even on these Rothamsted yields. By adding lots of ammonium nitrate fertiliser it is possible to grow over 10 tonnes of wheat and 50 tonnes of potatoes per hectare.

Generally the debate about nitrate fertilisers has been fought over which type is best: inorganic nitrate or organic nitrate. To the growing plant it matters not at all—they are chemically the same, and so is the nitrate from microbes in the soil, and that derived from rainwater.

Nitrate in natural waters

The phosphate and nitrate of artificial fertilisers have come in for a lot of adverse publicity over the years, and they were partly responsible for the eutrophication of rivers and lakes. The word eutrophication is derived from the Greek words for over-nourishment, and this happens when there is too much phosphate and nitrate entering a body of water. The species which most quickly uses these nutrients are the algae, and they multiply rapidly and choke the water with their slimy green scum. The living algae at the surface block out the sunlight for other plants, while the dead algae at the bottom use up dissolved oxygen as they rot away. Other creatures such as fish die because they are unable to breathe, and the system goes out of balance and may become a stinking mess. Nor is this only a setback for wildlife. Humans may be deprived of a source of drinking water and a place of recreation. Back in the 1950s and 1960s this happened to some of the Great Lakes of North America.

Because phosphate and nitrate are the main component of fertilisers the cause seemed obvious: streams and rivers draining water from intensively fertilised land were being over-supplied with these nutrients. Fertiliser use and eutrophication appeared to go hand in hand, and the link between them was often made by environmentalists. The chemical industry was held to be responsible for encouraging farmers to use more and more nitrate to get higher and higher yields. Of all salts, nitrates are the most soluble and the most likely to be leached from the land to pollute rivers and lakes.

In fact the effluent from sewage works was mainly to blame for eutrophication. The problem was worse than just eutrophication: nitrates were contaminating drinking waters, and this chemical was known to cause a life-threatening condition known as 'blue-baby' syndrome (see p. 228). Some people even blamed nitrate for causing cancer.

Leaching nitrate from the land

The nitrate in rivers and other natural waters comes mainly from the soil, of that there is no doubt. Nor is there any doubt that fertiliser nitrate is responsible for some of it, and sometimes for a lot of it, especially when it is washed from the land by heavy spring rains or floods. However, these are relatively rare events, and do not explain the normal levels of nitrate in natural waters. So what is the cause? There is no simple answer. Even if we can be certain from which soil the water has drained, we cannot be sure which type of fertiliser, organic or inorganic, is to blame.

Although nitrate fertilisers are used in large amounts, they do not account for the raised levels of nitrates in rivers. This comes mainly from organic sources such as soil microbes or animal manure. Environmentalists assumed that it was the fault of farmers for putting too much nitrogen fertiliser on their land. In fact it is more likely to have been caused by their forefathers spreading manure or simply ploughing up grassland. It can take decades for nitrate from soil to seep into underground water sources and find its way into rivers.

Ungrazed grassland is least likely to leach nitrate, even when inorganic fertiliser is added, provided this has been applied at the right time of year. Nitrate loss is accelerated if animals are put on the land because of their urine and dung. Urine is the main route for an animal to dispose of unwanted nitrogenous material from its body, and this tends to be deposited on a small patch of ground which is then over-fertilised. This local bounty of nitrogen exceeds plant uptake and so remains unused at the end of the season. A meadow of contented cows may look like a perfectly balanced organic system as the cows eat the grass and fertilise the soil, but it is a system out of balance. From such a field there will be a leaching of more nitrate in the autumn and winter than if the soil had been evenly fertilised in the spring with inorganic nitrates, and cattle kept off it.

The nitrate in farmed soil comes from four main sources:

1. fertilisers, i.e. inorganic nitrate

2. animal manure, i.e. organic nitrate

3. soil microbes, i.e. nitrate from microbial wastes, and

4. rainwater, which contains dissolved nitrogen oxides which are nitrate precursors.

All can contribute to nitrate loss, and this will happen if too much nitrogen fertiliser is applied in spring for the growing crop to use, or too much manure or slurry is spread in the autumn, or the microbes are disturbed by ploughing, or the rain falls through heavily polluted air from an urban area. Each contributes to the nitrate which leaches from the land.

Inorganic nitrate. The optimum amount of nitrogen to benefit a particular crop has been known for over a century. For example winter wheat needs 214 kg of nitrogen per hectare, so amounts in excess of this will simply be wasted. If it gets a little less fertiliser than this economic optimum, then the amount of residual nitrate left at the end of the season will be very small.

Computer programs have been developed to help farmers cut down the loss of nitrate from their land. Input the crop, the time of year, and the existing natural nitrogen content of the soil, and the program will calculate the right amount of nitrogen fertiliser to add to maximise crop yield and minimise waste. Of course a big unknown factor in all this is the weather, and in particular the rainfall, although irrigation can redress a dry season.

Organic nitrate. Adding manures also leads to greater yields. In the very long term, organic matter added as fertiliser increases the store of organic nitrogen in the soil, and this in its turn breaks down to nitrate at a later date, and may then be leached. Any agriculture that builds up soil fertility and organic matter will increase leaching of nitrate if it is not properly managed.

Organic manures come in the form of semi-liquid slurry from livestock that is housed, and solid matter from farmyard manure and poultry. In many countries these sources of nitrogen make up about a third of all fertilisers applied to the land. Unfortunately they are not necessarily applied at the best time for a growing crop. Indeed, a traditional time for spreading muck is the autumn, on the stubble of a previous crop, and this leads to nitrate leaching during the coming winter because there is rapid degradation of the nitrogen compounds to nitrate. Experiments have shown that pig slurry will lose a third of its nitrogen as nitrate in this way. It is possible to slow down this loss by controlling the bacteria that cause the breakdown. This can be done with **dicyandiamide**, which will suppress the microbial action that causes the conversion of the ammonia in the manure to nitrate.

Even organic farming can cause leaching of nitrate to rivers. Crop rotations in which the land is fertilised by growing a nitrogen-fixing legume crop, and then killing this by ploughing it in, can add several hundred kilograms of nitrogen to a hectare of land, but a lot of this may be leached away over winter and be gone before the next crop can use it.

Microbial nitrate.   In the top 25 cm (10 inches) of arable soil, known as the topsoil, there may be 5 tonnes (5000 kg) of nitrogen per hectare, locked up in humus and living things. Most of this is unaffected by rainwater. In undisturbed grassland and forest there may be as much as 20 tonnes (20 000 kg) of nitrogen per hectare. It can be slowly released as nitrate by the action of enzymes.

This natural fertilising action can provide 45 kg of nitrogen as nitrate per hectare per year. We can upset the natural ecosystem by ploughing it up, which stimulates the microbial activity, and this is probably the most important cause of nitrate loss from any soil. When permanent grassland is ploughed up for arable farming it releases a huge amount of nitrate, eventually up to 4 tonnes (4000 kg) per hectare. This loss is far in excess of any amounts from nitrate fertilisers. The best course of action to prevent nitrate loss is to leave old-established grassland well alone.

Rainwater nitrate.   We can also blame rain for adding to the nitrate run-off from farms. The gases dissolved in the rain, along with dust particles washed out of the air, can add up to 50 kg per hectare per year of nitrogen to the land, but most of this cannot be used by plants because it falls out of season.

Nitrate loss to rivers also depends upon the rock below the soil. If this is impervious then the water in the soil drains away into ditches or streams, but if it is porous rock, such as limestone or sandstone, then the water, and the nitrate dissolved in it, trickles slowly through and accumulates in the water table below. If we use this for drinking water by sinking a well or drilling a borehole, then we may be consuming nitrate carried there a century or more ago.

On a typical modern farm most of the useable nitrogen comes from inorganic fertilisers. The next largest amount comes from manures, then organic soil residues, and finally a small amount from rainwater. The nitrate that is leached from the soil also comes from these sources, but not in the same order. Organic soil residues provide most, then manures, then rainwater, and finally a small amount from unused inorganic fertilisers. This order is the opposite of what we might expect, and indeed it is contrary to the claims of those who condemn inorganic fertilisers. You may be wondering how we know that inorganic nitrate is the least to blame. Earlier I stressed that nitrate is nitrate, no matter what its source. There is no different between the nitrate of inorganic fertilisers and that from manures, humus, or rainwater. So how can we differentiate inorganic fertiliser nitrates from the organic ones?

Analytical chemists constantly monitor water taken from rivers, lakes, streams, ditches, wells and boreholes, and measure its nitrate content. If the source of water can be linked to a particular stretch of land then it may be possible to say how much nitrate per hectare is being leached. A more meaningful analysis is to measure the water as it actually drains from the soil itself. In Europe and the USA this is done by inserting porous suction cups and sucking out soil water. This is easy and cheap to do, but even then we cannot be certain that water sucked out this way is the same as water which would be leached from the soil. Another way is to take samples of soil and extract all the soluble nitrate, including that which is sticking to the soil particles themselves. But again, we can not know for certain if this method of extraction removes the same nitrate as natural leaching.

A better, but more expensive, way is to cut out blocks of soil and encase them in plastic so that the water leaching from them can be collected. The most expensive method of all is to isolate whole areas with plastic barriers and measure the nitrate run-off while leaving the soil as part of a field. In all these ways we can assess nitrate loss, but none of these methods conclusively proves where the nitrate is coming from.

In order to do this, analytical chemists use a method of labelling the nitrogen atoms with the nitrogen isotope N-15. Nitrogen consists predominantly of isotope N-14, with seven protons and seven neutrons in the nucleus of the atom, giving a mass number of 14. Indeed,

99.63% of nitrogen atoms are of this kind. The remaining 0.37% of nitrogen atoms have eight neutrons in the nucleus, making them slightly heavier with a mass number of 15. If we enrich a nitrogen compound, like ammonium nitrate, with more of the heavier N-15 isotope then we can follow its progress by taking samples and seeing where the N-15 is going. The N-15 isotope is easily detected by an analytical technique known as mass spectrometry.

At Rothamsted they fertilised crops with ammonium nitrate that was enriched with the N-15 isotope and showed that up to 70% of the nitrogen applied as fertiliser was taken up by the crop and harvested in the year it was applied. Of the remainder some was taken up by soil microbes, and some was decomposed back to nitrogen gas by bacteria. Only 5% was leached away into ground water or drained from the land. This loss was higher in the winters following a summer of drought, when the crop did not grow so well and so could not use all the nitrate provided in the fertiliser.

Despite these research findings there is still a call to limit nitrogen fertilisers, maybe because this is the only nitrate input over which we have any real control. There are those who advocate a tax on nitrate fertilisers as a way of discouraging their use, and some have even suggested a tax rate of 50%. Calculations have shown that even with such a tax it would still be worthwhile for a farmer to use nitrate fertiliser, and the price of wheat would need to halve to wipe out the benefits of fertiliser use. A tax might check misuse, especially by those farmers who add more than the recommended amount. A better way to prevent nitrate leaching away would be to make it illegal to apply fertilisers (organic or inorganic) in the autumn, and at the same time to encourage farmers to plant another crop for winter, instead of leaving the land bare and exposed to weathering and run-off.

Removing nitrate from drinking water

Nitrate in drinking water has been described by environmentalists as a 'biological time-bomb' and 'cancer on tap'. Both are alarming phrases, but there is little scientific backing to support them. Nevertheless, they have been the rallying cry of campaigns for the removal of nitrate from public water supplies, even though such nitrate has never killed anyone. Nor is it ever likely to. The World Health Organisation (WHO) has set a limit for nitrate in drinking water of 50 mg per litre (50 ppm), and in 1980 the European Community issued its *Directive on the Quality of Water Intended for Human Consumption* which set the same permitted maximum. This limit is well below the level at which nitrate would pose a risk to health. In those regions where river water is found to contain more than 50 ppm of nitrate, as it does in certain agricultural areas, then it must be treated before it can legally be supplied for human use.

There are two ways of removing nitrate from drinking water. It can be done by biological (organic) methods, or chemical (inorganic) methods. The biological process uses the denitrifying bacteria *Pseudomonas denitrificans* which, in the absence of oxygen from the air, attacks nitrate as a source of oxygen. Having stripped off its oxygen atoms, the bacteria then release the nitrogen to the atmosphere as N_2. Denitrification plants that work in this way are already in operation in parts of Europe where local nitrate levels exceed 50 ppm, and by the end of the century there will be dozens of them in operation. A typical plant treats groundwater, the type that is more likely to exceed the guidelines, and it may process over 6 million litres a day (1.5 million gallons). The denitrifying bacteria need to be supplied with other nutrients, and these can be added in the form of hydrolysed straw[5] and traces of minerals. This requires another treatment of the water after denitrification, in which the organic debris is filtered out. The biological method of nitrate removal appeals to our sense of environmental economy, even though it is costly.

There is a cheaper way of denitrification based on a chemical method called ion exchange, and this is preferred in the USA. As its name suggests, one type of ion, in this case unwanted nitrate (NO_3^-) is replaced with another, such as the safer chloride ions (Cl^-). As the nitrate-rich water filters through the ion-exchange resin the swop takes place in a quick, efficient and easy process. Eventually the ion-exchanger becomes exhausted and has to be recharged with more chloride, and this can be done with a strong

[5] The cellulose of straw can be broken down to its glucose components by chemical reaction with water, and this is what the term 'hydrolysed' means.

solution of brine (sodium chloride). This leaves behind a concentrated nitrate solution which has then to be disposed of separately.

Nitrate in the diet

Nitrate in drinking water does not affect its taste, but just knowing it is there worries some people. Those who believe it is a danger to their health think that they can reduce the risk by drinking bottled water. However, not all such waters are free of nitrate. The world's most popular mineral water is Perrier, renowned for the 'purity' of its source, which is at the village of Vergeze near Nîmes in southern France. If you examine the label of a bottle of Perrier you will discover that it contains 17 mg of nitrate per litre. In many areas you would get less nitrate if you drank water from the kitchen tap. Nitrate is to be found in other bottled waters, although generally at much lower levels than this.

Despite the alarms about nitrate we are in no real danger from it, and even if you find a source of water that is nitrate-free, you still cannot avoid nitrate because we produce this chemical naturally in our own body. If you eat a lot of greens, and particularly spinach and lettuce, you may be getting a lot of nitrate.[6] It is not clear why some vegetables take in much more nitrate than they need. Some can have over 2000 parts per million (ppm) of nitrate; for example beetroot can have up to 6000 ppm, and radishes have been found with more than 13 000 ppm, which is 0.13%. These are exceptional examples, and there is no cause to be alarmed by this last figure, which is the highest value recorded in a vegetable, because the amount you eat at any one time will be small. The table opposite shows the more likely amounts in vegetables. The level depends on the soil in which they are grown, and on the time of year: winter-grown vegetables have higher nitrate levels.

Nitrate also comes in foods such as bacon and ham which are cured by being immersed in brines made of sodium or potassium nitrate. The solutions which are used for this have 500 ppm of sodium nitrate or 600 ppm of potassium nitrate, and these figures are low compared

---

[6] It is possible to imagine some people, such as vegetarians, exceeding acceptable limits by eating lots of those foods which have high levels of nitrate.

Nitrate in vegetables

Vegetable	Nitrate/ppm*
Spinach	3000
Lettuce	1600
Red cabbage	600
Carrots	500
Beetroot	500
Celery	400
Green cabbage	200

*Typical values measured in parts per million (ppm), which is the same as milligrams per kilogram.

---

to the level of 30 years ago when 5000 ppm was the norm. Beer often contains a small amount of nitrate, and because those who drink beer often consume several glasses at one session, they may take in a lot of nitrate.[7]

Sodium and potassium *nitrites* are also used to cure pork and ham, and the use of these is strictly governed by law. In the USA the limits are 120 ppm for sodium *nitrite* and 148 ppm for potassium *nitrite*. *Nitrite* is added to tinned meats, cooked meats, and sausages, not only to preserve them, but also to give them the attractive pink colour that makes them sell better.[8] Adding *nitrite* prevents the bacterium *Clostridium botulinum* from multiplying, which it might otherwise be able to do inside a sealed can of meat or fish. Those eating food from an infected can will get botulism, the deadly paralysing disease that is caused by a toxin which the bacteria produce. *Nitrite* is thought to interfere with the bacteria by cutting off their supply of iron, which is as essential for them as it is for any form of life. *Nitrite* binds chemically to the iron in the meat or fish and prevents it being used by the bacteria.

The amount of nitrate we take in with our food each day depends very much on what we eat. The average person consumes around 75 mg daily, and vegetarians about 200 mg. On top of this there could well be another 30 mg from the things we drink. To make matters worse, our own body produces about 50 mg of nitrate as part of its natural processes, giving a grand daily total intake of around 170 mg

---

[7] It may even do them some good, since nitrate helps some kinds of kidney stones to dissolve.

[8] *Nitrites* even improve the flavour.

for most people, and 300 mg for vegetarians. Moreover, if we have certain bowel disorders the production of nitrate by bacteria in the gut goes up dramatically.

Should these facts and figures worry us? Thankfully our body can deal with such quantities of nitrate—even 300 mg per day presents no problem. Nitrate passes from our gut to our bloodstream and is quickly filtered out by our kidneys, so that within a day of taking in a large dose we have excreted most of it. We cannot store nitrate within our body so there is no build-up that threatens to be released suddenly, and in any case it is almost impossible to poison someone by giving them nitrate. There is absolutely no need for people to become alarmed about nitrate in drinking water if their supply is within legal limits.

You might still be wondering: why has the WHO set a limit of 50 ppm, if nitrate is not a serious health hazard? And why is this limit being enforced in developed nations? The answer is that *excessive* amounts of nitrate are a health hazard, as we have seen, and tap water contributes to the nitrate which we take in each day. It is really the only source over which we have any control. An upper limit of 50 ppm for water supplies represents a generous safety margin that will protect everyone, even if it is occasionally breached.

Nitrate and human health

People are worried because of what they are told nitrate can do to them or their children. There are two commonly cited ways in which nitrate is said to pose a threat to humans: blue-baby syndrome and stomach cancer.

Blue-baby syndrome

It takes a lot of nitrate to poison a baby. Even if babies were fed water with 100 ppm of nitrate—twice the recommended limit—they would come to no harm. So why has there been concern over nitrate and babies? In fact nitrate has caused the deaths of babies who were fed on milk powder made up with water from wells that had very high levels of nitrate. The circumstances were rather exceptional. The babies turned blue and died because of excess nitrate.

The last case of blue-baby syndrome[9] in Britain was in 1972, and the baby's life was saved. The last fatal case of the disease was in the 1950s. Those at risk were babies in rural areas whose feed was made with water from wells where it was later discovered the level of nitrate could be as high as 500 ppm, ten times the level set by the World Health Organisation. In addition the well-water was contaminated with bacteria which could have exacerbated the problem by causing more nitrate to be produced in the baby's intestines.

If we follow the fate of a nitrate ion when it enters the human body we can understand why babies were at risk. The nitrate itself is harmless, as we have seen, and most nitrate passes easily through. It is the nitrate that undergoes a chemical change which does the damage. Bacteria are to blame, and these remove one of the nitrate's oxygens and so turn NO_3^- into *nitrite*, NO_2^-.

Bacteria in our gut produce about 5 mg of *nitrite* each day. Microbes in our mouths begin the process, which is continued in our stomach and intestines. White blood cells, which engulf and break down invading organisms, also make nitrate and *nitrite*. They use the amino acid **L-arginine** as their source of nitrogen, and they are stimulated to make nitrate by carbohydrate from bacteria. White blood cells are thought to produce nitrate and *nitrite* as intermediates in their production of nitric oxide. This molecule has several uses in the body, from relaxing muscles in our arteries to causing erections in men. It may also be used in the fight against infection. But there can be too much of a good thing, and this is true of *nitrite*.

All animals, including humans, have evolved to cope with a surplus of *nitrite* since it could occur quite naturally. Our first line of defence is vitamin C, which can snatch another oxygen from *nitrite* and so convert it into nitric oxide. We can not destroy all the *nitrite* in this way, and some escapes. It then targets certain of the body's metals, indeed it positively seeks them out and clings to them very strongly. In our bloodstream *nitrite* attaches to the iron atoms at the heart of haemoglobin, the molecule which carries oxygen from the lungs to where it is needed to generate energy. When *nitrite* meets haemoglobin it blocks its active iron site and turns it into methaemoglobin. Still

---

[9] Blue-baby syndrome is known as well-water methaemoglobinaemia in the USA.

we need not worry because we have enzymes to deal with this, and these remove the *nitrite* and so free the haemoglobin.

All these things happen in babies as well, but in relation to their fluid intake, a baby's blood volume is much smaller than that of an adult. An excess of nitrate, and the *nitrite* that is formed from it, will stress their metabolism much more severely. Up to 2% of a normal person's blood may be in the methaemoglobin form. If the level of methaemoglobin exceeds 10% we begin to suffer, and our skin turns a blue-grey. This is what happened with some babies, and hence the name 'blue baby' for those suffering this condition. When the level reaches 40% the baby's life is in danger, and there have been a few rare cases of bottle-fed babies dying.[10]

Breast-feeding is still the best way to nourish and protect a baby, but there is no threat to babies fed on formula foods if the level of nitrate in the water used to make them up is below 50 ppm, the legal limit. The introduction of ready-for-use formula feeds made with nitrate-free water will finally put an end to all worries about blue babies. By the year 2000 these feeds may well have displaced powdered formulas.

Cancer

The other charge levelled at nitrate is that it threatens the health of adults by causing cancer, and especially stomach cancer. The threat comes not from nitrate itself, which is not a cancer-forming chemical, nor from *nitrite* which is also not a carcinogen. The threat comes from nitrosamines, which are a group of known potent carcinogens. These can be produced in the laboratory by reacting *nitrite* with so-called amines, and because nitrosamines are present in some foods it seems likely that the same chemical reaction is producing them there too. **Dimethylnitrosamine** is the most common nitrosamine and is a powerful carcinogen. It is detectable in several foods, although levels vary as the table opposite indicates.

Nitrosamines are extremely reactive and will attack almost any other molecule, including DNA, and this is why they are so dangerous. The table shows what appear to be high levels of these in

[10] Boiling the water to make up a formula feed does not remove the nitrate, but concentrates it.

Nitrosamines in foods

Food	Nitrosamine/ppb*
Hot dog	0–84
Salami	10–80
Bacon	1–60
Smoked fish	4–26
Fried fish	1–9
Cheese	1–4

*Ranges given in parts per billion (ppb), which is the same as millionths of a gram per kilogram.

commonly eaten foods, but the amounts are really tiny, and our body's defences will easily cope with them at the normal daily intake. If you ate a rasher of bacon (50 g) every day for 50 years, and even assuming it had the highest level of 60 parts per billion of nitrosamine, you would still only consume 0.05 g of nitrosamine in all that time.

Nitrosamines are very reactive molecules and the danger is that they will reach the heart of a living cell and attack the DNA. If this happens the damage has to be repaired. This is a relatively simple job that a cell often has to do because of the presence of other more dangerous chemicals called **free radicals**. If the cell's defences are overwhelmed, then the repair job may not be perfect. If this happens we have a potentially cancerous cell. Once this cell starts to replicate itself, and not be recognised as alien, we are in trouble. Luckily we have evolved a whole defence system to protect us against free radicals, and they are quickly rendered harmless by molecules such as vitamins C and E, and these also protect us against nitrosamines.[11]

As we have seen, nitrate is a perfectly normal and natural part of many vegetables, but that does not mean that it could not be a factor in causing cancer. If the sequence: nitrate → *nitrite* → nitrosamines → cancer, really does operate in our gut, then an increase of nitrate in

---

[11] If you like to start the day with fried bacon and are still worried about nitrosamines, then you can take some evasive action. Microwave your bacon rather than fry it: this produces less nitrosamine because it is quicker and allows less time for them to form. If you fry your bacon, don't dip your bread into the bacon fat because this is where most of the nitrosamines end up. Also drink fresh orange juice (rich in vitamin C), or have some wheat germ (rich in vitamin E).

our diet could lead to an increase of cancers in those parts of the body such as the stomach and intestines.

There are those who seek to link high levels of nitrate in the water supply to the incidence of stomach and colon cancers in particular regions. Attempts to show such a link have met with little success. We might have expected that those most at risk would be the workers making nitrate fertilisers in the chemical industry. This employs a large number of people, and an analysis of their health should indicate whether high exposure to nitrate has led to an increased incidence of cancer. In 1986, the 1300 men who had worked at a fertiliser plant between 1946 and 1981 were studied. Their saliva was sampled and, as we might expect, it showed them to have double the level of nitrate of the rest of the population. Nevertheless they suffered no more cases of cancers of the stomach, oesophagus, bladder or liver than expected. In fact, they were generally healthier than average.

In another investigation, the saliva from patients admitted to hospital with cancer was tested for nitrate, and so was saliva from their families and friends who came to visit them. This ingenious test was designed to measure the nitrate levels in people who were likely to have been exposed to the same levels of nitrate in the drinking water as the cancer patients. The results of this survey revealed that people in areas with high nitrate levels suffered *fewer* cases of stomach cancer than those in areas of low nitrate in drinking water. So much for the nitrate → *nitrite* → nitrosamines → cancer theory, yet the remark that nitrate leads to cancer is still frequently made by those who oppose the use of nitrate fertilisers. We have seen that there may be reasons for opposing the overuse of nitrate fertilisers in farming, but persuading us that this will prevent cancer is not one of them.

Conclusions

Inorganic nitrate fertilisers double or treble crop yields and make farming profitable, and there is no getting away from this fact. If any country were to abandon their use there would be a dramatic fall in crop production and a concomitant rise in food prices. The vulnerable sections of society—the unemployed, the poorly paid, and the old—would be worst affected, since a larger proportion of their income is spent on food.

Longer-term alternatives to nitrate fertilisers are possible. With biotechnology we may even be able one day to design all food crops so they are like legumes, and can fix atmospheric nitrogen. No nitrate fertiliser would then be needed. The prospects of doing this are still very remote.

Nitrate is a perfectly natural part of the world around us. We take it into our bodies, we make it there, and we dispose of it easily. Even that which turns into *nitrite* appears to pose no real threat, although this is the precursor of nitrosamines in some foods. Nor are babies at risk from nitrates, even if they are bottle-fed, as long as the water does not exceed the WHO limit of 50 ppm, and it rarely does.

You may still want to take some action as an individual that might help reduce nitrate levels in rivers, and thereby prevent their being choked with water weeds and algae. I can give you no easy advice. The best course of action might seem to be to stop eating meat. Growing crops to feed farm animals for slaughter is a very inefficient process. Less nitrate would be used if humans took in more of their protein as vegetable protein rather than animal protein. Yet to grow more crops we need to plough up more grassland, and as we have seen that results in even more nitrate draining into rivers. And if you become a vegetarian you take in more nitrate anyway. Happily, this sacrifice would appear to pose no serious threat to your health.

CHAPTER NINE

Carbon Dioxide

Carbon dioxide, CO_2; greenhouse gases; the global CO_2 budget; global warming; the good side of carbon dioxide

IF you ask someone which chemical presents the greatest threat to the environment, they would probably reply 'carbon dioxide'. Which would not surprise us, because we are continually warned that this is the greenhouse gas which will cause global warming in the next century, and in so doing will make parts of the Earth uninhabitable. Most people are probably not aware that such warnings and predictions are based solely on computer simulations, nor are they told that there has already been an increase of over 25% in the level of atmospheric carbon dioxide this century, with no reliable signs of global warming. Although some environmentalists find this rather puzzling, we can explain the anomaly with a little chemical understanding.

Carbon dioxide is produced every time we burn something containing carbon, whether it be a cigarette, a bonfire in the back garden, gas in our heating system, or petrol in our car. If we switch on a light we produce it because we consume electricity, and this is generally produced by burning coal, oil or gas in a power station. Almost everything we do produces more CO_2.

Carbon dioxide is a greenhouse gas, of that there is no doubt. But if we take a closer look at the gases of the atmosphere, including carbon dioxide, we discover that CO_2 has already contributed almost all it can to global warming and is really a spent force. Its ability to cause further warming is debatable. This chapter will take a closer look at carbon dioxide itself, and explain why it, along with other molecules, is called a greenhouse gas. We will consider the various issues which surround this controversial chemical. How much of this gas is there in the atmosphere? How much are we adding each year? Where does it all go.

We will also look at other less well-known aspects of this chemical, such as its role as an industrial resource.

Carbon dioxide, CO_2

There is a lot of carbon dioxide in the Earth's atmosphere—about 2750 billion tons in total—but the concentration in air is quite low, about 0.035% or, as it is more usually reported for amounts this small, 350 parts per million (ppm) by volume. Most CO_2 in the atmosphere is released from natural sources such as the soil, the sea and subterranean depths. Indeed, the human contribution to atmospheric CO_2 is small by comparison. At the beginning of the Industrial Revolution 250 years ago the concentration was around 280 ppm. This amount did not change significantly until about a century ago when we began to exploit oil. It started going up more steeply about 40 years ago with rapid industrialisation around the world and the growing popularity of the motor car, of which there are now over 400 million. Atmospheric CO_2 levels are rising by about 1 ppm per year, but only a fraction of the CO_2 we emit to the atmosphere each year remains there: some is taken up by plants, some is absorbed by the sea, and a lot dissolves in rainwater. It becomes part of the carbon cycle of Nature.

The amount of CO_2 extracted from the atmosphere by living plants is estimated to be about 350 billion tonnes per year, with a roughly equal amount passing back as these are eaten by animals, or as they die and decay. A similar amount of around 350 billion tonnes of CO_2 probably moves back and forth between the atmosphere and the sea each year. It is against these massive changes that the human release of 22 billion tonnes a year from fossil fuels seems relatively unimportant, but over a century or so this could become significant and might make all the difference in tipping the global environment into an unstable state. Later in this chapter we will look at the various compartments of the environment and the amount of carbon each contains.

Carbon dioxide is not in itself a dangerous chemical. Indeed, as a refrigerant it has probably saved many lives, and those who have died from CO_2 have been killed by natural CO_2 erupting from deep below the surface of the Earth. It was from a subterranean source, below Lake Nyos in western Cameroon, that massive bubbles of CO_2 suddenly surfaced one night in August 1986. Hundreds of sleeping villagers living near the lake, and thousands of their animals, died from asphyxiation as tonnes of the gas emerged from the lake and rolled over the surrounding countryside.

Less threatening is the underground 'lake' of CO_2 a mile below the surface near the extinct volcano Mount Gambier, in South Australia, which is being commercially exploited. In the USA many wells of CO_2 have been discovered while drilling for oil, and the gas from some of these wells has been put to use. It is piped hundreds of miles to oil fields where it is re-injected into oil-bearing rocks to force out more oil from wells that were thought to be exhausted. The Western Texas oil-field will eventually yield an extra 56 billion barrels of oil this way.

You might wonder why there should be large deposits of CO_2 underground. Part of the answer is a natural release of gases from the molten rock deep below the crust, and which we observe when a volcano erupts. However, a lot of CO_2 in the Earth's crust is of biological origin, and comes from prehistoric plants. Their organic matter that gave rise to coal, oil and natural gas was mainly carbohydrate, which consists of carbon, hydrogen and oxygen. It underwent the chemical transformation due to the heat and pressure in the Earth's crust, when some of the carbohydrate ended up as hydrocarbons, and some as CO_2.

Billions of tons of carbon are cycling through all parts of the environment, and have been doing so for hundreds of millions of years. In our pre-industrial state the human race was a part of the natural order, but then we started tapping the energy of fossil carbon that was locked away in the Earth's crust. Since the Industrial Revolution began in the mid-18th century, we have unlocked vast reserves of fossil carbon, almost always to burn it. We have done this on such a large scale that we have increased the amount of CO_2 faster than other natural processes in the cycle could dispose of it.

Early analytical chemists who measured the concentration of CO_2 in the air found it varied considerably with the time of year and the location. The limits of accuracy of their analyses were such that they could not register small global changes. An agreed reference point was needed and this is now the value published regularly by the monitoring facility at Mauna Loa in Hawaii.[1] This started reporting CO_2 levels in the 1950s, and for almost 40 years scientists there have observed the seasonal ups and downs in the level of CO_2 in the atmosphere of the mid-Pacific. These have shown an overall upward trend, rising from 315 ppm in 1958 to over 350 ppm today. Environmentalists blame this increase in CO_2 on two main factors: industrialised nations using fossil fuels, and Third World countries burning forests to clear land for agriculture. As the change seemed always to be upwards, people quite naturally began to wonder what effect it might be having.

Greenhouse gases

Of the energy from the Sun which falls on the Earth, less than half warms the surface. The clouds and oceans reflect about 30% straight back into space. Another 25% is absorbed by the atmosphere itself. The remaining 45% which heats the planet also has eventually to be reflected back into space as radiant heat (more correctly called infrared rays), otherwise as more and more heat is trapped the planet would get hotter and hotter. The radiated heat, however, has to pass back through the atmosphere, and molecules in the air are able to trap it and reflect some of it back down again. This is the greenhouse effect, and the molecules which behave this way are called greenhouse gases, of which CO_2 is the best known. But CO_2 is not the most important—water vapour is.

The effect of trapping the Sun's energy for heat is one that we are familiar with in a normal greenhouse. The glass allows rays from the Sun to enter, but prevents the warm air from escaping. An analogy

---

[1] Some scientists have questioned the wisdom of siting such an important global facility at Mauna Loa, because it is located on the side of a volcano which erupts on average every three and a half years, and it is only 27 km from the largest active volcanic crater in the world.

can be made with the planet; if molecules in the atmosphere stop radiant heat escaping, this too will warm up. It was a little misleading of the proponents of global warming to speak as if releasing CO_2 was the equivalent of building a greenhouse round the planet, although this was the image often used to drive home their message. In fact we *need* the atmosphere to act as a greenhouse, to prevent too much heat escaping into space, otherwise we would experience daily fluctuations of temperature like those of the Moon, and that would make life impossible.

The atmosphere consists of several gases, of which **nitrogen**[2] and **oxygen** account for 99% of the total volume, and **argon** accounts for most of the remaining 1%. The other gases are there in only tiny amounts, and for this reason we do not talk of them in percentage terms but in units of parts per million (ppm). Of the lesser gases, the most abundant appears to be CO_2 at 350 ppm, and this is what you will find if you consult tables which give the composition of the atmosphere. You will not find water vapour mentioned because such tables will be referring to samples of *dry* air. Water vapour is excluded because the amount varies so markedly, and it ranges from a fraction of 1% on a very cold day, to 4% on a hot, humid day. The table opposite gives two sets of data for the gases of the atmosphere: the 'dry air' one which is commonly quoted, and a 'normal air' one in which I have recalculated the concentrations assuming there is 2% water vapour present. You will see that water vapour is really the third most abundant gas in the atmosphere. It is also the most powerful greenhouse gas.

The Earth's atmosphere keeps the temperature reasonably stable, smoothing out the daily changes, and the seasonal ones. The vapour which does this so effectively is water. Without water, the average temperature of the planet would be about 33 °C colder than it is. Water is very good at trapping a lot of the infrared rays which would otherwise be lost to space, and water vapour alone is responsible for a warming of roughly 32 °C, or about 97% of the greenhouse effect. Carbon dioxide helps a little bit as well, accounting for about 1 °C.

---

[2] A reminder that when the name of a substance appears in **bold** type, it means that there is more about its chemistry in the Appendix.

The composition of the atmosphere (parts per million by volume)*

	dry air	normal air**
nitrogen	781 000	766 000
oxygen	209 500	205 000
water	0	approx. 20 000
argon	9500	9000
carbon dioxide***	350	340
neon	18.2	17
helium	5.2	5
methane	1.7	1
krypton	1.1	1
hydrogen	0.6	0.5
nitrous oxide	0.3	0.3
carbon monoxide***	0.2	0.2
xenon	0.1	0.1
ozone***	0.03	0.03
CFCs	0.000 76	0.000 76

*The figures in these columns do not total to exactly 1 000 000 because of variations in the values of some of the gases and limitations to the number of significant figures for the more abundant gases. **For normal air I have assumed a figure of 20 000 for water vapour and adjusted the figures for nitrogen, oxygen, argon, etc. accordingly. ***There are seasonal variations in the amounts of these gases.

What makes a molecule act as a greenhouse gas? The answer to this question is one of chemistry: a molecule can absorb radiant heat (infrared rays) only if it has a certain kind of structure. To be a greenhouse gas, a molecule needs to have chemical bonds, because these vibrate with the same frequencies as infrared rays and can absorb them. A gas like argon (9000 ppm) consists of just single atoms and has no chemical bonds, so it cannot interact with infrared rays. The same is true of the other gases which consist of single atoms: **neon** (17 ppm), **helium** (5 ppm), **krypton** (1 ppm) and **xenon** (0.1 ppm).

Even if a molecule has a chemical bond it does not necessarily mean that it will absorb infrared rays. Those gases in which there is a single bond between two atoms of the same element can not interact with radiant heat, and this is why nitrogen N_2 (766 000 ppm), oxygen O_2 (205 000 ppm), and hydrogen H_2 (0.5 ppm) are not greenhouse gases either.[3] They have chemical bonds, but not the right kind.

---

[3] When a molecule like these vibrates there is no change in the electric field surrounding it. Without such a change it can not absorb infrared rays.

To absorb infrared rays, a molecule of two atoms must have both atoms different, such as carbon monoxide, or it must have three atoms or more. The ones in the Earth's atmosphere which therefore qualify as the chief absorbers of heat are: water (H_2O), **carbon dioxide** (CO_2), **methane** (CH_4), **nitrous oxide** (N_2O), **carbon monoxide** (CO) and **ozone** (O_3). There are lots of other molecules which qualify, such as **sulfur dioxide**, **methyl sulfides**, and the **CFCs**, but these are present only in tiny amounts.[4]

The wave band of the infrared range spans the wavelengths from 1 micron to about 40 microns (a micron is a millionth of a metre). How well a greenhouse gas reflects back radiant heat depends on how much of this range it covers. Different vibrations of a molecule occur at different wavelengths, and for a particular molecule we get a particular pattern of bands. These bands are determined by the chemical structure and are unique to each molecule. Water has many bands at many wavelengths. CO_2, on the other hand, has only two.

The infrared absorbance of the atmosphere can be recorded by passing a beam of infrared light through a sample of air and noting the wavelengths that are being absorbed by the greenhouse gas molecules. When we examine the spectrum we discover that at many wavelengths the energy is being absorbed mostly by water, whose bands blot our whole ranges of the spectrum. CO_2 absorbs radiant heat very well, but only at 4.3 microns and 15.0 microns. It traps almost all the heat being emitted at these wavelengths, but only at these wavelengths—which is why it contributes relatively little to global warming. There is a 'window' in the spectrum through which radiant heat can escape, and this is the 8–13 micron range. None of the natural greenhouse gases absorbs at these wavelengths.[5]

Once we understand that the absorbing capabilities of CO_2 are rather restricted by its chemistry, we should not be surprised that

---

[4] Even the HFCs make excellent greenhouse gases, and these are the hydrofluorocarbons that are being introduced to replace the CFCs which damage the ozone layer. The concentrations of HFCs are too small to be included in the table on p. 239.

[5] On the other hand the CFCs do absorb in this region. For example CFC-12 absorbs mainly in this region, as do most of the other molecules in which there are carbon-to-chlorine chemical bonds, such as the organochlorine solvents.

there is little relationship between the amount of this gas in the atmosphere and the average global temperature. This is why the 25% increase in CO_2 in the atmosphere during the past century can only have contributed a fraction of a degree to raising the average temperature of the Earth, and why this has not been detectable so far.

It would take about 200 years at the present rate at which CO_2 is increasing for the level of CO_2 to double to around 700 ppm. This will have an effect, but at most it will add another 1 °C to global warming. There is no way could it boost planetary temperatures by the 5 °C that some have predicted will happen in the next century. There is no way that CO_2 can behave like water as a greenhouse gas and absorb heat at many wavelengths—its chemistry will not allow it to do this.

So why was there so much alarm about CO_2? This arose through some data which seemed to show a strong link between this gas and previous global temperatures. Analyses of ice cores from deep within the polar ice-cap revealed that during the ice ages the amount of CO_2 fell, and was lowest during the coldest periods. Between the ice ages it rose, and so did the Earth's temperature. Supporters of global warming saw this as proof that the amount of CO_2 in the atmosphere was the main regulatory mechanism. The ice-core data provided what they badly needed: experimental evidence to support their computer simulations. Then in 1992 it was reported by a group of Norwegian and Japanese scientists that these ice-core data were flawed. The crude way in which the ice samples were taken meant that the chemical analysis of the CO_2 trapped in the ice was unreliable. More careful collecting of samples and more accurate analyses showed that the CO_2 trapped in the ice changes over time, and varies with the condition of the ice itself.

In the summer of 1992 more experimental results, reported in the journal *Nature*, further undermined the supposed relationship between CO_2 and global warming in the past. A new ice core had been drilled over 3000 metres down into the Greenland ice sheet, and its water had been analysed. This study had been carried out by a group of researchers from all over Europe under the auspices of GRIP, the Greenland Ice Core Project, and they had sampled snow that had fallen over the past 260 000 years, a period which included two Ice Ages and three interglacial warm periods, including the present one. The current warm period is called the Holocene era, and so far has lasted about 11 000 years. The previous ice age lasted about 100 000 years. This was preceded by the Eemian warm period of 20 000 years, and before that another Ice Age of 90 000 years.

The ice samples corresponding to the Eemian warm period were particularly revealing. During the hottest years of the Eemian period, the Earth was about 4 °C warmer than it is now, and there were lions and elephants roaming Europe. During that era temperatures sometimes fell dramatically by as much as 10 °C over a period as short as 10 years, and then the Earth remained cold for several decades or centuries before suddenly warming again. Global warming came and went several times in the Eemian period, until finally there was a warm spell of 2000 years. Such rapid changes can not be linked to a doubling, a tripling, nor even a quadrupling of the amount of CO_2 in the atmosphere. But whatever the cause, it did not last. The Earth plunged into the last Ice Age, which it did with a rapid drop in temperature of about 14 °C in only ten years.

You may be wondering how the water molecules of compacted snow which fell a hundred thousand years ago could preserve a record of the Earth's temperature. This information is locked away in their oxygen atoms. The GRIP core was studied by measuring the isotopes of oxygen, a method developed by Willi Dansgaard of the Niels Bohr Institute at the University of Copenhagen. Oxygen consists of two isotopes, oxygen-16, which accounts for 99.8% of all oxygen, and oxygen-18, of which there is 0.2%. Oxygen-18, as its name implies, has a mass of 18 because it has two extra neutrons. Slightly more energy is needed to evaporate water with oxygen-18, and the result is that as the climate gets colder, the amount of this in snow decreases slightly. Chemists can measure the oxygen-18 to oxygen-16 ratio very accurately using a mass spectrometer, and relate this to the temperature of the winter in which the snow fell; the colder the winter, the lower this ratio.

Our present interglacial warm period, the Holocene, has not been without its ups and downs. A Little Ice Age from the sixteenth to the nineteenth centuries saw the Alpine glaciers advance and winter fairs held on a frozen Thames in London and ice-bound canals of Holland. Indeed, the threat of a new Ice Age was the concern of many environmentalists and meteorologists in the 1970s, who based their predictions on falling global temperatures recorded from 1940 to 1970. This happened despite the rising level of CO_2 in the atmosphere.

Nevertheless, in the 1980s the Earth appeared to be warming and the earlier ice-core CO_2 data seemed to be proof that this warming could cause a global climate change. In the 1990s it appears to be cooling, and there were several unusual happenings: Hudson's Bay stayed ice-bound throughout the cold summer of 1992. There were snowstorms in Florida in early 1993, followed by another cool, wet summer, and record low temperatures in the winter of 1993/4. Of course this kind of local evidence is as unrepresentative as the heat-waves and droughts of the 1980s. What is required is a *global* average.

It is easy to measure accurately the temperature of the Earth at any one point, but it is not easy to turn millions of such recordings into an average for the whole Earth, most of which is covered by sea. A satellite, on the other hand, can take a temperature picture of the whole planet, and much store was set on the data this would provide. In the summer of 1993 Dr John Christy of America's space agency, NASA, reported a 14-year study. Despite extensive searches using the most advanced technology, their satellite had found no global warming between 1979 and 1993. Apparently the rising level of CO_2 was still having no effect.

This is reassuring, but not unexpected from what we know of CO_2. However, we should not become complacent because there are other gases being added to the atmosphere that can absorb radiant heat at wavelengths in the 8–13 micron window which currently allows heat to escape from the Earth. One such gas is methane, which comes mainly from natural sources, but is also building up in the atmosphere as a result of human activity. Some of this gas escapes from leaks in gas pipelines, some is generated by rotting organic matter in landfill sites, some is given off by paddy fields, termite mounds, and some is produced in the stomachs of cows and in the intestines of many domestic animals. Indeed, humans also add to the methane in the atmosphere in this way.

Other volatile hydrocarbons will also absorb infrared heat in the same region of the spectrum, as will any gas with carbon–hydrogen bonds. When you fill up your car at a petrol station, the incoming petrol will displace the same volume of hydrocarbon-saturated air from the fuel tank, and this will then act as a greenhouse gas. Petrol companies are already alert to this danger and are now finding ways of reclaiming these lost hydrocarbons by installing air filtering units at fuel depots and even at service stations.[6]

Hydrocarbons cannot linger for long in the atmosphere because they are susceptible to reaction with the oxygen of the air. Other greenhouse gases that we are producing will linger longer, such as the CFCs. The countries who signed the Montreal Protocol of 1987 agreed to the phasing out of the CFCs by the end of the century, and they agreed to speed this up at their London meeting in 1990. These gases are being controlled not because of their contribution to global warming, but because the chlorine they contain threatens the ozone layer. The gases which are set to replace them, the **hydro-fluorocarbons** (HFCs), do not contain chlorine so at least they are not able to deplete the ozone. They could still contribute a little to global warming though.

The global CO_2 budget

Even though CO_2 may not be the greenhouse threat which we were led to believe, it is still pouring into the atmosphere. In some respects this is a measure of human folly. There are now far too many of us, and as we go about our business, building, farming, burning, and wasting, we are producing CO_2. Our great grandchildren may not blame us for global warming by doing this, but they might blame us for a global squandering of resources that has achieved little of which we can be proud.

All the carbon that is locked away in deposits of gas, oil and coal was once CO_2 in the Earth's atmosphere. We saw in the last chapter that there is a nitrogen cycle in Nature, and similarly there is a carbon cycle which circulates this element through the environment, and through all living things. We can trace the route of a carbon atom as it moves through this cycle. It starts with CO_2 in the atmosphere, and then with the help of sunlight and the chlorophyll in the leaves of plants it reacts with water to form carbohydrate. This may then move

---

[6] When they do they can trap the petrol that evaporates and sell it again.

through the cycle within a few weeks by being eaten and used as a source of animal energy, and as a result the carbon will be breathed out again as CO_2. On the other hand it may be incorporated into other molecules and remain locked away for a year, a century, or even a million years or more, before it returns to the atmosphere.

When humans evolved they had little impact on the environment until they started felling and burning trees, draining land and farming, but even then they only speeded up the cycle without increasing the amount of carbon moving through it. Humans started to make a significant contribution when we began burning fossil fuels and greatly increasing our numbers. What effect are we having?

Human activity generates CO_2 in six important ways. Three of these return the CO_2 whence it came, to the air, and the other three add CO_2 to the atmosphere from sources that were locked away underground. The first three are breathing, rearing farm animals and using wood. The second three are making cement, burning fossil fuels and draining land for cultivation. Together these add up to a yearly total of over three million litres of CO_2 per head of population. This is about the capacity of a large hall of $30 \times 10 \times 10$ metres (roughly $100 \times 30 \times 30$ feet). If you prefer to think in weights of CO_2 rather than volumes then this is six tonnes per person (see the Box). In some regions the release per person is less than a million litres per year, while in others, such as the USA and Europe, it is over ten million litres.

How to measure CO_2: units of volume or weight?

Gases, like liquids, are measured in volumes, and the litre is a convenient measure of volume that most people can understand since it is the size of a mineral water bottle. Americans may not be as familiar as Europeans with this quantity, but a rough equivalent is a quart. This is about 5% smaller than a litre. When volumes get larger it is more convenient to talk in terms of a cubic metre, which equals 1000 litres. The cubic metre is 1.307 cubic yards, and this volume is the same as 880 quarts. With even larger volumes the cubic metre measure is not adequate, for example when we are considering global totals of CO_2. Then it is easier to talk in terms of weight, in this case in metric tonnes. A tonne of CO_2 occupies 500 cubic metres or 500 000 litres. A tonne is about 10% larger than a US ton.

Let us begin by looking at the CO_2 which we produce in our own bodies. Most of the food we eat provides us with energy, and this comes mainly from carbohydrates and fat. The average person needs 2200 kilocalories of energy per day from food, and if this were all derived from carbohydrate then we would need to consume 550 grams (20 ounces). Our yearly requirement would be 200 kg. Of course we cannot live only on carbohydrate, but for the sake of our calculations let us assume that all our energy is coming from this source.[7]

The molecular weight of a carbohydrate, formula $C_6H_{12}O_6$, is 180 units, and when this is burnt or used as fuel in our bodies it ends up as six molecules of CO_2 which together weigh 264 units. Therefore if we consume 200 kg of carbohydrate a year this would end up as 300 kg of CO_2 expelled from our lungs. In volume terms this is 150 000 litres, which works out about at 17 litres per hour. This tallies with the observed rate of exhalation.

We could do the same sort of calculation for domestic animals, who owe their very existence to human needs. The number of these of course probably exceeds the number of humans by quite a margin, so it is not easy to estimate how much CO_2 they are breathing out each year. One reasonable estimate is that it amounts to an annual total of 2 billion tonnes, which is 370 kg, or 185 000 litres, for every human being on the planet.[8]

But the human activity which returns most CO_2 to the atmosphere is our use of wood. Again it is difficult to put a figure on the amount of wood that is cut down each year, and estimates vary between 3.5 billion metric tons and 7 billion metric tons. Most of this is harvested in the Third World where it is used for cooking, which of course returns it immediately to CO_2. Even the wood that is used in industrial countries as paper products and building material eventually ends up this way—fairly quickly if our waste goes to a municipal incinerator, more slowly if we recycle it, and very slowly if it ends up in

[7] We could do a much more sophisticated calculation based on our total diet, and we could actually measure the amount of CO_2 we evolved during the course of a whole day, but as we are only talking in round figures for the average human, precise measurements on an individual are not much help.

[8] These figures are not as exact as they appear, and are based on the conversion factors in the Box on p. 245. Another way of expressing them would be to the nearest round number, i.e. 400 kg or 200 000 litres.

landfill sites and decomposes over the centuries. We may delay its
return by using it for books, furniture or house-building, but even
these are finally burnt or rot away. If we assume the destruction of 5
billion metric tons of wood per year, this will turn to 7 billion tons of
CO_2 when burnt, or 1.3 tons per person, which in volume terms is
650 000 litres.[9]

The CO_2 from our food, our animals and our use of wood came
from the air in the first place, so all we are doing is putting it back. If
humans didn't do that other creatures might, so we are not upsetting
the carbon cycle by these actions: this release of CO_2 is merely
recycling it. The 'natural' CO_2 adds up to about a million litres per
person per year, and I have given these figures so that we can put into
perspective the 'new' CO_2 that we add to the atmosphere each year.

Let us now turn to the CO_2 we are releasing from carbon in the
Earth's crust, the CO_2 that has been long locked away. There are
large deposits of mineral carbonates such as limestone (which is
calcium carbonate) and **dolomite** (which is mixed magnesium
and calcium carbonate). Cement works roast a billion (1000 million) metric tons of limestone a year and this drives off 440 million
metric tons of CO_2. A further 200 million metric tons of limestone is
heated in kilns to make lime for agriculture and industry, and this adds
another 90 million metric tons, making a total of 530 million metric
tons of CO_2 in all. Consequently cement and lime manufacture is
adding about 50 000 litres per person per year to the atmosphere, and
this does not include the fuel burnt to do the roasting. That is
included in our next calculation.

The amount of CO_2 from fossil resources is easy to compute since a
careful tally is made of the natural gas, oil and coal that is used each
year. For example the BP Statistical Review of World Energy for 1993
reveals that together these totalled 7073 million metric tons of 'oil
equivalent'. This is made up of 3128 million tons of oil, 1781 million
tons of natural gas, and 2164 million tons of coal. Natural gas is mainly
methane, chemical formula CH_4, oil is a complex mixture of hydrocarbons of average chemical composition CH_2, and coal is even more
complex, has even less hydrogen, and is roughly CH. To have every-

---

[9] The calculation is the same as for carbohydrate, which is what wood mainly is.

thing reduced to 'oil equivalent' means our calculation of how much CO_2 is given off is easy. When CH_2 turns to CO_2, then 14 tonnes of 'oil equivalent' turns into 44 tonnes of CO_2.

The release of CO_2 from fossil reserves in a developed country comes in roughly equal proportions from power stations, transport, industry and heating. Of course, not all fossil fuel is burnt, but by far the major part is, and even that which is turned into plastics, textiles, and paints eventually suffers the same fate as the products from wood, and ends up as gas in the atmosphere. The average fossil fuel used per person is 1.75 metric tonnes per year, which converts to 4.1 tonnes of CO_2 or 2 050 000 litres—twice the amount we release from 'natural' sources. The amount of CO_2 per head of population from fossil fuel varies considerably from country to country. The countries with the highest totals are the US and Canada, where it is about 15 tonnes per person per year, and Europe and Japan, where it is in excess of 7 tonnes.

Finally there is an unknown amount of CO_2 we release by our draining of land for agricultural use. Wetland locks up a lot of organic matter as humus, which slowly turns to peat and eventually would end up as other fossil fuels if it were to experience pressure and temperature as a result of geological action over millions of years. As far as I am aware no one has yet put a figure on the CO_2 from the land itself, but intensive agriculture slowly reduces the organic content of soils, and this is mainly carbon based. The agricultural release of CO_2 from this source might indeed be quite large, but we can not include it in our calculations—all we can do is remember that what follows is an underestimate of the amounts of CO_2 released each year as a result of human activity.

If we total all the above sources we find the average human is responsible for not less than 3 million litres of CO_2 being emitted into the atmosphere each year. The inventory is as follows:

	litres
Breathing	150 000
Rearing farm animals	185 000
Using wood	650 000
Making cement	50 000
Using fossil fuels	2 050 000
Total per person	**3 085 000**

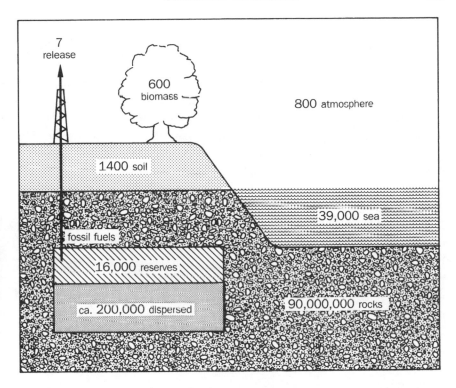

The Earth's carbon. The amounts shown are in billions of tonnes of carbon (10^9). The carbon in the atmosphere is mainly CO_2, that in the sea and rocks is carbonate, and the fossil fuel forms are mainly hydrocarbons or coal.

This works out at 6.2 metric tonnes per person, giving a grand total of 33 billion tonnes per year for the planet as a whole. At this point you may be getting a little weary of large numbers and you still do not know how this number compares with the overall distribution of carbon on the Earth. The diagram above shows the amounts of carbon in the major compartments of the environment. This information is expressed as weights of carbon to take into account all the varied forms in which carbon exists. For the atmosphere this means talking of carbon even though it is there as CO_2.[10]

[10] It is easy to convert from one to the other because a tonne of CO_2 contains 0.27 tonnes of carbon. The 2750 billion tonnes of CO_2 in the atmosphere represent 800 billion tonnes of carbon.

The amount released to the atmosphere from fossil fuels is 7 billion tonnes per year, adding to the 800 billion tonnes already there in the atmosphere. This is roughly 1%, and yet the amount in the atmosphere goes up only by less than a third of this each year. The reason is that CO_2 dissolves in the sea, and is washed out in rainwater. Most importantly of all, the plants of the planet, the so-called biomass, convert CO_2 to the chemicals that are needed by living cells. This also takes place in the upper layers of the sea and it is now thought that the amount of carbon dioxide these absorb has been greatly underestimated. The transfer of carbon to other compartments removes most of the extra carbon added from fossil fuels, but it is not clear where a lot of CO_2 is ending up. Some obviously could be going into increased growth by plants and especially the trees of the forests which still cover large tracts of the Earth. A fully mature forest does not have a net input of carbon dioxide because there is a balance between growth, which absorbs CO_2, and respiration and decay which release it. But if the level of CO_2 in the atmosphere increases, so does plant growth. This is one positive effect of CO_2 which is made use of in commercial greenhouses, as we shall see.

The level of CO_2 in the atmosphere is rising, and we can link the increase to the burning of fossil fuels. This can go on at the present rate for a long time yet, but reserves are finite, even though the success in finding new ones more than keeps pace with the rate at which they are being used up.[11] One day they will become too expensive to extract, however advanced our technology, but that might be a thousand years in the future. Then we may stand condemned for the sheer waste of so much of it. Future generations may well ask why we used these fossil reserves to such unworthy ends as heating buildings that were badly insulated, generating electricity in such an inefficient manner, or driving a car when we could walk or cycle.

---

[11] If the 1000 trillion tonnes of oxygen in the Earth's atmosphere all originated from photosynthesis by plants of CO_2 then we can calculate that the amount of carbon locked away in the crust could be an astounding 375 *trillion* tonnes. Much of it is too dispersed to use as a fuel.

Global warming

An Atmospheric Temperature Workshop held in the USA in 1991 issued a report which contained the following warning: 'The specific concern today is that the exponentially increasing concentrations of anthropogenically introduced greenhouse gases will, sooner or later, irreversibly alter the climate of the Earth and thereby disrupt global weather distribution, agricultural production, water supplies and other economic and social activities.' Put in plain language, this says that because humans are releasing greenhouse gases in ever-increasing amounts, sooner or later we will damage the Earth's climate, causing droughts, floods, famine and economic ruin. The authors made these doleful forecasts on the basis of calculations carried out on 'the most powerful supercomputers available.' The meeting concluded that the most pressing need was to run even bigger computer simulations, and to discuss the data from these at more workshop meetings around the world.

When computer modellers took it upon themselves in the late 1980s to predict what might happen if the level of CO_2 in the atmosphere were to double, they came up with a forecast of global warming of 5.2 °C. If the level of CO_2 were to rise by 1% per annum this might occur within 70 years, they said. Such a rapid change in climate, over so short a period, would melt polar ice and flood the low-lying areas of the globe.[12] The world was warned of the catastrophes that lay ahead. Only a few years earlier there had been alarms about global cooling and the imminent ice age. This was rather unfairly recalled by Douglas Story in a letter to the American Chemical Society's weekly magazine *Chemistry & Engineering News* in September 1993:

'I am concerned about our public integrity when I see the people who lectured in the early 1970s at my university about the coming environmental disaster of global cooling, now lecturing (and making a good living at it) about the coming disasters of global warming. It scares me to see other scientists and the media starting efforts ... to substantiate the theories of these guys. It petrifies me to know that government bureaucrats and politicians are developing social and business policies based upon this camera-lens science.'

[12] Only ice sheets on land can raise sea levels when they melt. If all the ice at the North Pole, which is sea-ice, were to melt, it would have no effect on sea levels. Ice floats on water because it is less dense than water and when the floating ice melts, the level of liquid does not change.

Those earlier warnings of an approaching ice age were overtaken by events when the global temperature, which had been falling from 1940 to 1970, suddenly went up a little. The message of doom changed accordingly: the world was now in danger, not of freezing in the next century, but of overheating. The prophets even suggested why this might happen: there was too much carbon dioxide going into the atmosphere.

The present concerns about global warming really began in the summer of 1988 when predictions based on computer-simulations were published. These forecast that the world was about to warm up rapidly. There would be worldwide floods as the ice at the poles melted and sea levels would rise by as much as 8 metres (25 feet). This message of a Second Flood was taken up by the media, and soon even politicians were voicing alarms of global warming. Paperback books appeared, explaining the message in graphic detail. Some environmentalists and meteorologists warned of mass evacuations of people as Pacific islands disappeared, and mass migrations of refugees from Bangladesh and other low-lying regions of Asia, which are among the world's most populated regions.

The main protagonist behind all this agitation was The Intergovernmental Panel on Climate Change (IPCC). In 1988, members of the World Meteorological Organization and the United Nations Environment Programme set up the IPCC to assess the available scientific information on climate change, and the environmental impact this might have. The IPCC formed itself into three committees, one to look at the evidence for climate change, a second to forecast the results of such changes, and a third to suggest what could be done.

The first of the committees was the most important because its findings would determine the validity of the others. The so-called Working Group I published its deliberations in July 1990. The report was the work of 170 scientists in 25 countries.[13] The IPCC blamed CO_2 for being the main contributor to the enhanced greenhouse

[13] The report admitted that there were some scientists who did not agree with the IPCC findings. Their views were ignored. However, a survey of climatologists in 1991 showed that fewer than 20% of them believed in imminent global warming.

effect, along with other gases such as methane, nitrous oxide and the CFCs, and concluded that an immediate 60% reduction in the emissions of these gases was necessary to prevent them from further increasing in the atmosphere. The IPCC predicted that if we continued to emit these gases at the present levels, then the temperature of the Earth would rise by 3 °C in the next century, and this would lead to a rise in sea level of 65 cm. The report admitted there were uncertainties in their predictions because their computer simulations could not take into account clouds, oceans and polar ice sheets.

The doubts and uncertainties were ignored by environmental pressure groups and their supporters, who promoted the message of the IPCC with gusto. No publicity was given to the warning in the IPCC report that it was 'neither an academic review, nor a plan for a new research programme.' The environmentalists behaved as if the report was an official document issued jointly by the world's governments, as its very name seemed to imply. Coming on top of a series of warm winters and hot summers in the Northern Hemisphere, the IPCC report seemed to confirm what people were really experiencing: the world was rapidly warming up. Regrettably the scientists of the IPCC did nothing to check this alarmist scenario; indeed, by not refuting their wilder supporters they appeared to agree with them. Some popular science writers gave their imaginations full throttle, and talked of runaway global warming with the world eventually heating to almost 500 °C (the 'Venus scenario')[14], while others spoke of the Western Antarctic ice sheet suddenly sliding into the sea causing an instant tidal wave that would sweep the world and cause the sea level to rise by 9 metres (30 feet).

The 1990 IPCC report calculated that as more CO_2 from fossil fuels forced up the temperature, water vapour would become a threat in that it would provide positive feedback, thereby enhancing global warming. As the temperature went up, more water would evaporate from the oceans. This would increase the greenhouse effect, which in turn would encourage more water to evaporate, and so on.

Other effects were also taken into account, such as increased plant growth and decay, and the loss of soil moisture, but again these were

[14] Venus's atmosphere is 96% CO_2 and with a pressure of 90 times that of the Earth's. Under such conditions the two infrared bands of CO_2 experience pressure broadening, enabling tham to trap a wider range of radiant heat than on the Earth.

assumed only to make matters worse. All these factors were duly allowed for in the IPCC's model of the Earth's atmosphere, using a program referred to as the General Circulation Model (GCM). The output from this computer simulation was the foundation on which their predictions were based. The 1990 report also contained a rather misleading diagram that was to be reproduced many times. This showed that greenhouse gases produced from human activity contributed to the change in global warming in the proportions: CO_2 55%, CFCs 24%, methane 15%, and nitrous oxide 6%. It was not surprising that people began to read and hear that CO_2 was the single most important greenhouse gas.

Perhaps aware of what was to follow, the IPCC belatedly tried to maintain its credibility within the scientific community by stressing the uncertainty inherent in its predictions, but these reservations were not given quite the same publicity as their earlier warning of calamitous global warming. The IPCC acknowledges the difficulty in measuring global average temperature before the mid-19th century, but it felt able to say that since 1860 there has been an increase of 0.4 Celsius, mainly from 1910 to 1940. At the end of its first report in 1990 IPCC stressed the need for more funding so that researchers could have access to the fastest possible computers. This would enable them to take into account the links between the atmosphere and the oceans, and also to make more detailed regional predictions. The funding was forthcoming.

In 1992 the IPCC published a Supplement, the text of which was agreed at a meeting of Working Group I at Guangzhou, China, in January 1992, which was attended by 170 delegates from 47 countries. New modelling studies had not confirmed the wilder claims of the 1990 report. The IPCC now came to the conclusion that global warming due to CO_2 was not likely to be a runaway process after all, would not exceed 4.5 °C, and may even be as little as 1 °C. The IPCC also said that the increase in global warming in the past 100 years fell within the usual climate variability and could even be due to other causes. Their most telling statement was that 'the unequivocal detection of the enhanced greenhouse effect from observations is not likely for a decade or more.' The computer model was now able to take into account ocean–atmosphere effects but still could not cope with clouds, which of course have a profound effect.[15]

Moreover, a new uncertainty had crept into the computer modelling: sulfate dust. Specks of sulfate from industrial emissions of sulfur compounds have a cooling effect, especially in the industrialised Northern Hemisphere. The link between global temperature and the 11-year cycle of activity of the Sun was acknowledged as likely to play a part, but it was not possible to include this factor in the model. And the IPCC modellers could still not find where 7 billion tonnes of atmospheric CO_2 were disappearing to each year. They also calculated that most global warming is occurring at night time in the Northern Hemisphere—if it is occurring at all.

They also noted that the part of the greenhouse effect which could be attributed to CO_2 did not relate to the amounts of CO_2 in the atmosphere. Again to quote the 1992 IPCC report: 'the estimates of warming over the last 100 years due to increases in greenhouse gases made in the original report may be somewhat too rapid.' The report concludes that much more work needs to be done, especially in conjunction with social scientists, to develop new scenarios. What is needed, the report says, are better computer simulations, more accurate temperature measurements, more support for climate research around the world, and yet more meetings.

Clearly something had to be done, and alarmed by all this, governments around the world continue to pour funds into meteorological research. (The US Government alone will have spent $2 billion by the year 2000.) Global warming research groups sprang up with proposals on ways in which this bounteous funding could be employed. Most proposals were based on the use of larger computers, although some came up with ingenious but ingenuous ways of disposing of the CO_2 (see the Box on the next page).

The global warming facts, figures, fantasies and fictions are neatly summarised in *The Heated Debate* by Dr Robert Balling Jr, director of The Office of Climatology at Arizona State University, which was published in 1992. This readable and balanced account explains the background to the alarms of the 1980s. Balling pleads for a more

---

[15] We are all aware how important clouds are. The hottest days and the coldest nights are those without a cloud in the sky. Cloud cover moderates both extremes very effectively.

rigorous approach to the discussion of climatic research, and a more balanced approach to the forecasting of climate change. Both have been sadly lacking in recent years.

How to dispose of CO_2

Assuming that CO_2 emissions to the atmosphere should be reduced, then one way would be to burn more of the fuel which produces the least CO_2. Another way is to collect the CO_2 that is being generated and put it somewhere other than into the atmosphere.

Burning coal produces more CO_2 than burning oil, but burning natural gas produces least of all. A rough guide is that for every million calories of energy produced, we release about 400 grams of CO_2 if we use coal, 300 g if we use oil, and 200 g if we use natural gas. This solution to the problem would only last for a few years until the supplies of natural gas were exhausted, and this will happen anyway within 50 years, after which we will be forced to use more oil and coal. Oil will run out in about 125 years, although supplies of coal will last for over 1000 years.

Alternatively we can trap the CO_2 emitted by the major users of fossil fuels, such as power stations, and prevent its release to the atmosphere. One suggestion is that we should liquefy the gas and pump it into the deep oceans. The chemistry behind such a suggestion shows it is feasible. Collecting and shipping CO_2 as a liquid presents no technological problems, nor will pumping it to the ocean depths where the temperature is about 2 Celsius. At such a temperature a pressure of 37 atmosphere is needed to keep CO_2 a liquid, and this pressure is reached below 400 metres.

In theory, then, we can dispose of CO_2 into the ocean, and since there is little mixing between the depths and the surface layers, the CO_2 would be safely locked away. But just how much of the 22 billion tonnes of CO_2 which comes from fossil fuels each year we could reasonably dispose of in this way is another question—it would take 1000 pressurised supertankers each carrying 500 000 tonnes and making one trip a week to transport this amount. There is also a risk that a sudden upwelling of CO_2 from the depths might roll over the surface of the sea and suffocate all in its path, just as it did from Lake Nyos (see p 236).

Another more fanciful method of storing CO_2 has been proposed, and that is to store it on land as giant snowballs of solid CO_2 (dry ice). Walter Seifritz of the Institute of Energy Economics of Stuttgart came up with the amusing idea of snowballs the height of the Eiffel Tower and wrapped in glass wool to insulate them. A country like Germany would need to build two such snowballs a year, although to do so would consume half the energy produced in their power stations.

If disposal of CO_2 was deemed to be necessary then the most likely method of disposal would be to pump it back underground into exhausted gas and oil wells, and in the latter it might do a useful job by forcing more oil to the surface.

The good side of carbon dioxide

There are some ways in which carbon dioxide serves to improve the quality of our lives, and in some rather unexpected guises. Apart from its well-known ability to put the fizz into drinks, it will keep food fresher, it makes aromas smell more alluring, it can take a lot of the fat out of fried snacks, it can decaffeinate coffee, and it can be used as a gas for greenhouses. It can also be turned into other molecules such as solvents, plastics and painkillers.

Carbon dioxide appears in the top twenty industrial chemicals produced by the chemicals industry. The gas is collected as a by-product of ammonia manufacture and from the fermentation of alcohol. In the USA over a million tons of CO_2 are collected each year and used as a resource for the chemicals and other industries. In the UK it is 40 000 tons. As a starting material for other chemicals, the industrial use of CO_2 is somewhat limited. A little is reacted with phenol to make aspirin. Much more goes into manufacturing poly-carbonate plastics, and even more into the manufacture of **urea**. The CO_2 can be converted to urea by reaction with ammonia, and this white solid can be used directly as a fertiliser, as an animal food supplement, or reacted further and turned into plastics. Some CO_2 can be turned into the solvent propylene carbonate, which is used in the polymer industry.

CO_2 is now used to boost greenhouse crops, and this is done simply by pumping CO_2 into glasshouses. If you tried to grow plants under glass without any ventilation they would quickly stop growing because they would use up all the CO_2. With 1000 ppm of CO_2 in the air it is possible to increase crop yields by 40%. Plants grow bigger where there is more CO_2, and this is also true in the wild. Research by Professor James Teeri of the University of

Michigan has demonstrated that if the amount of CO_2 in the atmosphere were to double, then tree growth would go up by 20%.

CO_2 is increasingly used as a solvent with remarkable properties. Liquid CO_2 has the ability to dissolve a large range of materials, and especially organic compounds, such as fats and oils. Unlike most industrial gases, CO_2 is not transported in heavy cylinders, but either as a solid, referred to as 'dry ice', or as a liquid. Solid CO_2 was formerly used in long-distance transportation of food before refrigerated trucks were developed. It is still used to cool processed food, and a blast of CO_2 snow will ensure the rapid refrigeration of frozen meals. It is delivered to food processors as a liquid, in heavy-gauge steel tankers carrying up to twenty thousand litres at a time, and is converted to CO_2 snow on site. Tankers carry their cargo at pressures of about 70 atmospheres.

At atmospheric pressure CO_2 can never be a liquid, and if we cool it we find that at -78 °C it freezes into a solid. On warming it reverts straight back to a gas. This physical process is called sublimation. To get CO_2 to behave as a liquid we need to apply pressure. The higher the temperature the higher the pressure needed to keep it in the liquid state. It is possible to have liquid CO_2 at room temperature, and even up to 31 °C, when a pressure of 73 atmospheres is needed. This is called the critical temperature for CO_2, because above this temperature no pressure, however great, can keep CO_2 a liquid. Yet in industry and research, chemists work with CO_2 up to 100 °C and 300 atmospheres. Under these conditions CO_2 has both the properties of a liquid and of a gas, and is correctly referred to as a supercritical fluid.

Carbon dioxide is ideal for processing materials which eventually come into contact with humans, because it is odourless and tasteless, it does not leave any unwanted residues, and, unlike many solvents, it is not flammable. Industry finds it attractive because liquid CO_2 is cheap and chemically unreactive, it has a low viscosity, and it will dissolve a wide range of materials such as oils, fats, caffeine, perfume essences and other plant extracts. Extracting the essential oils of plants, herbs, flowers and spices using supercritical CO_2 produces much improved essences, which reflect the natural composition more closely than extracts using traditional solvents. Moreover, liquid CO_2 has no smell of its own, unlike other solvents which can leave residues.

Many of the fragrances discussed in Chapter 1 can now be extracted using liquid CO_2. Hops have been extracted in this way since 1977 for use in making beers.

Other oils that can be extracted with liquid CO_2 are the edible oils from fried foods. Surface oil on potato snacks can be washed off to produce the 'reduced fat' varieties, which have 25% fat as compared to untreated snacks with 40% fat. Liquid CO_2 is the solvent of choice for decaffeinating coffee. Earlier methods of making this used organo-chlorine solvents such as chloroform, but these left behind minute residues of solvent which still worried people. The best-selling dec-affeinated coffees, such as Café Hag in Europe, are made using liquid CO_2. The process involves extracting the caffeine from the beans with superheated water, and then extracting the caffeine from the water with supercritical CO_2. The result is to reduce the amount of caffeine in a cup of instant coffee from 60 mg to only 3 mg. Tea can also be decaffeinated, but this is a more complicated process since there are subtle tea flavours extracted along with the caffeine. However these can be recovered and put back.

The most recent suggestion for using liquid CO_2 is as a solvent for dyeing. The effluent from textile dyeing works is particularly difficult to clean up, and although the amount of chemical waste may be relatively small it certainly looks like a great deal. Some dyes are very soluble in liquid CO_2 and this turns out to be an ideal dyeing medium. There is no water involved and the results are often much brighter shades of colour. If we are prepared to invest in new tech-nology we may find that CO_2 is one of the chemicals that in the next century is actually *protecting* our environment.

One day we may use CO_2 to *make* other fuels such as methane, methanol, and even petrol. This can easily be done provided we have a supply of hydrogen gas to convert the CO_2 to methane (CH_4). We could get the hydrogen by the electrolysis of water from power generated by windmills, hydroelectricity, tidal barrages or nuclear power. We might even use sunlight to split water directly into oxy-gen and hydrogen, a process that chemists have shown is feasible but not very efficient. When sunlight shines on **titanium dioxide** parti-cles in water it will work this little miracle, provided the titanium dioxide has a small amount of platinum metal incorporated into its surface. Currently we do not use hydrogen to turn CO_2 into methane: in our topsy-turvy world we convert methane to CO_2 and hydrogen. The hydrogen is used as a chemical resource to make ammonia for fertilisers and plastics.

In our everyday lives the most pleasant way in which we come into contact with CO_2 is in colas, sparkling wines, mineral waters and fizzy fruit drinks. Traditionally wine-makers added more yeast, and got the sparkle by letting the CO_2 build up naturally in the bottle. Today it is added from industrial sources, but it is no different, although there are some who say that 'natural' CO_2 in expensive champagne or Perrier water produces finer bubbles, and that this makes for a better drink.

Another way in which CO_2 will improve drink is in the treatment of municipal water supplies. Water can be clarified by adding aluminium salts which precipitate and carry down impurities, so making it crystal clear. This use of aluminium is not wanted by some people, who consider this metal to be toxic and harmful to health. The alternative way of treating drinking water is to make it slightly acidic with CO_2 and then add iron salts. This use of CO_2 is likely to grow in the next century.

We have focused in this chapter on the CO_2 gas which comes from fuel and ends up in the atmosphere, but for each molecule of CO_2 that is formed, there is a molecule of oxygen consumed. Even though CO_2 may not be the global threat we have been led to believe, could it be that we are overlooking another threat? Are we using up the Earth's oxygen? The answer is yes. The burning of 7 billion tonnes of carbon from fossil fuels each year means we are consuming 18 billion tonnes of atmospheric oxygen.[16]

But there is no need to worry. The amount of oxygen we are losing each year is so small as to be almost unmeasurable, because it is trivial compared to the total amount of oxygen that surrounds the Earth: there are a thousand *trillion* tonnes circling the globe. It would take over 2000 years, even at the present rate of depletion, for the oxygen level in the atmosphere to fall a mere 1%, from 21% to 20%. Even if we were to consume all 16 trillion tonnes of accessible fossil fuel

[16] The 100 million tonnes of O_2 that industry extracts from the atmosphere, by condensing and by distilling liquefied air, is trivial in comparison. This goes to producing steel, making ethylene oxide (which is turned into antifreeze or polyester for bottles and fabrics) or used as oxygen gas itself, in medical care, or to purify sewage.

(mainly coal) in one glorious conflagration we would only use up 4% of the planet's oxygen, although this would put us dangerously close to the 17% minimum that is required to support human life.

CHAPTER TEN

Take care

TODAY the word 'chemical' is used by many people to mean pollutant, unnatural, or dangerous. It once simply referred to something that was made and used by chemists. The odium which now surrounds the word 'chemical' is a symptom of a science in decline. Why has this happened to chemistry? When I was young, chemistry needed no one to defend it—its achievements spoke for themselves. In the 1960s, much of what was reported about chemicals in the media was positive, and this encouraged me to believe that my choice of subject to study at university had been the right one. Then in the 1970s and 1980s what I read became increasingly negative, until the very word 'chemical' became synonymous with danger, and was only used in that context. Like many of my fellow scientists I objected to this, especially so when what was being said about 'chemicals' was in fact wrong.

Chemists are puzzled by the way some people have a strong aversion to *all* things 'chemical', and there is even a word, chemiphobia, to describe this state of mind. Chemiphobia stems not from a fear of industrial accidents, but from the dangers which people see lurking in everyday materials. Nevertheless, our public image was not helped by a sequence of terrible chemical disasters in the 1970s and 1980s, such as the mass poisoning of the people of Bhopal, India, in 1984, or the killing of all the fish in the river Rhine in 1986. Tighter safety precautions followed, but the damage was done. The chemicals industry was to pay for appearing to be so uncaring; and because it was such a profitable industry there were those who extorted a heavy price.

In this respect it seems rather strange that other industries which inflict such damage on the public have suffered much less, and we rarely see protestors attacking the work places of car makers, tobacco companies and arms manufacturers. Their products kill and maim far more often than the chemicals industry. I find it hard to understand. Thousands of my fellow chemists work away in research laboratories, and with the best of motives, to make better healing drugs, stronger plastics, safer solvents, better cleaners, and tastier germ-free food. It is thanks to them that those same protestors will live richer and longer lives, and even enjoy a pain-free old age. But no matter how hard chemists toil, their public image seems fated not to improve.

It is not the chemicals industry as such that has led to chemiphobia, but the many alarms about 'chemicals' in everyday products which we are told could possibly be damaging our health or the environment. Additives, pollution, residues and side-effects are the issues that have led some people to question the use of 'chemicals' and to advocate 'natural' alternatives. It is just these areas that I have sought to tackle head on in *The Consumer's Good Chemical Guide*, and I hope that you will now see artificial sweeteners, dioxins, carbon dioxide, PVC and painkillers in a slightly less worrying light.

I have also looked at other areas where a little chemical understanding can make the issue seem less frightening than some would claim, and in this context I have dealt with aspects of our diet such as sugar, cholesterol, saturated fats and nitrates. And just to show that chemists are involved in areas that are not generally regarded as their province I have written about their role in making better perfumes and safeguarding our favourite relaxant, alcohol.

Chemists are saddened by the fact that our language has been hijacked and turned to our disadvantage—the words 'chemical' and 'drug' are the examples they cite most often. For many people 'drug' has become a four-letter word meaning a drug of abuse or addiction, as in the cruelly dismissive phrase 'drug addict'. Yet the word also means just the opposite, a drug that heals—and this was how it was once used. Most people do not confuse these different meanings, even though they do overlap, as we saw in Chapter 5.

The misuse of the word 'chemicals' is more worrying. We live in a world in which the ultimate cause of things can generally be traced to a chemical process, whether these be the shape of a snowflake, the smell of freshly ground coffee, the colour of blood or the warming of the Earth. The same is true of the human body, and when things go wrong with that we may look around for a chemical cause. If the threat of heart disease or cancer, the two grim reapers that eventually mow most of us down, can be linked to 'chemicals' we become alarmed. Yet chemicals are rarely the cause of disease, and the major factors remain the ones that have always been important: a hereditary tendency to heart disease or cancer; poor diet and lifestyle leading to overweight; lack of exercise; and smoking. Those who fear these illnesses and feel at risk are perhaps particularly open to the suggestion that the fault lies not within themselves or what they do, but in some hidden threat.

Because we find it hard to come to terms with death, we are particularly sensitive to things which threaten to bring it about prematurely, and yet we are illogical in our fears. It is no good my telling you that you are a million times more likely to die in a car accident than from drinking artificially sweetened drinks. You will find people taking action to remove the latter threat from their lives, while making no effort at all to change the way they drive.

Perhaps it is natural to look for an external threat, because we find it difficult to accept that internal ones are beyond our control. Thus we may be predisposed to believe someone who tells us that it is sugar or fats that cause heart disease, that PVC causes cancer, that dioxins lead to deformed babies, and that nitrates can kill. The language of those who make these charges is carefully framed, since the charges are not proven. They use carefully crafted phrases like: 'evidence suggests that', or 'environmentalists believe that', or 'medical data point to'. They speak the language of doubt while appearing to be sure. They use the words of uncertainty but with conviction, and say ' it is believed that ...', or 'indications are that ...' They talk of 'facts that are connected...' or 'factors which appear to be linked ...' Phrases like these should put us on our guard, because they warn us that there is no *scientific* proof for what is being suggested, and we would do well to question those who are making the claims.

If you ask a group of people about their health and behaviour you can do lots of statistical analysis on such a survey, and maybe even discover some relationships that at first sight are not obvious. This analysis may reveal that people in certain areas are more likely to suffer stomach cancer, and you may then look for things in their food or water supply to explain this. Given the recent dramatic advances in chemical analysis, you might discover there are things in our environment or diet of which we were previously unaware, and the temptation will be to fix on these 'new' threats for an explanation. Indeed, our current awareness of environmental issues rests on the achievements of chemical analysts, who can now detect and measure some substances that are present in only *trillionths* of a gram. These advances in chemical analysis rarely hit the headlines; but what is discovered often makes the news.

It is easy for someone to accuse a particular chemical of causing illness, but much more difficult for the chemist to prove that it is innocent. And even when this is done it will rarely be given the same coverage in the media as the original charge. This book has been an attempt to try and level the playing field a little. I have taken a different view of chemicals, not from the top down, but from the bottom up. I did not start with alarming statistics about heart disease or cancer, and possible links to unsuspected chemical causes; instead I tried to explain the chemistry and then see if this is consistent with the accusations being made against the chemical. This way we discovered that some of the most famous scares of the past few years had little substance, and that some of the 'chemicals' that people worry about pose no danger to their well-being at all. There are still many threats to our health, our sanity, our society, our world, and our children's future, but these threats are not to be found in 'chemicals'. In the next volume of *The Consumer's Good Chemical Guide* I hope to deal with other chemicals that have given rise to alarm, such as phosphates, MSG, preservatives, chlorine, nicotine, methanol and the HFCs, and some that have led to unrealistic hopes of improved health, such as vitamin C and calcium. I will also look at topics that reveal a more positive side to 'chemicals', such as colour.

Whenever a scare story starts, you trust that the right questions will be asked of those who are banging the warning drum. Up to now this questioning rarely seems to have happened, but then the alarmists are rarely cross-examined by a science-trained interviewer. If it is a health scare, as indeed most of them are, then they should be asked the following questions: 'Have you compared those affected with a control group?' 'Has the harm that you say is being done been confirmed by doctors?' 'Have you repeated your study and got the same results each time?' The answers to these questions should be our first line of defence if we want to be sure of the truth. Unfortunately, they rarely seem to be asked.

If you want to put the risks associated with 'chemicals' and 'drugs' into their proper context, I would advise you to read one of the books on risks listed in the Bibliography, such as *Living with Risk* by Michael Henderson. These will explain the risks we run in all walks of life. *Living with Risk*, for example, discusses the main causes of death, and the factors which have the most influence on our health. Read it and you will discover how tiny is the threat from chemicals.

Finally, a word to the members of my own profession, the chemists. We are now resigned to seeing the things we produce misrepresented as dangerous, even though we have tested them and proved that they are safe. Even we tend to forget that chemicals have saved more lives than surgeons, and created more wealth than bankers. Of course we have made mistakes, and this book has reminded you of some of them, but for every mistake there have been many more successes. The greatest danger for the future is that young people are turning away from chemistry. We should do all we can actively to promote our science. The time has come for us to come out of the bunker and fight back. We know that remarkable things can be achieved by chemistry, but only if we capture the best young brains of each generation and direct them to a career in research in the laboratory, or to manufacturing new materials and drugs in the chemicals and pharmaceuticals industries. Once upon a time this happened, and looking around us we can see how the achievements of that earlier generation of chemists changed the world. For the sake of the world in the next century, we must take care it happens again.

Chemical Data

The Consumer's Good Chemical Guide is all about chemicals, but not about their chemistry as such. If you are seeking that kind of information then here are some of the bare essentials. Compounds are listed in alphabetial order according to the common name used in the main body of the text. The formula is given next, followed by the other information; the molecular structure appears in the margin. In many instances I have given alternative names for the various chemicals mentioned, including the chemical name. You will need this if you want to look for further information by consulting the general chemistry reference works listed at the end of this Appendix. To find a particular chemical, ignore any single letter such as L-, D- or *N*- at the start of a word, and any numbers and Greek symbols. Acronyms such as PVC are in alphabetical order.

Where a zig-zag line is used this represents a chain of CH_2 groups, e.g. stearic acid on page 319.

acesulfam: $C_4H_4KNO_4S$, is the intensely sweet-tasting potassium salt of 6-methyl-1,2,3-oxathiazin-4-one 2,2-dioxide. It is also called acesulfam-K when used as an artificial sweetener

acetaldehyde: C_2H_4O, more correctly called ethanal. It is a colourless liquid with a pungent, fruity odour which boils at 2 °C. Normally it is available as a solution in water, and used as such. Acetaldehyde used to be produced on a large scale industrially since it is the forerunner of many other chemicals such as acetic acid and acetic anhydride, but these are now made by alternative methods.

acetanilide: C_8H_9NO, can be obtained as white, shiny, crystals which melt at 114 °C. It is used as a stabiliser for hydrogen peroxide and cellulose coatings. It is also used in the manufacture of pharmaceuticals, dyestuffs and antiseptics. (See **paracetamol**.)

acetate: the salt component of **acetic acid**.

acetic acid: $C_2H_4O_2$, more correctly called ethanoic acid. It is more popularly known in the form of vinegar which is a dilute solution of the acid in water. Pure acetic acid is a colourless, sharp-smelling liquid which boils at 118 °C and is produced industrially. The acetic acid in vinegar is manufactured by the action of bacteria on alcohol and the name vinegar comes from the Frnech *vin egar* meaning sour wine.

acetone: C_3H_6O, also known as dimethyl ketone, but is more correctly called propanone. Acetone is a volatile liquid which boils at 56 °C and is used widely as a solvent, both industrially and also domestically for such things as nail varnish remover.

acetylsalicyclic acid: See **aspirin**

N-acetylcysteine: $C_5H_9NO_3S$, the N-acetyl derivative of the naturally occurring amino acid, cysteine. It is used in medicine and biochemical research.

acids: see **carboxylic acids**

acrolein: C_3H_4O more correctly called 2-propenal. It is a colourless or yellow liquid which boils at 53 °C and has a disagreeable choking odour. It is produced when organic materials and plastics catch alight, and is a major cause of death of those suffocated in house fires. Acrolein is produced as an industrial chemical for the manufacture of plastics, resins, pharmaceuticals and herbicides.

acrylic acid: $C_3H_4O_2$, also more correctly known as propenoic acid. This is a colourless liquid which boils at 141 °C and has an acrid odour. It polymerises readily, and so does its esters which are used in surface coatings, emulsion paints and to treat paper and leather.

$$CH_2\!=\!CH\!-\!CO_2H$$

acrylonitrile: C_3H_3N, also known as vinyl cyanide or more correctly, propenenitrile. It is produced industrially on a large scale by the reaction of propylene, $CH_2\!=\!CH\!-\!CH_3$, ammonia and air at 400 °C in the presence of a molybdenum-based catalyst. Most acrylonitrile is polymerised to make fibres and plastics.

$$CH_2\!=\!CH\!-\!CN$$

alcohol: the general name for a class of chemical compounds which have a hydroxy group (OH) attached to a carbon atom. The simplest alcohol is methanol, CH_3OH, then ethanol, propanol, butanol etc. (See individual entries.)

aldehyde: the general name for the group CHO, and for the chemical compounds in which this group occurs. Alcohols are oxidised to aldehydes, which in turn are oxidised to acids, thus:
$$RCH_2OH \rightarrow RCHO \rightarrow RCO_2H$$
(R = an organic group)

alginates: any of several salts of alginic acid which is a polysaccharide consisting of long chains of joined units of mannuronic acid and guluronic acid. Alginates occur in all brown algae as a component of their cell walls, and

mannuronic acid

guluronic acid

the major source is the giant seaweed *Macrocystis pyrifera*. Alginates make excellent thickening agents and are used in many foods such as ice cream, salad dressing, and milk chocolate. They are also used to stabilise fresh fruit juice and the foam on beer.

alkane: general formula C_nH_{2n+2}, the name given to a series of hydrocarbons starting with the simplest, methane, CH_4, which has only one carbon atom, then going up through ethane, C_2H_6, propane, C_3H_8 and butane, C_4H_{10}, after which they are named after the corresponding Greek numbers: pentane, C_5H_{12} hexane, C_6H_{14}, heptane, C_7H_{16}, and so on. Some alkanes are given as separate entries in this Appendix. The early members of this series are gases, then come volatile liquids whose boiling points increase with increasing molecular weights. Eventually when there are many carbons we have thick oils, greases and finally waxes. In everyday life we encounter these hydrocarbons not as pure compounds but as mixtures which are called gasoline/petrol, diesel, kerosene/paraffin, white spirit and liquid paraffin. The old name for the alkanes was the paraffins.

$$CH_3—CH_3$$
ethane

$$CH_3—CH_2—CH_3$$
propane

etc.

allyl alcohol: C_3H_6O, more correctly known as 2-propen-1-ol, and is a colourless liquid with a pungent smell and boiling point of 97 °C. It is produced industrially on a large scale as the starting material for resins and plasticisers, and as an intermediate in the production of other chemicals.

$$H_2C=CH—CH_2OH$$

ambergris: $C_{16}H_{29}O$, the main aroma constituent of the balls of ambergris produced in the intestines of sperm whales.

amino acids: a collection of chemical compounds with the common grouping shown where R stands for a variety of other atoms and groups. The simplest amino acid is glycine

$$H_2N—CH—CO_2H$$
$$\overset{\displaystyle R}{|}$$

$$H_2N—CH_2—CO_2H$$

glycine

$$H_2N—CH—CO_2H$$

arginine

(coded gly) in which R is hydrogen. There are over 20 amino acids found in living things, some of which are essential to humans, such as **arginine** (arg) which has $R = NH_2C(NH)NH(CH_2)_3$. The other essential amino acids are histidine (his), isoleucine (ileu), leucine (leu), lysine (lys), methionine (met), phenylalanine (phe), threonine (thr), tryptophan (trp) and valine (val). Amino acids join together by reacting the amino group (NH_2) on one with the acid group (CO_2H) on another to form a peptide bond ($-CHR-CO-NH-$etc). Long chains are known as peptides, and very long chains as polypeptides. Proteins are polypeptides. Glutamic acid (glu), better known as its sodium salt, monosodium glutamate (MSG), is also an amino acid in which R is $CH_2CH_2CO_2H$.

ammonia: NH_3, a colourless gas with a strong odour. It condenses to a liquid at $-33\ °C$ which has the unique ability to dissolve metals like sodium without reacting with them. Ammonia is manufactured on a large scale industrially and used to make fertilisers, plastics and nylon. Ammonia gas dissolves readily in water to give a solution popularly known just as 'ammonia'.

ammonium nitrate: NH_4NO_3, a salt of nitric acid which is formed by reacting the acid with ammonia. It is a colourless, crystalline material which decomposes on heating to form nitrous oxide gas, N_2O, and water. Solid ammonium nitrate tends to cake into lumps and is treated with anti-caking powders to keep it free flowing. It is produced on a large scale worldwide, principally as a fertiliser, although some is used as an explosive when mixed with other materials.

α-amyl-cinnamaldehyde

α-hexyl-cinnamaldehyde

α-amyl-cinnamaldehyde, $C_{14}H_{18}O$, and **α-hexyl-cinnamaldehyde, $C_{15}H_{20}O$,** are both yellow liquids which can be synthesised from benzaldehyde. They have soft, floral odours with distinct jasmin notes.

androstenone: $C_{19}H_{28}O$, also known as 5α-androstenone, and more informatively as 16-androsten-3-one. It is a molecule consisting of four joined rings in an arrangement which is characteristic of a steroid. Its melting point is 103 °C. Androstenone is responsible for the smell referred to as 'boar taint' in pig meat.

Antabuse: the trade name for disulfiram, $C_{10}H_{20}N_2S_4$, more correctly called bis(diethylthiocarbamyl) disulfide. It can be given as part of the treatment of alcohol addiction, and it inhibits the enzyme aldehyde dehydrogenase. If alcohol is taken during treatment with the drug, which is prescribed as 200 mg tablets, then the patient will suffer unpleasant effects such as nausea and vomiting. One of its side effects is to produce bad breath, because of its high sulfur content.

antimony oxide: Sb_2O_3, also more correctly known as antimony trioxide. It is found as the ore valentinite, or it can be made by burning antimony in air. It is used to flameproof textiles, paper and plastics, especially **PVC**. It is also used to decolourise glass.

arabinose: $C_5H_{10}O_5$, also known as pectin sugar and gum sugar. Both the left and right hand forms of this sugar occur naturally and L-arabinose is common in vegetable gums, of which gum arabic is the richest source. Arabinose is a white crystalline material, which is soluble in water, and melts at 159 °C. It is used as a culture medium.

```
      CHO
       |
  H — C — OH
       |
 HO — C — H
       |
 HO — C — H
       |
     CH₂OH
```

L-arginine: see amino acids.

argon: element, atomic number 18, atomic mass 40, symbol Ar. This element is completely unreactive and as such exists in the air only as a gas composed of single atoms. It condenses to a liquid at −186 °C. Argon is 1% of the atmosphere, totalling 66 trillion tonnes (66×10^{12}). It is so abundant because it is being continually formed by the radioactive decay of one of the isotopes of potassium (^{40}K). About 700 000 tonnes are extracted each year from the air for lamps and high temperature metallurgy, where it is used to provide an inert atmosphere.

arsenic: element, atomic number 33, atomic mass 75, symbol As. Arsenic is used in alloys, semiconductors, glass and pesticides. The term 'arsenic' in literature refers to the oxide, As_2O_3, a white powder which is slightly soluble in water and acts as a deadly poison. The element occurs widely and is essential for some species including humans. Our daily diet provides between 5 and 50 mg of arsenic, and it is high in seafoods like plaice and prawns. We excrete arsenic rapidly. A small amount of arsenic can act as a tonic by speeding up our metabolic rate, and it has been used to rear livestock more quickly. However, too much arsenic over a long period can cause cancer.

asbestos: the name given to a family of fibrous minerals that are impure magnesium silicate. Their colours vary and some have individual names such as chrysotile, whose fibres are strong enough to be woven, and amphibole, which is very resistant to heat and chemical attack. Asbestos was once used for fireproof fabrics, brake linings, building panels, roofing components, rubber reinforcement, and chemical filters. It is still used in the diaphragm cells for chlorine manufacture. Exposure to asbestos dust in industry caused workers to be affected with the lung disease asbestosis and cancer. Its use is now strictly controlled.

aspartame: $C_{14}H_{18}N_2O_5$, (brand name NutraSweet) a white crystalline powder slightly soluble in water and alcohol.

$$H_2N-CH-CO-NH-CH-CO_2CH_3$$

with CH_2 and CO_2H on the left chain, and CH_2 attached to a benzene ring on the right chain.

aspartic acid: $C_4H_7NO_4$, a naturally occurring but non-essential amino acid. The common form is L-aspartic acid which can be obtained as colourless crystals from young sugarcane or sugar beet molasses.

$$CH_2CO_2H$$
$$H_2N-CH-CO_2H$$

aspirin: also known chemically as acetylsalicylic acid. It is a white crystalline material with a slightly bitter taste, and it melts at 132 °C. It is stable in dry air but in moist air it slowly breaks up into salicylic acid and acetic acid.

Structure: benzene ring with $OCOCH_3$ and CO_2H substituents.

auranofin: the correct chemical name for this anti–arthritic drug is 2,3,4,6-tetra-O-acetyl-1-thio-D-glucopyranosato-S-(triethyl-phosphine)gold.

$$CH_2OCOCH_3$$

CH₃OCO ... O

CH₃OCO ... S—Au—P(CH₂CH₃)₃

OCOCH₃

Bakelite: a trade name for a whole range of cross–linked co–polymers, made from phenol and formaldehyde. Leo Baekeland (1863–1944) discovered that when these chemicals reacted, and the product was heated under pressure, it turned into a useful resin which he called Bakelite. In 1910 he established a company to make products of the new plastic which became very popular, and he became very wealthy.

OH ... OH

CH₂ ... CH₂ ... CH₂—

CH₂ ... CH₂

CH₂ ... CH₂ ... CH₂—

OH ... OH

benzene: **C₆H₆**, the simplest of the so–called aromatic hydrocarbons. It is produced indust-rially on a large scale because it is the feedstock for many processes and is used in the manu-facture of a large number of chemicals that end up as polymers, plastics, detergents, drugs and dyes. Benzene itself is a colourless, volatile liquid which boils at 80 °C. It is easily ignited and burns with a smoky flame. It was commonly used as a solvent in industry and dry-cleaning, but is now strictly controlled because exposure to its vapour over a long period can cause certain types of cancer.

Bitrex: $C_{28}H_{34}N_2O_3$, the trade name for denatonium benzoate, and the bitterest substance known, according to the *Guinness Book of Records*. It is a white powder that is added to household and garden chemicals to deter young children from drinking them. It is also used to denature industrial alcohol, which requires only 10 mg per litre (only 10 parts per million).

butane: C_4H_{10} is a hydrocarbon gas under normal conditions, but it condenses easily under pressure to a liquid which is sold as camping gas or lighter fuel. It is increasingly being used as an aerosol propellant in place of CFCs. Butane is a by-product of petroleum refining and is a raw material for the chemicals industry, especially in the manufacture of butadiene which is turned into synthetic rubber. There are two kind of butane molecule: n-butane (the n stands for normal) with its carbon atoms in a row, which condenses to a liquid that boils at $-0.5\,°C$; and *iso*-butane, which has a branched chain, and boils at $-12\,°C$.

$$CH_3—CH_2—CH_2—CH_3$$
n-butane

iso-butane

2,3-butanediol: $C_4H_{10}O_2$, also known by its older name of 2,3-butylene glycol. It is derived from starch and sugar beet molasses.

CH₃
|
CHOH
|
CHOH
|
CH₃

$CH_3-CH_2-CH_2-CH_2OH$

butan-1-ol

$CH_3-CH_2-CH-CH_3$
|
OH

butan-2-ol

CH₃
|
CH_3-C-CH_3
|
OH

tertiary butanol

2,3-Butanediol is a colourless crystalline material, but because it melts at 23 °C it is often found as a liquid. It boils at 179 °C and is soluble in water and alcohol. 2,3-Butanediol is used in resins and as a solvent for certain dyes.

butanol: $C_4H_{10}O$. There are three forms of butanol: butan-1-ol, which boils at 118 °C; butan-2-ol, which boils at 100 °C; and tertiary butanol (more correctly called 2-methylpropan-2-ol), which boils at 83 °C. The liquids are similar in physical properties, but in their chemical reactions they lead to very different products. They are used as intermediates in synthesising other chemicals.

caffeine: $C_8H_{10}N_4O_2$, also known as methyltheobromine and 1,3,7-trimethyl-xanthine. When pure it consists of white, long, flexible crystals which melt at 237 °C. It is soluble in chloroform, and is extracted from coffee beans or kola nuts. Caffeine is the active ingredient in coffee, tea and colas, and is used medicinally in the treatment of asthma. Its effect on the body is to stimulate metabolism. Despite claims to the contrary research has shown that it is not addictive.

calcium: element, atomic number 20, atomic mass 40, symbol Ca. It is a soft silvery metal that reacts slowly with air and water. It does not exist as such in Nature, where the only stable form is the calcium ion, Ca^{2+}, in which the calcium atom has lost two of its negatively charged electrons. This is also the form in which calcium occurs in food and in the body, and as such it is essential to all living things. The average person contains about a kilogram of calcium, most being in the skeleton as calcium phosphate. Rich sources of dietary calcium are sardines, dairy products such as milk and cheese, and white bread. Calcium is the fifth most abundant element in the Earth's crust, and there are vast deposits of **calcium carbonate** (limestone), **calcium phosphate** (apatite) and **calcium sulfate** (gypsum).

calcium carbonate: $CaCO_3$, commonly referred to as limestone. This sedimentary rock takes many forms, including marble. Calcium carbonate as a pure chemical is a colourless solid. It evolves carbon dioxide when heated strongly to give lime (CaO):

$$CaCO_3 \rightarrow CaO + CO_2$$

Calcium carbonate is used in smelting iron, and for manufacturing glass and cement. It is also used to absorb acidic gases, and to neutralise acid solutions (for example in indigestion tablets.)

calcium oxalate: CaC_2O_4, the calcium salt of oxalic acid. It is a white crystalline powder that finds some use in making glazes and in chemical research.

calcium phosphate: $Ca_3(PO_4)_2$. There are several types of calcium phosphate, but all consist of a lattice of positive calcium ions (Ca^{2+}) and negative phosphate ions (PO_4^{3-}). One form of calcium phosphate, called apatite, has the formula $Ca_5(PO_4)_3(OH)$ and is the main component of tooth enamel. Another, called fluoroapatite, has the formula $Ca_5(PO_4)_3F$ and occurs as vast mineral deposits.

camphor: $C_{10}H_{16}O$, a white solid with a characteristic medicinal smell. It occurs naturally in the roots and branches of the camphor tree, *Cinnamomum camphora*, which grows in China and Japan. It melts at 179 °C. It was previously much used in medicine, and as a plasticiser for cellulose nitrate, and in making lacquers.

caramel: this is a food colourant of indeter-
minate chemical composition, made by melting and heating sugar. It can also be made
from liquid corn syrup by heating it in the
presence of catalysts at 120 °C for several
hours. Caramels can be designed for use as
either flavours or colourants. In the latter case
the reaction is done in the presence of
ammonia.

carbon dioxide: CO_2, a colourless, odourless, gas which is 1.5 times as dense as air. It is
produced in large quantities as a by-product of
fermentation or fertiliser production. When
CO_2 is cooled it does not condense to a liquid
but to a solid, popularly known as 'dry ice'.
When a piece of this is warmed it sublimes at
−78 °C, which means that it evaporates from
the solid to the gas without going through a
liquid form. CO_2 is soluble in water to the
extent of 760 ml per litre, and this can be
increased by raising the pressure when the
product is called soda water or carbonated
water. This is the basis of 'sparkling' mineral
waters, colas, and other soft drinks.

O=C=O

carbon monoxide: CO, a colourless, odourless and deadly gas, discovered by Joseph
Priestley in the USA in 1799. It is highly
toxic because it binds to the haemoglobin in
the blood 200 times more strongly than
oxygen and thereby prevents red blood cells
from carrying out their vital function. CO will
condense to a liquid at −190 °C. It is produced on a large scale in industry by the action
of steam on hot coke or natural gas, and is
turned into methanol. CO is flammable, and
can be used as a fuel—it burns with a pale
violet flame.

carvone: $C_{10}H_{14}O$, a pale yellow liquid which boils at $230\,°C$. Its correct chemical name is 2-methyl-5-(1-methylethenyl)-2-cyclohexene-1-one. The molecule is found in its mirror image forms, with D-carvone being present in caraway seeds and dill, while L-carvone is the flavour component of spearmint.

caustic soda: **NaOH**, often referred to simply as 'caustic' or by the old name of 'lye', but more correctly called sodium hydroxide. It is a white compound that becomes moist when exposed to the air. It is sold as a household chemical for unblocking drains. Caustic soda is produced on a large scale along with chlorine by the electrolysis of brine, and it is used industrially in the manufacture of rayon, pulp and paper, aluminium, soaps and detergents, textiles and vegetable oils. It is highly corrosive.

cellulose: $(C_6H_{10}O_5)_n$, a long chain carbohydrate polymer more correctly known as a polysaccharide. It consists of glucose units interconnected through oxygens. The cellulose from wood has about 1000 units while that from cotton has about 3500. Cellulose is the most abundant organic material in the world. It is a colourless solid which is insoluble in both water and organic solvents. As the raw material, its most important uses are in paper and clothing, but it is also chemically modified and turned into **cellulose nitrate** and **cellulose acetate**.

cellulose acetate: when **cellulose** from wood pulp or cotton is treated with acetic anhydride and acetic acid, it forms the acetate. Not all of the three replaceable hydrogens of a glucose unit of cellulose are replaced by acetate, only two of them on average. The product is a polymer that has a nice feel against the skin, and it has many outlets: fibre for clothing and furnishings; lacquer;

transparent sheeting (Cellophane); cigarette filters; magnetic tape; spectacle frames and screwdriver handles.

cellulose nitrate: also known as nitrocellulose or gun cotton. Replacing some or all of the reactive OH groups of the glucose rings of cellulose with nitrate groups, NO_3, gives cellulose nitrate, and its formula is approximately $C_6H_7N_3O_{11}$. It is made from cellulose using a mixture of nitric and sulfuric acids, and the product can vary from a pulpy solid to a liquid, depending upon the conditions of the reaction. Cellulose nitrate is highly flammable, but was widely used for fast-drying paints for car bodies, in explosives, and in Celluloid. Collodion was a solution of cellulose nitrate in ether and ethanol, and this was used in model making, for removing corns, and in engraving and photography. Because it is dangerously flammable it is no longer available.

CFCs: this is the acronym for chlorofluorocarbons, which are compounds with one or two carbon atoms to which are bonded only chlorine or fluorine atoms. They were once used in aerosols and are still used in refrigerators, but they are now being phased out around the world because of the damage they can inflict on the ozone layer. The most important ones, and the ones still present in the atmosphere, are CFC-11 (which has the chemical formula $CFCl_3$), CFC-12 (CF_2Cl_2) and CFC-113 ($C_3F_3Cl_3$).

chlorine: element, atomic number 17, atomic mass 35.5, symbol Cl. The element occurs as a pale yellow-green gas of formula Cl_2. It is highly toxic. Chlorine gas can be condensed to a liquid either by applying pressure (8 atmospheres), or cooling to $-39\,°C$. Chlorine is produced on a large scale industrially and used for making plastics, especially PVC, and in water purification.

Many of its uses have been curtailed, such as the manufacture of **DDT**, **CFCs**, and solvents such as carbon tetrachloride. The manufacture of chlorine is carried out in a so-called chlorine cell. In this an electric current is passed through concentrated brine (sodium chloride solution) which releases chlorine at the positive electrode and sodium at the negative electrode. The chlorine that comes off has to be kept isolated from the sodium, and the older method of doing this was called the amalgam process which used liquid mercury as the negative electrode. This dissolves the sodium as it is formed to give a sodium—mercury amalgam, and this is run out of the cell to a separate compartment. There it comes in contact with water and immediately reacts to form **caustic soda**. Having given up its sodium the mercury is then pumped back to the electrolysis cell to go round the cycle again.

cholesterol: $C_{27}H_{46}O$, the most common animal sterol (steroid alcohol). It can be isolated as white pearly granules which melt at 149 °C. It is only sparingly soluble in water but soluble in oils, fats and solutions of the bile salts. Cholesterol as a chemical has been used as an emulsifying agent in cosmetics and pharmaceuticals, and the main commercial source has been from the spinal cord of beef cattle.

cinnamic aldehyde: C_9H_8O, also known as cinnamaldehyde. It is a yellow liquid with a powerful odour, which can be synthesised from benzaldehyde (C_6H_5CHO) and acetaldehyde (CH_3CHO). It is the main component of cinnamon bark (*Cionnamomum zeylanicum*) and cassia oils. It is more correctly named 3-phenylpropenal.

cis-**3-hexenol:** $C_6H_{12}O$, a colourless liquid also known as leaf alcohol which in the pure form has a very powerful, leafy-green smell of newly cut grass. It occurs naturally in various extracts such as geranium, thyme, mulberry leaf, violet and tea.

citric acid: $C_6H_8O_7$, more correctly called 2-hydroxy-1,2,3-propanetricarboxylic acid. It is a colourless crystalline material which melts at 153 °C, dissolves readily in water, and has a strongly acid taste. It is present in citrus fruits and can be produced by the fermentation of carbohydrates. Citric acid is used as a flavouring and a food additive (it acts as an antioxidant), and is the acid component of many soft drinks and effervescent tablets. It is also sold as a descaler to remove 'lime' (**calcium carbonate**) deposits. It is non-toxic, and is part of all living cells.

citronellol: $C_{10}H_{20}O$, a colourless liquid that can be obtained by the distillation of geranium or citronella oils. It occurs naturally in these plants and in roses. It is more correctly called 3,7,7-trimethyl-6-octen-1-ol.

civetone: $C_{17}H_{30}O$, consists of a ring of 17 carbon atoms with an oxygen atom attached to one of them, and a double bond between two of them. It is the main odour chemical of civet, produced by the civet cat. Civetone is able to mould itself to different shapes and this probably enables it to fit different types of odour receptors, hence its tantalising and evocative smell.

cocaine: $C_{17}H_{21}NO_4$, a white crystalline powder which melts at 98 °C and is slightly soluble in water. It is extracted from the leaves of the *Erythroxylon coca* and was once used as a local anaesthetic in dentistry and in so-called tonic wines. It is still widely used illegally as a drug of abuse.

codeine: $C_{18}H_{21}NO_3$, also known as methylmorphine. It is a narcotic alkaloid and is a white solid which melts at 155 °C. Codeine is made from morphine which is extracted from opium, and it is sold as an over-the-counter painkiller, mostly used in conjunction with other painkillers. It is also used in cough syrups.

coumarin: $C_9H_6O_2$, a white crystalline powder, melting point 69 °C, also known as benzopyrone. It can be synthesized from salicylic aldehyde and it occurs naturally in many plants and fragrance oils, especially the tonka bean (*Dipteryx odorat*). Coumarin is also found in cassia (Chinese cinnamon tree, *Cinnamomum cassia*) and lavender. It is not permitted in food products because it is a known carcinogen. Coumarin has a sweet, herbaceous, warm, somewhat spicy, odour which when diluted also has the aroma of new mown hay. It is used in deodorising products.

cyclamate: $C_6H_{13}NO_3S$, a white, sweet-tasting crystalline powder once used as an artificial sweetener but now prohibited in some countries.

3-cyclohexenyl-1,3-dioxan: the 'parent' molecule for a new group of synthetic ambergris odorants. These derivatives vary according to the other chemical groups attached to the molecule, but they all have the same basic chemical structure.

parent

derivative

DDT: short for dichlorodiphenyltrichloroethane, $C_{14}H_9Cl_5$, and more correctly called 1,1-bis(4-chlorophenyl)-2,2,2-trichlorothane. DDT comes as colourless crystals which are insoluble in water, and is made from chloral hydrate and chlorobenzene. DDT was first discovered in the 19th century, but its insecticide properties were only discovered by accident in 1939. DDT was the first of the new generation of organochlorine insecticides which were much safer than the older variety because they required relatively little to be effective, and they were not toxic to animals. In the 1940s and 1950s they achieved spectacular success in controlling mosquitos and lifting the threat of malaria from a large part of the globe. Its success led to farmers using it on a wide scale. However, DDT is biodegraded only slowly, and so it built up in the environment and passed along the food chain until it threatened to wipe out some birds of prey. It also gave rise to DDT-resistant insects, and in the 1970s the USA banned its use at home, although not its manufacture for export.

DEHA: this is short for di(2-ethyl-hexyl)adipate which is used as a plasticiser for PVC thereby turning a rigid plastic into one that is supple and suitable for a wide range of applications such as wire insulation, tubing and transparent film.

DEHP: this is short for di(2-ethyl-hexyl)phthalate and is an alternative plasticiser for PVC (see **DEHA**).

diazepam: $C_{16}H_{13}ClN_2O$, also known as Valium, but its chemical name is 7-chloro-1,3-dihydro-1-methyl-5-phenyl-1,4-benzo-diazepin-2-one. It is a pale yellow powder which melts at 132 °C. It is prescribed as an anti-depressant because it calms the central nervous system, but over-use may lead to addiction. If the chlorine atom in the molecule is replaced by a nitro (NO_2) group then the compound is nitrazepam, better known as the sleeping pill Mogadon.

2,4-D: $C_8H_6Cl_2O_3$, the abbreviation for 2,4-dichlorophenoxyacetic acid, where the numbers refer to the positions of the two chlorine atoms attached to the benzene ring. It is a pale yellow/tan solid which melts at 138 °C. It was widely used as a selective weedkiller and also to prevent fruit drop. However, as it was originally manufactured, 2,4-D was contaminated with dioxins. See also **2,4,5-T**.

2,4-dichlorophenol: $C_6H_4Cl_2O$. The numbers in the name refer to the positions of the two chlorine atoms attached to the benzene ring. It is a white solid which melts at 45 °C and is produced by the reaction of chlorine gas and phenol, and is used as an intermediate in the manufacture of other compounds.

dicyandiamide: $C_2H_4N_4$, used in agriculture to prevent the loss of nitrogen from animal manures. These are susceptible to denitrifying bacteria which end up releasing the nitrogen compounds as soluble nitrates, etc. Dicyandiamide suppresses this microbial action.

diethylene glycol: $C_4H_{10}O_3$, also known as DEG and dihydroxydiethyl ether. This is a colourless, syrupy liquid with a sweetish taste which is used as an antifreeze because when mixed with water it prevents it freezing at temperatures below 0 °C. Diethylene glycol is also used as an industrial intermediate in the production of polymers and resins. It is also used as a plasticiser, a wetting agent, and as a humectant for tobacco (it keeps it moist), cork and sponge.

$$HO-CH_2-CH_2-O-CH_2-CH_2-OH$$

dimethylnitrosamine: $(CH_3)_2NNO$, formed by the chemical reaction of *nitrite* with dimethylamine. As a pure compound it is a dangerous carcinogen. It is also present in

minute traces in several foods, especially
cooked meats.

dimethyl sulfide: C_2H_6S, also known as
methyl sulfide. It is a foul-smelling volatile
liquid which boils at 38 °C and is produced
naturally by bacteria, along with the gas $CH_3—S—CH_3$
methyl mercaptan, CH_3SH. Together they
are responsible for bad breath. Dimethyl
sulfide is sometimes used to 'stench' natural
gas so that leaks can be readily detected.

dioxin: this is the general name for a whole
range of compounds whose framework consists of two benzene rings connected via one
or two oxygen atoms. Those with two linking
oxygens are called dibenzo–dioxins, and those
linked through one oxygen are called
dibenzo–furans. Each benzene ring can have
up to four chlorine atoms, and these are
numbered according to the carbon atoms to
which they are attached:

dibenzo-dioxin   dibenzo-furan

There are many ways of attaching between one
and eight atoms to these molecules. For
dibenzo dioxin there are 75 possible combinations, and for dibenzo furan there are 135
combinations, making a total of 210 compounds for which the generic term 'dioxins' is
used. Of the 75 dibenzo dioxins seven are
toxic, and of the 135 dibenzo furans ten are
toxic. The most dangerous of all is 2,3,7,8–
tetrachlorodibenzodioxin, or 2,3,7,8–TCDD
for short, and this is often abbreviated to
TCDD. The toxicity of TCDD is the benchmark for all the other dioxins, most of which

are only mildly toxic. The key to TCDD's toxicity is the chlorine atoms attached to carbons 2, 3, 7 and 8. Adding one more chlorine atom reduces its toxic action by half. Moving a chlorine from atom 7 to atom 1 reduces it to a thousandth of its original toxicity. When there are the maximum eight chlorine atoms attached to either dibenzo-dioxin or dibenzofuran do we find that the toxic action is negligible. We can see a chemical explanation for this: if 2,3,7,8-TCDD is the key which exactly fits a receptor lock and blocks it, then any changes to the key are bound to make it fit less well.

dolomite: $CaCO_3.MgCO_3$, a naturally occurring mineral that is a mixed calcium magnesium carbonate. It can vary in colour from white to pink to grey. It is from this that magnesium metal is obtained. Dolomite is also used for ceramics, paper making, and as a building material.

epibatidine: $C_{11}H_{13}N_2Cl$, discovered in 1992 in the skin of the Ecuadorean frog *Epipedobates tricolor*. It is 200 times as potent as a painkiller as morphine.

erythritol: $C_4H_{10}O_4$, also known as tetra-hydroxybutane, and more correctly as butane-1,2,3,4-tetrol. This is a white, sweet-tasting, crystalline powder, which melts at 121 °C. It is stable in air, and soluble in both alcohol and water. It is found naturally in *Protocaccus vulgaris* and other lichens.

esters: general formula RCO_2R. This is the name given to the products of the reactions between acids (RCO_2H) and alcohols (ROH) where R stands for the rest of the organic molecule. Esters are generally colourless liquids that have smells characteristic of fruit, and they are often present in fruit.

ethane: C_2H_6, a natural gas which condenses to a liquid at $-89\,°C$. It is the precursor to **ethylene**.

CH_3—CH_3

ethanol: C_2H_6O, also known as ethyl alcohol, or just as alcohol. Ethanol is a colourless liquid with a sharp smell. It boils at $78\,°C$ and freezes at $-115\,°C$, which is why it is used in thermometers for measuring low temperatures. It is produced on a large scale, not only by brewing and fermentation but also from **ethylene**, and it is used industrially as a solvent, a fuel, and in the manufacture of paints, plastics, etc. The density of pure ethanol is 0.789 grams per ml, and the density of mixtures of alcohol and water, referred to as the specific gravity, is used as a quick measure of the alcohol content of a liquid.

CH_3CH_2OH

ethyl chloride: C_2H_5Cl, more correctly called chloroethane. This is normally a gas which condenses to a liquid at $12\,°C$, and is used to manufacture tetraethyl-lead, which is the additive of leaded petrol. It has other industrial uses, and once had commercial outlets as an anaesthetic and refrigerant, but along with other chlorine-containing gases it is considered to be potentially damaging to the atmosphere.

CH_3—CH_2—Cl

ethylene: C_2H_4, more correctly called ethene, but this name is little used other than in textbooks. Ethylene is a colourless gas (it condenses at $-104\,°C$) which is produced from oil on a vast scale industrially, and is used as the starting point for hundreds of products such as paints, solvents, antifreeze and especially polymers. Linking the two carbon atoms of ethylene is a double bond, and this is the key to its ability to polymerise when heated under pressure, and in the presence of a catalyst:

$$CH_2{=}CH_2 \xrightarrow{\text{polymerise}} {-}CH_2{-}CH_2{-}CH_2{-}CH_2{-}\text{etc.}$$

ethylene   polyethylene
monomer   polymer

Polyethylene comes in two types, low density polyethylene (LDPE) and high density polyethylene (HDPE), which differ in the length of their chains and in the ways in which they pack together. The conditions of manufacture determine which form is produced. LDPE is used for transparent film and carrier bags, whereas HDPE is used to make plastic containers. Ethylene is produced from natural gas and by ' cracking' oil.

ethylene dichloride: $C_2H_4Cl_2$, has a variety of names including the chemically correct one of 1,2-dichloroethane. It is a colourless, oily liquid which boils at 84 °C, and is the precursor of **vinyl chloride**, which in turn is the precursor of **PVC**. Ethylene dichloride has found several other uses: in leaded petrol, as a paint remover, as a metal degreaser, and as a penetrating agent.

ethylene glycol: $C_2H_6O_2$, also known as glycol, but more correctly called 1,2-ethanediol. This is a clear, colourless, syrupy liquid, which lowers the freezing point of water and is used as an antifreeze. There are many other industrial uses, the principal one being as a solvent for such things as lacquers, resins, printing inks, and adhesives. Despite its wide application, ethylene glycol is toxic, and as little as 100 ccs can kill if consumed.

ethyl heptanoate: $C_9H_{18}O_2$, the ethyl ester of heptanoic acid. It can easily be prepared from ethanol and heptanoic acid. It has a brandy-like aroma.

2-ethyl-3-methylbutanoic acid: $C_7H_{14}O_2$, the strong-smelling molecule which gives rum its characteristic aroma.

$$CH_3-CH-CH-CO_2H$$
$$\quad\;\; | \quad\;\; |$$
$$\quad CH_3 \; CH_2CH_3$$

eugenol: $C_{10}H_{12}O_2$, a colourless or pale yellow liquid which boils at 255 °C. It is more correctly called 2-methoxy-4-(2-propenyl) phenol. Eugenol occurs naturally in cloves and is obtained by distilling clove leaf or clove stem oil which can be 80% eugenol. It is also present in cinnamon, pimento and bay leaf. Eugenol has a warm-spicy odour with a slight medicinal hint.

formaldehyde: CH_2O, also known as oxymethylene and more correctly called methanal. It is a gas with a pungent odour which condenses at -19 °C when it rapidly polymerises by reacting with itself. It is generally available as formalin, a 37% solution in water with up to 15% methanol added to prevent polymerisation. This is used as a preservative for biological and medical specimens, and as an embalming fluid. Formaldehyde is produced industrially on a large scale and used to make urea-formaldehyde resins (e.g. melamine), dyes and drugs.

formic acid: H_2CO_2 or HCO_2H, also more correctly called methanoic acid. It is a colourless liquid with a penetrating odour, which boils at 101 °C. It gets its name from *formica*, the Latin word for ant, and it is the main component of the irritant fluid emitted by certain types of stinging ant. Formic acid is produced industrially and used in dyeing, textile-finishing, leather treatment, and the manufacture of fumigants, insecticides, lacquers and solvents. Formic acid is used in electroplating and for silvering mirrors, when it reduces silver nitrate solution to silver which deposits out on the glass surface.

free radicals: these are chemicals that have an unattached electron, and this makes them extremely reactive since the whole object of chemical bond formation is to pair off electrons. Often when a free radical reacts with another molecule it produces yet another free radical among the reaction products. Living systems have to protect themselves against free radicals, and they do this by mopping them up with so-called free radical 'sinks', which are chemicals that will react with a free radical and destroy it, without producing another free radical in its place. We need such defences because the oxygen gas we breathe is prone to reacting to form free radicals.

fructose: $C_6H_{12}O_6$, also known as levulose and fruit sugar. It occurs in several fruits and in honey, and is the sweetest of all the natural saccharides. It is a component of nectar. Fructose can be separated as white crystals which melt at 103 °C and decompose, and is obtained commercially from beet sugar or cornstarch by enzyme action. Fructose is the source of energy which powers the movement of sperm.

galactose: $C_6H_{12}O_6$, a monosaccharide that is common in milk and other polymeric saccharides. It can be produced from lactose. Galactose is sweet to taste, with a relative sweetness about half that of sugar. It is readily absorbed by the body where it changes to glucose and so raises blood sugar levels.

geraniol: $C_{10}H_{18}O$, a colourless liquid which can be made synthetically from pinene or isolated from natural oils of Javanese citronella grass. It is found in geranium, and as geranyl acetate in Eucalyptus oil. Geraniol has a sweet, floral-rose odour with dry undertones.

gluconic acid: $C_6H_{12}O_7$, is widely distributed in both animals and plants, usually occurring as part of a larger molecule, as in various gums. It is derived from gum acacia, and separates as needle–like crystals which melt at 165 °C. It is soluble in water and alcohol.

$$
\begin{array}{c}
CO_2H \\
| \\
H-C-OH \\
| \\
HO-C-H \\
| \\
H-C-OH \\
| \\
H-C-OH \\
| \\
CH_2OH
\end{array}
$$

glucose: $C_6H_{12}O_6$, more commonly called blood sugar, starch sugar, grape sugar or corn sugar, depending on its source. It exists in two main forms, α-D-glucose and β-D-glucose, of which the former is stable below 50 °C. There is a third form which is a five-membered ring. Glucose occurs in ripe fruits. In the body it represents immediately available energy and circulates in the blood to where it is needed.

α-D-glucose

glutathione: $C_{10}H_{17}N_3O_6S$, γ-L-glutamyl-L-cysteinyl-glycine, a peptide composed of the **amino acids** glutamic acid, cysteine and glycine. It is a component of the living cell and acts as a co-enzyme; it is also involved in transporting amino acids, and in redox-type reactions. Glutathione can be separated as a white crystalline powder which melts at 190 °C and has a mild sour taste. It is used in nutritional and biochemical research.

glycerol: $C_3H_8O_3$, also known as glycerin or glycerine, but more correctly called propane-1,2,3-triol. It is a clear, colourless, oily liquid which will solidify at 18 °C, boil at 290 °C, and is soluble in water and alcohol. Glycerol is a by-product of soap manufacture

$$
\begin{array}{c}
CH_2OH \\
| \\
H-C-OH \\
| \\
CH_2OH
\end{array}
$$

when oils and fats (**triglycer-ides**) are heated
with alkalis to give long chain fatty acids and
glycerol. It can also be manufactured chemically. Glycerol is used to make many products,
among which are resins, pharmaceuticals,
cosmetics, emulsifiers, inks, lubricants and
antifreeze mixtures.

helium: element, atomic number 2, atomic
mass 4, symbol He. This element is completely unreactive and as such exists in Nature
only as single atoms. It condenses to a liquid at
$-269\,°C$, and behaves like no other fluid in
that it can flow up the walls of a container.
Helium is part of the atmosphere and is
formed in the Earth by radioactive decay—
an alpha particle is in effect the nucleus of a
helium atom. Helium constitutes 5.2 ppm of
the atmosphere, totalling 3.7 billion tonnes
(3.7×10^9), but it is slowly escaping away into
space. The helium that is used in deep-sea
diving, weather balloons and low temperature
research instruments comes from natural gas
wells, some of which may contain up to 7%
helium. World production of helium is about
4500 tonnes a year.

heroin: $C_{21}H_{23}NO_5$, also called diamorphine, or more correctly diacetylmorphine.
It is a white, bitter, crystalline compound
which melts at $173\,°C$, and is obtained from
morphine. Heroin is an illegal drug of abuse
which is quickly habit forming and can be
fatal in small doses.

HFCs: this is short for hydrofluorocarbons. These are like the **CFCs**, but they contain no chlorine; only hydrogen and fluorine atoms are attached to the carbon atoms in these molecules. HFCs are replacing CFCs in such uses as refrigerants because even if they eventually escape into the atmosphere they will not affect the ozone layer. Difluoromethane, CH_2F_2, which is being manufactured for use in refrigerators, has a boiling point of $-52\,°C$.

hydrocinnamaldehyde: $C_9H_{10}O$, also known as 3-phenylpropanal. This is a colourless liquid with the odour of hyacinths.

hydrogen: element, atomic number 1, atomic mass 1, symbol H, which exists as a gas of formula H_2. It is colourless, odourless, burns in air, and forms explosive mixtures with oxygen. It is produced on a large scale industrially to the extent of 350 million cubic metres per year, from the controlled reaction of natural gas and oxygen. It is also produced as a by-product of caustic soda manufacture. H_2 gas condenses to a liquid at $-253\,°C$, and can be stored and transported as such. It is used as a rocket fuel and has even been tried as a fuel for buses and cars. Some scientists believe that when natural gas and oil supplies are exhausted, a 'hydrogen economy' will be developed instead.

hydromorphone: $C_{17}H_{19}NO_3$, also known as dimorphone and Novolaudon. It is a narcotic alkaloid and is a white solid which melts at 266 °C. Hydromorphone is made from morphine by reacting it with hydrogen gas in the presence of a palladium catalyst. It is the most potent of the opiate painkillers, and like morphine and diamorphine (heroin) it may be addictive.

OH
|
$CH_3—CH—CH_2—CO_2H$

3-hydroxybutyric acid: $C_4H_8O_3$. This is the parent acid from which **polyhydroxybutyrate** polymer (**PHB**) is derived.

ibuprofen: $C_{13}H_{18}O_2$, more correctly called 4-isobutyl-α-methylphenylacetic acid. It is a white powder which melts at 51 °C. it is one of the best-selling over-the-counter pain-killers.

$$(CH_3)_2CHCH_2— \hspace{2cm} —CHCO_2H$$

CH₃ (above CHCO₂H)

invert sugar: derived from ordinary sugar by the action of acid or enzymes. It gets its name from the effect it has on a beam of plane-polarised light. Ordinary sugar solution will rotate such a beam of light clockwise, a process which chemists call *dextro* (*d*), meaning to the right. When sugar has reacted with water it rotates the beam in the opposite direction, and it is called *laevo* (*l*), meaning to the left. Put another way, it has 'inverted' the light, and so we have the old name of invert sugar.

α-ionone

β-ionone

ionone: $C_{13}H_{20}O$, a mixture of two forms, α-ionone and β-ionone. These can be synthesised from citral and acetone. Ionone occurs naturally in *boronia megastigma* which grows wild in Western Australia, and in the oil of violets (*viola odorata*). Synthetic ionone is a pale yellow liquid first made in 1893, and used ever since as a fragrance chemical. α-ionone has a sweet, violet odour, while β-ionone has a green-woody fruity odour reminiscent of cedarwood and raspberries. It also smells of freesias when diluted.

iron: element, atomic number 26, atomic mass 56, symbol Fe (from the Latin *ferrum*). It is a lustrous, workable metal, but rusts readily in damp air. This can be controlled by adding a small amount of carbon (up to 1.7%), and thereby turning it into steel. By adding a lot of nickel and chromium, and traces of other metals, it is possible to turn iron into stainless steel. Iron is not found as the metal itself on Earth (although it is found as such in meteorites). It occurs as the ions, Fe^{2+} and Fe^{3+}, in which the iron atom has lost two or three of its negatively charged electrons. These are called the reduced (Fe^{2+}) and oxidised (Fe^{3+}) forms of iron, and it is as these ions that iron is incorporated into all living things. The average human contains about 4 grams of iron, most being in the blood because this is the element which is at the heart of haemoglobin. Rich sources of iron in the diet are liver and kidney, sunflower seeds, soyabeans, wheat germ, bran and red wine. Iron is the fourth most abundant element in the Earth's crust, and there are vast deposits of haematite (Fe^{3+} oxide), magnesite (Fe^{2+}/Fe^{3+}, oxide), and siderite (iron carbonate).

jasmone: $C_{11}H_{16}O$, which exists in two forms, *cis*-jasmone and *trans*-jasmone. Only the former occurs naturally in jasmin extracts, whereas the synthetic variety contains both. This means that if *trans*-jasmone is detected in a sample of the fragrance, then the material is not solely of plant origin. Jasmone is a pale yellow liquid with a fruity, celery-like odour that changes on dilution to a sweet-floral odour reminiscent of jasmin and cherry blossom. There are several versions of methyl *cis*-jasmonate, because in addition to the *cis* and *trans* forms there can also be variants in which the ester group is on the same side of the five-membered ring as the long chain, or on the opposite side. (There are also mirror-image molecules.) In addition to jasmone there are the methyl jasmonates, also used as fragrances.

cis-jasmone

trans-jasmone

methyl *cis*-jasmonate

krypton: element, atomic number 38, atomic mass 84, symbol Kr. This element is unreactive and as such exists in the air only as a gas composed of single atoms. It condenses to a liquid at $-152\,°C$. Krypton is a trace component of the atmosphere (1.14 ppm) and a small amount is reclaimed from liquid air plants for use in research. An orange–red line in the atomic spectrum of krypton is used as the fundamental standard of length to define the metre; 1 metre is exactly 1 650 763.73 times the wavelength of this line.

lead acetate: $(CH_3CO_2)_2Pb$, once known as sugar of lead. It is one of the few lead salts which is soluble in water, to which it imparts a sweet taste. It is formed by the chemical reaction of acetic acid on lead and was a common, but unsuspected, additive in many alcoholic drinks in former times.

limonene: $C_{10}H_{16}$, a terpene hydrocarbon found in many essence oils from which it can be produced by distillation. It is a colourless liquid with a bright, fresh, clean odour, typical of citrus fruits. It occurs in two mirror–image forms, D-limonene and L-limonene, of which the former predominates.

linoleic acid: $C_{18}H_{32}O_2$, more correctly called 9,12-octadecadienoic acid. It is a doubly unsaturated fatty acid, and is an essential fatty acid in the diet. It is a colourless liquid which freezes at $-12\,°C$ and decomposes on heating to boiling.

$$CH_3(CH_2)_3 \diagdown \diagup = \diagdown \diagup = \diagdown \diagup (CH_2)_6CO_2H$$

γ-linolenic acid: $C_{18}H_{30}O_2$, more correctly called 6,9,12-octadecatrienoic acid. It is a polyunsaturated fatty acid which occurs as the glyceride in many seed fats, and is an essential fatty acid in the diet. Linolenic acid is a colourless liquid which freezes at $-11\,°C$ and boils at $230\,°C$.

$$CH_3(CH_2)_4 \qquad\qquad (CH_2)_4CO_2H$$

lovastatin: a white crystalline material which melts at $175\,°C$. It is given as a treatment to control high cholesterol levels in the body.

mercury: element, atomic number 80, atomic mass 201, symbol Hg (from the Latin *hydrargyrum*, meaning liquid silver). This liquid metal has been known since ancient times, and is still in production because of its use in industry, street lighting, pesticides and electrical apparatus. Mercury salts are poisonous, and methyl mercury, which can be produced by micro–organisms, is particularly dangerous. This compound is volatile and explains why mercury is widely diffused throughout the environment. Every mouthful of food we eat contains a minute amount of mercury, and some fish such as tuna concentrate it naturally. Humans take in about 5 micro–grams of mercury daily, but even if we retained all this within our body we would not accumulate a fatal dose during our life–time—provided it was in the inorganic form.

methadone: $C_{21}H_{27}NO$, more correctly called 6–dimethylamino–4,4–diphenyl–3–hep–tanone. This is a synthetic narcotic, usually supplied as its hydrochloride salt. It is a white solid with a bitter taste which melts at $232\,°C$. Methadone is used in the treatment of heroin addiction, and whereas heroin addiction begins within five days, methadone takes about a month. It can therefore be prescribed

$$(CH_3)_2N-CH-CH_3$$
$$|$$
$$CH_2$$
$$|$$
$$C-CO-CH_2CH_3$$

to help control the withdrawal symptoms of heroin without itself causing addiction. Methadone can exist in two mirror-image forms, but only the left-hand one is physiologically active.

methane: CH$_4$. This was once called marsh gas because it is the gas given off when organic matter rots under anaerobic conditions. It is the main component of natural gas. Methane is odourless and dangerous, because it can explode in air if sparked. Vast deposits of methane are found in the Earth's crust, and are tapped as an industrial and fuel resource. Industry uses methane mainly as a source of hydrogen, which can be generated by reacting the methane with a limited amount of oxygen. This produces so-called synthesis gas, a mixture of **carbon monoxide** and **hydrogen** which is used to make **methanol**. Methane is formed naturally by certain bacteria living in cows, which explains why these animals and other ruminants contribute to global warming since methane is an atmospheric greenhouse gas.

methanol: CH$_4$O, which is more informatively written as CH$_3$OH to emphasise that one of the hydrogen atoms is attached to the oxygen as an hydroxy (OH) group. Originally methanol was known as wood alcohol because it is given off when wood is heated, and this was how it was once made. Today it is manufactured on a large scale from synthesis gas, a mixture of **hydrogen** and **carbon monoxide** gases. Methanol is used as a solvent, and in some states of the USA as a replacement fuel for petrol because it is cleaner burning. Methanol is also used as a chemical in the manufacture of other compounds such as adhesives and protective coatings.

3-methyl-2-hexenoic acid: $C_7H_{12}O_2$, the unpleasant smelling chemical which is produced in the human armpit.

$$CH_3-CH_2-CH_2-\overset{\overset{\displaystyle CH_3}{|}}{C}=CH-CO_2H$$

methyl mercaptan: CH_4S, more informatively written as CH_3SH and more correctly known as methanethiol. This is a gas which condenses to a colourless liquid at 6 °C, and is one of the vilest smelling chemicals known. It is produced as the by-product of bacterial decay of protein under anaerobic conditions, and as such is responsible for bad breath. It is also an industrial chemical that can be made from methanol and hydrogen sulfide, and is an intermediate in the manufacture of methionine (used as a dietary supplement for animals), and in the making of pesticides, catalysts for industry, and the sulfur-based compounds that are used to 'stench' natural gas, so that leaks can be readily detected.

$$CH_3-SH$$

methyl methacrylate: $C_5H_8O_2$, a derivative of ethylene which can be polymerised to form poly(methyl methacrylate), which is also known as Perspex and Lucite. Methyl methacrylate itself is a liquid which boils at 101 °C.

2-methylundecanal: $C_{11}H_{24}O$, also known as aldehyde C12 MNA, short for methyl nonyl acetaldehyde. It is a colourless liquid with a dry, slightly fruity odour reminiscent of ambergris and incense, with floral notes.

$$CH_3(CH_2)_7\overset{\overset{\displaystyle CH_3}{|}}{CH}-CHO$$

mevalonic acid: $C_6H_{12}O_4$, more correctly called 3,5-dihydroxy-3-methylpenantoic acid. This is a precursor to cholesterol formation in the body. It is an oil which occurs as a mixture of two interchanging molecules.

mevastatin: $C_{23}H_{34}O_5$, given as a treat-ment to control high cholesterol levels in the body.

morphine: $C_{17}H_{19}NO_3$, the active consti-tuent of opium, which oozes as a milky juice from unripe poppy seeds of the *Papaver somniferum*. Pure morphine is a white solid, slightly soluble in water. It is among the most powerful painkillers known, but it is addic-tive.

muscone: $C_{16}H_{30}O$, a white or colourless crystalline solid with a very soft, sweet, musky, erogenous odour. It is the main aroma com-ponent of natural musk, but is now made synthetically from diacetyldodecane. It is chemically similar to **civetone**.

N-acetylcysteine: see acetylcysteine.

neon: element, atomic number 10, atomic mass 20, symbol Ne. This element is com-pletely unreactive and as such exists in the air only as a gas composed of single atoms. It condenses to a liquid at $-246\,°C$. Neon is not very abundant on Earth and constitutes 18 ppm of the atmosphere, although this adds up to a total of 65 billion tonnes (65×10^9). About one tonne is extracted each year from liquid air for use in ornamental lighting (neon signs).

nicotine: $C_{10}H_{14}N_2$, chemical name β-pyridyl-α-N-methylpyrrolidine. Nicotine is an alkaloid which is present in tobacco and can be extracted as a viscous colourless oil which turns brown on exposure to air. In the small amounts taken in by smoking tobacco, nicotine has a pleasurable effect on the brain, but it is nevertheless a highly toxic chemical, and is addictive. In the form of its salts, nicotine has been used as an insecticide and fumigant.

nitrate: NO_3^-, the negative ion in which a central nitrogen atom is surrounded by, and chemically bonded to, three oxygen atoms. Nitrates are salts of nitric acid in which the hydrogen of HNO_3 has been replaced by a positive metal ion, leaving the nitrate as the negative ion, NO_3^-. The best known salts are sodium nitrate, $NaNO_3$, which is found as large deposits in Chile and called Chile nitre or Chile saltpetre, and potassium nitrate, KNO_3, which is the original saltpetre. All nitrates are very soluble in water.

nitric acid: HNO_3, a strong, oxidising acid. In its concentrated form, it gives off brown fumes of **nitrogen dioxide** (NO_2). This acid is very dangerous and will rapidly char any organic material it comes in contact with. Nitric acid is made in large quantities by the oxidation of ammonia to form **nitric oxide**, NO, and then reacting this with air and water to form HNO_3. Most nitric acid is used in the manufacture of **ammonium nitrate**, and the rest is used to make plastics, dyes and explosives.

nitrite: NO_2^-, a molecular ion and technically the salt of nitrous acid HNO_2, although this is very unstable. Of the nitrite salts, sodium nitrite, $NaNO_2$, and potassium nitrite, KNO_2, are the most common, and are used in curing meat and as chemical reagents in the laboratory. Nitrite is radically different from nitrate in its chemical beha-

viour; for example, whereas nitrate is relatively indifferent towards metals, preferring to
exist independently as NO_3^-, nitrite is
attracted to metals such as iron, and bonds
to them very strongly.

nitrogen: element, atomic number 7, atomic
mass 14, symbol N. It occurs in the air as N_2,
and is more correctly known as dinitrogen. It
is a colourless, unreactive gas which comprises
79% of the atmosphere. It is produced on a
large scale industrially by liquefying air, and is
shipped as liquid nitrogen which boils at
$-196\,°C$. It is used in metallurgy, food
packaging, refrigeration, and to manufacture
ammonia.

nitrogen oxides: most likely to be encountered as pollutants, because they form during
combustion and are generally labelled
together as NO_x. There are three gases:
nitrous oxide, N_2O, was once known as
laughing gas, following its use as an anaesthetic in dentistry, when it led to some
patients becoming euphoric. It occurs naturally in the atmosphere in low concentration
and it is a relatively unreactive gas. Nitric
oxide, NO, is produced in the human body
which uses it as a chemical messenger. Its best
known role is in securing an erection in males,
but it has several other roles to play, such as
relaxing arteries. Nitric oxide is chemically
very reactive, and is easily oxidised by oxygen to nitrogen dioxide. It has a powerful
affinity for metals. Nitrogen dioxide, NO_2, is
a brown gas with a choking effect if breathed
in large amounts due to its instant reaction
with water in the lungs to form nitric acid. It
is very reactive towards organic molecules,
and under atmospheric conditions is a key
factor in producing smog because it combines with unburnt hydrocarbon emissions in
the exhaust gases of cars.

nylon: now a general name for a family of polymers which are polyamides, meaning they have the molecular amide unit, $-CO-NH-$, along the backbone of the polymer. The best known nylon is nylon-6,6 in which amide units are linked by chains with six carbon atoms. This was the nylon discovered by Wallace Carothers in 1935. Other nylons have carbon chains of different lengths. Nylon is strong and versatile and finds use in tyres, hosiery (for which it is spun so fine that its inherent strength is nullified), bristles, ropes, fishing nets, sails, carpets, clothing, upholstery, membranes, gears and bearings.

$$\left[-\overset{\overset{\displaystyle O}{\|}}{C}-(CH_2)_4-\overset{\overset{\displaystyle O}{\|}}{C}-NH-(CH_2)_6-NH- \right]_n$$

octanol: $C_8H_{18}O$, more correctly called 1-octanol, and also known as *n*-octyl alcohol. It is a colourless liquid which boils at 195 °C. It is used in perfumery, cosmetics and in industry as a solvent and anti-foaming agent. It is also an intermediate for making other chemicals.

$$CH_3(CH_2)_6CH_2OH$$

Opren: $C_{16}H_{12}ClNO_3$, has the generic name benoxaprofen, and the chemical name 2-(4-chlorophenyl)-α-methyl-5-benzoxazole acetic acid. It is an anti-inflammatory analgesic, which is now banned in some countries.

oxygen: element, atomic number 8, atomic mass 16, symbol O, which exists as a gas of formula O_2 and is more correctly called dioxygen. It is colourless, odourless, very reactive, and forms oxides with almost every other element. Despite this it accounts for 21% of the Earth's atmosphere. There are limitless supplies of the gas to be obtained from liquid air and about 100 millions tonnes are extracted from this source every year for use in steel making, metal cutting, in the chemicals industry and for medical applications.

ozone: the other gaseous form of elemental oxygen, with formula O_3. It is an unstable blue gas with a pungent odour that can be detected near electric sparks and UV lamps. It will liquefy at $-12\,°C$ but is highly dangerous as such. The gas is produced in ozonisers which work by passing an electric discharge through air and converting a few per cent of the O_2 to O_3. The gas is then used as an oxidising agent in industry, and as a disinfectant for swimming baths and public water supplies. Ozone is a natural part of the upper atmosphere and serves to filter out dangerous ultraviolet light from the Sun's rays. Ozone is sensitive to chlorine atoms which can destroy it, and hence the concern about long-lived organochlorine vapours in the atmosphere, such as the CFCs. In the lower atmosphere ozone is produced as part of photochemical smog, and as such is damaging to plants and human lungs.

paracetamol: $C_8H_9NO_2$, also known as N-acetyl-*para*-aminophenol or N-acetyl-4-aminophenol. It exists as colourless crystals which melt at $168\,°C$. Paracetamol is slightly soluble in water, and has a bitter taste. Although it is best known as a painkiller, it is also used as an intermediate in the production of pharmaceuticals, dyes and photographic chemicals.

NHCOCH₃

OH

PCB: the abbreviation for polychlorinated biphenyl, and refers to a collection of molecules that have the common biphenyl (also known as diphenyl) framework. In the middle years of this century the PCBs were produced on a large scale as a solvent and particularly as an insulating fluid for electrical transformers. Their escape into the environment has given cause for concern because, like dioxins, these chemicals are long-lived and slightly carcinogenic.

biphenyl

PCDD: the abbreviation for pentachlorodibenzodioxin, in which there are five chlorine atoms attached to the dibenzodioxin molecule (see **dioxin**).

PET: the abbreviation for polyethylene terephthalate, which is the chemical name for the polymer often referred to simply as polyester. PET can be spun into fibres (Terylene, Dacron) which produce fabrics that resist creasing, and are used for clothing. The polymer can also be used to make transparent film and containers, such as bottles.

PHB: the abbreviation for polyhydroxybutyric acid, a natural polymer made by a wide range of micro-organisms, such as the bacterium *Alicaligenes eutrophus*, as a convenient way of storing energy. PHB consists of chains of **3-hydroxybutyric acid** which has an acid group CO_2H at one end of the molecule and a hydroxyl group OH at the other. When these react they form a chemical bond called an ester link, and in this way they can join head–to–tail to form long chains thousands of units long, in other words a polymer.

phenol: C_6H_6O, also known as carbolic acid and once commonly used as an antiseptic. It is now considered too dangerous for general use, because it is an irritant to skin. Phenol is a pinkish crystalline solid (although white when pure) which melts at 43 °C and has a distinctive odour. It is still manufactured on a large scale and used to produce products ranging from aspirin to resins. The term phenol also applies to the group of compounds characterised by a hydroxyl group (OH) attached to a benzene ring.

phenylacetic acid: $C_8H_8O_2$, also known as α-toluic acid, and consisting of white crystals which melt at 76 °C. It has a sweet, floral odour and is the main aroma associated with honey, in which it occurs as the ethyl ester. It is made synthetically from benzyl cyanide and hydrochloric acid. It is used as a flavouring, and in the manufacture of penicillin G.

acid

ester

phenylalanine: $C_9H_{11}NO_2$, an essential amino acid also named α-amino-β-phenyl-propionic acid. It is soluble in water, from which it can be obtained as plate-like and leaf-like crystals; it decomposes at 283 °C. Phenylalanine is isolated commercially from proteins and is used in biochemical research and sometimes as a dietary supplement.

2-phenylethanol: $C_8H_{10}O$, a colourless liquid alcohol which can be synthesized from benzene and ethylene oxide. It occurs naturally in rose, geranium and neroli oils and has a mild, warrm, rose-like odour with green, hyacinth undertones.

phenylethylamine $C_8H_{11}N$, also known as 2-phenylethylamine or 1-amino-2-phenyl-ethane. This is a liquid which boils at 195 °C, and has a fishy odour in the concentrated state. It occurs naturally in chocolate and a 100 gram bar can contain as much as 0.7 grams of phenylethylamine. This chemical is believed to raise blood pressure, producing a heightened sensation and a feeling of well-being.

$CH_2CH_2NH_2$

polyethylene: sometimes abbreviated to PE. This polymer consists of endless chains of carbon atoms, each carrying two hydrogens (see **ethylene**).

$$\left[CH_2-CH_2 \right]_n$$

polyhydroxybutyrate (PHB): a biodegradable polymer sold under the trade name of Biopol (see **PHB**).

polystyrene: $(C_8H_8)_n$. This is a thermoplastic resin, which means that it softens when heated but hardens again when it cools. It is hard and strong, with excellent electrical resistance. Expanded polystyrene foam finds use as thermal insulation. However polystyrene has two drawbacks: it is attacked by organic solvents, and it needs additives to protect it against sunlight (see also **styrene**).

$$\left[\overset{O}{\overset{\|}{C}}-(CH_2)_4-\overset{O}{\overset{\|}{C}}-NH-(CH_2)_6-NH \right]_n$$

6,6-nylon

polyvinyl chloride: see PVC.

propane: C_3H_8, the third member of the **alkane** series after **methane** and **ethane**. It is also a gas, but with a higher boiling point (−43 °C) than its lighter fellows. It is used as an industrial resource, a fuel, a refrigerant and an aerosol propellant. It is highly flammable.

$CH_3-CH_2-CH_3$

CH₃—CH—CH₂OH — represented as:

$$CH_3-CH-CH_2OH$$
$$\qquad |$$
$$\qquad OH$$

$$CH_3-CH_2-CH_2OH$$
1-propanol

$$CH_3-CH-CH_3$$
$$\qquad |$$
$$\qquad OH$$
2-propanol

propane-1,2-diol alginate: this is the ester of alginic acid (see **alginate**). Propane-1,2-diol has the formula shown.

propanol: C_3H_8O, formerly known as *n*-propyl alcohol, but more correctly called 1-propanol. There is also the related chemical 2-propanol. Both alcohols are colourless liquids which boil at 97 °C (1-propanol) and 82 °C (2-propanol), and both are used industrially as intermediates in the manufacture of other chemicals.

prostaglandins: these are a group of physiologically important compounds derived from arachidonic acid, which is a 20-carbon fatty acid that is found in glands and in the liver. Prostaglandins have a role to play in hormones, reproduction, blood pressure, digestion, smooth muscle stimulation and labour. They are particularly abundant in semen. Prostaglandins have been intensively studied and they can be made synthetically, although the most prolific source is from other organisms such as the gorgonian sea whip which is abundant in the Caribbean.

prostaglandin E₁

arachidonic acid

$$\left[CF_2-CF_2-CF_2-CF_2\right]_n$$

$$\left[\begin{array}{c} CH-CH_2-CH-CH_2 \\ | \qquad\qquad | \\ Cl \qquad\qquad Cl \end{array}\right]_n$$

PTFE: $(C_2F_4)_n$, poly(tetrafluoroethylene). This polymer is known by a variety of trade names such as Teflon. It has a very low coefficient of friction and this makes it an ideal coating for non-stick pans and skis.

PVC: $(C_2H_3Cl)_n$, poly(vinyl chloride). This polymer is made from vinyl chloride, and is a thermoplastic material. It is an excellent water repellent and resists weathering, so finds many outdoor uses. It is easily coloured and shaped and can be produced as fibre, foam or film.

quinine: $C_{20}H_{24}N_2O_2$, an alkaloid extracted from the bark of the *cinchona* tree of South America. It can be obtained as a white powder with a bitter taste. It is slightly soluble in water and is the flavouring used to make tonic water. It was the original antimalarial drug and it operates by inhibiting replication of DNA.

quinoline: C_9H_7N, a colourless liquid that darkens with age and boils at 238 °C. It can be obtained from coal tar. When used in fragrances it is most likely to be as its *iso*butyl derivative, which has an intense leather odour with wood and dry undertones, and is employed in chypre-type perfumes.

quinoline   6-*iso*-butylquinoline

saccharin: $C_7H_5NO_3S$, a white powder, stable in air, soluble in water, and about 300 times sweeter than sucrose.

salicylic acid: $C_7H_6O_3$, more correctly called 2-hydroxybenzoic acid. It is a white powder with an acrid taste which melts at 158 °C. Although it can be obtained from natural sources it is made from the sodium salt of phenol by reacting with carbon dioxide. Salicylic acid is an intermediate in the production of aspirin, resins, dyestuffs, and fungicides.

salt: **NaCl**, also known as sea salt, rock salt, table salt and the mineral halite. The chemical name is sodium chloride. Large crystals are colourless, although they look white when small. Salt is an essential dietary component, and it has many general uses. Large deposits are mined, and salt is a major resource for the chemicals industry because it is used to make **chlorine** gas and **caustic soda** (sodium hydroxide).

silicon dioxide: SiO_2, occurs naturally in various forms such as common sand, quartz, flint, and even as semi-precious gemstones such as rhinestones (found in the River Rhine, hence the name). Silicon dioxide is not a simple molecule, but consists of an array of silicon atoms each surrounded by four oxygens which link to other silicons.

sodium alginate: see alginate.

sodium bicarbonate: $NaHCO_3$, a white solid that is also known as baking soda, and more correctly as sodium hydrogen carbonate. It is soluble in water to give an alkaline solution, and is commonly taken as an antacid. Its reaction with acids generates carbon dioxide, and the reaction is also used to make fizzy tablets. $NaHCO_3$ is made by passing carbon dioxide into a solution of sodium carbonate, Na_2CO_3. It is produced on a large scale and most is used in the food industry.

Sorbic acid: $C_6H_8O_2$, more correctly called 2-*trans*-4-*trans*-hexendienoic acid. This is a white crystalline solid which melts at 135 °C and is only slightly soluble in water, although its salts, such as potassium sorbate, are much more soluble. Sorbic acid and sorbates are used as food preservatives since they kill fungi and inhibit moulds.

sorbitol: $C_6H_8(OH)_6$, also known as hexahydric alcohol. It is a white crystalline powder with a faint sweet taste, and which absorbs moisture from the air. It is soluble in water and organic solvents, and melts at 95 °C.

Sorbitol is present in some fruits and berries, but is manufactured from glucose by reacting it with hydrogen under pressure. It is used in cosmetic creams, toothpaste, candy, and in industry as a stabiliser for resins, a thickener, an emulsifier, and an anticaking agent.

steroids: this is a group of biologically important chemicals which share the same basic structure of four inter–linked rings. An example is **androstenone**.

streptomycin: $C_{21}H_{39}N_7O_{12}$, an antibiotic. The term is also used for a group of antibiotics produced by actinomycetes. Streptomycin itself is got from *streptomyces griseus*, and is active against gram–negative bacteria and the tubercule bacillus.

styrene: C_8H_8, more correctly called phenyl–ethene. It consists of ethylene with a benzene ring attached to one of the carbon atoms. It is a colourless, oily liquid which boils at 145 °C, and which readily undergoes polymerisation to **polystyrene**.

Sucralose: $C_{12}H_{19}Cl_3O_8$, more correctly called 1,6–dichloro–1,6–dideoxy–β–D–fructo–furanosyl 4–chloro–4–deoxy–α–D–galactopyrano–side. Sucralose is the trade name for a type of chlorinated saccharide in which three chlorine atoms have replaced hydroxy groups of **sucrose**.

sucrose: $C_{12}H_{22}O_{11}$, more correctly called saccharose; its full chemical name iso-β-D-fructofuranosyl-α-D-glucopyranoside. It is also known as cane sugar, beet sugar, or just sugar. It melts when heated above $160\,^{\circ}C$ and caramelises above $200\,^{\circ}C$.

sulfanilimide

sulfanilimide: $C_6H_8N_2O_2S$. This is the simplest member of a group of 50 or so drugs which go under the general name of the sulfanilamides or sulfa drugs. They share the common chemical grouping shown in the parent compound.

sulfur dioxide: SO_2 is formed when any sulfur-containing compound burns. It is a colourless gas with a choking odour, and it is soluble in water forming a solution of a weak acid, sulfurous acid, H_2SO_3, which is used as a preservative in food processing, especially for fruit, and to prevent bacterial infection in grape juice prior to fermenting. The SO_2 which escapes to the air from coal-fired power stations is partly responsible for acid rain. Industrially SO_2 is made by burning sulfur, or 'roasting' iron pyrites (FeS). Most SO_2 is used to make sulfuric acid, by first oxidising SO_2 to sulfur trioxide, SO_3, and then dissolving this in water:

$$SO_3 + H_2O \rightarrow H_2SO_4 \text{ (sulfuric acid)}$$

Other uses of SO_2 include paper manufacture, bleaching, and in the production of solvents and detergents.

tannin: this is the general name for a large group of phenol compounds derived from plants. They are bitter tasting and occur in small amounts in alcoholic drinks which have been left to mature in oak casks, from which the tannins are extracted. The tannins are derivatives of tannic acid, also known as gallotannic acid, $C_{76}H_{52}O_{46}$, and this can be used to clarify wine and beer. Tannic acid was once used to denature industrial alcohol. Tannins are used to tan leather, which used to involve soaking hides in a solution derived from tree bark, thereby allowing tannic acid to permeate the skin. The result was that it became supple and immune from bacterial attack.

tartrate: the salts of tartaric acid, $C_4H_6O_4$, are called tartrates. Potassium tartrate is called cream of tartar. The acid itself consists of colourless, transparent crystals that are soluble in water. Tartaric acid occurs naturally in wine lees, and it can be made synthetically in other ways. It is a traditional ingredient in baking powder, and is used as the solid acid in fizzy indigestion and headache tablets. When these are put into water, the acid dissolves and reacts with sodium bicarbonate to release carbon dioxide gas. Tartaric acid occurs in two molecular forms which differ only in that

L-tartaric acid   D-tartaric acid

one is the mirror image of the other. The D-form is the natural one produced in the wine industry.

TCDD: the abbreviation for 2,3,7,8-tetra-chlorodibenzodioxin, in which there are four chlorine atoms attached to the dibenzo–dioxin molecule (see **dioxin**).

tetrafluoroethylene: C_2F_4, also known as TFE and perfluoroethylene, and more correctly as tetrafluoroethene. It is a gas, with boiling point $-78\,°C$, and is the starting material from which polytetrafluoroethylene is made (see **PTFE**).

thalidomide: $C_{13}H_{10}N_2O_4$. There are two forms of thalidomide which have identical chemical formulae, and which consist of exactly the same groups of interlinked rings of atoms. The difference is that one molecule is the mirror image of the other, and they are labelled S (from the Latin *sinister*) or R (*rectus*). R-thalidomide is safe, but if the S form is taken on certain days of a pregnancy, it will interfere with the replicating DNA and deform the foetus. As it was originally manufactured, thalidomide consisted of both R and S molecules in equal amounts.

titanium dioxide: TiO_2, a brilliant white solid that is produced on a large scale and used as the chief pigment in paints because of its covering power. It occurs naturally as the minerals anatase and rutile, but the TiO_2 used commercially has to be pure and is obtained, for example, by converting the titanium to its chloride $TiCl_4$ and then reacting this with water. TiO_2 is non–combustible and non–toxic to humans and is used in a variety of ways as a 'filler' (inert bulking agent) for paper and plastics. It is also used in cosmetics, glassware, ceramics, and printing inks.

toluene: C_7H_8, an aromatic hydrocarbon which consists of a methyl group attached to a benzene ring, and sometimes called methyl-benzene. Toluene is a colourless liquid which boils at 111 °C and has a density of 0.867 grams per millilitre. As a solvent it has all the dissolving power of benzene, and is used in industry and research instead of benzene.

2,4,6-trichlorophenol: $C_6H_3Cl_3O$.   The numbers refer to the positions of the three chlorine atoms attached to the benzene ring. It is a yellow solid which melts at 61 °C and is produced by the reaction of chlorine gas and phenol. It is a plant fungicide, herbicide, and wood preservative, although it is now little used because it is contaminated with dioxins.

2,4,5-T: $C_8H_5Cl_3O_3$, also known as 2,4,5-trichlorophenoxyacetic acid, where the numbers refer to the positions of the three chlorine atoms attached to the benzene ring. It is a pale brown solid which melts at 151 °C. 2,4,5-T has been widely used as a plant hormone, herbicide and defoliant, although it is contaminated with dioxins. See also **2,4–D.**

triglycerides: these are any naturally occurring esters of glycerol to which are attached long chain fatty acids. One such fatty acid is stearic acid with the formula $C_{17}H_{35}CO_2H$, which has a long chain of 17 carbon atoms that is saturated. If three of these are attached to **glycerol** it forms tristearin, which is a major component of beef fat and cocoa butter. The fatty acid oleic acid has the formula $C_{17}H_{33}CO_2H$, and its chain of 17 carbon atoms has a double bond about half way along. Oleic acid is an unsaturated acid, and is the principal acid component of olive oil.

stearic acid

oleic acid

trinitrotoluene (TNT): the basic molecule which can give rise to musk-like fragrances such as *tert*-butyl-trinitrotoluene and musk ketone, $C_{14}H_{18}N_2O_5$, which have warm, sweet, erogenous musk-like odours.

TNT

musk ketone

urea: CH_4N_2O, a stable, white, crystalline solid that is one of the waste products of nitrogen metabolism in animals and one of the main components of urine. It makes a good fertiliser and can be manufactured from ammonia and carbon dioxide.

Valium: the tradename for **diazepam**.

vanilla: $C_8H_8O_3$, also known as vanillin, a creamy white crystalline material which has the chemical name 3-methoxy-4-hydroxy-benzaldehyde. It is manufactured from the lignin waste of the wood pulp industry. It occurs naturally in the vanilla pod, in balsams and in benzoins. Vanillin is used in perfumes for its intense, sweet, creamy odour. It is also used in food flavours and to make L-dopa (L-dihydroxyphenylalanine), the amino acid used in treating Parkinson's disease.

vinyl acetate: $C_4H_6O_2$, a derivative of ethylene and the basic building block of poly(vinyl acetate) or PVA.

vinyl chloride: C_2H_3Cl, also known as vinyl chloride monomer, and abbreviated to VCM, but more correctly known as chloroethene. This is the starting material from which **PVC** is made.

xenon: element, atomic number 54, atomic mass 131, symbol Xe. This element is very unreactive and in the air it is found only as a gas composed of single atoms. It condenses to a liquid at $-107\,°C$. Xenon is rare and accounts for only 0.09 ppm of the atmosphere, although this in total comes to about 2 billion tonnes (2×10^9). A little is extracted each year from liquid air and used for chemical research. Although xenon is completely inert towards most other materials, it can be made to react with fluorine gas (F_2) to form solid compounds such as XeF_2, XeF_4 and XeF_6. These are highly reactive.

xylitol: $C_5H_{12}O_5$, a white, sweet-tasting, crystalline powder, stable in air, soluble in alcohol and very soluble in water. A litre of water will dissolve 1.6 kg of xylitol.

xylose: $C_5H_{10}O_5$, also known as wood sugar or birch sugar, and more correctly as α-D-pyranose. It is a white crystalline powder which is stable in air and soluble in water.

yohimbine: $C_{21}H_{26}O_3N_2$, also known as aphrodine, corynine and quebrachine. It is a member of the group of chemicals known as alkaloids, and forms needle–like crystals when pure which melt at $234\,°C$. It is extracted from the bark of the *Corynanthe yohimbe* tree which grows in Cameroon.

BIBLIOGRAPHY

This bibliography contains the main sources of information I have used in writing the book. Under each chapter heading I have included a few titles that give good general coverage and which are written for people without specialist chemical training. The other references do assume a specialist knowledge in the area, and these are sources that you would probably only find in a reference or college library.

Chapter 1   Perfumes
General reading
A. Birchall, 'A whiff of happiness', *New Scientist*, p. 44, 25 August 1990.
P. M. Muller and D. Lamparsky, eds, *Perfumes: Art, Science and Technology*, Elsevier, Amsterdam, 1991.
D. M. Stoddart, *The Scented Ape*, Cambridge University Press, 1990.
S. Van Toller and G. H. Dodd, eds, *Perfumery: the Psychology and Biology of Fragrance*, Chapman and Hall, London, 1991.

Specialist reading
J. Ayres, 'Uses of fine chemicals in flavours and fragrances', *Chemistry & Industry*, p. 575, 19 September 1988.
R. J. Kutsky, *Handbook of Vitamins, Minerals and Hormones*, 2nd edition, Van Nostrand Reinhold, New York, 1981.
J. Müller *et al.*, *The H&R Book of Perfume: Understanding Fragrance, Origin, History, Development and Guide to Fragrance Ingredients*, Glöss Verlag, Hamburg, 1992.
C. S. Sell, 'Organic chemistry in the perfume industry', *Chemistry in Britain*, p. 791, August 1988.
C. S. Sell, 'The chemistry of ambergris', *Chemistry in Britain*, p. 516, August 1990.

Fragrance Guide, Feminine Notes and Masculine Notes, Glöss Verlag, Hamburg, 1991.

Chapter 2 Sweetness and light

General reading

H. Hobhouse, *Seeds of Change: Five Plants that Transformed Mankind*, Sidgwick & Jackson, London, 1985. This has a chapter on the history of sugar.

R. Tannahill, *Food in History*, revised edition, Penguin, 1988.

H. D. Belitz and W. Grosch, *Food Chemistry*, 2nd edition, translated by D. Hadziyev, Springer Verlag, Berlin, 1987.

J. Emsley and L. Hough, 'Sweeter by far?' *New Scientist*, p. 48, 19 June 1986.

J. Yudkin, *Pure White and Deadly*, updated edition, Viking, London, 1986.

Specialist reading

L. O'Brien Nabors and R. C. Gelardi, eds, *Alternative Sweeteners*, Marcel Dekker, New York, 1986.

L. Oxdale, 'The sweet taste of success', *Chemistry in Britain*, March 1991.

T. H. Grenby, 'Prospects for sugar substitutes', *Chemistry in Britain*, April 1991.

H. Schiweck, K. Rapp and M. Vogel, 'Utilization of sucrose as an industrial chemical, state of the art and future applications', *Chemistry & Industry*, 4 April 1988.

B. Crammer and R. Ikan, 'Sweet glycosides from the stevia plant', *Chemistry in Britain*, October 1986.

Developments in Sweeteners, Elsevier Applied Science, London, 1979 – An on-going series of volumes edited by various people, and containing articles written by authorities in each area.

Chapter 3 Alcohol

General reading

T. Parratt, *Name Your Poison, A Guide to Additives in Drinks*, Robert Hale, London, 1990.

E. Maury, *Your Good Health, The Medical Benefits of Wine Drinking*, Souvenir Press, London, 1992.

J. Postgate, *Microbes and Man*, 3rd edition, Penguin, London, 1992.

Specialist reading

H.-D. Belitz and W. Grosch, *Food Chemistry*, 2nd edition, translated by D. Hadziyev, Chapter 20, Springer Verlag, Berlin, 1987.

R. Boddey, 'Green energy from sugar cane', *Chemistry and Industry*, 17 May 1993, p. 355.

F. A. Lowenheim and M. K. Moran, *Faith, Keyes, and Clark's Industrial Chemicals*, 4th edition, Wiley-Interscience, New York, 1975.

The Essential Chemical Industry, Chemical Industry Education Centre, University of York, 1989.

R. Muller, 'Flavour in low-alcohol beers', *Chemistry Review*, September 1993.

G. Winger, F. G. Hofmann and J. H. Woods, *A Handbook on Drug and Alcohol Abuse, Biomedical Aspects*, 3rd edition, Oxford University Press, 1992.

Chapter 4 Cholesterol, fats and fibre

General reading

A. E. Bender, *Health or Hoax?* Sphere, London, 1986.

S. Bingham, *The Everyman Companion to Food and Nutrition*, J. M. Dent, London, 1987.

Robert, L. Ory, *Grandma called it Roughage, Fiber Facts and Fallacies*, American Chemical Society, Washington DC, 1991.

A. Eyton, *The F-plan Diet*, Penguin, 1982.

R. E. Kowalski, *The 8-Week-Cholesterol Cure*, Bantam, Sydney, 1988.

C. A. Rinzler, *Food Facts and What They Mean*, Bloomsbury, London, 1987.

Specialist reading

H.-D. Belitz and W. Grosch, *Food Chemistry*, Springer Verlag, Berlin, 1987, Chapter 14.

T. P. Coultate, *Food, the Chemistry of its Components*, 2nd edition, Royal Society of Chemistry, London, 1988.

J. Davies and J. Dickerson, *Nutrient Content of Food Portions*, Royal Society of Chemistry, London, 1991.

R. Passmore and M. A. Eastwood, *Davidson and Passmore, Human Nutrition and Dietetics*, 8th edition, Churchill Livingstone, Edinburgh, 1986.

A. A. Paul and D. A. T. Southgate, *McCance and Widdowson's The Composition of Foods*, 4th edition, Her Majesty's Stationery Office, London, 1988.

Chapter 5   Painkillers and painful decisions

General reading

Living with Risk: the British Medical Association Guide, John Wiley, Chichester, 1987.

B. Selinger, *Chemistry in the Market Place*, 4th edition, Harcourt Brace Jovanovich, Sydney, 1988, Chapter 9, pp. 300–344.

M. Weatherall, *In Search of a Cure, a History of Pharmaceutical Discovery*, Oxford University Press, 1990.

Specialist reading

S. Adams, 'The discovery of brufen (ibuprofen)', *Chemistry in Britain*, December 1987.

A. Albert, *Xenobiosis, Food, Drugs and Poisons in the Human Body*, Chapman and Hall, London 1987.

S. Stinson, *Better Understanding of Arthritis Leading to New Drugs to Treat it*, Product Report, *Chemical & Engineering News*, 16 October 1989.

J. A. Timbrell, *Introduction to Toxicology*, Taylor & Francis, London, 1989.

Chapter 6   PVC

General reading

H. G. Elias, *Mega Molecules*, Springer Verlag, Berlin, 1985.

N. R. Kamsvåg and J. Baldwin, eds, *PVC and the Environment*, Norsk Hydro, 1992. This is a comprehensive 220-page book for the general reader. It gives a pro-industry view, but much was written by academic experts in the field. The book also tries to carry out a full cradle-to-grave analysis of PVC, including an environmental and health audit. Norsk Hydro also publishes a 24-page colour brochure *Facts about PVC*, which is available from their Petrochemical Division, P. O. Box 2594, Solli, 0203 Oslo 2, Norway.

Specialist reading

C. A. Heaton, ed., *The Chemical Industry*, Blackie, Glasgow, 1986.

D. Houndshell and J. Kelly Smith, *Science and Corporate Strategy, DuPont R&D 1902–80*, Cambridge University Press, 1988.

C. Kennedy, *ICI, the Company that Changed our Lives*, Hutchinson, London, 1986.

R. J. Lewis Sr, *Carcinogenically Active Chemicals*, Van Nostrand Reinhold, New York, 1991.

P. J. T. Morris, *Polymer Pioneers*, The Center for History of Chemistry, publication No. 5, Philadelphia, 1986.

M. P. Stevens, 'Polymer additives', *Journal of Chemical Education*, p. 444, Volume 70, 1993.

W. Tötsch and J. Gaensslen, *Polyvinylchloride. Environmental Aspects of a Common Plastic*, Elsevier, 1992.

Chapter 7   Dioxins

General reading

H. D. Crone, *Chemicals & Society*, Cambridge University Press, 1986.

M. A. Ottobone, *The Dose Makes the Poison*, 2nd edition, Van Nostrand Reinhold, New York, 1991.

Specialist reading

The journal *The Science of the Total Environment* published a special issue, Volume 104, entitled 'Dioxins. Chemistry and Health Effects' in 1991. Some of the key papers are included below.

B. N. Ames, 'Natural carcinogens and dioxin', *The Science of the Total Environment*, 1991. Volume 104, pp. 159–166.

T. Colborn and C. Clement, eds, *Chemically-Induced Alterations in Sexual and Functional Development: The Wildlife/Human Connection*, in the series *Advances in Modern Environmental Toxicology*, Volume XXI, Princeton Scientific Publishing, New Jersey, 1992.

Dioxins in the Environment, Pollution Paper No. 27, Department of the Environment, Her Majesty's Stationery Office, 1989.

G. H. Eduljee, 'Dioxins in the environment', *Chemistry in Britain*, December 1988.

H. Fiedler, O. Hutzinger and C. W. Timms, 'Dioxins: sources of environmental load and human exposure', *Toxicological and Environmental Chemistry*, Volume 29, 1990, pp. 157–234.

M. A. Gallo, R. J. Scheuplein and K. A. Van der Heijden, eds, *Banbury Report 35: Biological Basis for Risk Assessment of Dioxins and Related Compounds*, Cold Spring Harbor Laboratory, 1991.

M. Gough, 'Human health effects: what the data indicate', *The Science of the Total Environment*, 1991. Volume 104, pp. 129–158.

G. W. Gribble, 'Naturally occurring organohalogen compounds—a survey', *Journal of Natural Products*, 1992, Volume 55, pp. 1353–1395.

D. Hanson, 'Dioxin toxicity: new studies . . .', *Chemical & Engineering News*, 12 August 1991.

S. J. Harrad and K. Jones, 'Dioxins at large', *Chemistry in Britain*, December 1992.

C. A. Heaton, ed., *The Chemical Industry*, Blackie, Glasgow and London, 1986.

O. P. Kharhanda and E. A. Stallworthy, *Safety in the chemical industry*, Chapter 11, Heinemann, London, 1988.

L. O. Kjeller, K. C. Jones, A. E. Johnston and C. Rappe, 'Increases in the polychlorinated dibenzo-*p*-dioxin and -furan content of soils and vegetation since the 1840s; *Environmental Science and Technology*, Volume **25**, pp. 1619–1627, 1991.

R. Bate and J. Morris, *Apocalypse or Hot Air?*, Institute of Economic Affairs, London, 1994.

N. Fell and P. Liss, 'Can algae cool the planet?' *New Scientist*, 21 August 1993.

J. Gribbin, *Hothouse Earth: the Greenhouse Effect and Gaia*, Black Swan, London, 1989.

J. Leggett (ed.), *Global Warming, the Greenpeace Report*, Oxford University Press, 1990.

J. Mason, 'The greenhouse effect and global warming', Royal Institution lecture, London, November 1990. Available from British Coal, Coal Research Establishment, Stoke Orchard, Cheltenham, Gloucestershire GL52 4RZ, UK.

F. Pearce, 'The high cost of carbon dioxide', *New Scientist*, 17 July 1993.

Specialist reading

T. E. Graedel, D. T. Hawkins and L. D. Claxton, *Atmospheric Chemical Compounds, Sources, Occurrence and Bioassay*, Academic Press, Orlando, Florida, 1986.

The Hadley Centre Transient Climate Change Experiment, August 1992. Report from the Hadley Centre for Climate Prediction, Meteorological Office, London Road, Bracknell, Berks RG12 2SY, UK.

J. T. Houghton, G. T. Jenkins, and J. J. Ephraums (eds), *Scientific Assessment of Climate Change*, WMO/UNEP Intergovernmental Panel on Climate Change, Geneva, 1990, also published by Cambridge University Press. A summary booklet is available as the *1990 IPCC Scientific Assessment of Climate Change*, Submission from Working Group 1 to the Intergovernmental Panel on Climate Change (IPCC), World Meteorological Organization, United Nations Environment Programme, 1990.

1992 IPCC Supplement Scientific Assessment of Climate Change, Submission from Working Group 1 to the Intergovernmental Panel on Climate Change (IPCC), World Meteorological Organization, United Nations Environment Programme, 1992.

Z. Jaworowski, T. V. Segalstad and N. Ono, 'Do glaciers tell a true atmospheric CO_2 story?' *The Science of the Total Environment*, Volume 114, pp. 227–284, 1992.

Z. Jaworowski, T. V. Segalstad and V. Hisdsal, *Atmospheric CO_2 and Global Warming: a Critical Review*, 2nd revised edition, Norsk Polar Institutt, Oslo, 1992.

R. H. Nielsen, 'Chill warnings from Greenland', *New Scientist*, 28 August 1993. Based on two articles in *Nature*, Volume 364, pp. 203 and 218, 1993.

P. Warneck, *Chemistry of the Natural Atmosphere*, Academic Press, San Diego, California, 1988.

R. P. Wayne, *Chemistry of Atmospheres*, 2nd edition, Clarendon Press, Oxford, 1991.

Chapter 10   Take care

General reading

If you want to read further about the role of chemistry and chemicals in every day life, then the following books are highly recommended.

P. W. Atkins, *Molecules*, Scientific American Library, New York, 1987.

H. D. Crone, *Chemicals and Society*, Cambridge University Press, 1986.

Living with Risk: the British Medical Association Guide, John Wiley, Chichester, 1987.

J. Lenihan, *The Crumbs of Creation*, Adam Hilger, Bristol, 1988.

M A. Ottoboni, *The Dose Makes the Poison*, 2nd edition, Van Nostrand Reinhold, New York, 1991.

J. V. Rodricks, *Calculated Risks, Understanding the Toxicity and Human Health Risks of Chemicals in our Environment*, Cambridge University Press, 1992.

B. Selinger, *Chemistry in the Market Place*, 4th edition, Harcourt Brace Jovanovich, Sydney, 1989.

Appendix   Chemical Data

General reading

A. Nickon and E. F. Silversmith, *Organic Chemistry, The Name Game, Modern Coined Terms and Their Origins*, Permanon Press, New York, 1987.

Specialist reading

H.-D. Belitz and W. Grosch, *Food Chemistry*, Springer Verlag, Berlin, 1987.

S. Budavari, ed., *The Merck Index*, 11th edition, Merck, Rahway, New Jersey, 1989.

J. Emsley, *The Elements*, 2nd edition, Oxford University Press, 1992.

G. G. Hawley, *The Condensed Chemical Dictionary*, 10th edition, Van Nostrand Reinhold Company, New York, 1981.

R. C. Weast, editor-in-chief, *CRC Handbook of Chemistry and Physics*, 70th edition, CRC Press, Boca Raton, Florida, 1990.

Dictionary of Organic Compounds, 5th edition, Chapman and Hall, London and New York, 1982, plus supplements.

Dictionary of Inorganic Compounds, Chapman and Hall, London and New York, 1992, plus supplement.

INDEX

Chemical compounds are listed alphabetically, but not including single letter Greek and Roman prefixes.